Cross-Border Debt Recovery in the EU

Elena Alina Onţanu

Cross-Border Debt Recovery in the EU

A Comparative and Empirical Study on the Use of the European Uniform Procedures

intersentia

METRO

Ius Commune Europaeum

Intersentia Ltd
Sheraton House | Castle Park
Cambridge | CB3 0AX | United Kingdom
Tel.: +44 1223 370 170 | Fax: +44 1223 370 169
Email: mail@intersentia.co.uk
www.intersentia.com | www.intersentia.co.uk

Distribution for the UK and Ireland:
NBN International
Airport Business Centre, 10 Thornbury Road
Plymouth, PL6 7 PP
United Kingdom
Tel.: +44 1752 202 301 | Fax: +44 1752 202 331
Email: orders@nbninternational.com

Distribution for Europe and all other countries:
Intersentia Publishing nv
Groenstraat 31
2640 Mortsel
Belgium
Tel.: +32 3 680 15 50 | Fax: +32 3 658 71 21
Email: mail@intersentia.be

Distribution for the USA and Canada:
International Specialized Book Services
920 NE 58th Ave. Suite 300
Portland, OR 97213
USA
Tel.: +1 800 944 6190 (toll free) | Fax: +1 503 280 8832
Email: info@isbs.com

Cross-Border Debt Recovery in the EU. A Comparative and Empirical Study on the Use of the European Uniform Procedures

This research was made possible with the support of the Netherlands Organisation for Scientific Research (NWO) within its Innovational Research Incentives Scheme (VIDI).

ISBN 978-1-78068-609-7
D/2017/7849/117
NUR 727

British Library Cataloguing in Publication Data. A catalogue record for this book is available from the British Library.

ACKNOWLEDGEMENTS

The present research is part of the project 'Securing Quality in Cross-Border Enforcement: Towards European Principles of Civil Procedure?', and was made possible by a VIDI research grant awarded by the Dutch Organisation of Scientific Research to Professor Xandra Kramer.

This project has been a unique journey, for which I would like to thank my two supervisors: Professor Xandra Kramer for her trust in me and in my capabilities, and for the tremendous opportunity she gave me to develop as a researcher and as a lecturer, and Professor Christopher Hodges for agreeing to become my supervisor, for our productive discussions, and for his assistance in conducting empirical research in England. I also want to thank them both for their encouragement in finalising this thesis. In addition, I would like to thank the members of my doctoral committee, Professors Marta Pertegás Sender, Elisabetta Silvestri, and Emese von Bóné for kindly agreeing to take on the task of reading this thesis, and for their constructive evaluation.

A number of researchers and professors have welcomed me at universities and institutes abroad, and I am grateful to each of them. I want to thank Professor Neil Andrews for his kind invitation to conduct research on English law at Clare College, University of Cambridge. I am also indebted to Marco Fabri for welcoming me to the Research Institute on Judicial Systems – National Research Council (IRSIG-CNR) in Bologna, and to Marco Velicogna, Marco Mellone, Luca Verzelloni, Giampiero Lupo, Daniela Cavallini, and Francesco Contini for their support in conducting empirical research in Italy, and for the extensive discussions we had on European procedures and Italian law. I am deeply grateful to Professor Burkhard Hess for the rewarding period I spent as a visiting researcher at the Max Planck Institute for International, European and Regulatory Procedural Law in Luxembourg, and for the discussions I had with researchers there, especially Professor Marta Requejo Isidro, Matteo Gargantini, Katharina Raffelsieper, Adriani Dori, and Vincent Richard. I also want to thank Professors Elaine Mak, Vincent Buskens, Urszula Jaremba, John Sorabji, Robert Turner, Emmanuel Guinchard, Carla Crifò, Gilles Cuniberti, Camelia Toader, Pietro Franzina, and to Eral Knight, Octavia Spineanu-Matei, and Walter Gaetano Caglioti for the helpful discussions, for their advice, and for the materials they chose to share with me during my doctoral research.

A special thank you goes to Francesco Contini at IRSIG-CNR for our collaboration on a different project during the completion of this research, and for our valuable discussions. It has been a great pleasure to work with him.

My research would not have been as rich without the help and assistance of Nicolas Wintz (Bibliothèque Universitaire Droit et Sciences Économiques, Université de Lorraine) and of Allan Mulondo, Irina Kühn, and Esther Sánchez Coro (Max Planck Institute for International, European and Regulatory Procedural Law). Their support in tracking down my much-needed bibliographical references has been invaluable.

I am grateful to all the judges, clerks, lawyers, legal advisors, and bailiffs who took time to participate in this research, and to share their views and experience in applying the European uniform procedures. They have made a very important part of this study possible, and I hope the outcome of this project will contribute to their daily activities in applying EU law.

My colleagues and fellow PhDs at Erasmus School of Law, Denise Korthals Altes Biemans, Abiola Makinwa, Irma Mosquera, Ekaterina Pannebakker, Monique Hazelhorst, Erlis Themeli, Piotr Wilinski, Marta Kolacz, Steven Stuij, Yahan Wang, Priskila Penasthika, Ryan Gauthier, Jing Hiah, Thomas Riesthuis, and Petra Gyongyi, have made this whole experience richer. A special thank you goes as well to Laura van Bochove for making me feel so welcome in Rotterdam, for her friendship, and for her support throughout my PhD journey. I am grateful to Renate Buijze, Jing Hiah, and Alexandre Biard for our discussions on empirical research and data analysis. And I want to thank the former student assistants Nadia Ayrir, Sander Rijsterborgh, Ramses de Leeuw, Tom Vleeschhouwer, and the secretariat of the Private Law Department for their technical support.

My final words of gratitude are for my close family and friends, who have supported me through many moments of difficulty and extreme exhaustion, who have been so understanding when I needed to spend time away from them, and who have been able to make me laugh and to enjoy this journey. I owe a very special thank you to my mother for her unconditional support and encouragement from the moment that I started primary school, and to Luca Catano who, patiently and with dedication, has listened to me talk for so many hours about my research and my dilemmas. I am grateful beyond words for their advice, their patience, and their cheerful optimism.

Rotterdam, August 2017

CONTENTS

ABBREVIATIONS

ABI	Association of British Insurers
ALI	American Law Institute
APIL	Association of Personal Injury Lawyers
AUGE	Associazione Ufficiali Giudiziari in Europa
Blackstone's Civil Practice	Maurice Kay (ed.-in-chief), Blackstone's Civil Practice (2015)
CA	Cour d'appel
Cass	Cour de cassation
CBI	Confederation of British Industry
CEPEJ	the European Commission for the Efficiency of Justice
Charter	Charter of the Fundamental Rights of the European Union
COJ	Code de l'organisation judiciaire
Commission EOP Report	European Commission, Report from the Commission to the Commission to the European Parliament, the Council and the European Economic and Social Committee on the application of the Regulation (EC) No. 1896/2006 of the European Parliament and of the Council creating a European Order for Payment Procedure, COM(2015) 495 final
Commission ESCP Report	European Commission, Report from the Commission to the European Parliament, the Council and the European Economic and Social Committee on the application of the Regulation (EC) No. 861/2007 of the European Parliament and of the Council establishing a European Small Claims Procedure, COM(2013) 795 final
CPC	Claim Production Centre (English Chapter)
CPC	Code de procédure civile (French Chapter)
CPC	Codice di procedura civile (Italian Chapter)
CPC ex.	Code des procédures civiles d'exécution

CPLR	Civil Practice Law Reports
CPR	Civil Procedure Rules
CSM	Consiglio superiore della magistratura
Deloitte Report	Assessment of the socio-economic impacts of the policy options for the Future of the European Small Claims Regulation, Final Report, RDT-L05–2010, Deloitte, Brussels, 19.07.2013
DTI	Department of Trade and Industry
EAPO	European Account Preservation Order
ECC	European Consumer Centre
ECC France	Centre Européen de la Consommation, Zentrum für Europäischen Verbraucherschutz e.V.
ECC Italy	European Consumer Centre Italy
ECC-Net	European Consumer Centres Network
ECC Romania	Centrul European al Consumatorilor România
ECC UK	European Consumer Centre UK
ECHR	European Convention for the Protection of Human Rights and Fundamental Freedoms
ECtHR	European Court of Human Rights
EC Treaty	European Community Treaty
EEO	European Enforcement Order
ELI	European Law Institute
EOP	European Order for Payment
ESCP	European Small Claims Procedure
EWCA	Court of Appeal
EWHC	High Court
HMCTS	Her Majesty's Courts and Tribunals Service
ICT	Information and Communication Technology
IRSIG-CNR	Research Institute on Judicial Systems – National Research Council of Italy
JP	Juridiction de proximité
LACORS	Local Authorities Co-ordinators of Regulatory Services
Law Society	Law Society of England and Wales
LRC	Law Reform Committee of the Bar Council
MCOL	Money Claim Online
NACAB	National Association of Citizens Advice Bureaux
NCC	National Consumer Council
NCPC	Noul Cod de procedură civilă
OJ	Official Journal of the European Union
PCT	Trial On-Line system (Processo Civile Telematico)
PD	Practice Direction, Civil Procedure Rules

PEC	Certified e-mail address (indirizzo di posta elettronica certificate
PIQR	Personal Injury and Quantum Reports
QB	Law Reports: Queen's Bench Division
TC	Tribunal de commerce
TFEU	Treaty of the Functioning of the EU
TGI	Tribunal de grande instance
TI	Tribunal d'instance
UNEP	Uffici Notificazioni, Esecuzioni e Protesti
UNIDROIT	International Institute for the Unification of Private Law
WLR	Weekly Law Reports

Chapter 1

INTRODUCTION

'La libre circulation des jugements est illusoire si le titre ne se concrétise pas avec la même efficacité dans les États membres.'[1]

'Basically, the main problem associated with execution is that of making it effective.'[2]

1.1. A Union of Law and Uniform European Procedures

Access to justice and effective enforcement mechanisms are crucial for a European Union built on the rule of law,[3] aimed at protecting citizens' rights, and supporting economic activities undertaken on the basis of the four fundamental freedoms.[4] The free circulation of judgment, which can be 'held to be a fifth freedom'[5] can enhance the outcomes of these freedoms for citizens and businesses within the EU. Well-developed legal mechanisms are necessary to increase enforcement efficiency and to discourage bad faith debtors from channeling their activities and funds into Member States where they can escape enforcement.[6] Cross-border litigation can be particularly cumbersome for parties due to the diversity of applicable rules, lengthy proceedings, and significant costs that can easily reach disproportionate levels. The complexity of a national procedural system, the lack of transparency of applicable national procedural rules, the limited familiarity with other justice systems, and slow and ineffective enforcement mechanisms can be a serious disincentive for creditors to take action and defend their rights. The diversity of procedural rules in cross-border litigation places litigants in an unequal position, having to accept diverse handling and varying costs for the same type of claim in different Member States.

The purpose of procedural law is to insure the effectiveness of law (substantive norms) and to provide judges with appropriate instruments to interpret and apply the law.[7] It determines how substantive legal rights and duties 'must be established, effected or

1 de Leval (1996), at 595–626.
2 de Leval (1998), at 45–56.
3 Preamble to the Treaty on European Union (TEU) and Article 2 and Article 3(1) TEU.
4 Velicogna, Lupo & Onțanu (2017).
5 Storskrubb (2016), at 302–303.
6 Berglund (2009), at 2.
7 Jolowicz (2000), at 71.

shaped in legal proceedings'.[8] Civil procedure rules 'are the expression of fundamental rights', as recognised by national constitutions, the Charter of Fundamental Rights of the European Union (Charter), and international treaties.[9] They 'maximize efficiency of justice systems while at the same time not limiting fundamental rights of litigants'.[10] Securing access to justice and, in particular, to 'equally efficient justice throughout the European Union'[11] is crucial for safeguarding the right to a fair trial,[12] as laid down by Article 6 European Convention for the Protection of Human Rights and Fundamental Freedoms (ECHR) and Article 47 Charter.[13] This also includes a right to an effective means to enforce the judgments obtained.[14]

Within the national systems of the Member States, however, enforcement of the judicial decisions is a bottleneck. Following the Amsterdam Treaty, the EU sought to address this issue through ambitious programmes and the adoption of measures to enhance the enforcement of judicial decisions.[15] The treaty provided the legal basis to adopt instruments to tackle the implications of cross-border litigation. Article 65 European Community Treaty (EC Treaty), included now in Article 81 Treaty of the Functioning of the EU (TFEU), empowered the Community (now the European Union) to adopt measures in the area of judicial cooperation in civil matters having cross-border implications.[16] The need to establish a 'well-functioning legal system within the European Union' opened the door to new legislation,[17] and the aim of improving cross-border enforcement took shape in the enactment of different regulations dealing with civil procedural matters (e.g. jurisdiction, recognition and enforcement, and service of documents).[18] These instruments primarily coordinate national procedures.[19] This was followed by 'second generation instruments' eliminating exequatur and relying on the principle of mutual recognition:[20] namely, the European

8 van Rhee (2000), at 589–611.

9 Tulibacka (2009), at 1538.

10 *Ibidem.*

11 Tenereiro & Seoane (2003), at 461–472.

12 See Golder Case in which the ECtHR confirmed access to justice as one of the fundamental guarantees of the right to a fair trial in accordance with Article 6 ECHR. ECtHR, *Golder v. UK*, 4451/70, 21 February 1975, Series A No. 18.

13 European Convention of Human Rights and Fundamental Freedoms as amended by Protocols No. 11 and No. 14, Rome, 4 November 1950; Charter of the Fundamental Rights of the European Union, OJ C 83/389, 30.3.2010.

14 ECtHR, *Hornsby v. Greece*, 18357/91, ECHR 1997-II, para. 40. See further on the discussion of the right to enforcement in the context of free movement of civil judgments, Hazelhorst (2016), at 162–164.

15 Kramer (2010), at 17–18.

16 Onţanu & Pannebakker (2013), at 169.

17 Tulibacka (2009), at 1527.

18 Regulation (EU) No 1215/2012 of the European Parliament and of the Council of 12 December 2012 on jurisdiction and the recognition and enforcement of judgments in civil and commercial matters, in OJ L 351/1, 20.12.2012; Regulation (EC) No 1393/2007 of the European Parliament and of the Council of 13 November 2007 on the service in the Member States of judicial and extrajudicial documents in civil or commercial matters (service of documents), and repealing Council Regulation (EC) No 1348/2000, in OJ L 324/79, 10.12.2007.

19 Kramer (2008a), at 253.

20 Hess (2016), at 3; Mańko (2015), at 3.

Enforcement Order (EEO),[21] which paved the way to the European Order for Payment (EOP) and the European Small Claims Procedure (ESCP), and – more recently – to the European Account Preservation Order (EAPO).[22]

Uniform procedural rules at the European level can ease the parties' tasks in cross-border litigations by applying the same set of rules in any Member State. Despite the intention of the European legislator, the European uniform procedures rely to a certain extent on national procedural rules, which are applied by national courts in domestic justice systems. National legal systems are the result of the development and construction of the society in question[23] – the framework in which litigation takes place – and the procedural structures and practices are shaped by many centuries of application. In this context, a number of questions arise. How do the European uniform procedures fit within this national procedural framework? What is the status and place of national civil procedural rules in an evolving European area harmonising civil justice? How do the two levels of legislation interact and coordinate with each other? Are national courts encountering difficulties in applying these European procedures? Do the EOP and the ESCP achieve the goals for which they were enacted, or must further steps be taken to secure proper enforcement mechanisms in cross-border litigation?

1.2. Harmonisation of Procedural Rules in the European Union

The harmonisation of civil procedure was not one of the key initial aims of the EC Treaties. The process emerged gradually, based on increased interest and the desire to improve access to justice and create a European area of freedom, security, and justice.[24] The first concrete document on the approximation of judiciary law in the EU was issued by the Storme working group in 1994. This group laid down a series of proposals on procedural matters, including provisions with respect to the enforcement of judgments.[25] However, the harmonisation approach came later with the 1999 Tampere Council Conclusions, which voiced the need to improve access to justice, to encourage

[21] Regulation (EC) No 805/2004 of the European Parliament and of the Council of 21 April 2004 creating a European enforcement order for uncontested claims, OJ 2004 L 14315, 30.4.2004.

[22] Regulation (EC) No 1896/2006 of the European Parliament and of the Council of 12 December 2006 creating a European order for payment procedure, in OJ L 399/1, 30.12.2006; Regulation (EC) No 861/2007 of the European Parliament and of the Council of 11 July 2007 establishing a European Small Claims Procedure, in OJ L 199/1, 31.7.2007; Regulation (EU) No 655/2014 of the European Parliament and of the Council of 15 May 2014 establishing a European Account Preservation Order procedure to facilitate cross-border debt recovery in civil and commercial matters, in OJ L 189/59, 27.6.2014.

[23] The national legal system mirrors the needs and developments in a society, considering economic, social, cultural, political, ideological, institutional factors, constitutional reality, and traditions. See also Taruffo (2008), at 48; Tulibacka (2009), at 1532.

[24] *De facto* harmonisation of certain procedural rules existed before the enactment of specific procedural regulations by the European institutions in relation to EU substantive law (e.g. consumer protection directives, intellectual property regulations, and insolvency regulations).

[25] Such as the moment when a judgment becomes enforceable, the stay of execution, the issuance of an order for the preservation of assets, the recognition of the titles of execution in the state of execution, grounds for objection to execution, disclosure of the debtor's assets, and assets that are exempted from seizure and sale. Storme (1994).

mutual recognition of judicial decisions, and to facilitate greater convergence in civil law.[26]

As expressed previously in the Storme Report, the approximation of rules of procedure can lead to 'a common legal culture in Europe',[27] but such a process is difficult to attain, as it requires time and an advanced application of the principle of mutuality. Enforcement rules are still quite different between national legal systems in the EU. Following the Amsterdam Treaty, the EU acquired the legal grounds to address this matter, and actions materialised in the adoption of a number of instruments that seek to facilitate enforcement for businesses and citizens. In this context, the harmonisation of enforcement procedures can contribute to the 'free circulation of courts judgments' by encouraging the establishment of and compliance with mutual procedural standards between Member States. Judgments would be 'illusory if enforcement instruments were not equally effective in all the Member States'.[28] The harmonisation of procedural rules in cross-border litigation can reduce differences, encourage convergence in civil law, and promote the compatibility of procedural legislation applicable in the Member States. This can enhance free movement of judgments by simplifying formalities, addressing the cross-border aspect of proceedings in a manner that can facilitate enforcement, and abolish interim procedures for recognition and enforcement of judgments (*elimination of exequatur*). It can create common grounds and guarantees in the administration of justice in civil and commercial matters without impairing the specificities of the legal systems of the Member States.

In consideration of the reliance of European harmonised instruments on national procedural rules for certain aspects related to their application (e.g. territorial competence of courts, valid methods of service, court fees, and means of execution), there is a certain obligation for national legislators to provide the rules relating to implemention and coordination in accordance with the principle of sincere cooperation.[29] This leads to a certain *autonomie encadrée* of the national procedural rules. These are set up to secure judicial cooperation in accordance with the provisions of the regulation, and to comply with the high standard of protection of rights that EU law grants. The process does not seek to limit application of the national procedural law when the rules need to supplement the European instruments, but to establish a common procedural standard, a shared approach that facilitates access to justice and guarantees a fair trial in accordance with Article 6 ECHR and Article 47 Charter.

The legislative process of harmonisation needs to be matched by a unitary approach to the application of available European procedures, by a convergence of practices, and by a common understanding and interpretation of their provisions in accordance with the *effet utile* principle. In this regard, questions can be raised as to the elements that can secure a proper and effective application of these harmonised European procedures. A

26 See Tampere European Council 15–16 October 1999, Presidency Conclusions, (available at www.europarl.europa.eu/summits/tam_en.htm).

27 Storme (1994), at 52.

28 Commission Communication to the Council and European Parliament, *Towards greater efficiency in obtaining and enforcing judgments in the European Union*, COM (97) 609 final, Recital 42.

29 Article 4(3) Treaty on European Union. See Hess (2016a), at 7–8 (available at www.europarl.europa.eu/RegData/etudes/IDAN/2016/556971/IPOL_IDA(2016)556971_EN.pdf).

coherent step-by-step process of harmonisation at the EU level appears to be the way to secure a more transparent legislation and to create a balance with the particularities, traditions, and cultures of national legal systems. These systems need to adapt and accommodate the application of harmonised European procedures. These European instruments require the application of two sets of procedural rules in a unitary manner, but because this is a procedural novelty, additional measures need to be identified and adopted in order to secure similar results across Member States.

1.3. Securing Access to Justice and Building Trust in National Legal Systems

The national civil procedural rules together with the present fragmented EU procedural framework have the task of assuring that parties have proper access to justice, protecting their rights as well as providing expeditious and efficient mechanisms to enforce court decisions in order to preserve *l'effet utile* of the law at the European and national level. Overly complicated mechanisms or no instruments to enable a creditor to enforce a judgment he was awarded may become equivalent to a denial of justice,[30] especially in the case of weaker parties such as consumers and small businesses.

The Council identified this need to facilitate access to justice in cross-border matters, and – by building up confidence between the jurisdictions of Member States – its programmes established periodic objectives with regard to achieving better access to justice, easier enforcement instruments, mutual recognitions of judgments, and enhanced judicial cooperation.

Mutual recognition is based on mutual trust among national legal systems, judges, legal professionals, businesses, and citizens.[31] In the 1999 Tampere Conclusions, the principle of mutual recognition was identified as the cornerstone for the creation of a European judicial area.[32] The importance of the principle of mutual recognition of judgments was then confirmed by the 2005 Hague Programme.[33] The 2009 Stockholm Programme reiterated the principle as a way to protect rights and to secure cross-border enforcement in Europe, while the EU Justice Agenda for 2020 enhanced its importance.[34] Mutual recognition and mutual trust are 'core concepts' in seeking to achieve a free circulation of judgments.[35]

According to the principle of mutual recognition, no matter in which Member State the judgment is issued it should be treated as being equal to a national judgment. In order for this principle to function according to its aims, there should be mutual trust between the Member State justice systems, independence of the judiciary, observance of the rule

30 See Andenas (2005), at 7–23.

31 European Commission Action Plan Implementing the Stockholm Programme, COM(2010) 171 final, para. 4. On mutual recognition and mutual trust, see also Kramer (2011a), at 633–641.

32 Tampere European Council 15–16 October 1999, Presidency Conclusions, para. 33–34.

33 European Council, *The Hague Programme: Strengthening freedom, security and justice in the European Union*, OJ 2005, C53/1.

34 European Council, *The Stockholm Programme – An Open and Secure Europe Serving and Protecting Citizens*, OJ 2010, C115/1; European Commission, *The EU Justice Agenda for 2020 – Strengthening Trust, Mobility and Growth within the Union*, COM(2014)144 final.

35 Linton (2016), at 247.

of law, and fundamental rights as well as a high quality of judgments.[36] In such circumstances, safeguards at the stage of recognition and enforcement are no longer necessary to protect parties' procedural rights.[37]

The EOP and the ESCP seek to achieve mutual trust by laying down certain minimum procedural standards to create certainty and to guarantee that parties' procedural rights have been observed. Common rules setting clear requirements for high procedural standards to be complied with by all European jurisdictions should secure a high quality of justice and not lead to suspicions regarding the standard of the judicial act of another national court. Further, judicial cooperation and communication between Member State courts and professional organisations can contribute to a better understanding and knowledge of national procedural systems, and smooth the path to mutual trust and to the mutual recognition of decisions. However, questions are raised as to whether the mechanisms and safeguards set by the EOP and the ESCP are sufficient to protect the parties' – and especially the defendant's – access to justice and to a fair trial.

A prompt and efficient system for enforcing judgments is vital for accessible justice.[38] The 'cornerstone of effective cooperation'[39] in enforcing judgments between Member States comprises the principle of mutual recognition of judicial decisions. Setting up common minimum procedural standards contributes to legal certainty. Further, by establishing clear procedural rules for the parties to follow, and a predictable process that secures the protection of individual rights in the European Union,[40] cross-border litigation and enforcement can be simplified, and access to a fair trial guaranteed without constraining the Member States to unify their procedural laws.[41]

The EOP and the ESCP create a uniform framework of rules for uncontested and small value claims in cross-border litigation, but are still forced to rely on national procedural rules for a number of aspects such as valid service methods, court fees, appeals and transfer following opposition, and enforcement. The latest European uniform procedure, the EAPO, also relies on domestic rules for its application. Hence, it remains to be seen whether the standards that these European procedures set and the guarantees the national procedural rules have to provide are sufficient to secure access to justice. In addition, it is still uncertain as to whether their template could be considered a model for other European procedures seeking to simplify cross-border enforcement and harmonise civil procedure.

36 *Ibidem.*

37 The exequatur procedure creates certain safeguards and protection for the rights of the defendant, but it also slows down the process of enforcement, creating restrictions and disincentives for trade and the free movement of persons, goods, and services between the Member States, and for the 'unhindered movement of judgments'. Andersson (2005), at 248.

38 Commission Communication to the Council and European Parliament *Towards greater efficiency in obtaining and enforcing judgments in the European Union*, COM (97) 609 final, http://eur-lex.europa.eu/LexUriServ/LexUriServ.do?uri=COM:1997:0609:FIN:EN:PDF, point 42.

39 Andenas (2005), at 11.

40 Andersson (2005), at 245–251.

41 The term 'unified procedural rules' refers to the process of adopting a common set of procedural rules in all the Member States (i.e. a code of civil procedure) and giving up the national particularities of procedural law in order to achieve mutual trust and the recognition of judicial decision in cross-border cases.

1.4. Research Question

The research aims to investigate the functioning of the first two European uniform procedures almost ten years into their application, seeking to understand the way these procedures function in interaction with national procedural rules, and whether they manage to achieve the purpose for which they were adopted. To this end, the study is conducted in four European jurisdictions: England and Wales (hereafter England), France, Italy, and Romania.

The central question this research seeks to answer is whether the first European uniform procedures – the EOP and the ESCP – improve cross-border litigation in terms of securing effective enforcement mechanisms while protecting parties' procedural rights.

The notion of 'enforcement' is to be understood broadly, comprising the process of obtaining an enforceable title as well as the execution stage, as access to justice 'would be illusory if [...] a final, binding judicial decision [...] remain inoperative to the detriment of the party'.[42]

In order to answer the main research question, the following five sub-questions will be addressed in Chapters 3–7:

1) Which national instruments serve a purpose similar to that of the EOP and the ESCP, and how do they function in practice?[43]
2) How are the European uniform procedures implemented within the legal framework of the analysed national systems?
3) How are these European procedures perceived and applied in practice?
4) To what extent do the EOP and the ESCP succeed in providing effective alternative instruments in cross-border litigation?
5) Do the European uniform procedures offer sufficient guarantees for parties' procedural rights?

A complementary question will be based on the answers to and findings from the main questions considering whether the template established by the EOP and the ESCP can represent a model for future procedures simplifying cross-border enforcement and harmonising civil procedure. In investigating the validity of the model of the first European uniform procedures for future procedures simplifying cross-border enforcement and harmonising civil procedure, the third European uniform procedure – the EAPO – will be referred to and used as a perspective on possible developments and future projects concerning the area of civil justice.

1.5. Aims and Limitations

The research focuses on the EOP and the ESCP, which are an alternative to national procedures in recovering uncontested and small value claims in cross-border litigation. This study aims to make an additional contribution to the discussion on the European

42 ECtHR, *Hornsby v. Greece*, 18357/91, ECHR 1997-II, para. 40.

43 The EOP and the ESCP are optional instruments that parties can choose as an alternative to national procedures in seeking to recover uncontested or small value debts in cross-border situations.

civil procedures, providing a broader picture of the way such instruments function within national procedural systems and how they relate to national rules and procedures. The research was initiated a few years after the EOP and the ESCP became applicable because it was not clear how these procedures were functioning and what their outcome was in achieving simpler, cheaper, and faster justice for parties without neglecting their procedural rights and access to a fair trial.

In evaluating results of the enactment of the European uniform procedures in England, France, Italy, and Romania, this multi-level comparative analysis of four EU legal systems can contribute to a better understanding of the way these uniform procedures function in providing a harmonised enforcement mechanism that can facilitate access to justice for citizens and businesses seeking – by way of cross-border litigation – to recover monies owing to them.

At the legislative level, the last few decades have seen a surge of instruments in the area of justice, and a growing importance of procedural law. The making of laws, however, has been mainly sectorial and has involved a piecemeal approach. An in-depth understanding of the way the existing instruments are applied and used, in addition to their interaction with national law and practices, is key to achieving coordination between European procedural instruments as well as better implementation and smoother coordination with national procedural rules.[44] The information provided by this research can be used further to identify and address the needs related to developing the European area of justice: for instance, by helping to focus on aspects that require additional action at the national and European level. This can assist not only in developing new procedural instruments that harmonise civil procedure and simplify enforcement in cross-border litigation but also in consolidating the present framework, enhancing coherence, and raising the awareness of small claims litigators and legal professionals. Furthermore, in implementing the EAPO, the experience of the EOP and ESCP application may prove to be a useful tool.

The concrete way in which EOP and ESCP procedures function and interact with national procedural instruments and rules in the selected jurisdictions is of significant value for courts and practitioners as well as for legislators. This allows all stakeholders to have useful information on how European uniform procedures are applied by their colleagues in other Member States, to gain understanding of the encountered difficulties, and to share solutions for overcoming procedural intricacies in guaranteeing access to justice and parties' procedural rights. In addition, this can facilitate an exchange of good practices and enhance judicial cooperation. It is crucial to understand the strong points and the difficulties encountered in applying the EOP and the ESCP in order to address the needs of users and legal professionals.

The research seeks to assess EOP and ESCP contributions to securing easy access to justice instruments, and to engendering the much-needed mutual trust between Member State judicial systems in the context of free movement of judgments. Overall, as well as furthering the academic debate, the analysis will provide invaluable information for national and European stakeholders as to the functioning and effectiveness of such European instruments.

44 See Regulation (EU) No 1382/2013 of the European Parliament and the Council of 17 December 2013 establishing a Justice Programme for the period 2014 to 2020, OJ L354/73, 28.12.2013.

This study includes and analyses all available national EOP and ESCP decisions issued by English, French, Italian, and Romanian courts, as well as the EOP case law of the Court of Justice of the European Union.[45] The case law research was concluded on 1 October 2016 to allow a thorough analysis of the cases. For the same reason, the empirical research ended in March 2016. Relevant literature and legislation were taken into account until October 2016, while later reports and materials were considered as far as possible.

The EEO is not part of the present study although it 'marks the beginning of a new era for recognition and enforcement of decisions as well as for European civil procedure'.[46] The instrument does not establish a self-standing European procedure but a means to facilitate enforcement through a certification procedure for uncontested claims judgments, court settlements, and authentic instruments.[47] The EAPO became applicable on 18 January 2017, and is therefore only addressed incidentally following upon the procedural model represented by the EOP and the ESCP for future procedures simplifying cross-border enforcement and harmonising civil procedure.

Lastly, this research does not focus on the right to a fair trial and access to justice as laid down by Article 6 ECHR and Article 47 Charter as such, but will address them in relation to the EOP and the ESCP when required for the purpose of the analysis.[48]

1.6. Methodology

For a number of years following the entrance into force of the EOP and the ESCP, most scholarly contributions have addressed the European uniform procedures from a theoretical perspective, debating particular procedural elements and providing limited insight into national case law, or into a cross-border perspective. Information on the application of the EOP and the ESCP and the assessments available has often reflected the consumers' perspective or that of certain Member States.[49] Little is known about national EOP and ESCP case law, the way courts and professionals handle these claims,

45 See Chapters 2–6.

46 Kramer (2008a), at 257.

47 Article 3 EEO.

48 For an extensive analysis on the right to a fair trial and cross-border litigation, see Hazelhorst (2016).

49 See *inter alia Assessment of the socio-economic impacts of the policy options for the future of the European Small Claims Regulation* (RTD-L05–2010), prepared by Deloitte for the European Commission, July 2013; The Special Eurobarometer 395, *European Small Claims Procedure Report*, published by the European Commission, April 2013; ECC-Net, *The European Small Claims Procedure Report*, September 2012; Kačevska (2012); *Cross-border Alternative Dispute Resolution in the European Union* (IP/A/IMCO/ST/2010–15, PE464.424) a study commissioned by the European Parliament, 2011; Lithuanian Consumer Institute, *Consumers' cross-border dispute resolution: European Order for Payment and European Small Claims Procedure*, Vilnius 2011; Dockers (2010), at 111; ECC-Ireland, *European Small Claims Procedure. First Year of Operation in Ireland*, November 2010; M. E. Storme, *Le rapport entre les Règlement européens en matière de procedure (en particulier celle relative aux petites créances) et le droit judiciaire interne belge* (available at www.academia.edu/11398039/Le_rapport_entre_les_Re_glements_europe_ens_en_matie_re_de_proce_dure_en_particulier_celle_relative_aux_petites_cre_ances_et_le_droit_judiciaire_interne_belge).

and whether the enforcement of obtained judgments is effective. In analysing the functioning of the EOP and the ESCP, this research brings together several perspectives by intertwining multilevel comparative and empirical research to create a scenario that depicts what European uniform procedures contribute to cross-border debt-recovery litigation.

1.6.1. Choice of Research Method and Sources

The project follows a mixed research methodology combining classical doctrinal legal research with social science methods in order to answer the main research question. The classical research combines doctrinal research, analysing primary and secondary legislation, policy papers, guidelines, legislative history, the literature, and national and European case law along with empirical data gathered for this thesis.[50]

The nature of the analysed procedure – alternatives to national instruments in cross-border claims – and the main research question indicate that a comparative research methodology is the appropriate choice for this project. First, the comparative law approach can clarify 'how legal institutions are connected, [...] and transposed'.[51] A comparative analysis of civil procedure across different Member States can better assess the effects of a procedural harmonisation process[52] and contribute to building on mutual trust between national legal systems, encouraging communication and an exchange of information. The European uniform procedures apply in a national framework, and rely to a significant extent – directly or indirectly – on national procedural rules and practice. Thus, domestic legislation has to accommodate their application and provide the necessary supplanting rules for their functioning. This can facilitate an understanding of the national legal mechanisms and improve the application of EU procedural law, especially with regard to enforcement measures, which are traditionally limited to the territory of a Member State.[53] Further, it can plant the seeds that will grow into a common approach to the application of uniform procedural rules and lay the foundation of a EU legal culture.

Second, comparative research can provide valuable insight into the solution chosen at the domestic level in order to accommodate the EOP and the ESCP within the national legal system and practice: namely, the way national procedural rules are interpreted when needing to supplement the provisions of the regulation. Such information can contribute to raising awareness as to how similar difficulties have been dealt with by different justice systems. This will make discussions possible with regard to chosen approaches and to an exchange of ideas that can contribute to building a common harmonised approach to applying the European uniform procedures.

Third, the comparative approach also has an educative function, offering courts and practitioners a way to learn about each other's experiences with the EOP and the ESCP,

50 Section 1.6.3 will elaborate in more detail on the empirical sources.

51 Örücü (2002), at 15.

52 See van Gerven (1995), at 679–702.

53 Hess (2005), at 25.

and to learn how their colleagues in other Member States apply these procedures. This allows a sharing of information, knowledge, and approaches.[54]

Fourth, the comparative study can help clarify certain aspects of the European uniform procedures that create doubt or lead to diverse interpretations in practice; this will contribute to the establishment of an autonomous and uniform interpretation of the EOP and the ESCP in view of the *effet utile* principle.

The possibility of comparing the functioning of the EOP and the ESCP in the chosen jurisdictions as well as to the national procedures fulfilling a similar function depends on the 'existence and availability of data'.[55] According to Örücü, data can best be obtained through social science methodology.[56] In this context, the empirical research adds an extra layer of data to the multilevel comparative analysis, offering the information necessary to assess the functioning in practice of the EOP and the ESCP, and discovering similarities and differences as well as the interrelation between domestic and European procedural rules.

1.6.2. *Selection of Legal Systems*

The multilevel comparative analysis and the empirical study were carried out in England and Wales,[57] France, Italy, and Romania. This choice was based on a number of considerations:

- national systems to represent the civil law and the common law tradition;
- older as well as younger Member States;
- countries that have experience in applying national instruments similar to the ones enacted by the European regulations or that have introduced national procedures to match the EOP and ESCP; and
- countries that have different approaches to the implementation of European uniform procedures within their national justice system.

England is a common law tradition, and over the years the United Kingdom has had a more reserved attitude towards European developments. At the national level, courts have considerable experience in using standard forms and simplified procedures that allow the creditor to obtain a decision in the early stages without the case proceeding to a trial when claims are undisputed or of small value. The English legislator chose to adopt internal provisions for implementation of the European uniform procedures. While this research was being completed, however, the United Kingdom decided to leave the European Union by invoking Article 50 TFEU. Nevertheless, the experience of English legal practitioners and courts with the application of these instruments remains valuable in terms of the further development of European civil procedure and possible future forms of collaboration.

54 On the interest expressed by practitioners in the experience of their colleagues from other Member States with the EOP and the ESCP, see Onţanu (2017).

55 Örücü (2012), at 565.

56 *Ibidem.*

57 The present research does not include an analysis of the systems in Scotland, Northern Ireland, and Gibraltar.

France, Italy, and Romania are all civil law systems. They share different characteristics of national procedures and strategies regarding the European uniform procedures. While France and Italy are two founding countries of the European Union, Romania is one of the newer Member States. Another reason for choosing these three countries is that they have various approaches to the implementation of European uniform procedures within their national system. France, for instance, amended its Code of civil procedure to accommodate the EOP and the ESCP within its legal system. Italy adopted punctual clarifications. Romania considered the text of the two regulations when amending its Code of civil procedure, but relied on the direct effect of regulations for their application. Furthermore, France and Italy have national procedures matching the function of the EOP, as well as a simplified ordinary procedure for smaller value claims, while Romania has unified its domestic order for payment procedure and adopted a national procedure inspired by the ESCP Regulation.

Although the systems are different, there is a presumption that all four jurisdictions are required to apply the European uniform procedures in a similar manner, and that they encounter similar needs. A comparative analysis of the way the two regulations are applied and function will shed more light on the positive outcomes resulting from the implementation and application of these new-generation European procedures. It will also highlight the existing difficulties experienced by practitioners and parties, and which should be further addressed.

1.6.3. Functional Comparison

The functional comparative method is used in assessing the way the EOP and the ESCP improve the process of cross-border litigation in securing effective enforcement mechanisms while protecting parties' procedural rights. This choice relies on the principle that procedures that fulfil the same or a similar function are comparable: namely, they facilitate the recovery of cross-border uncontested and small value claims.

According to Zweigert and Kötz, 'the legal systems of every society faces essentially the same problems, and solves these problems by quite different means though very often with similar results'.[58] An assessment of the English, French, Italian, and Romanian systems indicates that the national procedures do not always provide direct equivalents to the EOP and the ESCP. National procedures can be vastly different from a procedural model perspective, although they may perform similar functions or respond to the same need when it comes to the recovery of uncontested or small value debts in domestic and cross-border claims. This is the case in England for the EOP and in France and Italy for the ESCP. Functionally equivalent procedures represent an alternative for parties in seeking to recover their uncontested or small value debts. The underlying assumption is that the domestic procedures and European uniform procedures analysed share a common purpose – that of securing a solution to the problem of cross-border debt recovery. Furthermore, the functioning and use of similar domestic procedures has the potential of influencing the use and functioning of the EOP and the ESCP and the way

[58] Zweigert & Kötz (1998), at 34.

these procedures are applied. The research does not intend to verify the legal transplant theory as such, but findings might point to the difficulties of importing European uniform procedures into national procedural law and practice.[59] Uniform procedures can be interpreted differently by national courts across Member States, as the rules are applied according to local circumstances, though users expect a harmonious set of requirements and uniform application of the European procedures.[60] These assumptions will be verified on the basis of the national literature and findings.

Knowledge of national practices and solutions to similar difficulties in the application of the EOP and the ESCP can lead to a diffusion of certain domestic approaches beyond the legal system analysed. The EOP and the ESCP leave directly or indirectly a number of aspects that are relevant for their application to national procedural rules. However, this does not automatically lead to harmonised solutions in the application of European uniform procedures. As noted by Örücü, 'in the context of the European Union, [...] where comparative law is a driving force and has a decisive role in the harmonisation process, the "functional comparative analysis method" shifts the focus from the "vertical" to the "horizontal" and provides the potential for convergence in both the legal systems and the legal methods of the member states, leading to a gradual and eventual legal integration'.[61] In a significant number of aspects, the EOP and the ESCP rely on domestic procedural rules. A functional comparison involves an examination of the national systems' requirements for the implementation and application of European uniform procedures. The comparative analysis can identify existing national practices, difficulties related to the application of these European procedures, solutions chosen to address these difficulties, and methods to single out good practices. Being aware of the responses chosen by different legal systems is a first step in being able to discuss them and consider their use. An exchange of solutions and ideas and discussions with regard to national practices can set the way for potential converging approaches and for the sharing of best local practices in the application of European uniform procedures. This can further encourage cross-border cooperation, enhancing mutual trust, and improving knowledge and understanding of European legislation as well as that of other Member States. Another assumption that this research seeks to verify is whether the application of European uniform procedures encounters similar problems and requirements in the analysed systems, and whether functionally equivalent solutions or approaches are chosen.

The comparative analysis is carried out on several levels. The first level concerns the interaction between the national procedures and the European instruments. The analysis focuses on characteristics of the national functionally equivalent procedures and their use in comparison with the EOP and the ESCP, looking at existing similarities and differences between the two categories of instruments. The second step remains at the national level, and compares the way the EOP and the ESCP are implemented, perceived by stakeholders, used, and function within the analysed jurisdiction. The third level

59 See Nelken (2002), at 26–27.

60 See Arvind (2010), at 65, 78–81; Graziadei (2006), at 441–475; Berrowitz, Pistor & Richard (2003), at 177–179.

61 Örücü (2012), at 563.

relies on the domestic findings in England, France, Italy, and Romania. The way the EOP and ESCP function and are applied in these four systems is compared. The goal is to identify similarities and differences that contribute to the way the European procedures are applied, and to the practices they establish, as well as to determine whether they achieve their aims in terms of securing effective enforcement mechanisms while protecting parties' procedural rights. Based on the empirical data gathered, the research will investigate whether the information reveals significant differences in experiences and perceptions with regard to the European uniform procedures between different groups of practitioners (i.e. judges, clerks, lawyers, and bailiffs/enforcement officers). In assessing the functioning of the EOP and the ESCP in the selected jurisdictions, a set of pre-determined evaluation criteria is used, and is presented in Section 7.1.3.

A comparative analysis of the application of the EOP and the ESCP is an indispensable tool for building a dialogue between practitioners called upon to implement these regulations. This can lead to a common approach to the application and interpretation of the European uniform procedures. Furthermore, the results of the comparative research can be of significant value to European and national legislators in assessing the need for additional actions that can contribute to a unitary application of the EOP and the ESCP.

1.6.4. Empirical Research

In order to provide an answer to the main research question – namely, whether the EOP and the ESCP improve cross-border litigation in terms of securing effective enforcement mechanisms while protecting the parties' procedural rights – empirical research methods are necessary to understand how the EOP and the ESCP are applied and function in the chosen systems. For this purpose, social science methods are used.

No detailed national data on how the EOP and the ESCP are implemented is generally available across the EU. This is also the case for the four selected justice systems. Annual reports published by the Ministry of Justice or the Council of the Judiciary on the activity of the judiciary and courts in England, France, Italy, and Romania do not contain information on the use of these first European uniform procedures. During the period of this research, certain studies carried out or commissioned by the European Commission and the ECC-Net were published,[62] and

[62] See Centre Européen de la Consommation, Zentrum für Europäischen Verbraucherschutz e.V., *Procédure européenne de règlement des petits litiges et injonction de payer européenne. Des procédures simplifiées pas si simples dans la pratique*, 2011; European Parliament, Cross-Border Alternative Dispute Resolution in the European Union, IP/A/IMCO/CT/2010-15, PE464.424; June 2011; ECC-Net, *The European Small Claims Procedure Report*, September 2012; European Parliament, *Mise en œuvre des instruments optionnels dans le domaine du droit civil en Europe*, Étude, PE462.425, 2012; Special Eurobarometer 395, *European Small Claims Procedure*, Report, April 2013; *Assessment of the socio-economic impacts of the policy options for the Future of the European Small Claims Regulation*, Final Report, RDT-L05-2010, Deloitte, Brussels, 19.07.2013; European Commission, *Report from the Commission to the European Parliament, the Council and the European Economic and Social Committee on the application of the Regulation (EC) No 861/2007 of the European Parliament and of the Council*

they offer valuable data for some of the matters the present study investigates. Those results are taken into consideration as additional sources of information or for triangulation purposes, by cross-checking them with the data gathered for this research. In comparison with published studies, the present research has a broader object with regard to the application and functioning of the EOP and the ESCP, and combines different perspectives in seeking to create a holistic image of the results of the European uniform procedures.

The empirical research is based on mixed methods, combining quantitative and qualitative approaches for the collection of data.[63] The reasons for the use of this combination are:

- the quantitative data is indicative of the use for, interest in, and familiarity that parties and practitioners have with European uniform procedures;
- quantitative data is limited, and data series are sometimes incomplete;
- the level of details provided by the available quantitative data across the analysed jurisdiction is inconsistent;
- qualitative data is complementary to the quantitative findings, and offers a more comprehensive picture of the EOP and the ESCP and their outcome in securing effective enforcement mechanisms in cross-border litigation; and
- triangulation allows a combination of the qualitative method and quantitative data in order to cross-check the consistency of results and to increase confidence in the overall validity of the findings.

The methods used will be discussed in sub-sections 1.6.4.1 and 1.6.4.2. Details with regard to specific steps taken in each of the four justice systems are provided in the dedicated sections of Chapters 3–6. Section 1.6.4.3 focuses on the methods used for the analysis of the data gathered.

1.6.4.1. Quantitative Research

The quantitative research is based on the use of official statistics and quantitative data collected by way of self-administered surveys filled in by practitioners (i.e. judges, clerks, lawyers, bailiffs, and ECC offices) in England, France, Italy, and Romania.

The official statistics provided by national authorities as well as data published in the European Commission reports were used as a starting point in the collection of data and the development of the research approach. As historical data series are not always available for both European procedures, and are at times incomplete, additional research methods had to be considered.

establishing a European Small Claims Procedure (Commission ESCP Report), COM(2013) 795 final, Brussels, 19.11.2013; European Commission, *Report from the Commission to the European Parliament, the Council and the European Economic and Social Committee on the application of the Regulation (EC) No 1896/2006 of the European Parliament and of the Council creating a European Order for Payment Procedure* (Commission EOP Report), COM(2015) 495 final, Brussels, 13.10.2015; Velicogna, Lupo & Mellone (2016); Hess (2017).

63 On the mixed method of research combining qualitative and quantitative methods, see Bryman (2012), at 627–650; Spicer (2012), at 479–490.

The surveys seek to collect additional data to be added to information provided by official statistics. This regards the frequency with which the EOP and the ESCP are used by practitioners and applied by the courts in the analysed jurisdictions, as well as a number of related aspects (e.g. appreciation of familiarity with the EOP/ESCP, procedural timeframe, service method used, challenge of the decision, representation, and appreciation of the procedures). For this purpose, the surveys rely partly on closed questions. In these cases, the respondent is required to provide a quantitative reply or to choose between pre-determined answers (i.e. Likert scale).

In preparing the survey questionnaires, a trial was conducted as part of a field research project on the use of the ESCP in the Netherlands.[64] The research was carried out in 2012 with a number of Dutch courts, and led to an adjustment of the questionnaires' format.

The EOP and ESCP surveys were made available online through a dedicated website, with a version in the official language of each of the investigated legal systems being made available.

Initially, the research design aimed to administer the surveys on the basis of a representative sample of courts and practitioners. They should have been chosen with the assistance of the Ministry of Justice and/or professional bodies, but this approach was impossible because the Ministry of Justice and the Councils of the Judiciary[65] as well as other professional bodies in the selected jurisdictions were unable to assist in the sampling.

Based on the available official statistical data that the Ministries of Justice or Councils of the Judiciary were able to provide, the use of the EOP and the ESCP in England, France, Italy, and Romania is quite modest in comparison to other domestic procedures employed in uncontested or small value debt recovery. Hence, addressing a random selection of courts and/or practitioners did not make sense. Replies were often negative, as courts or practitioners often indicated that they had no or very little experience with these EU instruments. For this reason, invitations to participate in the research were sent to all national professional organisations. Their assistance was requested to disseminate the research-related information to their members, who in turn were asked to share their views and experiences. In addition, personal invitations were sent to individual practitioners and courts for which there was an indication or reference that they had experience with these European uniform procedures. With regard to courts, the choice was often based on criteria such as the size of the court, the importance of the region where the court is situated for economic activities, and the geographical location.

The quantitative data included are documented as well as possible according to national realities, but their soundness and their limitations do not allow any inferences. As a result, the research focuses particularly on the qualitative results.

64 On this research approach and results, see Kramer & Onţanu (2013), at 323–327; Kramer & Onţanu (2014), at 10–12.

65 The notion of 'Council of the Judiciary' is used in a general manner to designate the professional body that represents the interest of judges and/or clerks within the national legal systems.

1.6.4.2. Qualitative Research

The qualitative research relies on the surveys' open questions, the semi-structured interviews, the correspondence exchanges with English, French, Italian and Romanian practitioners, and case files analysis in Romania.[66]

The open questions included in the online surveys offered respondents the possibility of providing additional input and comments. This choice was made in order to maximise the amount of data that could be collected from national courts, practitioners, and the ECCs.

The semi-structured interviews were conducted mostly over the phone or by ICT means, and, occasionally, in person by the researcher.[67] This choice of telephone or ICT for interviews was determined by the ease of making arrangements in this format, thereby avoiding special approvals to visit institutional premises in some instances as well as keeping travel costs low and taking into account time constraints. The interviews targeted practitioners who are experienced in using and applying the EOP and/or the ESCP. The interviews are based on an interview guide that was adjusted prior to each interview based on the competences of the interviewees and their experience with one or both European uniform procedures. This laid the basis of the discussion that was always conducted in the official language of the justice system in which the interviewee carried out his professional activity (English, French, Italian, or Romanian). During the interviews, the researcher made notes on the discussion and answers provided. When permission was given by the interviewee, the discussion was recorded and later transcribed.

1.6.4.3. Method of Analysis

The quantitative and qualitative data collected through various methods are not reasonably large enough to allow a meaningful analysis through statistical methods. Additionally, the sample of participants is not suitable for making inferences that would extend the obtained results to the entire territory of the analysed jurisdictions and for all the members of a particular legal profession.

In order to analyse the empirical data gathered, qualitative analysis software – ATLAS.ti – was used. Surveys, interview notes and transcripts, correspondence exchanges, and case file notes were uploaded into the software. Before the data began to be coded,[68] a series of thematic codes were established and defined. During the coding process, an additional number of open codes were established and defined. The open codes are relevant aspects of the analysis, although they were not part of the initial coding framework; however, they provide additional information and perspectives with regard to the analysed topics, and they enrich the findings. During the coding process,

66 On the reasons that triggered a different approach in Romania, see Section 6.7.3.1.

67 For additional methodological aspects regarding research based on semi-structured interviews, see Bryman (2012), at 468–496; Lawless, Robbennolt & Ulen (2010), at 80–82.

68 On data coding, see Rivas (2012), at 365–371; Bryman (2012), at 565–578; Yin (2011), at 176–190; Boeije (2010), at 93–114.

memos and notes were also drafted to facilitate subsequent analysis of the data. These included comments, impressions, and connections that appeared during the coding process and that were relevant for analysis of the data.

The results of the empirical research are presented in a descriptive manner, seeking correlations between findings in each national system as well as in a comparative approach. Possible explanations and interpretations of the findings are explored. The results of the data analysis are then triangulated in two steps: first, with the findings resulting from the domestic case law analysis and statistical data; and second, with results from other studies regarding different aspects of the EOP and the ESCP that had been published during the data collection and analysis period of the present research. Triangulation is used in order to cross-check and corroborate the results from different sources for consistency.[69] This can further strengthen the validity of the findings, as the sample of respondents is relatively modest and cannot be the basis for any inference regarding generalisation.

Lastly, for the purpose of simplicity, the pronoun 'he' is used throughout the analysis of the empirical data, although women were well represented among legal practioners who responded to the surveys and/or who were interviewed.

1.7. Outline

This book seeks to create a clearer image as to how the EOP and the ESCP function in practice in the selected Member States, and the extent to which they succeed in providing effective enforcement mechanisms that do not trade off the procedural rights of parties involved in cross-border litigation.

Chapter 2 focuses on the features of the EOP and the ESCP, analysing their characteristics, the standards they establish in cross-border litigation, and their interaction with national procedural rules from an EU perspective. It also provides an overview of the political background that led to the adoption of the first two European uniform procedures.

Chapters 3–6 carry out a multi-level comparative and empirical analysis on the implementation and application of the EOP and the ESCP in England, France, Italy, and Romania. The functioning of the European uniform procedures is explored within the national procedural systems, and in relation to functionally equivalent domestic procedures. The analysis focuses on the implementation of the EOP and the ESCP within the domestic procedural system and practice, on the perceptions and expectations of stakeholders and scholars with regard to the European procedures, and on the use of the instruments in practice. Statistical data, case law, and empirical data are scrutinised together. The findings are triangulated to provide a wider picture of the way the EOP and the ESCP function and manage to secure the protection of parties' rights.

Chapter 7 compares the national findings from Chapters 3–6. It analyses whether the EOP and the ESCP improve the process of cross-border litigation in providing

[69] Triangulation is an analytical technique used to corroborate findings with evidence from two or more different sources. See Yin (2011), at 81–82 and 313.

effective and efficient enforcement mechanisms while protecting parties' procedural rights. The analysis criteria and the perspective of the assessment are explained in this chapter.

Chapter 8 contains a synthesis of the findings as well as a follow-up on the implications that the legal standards established by the EOP and the ESCP have for future developments aimed at simplifying cross-border enforcement and harmonising civil procedure in the European Union. In concluding, the chapter addresses ongoing developments in the area, and their importance for simplifying cross-border enforcement, facilitating parties' access to justice, and consolidating European civil justice.

Chapter 2

A EUROPEAN PERSPECTIVE ON THE EOP AND THE ESCP

2.1. Historical Background

The European Union has adopted a number of regulations in the area of civil justice with the aim of simplifying cross-border litigation, reducing its costs, and providing legislative tools that will facilitate access to justice for businesses and consumers. The regulatory and procedural diversity among the national systems can lead to an 'enforcement deficit' within the internal market.[70] In cross-border litigation, the diversity of civil procedure rules may result in significantly lengthier proceedings, disproportionate costs of court actions, and cumbersome procedures. In addition, it may also require the employment of legal practitioners in more than one jurisdiction. The situation is even more challenging for creditors when cross-border cases face more procedural requirements, while purely domestic claims benefit from rapid recovery instruments. Consumers and small- and medium-sized businesses are particularly sensitive to these hurdles related to cross-border litigation. This can easily dissuade them from taking action, thus limiting their access to justice, especially for uncontested and small value claims.

The Conclusions of the Tampere European Council emphasised the need for improved access to justice, mutual recognition of judicial decisions, and greater convergence in civil law.[71] For this purpose, the adoption of new procedural legislation for cross-border cases, including for uncontested and small value claims, was considered.[72] The Council Draft Programme for Mutual Recognition underlined the priority of abolishing the exequatur for uncontested claims in order to promote the rapid recovery of outstanding payments and to simplify and speed up cross-border litigation in small claims, especially for consumers.[73] The 2002 Green Paper argued that there is a need for EU procedures concerning these type of claims, pointing to the excessive costs, delays, and complexity of domestic procedures when the claims are not disputed as to their merits or are of small

70 Tulibacka (2009), at 1529; Andenas (2005), at 8.
71 Tampere European Council, 15–16 October 1999, Presidency Conclusions, no. 28–39.
72 Tampere European Council, 15–16 October 1999, Presidency Conclusions, no. 30. See also Kramer (2010), at 18.
73 European Council, Draft Programme of Measures for Implementation of the Principle of Mutual Recognition of Decisions in Civil and Commercial Maters, OJ C12/1, 15.01.2000.

value.[74] Further, as well as the available national solutions, the Paper investigated the possible features and procedural models that would be suitable for the new procedures. This formed the basis for the European Commission proposal for the adoption of two regulations in 2004 and 2005. The Regulations seek to address some of the bottlenecks in cross-border litigation (e.g. complexity, costs, lengthy proceedings, the need for legal representation in various systems, and enforcement) in order to create a level playing field in this area of law and to enhance effective enforcement.[75] Recital 6 EOP emphasises that the swift and efficient recovery of outstanding uncontested debt is of 'paramount importance for the economic operators' in the EU, as late payments threaten the survival of their businesses, especially in the case of small and medium-size companies. In the same way, Recitals 7 and 8 ESCP underline the need to provide access to justice by introducing a procedure that will limit the obstacles and complexities that small value claims can incur in cross-border litigation, especially as these may be relevant for consumer actions.

The EOP and the ESCP became applicable on 12 December 2008 and 1 January 2009, respectively.[76] The Regulations do not replace or harmonise national procedures, but coexist with them.[77] Through the abolition of exequatur, these optional procedures sought to simplify, speed up, and reduce the costs of litigation, as well as to secure the free circulation of judicial decisions issued between Member States. The latter aim has lost its significance, however, now that the exequatur has been abolished in the meantime under the Brussels *Ibis* Regulation as well.

Following several years of EOP and ESCP application, the European Commission initiated an assessment of the impact and the implementation of these two European uniform procedures in the Member States.[78] The evaluation focused on the achievements reached in facilitating cross-border enforcement, in guaranteeing the parties' procedural rights, in securing access to justice, and in identifying aspects that can further improve the functioning of these procedures. The 2013 Deloitte Report on the ESCP revealed that despite the expected benefits the procedure might bring, the instrument is underused and still little known.[79] The subsequent European Commission Report stated that the regulation generally improved, simplified, and accelerated the handling of small cross-border claims, but shortcomings remained. Users need to be become more familiar with the procedure. The identified deficiencies and difficulties have to be remedied (e.g. lack of free assistance for the parties, difficulties in filling in the forms, type of methods available

74 Green Paper on a European Order for Payment Procedure and on measures to simplify and speed up small claims litigation, COM(2002) 746 final, Brussels, 2012, 2002, at 10–11 and 59–60.

75 European Commission, Proposal for a Regulation of the European Parliament and of the Council creating a European order for payment procedure, COM(2004) 173 final, Brussels, 19.03.2004, at 6; European Commission, Proposal for a Regulation of the European Parliament and of the Council establishing a European Small Claims Procedure, COM(2005) 87 final, Brussels, 15.03.2005, at 3–5.

76 Article 33 EOP, Article 29 ESCP.

77 See also Tulibacka (2009), at 1544.

78 In 26 Member States. The EOP and the ESCP do not apply to Denmark (Recital 32 EOP and Recital 38 ESCP). Lastly, Croatia became a Member State only in July 2013.

79 *Assessment of the socio-economic impacts of the policy options for the Future of the European Small Claims Regulation* (Deloitte Report), Final Report, RDT-L05–2010, Deloitte, Brussels, 19.07.2013.

to pay the court fees, and deficiencies in practical information regarding application of the procedure).[80]

Like the earlier ESCP Reports, the 2015 EOP Report recognises a limited use of the procedure. The European Commission remains nonetheless highly positive as to the function of the EOP, stating that it functions 'in a sound and satisfactory manner'.[81] However, in practice, difficulties are encountered at different levels, as revealed by national findings in the following chapters and in CJEU case law. Various national courts have referred preliminary questions to the CJEU on the interpretation of provisions of the EOP Regulation and their interaction with national procedural rules.[82] Surprisingly, the report only acknowledges them indirectly by underlining a need to improve the function of the procedure through 'non-legislative and implementation measures'.[83]

Acknowledging the difficulties, the European Commission proposed structural amendments of the ESCP, while only marginally addressing the EOP, which underwent a single technical modification. Regulation 2015/2421 explicitly links the EOP to the ESCP, enabling a transfer of an opposed order to the ESCP for a continuation of the proceedings.[84] The Commission seized the moment to bring back into discussion earlier points concerning the ESCP negotiations (e.g. extending the material scope, increasing the threshold, and extending the cross-border definition) as well as taking steps to further the provisions of the Regulation (e.g. making use of the distance communication means compulsory, use of electronic filing, introducing a limitation with regard to court fees, and diminishing the use of translation for Form D).[85] However, many of the proposals were not adopted, while others were set aside for future assessment and review (e.g. considering an extension of the scope of the ESCP to claims for remuneration in cross-border employement disputes).[86] The most substantial reform is that the ESCP will apply to claims up to €5,000.[87] Other changes concern (1) court fees; (2) the use of communication

80 European Commission, *Report from the Commission to the European Parliament, the Council and the European Economic and Social Committee on the application of the Regulation (EC) No. 861/2007 of the European Parliament and of the Council establishing a European Small Claims Procedure* (Commission ESCP Report), COM(2013) 795 final, Brussels, 19.11.2013.

81 European Commission, *Report from the Commission to the Commission to the European Parliament, the Council and the European Economic and Social Committee on the application of the Regulation (EC) No. 1896/2006 of the European Parliament and of the Council creating a European Order for Payment Procedure* (Commission EOP Report), COM(2015) 495 final, Brussels, 13.10.2015, at 12.

82 No preliminary request regarding application of the ESCP rules was referred to the CJEU until October 2016.

83 Commission EOP Report, COM(2015) 495 final, Brussels, 13.10.2015, at 12.

84 See Payan (2014), at 273–274; Guinchard (2014), at 479.

85 Proposal for a Regulation of the European Parliament and of the Council emending Regulation (EC) No 861/2007 of the European Parliament and the Council of 11 July 2007 establishing a European Small Claims Procedure and Regulation (EC) No 1896/2006 of the European Parliament and of the Council of 12 December 2006 creating a European order for payment procedure, COM(2013) 794, Brussels 19.11.2013.

86 Regulation (EU) No 2015/2421 of the European Parliament and of the Council of 16 December 2015 amending Regulation (EC) No 861 establishing a European Small Claims Procedure and Regulation (EC) No 1896/2006 creating a European order for payment procedure, OJ L34, 24.12.2015, at 1.

87 The European Commission initial proposal sought to raise the ESCP threshold to €10,000, but a consensus on this amount could not be reached. Explanatory Memorandum, European Commission

technology, electronic payment of court fees, and the electronic service; (3) minimising translation needs and costs associated with this; (4) providing practical assistance and general information for the parties; and (5) the review procedure. The provisions seek to address the deficiencies and problematic aspects revealed in the ESCP Reports. Regrettably, some amendments that would have been beneficial also in relation to the EOP were not extended to this procedure as well (e.g. minimising translation needs for Form G; general information for the parties; and the review procedure).[88] It remains to be seen whether in practice the new ESCP provisions will achieve the desired results. A positive outcome could create grounds for a similar modification of the relevant EOP provisions. However, for the moment, the amended provisions applying from 14 July 2017 require action at the national level in order to facilitate their application and coordination with national procedural rules.[89] This is paramount for an effective functioning of both European uniform procedures, which until now have registered little use.

2.2. Main Features of the EOP and the ESCP

The EOP and the ESCP are the first uniform procedures created as an alternative to national procedures for parties seeking to recover uncontested monetary and small value claims in cross-border litigation. Though different procedures, both Regulations share a number of common features that contribute to their aim of simplifying and speeding up litigation in cross-border cases, and reducing the associated costs.[90] This section will discuss these points, analysing their impact on the application of these instruments and the expected developments.

2.2.1. Scope

Irrespective of the nature of the court or tribunal, the application of EOP and ESCP procedures is limited to civil and commercial matters. The EOP is available for the collection of pecuniary claims that have fallen due at the time of the application. The ESCP is not limited to monetary claims, but non-monetary claims have to be valued for the court to be able to assess whether the application falls within the scope of the Regulation.[91] In contrast to the EOP, the ESCP is limited to claims whose value does not exceed €2,000 at the time the court receives the application.[92] This threshold increased to €5,000 from 14 July 2017,[93] as the present value was perceived to 'severely' limit the

Proposal for a Regulation amending Regulation (EC) No 861/2007 of the European Parliament and the Council of 11 July 2007 establishing a European Small Claims Procedure and Regulation (EC) No 1896/2006 of the European Parliament and of the Council of 12 December 2006 creating a European order for payment procedure, COM(2013) 794 final, Brussels, 19.11.2013, at 5–6.

88 See Payan (2014), at 241–281; Guinchard (2014), at 479–481.

89 Article 3 Regulation 2015/2421.

90 Recital 9 and Article 1(1) EOP; Recital 8 and Article 1 ESCP.

91 Article 5(5) ESCP. See also Kramer (2011), at 121.

92 Article 2(1) ESCP. This excludes interests, expenses, and possible disbursements.

93 As the €2,000 limit, the new threshold is the result of a compromise. Council of the European Union, Information Note, 12357/15, Brussels, 12 October 2015, Interinstitutional File 2013/0403 (COD). The

availability of the procedure for SMEs.[94] The increase corresponds to a national trend regarding domestic small claims that saw their thresholds increase after adoption of the first text of the ESCP Regulation.[95] This increase could also help parties retain some interest with regard to the ESCP compared to domestic small claims procedures that have a broader scope.[96]

The material scope of the two Regulations corresponds largely to that of the Brussels I Regulation (now Brussels I*bis*).[97] They do not apply to revenues, customs, or administrative matters, or to the liability of the State for acts and omissions in the exercise of the State authority (*acta iure imperii*).[98] Further, both Regulations exclude from their scope the (1) rights in property arising out of matrimonial relationship, wills, and succession; (2) bankruptcy; and (3) social security. In addition, the EOP does not apply to claims arising from non-contractual obligations, unless these have been subject to an agreement or an admission of debt, or they relate to liquidated debts arising from the joint ownership of property. Similarly, the ESCP does not apply to matters related to (1) the status or legal capacity of natural persons; (2) arbitration; (3) employment law; (4) tenancies in immovable property, with the exception of actions on monetary claims; and (5) violation of privacy and of rights relating to personality, including defamation, are excluded from its scope.[99] The exclusion from the scope of the EOP of claims arising from non-contractual obligation, unless subject to an agreement or an admission, or debts arising from joint ownership, has been considered 'unnecessarily complicated'.[100] Practice data do not provide any evidence as to the use of the EOP in relation to fixed tortuous claims.[101] As regards the ESCP, the amendment resulting from Regulation 2015/2421 achieved only an increase in the procedure threshold. In addition, it detailed some of the matters excluded from its scope (i.e. matters arising out of relationships that are considered to have effects similar to matrimonial relations, maintenance, and succession). The rapporteur of the European Parliament on the Commission's proposal recommended an extension of the material scope of the Regulation to claims for violation

initial proposal for amending the text aimed to establish the limit of ESCP to €10,000. Subsequently, an agreement was reached within the Council to increase the threshold to €4,000. See Proposal, Interinstitutional File 2013/0403 (COD), COM(2013) 794 final; Council of the European Union, Note, General Approach, 15841/14, Brussels, 24 November 2014, Interinstitutional File 2013/0403 (COD), at 3.

94 Commission ESCP Report, COM(2013) 795 final, Brussels, 19.11.2013, at 3. The threshold was previously considered insufficient also by the European Economic and Social Committee in view of the value of goods and services. Opinion of the European Economic and Social Committee on the Proposal for a Regulation of the European Parliament and of the Council establishing a European Small Claims Procedure, OJ C88/61, 11.4.2006, point 6.1. The value was a significant point of debate during negotiations involving the first text. See Kramer (2011), at 121; Kramer (2008), at 360–361.

95 Commission ESCP Report, COM(2013) 795 final, Brussels, 19.11.2013, at 3; Explanatory Memorandum, COM(2013) 794 final, Brussels, 19.11.2013, at 6.

96 See also Guinchard (2016), at 436–437.

97 The EOP and the ESCP are more limited in scope than the Brussels I*bis* Regulation. See Berthe (2014), at 303–306; Oro Martinez (2016), at 105–106.

98 Article 2(1) EOP. Article 2(1) ESCP.

99 Article 2(2) EOP. Article 2(2) ESCP.

100 Kramer (2010), at 21; Kramer & Sujecki (2006), at 368.

101 On national practice, see further Sections 3.7, 4.7, 5.7 and 6.7.

of privacy and the right of personality. An extension of the material scope of the ESCP would have been particularly beneficial for weaker parties (e.g. violation of privacy and rights related to personality, or for employees bound by cross-border employment agreements),[102] but no political agreement in this regard could be reached. However, the text does set a duty on the Commission to evaluate this possibility by 2022, particularly in relation to employment law matters.[103]

As will be clear from the next chapters, the material scope of the European uniform procedures is generally more limited than that of similar national procedures in England, France, Italy, and Romania.

2.2.2. Cross-Border Claims

The EOP and the ESCP apply only to cross-border cases.[104] This limitation is a consequence of Article 65 EC Treaty (present Article 81 TFEU), according to which measures have to concern cases having 'cross-border implications'. Although in the initial proposals the European Commission sought an application of the EOP and the ESCP to cross-border as well as domestic cases, the European Parliament and the majority of the Member States did not favour a solution that would extend to purely internal cases.[105] In practice, this results in cross-border and domestic claims being handled differently.

The Regulations contain an identical definition of 'cross-border cases'. The Commission proposal intended to broaden this definition in relation to the ESCP,[106] but negotiations in this regard were not successful, and the provision in Regulation 2015/2421 remained unchanged. Hence, at the moment that a court is seised at least one

102 The rapporteur for the Committee of Affairs of the European Parliament proposed in the draft report of 7 November 2014 the extension of the material scope of the ESCP Regulation to claims for violation of privacy and the right of personality as proposed by the European Commission. Committee of Legal Affairs, European Parliament, Draft Report on the proposal for a regulation of the European Parliament and of the Council amending Regulation (EC) No. 861/2007 of the European Parliament and the Council of 11 July 2007 establishing a European Small Claims Procedure and Regulation (EC) No. 1896/2006 of the European Parliament and of the Council of 12 December 2006 creating a European order for payment procedure (COM(2013)0794 – C7–0414/2013 – 2013/0403(COD)), 2013/0403(COD), 7 November 2014 (available at www.europarl.europa.eu/sides/getDoc.do?pubRef=-//EP//NONSGML +COMPARL+PE-539.630+01+DOC+PDF+V0//EN&language=EN).

103 Article 28 Regulation 2015/2421.

104 Article 3(1) EOP and Article 3(1) ESCP.

105 European Commission, Proposal for a Regulation of the European Parliament and of the Council creating a European order for payment procedure, COM(2004) 173 final, Brussels, 19.03.2004, at 7–8; European Commission, Proposal for a Regulation of the European Parliament and of the Council establishing a European Small Claims Procedure, COM(2005) 87 final, Brussels, 15.03.2005, at 6. Storskrubb (2008), at 203–208 and 220–223; Kramer (2010), at 22.

106 European Commission, Proposal for a Regulation of the European Parliament and of the Council emending Regulation (EC) No. 861/2007 of the European Parliament and the Council of 11 July 2007 establishing a European Small Claims Procedure and Regulation (EC) No. 1896/2006 of the European Parliament and of the Council of 12 December 2006 creating a European order for payment procedure, COM(2013) 794, Brussels 19.11.20113, Explanatory Memorandum, at 6–7. See also Kramer (2016a), at 95; Oro Martinez (2016), at 106–108.

of the parties has to be domiciled or habitually resident in a Member State other than that of the court.[107] This definition raised serious concerns with stakeholders and legal scholars in some of the analysed jurisdictions, and was criticised for being too narrow in the category of cross-border cases.[108] In practice, the feared adverse effects do not seem to have materialised in the analysed jurisdictions, as case law provides no indication of forum shopping in this respect. The Commission ESCP Report has pointed to the uncertainty the cross-border definition creates for some users who expected more cases to be covered by the text (e.g. contracts carried out in a different State, or enforcement in a different Member State).[109] As a consequence, there have been reports of situations in which a cross-border scenario was created artificially in order to benefit from the ESCP by assigning claims to foreign companies. The following chapters do not point to a generalised practice in this regard across the analysed jurisdictions, but there have been situations where the claimant thought to demonstrate that the defendant was actually domiciled in a different Member State in order to make use of the EOP procedure.[110]

2.2.3. *Optional Nature*

The EOP and the ESCP are procedures that are alternatives to available national instruments,[111] in accordance with the principle of proportionality and subsidiarity.[112] They do not seek to harmonise domestic procedures or to take precedence over them. The Regulations do not prevent the claimant from pursuing a claim by making use of any national or European procedure in order to recover the amount owed to him. Hence, when conditions for the application of an EOP or an ESCP are complied with, the creditor may choose to use either of the two procedures, or any national instrument he considers best suited to his claim. The European uniform procedures and the national procedures apply in parallel with regard to cross-border claims. In some jurisdictions the non-compulsory nature of the procedures was a point of discussion and criticism, while in

107 Article 3 EOP and Article 3 ESCP.

108 Kramer (2010), at 22. See further Sections 3.4.2, 4.4.2, and 5.4.2. With regard to the narrow definition of cross-border cases, see Oro Martinez (2016), at 106 and 115. On an opposing perspective on the EOP, see Farina (2012), at 218–220; Lupoi (2010), at 402–403; Bonato (2007), at 210–212; Lopez de Tejada & d'Avout (2007), at 738–743.

109 Commission ESCP Report, COM(2013) 795 final, Brussels, 19.11.2013, at 3–4. A study carried out by the Max Planck Institute identified a case where an Austrian Court applied the ESCP cross-border definition beyond its limits. The parties were domiciled in the same country, but the place of arrival of an international flight was in a different Member State. See Judgment of Bezirksgericht Schwechat of 12 October 2014, 4C 580/11v – 10, in Oro Martinez (2016), at 106–107.

110 See Section 6.7.3, particularly in relation to Tribunalul Bucureşti Files No. 4787/3/2013, 7419/3/2013, 7422/3/2013, 7426/3/2013, 7430/3/2013; and Judecătoria Sectorului 2, Bucureşti, File No. 49185/300/2012.

111 The Commission 2002 Green Paper carried out a comparative analysis of the available national order for payment and small procedures, and of their optional or obligatory nature. See Green Paper on a European Order for Payment Procedure, and on measures to simplify and speed up small claims litigation, COM(2002) 746 final, Brussels, 2012, 2002, at 22 and 53–54.

112 Recital 29 EOP and Recital 36 ESCP.

others, scholars did not perceive it as a problematic aspect.[113] Considering the Member States' sensitive reaction to aspects that could touch upon their sovereignty and procedural autonomy, and in view of the principle of proportionality and subsidiarity on which the European Commission justified its action, it would simply have been impossible to make these procedures compulsory.[114] A proposal aiming to establish compulsory European procedures would never have been accepted. Furthermore, this would have given rise to many discussions and significant problems concerning the adaptation of diverse national procedural systems and the delimitation of competences between the EU and Member States.

2.2.4. Use of Standard Forms

The EOP and the ESCP are meant to be conducted mainly by means of standard forms, with the particularity that a hearing can be held in accordance with the the ESCP procedure when this is required and if the courts consider it necessary. The EOP procedure is based on seven standard forms,[115] and the ESCP on four.[116] For each procedure, the forms have been designed carefully to make them user-friendly. Additionally, the forms include guidelines and short explanations geared to facilitate their being filled in.[117] The model of standard forms chosen for the two procedures differs. The EOP combines the use of open-question boxes with fields containing code boxes that parties have to choose from for specific information, while the ESCP relies on a system of open fill-in and tick boxes. Nonetheless, in both cases the forms rely to a maximum extent on standard text available in all EU official languages. However, the forms sometimes prove to be difficult for laypersons. In practice, the difficulty appears to be most often related to the information and technical details the party needs to provide or choose from rather than to the format of the standard forms.[118]

113 See, for example, the discussion regarding the ESCP in Italy (Section 5.4.2), Pietra (2011), at 311–316; Castellaneta (2009), at 66. On a different perspective, see Kramer (2007), at 35–36 and 61; Haibach (2005), at 596.

114 Recital 29 EOP, Recital 36 ESCP.

115 Annex I, Form A – Claim Form; Annex II, Form B – Request by the Court or Tribunal to Complete and/ or Rectify the Claim Form; Annex III, Form C – Answer Form; Annex IV, Form D – Decision to Reject the Application for a European Order for Payment; Annex V, Form E – European Order for Payment; Annex VI, Form F – Opposition to a European Order for Payment; Annex VII, Form G – Declaration of Enforceability. The forms are attached to the EOP Regulation.

116 Annex I, Form A – Claim Form, Annex II, Form B – Request by the Court or Tribunal to Complete and/ or Rectify the Claim Form, Annex III, Form C – Answer Form, Annex IV, Form D – Certificate concerning a Judgment in the European Small Claims Procedure. The forms are attached to the ESCP Regulation.

117 Kramer (2010), at 23; Kramer (2008), at 362. See also, European Commission *Practice Guide for the Application of the Regulation on the European Order for Payment*, 2011; European Commission, *Practice guide for the application of the European Small Claims Procedure under Regulation (EC) No 861/2007 of the European Parliament and of the Council of 11 July 2007 establishing a European Small Claims Procedure*, 2013.

118 Centre Européen de la Consommation, Zentrum für Europäischen Verbraucherschutz e.V., *Procédure européenne de règlement des petits litiges et injonction de payer européenne. Des procédures simplifiées pas si simples dans la pratique*, 2011, at 5 (available at www.europe-consommateurs.eu/uploads/media/ 4.4.3_procedure_de_reglement_des_petits_litiges.pdf); sections 5.7.2 and 6.7.2. On an opposing

2.2.5. *Non-Mandatory Representation*

Representation by a lawyer is not mandatory in EOP and ESCP procedures.[119] In practice, however, it appears that the services of a legal representative are often used, and professional guidance remains necessary for parties choosing to use these alternative European procedures. Available national case law and studies undertaken regarding the application of these two procedures provide evidence in this regard, and are confirmed by the present study.[120] For example, the Special Eurobarometer 395 found that one third of the respondents who used the ESCP made use of legal representation,[121] even if in this procedure national free assistance should be available for the filling in of forms.[122] This outcome might be influenced by a series of practical matters and/or difficulties such as the impossibility of paying the court fees by distance means;[123] the actual lack of free assistance available for parties in the ESCP procedure; or parties being accustomed to generally using legal representation when compulsory in domestic procedures. The implementation within the national procedural system of free assistance services for the parties has proven problematic, creating tensions between the European provision and internal procedural rules and principles. The Commission ESCP Report reveals that only a few specific arrangements were made in this regard at the national level, and Member States do not consistently provide free-of-charge assistance.[124] The amended Article 11 ESCP rightfully tries to improve this situation by mentioning expressly the type of assistance and information the parties must be provided with by national authorities or organisations. Furthermore, in seeking to eliminate the possible conflicting situation between the ESCP provision and the principle of impartiality that the national judges have to comply with, the text of the new article expressly recognises this is not to take the form of a legal assessment of a particular case or of a duty to offer legal aid.[125]

2.2.6. *Abolition of Exequatur*

Both procedures seek to facilitate the free circulation of judgments between Member States by laying down minimum standards that would render intermediary enforcement-related activities unnecessary. The abolition of exequatur was an important development

result, with respondents considering use of the ESCP application form easy, see Special Eurobarometer 395, *European Small Claims Procedure*, Report, April 2013, at 76.

119 Article 32 EOP and Article 10 ESCP.

120 See further Sections 3.7, 4.7, 5.7, and 6.7 for the national perspective in the analysed jurisdictions. See also studies by Ng (2012) (available at www.irsig.cnr.it/BIEPCO/documents/case_studies/EPO_Simulation_Gar_Yein.pdf); Centre Européen de la Consommation, Zentrum für Europäischen Verbraucherschutz e.V., *Procédure européenne de règlement des petits litiges et injonction de payer européenne. Des procédures simplifiées pas si simples dans la pratique*, 2011 (available at www.europe-consommateurs.eu/uploads/media/4.4.3_procedure_de_reglement_des_petits_litiges.pdf); Commission ESCP Report, COM(2013) 795 final, Brussels, 19.11.2013, at 8.

121 Special Eurobarometer 395, *European Small Claims Procedure*, Report, April 2013, at 78.

122 Article 11 in conjunction with Recital 11 ESCP.

123 Commission ESCP Report, COM(2013) 795 final, Brussels, 19.11.2013, at 8.

124 *Ibidem*, at 7.

125 Regulation 2015/2421. See also Sections 4.4.2, 4.7.2, 5.4.2, and 6.4.2.

for the EOP and the ESCP, and a step forward in comparison with the Brussels I Regulation, which at the time of the Regulations' adoption still required an exequatur procedure to be applied. This allowed the judgments issued on the basis of these European procedures to be enforceable in other Member States (except Denmark) without the need for a declaration of enforceability or for a possibility of opposing recognition.[126] The formulation regarding enforcement and recognition is identical in the two Regulations, as well as in the one contained by the European Enforcement Order.[127] In contrast to the Brussels *Ibis* Regulation, which maintains the grounds for refusal at the recognition and enforcement stage, these regulations abolished them, except for the ground pertaining to the irreconcilability of judgments that can be still invoked by an interested party.[128] A certification of the ESCP judgment or a Declaration of enforceability for the EOP will be issued by the court in the Member State of origin.[129] The execution of the decision will be carried out in accordance with the national law of the Member State in which this is enforced, similar to a national judgment. The European Commission EOP and ESCP Reports make no reference to any problems that have been reported following the abolition of exequatur.[130]

2.2.7. Functioning within the National Procedure Context

The EOP and the ESCP are applied and function within the national procedural context. The Regulations establish the main structure of the procedures and the minimum standards that have to be complied with to guarantee a fair trial for the parties. In both cases the text refers to national legislation for a number of procedural aspects that need to be supplemented as well as for matters that are not dealt with specifically by the Regulations.[131] Hence, the procedural law of the Member State in which the claim is filed will continue to govern a number of procedural aspects for which the provisions of the European procedures do not establish a unitary rule or allow for diverse solutions in accordance with the applicable domestic law. This leaves room for national specificities to continue to exist within the framework of a uniform European procedure, maintaining some of the differences it vows to eliminate. However, these differences are not immediately visible to the user, especially a first-time user, as information presented by citizens' guides give a much-simplified vision of the procedure and its implications for the party.[132]

126 Article 1(1)(b) and Article 19 EOP; Article 1(2) and Article 20 ESCP.

127 Mańko (2014), at 17.

128 Article 21 EEO, Article 22 EOP, and Article 22 ESCP. Article 45 Brussels *Ibis* Regulation.

129 Article 18(1) EOP, Article 20(2) ESCP.

130 Commission EOP Report, COM(2015) 495 final, Brussels, 13.10.2015, at 10; Commission ESCP Report, COM(2013) 795 final, Brussels, 19.11.2013, at 6.

131 Article 26 EOP, Article 19 ESCP. Payan (2014), at 246–247; Kramer, (2011), at 128; Oro Martinez (2016), at 111–112; Lopez de Tejada & d'Avout (2007), at 724–725.

132 European Commission, *A Citizens' Guide to Cross-Border Litigation in the European Union*, at 5 and 10–11 (available at http://ec.europa.eu/civiljustice/publications/docs/guide_litiges_civils_transfrontaliers_en.pdf). Further, information presenting the EOP on the e-Justice website mentions that the procedure 'does not require presence before the court. The claimant only has to submit his application,

In seeking to facilitate the access of potential users to relevant aspects that are supplemented by national provisions, the Regulations set a duty on the Member States to communicate a wide range of relevant information (e.g. courts having jurisdiction, means of communication accepted, language requirements for enforcement purposes, and enforcement authorities) to the European Commission, which undertook the task of securing their publication on European dedicated websites. The co-existing various websites on which information on diverse aspects of these European procedures can be found (e.g. courts having jurisdiction, forms, court fees, service of document requirements, and enforcement) as well as the general problem of finding up-to-date information in all official languages of the Member States has created a constant bottleneck for potential users. The latest action in this regard, the continuous adding of information to a single portal – e-Justice Portal – has again affected the availability of information for parties and practitioners who have to identify additional ways to find references to the national procedural law of one or more Member States that are relevant for their case.[133] This is unfortunate for users who for significant periods of time are deprived of straightforward access to necessary information, particularly regarding the national rules that are essential for the initiation of an EOP or an ESCP claim with a local court.

Moreover, the way the EOP and the ESCP are implemented within the analysed jurisdictions is of considerable importance for the way the European uniform procedures function and are applied within the national context. For the ESCP, which is less used than the EOP, the difficulties posed by the differences in its application between Member States have thus far been less visible.[134] A significant EOP example addressing aspects of interaction between the two levels of legislation is the *Szyrocka* case.[135] The case reveals the tension existing between the two levels of legislation, and the importance of the way the EOP is implemented in the national procedural system. This type of interaction and tension also surfaces in the following chapters, indicating the way national courts sometimes have a tendency and feel the need to supplement the requirements set by the Regulation for the issuance of an EOP with additional national requirements. Thus, they transfer onto the EOP the characteristics of an instrument with which they are familiar and with which they assimilate the European uniform procedure in the national procedural system. The judgment of the CJEU is of particular importance, as it affirms the exhaustive nature of the requirements an application has to comply with for the

after which the procedure will lead its own life. It does not require any further formalities or intervention on the part of the claimant' (available at https://e-justice.europa.eu/content_european_payment_order-353-en.do).

133 The updated information was for a significant period not available in all official languages of the EU, being limited mainly to the official language of the Member State concerned. Additionally, the research engines regarding the competent courts in the EOP and ESCP were also not immediately migrated and made available on the e-Justice portal. (available at https://e-justice.europa.eu/content_european_payment_order-353-en.do and https://e-justice.europa.eu/content_small_claims-354-en.do?init=true). A European Court Database is expected to improve the accuracy of the process for the parties to determine the competent court to which the claim should be submitted. However, the service was not operational at EU level on 1 October 2016. Commission EOP Report, COM(2015) 495 final, Brussels, 13.10.2015, at 7.

134 See Deloitte Report, RDT-L05–2010, Part I, Brussels, 19.07.2013, at 63 and 66–67.

135 Case C-215/11, *Iwona Szyrocka v. SiGer Technologie GmbH*, 13 December 2012, ECLI:EU:C:2012:794.

issuance of an EOP. This means that the national judge cannot request the claimant to submit the evidence described in the application form (Form A) on the basis of national legislation,[136] an aspect that is not foreign to national practices in relation to the EOP. Recognising the possibility of adding additional requirements in accordance with national law for the issuance of an EOP would be contrary to the aims of the Regulation and the literal interpretation of the text, and would result in increasing the complexity of the procedure as well as its duration and costs.[137] The reasoning of the CJEU in the *Szyrocka* case – interpreting the provisions of the EOP in the light of preserving the *effet utile* – has been inspiring for some national judges who subsequently followed this reasoning and refer to it in issuing EOP decisions, or in relation to enforcement requests. They have sought in this manner to create a bridge between the two levels of legislation in order to guarantee an effective application of the European procedure in accordance with the aim for which it was established.

2.3. EOP and ESCP: Conduct of Proceedings

2.3.1. The EOP

2.3.1.1. Application

Prior to submitting an application for the issuance of an EOP, the claimant has to identify the court having jurisdiction in accordance with the general rules of the Brussels I Regulation (now Brussels I*bis*). However, a special, more favourable rule was added in the event that the defendant is a consumer. In such cases, only those courts in the defendant's Member State will have jurisdiction.[138] Further, the jurisdiction of the national courts is determined by the internal legislation of the Member State concerned.

An EOP application has to be made in accordance with the requirements set by Article 7 EOP using standard Form A. The CJEU *Szyrocka* judgment is of particular significance for the interpretation of the provisions of Article 7 and the content of the standard forms.[139] Rightfully, as previously mentioned, the Court affirms the exhaustive nature of the requirements with regard to the information the application has to contain and to the way in which the form has to be used.[140] This means that the national judge cannot request the claimant to comply with additional conditions in accordance with national law for the issuance of the order, such as submitting the evidence described in Form A.[141] The possibility of applying national law is expressly referred to in some paragraphs of Article 7 ((2)(c), (3), (5), and (6) EOP).[142] The Regulation is meant to

136 Guinchard (2013a), at 335; Payan (2014), at 264.

137 Case C-215/11, para. 31; Opinion C-215/11, para. 33; Bochove & Onţanu (2013), at 291; Idot (2013), at 50.

138 Article 6(2) EOP. See Guinchard (2012), at 567–568.

139 Case C-215/11.

140 Case C-215/11, para. 36. Bochove & Onţanu (2013), at 335.

141 Guinchard (2013a), at 336.

142 Case C-215/11, para. 28 and 36. See also the Opinion of Advocate General Mengozzi, Case C-215/11, *Iwona Szyrocka v. SiGer Technologie GmbH*, ECLI:EU:C:2012:400, para. 27. See Bochove & Onţanu (2013), at 291; Porchia (2009), at 57.

establish 'a complete and exhaustive list of the requirements' for the delivery of an EOP.[143] However, the text does not harmonise all procedural aspects; hence, based on the principle of procedural autonomy, the court will have to determine a number of procedural matters in accordance with the applicable national law (Article 25(2) EOP), such as the amount of the court fees.[144] Furthermore, in compliance with the principle of effectiveness and equivalence, the national law should not put the claimant in an excessively difficult situation or make it impossible for him to exercise his right.[145] Accordingly, the format of the standard Form A should be interpreted in a manner that would allow the procedure to attain its full effects and purpose.[146] The CJEU interpreted the provisions of Article 7(2)(c) EOP in the light of the objectives of the Regulation. A restrictive interpretation of the standard forms would have deprived the claimant of the possibility of demanding and recovering the entire amount of interest owed on the principal amount, thus dissuading him from using the EOP. This could also possibly force the creditor to launch additional claims or to shift to domestic instruments allowing such a request.[147] Article 7(2)(c) sets no limitations to the associated timeframe. The 'Practice Guide for the European Order for Payment' contains a similar interpretation.[148]

Once the standard application form (Form A) is filled in, it has to be submitted in paper format or by other means of communication accepted by the Member States and available to the courts, as notified to the European Commission.[149] This aspect is regulated by national procedural rules and possible implementation measures adopted for this purpose. According to the European Commission EOP Report, many Member States allow electronic submission of the application,[150] or envisage developing this possibility for the competent courts.[151] In practice, in the analysed jurisdictions, electronic filing is not yet used extensively in the EOP procedure, even when it is available within the ordinary or special national procedures. The reasons for this have mainly to

143 See Explanatory Memorandum, Proposal for a Regulation of the European Parliament and of the Council creating a European order for payment, COM(2004) 173, at 11.

144 Case C-215/11, para. 34.

145 See Bochove & Onţanu (2013), at 291–292; Prechal & Shelkoplyas (2004), at 589–611.

146 Case C-215/11, para. 45. See also Idot (2013), at 50; Bochove & Onţanu (2013), at 292.

147 Case C-215/11, para. 47. Mondini (2014), at 283–284; Idot (2013), at 50; Guinchard (2013a), at 335; Bochove & Onţanu (2013), at 292.

148 Interest can be claimed for a period 'up to the date of payment'. *Practice Guide for the Application of the Regulation on the European Order for Payment*, European Commission, Directorate General for Justice, 2011, at 19 (available at http://bookshop.europa.eu/en/practice-guide-for-the-application-of-the-regulation-on-the-european-order-for-payment-pbDS3211946/?CatalogCategoryID=oDoKABstRQgAAAEj1JEY4e5L). Bochove & Onţanu (2013), at 292.

149 Article 7(5) in conjunction with Article 29(1) c) EOP. For facilitating access to information, the relevant references contained previously by the Judicial Atlas website have been added to the European e-Justice portal. This process temporarily limits the availability of information, an aspect that can lead to difficulties for interested parties until all linguistic versions become available.

150 Czech Republic, Germany, Estonia, France, Lithuania, Austria, Slovenia, Slovak Republic, Finland, Sweden, UK and Cyprus. See Commission EOP Report, COM(2015) 495 final, Brussels, 13.10.2015, at 6.

151 Ireland, Italy, Malta, Portugal. See Commission EOP Report, COM(2015) 495 final, Brussels, 13.10.2015, at 6.

do with technical difficulties. The ICT systems used at the national level are often not designed for non-resident users.[152] The e-Codex pilot project has been testing the filing of EOPs electronically, but at the moment not all Member States have an operational system that allows the electronic sending of an EOP application.[153] Thus, paper-based applications remain the only way to submit EOP applications, due to the technical difficulties and different levels of ICT development in the Member States.

The forms are available on the e-Justice Portal and can be filled in electronically or downloaded to be fill in by hand. To minimise the need for translation and the costs this can involve, the forms' standard text can be translated automatically from one EU language to another in accordance with the requirements of the procedure. Nonetheless, the descriptive parts on evidence, the explanatory statements, and additional information in Form A will still require translation, which can be burdensome for the claimant.

The EOP is a single-sided procedure of a primarily administrative nature. The adopted format is a compromise situated at the crossroads between the 'evidence' and 'non-evidence' national models,[154] seeking to provide maximum efficiency for a speedy, simple, and less costly procedure. Hence, on the basis of the 'non-evidence model', the Regulation does not require the filing of evidence together with the standard application form, but only a description of the evidence available in support of the claim.[155] However, the practice of the national courts has been contradictory in this respect.[156] The national order for payment models or equivalent instruments used in the analysed jurisdictions often clash with the 'non-evidence' procedural model chosen for the EOP.

Lastly, together with the application form, the claimant often needs to provide evidence of having paid the court fees. This is problematic, as court fees and payment methods vary considerably between Member States. This aspect is discussed in the following chapters dedicated to the national practices in England, France, Italy, and Romania. The transparency of the information in this regard has also been problematic,[157] and more efforts are being made at present to make this information available in all EU official languages on the e-Justice Portal.[158] It remains to be seen, however, whether in practice the EOP court fees remain within the limits set by Article 25(1) EOP: in other words, not exceeding the court fees for ordinary civil proceedings.

152 Velicogna, Lupo & Onţanu (2017); Velicogna, Lupo & Mellone (2016); Kramer (2016), at 351; Velicogna, Lupo & Onţanu (2015); Mellone (2014), at 91–92.

153 Some 'sending' Member States part of the project allow an electronic submission of the EOP application for certain potential users (e.g. lawyers, banks, insurance companies, and social security institutions). The possibility is not yet open to the general public.

154 Kramer (2010), at 23; Fiorini (2008), at 455; Lopez de Tejada & d'Avout (2007), at 722–724.

155 Point 10 EOP standard Form A, Annex I EOP. The proof model chosen is to a certain extent softened by the fact the claimant has to provide a description of the evidence on which he bases his claim. See Ferrand, (2005a), at 193–195.

156 See further in Chapters 3, 4, 5, and 6.

157 Commission EOP Report, COM(2015) 495 final, Brussels, 13.10.2015, at 8.

158 https://e-justice.europa.eu/content_court_fees_concerning_european_payment_order_procedure-305-en.do. However, on 1 October 2016 the information was not yet available in all official EU languages, and did not concern all 27 Member States.

2.3.1.2. Examination of the Application

The court seised will have to proceed as soon as possible to examine the form and assess whether it complies with the requirements of Articles 2, 3, 4, 6, and 7 of the Regulation, and whether the claim appears to be founded.[159] Article 8 EOP requires the judge to perform only a compliance check with certain formal requirements (in particular regarding scope, cross-border case, claim for a specific amount that has fallen due, and jurisdiction) and the provision of particular standard information regarding the parties, the type of claim, and the evidence on which the party relies. This will be carried out in accordance with national rules regarding the activity of the judiciary; hence, based on the internal arrangements of each Member State. The competence of the court will be assessed on the basis of the information contained in the application form. Examining the validity of a jurisdiction clause when the claimant indicated in his request the place of performance as basis for jurisdiction of the court may give rise to complex points of law (Article 5(1) Brussels I, now Article 7(1) Brussels I*bis*). As retained by the CJEU and the Advocate General in the *Thomas Cook* case, such a thorough examination can easily go beyond what is required from an examination under Article 8 EOP.[160] In these circumstances, a defendant who is most probably aware that the information in the application form is false has to act within the time limit set for contesting the claim (Article 16 EOP).[161]

Though the assessment can take the form of an automated procedure, verification of the application appears not to be limited to a compliance with the formalities, but will also imply a *prima facie* appreciation of the merits of the claim, and will *inter alia* exclude clearly unfounded claims or inadmissible applications.[162] The way the evaluation of the claim is to be carried out creates tension and uneasiness for practitioners in certain Member States, as it does not fit within the traditions of the national procedural system where generally the judge is reviewing the evidence. Nevertheless, according to the Regulation, a judge should not necessarily carry out the task. The European Commission considers the EOP suited for a full electronic processing that would influence positively the amount of time necessary for the procedure to be conducted.[163] It is questionable though whether the opposition procedure can duly guarantee the defendant's procedural rights and a fair trial in a full electronic processing, considering the problems related to effective service exposed by the *eco cosmetics* case.[164] Furthermore, there is a perception that the right of defence is not sufficiently protected by the EOP.[165] This unease leads to

159 Article 8 EOP.

160 Case C-245/14, *Thomas Cook Belgium NV v. Thurner Hotel GmbH*, 22 October 2015, ECLI:EU:C:2015:715, para. 42. Opinion of Advocate General Cruz Villalón, Case C-245/14, *Thomas Cook Belgium NV v. Thurner Hotel GmbH Case*, 2 July 2015, ECLI:EU:C:2015:442, para. 33.

161 Case C-245/14, para. 39–41.

162 Article 8 in conjunction with Recital 16 EOP.

163 Commission EOP Report, COM(2015) 495 final, Brussels, 13.10.2015, at 7.

164 Joined Cases C-119/13 to C-120/13, *eco cosmetics GmbH & Co. KG v. Virginie Laetitia Barbara Dupuy, Raiffeisenbank St. Georgen reg. Gen. mbH v. Tetyana Bonchyk*, 4 September 2014, ECLI:EU:C:2014:2144.

165 Guinchard (2014), at 480; Lopez de Tejada (2014), at 145; Lopez de Tejada & d'Avout (2007), at 722–723.

claimants being requested to submit the evidence described in Form A as well as a translation in order for the judge to be able to determine whether the claim appears to be founded. Such interpretations and application of the EOP annuls the benefits of the European uniform procedure. This shows a lack of familiarity and understanding of the aims and purpose of this procedure, an aspect that may also be partially triggered by the limited experience of the courts with the EOP in the first years of its application.[166] The European Commission EOP Report denotes a high level of requests to complete or rectify the application (Form B) in some Member States, due to inaccuracies or incomplete information and unpaid court fees.[167] If the requirements set by Article 7 EOP are not met or the ones referred to by Article 8 EOP are complied with only partially, the claimant will be requested to complete or rectify Form A or, respectively, the court may offer to issue the EOP for part of the claim. In setting the time limits for completing or rectifying the claim or establishing the legal consequences for the remaining part of the claim, the provisions of the national law will prevail. Hence, the results of the uniform procedure will unfortunately vary or depend on the national implementation arrangements and/or on the practice of the local courts. Inevitably, this will maintain a diverse handling for similar claims based on the court having jurisdiction, an aspect the EOP sought to overcome.

2.3.1.3. Rejection or Issue of the EOP

The court can reject the claim for a limited number of reasons set by Article 11(1) EOP. As rightfully emphasised by the CJEU in the *Szyrocka* case, additional requirements applicable to similar national procedures are not part of the grounds established by this article for refusing the claimant's application for an EOP (in this case indicating the value of the subject matter in Polish currency for the court to establish the level of court fees in accordance with domestic rules).[168] The rejection will be communicated to the claimant on standard Form D, and will include the reasons as well as further information if the court considers it necessary. This decision is not subject to appeal, but the claimant is not precluded from filing a new EOP or another domestic procedure available within the Member State where the court is situated. Unfortunately, in its evaluation the Commission EOP Report did not take rejected applications into consideration. In fact, no quantification of rejected claims is available at the EU level, although in some jurisdictions (e.g. France) statistics do keep track of them. Sometimes national case law can offer a glimpse into what the reasons were for this outcome, and whether the requirements of national legislation have played a role in it. The way the criteria set by Article 11(1) EOP is interpreted is subject to interaction with national procedural rules. In practice, though seldom, courts have reached unexpected outcomes by interpreting the uniform rules in the light of their own national legislation and proceedings, thereby depriving the claimant of an EOP award (e.g. Romania).

166 Commission EOP Report, COM(2015) 495 final, Brussels, 13.10.2015, at 3–4 and 13–15.

167 *Ibidem*, at 6–7.

168 See Case C-215/11, para. 35. According to Mondini, a practical approach of the court would have been to make use of standard Form B requesting the claimant to convert the amount of the principle from euro into the national Polish currency, zloty. Mondini (2014), at 283. Bochove & Onţanu (2013), at 291.

When the requirements referred to in Article 8 EOP are met, the court has to issue the EOP (Form E) as soon as possible, and normally within a period of 30 days from the lodging of the application. The Commission EOP Report shows that the 30-day period is complied with only by some Member States (Malta, Belgium, Ireland, Germany, Bulgaria, and Lithuania).[169] Of the analysed jurisdictions for this research, France is the Member State that comes closest to this requirement. Reasons for this outcome are revealed in the following chapters, which provide a more detailed picture of the national situation and the evolution of the length of the proceedings.[170] Achieving speedier court proceedings is one of the Regulation's aims, and a positive evolution in this regard can be observed in comparison with the length of the national procedures in the researched jurisdictions. Nonetheless, additional steps need to be taken in order to achieve a further reduction of the timeframe necessary for the issuance of an EOP. The Commission considers this 'absolutely necessary', as a quick recovery of an uncontested monetary claim is seen as having a significant impact on the cash flow of legal entities, especially SMEs.[171] The electronic processing of the claim is seen as a possible solution that will streamline the speedy issuance of the decisions. However, this does not appear to be a feasible solution in the immediate future. This is due to the significant existing difference between the Member States with respect to the use of information technology in submitting applications and handling court proceedings, and the limited access for non-resident users.[172]

The EOP has to contain clear information with regard to the principal, interests, costs, and possible penalties the debtor is required to pay. In the *Szyrocka* case, the CJEU underlines the minimum requirements that need to be provided by the EOP in relation to the interest rate: namely, it has to state clearly the date from which it is claimed and the moment up until which it will accrue. This information will enable the defendant to make an informed decision about the claim. The exact way in which the form is exactly completed in practice remains a matter for the national court to freely decide,[173] giving it the possibility of interpreting the content of the forms in order to preserve the *effect utile* of the procedure, and thereby allowing some level of flexibility in handling the case.[174]

When the requirements referred to in Article 8 EOP are only partly met, the judge will propose an EOP for a smaller amount.[175] In the event the claimant accepts the proposal, the court will issue the EOP for that amount, leaving the remaining amount of the initial claim to be governed by national law. This aspect of Article 10(2) EOP creates different solutions for an aspect that should have been addressed uniformly by the regulation.

169 The report has partial or complete statistical data for the 23 Member States. No information was communicated for Italy, Latvia, and Romania. Croatia became a Member State on 1 July 2013. Commission EOP Report, COM(2015) 495 final, Brussels, 13.10.2015, at 7 and 13–15.

170 An exception is England, where the limited information regarding case law and the lack of detailed statistical information make this difficult to investigate.

171 Commission EOP Report, COM(2015) 495 final, Brussels, 13.10.2015, at 7.

172 Velicogna, Lupo & Onţanu (2015); Velicogna, Lupo & Onţanu (2017).

173 Case C-215/11, para. 58. Opinion C-215/11, para. 87–90.

174 Bochove & Onţanu (2013), at 293.

175 Article 10(1) EOP.

Further, the EOP will need to be served on the defendant, who will be provided with a copy of Form A and Form E together with Form F for opposition purposes. In addition to this, the defendant has to be informed that the EOP was issued based only on the information provided by the claimant, and that he has a choice of paying it or opposing it within a period of 30 days from the moment of service. He will be made aware of the consequences of lodging an opposition.[176] Articles 13 and 14 EOP set two categories of minimum requirements that a valid service has to comply with when carried out in accordance with national law. Notwithstanding that these rules seek to achieve some uniformity as well as to eliminate the use of methods that do not provide sufficient guarantees that service effectively took place, the plethora of methods to choose from can pose problems in practice. National case law and the CJEU *eco cosmetics* judgment are proof of this difficulty.[177] If these minimum rules are not complied with, the balance between the objectives of establishing a speedy and efficient procedure and the rights of defence is undermined.[178]

When documents are not served effectively, the defendant does not have all the information necessary to enable him to decide on the action to take. This is incompatible with the right of defence, and the opposition procedure in Articles 16–17 EOP is inappropriate. Considering these situations, the Commission EOP Report appears overly optimistic when declaring that no major problems were registered, apart from complaints related to the costs of the cross-border service.[179] The implementation measures that accommodated the EOP within the domestic legal systems as well as the practice of the national courts have continued to favour the EOP methods of service that best resemble the familiar national means.[180] This does not appear 'highly effective' in a uniform procedure seeking to simplify and facilitate cross-border litigation.[181] Moreover, information should be clearly provided to indicate that not all methods of service contained in Article 13 and 14 are recognised as valid within all Member States, as well as the fact that in some jurisdictions the claimant himself will be required to arrange service of the EOP on the defendant (e.g. France, Italy). Such national developments and differences are certainly difficult to envisage before initiating the procedure, as the EOP is generally presented as a quick and simple procedure that only requires the claimant to submit the application.[182] Regulation 2015/2421 would have been a good opportunity to simplify this aspect of EOP procedure and to limit the methods of service to ones that

176 Article 12(3)-(4) EOP.

177 Recitals 19–20 EOP. Joined Cases C-119/13 to C-120/13. Velicogna, Lupo & Onţanu (2015); Mellone (2014a), at 282–283; Cultrera (2008), at 714; Romano (2009), at 126–127.

178 Joined Case C-119/13 to C-120/13, para. 37; Opinion of Advocate General Bot, 9 April 2014, Joined Cases C-119/13 to C-120/13, *eco cosmetics GmbH & Co. KG v. Virginie Laetitia Barbara Dupuy, Raiffeisenbank St. Georgen reg. Gen. mbH v. Tetyana Bonchyk*, ECLI:EU:C:2014:248, para. 36–41.

179 Commission EOP Report, COM(2015) 495 final, Brussels, 13.10.2015, at 7.

180 Crifò (2011), at 294; Velicogna, Lupo & Mellone (2016); Velicogna, Lupo & Onţanu (2015).

181 Kramer (2010), at 25; Velicogna, Lupo & Onţanu (2015).

182 EOP general presentation page on the e-Justice website: 'The claimant only has to submit his application, after which the procedure will lead its own life. It does not require any further formalities or intervention on the part of the claimant.' (available at https://e-justice.europa.eu/content_european_payment_order-353-en.do?init=true); European Commission, *A citizens' guide to cross-border litigation in the*

offer full certainty that the order had reached the defendant.[183] Further, when service needs to be carried out abroad, this has to comply with the provisions of the Service Regulation. The language requirements have to be observed for the defendant to be effectively informed in the light of the principle of equality of arms, guaranteeing his right to defence and access to justice, as recognised by Article 6 ECHR and Article 47 of the Charter.[184]

Available case law does not actually provide significant information on the way in which national courts proceed in forementioned case, and whether the compliance with language requirements is accordingly fulfilled. A preliminary request received by the CJEU in January 2017, the *Catlin Europe* case, indicates that at times the defendant might not always be provided with all the necessary information regarding his right to refuse to accept the EOP served when this is drafted in a language the party cannot understand.[185]

Complaints received by the European Commission regarding the costs of cross-border services could be well related to translation expenses and other unexpected costs such as the claimant having to take the necessary steps to serve the defendant. With regard to electronic service of the EOP on the defendant, the report rightfully underlines that this has not become a reality both for legal and technical reasons.[186] The e-Codex pilot project has been testing the electronic filing of EOP applications, and has considered the national differences.[187] However, as long as national procedural rules on electronic service are not in place and functioning, an implementation of EOP provisions in this regard seems precluded, as national rules are the basis on which the European Regulation operates.

Lastly, the court has to ensure that service of the order is carried out in compliance with national law and the minimum standards set by Article 13–15 EOP.[188] This double assessment can be problematic and difficult to carry out by the national judge, especially when the service is carried out cross-border, when the claimant has the duty to serve the EOP, and when the methods provided for in Article 14 EOP have been used. This was the situation in the *eco cosmetics* case, in which the CJEU rightfully pointed out that if service of the order is not carried out in accordance with the minimum standards, the period of 30 days for lodging an opposition does not start to run,[189] and the validity of the declaration of enforcement is affected. Observance of these two standards plays a key role in guaranteeing an equal protection of parties' rights and interests, thus securing

European Union, at 5 and 10–11 (available at http://ec.europa.eu/civiljustice/publications/docs/guide_litiges_civils_transfrontaliers_en.pdf). See further Velicogna, Lupo & Onţanu (2015).

183 However, the European Commission focused primarily on amending the ESCP procedure and, at the moment of its publication, the EOP Report was not yet available. The proposal aimed to link together the EOP and the ESCP in order to facilitate to a certain extent application of the ESCP.

184 Onţanu & Pannebakker (2012), at 176–177.

185 Article 8(1) Service Regulation. Case C-21/17, *Catlin Europe SE v O.K. Trans Praha spol. s.r.o.*, 18 January 2017, Application.

186 Commission EOP Report, COM(2015) 495 final, Brussels, 13.10.2015, at 8.

187 Velicogna, Lupo & Mellone (2016).

188 Article 12(5) EOP. See Lopez de Tejada & d'Avout (2007), at 726–727.

189 See in this respect the Joined Cases C-119/13 to C-120/13, para. 41–43.

their access to justice.[190] The CJEU decision stresses the importance of this verification by the national court before declaring the EOP enforceable, assuring itself at least of the fact that the method of service used was properly employed, if not of the effective informing of the defendant.[191]

2.3.1.4. Opposition and Review

Opposition is an essential mechanism for a defendant who is not made aware of the request for an EOP before the order is served on him. As underlined in *Goldbet Sportwetten GmbH v. Massimo Sperindeo*,[192] considering the non-adversarial nature of the EOP, the opposition is 'to compensate for the fact that the system established by Regulation No. 1896/2006 does not provide for the defendant's participation in the (...) procedure'.[193] Hence, this creates a balance between the rights and interests of the two sides.[194]

Following service of the EPO, the defendant has 30 days to send Form F back to the court, opposing the order.[195] The form has to be submitted to the court in the same manner as the application form.[196] Form F has a fully standardised text that should not create any difficulty for the defendant, irrespective of the language of the proceedings. The e-Justice Portal automatically translates the forms that are available in all the EU official languages. The defendant only needs to fill in data not affected by translation requirements (i.e. his personal details, the statement of opposition, the date of opposition, and his signature). No reasons for the opposition have to be provided at this stage. However, even if together with the form the defendant has put forward arguments related to the substance of the case, the opposition cannot produce effects other than those deriving from Article 17(1) EOP, termination of the European procedure, and transfer to the ordinary civil proceedings, unless the claimant has explicitly requested that proceedings be terminated. The format of the standard opposition form (Form F) is relevant in this regard. Additionally, Article 16(2) EOP expressly provides that the defendant does not have 'to specify the reasons' for opposing the order. A simple action is sufficient, as underlined in *Thomas Cook Belgium NV v. Thurner Hotel GmbH*.[197] The CJEU ruled in *Goldbet* and *Flight Refund Ltd v. Deutsche Lufthansa AG*[198] that a contrary

190 Velicogna, Lupo & Onţanu (2015); Velicogna, Lupo & Onţanu (2017).

191 Payan (2014a), at 298–299.

192 Case C-144/12, *Goldbet Sportwetten GmbH v. Massimo Sperindeo*, 13 June 2013, ECLI:EU:C:2013:393.

193 Case C-144/12, para. 29–30. Opinion of Advocate General Bot, 6 March 2013, Case C-144/12, *Goldbet Sportwetten GmbH v. Massimo Sperindeo*, ECLI:EU:C:2013:136, para. 30–31.

194 Lopez de Tejada (2014), at 145; Payan (2013); Nourissat (2013), at 15–16.

195 However, Recital 23 EOP invites courts to consider any other form of written opposition if it is expressed in a clear manner. This is in line with the aim of the Regulation, but might prove difficult to achieve in practice, as national practice has shown (see Sections 4.7.3 and 5.7.3). Guinchard (2012), at 577.

196 Article 16(4) EOP. See also Section 2.3.1.1.

197 Case C-245/14, *Thomas Cook Belgium NV v. Thurner Hotel GmbH*, 22 October 2015, ECLI:EU:C:2015:715, para. 40.

198 Case C-144/12, para. 38, 41 and 43; Case C-94/14, *Flight Refund Ltd v. Deutsche Lufthansa AG*, 10 March 2016, ECLI:EU:C:2016:148, para 47.

interpretation – considering the opposition as an entrance into appearance within the meaning of Article 24 Brussels I (now Article 26(1) Brussels I*bis*), when not containing a challenge of the jurisdiction of the court – would extend the effects of the statement of opposition beyond those established by the Regulation.[199] This would have an effect contrary to the simplification the EOP aims to achieve, and create uncertainty as to the effects of the opposition on the basis of its content and format.[200] In the *Goldbet* ruling, the CJEU insists on the difference that has to be made between EOP procedure and ordinary court proceedings in the Member State of origin.[201] The subsequent proceedings following opposition might even be conducted before a court different than the one competent to handle the EOP application. Thus, a challenge of the jurisdiction of the court should be possible after the opposition, and should be carried out before the court handling the second procedure. A statement of opposition including arguments on the substance of the case is not 'intended to serve as a framework for a defence on the merits (…) but to enable the defendant to contest the claim'.[202] An opposite interpretation would be contrary to the objectives of this mechanism and its purpose. In practice, the Commission EOP Report reveals a limited use of the opposition, although the levels differ between Member States.

After the opposition, and unless the claimant has explicitly requested that the proceedings be terminated, they will continue before the competent court in accordance with the rules of ordinary procedure.[203] As ruled by the CJEU in the *Flight Refund* case, and noted by the Advocate General, neither Article 17(1) EOP nor any other article of the Regulation establishes the powers and obligations of the national court, and particularly in relation to determining the competent courts in the Member State of origin. Based on Article 26 EOP, this transfer is governed by the law of the Member State where the procedure is taking place.[204] The implementation paths undertaken by the national legislators have led to various arrangements in the 27 Member States. This concerns the activities the parties and the court are required to undertake, the way the transfer operates, whether this is subject to specific rules or whether national legislation is applied by analogy, and deciding upon their international jurisdiction in the light of the provisions of the EOP and Brussels I*bis* Regulations. This diversity does not appear highly effective for a uniform procedure, however, especially as the information available for the parties is limited, and the Member States have no specific duty to provide clear updated references on this aspect. Though Regulation 2015/2421 was not intended to review the EOP Regulation as such, it would have been a good opportunity to address these aspects and to provide additional clarifications. The amended Article 17(1)(b) providing for a transfer of the opposed EOP to 'any appropriate national civil procedure'

199 Case C-144/12, para. 32. Payan (2014), at 272–273.

200 See also the reasoning on the principle of legal certainty made by Advocate General Bot, Opinion C-144/12, ECLI:EU:C:2013:136, para. 43–45.

201 They do not represent 'the same procedure'. Case C-144/12, para. 39. For a similar view, see Opinion C-144/12, para. 32, 36. See also Payan (2013); Payan (2014), at 273; Lopez de Tejada (2014), at 143–144.

202 Case C-144/12, para. 40.

203 Article 17(1) EOP.

204 Case C-94/14, para. 56; Opinion of Advocate General Sharpston, 22 October 2015, Case C-94/14, *Flight Refund Ltd v. Deutsche Lufthansa AG*, ECLI:EU:C:2015:723, para. 72.

has the potential of leading to even more diverse national approaches, which will add to the complexity confronting a claimant in a procedure that is supposed to be simple and uniform across Member States. Practices may also be at variance with each other at the national level if the implementation and accommodation of the EOP within the national procedural system has been accompanied by clear rules and guidelines for the courts to follow. Although the transfer following opposition has proven highly problematic in some jurisdictions (e.g. Italy), the Commission EOP Report surprisingly fails to recognise and address this aspect.[205] Such difficulties, coupled with the diversity of national solutions and arrangements, tend to have a hindering effect on parties' access to justice rather than actually achieving a simplified and unitary practice across the European Union.

After expiry of the opposition period, in exceptional instances the defendant will be entitled to a review, as is listed exhaustively in Article 20 EOP.[206] The national law governs the review procedure and establishes the courts competent to handle it.[207] Thus, the implementation of this mechanism is sensitive to the particularities of the national procedural rules[208] and format.[209]

The CJEU has interpreted Article 20 EOP strictly.[210] Failure to observe the time limit for lodging a statement of opposition due to the negligence of the defendant's representative is neither an 'extraordinary' nor an 'exceptional' situation within the meaning of Article 20(1)(b) or Article 20(2) EOP.[211] Allowing a review in such circumstances would be equivalent to giving the defendant a second opportunity to oppose the claim within the meaning of Recital 25 EOP.[212] Further, the CJEU did not agree with the application by analogy of the review procedure (Article 20 EOP) in order to safeguard the right of defence in the *eco cosmetics* case.[213] It chose instead to stress that the review procedure is applicable 'in exceptional cases' as enumerated exhaustively in Article 20, and a failure to secure an effective service was not listed among these. Consequently, national law should provide the defendant with a mechanism that would allow him to raise such an irregularity in accordance with Article 26, as the EOP Regulation is silent in this regard.[214] Regrettably, this decision sends parties to the fragmented remedies provided by national law, under which it does not automatically

205 Commission EOP Report, COM(2015) 495 final, Brussels, 13.10.2015, at 9.

206 Joined Cases C-119/13 to C-120/13, para 44. The review does not mean the defendant is given a second opportunity to oppose the claim (Recital 25 EOP).

207 Article 29(1)(b) EOP.

208 Guinchard (2012), at 580.

209 A standard form for review could be a welcome development for a uniform procedure, but this might be difficult to achieve if various national approaches govern this mechanism.

210 Case C-324/12, Novotech-Zala, Order of the Court of 21 March 2013, ECLI:EU:C:2013:205; Joined Cases C-119/13 to C-120/13; Case C-245/14.

211 Case C-324/12. According to Nourrisat, the three cumulative conditions that 'extraordinary circumstances' must comply with are: the party is prevented from opposing the EOP within the time limit, there is no fault on his part, and he acts promptly. Nourrisat (2013a), at 16.

212 Case C-324/12, para. 21–22.

213 See Hess & Raffelsieper (2015), at 401–402.

214 Joined Case C-119/13 to C-120/13, para. 46.

guarantee a higher level of protection of the defendant's procedural rights.[215] This is another blow to the uniformity and efficiency of the procedure. In practice, it is likely that the defendant will need to employ the services of a legal representative, as no specific information on this aspect of the procedure is available on the dedicated websites.[216]

An alternative interpretation by the Court, possibly based on the provision in Article 20(1)(b) EOP ('extraordinary circumstances without fault' on the part of the defendant), would have facilitated a uniform application of the EOP, common to all 27 Member States, and would not have resulted in a practical difficulty in individualising the correct national procedure to use for this purpose.[217] There is a high probability that the implementation process of the European uniform procedure within the national procedural system has not considered *a priori* such situations; hence, it will be up to the judges and legal representatives to find a common solution within their national legislation in order to provide the protection required by the CJEU Judgment. Furthermore, as the Regulation does not recognise, according to the CJEU, the right of the defaulting defendant to request the re-opening of a case on the basis of a faulty service, an amendment of the EOP would be desirable in order to ensure a uniform mechanism for the parties to raise such irregularities.[218] In this regard, the decision of the CJEU in the *Catlin Europe* case might be able to provide additional clarification.[219]

Though this step would have enhanced the consistency of the European procedure, Regulation 2015/2421 was not meant to clarify the review conditions for the EOP, nor to stream the methods of service and thereby eliminating the ones most criticised.[220] In *Thomas Cook Belgium NV v. Thurner Hotel GmbH*,[221] the CJEU interpreted the concept of 'exceptional circumstances' within the meaning of Article 20(2) EOP. In conformity with the previous judgments concerning Article 20 EOP, the Court follows a strict line of interpretation of the review provisions.[222] An EOP issued by a court other than the one indicated within the parties' agreement is not 'clearly' wrongly issued due to 'other exceptional circumstances'.[223] The defendant – who was most likely aware of the clause – could have opposed the EOP.[224] By not doing so, he is precluded from using the review

215 See Hess & Raffelsieper (2015), at 401–402; Romano (2015), at 808–810. Hazelhorst (2016), at 357. This appears to be a stricter sanction for non-compliance with the minimum standards. See further, Payan (2014a), at 301–302; Guinchard (2015), at 879.

216 See also criticism by Romano (2015), at 810.

217 See Romano (2015), at 808–809; Penasa (2015), at 5–6.

218 Commission EOP Report, COM(2015) 495 final, Brussels, 13.10.2015, at 9–10; Hess & Raffelsieper (2015), at 401–402; Payan (2014a), at 302–305.

219 Case C-21/17, *Catlin Europe SE v O.K. Trans Praha spol. s.r.o.*, 18 January 2017, Application.

220 Regulation 2015/2421 sought to amend and clarify only the ESCP review procedure. For this purpose, it took inspiration from the Maintenance Regulation as suggested by the Commission in relation to the EOP in the EOP Report. An amendment setting a clearer timeframe for the lodging of the review, clarifying the situations that fall under the exceptional and extraordinary circumstances and the limitation period, would also have been beneficial for the EOP Regulation.

221 Case C-245/14.

222 Case C-245/14, para. 45 and Recital 25 of the Amended proposal for an EOP Regulation, COM(2006) 57 final.

223 Case C-245/14, para. 48–49.

224 Case C-245/14, para. 47.

procedure as provided by Article 20(2) EOP to claim that the court of origin held its jurisdiction incorrectly on the basis of allegedly false information. *De lege ferenda*, a uniform definition of 'exceptional circumstances' provided by the EOP Regulation, would be a welcome clarification for the present text, considering its importance in safeguarding parties' procedural rights and the effective use of the European instrument. Further, in *Flight Refund Ltd v. Deutsche Lufthansa AG*[225] the CJEU abides by its strict interpretation of Article 20 EOP. Therefore, Article 20 EOP does not automatically apply to review an order opposed validly by the defendant when courts of the Member State of origin do not have jurisdiction (including the court that issued the EOP) according to Brussels I (now Brussels I*bis*). The provision applies only when the defendant has failed to enter a statement of opposition within the time limit established by Article 16.[226] The Hungarian Supreme Court has to examine the question of international jurisdiction on the basis of Brussels I*bis* in accordance with applicable national rules, or to designate a national court having jurisdiction to hear the substance of the claim as the court having territorial jurisdiction to rule on its international jurisdiction in the light of the aforementioned Regulation.[227] As rightfully indicated by the CJEU, in doing so the national court is not limited to the information provided by the claimant in the application form. Such an approach would not guarantee 'the effectiveness of the rules of jurisdiction (...) nor the rights of the defence to which the defendant is entitled'.[228] Therefore, the national court should use all the information it deems necessary for the purpose, including, if required, hearing the parties' submissions on the matter.[229]

Considering the difficulties that have been encountered thus far in relation to the interpretation and application of Article 20 EOP, it appears that the provisions of this article would benefit from further clarification, especially with regard to the meaning of exceptional circumstances that can justify a review.[230] This would facilitate a consistent interpretation of the provision, regardless of the national mechanisms that are to secure its application. Furthermore, a convergent practice of the national courts would contribute to a uniform application of the text. Regulation 2015/2421 amending the ESCP and the EOP Regulations has not considered it necessary to modify this Article. Nevertheless, clearer uniform criteria for the national courts to assess the prompt acting of the defendant would have been beneficial, as well as including a common provision regarding the interruption of the prescription or limitation period.[231]

In the event the review request is successful, the EOP will be declared null and void; otherwise, if the court rejects the request, the order remains in force and will be subject to enforcement proceedings.

[225] Case C-94/14.

[226] Case C-94/14, para. 69–71.

[227] Case C-94/14, para. 63–64.

[228] Case C-94/14, para. 62.

[229] Case C-94/14, para. 63. Opinion of Advocate General Sharpston, 22 October 2015, Case C-94/14, para. 63.

[230] See further Kramer (2010), at 26–27; Guinchard (2012), at 581–582.

[231] For criticism on the lack of express provisions regarding the limitation period, see Crifò (2009), at 359–378; Crifò (2009a), at 136–138.

2.3.1.5. Enforcement

The court declares the EOP enforceable after the opposition period has lapsed. Form G is used for this purpose. Before the Declaration of enforceability is issued, the court has to verify the date of service and allow sufficient time to pass for a possible statement of opposition to arrive. Although this verification is of significant importance to guarantee the defendant's procedural rights in compliance with the provisions of Article 6 ECHR and Article 47 Charter, there are some doubts as to whether this amounts to a sufficient degree of protection for the party against whom the EOP is issued.[232]

Once the EOP is declared enforceable in the Member State of origin, it will be recognised and enforced in all Member States (except Denmark), without any possibility of opposing its execution.[233] The enforcement will be carried out under the same conditions as a national decision.[234] The claimant will be required to provide the enforcement authorities with a copy of the order and, where necessary, a translation in the official language of the Member State of enforcement. The execution can be refused only in one of the situations set by Article 22 EOP. Additionally, if the defendant has applied for a review, enforcement may be stayed or limited upon his request.[235]

Although effective enforcement is a crucial stage in guaranteeing a fair trial,[236] little information is available about this final stage of the EOP procedure. The Commission EOP Report does not give any details on the success rate or outcome of enforcement proceedings in the Member States. The only obstacle identified for this final step of the procedure is the lack of transparency of the debtor's assets, an aspect that is common for cross-border as well as national execution proceedings. Enforcement is governed by national law, which gives rise to 27 EOP execution regimes that the claimant needs to discover within a uniform European procedure. The enforcement in another Member State will inevitably take time and result in costs for engaging national enforcement authorities and for necessary translations. However, eliminating the administrative steps for the recognition of the court decision (*exequatur*) diminishes the period needed to initiate the execution process in a different Member State, and eliminates the costs associated with it.

2.3.2. The ESCP

2.3.2.1. Application

In order to initiate an ESCP procedure, the claimant first has to identify the competent court. The Regulation does not contain any specific provisions regarding international

232 Kramer (2010), at 27.

233 Article 19 EOP.

234 Article 21(1) EOP.

235 Article 23 EOP.

236 ECtHR, *Hornsby v. Greece*, 18357/91, ECHR 1997-II: The 'right to a court… would be illusory if a Contracting State's domestic legal system allowed a final, binding judicial decision to remain inoperative to the detriment of one party'. On this decision, see van Rhee & Uzelac (2009), at 2.

jurisdiction. However, Form A refers to the application of Brussels I (now Brussels I*bis*) rules in order to determine the court having jurisdiction. As rightfully pointed out by scholars, this means that small-claims litigants will need to be aware of these rules,[237] which might create difficulties for non-repetitive lay users. This is made more difficult when the information is either not fully available in all EU languages or is not accurate.[238] Unfortunately, there have been reports of wrongful information available on the Judicial Atlas regarding competent courts. This complicates the situation, as the claimant is often left guessing which court has jurisdiction from among the several that are usually listed for the same territorial unit.[239] The amended Article 11(1) ESCP seeks to resolve this by expressly establishing that the assistance to be made available to the parties should also cover general information as to which courts in a Member State have jurisdiction.[240]

After identifying the appropriate court, the claimant has to fill in the standard claim form (Form A)[241] and lodge it together with the supporting documents. As regards the EOP, this can be done in person, by post, or by any other means of communication accepted under the procedural rules of the Member State in which the procedure is initiated.[242] Based on the implementation arrangements and provisions of the national rules, the Member States communicate this information to the Commission in order that it be publicly available.[243] The access to relevant information on various aspects of the procedure has been problematic and limited at certain points. More recently, this has been related to the transfer of information to a single dedicated portal, the e-Justice Portal, where for a significant period of time the information was not available in all EU official languages, or did not always contain updated references to applicable national rules. Such relatively long transition periods are worrying, since they deprive the potential user of updated information on various aspects of the proceedings (e.g. accepted means of communication, identifying the courts having jurisdiction) that are crucial for

237 Kramer (2011), at 123; Storskrubb (2008), at 224.

238 The court research engine on the e-Justice Portal was available for a significant period only in relation to some of the Member States. During the transfer of data to a single portal, the e-Justice Portal, the relevant information and the court research tool was not available in all EU official languages for all Member States.

239 *Comment ce faire rembourser un achat à l'étranger*, available at http://sosconso.blog.lemonde.fr/2014/01/17/comment-se-faire-rembourser-un-achat-a-letranger/. According to the checks carried out by Rivais, a foreign party that searches for the competent court for the 13th arrondissement in Paris will find two results: these are TI de Paris 13ème (Marie 3 Rue Philippe de Champagne; 75013 Paris) and TC de Paris (1 Quai de Corse, 75181 Paris). But when the claim is for less than €4,000 the competence lies with the Juge de proximité, which is not mentioned. Further, not only were not all the arrondissements provided by the list but it also contains some imaginary arrondissments 'Paris l'Hôpital', for which the courts would be located at Creusot (Saône-et-Loire) and another one called 'Parisot', for which the courts would be located at Montauban (Tarn-et-Garonne). Such situations make it virtually impossible for the party to lodge a valid application. See Rivais (2014).

240 Oro Martinez (2016), at 115.

241 The parties do not need to make any legal assessment of the claim (Article 12(1) ESCP).

242 Article 4(1) ESCP.

243 Article 4(2) ESCP. Information was available at first on the Judicial Atlas, but was subsequently transferred to and updated on the e-Justice Portal (available at https://e-justice.europa.eu/content_small_claims-354-en.do?init=true).

initiating an ESCP claim. Furthermore, these aspects differ in accordance with the legislation of each Member State. According to the Commission ESCP Report as well as the Deloitte Report, electronic submission of an application is possible in some Member States, although in practice this is still not operational or only partially available to national courts.[244] The Commission is optimistic about further development in this area, in the context of the e-Codex pilot programme on e-Justice,[245] although technical constraints are similar to those mentioned in relation to the EOP.

The forms are available in all official languages of the EU, and can be filled in electronically or downloaded for filling in by hand. The need for translation is to a certain extent minimalised by the automatic translation function provided by the e-Justice portal. However, this concerns only the standard text on the forms. Translation remains necessary for the descriptive parts and/or for the supporting documents drafted in a language other than that of the court when they appear to be necessary for giving the judgment.[246] This aspect of the procedure needs particular attention, as on a usual basis the courts do not accept applications lodged in a language different than that of the proceedings.[247] Submission of the forms in a different language may have a significant negative impact upon the procedure, as shown in some EOP cases.[248] More concrete information regarding the languages in which the forms can be filed with courts in various Member States would be welcome on the e-Justice Portal, since parties may be easily confused with regard to the languages accepted for enforcement purposes.[249]

In practice, various reports acknowledge a limited use of the ESCP compared to its potential in cross-border claims.[250] It seems that parties and especially consumers fail to find their way to this procedure, and sometimes encounter operational difficulties in employing this optional instrument. Additionally, the level of court fees the claimant has to pay upfront may have a deterrent effect. Various reports have qualified court fees as

244 This concerns ten Member States (Austria, Estonia, Cyprus, Czech Republic, Finland, France, the Netherlands, Portugal, Slovenia, and the UK – England and Wales) and five Länder in Germany (Berlin, Brandenburg, Bremen, Sachsen, Hessen). In France and the Netherlands, the practical means still need to be put into place, while in the Czech Republic electronic filing must be followed by submission of the original document to the court. Deloitte Report, RDT-L05–2010, Part I, Brussels, 19.07.2013, at 76–78; Commission ESCP Report, COM(2013) 795 final, Brussels, 19.11.2013, at 5.

245 Commission ESCP Report, COM(2013) 795 final, Brussels, 19.11.2013, at 5; e-Codex project for the ESCP, see www.e-codex.eu. On the ESCP first pilot in 2015, see www.e-codex.eu/e-codex-news letter-no-1–2015–0.

246 Article 6(1)-(2) ESCP.

247 In most cases the courts accept standard forms only in their national official language, as this aspect is often specifically regulated by national Constitutional or procedural rules. Exceptionally, national courts may accept forms in a language they can understand without requiring a translation. On this approach, see Kramer & Onţanu (2013), at 326. See also Commission ESCP Report, COM(2013) 795 final, Brussels, 19.11.2013, at 6–7; Guinchard (2014), at 483–484.

248 See Sections 4.7.2 and 5.7.2.

249 See further Onţanu & Pannebakker (2012), at 177–180.

250 See Commission ESCP Report, COM(2013) 795 final, Brussels, 19.11.2013, at 2–3; Deloitte Report, RDT-L05–2010, Part I, Brussels, 19.07.2013, at 66–67; Eurobarometer 347, *Business – to – Business Alternative Dispute Resolution in the EU*, at 31 (45% of businesses do not go to court because the cost of court proceedings would be disproportionate to the claim) (available at http://ec.europa.eu/public_opinion/flash/fl_347_en.pdf). See also Oro Martinez (2016), at 104.

disproportionate compared to the value of the claim.[251] These vary significantly among the Member States, and are based on different calculation methods. As for the EOP, the transparency of this information regarding the Member States has been problematic, but it is hoped that publication of the information in a dedicated section of the e-Justice Portal will improve the situation.[252] Although the information is not yet complete, the amendment brought by Regulation 2015/2421 to Article 25(f) ESCP requests Member States to communicate the applicable court fees, the way these are calculated, and the methods of payment accepted, thus establishing a legal duty for exhaustive information to be made available to litigating parties.[253]

2.3.2.2. Examination of the Application

In examining the application, the court may use Form B to request the claimant to complete or to correct Form A if it is not properly filled in or when the information is insufficient or inadequate. Together with this, the claimant may provide supplementary information or documents.

In seeking to speed up litigation, the ESCP Regulation sets specific time limits for various stages of the proceedings. The court has a period of 14 days to serve and communicate copies of the standard forms and documents to the parties. Subsequently, the defendant has 30 days from the moment of service to fill in Form C and return it to the court, accompanied by any relevant supporting documents.[254] In the event of a counterclaim, the claimant shall also have 30 days to send a response to the court.[255] The judge is expected to give a decision within a period of 30 days from (1) the moment of receiving the parties' answers, or (2) after receiving all the information required to issue the judgment, or (3) from the oral hearing, when this is considered necessary.[256] The text of the Regulation as well as the recent amendment do not foresee any sanctions for exceeding the time limit, apart from the foreclosure sanction for parties not complying with their duties within the set procedural time.[257] By making use of the uniform European procedure, the Commission ESCP Report points to a significant decrease in the timeframe for small claims litigation. This amounts to an average of approximately 5 months: namely, five times shorter than the period considered necessary before the regulation was adopted.[258]

[251] Deloitte Report, RDT-L05-2010, Part I, Brussels, 19.07.2013, at 28–30 and 87–91; Commission ESCP Report, COM(2013) 795 final, Brussels, 19.11.2013, at 7.

[252] Available at https://e-justice.europa.eu/content_court_fees_concerning_small_claims_procedure-306-en.do. However, for a considerable time the information has not been available in all official EU languages and does not include all twenty-seven Member States.

[253] See also Guinchard (2016), at 437–438.

[254] The defendant may also choose to respond to the court in any other appropriate way without using the standard answer form (Article 5(3) ESCP).

[255] Article 5(2)-(4), (6) ESCP.

[256] Article 5(2)-(6) and Article 7 ESCP.

[257] Article 14 ESCP.

[258] The document uses a sample of ten Member States where the period of the procedure varies between 3 to 8 months.

The express language requirements in Article 6(3) ESCP allow a party to refuse the documents he is served if these are not in the language of the Member State addressed or in a language he understands. This is an important guarantee for parties' procedural rights and a fair trial.

The ESCP is mainly a written procedure, but the court can decide to hold an oral hearing if it considers it impossible to give the judgment on the basis of the written evidence, or if a party requests it.[259] However, the request can be refused if it is obviously not necessary for the fair conduct of the proceedings. The court will provide the reasons in writing. This limitation of holding an oral hearing is not inconsistent with the provisions of Article 6 ECHR.[260] Considering the future increase in the ESCP threshold, which will make the procedure more attractive for commercial litigation, there are opinions that the limitation of oral hearings should be 'seriously reconsidered', as the lack of a hearing could reduce the possibility of determining the real problem giving rise to the litigation.[261] Furthermore, the ESCP Report, as well as the amended text of the Regulation, encourages the use of distance communication technology when it is available to the court. The new provisions allow a summoned party to request the use of such technology on the grounds that – compared to the value of the claim – his physical presence would result in disproportionate costs for the procedure.[262] However, the use of such means is also dependent on the provisions of national procedural rules, the implementation arrangements chosen for the ESCP,[263] and, possibly, language competences. Additionally, the amended provisions expressly link the procedure of hearing parties who are resident or domiciled abroad to the rules of the Taking of Evidence Regulation. This express reference provides clarity and certainty with regard to the way national courts should proceed in these cases.

The court will also have to decide on the extent of evidence necessary for its judgment, and on the means to be used. In keeping with the aims of simplifying the procedure and diminishing costs, 'the simplest and less burdensome' methods have to be chosen. Written statements of witnesses, experts, or parties are allowed, as well as hearings through distance communication technology.[264] Considering the primarily written nature of the procedure, the use of oral testimony is limited to situations in which it is impossible for the court to give a judgment on the basis of other evidence.[265] Furthermore,

259 Article 5(1) ESCP.

260 ECtHR, *Döry v. Sweden*, 28394/95, ECLI:CE:ECHR:2002:1112JUD002839495 para. 37; ECtHR, *Saccoccia v. Austria*; 69917/01, ECLI:CE:ECHR:2008:1218JUD006991701, para. 73. See Kramer (2011), at 124; Kramer (2008), at 364.

261 Oro Martinez (2016), at 109–110.

262 New Article 8(2) ESCP. In contrast, the party summoned to attend a hearing through distance communication technology may request to be physically present at the hearing (new Article 8(3) ESCP). However, the costs are subject to the conditions of Article 16 with regard to costs not being unnecessary or disproportionate to the claim.

263 On the limited availability of the use of such means in courts of the Member States, see Commission ESCP Report, COM(2013) 795 final, Brussels, 19.11.2013, at 4–5; Hazelhorst (2016), at 363–364.

264 When distance hearings are used, the conditions regarding oral hearings have to be complied with. New Article 9(3) in conjunction with new Article 8 ESCP. On a negative impact of the restrictive approach regarding the oral hearings on 'taking personal evidence', see Oro Martinez (2016), at 111–112.

265 New Article 9(4) ESCP.

in order to reduce costs, the ESCP has opted for a uniform mandatory rule of service by post when this is possible. Thus, the service has to be carried out primarily by post with an acknowledgement of receipt, including the date. In view of the developments in some Member States regarding the electronic service of documents in domestic procedures, the amended text of the ESCP puts this new method on the same level as postal service. Provided that service by electronic means is available, and the party to be served has expressly accepted in advance that documents may be served by electronic means, he is under a legal obligation to accept this method of service.[266] This second mandatory service rule is unfortunately highly dependent on and influenced by the provisions of national procedural rules and ESCP implementation arrangements. This will give way to more regimes of application within what is expected to be a uniform procedure. The other modification regarding alternative methods of service to be used when postal or electronic service is not possible makes a switch from the provisions of the EEO to the methods provided by Article 13 and 14 EOP.[267] This is possibly meant to consolidate coordination between the provisions of the two texts.

2.3.2.3. Dismissal or Issue of the ESCP Judgment

When the claim appears to be clearly unfounded or inadmissible, or the claimant fails to complete or rectify the claim within the set period, the application will be dismissed.[268] Alternatively, if the claim falls outside the scope of the ESCP, the court informs the claimant. The claimant may choose to withdraw the claim or let the case proceed in accordance with national law.[269] A counterclaim exceeding the ESCP threshold (€5,000 as of 14 July 2017) will also result in the entire claim being dealt with in accordance with the relevant national law.

As previously mentioned, the court will give a judgment within 30 days of receiving the parties' responses or of the hearing. In the event the court does not receive an answer from the relevant party, the judgment will be issued on the basis of the claim or the counterclaim.[270] The Regulation provides that the judgment will be served on the parties in accordance with Article 13 ESCP. However, the service duty remains under the influence of national procedural rules and ESCP implementation arrangements, thus creating a diverse national outcome for the European procedure.

When it seems appropriate, the court may also seek to reach a settlement between parties.[271] This aspect, however, seems particularly difficult to achieve in a primarily written procedure. Additionally, the occasional use of the procedure does not facilitate the establishing of a practice in this regard in the analysed jurisdictions. The amended

[266] New Article 13(1) ESCP. Such acceptance will be possible on the basis of standard Form A and Form C (new Article 13(3) ESCP). See also Guinchard (2014), at 482–483.

[267] New Article 13(4) ESCP.

[268] Article 4(4) ESCP. The national law is to determine the criteria according to which a claim is unfounded or an application inadmissible. The Regulation does not provide specific evaluation criteria in this regard.

[269] Article 4(3) ESCP.

[270] Article 7 ESCP.

[271] Article 12(3) ESCP.

ESCP text seeks to reinforce this mechanism by extending its application. From July 2017, the courts will be able to approve a settlement reached by the parties or a settlement reached before the court in the course of a proceeding. The decision will benefit from the same recognition and enforcement conditions of an ESCP judgment.[272] Time will determine whether the possibility of making use of distance communication technology as well as for the court to approve a settlement reached by the parties themselves can give an additional boost to the application of this uniform procedure, thereby contributing to the simplification and speeding up of the litigation process for small cross-border claims.

2.3.2.4. Appeal and Review

The Regulation does not contain a uniform rule on appeal.[273] Regrettably, in view of the substantive differences existing between domestic legislations, the solution was left to national law. This choice weakens the uniform procedure and leads to an unequal level of protection of parties' rights across the European Union.[274] Different national rules apply to a procedure that is intended to be simple, speedy, and less costly. This aim is affected by the multitude of available arrangements (e.g. two levels of appeal procedures are applicable in France and Italy, and an appeal was communicated for England and Romania). Moreover, as pointed out in the literature, the Regulation does not clarify whether the procedural rules it establishes apply to the appeal proceedings as well or whether the appealed judgment qualifies as a European title enforceable without the need of an exequatur.[275] With the coming into application of Brussels I*bis*, the exequatur as a general mechanism for recognition and enforcement was eliminated. Hence, this issue becomes less relevant, apart from the possibility of invoking – or not invoking – the grounds of refusal maintained under Brussels I*bis*. However, it is expected that the ESCP appeal will qualify as a European title in the light of the uniform procedure the regulation seeks to provide. The amended Regulation would have been a great opportunity to achieve a uniform rule on the availability of an appeal for this European procedure,[276] but the national approach continues to prevail. However, the extension of provisions regarding court fees and methods of payment to the appeal is a welcome development.[277] It has led to eliminating some of the possible disparities in terms of the proportionality of court fees, also in relation to the national simplified procedure that sometimes benefit from more advantageous court fees than the European procedure.

The review is an exceptional remedy that is meant to safeguard the defendant's procedural rights and to secure compliance with the requirement of a fair trial in accordance with Article 6 ECHR and Article 47 of the Charter. This regards situations in which the defendant was not aware of the proceedings initiated against him in the

272 Article 23a Regulation 2015/2421.
273 On the desirability of an appeal procedure being available in the ESCP, see Oro Martinez (2016), at 112–113 and footnote 56.
274 See also Oro Martinez (2016), at 112–113.
275 Kramer (2011), at 126–127.
276 The proposal for amending the ESCP Regulation did not address this issue. See also Oro Martinez (2016), at 113.
277 New Article 17(2) ESCP.

Member States of origin, and he therefore was unable to properly defend himself.[278] The Regulation establishes the conditions for its use, the minimum standards, but the way the procedure is applied is governed by national procedural law, just as for the EOP.[279] Implementation of the review procedure has created some difficulties and uncertainties at the national level.[280] The mechanism is not known to all EU procedural systems, and the interaction between the two levels of legislation may lead to tensions, particularly when the national procedure has more far-reaching effects than the review mechanism, or implies additional duties for the defendant. The amended text of the Article seeks to address some of these issues identified in the Commission ESCP Report by taking inspiration from the review provision in Regulation 4/2009 (Maintenance Regulation).[281] In accordance with this text, the review will be available if the defendant did not make an appearance due to the fact (1) he was not served with the claim form or he was not summoned to the oral hearing in sufficient time and in a way that would have enabled him to arrange for a defence, or (2) he was prevented from contesting the claim by reasons of force majeure or due to extraordinary circumstances. Moreover, he should not have failed to challenge the judgment if it had been possible for him to have done so.[282] The new Article 18(1) is broader than the previous rule, not being limited to situations in which the claim form or the summons to an oral hearing was served by methods without proof of receipt. The express requirement of non-faultier behaviour on the part of the defendant is eliminated from Article 18(1)(a). Disappointingly, the new provision does not explicate the situations covered by 'extraordinary circumstances', nor does it offer any criteria for appreciation.[283] This is left again to the provisions of the national procedural rules or to the interpretation of the judge, a situation that has the potential of resulting in different outcomes for similar situations across the Member States.

The interpretation of the review concept given by the CJEU in relation to the EOP in the *Thomas Cook* case might, however, give some support to the national courts in view of the similarity of the provisions and the purpose for which the mechanism was established. Further, the defendant has a period of 30 days to file a request for review from the moment he is made aware of the contents of the ESCP judgment and is able to react, at the latest, from the date of the first enforcement measure making his property non-disposable.[284] The explicit timeframe set for using this exceptional remedy is a welcome addition, taking into consideration the aim of providing a speedier procedure for small claims in cross-border cases and for securing a balance between the parties' procedural rights. Furthermore, this facilitates the task of the court in appreciating the prompt reaction of the defendant, and establishing objective criteria for calculation of

278 Article 18 ESCP.

279 See also Oro Martinez (2016), at 111.

280 Commission ESCP Report, COM(2013) 795 final, Brussels, 19.11.2013, at 6.

281 Article 19 Regulation (EC) No 4/2009 on jurisdiction, applicable law, recognition and enforcement of decisions, and cooperation in matters relating to maintenance obligations, O.J. L7/10.01.2009, at 1.

282 New Article 18(1) ESCP.

283 For criticism, see Kramer (2011), at 127.

284 New Article 18(2) ESCP.

the 30-day period. Based on the compliance with conditions set by Article 18(1) ESCP, the judgment will remain in force or be declared null and void.[285]

Finally, the new Article 18(3) ESCP partly clarifies the effects an ESCP judgment declared null and void will have for the claimant's rights.[286] Surprisingly, the interruption of the prescription or limitation period provision will benefit only the claimants in the Member State 'where such interruption applies under national law'.[287] Again, in similar situations the ESCP procedure will have different outcomes for the claimants based on the procedural law of the Member State of origin and for possible implementation measures that were undertaken by the legislator. This adds to the complexity of the procedure, as it is highly unlikely a lay user will be aware of this arrangement, especially with regard to the legislation of a different Member State. Furthermore, the new Article 25(1) ESCP does not set a duty for the Member States to communicate such information to the Commission, which means that the services of a legal representative will possibly be needed in this regard. This can be particularly problematic, creating tensions if interruption of the prescription is applicable within some of the national procedures while in others a more restrictive regime is chosen. This situation might create challenging situations for the national judge to assess.

2.3.2.5. Enforcement

The ESCP judgment is enforceable notwithstanding a possible appeal; no security is required for this purpose.[288] However, in the event that a party challenges the ESCP judgment (when this is possible in accordance with the national procedural law) or makes a request for review, the court, upon application by the party, may limit enforcement, make it subject to the provision of a security, or – under exceptional circumstances – stay enforcement.[289] To initiate enforcement proceedings in a different Member State at the request of one of the parties, the court will issue a certificate regarding the ESCP judgment without any additional costs. Various reports, however, reveal translation-related difficulties.[290] In seeking to address this issue, the amended Article 20(2) ESCP establishes that the party may request the court to provide him with a certificate in any other EU official language by making use of the multilingual dynamic form on the e-Justice Portal.[291] However, this does not include an obligation for the court to translate and/or transliterate the text contained in the free-text fields of the certificate.

285 New Article 18(3) ESCP.

286 The lack of express provision regarding the limitation period was previously criticised by Crifò in relation to the EOP Regulation. See Crifò (2009), at 359–378; Crifò (2009a), at 136–138.

287 Final provision New Article 18(3) ESCP.

288 Article 18(1) ESCP.

289 Article 23 ESCP.

290 It is usually necessary to provide a translation of Form D, as a limited number of Member States accept it in languages other than their own official language(s). The additional costs this implies for the party is one of the problems cited in relation to enforcement. ECC-Net, *European Small Claims Procedure Report*, September 2012, at 28 (available at http://ec.europa.eu/consumers/ecc/docs/small_claims_210992012_en.pdf); Commission ESCP Report, COM(2013) 795 final, Brussels, 19.11.2013, at 6–7.

291 Available at https://e-justice.europa.eu/content_small_claims_forms-177-en.do. On the use of multilingual forms in parallel, see Onțanu & Pannebakker (2012), at 181.

For this purpose, the interested party will still need to rely on the services of 'a person qualified to carry out translations in one of the Member States',[292] but the costs will be limited. The language and translation requirements for enforcement purposes would be further facilitated if more Member States were to accept Form D in languages other than their own official language(s).[293]

The provisions in Article 20–23 on enforcement match to a large extent the corresponding EOP articles. The law of the Member State of enforcement will govern the execution process.[294] The interested party will have to provide the enforcement authority with a copy of the judgment, the certificate (Form D), and a translation of this document in the official language of the Member State where execution is taking place, or in a language the authority will accept.[295] Available reports have revealed difficulties for the parties in finding information on the enforcement procedures and contact details of local enforcement officers.[296] Therefore, this will require additional time and effort, and will increase costs for the party, who might need to employ the services of a local legal representative for guidance.

The enforcement may be refused only when the ESCP judgment is irreconcilable with an earlier judgment given in a Member State or in a third country, provided it involves the same parties and cause of action.[297] Additionally, the judgment must either have been given in the Member State of enforcement or fulfil the requirements necessary for its recognition, and the irreconcilability can not have been raised as an objection in the Member State where the ESCP judgment was given.[298] Overall, enforcement will require additional action from the party if the debtor does not comply voluntarily with the judgment. The most significant achievement regarding this stage of the proceedings is the elimination of *exequatur* and of the additional administrative steps together with the costs these implied. Because Brussels I*bis* eliminated the exequatur process, the achievement of the ESCP is less relevant now apart from the elimination of the grounds of refusal.

2.4. Concluding Remarks

The EOP and ESCP Regulations are the first uniform European procedures, setting a procedural framework that aims to simplify cross-border litigation for uncontested and small claims. However, in their application the EOP and the ESCP still rely extensively

292 Article 21 (2)(b) ESCP.

293 At the moment, only nine of the swenty-seven Member States in which the ESCP applies agree to receive the certificate for enforcement purposes in other EU official languages as well. Most often this additional language is English: for example, Czech Republic (Slovak and English), Estonia (English), Ireland (English), France (English, German, Italian and Spanish), Cyprus (English), Malta (English), Slovenia (Italian and Hungarian, but only in the regions with Italian and Hungarian minority where these language are officially used in court), Finland (Swedish and English), Sweden (English). For a discussion on this, see Guinchard (2014), at 484.

294 Article 21(1) ESCP.

295 Article 21(2) ESCP.

296 ECC-Net, *European Small Claims Procedure Report*, September 2012, at 28; Commission ESCP Report, COM(2013) 795 final, Brussels, 19.11.2013, at 6.

297 Article 22(1)(a) ESCP.

298 Article 22(1)(b)-(c) ESCP.

on the use of national rules. The following chapters analyse how these European uniform procedures are implemented and function in the national procedural framework and practice. England, France, Italy, and Romania represent different institutional and procedural contexts in which the EOP and the ESCP are set to simplify and speed up litigation as well as to diminish its costs. Regardless of the national procedural model, the European uniform procedures should create a level playing field in cross-border litigation.

Important for the implementation of European uniform procedures is that Member States have provided the European Commission with a range of relevant information to be made generally available to the public (e.g. courts having jurisdiction, means of communication accepted, means of review and of appeal, and enforcement). However, this information does not always appear to be sufficient for the parties and the practitioners who decide to make use of the uniform procedures. Additional details are usually necessary. European websites and consumer organisations also seek to provide general as well as specific information regarding court proceedings in various Member States. The process is not yet perfect, however, and a great deal still remains to be done at the national level and by local practitioners. Analysing the choices made by national legislators and professional bodies in incorporating the EOP and the ESCP into the national procedural system and practice is the key to understanding the implications that the coordination or lack of clear coordination between the European and domestic procedural rules entail for the results of the European procedures.

The actions undertaken by Member States to adopt national implementation rules for the EOP and the ESCP have the potential to facilitate the application of these procedures.[299] The legislation enacted and the actions taken for the purpose of integrating the European uniform procedures into the national systems are highly significant for the functioning of these alternative instruments. The approach differs from Member State to Member State, but the difficulties and tension encountered between the two levels of legislation and national law seeking to accommodate the needs of the European uniform procedures might not be so different across jurisdictions. Similarly, the solutions chosen by Member States to address particular procedural matters might resemble each other.

As revealed by practice and case law in England, France, Italy, and Romania in the next chapters, integration of the EOP and the ESCP can be a challenging process. The EOP and the ESCP procedural model and institutions are not necessarily familiar to legal practitioners in all EU legal systems (e.g. the review procedure, service by post with acknowledgement of receipt), and can require a different approach from practitioners more used to familiar domestic procedures. As the analysis in this chapter shows, the CJEU has provided some guidance and uniform interpretation of certain EOP provisions in order to facilitate the task of the national courts in securing a unitary application of the Regulation across Member States (except Denmark). It remains then for national legislators and practitioners to undertake the subsequent steps to facilitate application of the European procedures and to secure a uniform and coordinated application of the EOP and the ESCP.

[299] Lack of proper implementation and interaction with domestic civil procedures are identified as problematic by judges and practitioners. See Kramer (2016a), at 94.

The following chapters will analyse the way EOP and ESCP procedures interact with national rules and procedures, identifying their integration needs as well as those of parties and practitioners in the selected jurisdiction, providing evidence of the effectiveness these instruments achieve and the steps that still need to be taken to further improve their application.

Chapter 3

ENGLAND AND WALES

3.1. Introduction

England and Wales (hereafter referred to jointly as England) share a common set of rules governing civil procedure.[300] England is a common law jurisdiction, relying not only on the application and interpretation of primary and secondary legislation but also on the use of precedent.[301] Theoretically, the courts 'merely interpret the law', but, in practice, judicial decisions contribute to the law, developing it and establishing binding interpretations of the legal provisions.[302] According to Andrews, the sources of English civil procedure are: (1) the primary legislation; (2) the statutory instruments (such as the Civil Procedure Rules); (3) practice directions; (4) the pre-action protocols; (5) judicial decisions; (6) court guides to practice (e.g. Chancery Guide, Queen's Bench Guide); and (7) inherent jurisdiction.[303]

The Civil Procedure Rules 1998 (CPR)[304] are the result of Lord Woolf's Reforms following the 1995 and 1996 Reports on Access to Justice.[305] They are the largest source of English procedural rules,[306] and govern the practice and procedure to be followed before the civil division of the Court of Appeal, the High Court, and the County Courts. These rules sought to address the complexity of the justice system and its funding, as costs of litigation had become unaffordable. They continued to be excessive, and the

300 The United Kingdom has four separate systems of law: England and Wales, Scotland, Northern Ireland, and Gibraltar. The term 'English law' refers to the law of England and Wales.

301 See Smith (2006), at 242; Jolowicz (2000), at 122–128; Jolowicz (1992), at 1–17.

302 See Andrews (2013), at 35–36; Haye & Prevett (2003), at 179–180.

303 Andrews (2013), at 33.

304 Civil Procedure Rules 1998, SI 1998/3123. The CPR applies since 26 April 1999. The 79 Parts of the CPR are supplemented by Practice Directions (PD) that establish details of the procedures, offering guidance on the interpretation and application of the law. See Kay (2015), at 43.

305 Access to Justice: Interim Report to the Lord Chancellor on the Civil Justice System in England and Wales (1995); Access to Justice: Final Report to the Lord Chancellor on the Civil Justice System in England and Wales (1996) (available at http://webarchive.nationalarchives.gov.uk/+/www.dca.gov.uk/civil/reportfr.htm). See also Jolowicz (2000), at 386–397.

306 See Andrews (2013), at 34.

reform was generally thought to have increased them.[307] Thus, subsequent steps were taken to address this concern. Sir Rupert Jackson's report on the cost regime[308] resulted in April 2013 in recommendations that introduced significant changes to a number of procedural topics in order to ensure the proper implementation and understanding of the Woolf civil justice review.[309] Nevertheless, successive increases in court fees and cuts in legal aids have led to a decrease in the number of cases and to an increase in litigants in person, which hinders case management and results in serious procedural delays. The English system is not designed for litigants in person. Therefore, a new action is being led by Lord Justice Briggs to redesign the system, which will allow many cases to be undertaken without lawyers and on the basis of information technology.[310] Reforms are far from over, however, and will surely continue in the effort to diminish litigation costs and to provide reasonable access to justice for ordinary people and small businesses that 'struggle to benefit from the strengths' of the English civil justice system.[311]

This chapter considers the choices creditors have in order to recover debts through English court procedures, focusing on the special instruments available to facilitate this process. The EOP and the ESCP are alternative solutions that have been added to these domestic instruments in cross-border litigation. The process of the UK's departure from the EU will very likely put an end to the application of these European uniform procedures in England, but the experience of English practitioners and courts with these instruments will be useful for the further development of European civil procedure and for possible future forms of collaboration. The chapter further underlines important aspects that need to be addressed and considered in the ongoing implementation and application of the instruments. Section 3.2 provides an overview of the English justice system and ordinary court proceedings. Section 3.3 gives a functional analysis of the special English court procedures available for debt recovery. The characteristics of the national instruments are examined in comparison to the EOP and the ESCP. Section 3.4 offers an insight into the perceptions and expectations of English stakeholders with regard to the EOP and the ESCP. Subsequently, Section 3.5 focuses on implementation of the European procedures within the national legal system. Section 3.6 analyses the main characteristics of enforcement proceedings in England and the execution of EOP and ESCP enforceable titles. Finally, Section 3.7 evaluates the functioning in practice of the European uniform procedures by using data provided by national statistics, available case law, and empirical research results.

307 Neuberger (2012), at 2 (available at www.judiciary.gov.uk/wp-content/uploads/JCO/Documents/Speeches/mor-speech-solicitors-cost-conference-lecture-feb2012.pdf).

308 Jackson (2010).

309 The reform sought to secure access to justice in a reasonable time and involving reasonable costs for parties, and to avoid a disproportionate use of the court's resources. Sorabji (2014), at 29–30. Schedule to the Civil Procedure (Amendment) Rules 2013, SI 2013/262. For an overview of the changes, see Andrews (2013), at 21–29.

310 Briggs (2016). See also Hodges (2016a), at 149–163.

311 Briggs (2015), para. 5.23.

3.2. The English Civil Justice System: An Overview

3.2.1. *General Aspects*

First instance civil proceedings in England are carried out in the County Court[312] and the High Court. Proceedings for which the High Court is competent are allocated to a particular division of the Court: in civil and commercial matters it is the Queen's Bench Division or the Chancery Division.[313] The County Court and the High Court have concurrent first jurisdiction over most types of claims.[314] Although the general rule is that the claimant is free to choose whether to start proceedings in the High Court or the County Court, a number of statutory provisions and practice directions address the distribution of jurisdiction and allocation of cases between the two.[315] The same rules apply to EOP and ESCP claims.

The CPR applies to all proceedings in the County Court, the High Court, and the Civil Division of the Court of Appeal.[316] The CPR rules aim to enable the courts 'to deal with cases justly and at proportionate cost'.[317] Justice is a limited resource, and therefore a court's resources and time need to be used in a proportional manner, maintaining a reasonable correlation with the seriousness or substantial value of the case.[318] The CPR provides template procedures applying to all cases: namely, the small claims track, the fast track, or the multi-track.[319] Allocation to one of the tracks is based on the complexity of the case and the amount claimed, and aims to ensure a suitable and fair use of judicial resources while maintaining a certain flexibility of proceedings, in accordance with the diversity and the individual elements of the case.[320]

312 Until 22 April 2014 there were about 180 county courts in England, each exercising its jurisdiction over a certain geographical district. The Crime and Courts Act 2013, Section 17 amended the County Courts Act 1984 to create a single County Court with national jurisdiction over England and Wales. The courts premises act as hearing centres. A list of all the County Court hearing centres can be found online at https://courttribunalfinder.service.gov.uk/search/.

313 The Queen's Bench Division handles claims for debt, damages, recovery of land, and recovery of goods ('claims seeking common law remedies'), including tort and contract claims. The Chancery Division is assigned cases regarding sale and property disputes, mortgages, execution of trust, administration of estates, competition, bankruptcy, tax partnership, execution of trust, intellectual property, probate claims, appointment of a guardian of a child's estate, and actions in contract or tort not expressly assigned to other divisions. See Blackstone's Civil Practice 2015, at 66.

314 Section 1, Courts and Legal Services Act 1990, High Court and County Court Jurisdiction Order 1991, SI 1991/724. See also Sime (2014), at 24; Zuckerman (2013), at 170.

315 Even when there is no compulsory requirement to commence the proceeding before a specific court, there might be further rules on trial venues to be considered. See 7A PD 1–2.

316 CPR 2.1(1).

317 CPR 1.1(1).

318 On this argument, see Andrews (2013), at 59.

319 See CPR 27–30.

320 Money claims up to £10,000 will be allocated to the small track (for personal injury and house repair claims the threshold is £1,000) (CPR 26.6(1) and CPR 27), while claims not exceeding £25,000 will be allocated to the fast track (CPR 26.6(4) and CPR 28). All other actions that are not dealt with under the small or fast track system will be handled in the multi-track by the County Court or the High Court (CPR 26.6(6) and CPR 29). These thresholds create a presumption that the case will be allocated to a

Although the English civil justice system is essentially adversarial, litigating parties are required to cooperate for the expeditious resolution of their dispute. This is supported by the use of pre-action protocols, the need to consider ADR, and a case management system through which a judge scrutinises from an early stage the conduct,[321] costs, and progress of litigation.[322] Parties are required to carry out the investigative work and to disclose information and documents early in the process.[323]

The representation of parties is not mandatory.[324] However, due to the complexity of court proceedings, parties are advised to seek advice and representation, especially in high value cases or complex claims. Due to the high costs of litigation, self-representation is becoming more common, and steps are being considered in order to adapt the English procedure to this approach.[325]

3.2.2. *The Ordinary National Procedure*

The regular claim procedure based on Part 7 CPR provisions begins with the claimant requesting that the claim form (NT) be issued by the court competent to hear the case (and by service of the claim upon the defendant).[326] Either the claimant or the court can serve the claim form on the defendant, but most often it is the court that handles the service.[327] The method most used is service by first-class post.[328] Other methods considered valid under CPR 6.3 are personal service, leaving the claim form at an address (e.g. at the defendant's solicitor's address, the residence of the defendant, or the principle office of the company), on a fax machine, or by other means of electronic communication or any other method authorised by the court.

Court proceedings in England rely extensively on the use of standardised forms tailored specifically for different procedures in order to achieve a degree of simplicity and uniformity.[329] Specific forms are available for making a claim, for the acknowledgement of service, and for the certification of service forms, response forms, and defence and counterclaim forms, as well as for allocating questionnaires, for case management directions, for judicial review forms, and for enforcement forms and so on.[330] Specific notes are available for guiding litigating parties in the compilation of these forms. This

specific track; however, particular features of the case might trigger a different allocation. For more details regarding the procedural tracks, see Zuckerman (2013), at 633–654; Andrews (2013), at. 94–96.

321 Case management aims to ensure that the action remains focused on the main issues and that the case does not lose direction or become blocked by side aspects of the claim. See Andrews (2012); Andrews (2013), at 199–202; Zuckerman (2013), at 551–566.

322 Blackstone's Civil Practice 2015, at 57. See also Andrews (2012).

323 Blackstone's Civil Practice 2015, at 57.

324 CPR 3.

325 Briggs (2016). See also Hodges (2016a), at 149–163.

326 CPR 7.2(1) and 7 PD 3.1 and CPR 7.5. Particulars of the claim can be served at the same time in a separate document or subsequently (CPR 16.2). Zuckerman (2013), at 168.

327 CPR 6.4(1).

328 PD 8A, 8.1. Blackstone's Civil Practice 2015, at 306.

329 On the use of forms in civil proceedings, see also Chapter 12 Practice and Procedure in Woolf (1996), at 116–136.

330 For a list of CPR Forms, see www.justice.gov.uk/courts/procedure-rules/civil/forms#general.

makes English courts extensively experienced in using standard forms for case handling, both for the ordinary claim procedure (Part 7 CPR) and for accelerated procedures for the recovery of monetary claims (e.g. default judgment, summary procedure, Part 8 Claims, and Money Claims Online). In principle, this characteristic of the English procedure should facilitate English courts in the task of handling EOP and ESCP forms.

In England, most proceedings terminate at a pre-trial stage, or when the parties agree to settle and to discontinue the claim in view of the significant level of costs involved. A small fraction of the registered claims reach trial (around 3% for the County Court in 2015).[331] In these cases, the court hears the parties' witnesses and pronounces a judgment on the merits. A number of steps need to be taken for this purpose: namely, preparing the witnesses, preparing trial bundles (especially for the fast track and multi-track trials), preparing skeleton arguments, case summaries, and reading lists. The procedural rules give the courts significant flexibility regarding how to deal with the trial, the timetable of the proceedings, and the evidence. Generally, the trials will be conducted in public,[332] though most civil claims are heard by judges sitting alone.[333]

Once all the aspects of fact and law have been clarified, a judgment can be pronounced. In accordance with CPR 40.7, the judgment takes effect as soon as it is pronounced by the judge. After the judgment is given by the court, it will need to be entered and perfected into a formal document.[334] This will be handed down in a public process in order to comply with the principle of publicity, and the court will normally serve a copy of judgment to each of the parties.[335] Judgments on the merits of the case are *res judicata*.[336] A money judgment must be complied with within 14 days of the judgment unless the court specifies otherwise (e.g. orders payment by instalments).[337]

Appeal procedures require court permission in England, which means that the interested party must submit a request. This is usually given by the first instance court (County Court or High Court) or the Court of Appeal if the appeal has a real chance of success or if there is a public interest in proceeding[338] – such as when the decision of the

331 Table 1.1 County Court activity, England and Wales, annually 2000–2015, Civil Justice and Judicial Review Tables; January to March 2016 (available at www.gov.uk/government/statistics/civil-justice-statistics-quarterly-january-to-march-2016-and-the-royal-courts-of-justice-2015). See also Andrews (2013), at 382; Zuckerman (2013), at 1006–1007; Sime (2014), at 420.

332 CPR 39.2(1).

333 Sime (2014), at 420.

334 The court is primarily responsible for drawing up the judgment, but it may also ask a party to do it (CPR 40.3). See Zuckerman (2013), at 1064–1065.

335 CPR 6.21 and CPR 40.4.

336 Courts emphasise the principle of finality of court decisions. See *Smith v. Brough* (2005) ([2005] EWCA Civ 26) in which Brooke LJ noted that [it] 'is a fundamental principle of our common law that the outcome of litigation should be final' (at [54]). On the same matter, see also Arden LJ at [35]: 'Interest in the closure of litigation is not only the interest of the public. Successful claimants also have an interest in finality and they are entitled to expect that if they have won at trial, and the time for appeal has passed, that that is the end of the matter.' Andrews (2013), at 465.

337 CPR 40.11.

338 CPR 52.3(1). The reason for this rests in the aim to avoid the waste of valuable court resources for hopeless appeals, and to focus on appellate issues that are of real significance for the parties and the general public. Court proceedings are expensive, an appeal will cause further delays, and it will lead to

first instance court is 'wrong' or 'unjust because of a serious procedural or other irregularity in the proceedings'.[339] The appeal is not meant to provide a second round of an adversarial process in which parties present their case a second time before a higher court. Instead, it is confined to the scrutiny of the lower court's decision. In practice, however, for judgments involving small value claims the right of appeal is rarely exercised.[340]

The duration of first instance court proceedings differs significantly between claims allocated to the small track and those allocated to the fast or multi-track. This period is around 8 months for small claim trials and 13.6 months for fast and multi-track trials.[341] According to official statistics published in 2016, the average time necessary to handle a claim at first instance (from its issuance to the trial) is around 6.5 months (183 days).[342]

3.2.3. *Costs of Ordinary Court Proceedings*

Litigation costs have a central place in the administration of civil justice in England, and are crucial with regard to parties' decision to litigate. Costs are high and often disproportionate to the amount of the claim, and attempts to control and diminish them have thus far not been successful.[343]

The main rules regarding costs of proceedings are contained in Parts 44–48 CPR and in the corresponding practice directions, as well as in the Her Majesty's Courts and Tribunal Services leaflet on Civil and Family Court Fees (EX50).[344] The costs of judicial proceedings also include the solicitor's fees (including those of the barrister), the witnesses' costs, and travelling and accommodation costs if necessary.

Court fees have increased several times during the last decade. At present, the court fee for initiating a claim varies from £35 (approx. €40) for claims of up to £300 (approx. €343) to £10,000 (approx. €11,460) for claims above £200,000 (approx. €229,205). If a hearing is organised, a hearing fee applies. The amount of the fees depends on the track to which the claim is allocated: namely, from £25 (approx. €28.65) for claims up to £300 (approx. €343) to £335 (approx. €384) for claims of more than £3,000 (approx. €3,438) in the small track, £545 (approx. €624.6) for the fast track, and £1,090 (approx. €1,249) for multi-track claims. Additionally, an application for a summons or an order for a witness to attend court

a certain duplication of proceedings. See further Andrews (2013), at 422–424; Zuckerman (2013), at 1113–1114. See also the explanation of Sir Andrew Morritt in *Colley v. Council for Licensed Conveyancers* at [32], [2001] EWCA Civ 1137; [2002] 1 WLR 160.

339 CPR 52.11(3). For the meaning of 'wrong' and 'serious procedural or other regularity', see Zuckerman (2013), at 1180–1188.

340 Fiorini (2008), at 458; Madge (2004), at 207.

341 Table 1.5 Number of trials and the average time to reach trial, England and Wales, annually 2000–2015. Civil Justice and Judicial Review Tables; January to March 2016 (available at www.gov.uk/government/statistics/civil-justice-statistics-quarterly-january-to-march-2016-and-the-royal-courts-of-justice-2015).

342 Ministry of Justice, Statistics Bulletin, Civil Justice Statistics Quarterly, England and Wales (Incorporating the Royal Courts of Justice 2015), January to March 2016, 2 June 2016, at 18.

343 Woolf (1996); Jackson (2010). For a new report addressing the issues, see Briggs (2016).

344 http://formfinder.hmctsformfinder.justice.gov.uk/ex50-eng.pdf.

entails a fee of £50 (approx. €57). Appellate proceedings are subject to additional fees. Fees relating to an appeal under Part 52 CPR are contained in Form 200.[345]

Recovery of the entire costs of litigation might prove difficult even though the losing party has to bear them. The court has discretionary power to determine to what extent and by whom the costs of proceedings should be paid. Additionally, the timing of payment puts significant pressure on the litigants.[346] In an assessment of the costs of the proceedings, the judge will consider in particular: (1) the conduct of the parties; (2) whether the party was only partly successful in his claim; and (3) any admissible offer to settle.[347]

3.3. National Tailored Solutions for the Recovery of Monetary Claims

In addition to the regular claim based on Part 7 CPR, the English system provides a diverse choice of instruments tailored to facilitate the recovery of contested or uncontested monetary and small value claims. The EOP procedure does not have a direct equivalent in English procedures,[348] as the same function can be fulfilled for example by the default judgment or summary judgment.[349] The ESCP, however, finds an equivalent in the small claims track. The English system has vast experience with small claims, the small track being 'one of the successful stories of the Woolf Reforms'.[350] Together with the default judgment, summary judgment, and small claims, in practice, parties also use procedures such as the Part 8 Procedure, Money Claim Online, and interim judgments. Orders obtained following these accelerated or summary procedures are the solutions preferred in many cases by 'bulk litigants' who use them to enforce commercial debts.[351] This section analyses these national procedures that parties apply in seeking to enforce their claims when needing to opt between domestic or European procedures.

3.3.1. Default Judgment

3.3.1.1. General Aspects

Default judgments as regulated by Part 12 CPR are judgments without trial where the defendant has failed to file an acknowledgement of service or to file a defence. Judgment by default is 'an important means of accelerating the legal process',[352] and it prevents the defendant from restricting the claimant's access to justice by a non-response to the claims.[353] Often the judgment is 'a purely administrative act, not involving any judicial determination of the merits of the claim'.[354] The procedure is available for claims such as

345 Form 200 is available at https://formfinder.hmctsformfinder.justice.gov.uk/form-200-eng.pdf.
346 CPR 44.2.
347 CPR 44.2 (4)-(5).
348 Jolowicz (2001), at 115; Crifò (2009), at 370; Crifò (2016), at 83.
349 See Jolowicz (2001), at 115–117; Crifò (2009a), at 152; Crifò (2009), at 359–378.
350 Crifò (2009), at 374–375.
351 Crifò (2005), at 203.
352 Andrews (2008), at 92.
353 Crifò (2009a), at 152; Zuckerman (2013), at 361–363.
354 Blackstone's Civil Practice 2015, at 407.

for specific sums, for unqualified damages or a combination of these, or for delivery of goods (with the alternative of paying their value), and for claims for remedy other than money claims, claims for costs (other than fixed costs), and in certain other cases where an application for judgment is made using Part 23 CPR.[355] The spectrum of claims for which this procedure can be used is wider than that of the EOP.[356]

3.3.1.2. The Procedure

In money claims, judgment is rendered following a request made by the claimant filing a standard form (N205A/B or N225 and N227). The judgment is issued by the court's administrative staff without any consideration of the merits of the claims.[357] This 'judgment by administrative process'[358] for money claims is different from the 'automated' form of examination provided for in Article 8 EOP. The EOP involves a prima facie examination of the merits of the claim to determine whether the 'claim appears to be founded' based on the information contained in the application form.[359] In claims only for costs other than fixed costs (CPR 12.9–12.11), the default judgment resembles the EOP examination, as the court will give a judgment to which the claimant appears to be entitled; thus, the merits of the claim are considered in a limited way, based on the statement of claim.[360]

In order to obtain a default judgment, a number of conditions have to be met.[361] First, the court must be satisfied that the defendant was served the particulars of the claim.[362] A certificate of service is usually considered to be sufficient evidence.[363] Second, the defendant has not filed an acknowledgement of service form or a defence, and the period for doing so has expired. The claimant can make a request for a default judgment following a period of 14 days after the service of the particulars of the claim on the defendant, who in turn has failed to acknowledge service or to file a defence.[364] This allows the claimant to obtain a judicial decision faster than in the EOP, where the court is to issue the order within 30 days or as soon as possible. Third, the defendant has not satisfied the claim, and fourth, he has not returned an admission to the claimant under CPR 14.4 (admission of the whole claim for a specific amount of money), or filed an admission with the court under CPR 14.6 (admission of liability to pay the whole claim for an unspecified amount of money).

The use and format of the standard form is similar to the EOP procedure, but there are also additional forms such as a service form to prove service of the claim upon the

355 CPR 12.4 and CPR 12.9–10. Claims for a 'specific amount of money' (CPR 12.4) are not limited to monetary debt, but include claims for damages or any claim on which the claimant is prepared to put a money value, claim for fixed costs or interest up to the date of the request judgment. 2012 White Book 12.4.3. Part 23 CPR – General rules about applications for court orders.

356 Article 4 EOP and Article 1(1)(a) EOP.

357 Andrews (2013), at 239.

358 Andrews (2008), at 92.

359 See Kramer (2010), at 24–25.

360 Blackstone's Civil Practice 2015, p. 407.

361 See Zuckerman (2013), at 363–367.

362 CPR 12.3(1)-(2) and 12 PD 4.1. Crifò (2005), at 220–221.

363 12 PD 4.3(1).

364 CPR 12.1 in conjunction with CPR 10.1 and CPR 10.3, and CPR 15.4.

defendant. In practice, most default judgments are entered in default of acknowledgement of service.[365]

For default judgments in which damages and/or interest, or the value of the goods, are to be decided by the court, a disposal hearing may be fixed for the court to assess the amount that needs to be paid.[366] However, generally in money claims the default judgment on request is obtained without a hearing. This is similar to the EOP procedure.

The enforcement of default judgments for specific amounts can be carried out immediately after the decision is issued by the court. In claims for specific sums of money, when the decision is to be executed abroad the claimant may need a judgment on the merits. In this case, he can request a summary judgment instead of a default judgment.[367]

Due to their purely administrative nature, default judgments, cannot be appealed by the defendant.[368] The exception is the default judgment by application where the court is required to undertake certain judicial considerations of the claim.[369] However, like the EOP, the domestic procedure provides for a challenging means in certain circumstances, provided the debtor acts promptly.[370] This is an application to set the default judgment aside or to vary it. The court has to consider whether the default judgment has been properly entered into, whether there are other reasons that require justice to set it aside, or whether the defendant deserves a second chance to contest the claim.[371] CPR 13.3 provides the criteria for the court's appreciation in setting aside or varying judgments. The defendant's application must be supported by evidence, showing a real prospect of defending the claim.

Judgments in default are perceived as 'procedurally fragile' due to the fact they are not the result of a decision 'after adjudication of the claim's merits', nor 'do they rest upon unequivocal acquiescence by a defendant',[372] giving the court the power to set it aside. In comparison, the means of challenge with regard to an unopposed EOP are more limited, leaving less room for the courts' appreciation.[373]

3.3.1.3. Costs of Proceedings

The court fees referred to in Section 3.2.3 apply accordingly to default judgments. Solicitor costs, witness costs, or other costs might apply. The claimant will be able to

365 CPR 12.3(1) and CPR 10.3(1). O'Hare & Browne (2013), at 277.

366 O'Hare & Browne (2013), at 280; Sime (2014), at 140.

367 When execution needs to be carried out abroad, default judgments may be refused enforcement. See Jolowicz (2001), at 115–116.

368 Zuckerman (2013), at 367.

369 However, this is not often used. Applications for judgments to be set aside are also rare. The defendant needs to show circumstances that are likely to produce a better outcome for him, or evidence that was not previously available (CPR 13.2–13.3). O'Hare & Browne (2013), at 283–287.

370 This means he has to act 'with all reasonable celerity' (*Regency Rolls Ltd v Carnall* [2000], EWCA Civ 379; *Mullock v Price* [2009], EWCA Civ 1222, [2010] at [2]).

371 CPR 13.2–3. The claimant can apply for the default judgment to be set aside if the decision is not to be enforced in a foreign jurisdiction where the assets of the defendant are located. See *Messer Griesheim GmbH v Goyal MG Gases PVT Ltd* [2006] EWHC 79, QB (Comm). Zuckerman (2013), at 367, Andrews (2008), at 93; Andrews (2013), at 240–242; O'Hare & Kevin Browne (2013), at 287.

372 Andrews (2003), at 497.

373 See Section 2.3.1.4.

recover fixed costs for the commencement of the claim and the entry of a judgment: namely, between £50 (approx. €57) and £110 (approx. €126) for the commencement of the claim,[374] and between £22 (approx. €25) and £35 (approx. €40) for the entry of a judgment variation.[375] The remaining costs will be borne by the claimant.

3.3.1.4. Use in Practice

In 2015, based on the Ministry of Justice statistics, 735,394 default judgments were issued in the County Court and 944 in the Queen's Bench Division of the High Court.[376]

3.3.2. Summary Judgment

3.3.2.1. General Aspects

Together with the default judgment, the summary judgment is the procedure by which creditors may seek to obtain an enforceable title without a full trial. The procedure allows the issuance of a judgment at an early stage of the proceedings, without the delay and additional expense of a trial.[377] The summary judgment was introduced in 1852 for the benefit of merchants, providing them with a means to enforce debts in a quick and efficient manner, and seeking to achieve results similar to those attained in other countries by 'summary' procedures. However, the summary judgment is not based 'upon a continental system of a court order to pay' that becomes a 'judgment' if this was not contested within a certain timeframe.[378] The current summary judgment procedure is available for claimants as well as defendants. Thus, judgments based on the domestic summary procedure may be issued not only against the defendant, as with the EOP, but also against the claimant. The procedure is suitable for cases in which it can be shown that the claim or defence has no real prospect of success,[379] and there is no other compelling reason for the matter to be disposed of at a trial.[380]

374 Table 1 CPR 45.2. Available at https://www.justice.gov.uk/courts/procedure-rules/civil/rules/part45-fixed-costs#rule45.4.

375 Table 2 of CPR 45.4. Available at https://www.justice.gov.uk/courts/procedure-rules/civil/rules/part45-fixed-costs#rule45.4.

376 Ministry of Justice, Civil Justice Statistics Quarterly, England and Wales (Incorporating The Royal Courts of Justice 2015), Statistics Bulletin, 2 June 2016, at 24; Civil Justice in the County Court, CSV Workload National Masked table (available at https://www.gov.uk/government/statistics/civil-justice-statistics-quarterly-january-to-march-2016-and-the-royal-courts-of-justice-2015). In 2011, the procedure accounted for around 70% of the specified money claims; Ministry of Justice, *Judicial and Court Statistics 2011*, 2012, at 17 (available at https://www.gov.uk/government/uploads/system/uploads/attachment_data/file/162459/judicial-court-stats-2011.pdf.pdf).

377 CPR 24.1. See Jolowicz (2001), at 115; Andrews (2008), at 86.

378 Crifò (2009a), at 152, 168.

379 The test of 'a real prospect of succeeding' has to be understood in the context of Lord Woolf's Access to Justice Report to promote a proportionate use of resources. Woolf (1996), Chapter 12, para. 31–32. Zuckerman (2013), at 380–382.

380 CPR 24.2, 24 PD 2(3)(b). This provision is a secondary test, a 'safety-valve provision' to safeguard the wider interest of justice. See Andrews (2008), at 87; Zuckerman (2013), at 384–385.

The spectrum of claims for which the summary judgment can be used is much wider than that of the EOP. Summary judgments against the claimant are available in any type of proceedings, including claims for specific sums of money, while summary judgments against the defendant are more limited, excluding certain matters.[381] The procedure may be used to test the legal as well as the factual merits of a claim or a defence, or a combination of these.[382] Furthermore, a summary judgment may dispose of the case as a whole or be confined to a particular issue, whereas the EOP deals with the entire case. Another particularity compared to the EOP is the fact that the summary judgment may also be initiated by the court, provided 'all the necessary materials are before the court and the parties have had adequate notice' of the issues the court proposes to process.[383] This allows the court to prevent weak cases from going to trial.[384]

3.3.2.2. The Procedure

The summary judgment allows a quick handling of a clear and undisputable claim where a full ordinary proceeding will not make any useful contribution to the just determination of the claim or its particulars.[385] The application for summary judgment should be made by the interested party as early as possible, preferably even before filing the allocation questionnaire – or at the same time – in order to avoid unnecessary costs.[386] The court may order a summary judgment on its own initiative at the allocation stage of the case, following an examination of the parties' statements.[387] The claimant may not apply for summary judgment before the defendant has served an acknowledgement of service or defence, unless the court gives permission or a practice direction provides otherwise.[388] If the application for summary judgment is dismissed, the court will give directions for the service of defence. The defendant may apply for summary judgment at any time after proceedings have started.[389]

The application for summary judgment is made by means of a notice (form N244). As with the EOP application form, the applicant has to identify the evidence on which he relies (24 PD 2(4)), and sign a statement of truth. The applicant relies on any written evidence contained in his statement of case or application notice, or on a witness statement confirmed by a statement of truth submitted to the court.[390] He has to show that on the basis of the evidence the respondent has no real prospect of succeeding with

381 CPR 24.3.

382 24 PD 1.2–1.3.

383 Zuckerman (2013), at 379; *Orford v Rasmi Electronics Ltd* [2000] EWCA Civ 1672.

384 According to CPR 3.3, the court has a general power to make orders on its own initiative, and based on the active case management duties (CPR 1.4(2)(c). This is an example of proportionality, a concept prominent within CPR 1.1(2)(c). See also Zuckerman (2013), at 379–380; Andrews (2003), at 506.

385 Zuckerman (2013), at 378.

386 26 PD 5.3.

387 CPR 24.4(3), 26 PD 5.1–2 and CPR 1.4(1)-(2).

388 CPR 24.4(1)-(2). When the claimant is allowed to apply for a summary judgment before the defendant has served a defence (e.g. for dishonoured cheques where the possible grounds of defence are very narrow), the defendant does not need to file a defence before the hearing of the application.

389 Zuckerman (2013), at 385.

390 Oral evidence cannot be used, unless the court allows it (CPR 32.6).

the claim or of successfully defending it, and that he knows of no other reason that disposal of the claim should await trial.[391] In contrast to the EOP, the procedure is adversarial, and can involve a hearing. The defendant wishing to rely on written evidence in return has to file a witness statement and serve copies on the other parties.[392]

Summary judgment hearings are not summary trials or 'mini-trials'[393] – they are simply hearings to dispose of cases for which there is no prospect of success. Thus, the summary judgment is not an uncontested claim. This is different than the EOP, which becomes enforceable when the claim is not contested.

When the summary judgment concerns the entire claim, the court will award the remedy sought. When the request refers only to part of the claim, the remaining issues will be handled according to common procedure.[394] It is the same for an EOP issued for part of the claim where the provisions of the national procedural law will regulate the remaining part.[395]

A summary proceeding involves a determination on the merits, and is a final judgment creating *res judicata*. This also concerns cases in which the summary judgment dismisses the claim. The judgment may be challenged only by way of appeal, except in situations in which it is issued against a defendant that did not appear at the hearing. In this second situation, the judgment may be varied or set aside, or the court may even decide to re-list the application. If the court dismisses the application for a summary judgment or does not dispose of the case entirely, it will give further directions regarding the trial.[396] As well as giving judgment or dismissing the claim, a solution common to the EOP as well, the court may issue a conditional order[397] if it appears the application might succeed but it is improbable that it will happen.[398]

3.3.2.3. Costs of the Proceedings

Court fees for summary proceedings vary according to the amount of the claim as mentioned in Section 3.2.3. Representation and other fees can be added to these costs. The creditor will be able to recover from the debtor only the fixed costs as provided for by CPR 45.2 and 45.3. The fixed costs for commencement of the claim depend on the value of the claim and on the service method chosen, and vary between £50 (approx. €57) and £110 (approx. €126).[399] The costs to be recovered for entry of judgment vary between £175 (approx. €200.55) and £2010 (approx. €2,303.5). The remaining litigation costs incurred are borne by the claimant.

391 24 PD 2(3). *E.D.&F. Man Liquid Products Ltd v Patel* [2003] CPLR 384; *Paseana Ltd v Lextrex Holdings Ltd.* [2010] EWCA Civ 1539; *Credit Suisse International v Ramot Plana OD* [2010] EWHC 2759 (Comm). Sime (2014), at 276.

392 CPR 24.5.

393 Lord Woolf M.R. in *Swain V. Hillman* [2001] 1 All E.R. 91. See also, Sime (2014), at 277–278.

394 24 PD 10.

395 For criticism of this solution, see Section 2.3.1.3.

396 24 PD 10 and 26 PD 12.

397 24 PD 4.

398 For the requirements, see 24 PD 5.2.

399 Table 1 CPR 45.2. Available at https://www.justice.gov.uk/courts/procedure-rules/civil/rules/part45-fixed-costs#rule45.4.

3.3.2.4. Use in Practice

Although the procedure seems to be a popular instrument due to its versatility, statistics published by the Ministry of Justice do not detail the number of cases that are handled annually in accordance with this instrument.

3.3.3. *Part 8 Claim*

3.3.3.1. General Aspects

A Part 8 Claim is an alternative procedure intended to provide a simple, speedy remedy regarding claims that do not involve 'a substantial dispute of fact',[400] raising clear, well-defined issues for the resolution of which there is no need to use the cumbersome ordinary claim procedure (e.g. exchange of particulars of the claims, defence, and disclosure).[401] A Part 8 Claim does not concern situations in which the defendant did not acknowledge service or did not respond to the claims.[402] Further, compared to the summary judgments, a Part 8 Claim does not involve factual disputes. The scope of the procedure is more limited than that of the default judgment or the summary procedure. This is appropriate for money claims concerning costs-only proceedings where parties have failed to agree on the amount of costs in the main proceeding; for applications seeking court approval of a settlement; or for applications for mediation settlement enforcement. In practice, a Part 8 Claim may involve cases in which the controversy between parties has been resolved at a pre-action stage, and this procedure regards only consequential matters such as failing to agree on the amount of the costs.[403]

3.3.3.2. The Procedure

Like the EOP application form, a Part 8 Claim is commenced by issuing a claim form (N208) containing details,[404] and includes a statement of truth. Unlike the EOP, however, the evidence supporting the claim must be filed and served with the claim form.[405]

The defendant takes part in the proceeding and can rely on written evidence to contest the claim, which he has filed with the acknowledgement of service and served on the claimant.[406] This is different than the EOP procedure, where the defendant only learns about the EOP after it has been issued.[407]

400 CPR 8.2(a).
401 Part 7 CPR. Blackstone's Civil Practice 2015, at 234; Zuckerman (2013), at 186–188, Sime (2014), at 87–88.
402 CPR 8(4). See Zuckerman (2013), at 188.
403 O'Hare & Browne (2013), at 183.
404 See the Notes for claimant on completing a Part 8 claim form (N208A) (available at www.justice.gov.uk/courts/procedure-rules/civil/forms).
405 CPR 8.5(1)-(2) – 8.6 and 8A PD 7.1–7.2.
406 CPR 8.5(3)-(6).
407 Article 12(2)-(5) EOP.

The court will automatically allocate the claim to the multi-track.[408] Generally, a hearing will be held, based on documentary materials, but the court may allow oral evidence or cross-examination.[409] However, cost-related proceedings may not require a hearing. In the light of Article 6 ECHR, in such a situation it is probable that the court will dispense with the hearing provided the parties agree to this.[410]

3.3.3.3. Costs of the Proceedings

Court fees for money-related claims apply for this type of Part 8 Claim, and depend on the amount of the claim. Representation and hearing costs can be added to these fees.

3.3.3.4. Use in Practice

The statistics published by the Ministry of Justice do not detail the number of cases that are handled each year in accordance with Part 8.

3.3.4. Money Claim Online and the Claim Production Centre

3.3.4.1. General Aspects

Money Claim Online (MCOL) and the Claim Production Centre (CPC) are regulated by a special practice direction to ordinary court proceedings: namely, PD 7C and PD 7E CPR. The MCOL procedure was established in 2001 to make justice more affordable and accessible with regard to domestic monetary claims in county courts,[411] and is not available for cross-border monetary claims. MCOL (7E PD) provides the possibility for a claim to be made online (7E PD 1.1) via Her Majesty's Courts and Tribunals Service website.[412] MCOL also requires parties to make use of standard forms that can be filed electronically in a procedure that can be conducted entirely online. This characteristic is only partially shared by the EOP and the ESCP, however. Although their forms are available and can be filled in electronically, they are not generally submitted to the court online.[413]

Previously known as the 'Summons Procedure Centre', the CPC was established in 1989 to enable county courts to deal more efficiently with the needs of institutions involved in bulk recovery claims (e.g. utility companies, credit card companies).[414] The procedure has features similar to MCOL, but in contrast to MCOL each user must obtain permission to use the CPC and comply with the Code of Practice issued by Her Majesty's Courts and Tribunals Service.[415]

408 CPR 8.9(c). Blackstone's Civil Practice 2015, at 237.
409 CPR 8.6.
410 Zuckerman (2013), at 188.
411 See www.gov.uk/make-money-claim-online.
412 www.moneyclaim.gov.uk/web/mcol/welcome.
413 EOP and ESCP claims can be filed online only as part of the e-Codex project. See further, Section 8.4.3.
414 2012 White Book 7.10.1.
415 7C PD 1.1. For the Code of Practice, see www.justice.gov.uk/courts/northampton-bulk-centre/claim-production-centre.

Both procedures are limited to claims for a specific amount of money less than £100,000, and can be brought against one or two defendants whose service address is within England. They cannot be used against the Crown or if either of the parties is a child or a protected party under Part 21, or if the claimant is publicly funded within the meaning of Legal Aid Act 1998. The procedures are limited to County Court claims. All claims filed according to MCOL and the CPC are submitted to the Northampton County Court Business Centre.

3.3.4.2. The Procedure

Particulars of the claim in MCOL must be set out in 1080 characters (including spaces), unless they are served and filed separately by the claimant.[416] This procedure is therefore available for 'relatively simple claims'.[417] The progress of the claim may be followed on the basis of an electronic record. The claimant must have a valid credit or debit card in order to pay the court fees.[418]

CPC bulk claims are submitted electronically to the court by the claimant or his solicitor. As with the MCOL claim, a statement of truth is to accompany each batch of claim forms.[419] This aspect is common also to the EOP procedure.[420] The court is to send the claim form and the response pack to the defendant. This characteristic is similar to the requirements of Article 5(2) ESCP, establishing a duty for the court to send the defendant a copy of the claim form together with the answer form. The defendant will be able to file a defence online.[421] The defence is governed by the ordinary court rules on defence (Part 15 CPR). Where a defence is filed against a CPC claim, the court asks the claimant whether he wishes to proceed with the claim. If in the affirmative, the proceedings will be transferred to the County Court hearing centre.[422] A defended MCOL will also be transferred to the defendant's County Court hearing centre.[423] Further, the case is to be handled according to the rules on track allocation, a feature that resembles the situation regarding an opposed EOP that is transferred to the ordinary civil procedure.[424]

If the defendant ignores or admits the claim, the claimant may request online a judgment in default or on admission, as the case may be. Together with this, the claimant may also request the issue of a warrant of execution.[425]

416 7E 5.2.

417 Sime (2014), at 64.

418 7E PD 3.1.

419 7C PD 1.4(4) and 7E PD 9.1–9.2.

420 Article 7(3) EOP.

421 7C PD 5.2A-5.2D and 7E PD 7.1–7.2.

422 7C PD 1.3(e).

423 7C PD 1.3(2)(e) and 7E PD 12.2.

424 Article 12(4)(c) EOP.

425 7C PD 5.6 and 7E PD 11.2. This can be done by completing an online request form and paying the appropriate fee electronically. *Money Claim Online (MCOL) – User Guide for Claimants*, HM Courts & Tribunals Service, at 20, (available at https://formfinder.hmctsformfinder.justice.gov.uk/mcol-guide-eng.pdf) and https://www.justice.gov.uk/newsite/courts/northampton-business-centre.

As with the European uniform procedures, representation by a lawyer is not compulsory with regard to MCOL or the CPC.[426]

3.3.4.3. Costs of Proceedings

MCOL court fees vary from £25 (approx. €28.65) for claims up to £300 (approx.€343.8) to 4.5% of the value of the claim for claims greater than £100,000 (approx. €116,402.7).[427] MCOL fees are overall lower than the court fees charged in other national procedures for the recovery of monetary claims. The same court fees appear to apply to the CPC, although in previous years they were lower than MCOL fees.[428]

If a defence or counterclaim is involved, additional fees apply. In the event that one or more hearings are held, the litigation costs will increase.[429]

3.3.4.4. Use in Practice

In 2010, 13% of the claims for a specific amount of money were issued through the MCOL procedure.[430] Subsequent statistics published by the Ministry of Justice do not mention the volume of MCOL cases handled yearly. This procedure appears to be attractive for cases in which the claim is admitted or is not disputed by the defendant. Additionally, the costs are lower than in the ordinary procedure, and the required forms may be filed online without parties generally needing to attend a hearing in court or to appear before a judge.

As regards the CPC, the Ministry of Justice does not publish statistical data on its use.

3.3.5. Interim Payments

3.3.5.1. General Aspects

An interim payment order enables the claimant to obtain advance payments from the defendant, often before the actual trial, on the basis of 'any damages, debt or other sum (except costs) which the court may hold the defendant liable to pay'.[431]

426 7C PD 1.1 and 1.3(2)(e)(ii), 7E PD 1.2–1.3. See Kramer, Tuil, Tillema, Hazelhorst & Onţanu (2012), at 146.

427 A detailed list of fees is available at www.gov.uk/make-court-claim-for-money/court-fees.

428 The court fees for institutional claimants involved in bulk recovery claims varied from £15 for claims not exceeding £300 to £550 for claims between £50,000 and £100,000.

429 *Money Claim Online (MCOL) – User Guide for Claimants*, HM Courts & Tribunals Service, at 4, (available at www.justice.gov.uk/downloads/courts/mcol-quickstart-guide.pdf); Kramer, Tuil, Tillema, Hazelhorst & Onţanu (2012), at 146.

430 *Judicial and Court Statistics 2010*, Ministry of Justice, 2011, at 10 (available at www.gov.uk/government/uploads/system/uploads/attachment_data/file/162482/judicial-court-stats.pdf.pdf). According to Table 1.2 (at 18) in the same document, 138,083 claims out of 1,040,589 specified 'money' claims were issued through Money Claim Online.

431 CPR 25.1(1)(k). The power to order interim payments is derived from Section 32 Senior Courts Act 1981 and Section 50 County Courts Act 1984. For an extended discussion on interim payments, see Andrews (2013), at 216–219; Zuckerman (2013), at 520–526.

Compared to other national procedures or to the European uniform procedure instruments, the interim payment order is not designed to provide a final resolution to the matter in dispute, although it may become final if the procedure is discontinued. The procedure seeks to ensure that a claimant who has a strong case will not suffer financial hardship or need to wait until after the trial for payment of the money to which he appears to be entitled.[432] Where the defence has no real prospect of success, it is common in practice to combine the application for summary judgment with an interim payment.[433]

The court can order an interim payment provided that: (1) the defendant has admitted liability but there are outstanding issues to be decided by the court and action must continue; (2) the court is satisfied that the claimant obtained judgment against the defendant with the amount of money or damages to be assessed (excluding costs);[434] or (3) the court is satisfied that, if the claim were to go to trial, the claimant would obtain a judgment against the defendant for a substantial sum of money (other than costs).[435]

3.3.5.2. The Procedure

Based on the claimant's application,[436] it is for the court to decide whether an order for payment is appropriate,[437] and, if this is the case, what is a 'reasonable proportion of the likely amount of the final judgment', taking into account contributory negligence and any relevant set-off or counterclaim.[438] The amount of the interim payment is discretionary, but the court will assess the amount that is likely to be awarded in the event of a success, reducing this then to a reasonable proportion of the determined amount.[439]

A copy of the application notice and the supporting evidence will be served on the respondent 14 days before the hearing, to which he can reply and rely on written evidence for the hearing.[440] This involvement of the parties, the timeframe, and the use of evidence is similar to the ESCP procedure. If the court refuses to order an interim payment, the claimant may appeal or apply for another order, provided that new evidence has emerged that would increase his chances of success.[441]

432 Blackstone's Civil Practice 2015, at 598–605; Zuckerman (2013), at 520.

433 Blackstone's Civil Practice 2015, at 602.

434 The judgment obtained may be a default judgment, a judgment on admission, or a summary judgment. If the sum representing the reasonable proportion to be awarded as an interim payment order is too small to justify the making of an order, the claimant's application may be dismissed. *Campbell v Mylchreest* [1999] P.I.Q.R. Q17, Auld L.J.; O'Hare & Browne (2013), at 407.

435 CPR 25.7(1)(a)-(c). Andrews (2008), at 77.

436 An application for an interim payment may be made by the defendant at any time after the claim form has been served on the defendant, and the time limit for the person to file an acknowledgement of service has expired (CPR 25.6(1)).

437 If the delay of assessment of damages is not considered to be substantial, the court may be reluctant to issue the order, unless the claimant has particular reasons for requesting it, such as hardship resulting from the loss of earnings. See O'Hare & Browne (2013), at 414–415.

438 CPR 25.7(4)-(5).

439 On the assessment factors, see Zuckerman (2013), at 524.

440 CPR 25.6(3).

441 CPR 25.6(2). See O'Hare & Browne (2013), at 416; Zuckerman (2013), at 525.

The awarding of an interim payment will not be disclosed to the trial judge until the questions of liability and the amount of money to be awarded have been decided, unless the defendant agrees.[442] The claimant cannot discontinue the proceedings except when the defendant gives his consent in writing, or if the court gives permission.[443]

3.3.5.3. Costs of Proceedings

The court fee the claimant has to pay is £155 (approx. €176.7). Other costs relating to money claims apply.

3.3.5.4. Use in Practice

In its statistics reports, the Ministry of Justice publishes no information with regard to the use of this procedure.

3.3.6. *National Small Claims Procedure*

3.3.6.1. General Aspects

Domestic small claims are handled within the small claims track. This is designed to provide a speedy, effective, and proportionate method of dealing with disputes of limited financial value: for instance, 'an expeditious and uncomplicated procedure for disposing of modest claims'.[444] The procedure was introduced in 1973, and was established as a means for adjudicating upon individual consumer complaints.[445] The process was reviewed as part of the Lord Woolf Reforms as an important instrument to increase 'access to justice for ordinary people'.[446] Due to its vast use in practice, the small claims track is one of the Reforms' most successful procedures.[447]

The procedure is regulated by 26 PD and Part 27 CPR and 27 PD. The small claims track is the usual track dealing with claims up to £10,000 (excluding personal injury and housing disrepair claims).[448] Cases allocated to the small claims track range from 'very modest consumer disputes (...) to technically complex disputes over credit hire and factually complicated disagreements over building extensions', as well as many road traffic accidents.[449]

442 CPR 25.9.

443 CPR 38.2(2)(b). Andrews (2008), at 77.

444 Zuckerman (2013), at 641; Sime (2014), at 302.

445 Lewis (2006), at 52–53; Madge (2004), at 202–203.

446 Lord Woolf believed that 'the small claims scheme provides the most effective protection for litigants who do not have the resources to pay for legal advice and representation and who are not eligible for legal aid'. Woolf (1995), Chapter 15, paragraphs 3 and 4 (available at http://webarchive.nationalarchives.gov.uk/+/http://www.dca.gov.uk/civil/reportfr.htm). Sorabji (2015), at 168.

447 See Turner (2009), at 85; Crifò (2016), at 83; Bello (2010), at 4 and 17.

448 On 1 April 2013 the threshold was increased from £5,000 to £10,000 (CPR 27.1(20)). Civil Procedure (Amendment) Rules 2013 Statutory Instrument 2013 No. 262.

449 Blackstone's Civil Practice 2012, at 657.

3.3.6.2. The Procedure

Small claims are initiated in a manner similar to other domestic procedures by the filing of a claim form (N1).[450] As with the ESCP, the claimant must provide particulars containing a concise statement of the facts on which he relies.[451] Also similar to the ESCP, once the claim is received by the court, it will be sent to the defendant.[452] If the defendant disputes the claim and the case is allocated to the track, the court will give directions. Like the ESCP, the national procedure is of an adversarial nature. Hearings in the small claims track are largely informal, taking place usually in the judge's room, and sometimes in a courtroom.[453] In practice, the hearing is expected to last around an hour, and the judge will question witnesses and parties, and direct the evidence considered to be appropriate.[454] The procedure has significant flexibility compared to ordinary court proceedings when it comes to evidence disclosure and expert evidence.[455] Under CPR 27.9(1) a party may request the court by written notice at least 7 days before the hearing to decide the claim in his absence. In this event, the court will consider the statement of case and any other documents submitted.[456] Furthermore, provided all parties agree, the claim can be determined by the district judge without a hearing, based on the written submissions to the court.[457] The parties' consent is essential in view of Article 6(1) ECHR.[458] In contrast, ESCP hearings are intended to be more of an exceptional nature if the court considers it necessary and the parties have requested it.[459]

There is a right to appeal small claims judgments,[460] just as for the ESCP.[461] However, the mechanism does not often seem to be exercised.[462] A party who wishes to appeal a small claim judgment must apply for permission, which will be granted only if the case has a real prospect of success or if there are other compelling reasons.[463] In contrast, the ESCP appeal is generally available, as the English legislator opted to make an appeal procedure available in the ESCP.[464]

450 See www.justice.gov.uk/courts/procedure-rules/civil/forms.

451 CPR 16.4(1)(a). Annex I, Form A – Claim Form, point 8 ESCP.

452 Article 5(2) ESCP.

453 CPR 27.4(1)(d), CPR 27.6 and 27 PD 4.2. Zuckerman (2013), at 641–642.

454 Sorabji (2015), at 169. Ministry of Justice, Civil Justice Statistics Quarterly, England and Wales, April June 2015, Statistics Bulletin, 1 September 2016, at 8–9 (available at www.gov.uk/government/uploads/system/uploads/attachment_data/file/549424/civil-justice-statistics-april-june-2016.pdf).

455 Sorabji (2015), at 169.

456 Blackstone's Civil Practice 2015, at 665.

457 CPR 27.10.

458 Sime (2014), at 304.

459 Article 5(1) ESCP. See also Section 2.3.2.2.

460 27 PD 8.1–8.2.

461 27 PD 8.1–8.3 CPR. The ESCP appeal will be treated as a claim allocated to the small track, and is subject to the provisions of Part 52 CPR (CPR 78.14(1)). Blackstone's Civil Practice 2015, at 750.

462 Madge (2004), at 207.

463 CPR 52.6.

464 78 PD 10 in conjunction with CPR 52. The English legislator was in favor of including a common rule on ESCP appeal on the grounds of error of law, but an agreement could not be reached between Member

In accordance with CPR 26 PD 8.1(1)(b), the procedure 'laid down in Part 27 for the preparation of the case and the conduct of the hearing are designed to make it possible for a litigant to conduct his own case without legal representation if he wishes'. The ESCP is also intended to be carried out in person, as representation is not mandatory.[465] The district judge is free to have 'an interventionist approach' in the way he sees fit,[466] considering that in most cases the parties are not represented, in order to 'elicit the relevant information in a quick and informal manner'.[467] In the same light, the ESCP Regulation provides for practical assistance for the parties, with the courts being able to offer information on procedural questions.[468] However, research carried out in England revealed that legally unrepresented parties in small claims procedures do less well than represented parties, since judges issue their decisions on the basis of legal provisions.[469]

3.3.6.3. Costs of Proceedings

The principle of proportionality plays a significant role in the national procedure. The costs of the case should not be disproportionate compared to the claim.[470] Court fees for starting a claim vary from £35 (approx. €40) for claims up to £300 (approx. €343.8) to £455 (approx. €521.4) for claims not exceeding £10,000 (approx. €11,460).[471] When a hearing is scheduled, a hearing fee has to be paid, and varies between £25 (approx. €28.65) for claims of up to £300 (approx. €343.8) to £335 (approx. €384) for claims that amount to more than £3,000 (approx. €3438). The 'no costs' for small claims rule encourages parties to represent themselves. The basic principle is that the litigation costs are not recovered by the winning party, except for routine expenses provided for in CPR 27.14 (i.e. court fees, costs for issuing the claim, witness expenses up to maximum £90 – approx. €103).[472] Further, the court has the power to order a party to pay further costs if he has behaved unreasonably.[473] This is one of the 'most important factors

States. Letter from Rt Hon Baroness Ashton of Upholland, Parliamentary Under Secretary of State, Department for Constitutional Affairs to the Chairman, 23rd Report: European Small Claims Procedure, 37th Report 2006–07, European Union Committee, House of Lords, at 87 (available at www.publications.parliament.uk/pa/ld200607/ldselect/ldeucom/182/18219.htm).

465 Article 10 ESCP.

466 The interpretation of the meaning of 'interventionist approach' varies with district judges. See Baldwin (2003), at 53–66.

467 Blackstone's Civil Practice 2015, at 738; Bello (2010), at 6 (available at www.consumerfocus.org.uk/files/2010/10/Small-claims-WEB-FILE.pdf).

468 Recital 21 and 22 in conjunction with Article 11 ESCP Regulation.

469 Cortes Dieguez (2008), at 86.

470 Andrews (2013), at 707; Lewis (2006), at 53.

471 EX 50, Civil and Family Court Fees, HM Courts & Tribunals Service, 6 March 2017, at 5.

472 Blackstone's Civil Practice 2015, at 738; Pearl & Goodman (2010), at 176–178.

473 CPR 27.14(2)(g). Blackstone's, Civil Practice, Oxford University Press, 2012, at 668; Pearl & Goodman (2010), at 182–184.

making the small claims procedure accessible'.[474] The is different than the ESCP where the loser-pays principle applies, except for costs that are incurred unnecessarily or are disproportionate.[475]

3.3.6.4. Use in Practice

The English small claims procedure is employed extensively in practice. Every year over 55,000 judgments relate to cases solved in the small claims track; in 2015, this amounted to 55,694 cases in the County Court and 72,524 cases in total.[476] Of the total number of small claims for a specific amount of money, 33,338 proceeded to a hearing at the County Court hearing centres.[477] Hence, unlike for the ESCP, the hearing is usually part of the national procedure. According to official statistics, the average time for handling a national small claim case was 32.4 weeks in 2015 (just above 8 months) from the moment of submission to the court to issuance of the judgment.[478]

3.4. National Attitudes towards EOP and ESCP Regulations

The negotiation and adoption of European accelerated summary procedures for the recovery of liquid and certain money debts in cross-border claims was generally welcomed in England. The following section analyses the views expressed with regard to the EOP and the ESCP at the national level.

3.4.1. The EOP

The UK decided to opt in to this Regulation. Nationally, the proposal was dealt with 'relatively swiftly', as the EOP retained some similarities to the European Enforcement Order (EEO), and civil justice was a high point in the programme of the British Presidency of the Council.[479] The EOP was perceived as a useful instrument that would enable the recovery of uncontested pecuniary claims in cross-border cases 'without the hassle, the delay and the expense of going and getting some further order' in the Member State where execution is sought.[480] The Government and Parliament did not favour an extended application of the EOP procedure to purely national cases.

474 House of Commons Constitutional Affairs Committee, *The Courts. Small Claims*, First Report of Session 2005–06, 6 December 2005, at 8 (available at www.parliament.uk).

475 Article 16 ESCP.

476 Ministry of Justice, Civil Justice Statistics Quarterly, England and Wales (Incorporating the Royal Courts of Justice 2015), January to March 2016, Statistics Bulletin, 2 June 2016, at 32 (Table 1.3) and Civil Justice in the County Courts (available at https://www.gov.uk/government/statistics/civil-justice-statistics-quarterly-january-to-march-2016-and-the-royal-courts-of-justice-2015).

477 *Ibidem*.

478 *Ibidem*, at 10.

479 Crifò (2005), at 215.

480 Committee on European Union Forty-Fifth Report, Annex A, Memoranda submitted by Baroness Ashton of Upholland, Examination of Witnesses (Questions 1 – 21), 30 November 2005 (available at https://www.publications.parliament.uk/pa/ld200506/ldselect/ldeucom/243/243251.htm).

However, stakeholders taking part in the domestic consultation on the EOP text had mixed reactions.[481] Similarly, scholars expressed mixed opinions with regard to adoption of the EOP and the procedure's features.[482]

EOP service provisions were also a cause of concern for judges' associations and for professional organisations. These concerns regarded the methods of service,[483] identifying the defendant's exact address,[484] the need to include an additional certificate of service form for situations when the creditor carries out the service on the defendant, and court staff access to service provisions applicable in other Member States.[485] For the securing of legal certainty, Crifò stresses the importance of setting minimum requirements of proof of notice. Also stressed is the importance of the existence of a general revocation remedy for cases in which the defendant is prevented from taking action and defending against the claim due to force majeure or exceptional circumstances.[486] Such a uniform approach, for instance, would have been a very welcome solution in situations such as those encountered in the *eco cosmetics* case.[487]

In view of the high costs of litigation in England, costs that could be claimed and additional fees triggered by the EOP due to the referral to the ordinary national procedure were part of the national discussion. The provisions of Article 25(1) were considered to hide 'a multitude of problems' because of the lack of an allocation of costs rule that can affect the parties' possibility of recuperating legal expenses, such as those incurred by relying on legal representation.[488] Hence, in the process of amending Article 25(1) EOP by Regulation 2015/2421, the UK played an active role. It sought to achieve a clear drafting of the provision concerning the court fees applicable to opposed EOPs, and to

481 Comments were received from the Senior Master of the Queen's Bench Division, the Council of Circuit Judges, the Association of District Judges, the Law Society, the Bar Council, the Civil Courts Users Association, National Association of Citizens Advice Bureaux (NACAB), the National Consumer Council, the Consumers Association, the Consumer Credit Association, CBI, the Forum of Private Businesses, the Department of Trade and Industry (DTI), the Federation of Small Businesses, Advice Services Alliance, the Trading Standards Institute, and Local Authorities Co-ordinators of Regulatory Services (LACORS). The responses of the Senior Master and the Association of District Judges considered various practical aspects of the proposal in connection with the existing national procedural rules, and the implications that such procedures would have on the workload of the judiciary and clerical members of the courts. See *Correspondence with the Ministers* in 4th Report Session 2005–06, European Union Committee, House of Lords, at 254.

482 James (2009), at 243; Sandbrook (2011), at 192; Crifò (2005), at 200–223; Crifò (2009), at 359–378; Crifò (2009a), at 117–147; Crifò (2011), at 283–303.

483 The House of Lords expressed its opinions on this matter of the EOP Regulation proposal. *Correspondence with Ministers*, 45th Report Session 2005–06, European Union Committee, House of Lords, at 406–416. Crifò (2005), at 217.

484 This aspect is of crucial importance as confirmed by the *eco cosmetics* case. On the importance of carrying out the service in accordance with the minimum standards set by the EOP Regulation, see Section 2.3.1.3.

485 Summary of consultation on the European Order for Payment in 4th Report of Session 2005–06, Correspondence with Ministers, European Union Committee, House of Lords, at 254.

486 Crifò (2005), at 217.

487 Joined Cases C-119/13 to C-120/13. See also Section 2.3.1.4.

488 Crifò (2009a), at 118–119.

make sure these fees would not exceed those applicable to other proceedings that were not preceding an EOP.[489]

Other references to national law have been identified as having the potential to create domestic variations and to affect the uniformity of the EOP procedure. This is the case for: (1) whether the claimant is precluded from resubmitting an application or making an ordinary claim for the part of debt not recovered by the EOP);[490] and (2) the transfer mechanism to the ordinary civil proceedings following opposition.[491]

Language differences and variations resulting from the translation of the EOP provisions also raised concerns among scholars,[492] as did the terminology used by the Regulation compared to that of the English procedure.[493] The lack of precision is seen as the result of multiple authentic linguistic versions, and of negotiations to reach common agreed principles to be translated into 'something that "fits" within the individual legal system' of each Member State.[494] Domestic procedural legislation is largely embedded in national realities and traditions, and political interference makes it more vulnerable to aspects that are incomplete, unsolved, or avoided in order to reach a common agreement.[495] Further, translation and possible language issues may arise in relation to the service of the application form and the EOP upon the defendant.[496]

The UK Government strongly supported the amendment of Article 17 EOP by Regulation 2015/2421 on continuation of the procedure following opposition in accordance with the ESCP or any appropriate national procedure, as did professional organisations that considered the amendment to benefit creditors.[497]

The EOP rules leaving enforcement to the domestic legislation of the place the assets are located was considered disappointing.[498]Further, the CPR 78 Rules that accommodate the EOP procedure in the English system were criticised because they do not contain actual specific enforcement rules.

3.4.2. The ESCP

The UK supported the adoption and revision of the ESCP, viewing it as a 'very practical measure' for ordinary citizens.[499] In the proposal, the Government saw a potential

489 Council of the European Union, Delegation of the United Kingdom, Interinstitutional File 2013/0403 (COD), 13498/14, Brussels, 24 September 2014, at 3; Council of the European Union, Delegation of the United Kingdom, Interinstitutional File 2013/0403 (COD), 14380/14, Brussels, 15 October 2014, at 3.

490 Form C read in conjunction with Article 26 EOP Regulation. See Crifò (2009a), at 127–130.

491 See discussion by Crifò (2009a), at 135–136.

492 Crifò (2009a), at 119, 122–123; Sandbrook (2011), at 192, 194.

493 2015 White Book, at 2014.

494 Crifò (2009), at 377.

495 Crifò (2009), at 377–379.

496 2012 White Book Part 78 – European Procedure, Annotation 78.2.2; Crifò (2009a), at. 123.

497 Council of the European Union, Delegation of the United Kingdom, Interinstitutional File 2013/0403 (COD),8530/14, ADD7, Brussels, 7 April 2014, at 8; House of Commons, European Scrutiny Committee, Thirty-third Report of Session 2013–14, 29 January 2014, at 47; Bar Council response to the European Commission's consultation on the European Small Claims Procedure, ETI 39850528734–23.

498 Sandbrook (2011), at 194.

499 23rd Report of Session 2005–06, *European Small Claims Procedure*, Report with Evidence, European Union Committee, House of Lords ('23rd Report on the European Small Claims Procedure'), at 10 and

instrument that 'could bring practical and immediate benefits to the citizens'.[500] The general feeling expressed by professional organisations and experts were met enthusiastically by the Government. Scholars views, however, were mixed.[501] The ESCP proposal stimulated national debates, attracting more attention than the EOP.[502] Parliament's consultations received opinions from various sources:[503] namely, the National Consumer Council (NCC); the Senior Master and Queen's Remembrancer Mr. Robert Turner; the Association of District Judges; the Law Society of England and Wales (the Law Society); the Confederation of British Industry (CBI); the Association of British Insurers (ABI); the Law Reform Committee of the Bar Council (LRC); the Association of Personal Injury Lawyers (APIL); and Which?.[504]

The limitation of the ESCP to cross-border claims was a welcome feature of the procedure, and the Government did not support a broadening of the definition by Regulation 2015/2421.[505]

The English Government favoured a primarily written ESCP procedure, with hearings being the exception and left to the appreciation of the court.[506] Additionally, the use of modern communication technology was to be encouraged for this purpose.[507]

14. House of Commons, European Scrutiny Committee, Thirty-third Report of Session 2013–14, 29 January 2014, at 45.

500 23rd Report on the European Small Claims Procedure, at 8; 1st Report 2005, European Small Claims Procedure, Committee on European Scrutiny, House of Commons referring to the Explanatory memorandum of 1 June 2005, the Parliamentary Under-Secretary of State, Department for Constitutional Affairs; Thirtieth Report of Session 2005–06, Report, together with formal minutes, European Scrutiny Committee, House of Commons, at 6.

501 ESCP was seen as the 'equivalent of small claims track for European money claims'. Sandbrook (2011), at 196; Crifò (2011), at 292. Crifò (2009), at 369–370 and 374–377. For a more reserved approach, see the 2012 White Book Part 78, Annotation 78.2.2.

502 See 23rd Report on the European Small Claims Procedure; First Report of Session 2005–06, *The Courts: small claims*, Report, together with formal minutes, oral and written evidence, Constitutional Affairs Committee, House of Commons; Thirtieth Report of Session 2005–06, Report, together with formal minutes, European Scrutiny Committee, House of Commons.

503 23rd Report on the European Small Claims Procedure. Partial Regulatory Impact Assessment on a EU proposal for a Regulation creating a European Small Claims Procedure, at 11 (available at http://webarchive.nationalarchives.gov.uk/+/www.dca.gov.uk/consult/smallclaims/smallclaims.htm).

504 An independent, non-profit consumer organisation (www.which.co.uk).

505 Letter from Rt Hon Baroness Ashton of Upholland, Parliamentary Under Secretary of State, Department for Constitutional Affairs to the Chairman, 12 June 2006, Government Response, 37th Report 2006–07, European Union Committee, House of Lords (available at www.publications.parliament.uk/pa/ld200607/ldselect/ldeucom/182/18219.htm). 23rd Report on the European Small Claims Procedure, at 19–23. The only organisation supporting the application of the ESCP to domestic cases was APIL. See for this *The European Small Claims Procedure*, A Response by the Association of Personal Injury Lawyers, CP(L) 12/05, APIL 10/05, at 5–6 (available at http://files.apil.org.uk/pdf/Consultation Documents/846.pdf). Bar Council response to the European Commission's consultation on the European Small Claims Procedure, ETI 39850528734-23, Council of the European Union, Delegation of the United Kingdom, Interinstitutional File 2013/0403 (COD),8530/14, ADD7, Brussels, 7 April 2014, at 2.

506 23rd Report on the European Small Claims Procedure, at 32–33. Council of the European Union, Delegation of the United Kingdom, Interinstitutional File 2013/0403 (COD), 8530/14, ADD7, Brussels, 7 April 2014, at 3.

507 New Article 8 as amended by Regulation 2015/2421. Council of the European Union, Delegation of the United Kingdom, Interinstitutional File 2013/0403 (COD), 8530/14, ADD7, Brussels, 7 April 2014, at

In-person representation and the costs of proceedings proportionate to the claim were also part of the procedural arrangements supported by the English legislator in the negotiations.[508]

The House of Lords expected a properly implemented ESCP to 'produce tangible benefits for individuals and business across the Union', providing a procedure 'specially designed to deal with cross-border cases, with common forms and simple enforcement across national boundaries'.[509] In practice, as shown in Section 3.7, the procedure has been less successful than expected several years into its application. Identified difficulties have been confirmed by empirical findings: namely, procedural costs, practical difficulties related to language and the use of information technology, and the need to clarify certain provisions in order to ensure a uniform application. The lack of knowledge and awareness contributes to the limited use of the procedure.[510] Furthermore, as noted by Crifò, a significant number of matters related to the ESCP are to be decided according to national procedural rules. Additionally, national courts retain extensive powers in deciding on certain procedural aspects such as the holding of a hearing, the extent of the evidence necessary and the means used, informing the parties about procedural questions, and seeking to reach a settlement between parties.[511]

The language requirements and costs related to translation were seen as problematic aspects by legal practitioners (i.e. the Association of District Judges, the Law Society, and the Civil Justice Council).[512] The consumer organisation Which? proposed the use of online translation based on a lexicon of general terms.[513] This idea has been taking shape with the Council of the European Union e-Justice Plan,[514] but no appropriate software

4; Council of the European Union, Delegation of the United Kingdom, Interinstitutional File 2013/0403 (COD), 13498/14, Brussels, 24 September 2014, at 1–2; Council of the European Union, Delegation of the United Kingdom, Interinstitutional File 2013/0403 (COD), 14380/14, Brussels, 15 October 2014, at 1–2; UK European Consumer Centre, Public Consultation on the European Small Claims Procedure.

508 See *Correspondence with Ministers*, 45th Report Session 2005–06, European Union Committee, House of Lords, at 416.

509 23rd Report on the European Small Claims Procedure.

510 Bar Council response to the European Commission's consultation on the European Small Claims Procedure, ETI 39850528734-23; The Law Society of England and Wales, European Small Claims Procedure Response to public consultation, Transparency Register No. 38020227042-38, June 2013; Civil Justice Council for England and Wales, Royal Courts of Justice, Public Consultation on the European Small Claims Procedure; UK European Consumer Centre, Public Consultation on the European Small Claims Procedure; Crifò (2016), at 89.

511 Crifò (2009), at 375.

512 23rd Report on the European Small Claims Procedure, at 46; *Correspondence with Ministers*, 40th Report of Session 2006-07, European Union Committee, House of Lords, at 347–348; Civil Justice Council for England and Wales, Royal Courts of Justice, Public Consultation on the European Small Claims Procedure.

513 This approach is favoured also by the Government. 23rd Report on the European Small Claims Procedure, at 45–46; 37th Report of Session 2006–07, *Remaining Government Responses Session 2004–05: Government Responses Session 2005–06*, European Union Committee, House of Lords, at 82–83.

514 Within the e-Justice Plan, aims have been expressed for the creation of legal glossaries and the establishment of an online automated translation portal. Implementation of the European e-Justice Action Plan – Roadmap, 9714/1/10, Brussels, 21 May 2010, at 5 and 10–11.

allowing an automatic translation of the open-text boxes on the standard forms on the e-Justice Portal is currently available.

The ESCP threshold of €2,000 was considered to be 'unrealistically low', and to undermine the value of the procedure.[515] Most professional organisations shared this view.[516] The Government as well as professional organisations and scholars welcomed the threshold's increase by way of Regulation 2015/2421, seeing it as an opportunity to increase use of the procedure and to facilitate access to justice.[517]

As regards standard forms, the English Government was in favour of simplifying the guidance notes included in the forms, as well as of improving the layout and format.[518]

The ESCP service rules are considered to be user-friendly and simple, with the court being 'in charge of most of procedural initiatives'.[519] However, 'postal service attested by an acknowledgement of receipt including the date of service' is not common in English law: that is, there is no such element as 'acknowledgement of receipt'. A proof of postage or delivery is possible under the 'registered signed for' postal service,[520] but the lack of precision in translation and terminology can create difficulties in practice.[521] Furthermore, when needing to depend on service methods established by the EEO Regulation (EOP following Regulation 2015/2421), it is expected that national courts will still rely on methods that best fit domestic practices, adapting European rules to the national instruments.[522] The Government and professional organisations supported the

515 Government Response to the Constitutional Affairs Select Committee's Report, 'The Courts: Small Claims', 2006, at 8. House of Commons, First Report of Session 2005–06, The Courts: small claims, Report, together with formal minutes, oral and written evidence, Constitutional Affairs Committee, House of Commons, at 23; Thirtieth Report of Session 2005–06, Report, together with formal minutes, European Scrutiny Committee, House of Commons, at 5–6.

516 23rd Report on the European Small Claims Procedure, at 28. For a different opinion see APIL, *The European Small Claims Procedure*, A Response by the Association of Personal Injury Lawyers, CP(L) 12/05, APIL 10/05, at 9 (available at http://files.apil.org.uk/pdf/ConsultationDocuments/846.pdf).

517 Bar Council response to the European Commission's consultation on the European Small Claims Procedure, ETI 39850528734–23; The Law Society of England and Wales, European Small Claims Procedure Response to public consultation, Transparency Register No. 38020227042–38, June 2013; Civil Justice Council for England and Wales, Royal Courts of Justice, Public Consultation on the European Small Claims Procedure; UK European Consumer Centre, Public Consultation on the European Small Claims Procedure; Council of the European Union, Delegation of the United Kingdom, Interinstitutional File 2013/0403 (COD), 8530/14, ADD7, Brussels, 7 April 2014, at 2; House of Commons, European Scrutiny Committee, Thirty-third Report of Session 2013–14, 29 January 2014, at 45–46. Crifò (2016), at 89.

518 European Small Claims Procedure (10160/06), Letter from Rt Hon Baroness Ashton of Upholland to the Chairman, *Correspondence with Ministers*, 30th Report of Session 2007–08, European Union Committee, House of Lords, at 295. In the public consultation for the amendment of the ESCP, the matter of improving the standard forms was taken up by The Law Society of England and Wales, European Small Claims Procedure Response to public consultation, Transparency Register No. 38020227042–38, June 2013.

519 Crifò (2011), at 292.

520 Crifò (2011), at 301.

521 2015 White Book, at 2014.

522 Article 13(2) ESCP in conjunction with Articles 13 and 14 of Regulation No 805/2004 (Articles 13 and 14 EOP from 14 July 2017). Crifò (2011), at 295.

use of electronic service as an alternative to postal service when available under national law and agreed by the parties, as well as the use of systems such as e-Codex.[523]

The loser-pays principle does not match the cost rule in the domestic small claims procedure, which was perceived to impair the attractiveness of the ESCP.[524] Potential users fear the risks of having to pay the other party's high legal fees, especially as they are unable to calculate them before deciding to bring or to defend a claim. Professional organisations and scholars expressed concerns as to the exposure of the parties to disproportionate levels of costs compared to the main claim.[525] However, in the ESCP's amendment the UK did not support capping the court fee. The applicable court fees in the majority of Member States are around or below 10% of the claim value, and below the threshold proposed by the European Commission.[526] The objective of making the payment of court fees available online received more support, but reservation was expressed regarding the fact that these means were not available in all Member States.[527]

In addition, the UK backed an increase in practical assistance to the parties, as well as limiting the translation of Form D to the substance of the judgment.[528]

Scholars expressed concern with respect to the domestic small claims procedure being a potential source of tension when domestic rules need to be applied differently (e.g. the ESCP contains a specific rule on costs that depart from established limits under the domestic procedure, along with postal service, evidence, disclosure of documents, and witness statements).[529] The research reveals that these concerns are grounded, but the extent of the phenomenon is difficult to assess due to the limited amount of data available.[530]

The absence of a common rule on appeals was considered disappointing, and added to the distortion the Commission was seeking to remove. Regrettably, this criticism could not be addressed by Regulation 2015/2421, as a consensus among the Member States could not be reached. The UK's proposal to include an express provision with regard to the prescription and limitation period in the event of a review has been upheld

523 Council of the European Union, Delegation of the United Kingdom, Interinstitutional File 2013/0403 (COD), 8530/14, ADD7, Brussels, 7 April 2014, at 5–6; The Law Society of England and Wales, European Small Claims Procedure Response to public consultation, Transparency Register No. 38020227042–38, June 2013.

524 First Report of Session 2005–06, *The Courts: small claims*, Report, together with formal minutes, oral and written evidence, Constitutional Affairs Committee, House of Commons, at 23. *The Courts: small claims*, Government Response to the Constitutional Affairs Select Committee's Report, 2006, at 8.

525 23rd Report on the European Small Claims Procedure, at 37–38; UK European Consumer Centre, Public Consultation on the European Small Claims Procedure; 2012 White Book Part 78 – European Procedure, Annotation 78.12.1.

526 Council of the European Union, Delegation of the United Kingdom, Interinstitutional File 2013/0403 (COD), 8530/14, ADD7, Brussels, 7 April 2014, at 6–7; House of Commons, European Scrutiny Committee, Thirty-third Report of Session 2013–14, 29 January 2014, at 46.

527 Council of the European Union, Delegation of the United Kingdom, Interinstitutional File 2013/0403 (COD), 8530/14, ADD7, Brussels, 7 April 2014, at 6.

528 House of Commons, European Scrutiny Committee, Thirty-third Report of Session 2013–14, 29 January 2014, at 46.

529 See 2012 White Book Part 78 – European Procedure, Annotation 78.12.1; Crifò (2009), at 377.

530 See Section 3.7.2.

by Regulation 2015/2421;[531] however, its reliance on the existence of such means under national law maintains a diverse handling of parties across the Member States.

Removal of the exequatur was seen as beneficial for the ESCP in view of the difficulties encountered in the enforcement process even for domestic claims.[532] Enforcement abroad was expected to create more difficulties and result in additional costs for the successful party,[533] a concern that has been hinted at by practice findings.[534] Moreover, the limited power to challenge ESCP enforcement is to add to the simplicity and certainty of the procedure.

3.5. Implementation of the EOP and the ESCP in National Practice

General Provisions

The procedures established by the EOP and ESCP Regulations were incorporated by an amendment into the CPR,[535] thus becoming part of the national procedural rules, together with the provisions accommodating these European instruments within the English system. Part 78 CPR and 78 PD contain additional rules concerning jurisdiction of the English courts, accepted means of communication, service of documents, transfer of proceedings, review, and enforcement. Most of the information had to be communicated to the Commission in accordance with Article 29 EOP, and Article 25 ESCP is included in 78 PD.

The English legislator's choice to add a new part to the civil procedure rules has the potential to increase the visibility of these procedures for practitioners and courts, as well as for the parties. According to statistics, however, the EOP and the ESCP have seldom been employed.[536] Nevertheless, as noted by Crifò, the English legislator chose a minimum approach implementation, with CPR 78 provisions referring numerous times to the text of the Regulations.[537]

Due to the CPR's flexibility, implementation of the European procedures gave rise to little controversy.[538] With its use of pre-printed forms and guidance notes, and its simplified approach, the EOP was considered to resemble the 'default summons', or Money Claims Online and the Claim Production Centre.[539] In the event of a transfer of the procedure, the application is to be treated as a Part 7 claim.[540] The ESCP procedure

531 Council of the European Union, Delegation of the United Kingdom, Interinstitutional File 2013/0403 (COD), 8530/14, ADD7, Brussels, 7 April 2014, at 7.

532 23rd Report on the European Small Claims Procedure, at 15 and 44–45.

533 See 2012 White Book Part 78 – European Procedure, Annotation 78.12.1.

534 The Law Society of England and Wales, European Small Claims Procedure Response to public consultation, Transparency Register No. 38020227042-38, June 2013; Civil Justice Council; The Creators' Rights Alliance, Public Consultation on the European Small Claims Procedure. See also Section 3.7.3.

535 The Civil Procedure (Amendment) Rules 2008 (SI 2008/2178) and the High Court and County Court Jurisdiction (Amendment) Order 2008 (SI 2008/2934), to which the full text of the regulations is appended.

536 See Section 3.7.1.

537 Crifò (2016), at 81 and 93–94.

538 Crifò (2009a), at 180–181.

539 *Ibidem*, at 181.

540 CPR 78.5. Crifò (2009a), at 181.

shares certain features in common with that of domestic small claims, and the rules applicable to the domestic procedure are to supplement the Regulation when necessary.[541] Furthermore, Part 78 CPR includes references to domestic law rules to supplement the provisions of the EOP and ESCP Regulations when these texts are silent on specific matters.[542] The jurisdiction of the EOP is shared in England between the County Court and the High Court (Queen Bench or Chancery Division),[543] while the ESCP procedure is handled by the County Court.

The Ministry of Justice website provides general information regarding the EOP and the ESCP, referring parties to the e-Justice Portal pages and to the national prepared leaflet on making cross-border claims in the EU.[544] The leaflet offers general guidance for parties considering starting a cross-border claim in the EU.[545] The Portal contains information on the type of procedure that might be suitable considering the type of claim, the entities offering legal advice to parties (particularly consumers), jurisdiction, defence, costs, and enforcement matters.[546] A special guide explaining the ESCP steps is also available from the UK European Consumer Centre.[547]

EOP Provisions

The EOP application form must be completed in English or accompanied by a translation into English, and can be filed at the court in person or by post.[548] Other forms may be filed by post or in person, and by fax or other electronic means where these are available.[549] If a deliberate false statement is made in an EOP application, it is to be treated as contempt of court in accordance with CPR 32.14.

Withdrawal of the EOP application by the claimant is possible at any stage prior to a statement of opposition (CPR 78.4), and not just in the event of a transfer to the national proceedings as provided by Article 17(1) EOP. The court is to notify the defendant of the withdrawal, and no order concerning the costs is to be made.[550]

The CPR contains special provisions to be followed in case the defendant wishes to dispute the court's jurisdiction when lodging a statement of opposition under Article 17 EOP.[551] A default judgment will be issued by the court if no acknowledgement of service is received or no defence is filed on the opposed EOP claim.[552] In the event of opposition to the EOP, CPR 78.5 states that the claim is to be treated as if it had been started under

541 CPR 78.14.
542 Part 78 CPR makes express reference to the domestic law provisions that are not applicable in the European procedures. For criticism of a few additional rules, see Crifò (2016), at 86.
543 78 PD 2.2.
544 www.justice.gov.uk/courts/european-union-cross-border-claims.
545 EX725, *Making a cross border claim in the EU,* HM Courts & Tribunals, 2013 (available at https://formfinder.hmctsformfinder.justice.gov.uk/ex725-eng.pdf).
546 For criticism of the general level of information in the leaflet, see Crifò (2016), at 86.
547 *Your Guide to the European Small Claims Court*, UK European Consumer Centre, Trading Standards Institute.
548 78 PD 2.1. For EOP, see also Kramer (2010), at 34–35.
549 78 PD 3 and 78 PD 14.
550 CPR 78.4.
551 CPR78.6(2). On the perspective of this solution and the *Goldbet* case (C-144–12), see Crifò (2016), at 95.
552 CPR 78.7.

Part 7 CPR (How to start Proceedings – the Claim Form). A request for review of the ESCP can be made at the court that issued the judgment in accordance with the provisions of Part 23 CPR on general rules on application for court orders A particularity of the review procedures for exceptional circumstances, stay or limitation, and refusal of enforcement in England is the possibility of oral hearings to be held by telephone or video conference.[553]

ESCP Provisions

As with the EOP, ESCP application forms must be drafted in English or accompanied by a translation into English. The form then has to be filed at the court in person or by post.[554]

CPR provisions concerning hearings state that these are normally to take place by telephone or video conference if considered necessary in the proceedings. This national provision is in line with the aims of the ESCP Regulation and Regulation 2015/2421, seeking to diminish the costs of cross-border litigation. Further, the provision has the potential to contribute to courts encouraging parties to reach a settlement in the ESCP (Article 12(3) ESCP), as is the case with ADR practices in domestic procedures. Generally, ESCP claims are to be treated as being allocated to the national small claims track, except for the rule concerning costs.[555]

An appeal is possible under the ESCP before the English courts.[556]A request for review of the ESCP can be made at the court that issued the judgment in accordance with the provisions of Part 23 CPR on general rules on application for court orders.

Costs

Cost relating to EOP and ESCP proceedings in England are similar to the fees applicable for ordinary proceedings. However, no online system is available for the payment of court fees for parties, although apparently credit card payment can be accepted over the telephone.[557] Court fees vary from £35 (approx. €40) for claims up to £300 (approx. €343.8) to £205 (approx. €233.7) for claims whose value is not higher than £5,000 (approx. €5,700), and to £10,000 (approx. €11,460) for claims greater than £300,000 (approx. €343,808). A hearing fee may be added in the event of an ESCP claim. Depending on the value of the claim, this may vary between £25 (approx. €28.65) for claims up to £300 (approx. €343.8) to £335 (approx. €382) for claims above £3,000 (approx. €3,420).[558] Representation fees and enforcement costs can be added to these.

553 78 PD 6.2.

554 78 PD 13.

555 CPR 78.14.

556 78 PD 10 in conjunction with CPR 52. The reference made by the e-Justice to Part 5.2 CPR might be confusing, as the provision does not refer to the appeal proceedings but to the preparation of documents in court proceedings (https://e-justice.europa.eu/content_small_claims-354-ew-en.do?member=1).

557 House of Commons, European Scrutiny Committee, Thirty-third Report of Session 2013–14, 29 January 2014, at 46.

558 See EX50, *Civil and Family Court Fees*, From 6 March 2017 (available at (https://formfinder.hmctsformfinder.justice.gov.uk/ex50-eng.pdf).

3.6. Enforcement in England: from National to European Judgments

The enforcement of judicial decisions in England is carried out in accordance with CPR provisions and with a number of additional legal acts. This section will provide an overview of the main characteristics of the enforcement, considering the applicable rules, the professionals involved in the process, and the costs it entails for the parties. The second part will focus on execution of the EOP and the ESCP in England.

3.6.1. Main Aspects regarding the Execution of Judicial Decisions in England

The rules on enforcement are contained in the CPR (Parts 70–74) and in a number of additional legal acts. These concern jurisdiction matters, rules regarding the activity of enforcement agents and officers, and enforcement procedures.[559] Enforcement in England has been part of a long-standing project to modernise it, and the Tribunals, Courts and Enforcement Act 2007 that came into force on 6 April 2014 introduced a major change.[560] In accordance with its provisions, enforcement against goods has been replaced with taking control of goods, and bailiffs have been replaced with enforcement agents.

Enforcement proceedings involve the courts in England – and by extension Wales – the competent courts being the County Court and the High Court. Enforcement proceedings with both courts are to a significant extent similar.[561] The execution of judicial decisions is not suspended in the event of an appeal, which removes the incentive of filing an appeal for obtaining a delay in the civil process.[562] Money judgments are to be honoured within 14 days of the effective date (CPR.40.11). If not, the successful party, on its own initiative, is able to proceed immediately to execution of the judicial decision, choosing from a range of available methods. The creditor has to trigger enforcement proceedings and apply for a court order to authorise enforcement. Judgments expressed in a foreign currency need to have the praecipe and the writ stated in the sterling equivalent on the date the writ was issued.[563]

Prior to deciding on the method of enforcement, a creditor who is not aware of the assets and duties of his debtor may choose to apply for a compelling order to obtain information under CPR 71.[564] The Tribunals, Courts and Enforcement Act 2007 (Section

559 The High Court and County Court Jurisdiction Order 1991 (SI 1991/724), the County Court Jurisdiction Order 2014 (SI 2014/503), the High Court Enforcement Officers Regulation 2004 (SI 2004/400), the Enforcement Agents Regulations 2014, SI 2014/421, the Tribunals, Courts and Enforcement Act 2007, the Charging Orders Act 1979, and the Attachment of Earnings Act 1971.

560 Blackstone's Civil Practice 2015, at 1387.

561 *Ibidem.*

562 2012 White Book 52.7(1): 'Neither the commencement of an appeal nor the grant of permission to appeal affects the enforceability of the judgment below. If the appellant desires a stay, they must apply for it and put forward solid grounds why such a stay should be granted.'

563 Queen's Bench Guide 2017, para. 23.4.16 (available at www.gov.uk/government/uploads/system/uploads/attachment_data/file/587836/qb-guide-2017-final5.pdf).

564 See EX324, *How do I apply for an order? An order to obtain information from a person who owes you money*, Her Majesty's Courts Services, 2013; Zuckerman (2013), at 1102–1103.

95–105) establishes new methods for obtaining information on debtors' assets and indebtedness (e.g. departmental information requests, information orders).[565] The application using standard form N316 must be made at the court that issued the judgment, unless a transfer is requested.[566] The creditor can request the debtor to be questioned before a judge and/or to produce specific documents (e.g. bank statements). The request will be dealt with by a court officer who will issue an order for the debtor to attend court, answer questions, and/or produce documents.[567] The order will be served personally on the debtor, usually by the creditor,[568] while the debtor is required to answer under oath questions directed to establish his financial situation. If the questioning is carried out by a judge, the creditor will have to attend the hearing,[569] where the evidence will be recorded and signed by the debtor.[570] Based on the information available, the creditor has complete freedom to choose the enforcement mechanisms that he considers most likely to be effective.[571] More than one method of enforcement can be used at the same time, or one after the other.[572]

Money judgments can be enforced by making use of the following methods:

- Writs of control or warrants of control (currently referred to as 'taking control of goods');[573]
- A third-party debt order;[574]
- A charging order, a stop order, or a stop notice;[575]
- By appointment of receiver;[576]
- An attachment of earnings order (only available in county courts);[577] and
- An administration order (only available in county courts).[578]

All requests are form based. If the claim is handled using Money Claim Online, a request for enforcement (i.e. warrant of control) can be filed online for an amount up to £5,000.[579] The court- based enforcement methods are based on a two-stage process. First,

565 See Andrews (2013), at 498–499.

566 CPR 71.2(2)(b)(i). Zuckerman (2013), at 1102–1103.

567 EX140 and EX 141 contain the list of standard questions. Blackstone's Civil Practice 2015, at 1390–1391.

568 PD 71.3.

569 CPR71.6. Zuckerman (2013), at 1103.

570 If the debtor fails to attend the court, refuses to take the oath, or refuses to answer the questions, a committal order can be issued against him. O'Hare & Browne (2013), at 675.

571 CPR 70.2(2).

572 CPR 70.2(2)(b).

573 Section 62–70, Schemes 12 and 13, Tribunals, Courts and Enforcement Act 2007. The writs or warrants are initially valid for 12 months, but they can be extended.

574 CPR 72. If a bank account is targeted, it will only concern the credit balance in the account at the time of service of the interim order; a further order is needed to attach money that is paid in subsequently. See Zuckerman (2013), at 1103–1106; O'Hare & Browne (2013), at 679.

575 A charging order is applicable against land property, a stop order concerns securities or funds in court, and the stop notice is against securities. CPR 73. See Zuckerman (2013), at 1106–1109.

576 RSC Orders 30 and 51, Scheme 1, CPR. Zuckerman (2013), at 1110–1111.

577 CCR Order 27, Scheme 2, CPR. Usually it is used as a last-resort method. No interest accrues while an attachment order is in force. J O'Hare & Browne (2013), at 682–683.

578 Part 5 Tribunals, Courts and Enforcement Act 2007.

579 See HMCTS, Money Claim Online (MCOL) – User Guide for Claimants, at 20–21 (available at www.gov.uk/government/uploads/system/uploads/attachment_data/file/520203/money-claim-online-user-guide.pdf).

the court issues an interim order that is purely paper based, and then a final order. The debtor might be invited to a hearing in order to put forward any reasons for the planned enforcement method not to be used or not to proceed (e.g. attachment of earnings orders, third-party debt orders), or served with the order to which he can object (e.g. charging order), but the hearing is not compulsory. The order of the court cannot be appealed. If the judgment on which the enforcement order is based is successfully challenged, the enforcement actions can be suspended on application of the debtor. Additionally, if the debtor is unable to pay or it is inexpedient to enforce the order, he can apply for a stay of execution.[580] Enforcement following the delivery of a court decision is problematic in England.[581]

A creditor seeking enforcement has to make an application to the court that has granted the judgment. However, based on the enforcement method chosen and on the characteristics of the debt, the case can or may need to be transferred or sent to a hearing centre for enforcement purposes.[582]

For debts exceeding £600, it is often advantageous for creditors to seek enforcement in the High Court.[583] On registration of an enforcement request in the High Court, the decision will involve interest in accordance with Judgments Act 1838.[584] A County Court judgment under £5,000 does not generally bear such an interest rate;[585] when it does, however, it ceases to apply as soon as the creditor commences any enforcement proceedings (e.g. information hearing, third-party debt proceedings), unless they fail to lead to any payment from the debtor.[586] In the High Court, interest will accrue during enforcement proceedings. At present the rate amounts to 8%,[587] which is generally the case for money judgments (e.g. orders for payment of money, default judgments).

The use of a lawyer or a legal professional to apply for enforcement is not compulsory, but in view of the complexity of the procedures, especially involving the High Court, creditors might choose to receive advice from a solicitor, a legal adviser, Consumer Advice, or Citizens Advice.

The High Court enforcement is carried out by authorised enforcement officers,[588] while county court enforcement activities are undertaken by enforcement agents (bailiffs).[589] Based on their abilities to undertake work, their financial standing,

[580] CPR 83.7. This will have to be made in accordance with Part 23 CPR. See Blackstone's Civil Practice 2015, at 1390.

[581] Baldwin & Cunnington (2004) at 305–328; Madge (2004), at 201–211; Bello (2010).

[582] Blackstone's Civil Practice 2015, at 1388.

[583] High Court and County Court Jurisdiction (Amendment) Order 1999, SI 1999/724.

[584] O'Hare & Browne (2013), at 673–674.

[585] Article 1(2), County Courts Order 1991/1184. County court judgments above £5,000 bear an 8% interest rate, Article 5, County Courts Order 1991/1184. See also Andrews (2013), at 516.

[586] O'Hare & Browne (2013), at 674.

[587] Judgments Act 1898.

[588] High Court Enforcement Officers Regulation 2004, SI 2004/400 and Courts Act 2003, Section 7, paragraph 2(1).

[589] Sections 63 and 64 Tribunals, Courts and Enforcement Act 2007 and Enforcement Agents Regulations 2014, SI 2014/421.

insurance standing, knowledge and so on, enforcement officers can be awarded a right to receive writs for enforcement in any or all of the 105 districts comprising England and Wales.[590]

Enforcement costs are added to the amount owed by the debtor, but the creditor has to advance them. The costs of enforcement depend on the methods used and on the actions undertaken to receive information concerning the debtor's assets and duties.[591] For example, in March 2017 the court fee for an application for an order for a debtor or other person to attend court to provide information was £55 (approx. €63). The fee is increased to £110 (approx. €126) in the event of a request for service by an enforcement agent or an order for a debtor to attend court for questioning. The application for the enforcement of an award for a sum of money by the County Court is £44, (approx. €50.4) and £66 (approx. €75.6) for the High Court. The issue of a warrant of control via Money Claims Online or the Country Court Business Centre will cost the creditor a court fee of £77 (approx. €88). A charging order, attachment of earnings, and third-party debt application entail a court fee of £110 (approx. €126) for each application. The writs require payment of a court fee of £66 (approx. €75.6), while the cost of a warrant is between £110-£121 (approx. €126–138.7). Enforcement officer or enforcement agent fees also apply to these court fees.[592] At the compliance stage, when the enforcement officer receives the writ and sends the debtor a notice of enforcement giving him 7 business days to pay the amount outlined in the notification, the statutory compliance fee amounts to £75 (approx. €85.95) plus VAT (£90). A similar fee of £75 is to be paid if the enforcement notice is sent by an enforcement agent.[593] If the debtor cannot pay in full, the enforcement officer will have to make a sensible payment proposal securing the goods. At this stage, a fee of £190 (approx. €217.75) plus 7.5% of the sums recovered over £1,000 (approx. €1,146) plus VAT applies. For example, for a debt of £2,500 (approx. €2,865), the 7.5% will be charged only for the difference: £1,500 (approx. €1,719). If the debtor defaults on the agreement, a second enforcement arrangement will be required to remove assets. For this, a higher fee of £495 (approx. €567) plus VAT applies. If goods have to be sold, a fee of £525 (approx. €601.66) plus 7.5% of sums above £1,000 (approx. €1,146) plus VAT applies.

When the services of a solicitor are used for enforcement purposes, additional costs will be incurred,[594] and might involve an hourly fee. Finally, if the debtor is requested to come to court for an information hearing, he can request that the creditor pay an amount that is reasonable to cover his travel expenses.[595]

590 Andrews (2013), at 515.

591 For a list of court fees applicable for enforcement purposes, see EX50, *Civil and Family Court Fees*, 6 March 2017 (available at http://formfinder.hmctsformfinder.justice.gov.uk/ex50-eng.pdf).

592 See http://bailiffadviceonline.co.uk/index/high-court-enforcement-debts/fee.

593 See www.civea.co.uk/bailiff-enforcement-agent-charges-fees.htm.

594 The fees depend on the contractual arrangements made, usually based on an hourly fee. Solicitors Remuneration Order 1994 and the Non-Contentious Probate Rules 1987 (SI 1987/2024). Zuckerman (2013), at 1447.

595 CPR 71.4.

3.6.2. *Executing EOP and ESCP Judgments in England*

National implementation rules regarding EOP and ESCP Regulations contain provisions on enforcement, but they are limited. The EX725 leaflet containing information on the use of EOP and ESCP procedure refers interested parties to the e-Justice Portal and to the EX321 leaflet on enforcement options in England. While useful, the information is not sufficiently detailed for the creditor to be able to proceed easily to the execution of his enforceable title. Most probably, the services of a solicitor or a Citizens or Consumer Advice body is necessary for a foreign creditor.

When the EOP or the ESCP are issued by an English court, the creditor will need to request the County Court or the High Court to issue the Declaration of enforceability to proceed to enforcement in accordance with national law as described in Section 3.6.1. In executing EOP or ESCP decisions issued by courts in other Member States, some minimum formalities need to be complied with in order to proceed in accordance with domestic enforcement arrangements. If the decision and the Declaration of enforceability are drafted in a language other than English, the creditor is required to translate the judgment into English and have it certified by a public notary or another qualified person who can confirm the accuracy of the translation.[596] In addition, when the amount of the EOP or the ESCP judgment is expressed in a foreign currency, the creditor is required to request a certificate of the sterling equivalent of the sum at the 'close of business on the date nearest preceding the date of the application'.[597]

The creditor is required to make an application to the court at which enforcement proceedings are to take place (County Court or the High Court), and to submit the documents required by Article 21 EOP or Article 21 ESCP together with the certificate of the sterling equivalent.[598] The provisions of CPR Parts 70–74 apply accordingly.

Any application for refusal of an EOP or ESCP judgment enforcement or of a stay or limitation of enforcement in England must be made in accordance with CPR 23 to the court that is enforcing the decision.[599] 78 PD 8.1–9.2 and 78 PD 20.1–21.4 establish the documents to be submitted by the debtor. Copies of the order issued by the English court for the refusal or stay or limitation of the aforementioned enforcement must be served by the debtor on any person that is affected by the order, and on any of the courts where the enforcement proceedings are pending. In the event of a request for refusal of enforcement, the proceedings will cease upon service of the order on the persons in question.[600] Similarly, the stay or limitation of enforcement will produce effects as soon as it is served on the court of enforcement and on the persons affected by the measures.[601]

596 For England, the United Kingdom notified the European Commission that the only language acceptable pursuant to Article 21(2)(b) EOP and Article 25(1)(d) ESCP is English.

597 CPR 78.9(2) and 78.20(2). However, without assistance from a local solicitor or legal advisor it might be difficult for a first-time user to figure out how to obtain the certificate of sterling equivalent. Information available online is difficult to find.

598 CPR 78.9(1) and 78 PD 7.1 for the EOP and 78.20(1) and 78 PD 18.1 for the ESCP.

599 Article 22 EOP in conjunction with CPR 78.10–11; Article 23 ESCP in conjunction with CPR 78.21–22.

600 CPR 78.10(3) and CPR 78.21(3).

601 CPR 78.11(2) and CPR 78.22(2).

The same methods that are available for enforcement under domestic law will be available for the enforcement in England of the EOP and ESCP issued in other Member States. Additionally, the same court fees and costs related to the proceedings will apply. Translation costs are added to these.

3.7. The EOP and the ESCP in Practice

3.7.1. Available Statistical Data

The annual statistics published by the Ministry of Justice on the courts' activities contain no specific information regarding application of the EOP and the ESCP. However, upon request, the Law, Rights and International Directorate of the Ministry of Justice provides information on applications made for the issuance of EOPs and ESCPs by English courts, as well as for enforcement purposes. The Directorate warns, however, that the data has been compiled manually by the courts' staff, and has not been subject 'to the rigorous quality assurance checks by Official Statistics'.[602] This is likely due to a lack of specific registration codes in courts' docket systems. Nevertheless, the existing information gives an indication of the use of the European uniform procedures, regardless of the data accuracy issue. Table 3.1 below presents information on the number of EOP and ESCP cases handled by the English courts between 2009 and 2014, as well as of requests to execute such decisions.

Application to issue	**2009**	**2010**	**2011**	**2012**	**2013**	**2014**
EOP	85	62	242	250	183	65
ESCP	200	105	176	45	69	217
Application to enforce						
EOP	38	196	47	37	107	65
ESCP	138	202	183	164	351	517

Table 3.1. Number of EOP and ESCP applications handled by English Courts, and of requests for enforcement received, according to statistics available from the Ministry of Justice, Source BMS & HM Courts & Tribunals Service Performance Database

The available statistics provide no indication as to the number of EOP cases handled by the County Court and the High Court. Additionally, no information is available as to the length of the proceedings.[603] The statistics also contain no details as to the number of

602 Number of EOPs and ESCPs issued in England and Wales between 2006 and 2012 (document on file with the researcher).

603 In addition, reports on the functioning of the EOP and the ESCP published at the EU level contain no relevant data on this aspect for the UK. See Commission EOP Report, COM(2015) 495 final, Brussels,

opposed EOPs or ESCPs that have been appealed, or whether the review procedure was used in either of the two instruments.

An analysis of the annual data on the number of applications filed indicates there has been no steady increase over the years in the use of the European instruments, and the significant difference between certain years raises doubts as to the soundness of the statistics. This for example is the case for the EOP. After a more or less similar rate of use in 2011–2013, in 2014 the number of EOP cases fell significantly from 183 to 65. The evolution of the use of the ESCP is also unexpected, with cyclical sequences of decrease and increase. For example, in 2011–2012 the number of applications fell by almost four times, while in 2013–2014 it increased by more than three times in comparison to the number of applications filed the previous year. The visual representation in Fig. 3.1 makes the evolution of the two European procedures easier to follow. One interesting observation is that the EOP and ESCP applications stay within similar upper and lower limits within the studied period. Specific registration codes would have been desirable in order to collect more detailed and accurate statistical data on the number of cases and the courts that handled them, as well as more general information (e.g. length of proceedings, opposition/appeal or review requests, number of rejected claims or settled ESCP). However, given the UK's pending departure from the EU, such data are currently of little interest to the English authorities.

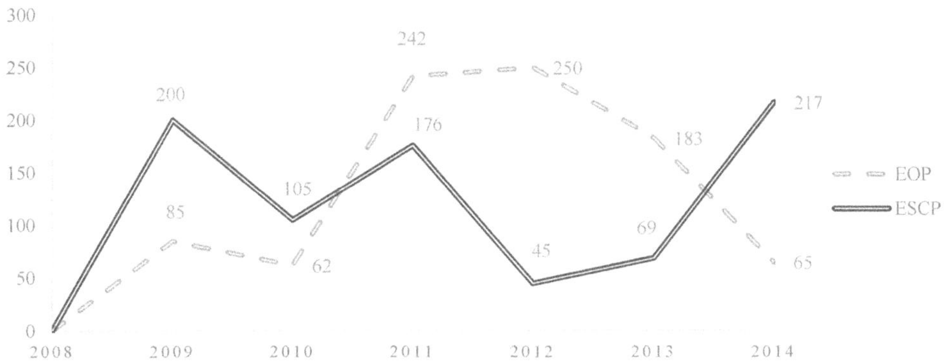

Fig. 3.1. Evolution of the number of EOP and ESCP cases in 2009–2014

Information regarding enforcement of the EOP and the ESCP in England also demonstrates a fluctuating trend. However, it is not clear how many of the enforcement requests were based on titles issued by courts in other Member States or by English counterparts. The data are not detailed enough to assess further the type of requests or origins of the titles.

13.10.2015, at 15; Deloitte Report, Final Report, Part I – Evaluation of the European Small Claims Regulation, 2013, at 67.

3.7.2. *Case Law*

3.7.2.1. Quantitative Data regarding Case Law

The EOP and ESCP cases are generally not published by legal databases or on dedicated websites that are open to public consultation.[604] County Court case law is not binding on other courts, although their decisions in relation to the EOP and the ESCP may prove relevant with regard to how these procedures are applied. For the High Court, there is no indication of reported cases that involved matters of fundamental principle.[605] Further, the literature does not refer to any such decisions issued by English courts. This limits significantly the information regarding how English courts handle these claims.

Only two ESCP cases were identified, and both were unreported. Information regarding one of the cases was provided by ECC France,[606] while the other was mentioned by a legal practitioner (*Puchala v Thomas Cook Airlines Limited*).[607] The Birmingham County Court handled the first case in 2011, while the Chichester County Court trialled the second in 2015. No relevant cases or information have been identified so far with regard to EOP claims.

3.7.2.2. Case Classification

The two analysed ESCP claims are C2B cases initiated by a foreign consumer against an English company. Both cases involve contractual claims. One is related to the reimbursement of car reparation costs under a duty of guarantee, while the other concerns compensation for a flight delay in accordance with Regulation (CE) No 261/2004.[608]

3.7.2.3. Conduct of Proceedings

The proceedings for one case took 4 months and 1 week, while for the second it took 6 months until delivery of the certificate (Form D). Information with regard to the holding of a hearing is available only for *Puchala v Thomas Cook Airlines Limited.* Because the defendant denied liability, the case was listed for trial in accordance with CPR Rules. However, the defendant, Thomas Cook Airlines, accepted liability before the hearing, and engaged in certain negotiations with the claimant's solicitors with regard to claimed

604 For example, Westlaw Database, www.bailii.org.

605 On the binding effect of the decisions of English courts, see Andrews (2008), at 17–18; Smith & Bull (2012), at 297.

606 Centre Europèen de la Consumation, Zentrum für Europäische Verbraucherschutz e.V (www.cec-zev.eu).

607 *Puchala v Thomas Cook Airlines Limited*, 12th May 2015, Chichester County Court, District Judge Ellis (Unreported) (transcript on file with the researcher).

608 Regulation (EC) No 261/2004 of the European Parliament and of the Council of 11 February 2004 establishing common rules on compensation and assistance to passengers in the event of boarding being denied and of cancellation or long delay involving flights, and repealing Regulation (EEC) No 295/91, OJ 2004, L 46/1.

costs. This practice is in line with national law whereby parties are encouraged to try to settle the case or settle issues as much as possible before the hearing.[609] In the Birmingham County Court, ECC France sought to mediate and to encourage the company to reimburse the amount stipulated in the invoice for reparation of the car, prior to the consumer initiating court proceedings.

In both cases, the claimants seem to have used the standard application form to file the claim. In *Puchala v. Thomas Cook Airlines Limited*, the judgment mentions that the defendant filed Form C. Information as to the issuance of Form D is available only for the Birmingham County Court case.

As regards the means of evidence, little information is available. In both cases, the judge appears to have proceeded to assess written evidence submitted by the parties. There is no indication of other means of evidence being used.

Finally, there is no information as to any appeal proceeding having been initiated.

3.7.2.4. Representation of the Parties

In *Puchala v Thomas Cook Airlines Limited*, both parties were represented, with the claimant having employed the services of two lawyers: an Austrian lawyer and subsequently an English solicitor. In the other case, the parties appear to have proceeded without representation.

3.7.2.5. Amounts and Costs Claimed

In both ESCP cases, information was available regarding the principle and the court fees. The principle amounted to £480 (approx. €550) and €714 (approx. £530), while the court fees were £50 (approx. €57) and £70 (approx. €80), respectively. In addition, the claimant seeking compensation for the flight delay also requested interest and additional costs amounting to £200 (approx. €229). These additional costs corresponded to legal assistance offered by lawyers. Proceeding by analogy with the domestic small claims allowing £50 (approx. €57) as fixed costs, the judge considered the £200 (approx. €229) request to be 'entirely excessive' for an 'entirely routine claim' in an 'entirely standardise procedure' where the only thing the claimant had to prove was the delay of the flight.[610] In view of the fixed costs awarded in the English procedure, the £200 (approx. €229) allows additional costs for the defence and the negotiation activities; thus, the second offer of the defendant was acknowledged by the judge as being reasonable, and the claimant should have accepted it.[611] The £200 (approx. €229) offer for costs was a 'reasonable and proportionate sum' consistent with both the European Small Claims Procedure and the level that would be awarded in English proceedings. An interesting aspect of this case is the fact that the judge concluded on a double appreciation of the costs in relation to the

609 The ESCP is treated as if allocated to the small claims track (CPR 78.14(1)); hence, in accordance with CPR PD 17 para 4, Appendix B point 4: 'The parties are encouraged to contact each other with a view to trying to settle the case or narrow the issues'.

610 *Puchala v Thomas Cook Airlines Limited*, 12th May 2015 (Unreported), para. 22.

611 *Puchala v Thomas Cook Airlines Limited*, 12th May 2015 (Unreported), para. 22 and 23.

ESCP Regulation and the national procedural rules.[612] Further, it is remarkable that the judge – although recognising the importance of the references contained in Article 16 as well as in Recitals 7, 8, and 29 for assessing the proportional and necessary costs incurred – proceeded to an appreciation in accordance with English procedure.[613] Although no direct reference was made to CPR 78.14(2) or PD 13.1 for the application of CPR78.14, the court correctly excluded the application of CPR 27.14 in determining the 'appropriate costs regime'. The interpretation was based on the general national provisions relevant for the matter. The judge qualified the ESCP provision on costs as 'entirely consistent with the English provisions, CPR 44.3, which refer to reasonable and proportionate cost'.[614] Hence, the judge proceeded to apply the reasonable and proportionate test in the national procedure to the necessary and proportionate test in Article 16 ESCP Regulation. It is not clear from the text of the judgment whether this was triggered by the provisions of Recital 29 ESCP that state 'the costs of the proceedings should be determined in accordance with national law', but the court did proceed to appreciate the costs to be awarded to the claimant in accordance with national provisions and practice. The proportionate element of the analysis does not create a problem *per se*, but the subsequent question is whether the meaning of the word 'reasonable' could be matched by the term 'necessary' used in the ESCP text. The reasoning appears to contradict Article 16 ESCP, which states that the court shall not award costs that are 'unnecessarily incurred or are disproportionate to the claim'.[615] The appreciation of the costs' proportionality should have been carried out in relation to the amount claimed and to whether they were necessarily incurred. Rightfully, in line with Recital 29, these can include the costs of legal representation or other costs related to the proceedings.

Further, with regard to interest, it appears from details of the case that it amounted to £39 when the parties were involved in a negotiation process seeking to achieve a settlement. The judge pointed out that interest was not part of the offer, and indicated not having enough elements of the parties' correspondence to consider that substantial costs had been incurred during negotiation (it 'seems that when the claim in relation to interest was made, an additional sum was allowed in relation to that figure').[616]

Only one of the ESCP cases refers to court fees amounting to £70 (approx. €80) being paid at the beginning of the proceedings.

3.7.2.6. Service and Language Aspects

There is no information regarding service of the documents of proceedings or requirements to translate any of the documents used in these two cases.

612 *Puchala v Thomas Cook Airlines Limited*, 12th May 2015 (Unreported), para. 24.

613 Part 44 CPR – General Rules about Costs.

614 *Puchala v Thomas Cook Airlines Limited*, 12th May 2015 (Unreported), para. 20.

615 As regards the disproportionate level of costs in ESCP claims, the Deloitte Final Report points to the fact that the average costs related to such a cross-border procedure are disproportionate because they often represent more than 25% of the value of the claim. See Final Report, 2013, Part I, 'Evaluation of the European Small Claims Regulation', at 28–30.

616 *Puchala v Thomas Cook Airlines Limited*, 12th May 2015 (Unreported), para. 23.

3.7.2.7. Enforcement

Based on information provided by ECC France, it took a period of around 6 months from the moment Form D was issued until the moment the company paid the amount owed (€714 plus the £70 costs – approx. €80). During this period, several steps were taken to convince the debtor to pay. The court, the consumer, and another person who acted in England in the name of the consumer contacted the debtor several times.[617]

3.7.2.8. Influence of the National Procedures

The two ESCP cases provide some general guidelines regarding the practice of the English courts. They point to an interpretation of the provisions of the Regulation in the light of national rules corresponding to similar special procedures. This results in a possible need to train the judiciary and members of the court in order for them to better understand the European uniform procedures, the reasoning behind such instruments, and their aims.

3.7.3. EOP and ESCP Procedures: Empirical Findings

3.7.3.1. Preliminary Aspects regarding Data Collection

The data analysed in the present section were collected through surveys, interviews, and correspondence exchanges with English legal practitioners and advisers providing support to foreign parties initiating legal actions before English courts.

In order to conduct research with the English courts with respect to their application of EOP and ESCP procedures, a first request was filed with the Judicial Office in July 2013. Due to the restrictions concerning foreign researchers obtaining clearance to conduct research involving English courts,[618] one of the supervisors of this project, Professor Christopher Hodges, filed the application.[619] The request was refused, allegedly due to the small number of cases across county courts – the national average was two to three cases per court annually. According to the Judicial Office, this would not have allowed a judge to provide a general overview response without straying into the merits of an individual case, and, moreover, it would have put undue weight on the courts. Further, the Judicial Office declared itself unable to identify which county courts actually handled such types of claims. The same refusal came to a similar request filed to Her Majesty's Courts and Tribunals Service (HMCTS) in order to obtain permission to address court staff. According to the HMCTS Performance, Analysis, Reporting Team,

617 This was a friend of the consumer and not a legal representative.

618 Judicial Office, 'Judicial participation in research projects. Guidance for researchers', January 2013, at 2 specifies nonetheless that the Office 'would not normally accept foreign research applications, unless there is some special reason for wishing to encourage comparative study in a particular subject'.

619 Professor dr. C.J.S. Hodges MA PhD FSALS was at the time Head of the Swiss Re/CMS Research Programme on Civil Justice Systems, Centre for Socio-Legal Studies, University of Oxford and Erasmus Professor of Fundamentals of Private Law, Erasmus University, Rotterdam.

it was unlikely that any county court had dealt with Part 78 CPR, and furthermore it would be impossible to identify which courts had handled such cases. In March 2014, an attempt was made to find an alternative way of reaching the English judiciary. A request for assistance was sent to the President of the European Commission for the Efficiency of Justice (CEPEJ), who forwarded it to the Judicial Office. Yet again, the request was refused, and for the same reasons. This put an end to the possibility of direct research involving the English judiciary.

The collection of empirical data continued, however, in relation to the other categories of practitioners. Several invitations were sent to professional organisations during 2013 and the beginning of 2014. These included various councils of the Law Society, the Wales Law Society, the London Solicitor Litigation Association, the Law Society of England and Wales, the Joint Brussels Office of the Law Societies, the Association of District Judges, the Association of Woman Judges, the Council of Bars and Law Societies of Europe, the High Court Enforcement Officers Association, Foreign Process Section of the Royal Courts of Justice, the Judicial College, and the Bar Council of England and Wales (the Brussels Office). However, only a few of these organisations replied to the invitation and the request for support. The London Solicitor Litigation Association responded that their members' activity was not geared towards the type of claims that would be handled in accordance with the EOP and the ESCP. The Joint Brussels Office of the Law Society agreed to publish the research information and to an invitation for practitioners with experience in handling EOP and ESCP claims to participate in the project. The newsletter was directed to its 6,000 subscribed members, and a notice of the research questionnaires was published in the October 2013 Brussels Agenda of the Law Societies. In addition, an invitation for practitioners to participate in this research and to share their views and experience was published in July 2015 on the Conflicts of Law website.[620] Individual requests to participate were also sent to barristers, solicitors, enforcement officers, and judges. These invitees – whose contact details were available through their professional association websites – appeared to have had experience with the application of EOP and ESCP procedures, or had previously expressed their opinions in relation to these instruments. The group consisted of 19 barristers and solicitors, 3 judges, and 23 enforcement officers.

To complete the framework of professionals' experience, ECC UK was invited to participate in the research and to share its experience from a consumer perspective.

Although numerous invitations and several reminders were sent, only a limited number of English legal practitioners participated in this research. Therefore, the data gathered offer only glimpses of the situation regarding application of the EOP and ESCP in England, and cannot be generalised for the whole jurisdiction. There are indications, however, that certain courts are more accustomed to CPR 78 instruments, while others are less familiar. The same applies with regard to the activities of lawyers and enforcement officers. The empirical findings together with the statistical data and the available case law create a certain framework to depict what the experience of English practitioners

[620] http://conflictoflaws.net/2015/surveys-on-european-order-for-payment-and-small-claims-procedures/.

might be in this area of law at a more general level. The difficulty in obtaining data and conducting research seems to indicate that the European uniform procedures are seldom used and/or are not a priority for English legal practice and most professional organisations.

3.7.3.2. Familiarity with European Procedures and Handling Practices

The eight EOP surveys together with the interviews and additional information gathered from correspondence with English professionals indicate that most of the respondents are aware of the EOP and the ESCP (Figs. 3.2–3.3). EOP and ESCP practitioners considered themselves to be familiar or aware of the European procedures, and they rated their knowledge as being between 2 and 3 on a scale of 1 to 5.[621] Solicitors, barristers, and enforcement officers often indicated they were aware or familiar with the procedures, but that they had had only limited involvement or no opportunity to apply the procedures in practice. Two practitioners (one barrister and one enforcement officer) indicated they had handled EEOs but not EOPs or ESCPs. Considering the very limited number of respondents who had actually applied the procedures in their daily professional activity, it is highly possible this scant involvement influences the perception that practitioners have with respect to their familiarity with the procedures. The respondents rating their knowledge as being 'significantly or very familiar' are practitioners that actually have had the opportunity to work several times with these procedures. Moreover, it appears that in most circumstances – including ones in which the practitioners had experience in applying the instruments – the respondents had not undergone any related training. However, some of the these practitioners had attended dedicated conferences and meetings. Moreover, the Law Society and the British Institute for International and Comparative Law (BIICL) have organised conferences and workshops on these European uniform procedures over the years.[622]

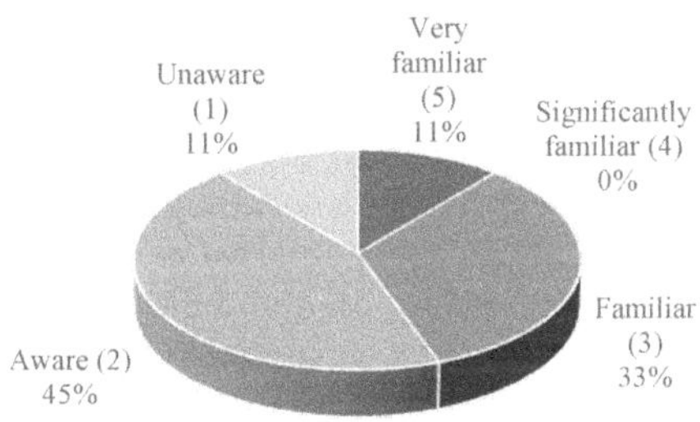

Fig. 3.2. Professionals' perception of their familiarity with the EOP (18 responses)

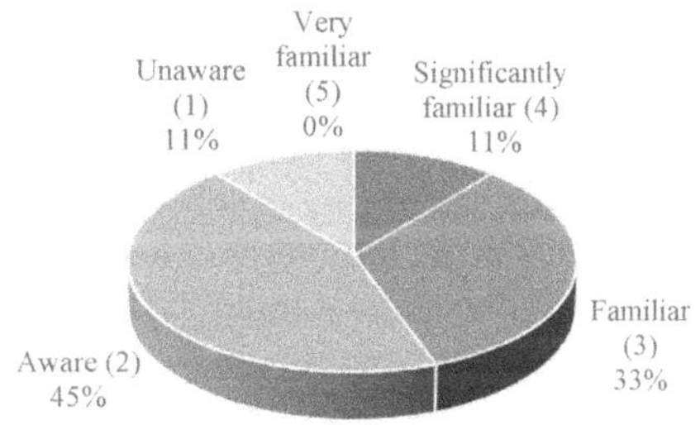

Fig. 3.3. Professionals' perception of their familiarity with the ESCP (17 responses)

621 With 1 meaning that the professional is 'not aware of the procedure' and 5 meaning that he is 'very familiar with the procedure' regarding which he is requested to provide information.

622 See also reference in Fauvarque-Cosson & Behar-Touchais (2012), at 363–365.

One of the responding solicitors remarked that there have been changes in the last few years with regard to practitioners' level of familiarity. He perceived the courts – after a 'shaky start' – to be more comfortable with the European procedures, especially the EOP. This might be related to possible organised training sessions and, in some courts, the allocation of EOP and/or ESCP cases to a particular judge.

As regards perceptions of general awareness of the instruments (Figs. 3.4–3.5), the results show a very similar level of appreciation regarding the respondents' personal knowledge.

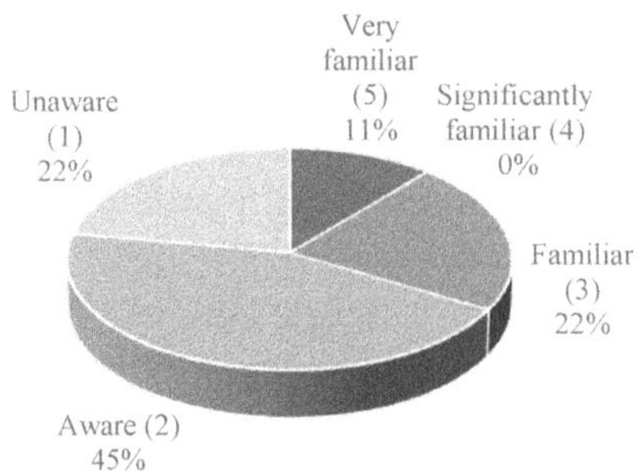

Fig. 3.4. Professionals' perception of general awareness of the EOP (9 responses)

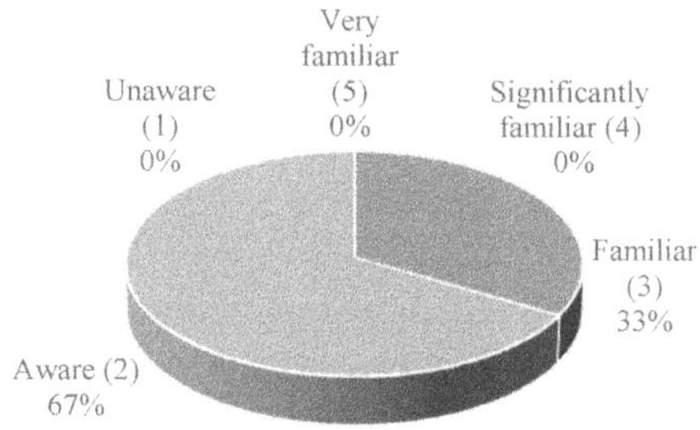

Fig. 3.5. Professionals' perception of general awareness of the ESCP (7 responses)

The level of awareness in relation to the ESCP is higher, but still remains at the lowest level of familiarity. Practitioners do point to a certain limited familiarity of the courts and practitioners with the European procedures. The lack of experience with their actual application is one of the aspects that influences the level of knowledge. As regards consumers, according to Special Eurobarometer 395, 1% of UK respondents indicated they had used the ESCP; 16% said they had heard of the procedure; and 82% said they had not.[623]

The limited practical experience of judges, court staff, and other practitioners, along with existing differences in the familiar national procedures, might create uncertainties as to the way the procedures need to be handled. This might be doubled in some cases by the decrease in the number of staff at certain courts, an aspect that could temporarily diminish their possibility of dealing smoothly with EOP and/or ESCP claims.

Further, according to some of the respondents there seems to be a certain preference for claims being handled by the courts in accordance with ordinary English procedure, default orders, and Money Claims (Online),[624] or even writing off the debt because litigation costs in a cross-border situation are considered too high in comparison to the debt. Figures 3.6 and 3.7 give an indication as to the national alternative procedures that are preferred over the EOP and the ESCP. The reason might be that the court staff, practitioners, and parties are more familiar with domestic instruments. This aspect is confirmed also by earlier studies regarding the use of optional European instruments.[625] Another element influencing this choice concerns the forms used. Some practitioners

623 Special Eurobarometer 395, *European Small Claims Procedure*, 2013, at 69.

624 This has also been used in paper format by cross-border claimants.

625 Fauvarque-Cosson & Behar-Touchais (2012), at 330 and 442–443.

consider the standard European Procedure forms unusual and odd at first in comparison to the domestic forms familiar to every court and practitioner.[626]

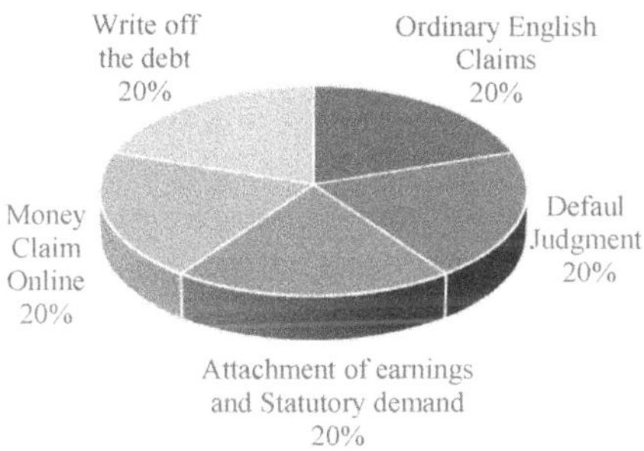

Fig. 3.6. National procedures chosen over the EOP (5 responses)

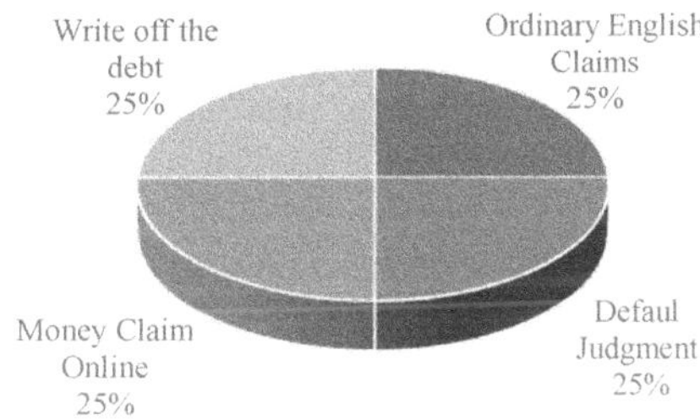

Fig. 3.7. National procedures chosen over the ESCP (4 responses)

The limited information provided by respondents indicates that there is a certain awareness with regard to the existence of the Part 78 European Procedures, but practitioners are uncertain as to how these function; hence, a preference for better known domestic procedures remains, as they are easier and faster to apply. Better training and the raising of awareness with regard to the European uniform procedures and their functioning would certainly be beneficial for courts, practitioners, and parties involved in cross-border litigation.

3.7.3.3. Case Classification

As to the type of claims for which the European procedures were used, the data available indicate the EOP has been employed in B2B cases, while the ESCP has been implemented in C2B cases. However, the data cannot be generalised, as input comes only from three respondents (2 referred to the EOP procedure and 1 to the ESCP). According to this information, EOP claims involved mainly litigation between private companies.

The information is limited also in relation to the type of contractual relationship on which the claim was based. The EOP procedure appears to be used more often in relation to contracts involving sale of goods, service, and real estate. For the ESCP, the claims seem to be based generally on sale-purchase agreements, service contracts, car rental agreements, air transportation contracts, and holiday package agreements.

3.7.3.4. Conduct of Proceedings and Encountered Difficulties

Handling of Cases

Very little information is available. A couple of respondents referred to particular judges being designated by some courts to handle this type of claim. The court staff appears to be

626 This finding is also confirmed by the results of the study published by Fauvarque-Cosson & Behar-Touchais (2012), at 442–443.

involved in offering support to judges with regard to procedural aspects and administrative matters. The court staff is the first to analyse the submitted standard forms; hence, it is important for them to be well aware of the European uniform procedures and the way they function. This will certainly avoid situations in which the application is rejected for lack of jurisdiction of the court, although according to the e-Justice Portal application the County Court is indicated as having jurisdiction. The courts in areas that are not so active in cross-border trade and commercial activities – or smaller courts – are possibly less likely to receive a significant number of EOP and ESCP cases; hence, their familiarity with the procedure might be less strong compared to London courts or other big cities across England. As indicated by respondents, other reasons that could contribute to the limited awareness and knowledge of the procedures are related to certain practical aspects. These are: (1) the significant workload the staff and courts have to handle in relation to domestic procedures, which gives them little time to dedicate to cross-border 'European flavour' instruments; (2) experienced court staff leaving without having a direct replacement to take up their tasks; and (3) traditionally, the county courts do not get involved in cross-border cases, which are left to the Foreign Orders Section of the Queen's Bench Division.

As to the possible existing tensions between the national and European procedural rules, only three survey respondents expressed their views in relation to the EOP, and two for the ESCP. This makes the results inconclusive. Some additional input is based on correspondence with the English practitioners. They also point to various difficulties: namely, (1) problematic service and the time needed to carry out procedures in cross-border situations; (2) the language of the regulations is difficult to follow, and there could be problems regarding what is actually covered by the provisions; (3) making decisions based on the standard form without disclosure of documents, along with the use of witness statements in relation to the EOP, can be perceived as a difficult task compared to domestic procedures; (4) video or telephone conferences, especially in relation to the ESCP, appear difficult to arrange, including determining when an interpreter might be necessary;[627] (5) the application to set aside the decision or stay proceedings seems complicated in relation to domestic procedures; and (6) there are difficulties related to enforcement when the recognised decision is challenged.[628] Some respondents also suggested that, in practice, courts feel to a certain extent uncomfortable in handling procedures that 'look similar to their own [n.n. domestic procedures], but are different in some ways'.

Forms

Standard forms are a common feature of English court proceedings, and courts and practitioners are familiar with their use. However, some respondents remarked that the European procedure forms differ from the familiar ones or that at first they appear odd. This might also be the result of the limited opportunities to handle EOP and/or ESCP claims. Figure 3.8 reveals the difficulties encountered most often in relation to the forms. These include the lack of legal knowledge as well as the way provisions are drafted in the

627 Nevertheless, the Deloitte Report on the ESCP mentions that videoconferencing is available in more than 50% of the English courts. Deloitte Report, Final Report, Part I, at 79.

628 According to the respondent, appeals procedures against registered judgments could take around 18 months.

forms requesting specific information from the party. The latter seems to be particularly problematic for litigants appearing in person.

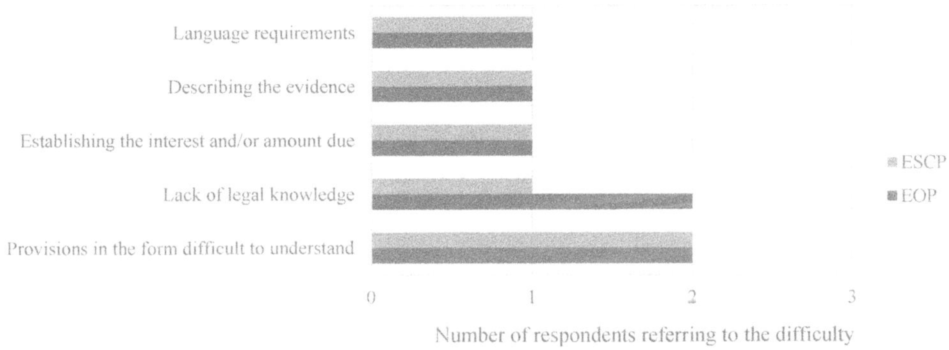

Fig. 3.8. The most common difficulties encountered by parties using the EOP and/or the ESCP

Assistance to the parties does not generally seem to be offered by court staff. In some cases, the county courts (currently referred to as 'hearing centres') even repeatedly refused EOP and ESCP applications by claimants, and referred them to domestic procedures with which they were familiar. In such circumstances, they can offer little assistance to claimants. Consumers sometimes revert to ECC UK for assistance and advice, as the organisation does offer information with regard to the European uniform procedures. However, it does not provide assistance on a usual basis for filling in the forms or help with translating the application forms into the required language of the proceedings, as it considers its main goal to be to help parties reach a solution outside the court. Further, ECC UK is of the opinion that courts themselves need to be more efficient and effective in helping consumers.

The respondents do not indicate a significant use by the courts of Form B to request a completion and/or rectification of the application. The input is available only from three respondents in relation to the EOP and two respondents for the ESCP. In the EOP, the reasons for the judge to request completion of standard Form A was related to: (1) incomplete information regarding the defendant; (2) the claimant not describing the evidence on which his claim was based; and (3) establishing interest on the amount owed. In relation to the evidence on which the EOP claim was based, one of the respondents indicated that he always includes the evidence documents with the standard form in order to avoid delays and additional exchanges with the court that might want to see the documents referred to in Form A. Another respondent mentioned that requests for providing a copy of the evidence documents are frequent, as judges 'seem to understand that it is part of their remit to robustly review the cases to make sure there is evidence of any and all losses', and have gone as far as challenging certain evidence elements. In relation to the ESCP, a translation of all documents attached to the standard application form would not come as a surprise.

Further, the Declaration of enforceability (EOP Form G) is issued upon the claimant's request, which is also confirmed by the e-Codex WP7 Study.[629] No additional information

629 Velicogna, Lupo & Mellone (2016), at 14.

is available as to the use of standard forms in England, or to what extent particular forms are used. Discussion with practitioners showed that the standard EOP and ESCP forms are not generally available from the courts, nor was it known whether these are available on other portals apart from the European websites.

Language
Translation and language requirements do not appear to cause significant difficulties for parties using the EOP and the ESCP, other than increasing the costs of the proceedings. One practitioner even refers to the online multilingual forms and the possibility of using them as a 'resounding success'. If any documents of the proceedings are gained as evidence for the case, the party is required to translate them. According to one respondent, the difficulty in such cases is that translation services are very expensive in England, more than in other Member States. ECC UK stresses that this problem also remains when consumers file a claim with a foreign court; the court will always require them to provide the documents in the language of the local court. Additionally, ECC UK emphasises that in small claims cases, consumers that seek to recover £30–40 will not spend additional money for translation purposes – they will simply give up the court procedure. In practice, the organisation does not actually provide assistance in filling in forms in the language of the proceedings. A small number of language-related difficulties were also identified in relation to the language in which the documents of the proceedings were served on the defendant in the ESCP procedure. This factor can hinder the party's access to justice.

Service
As regards the EOP, the few survey respondents point to a variety of means being used for the service of documents of the proceedings (Fig. 3.9).

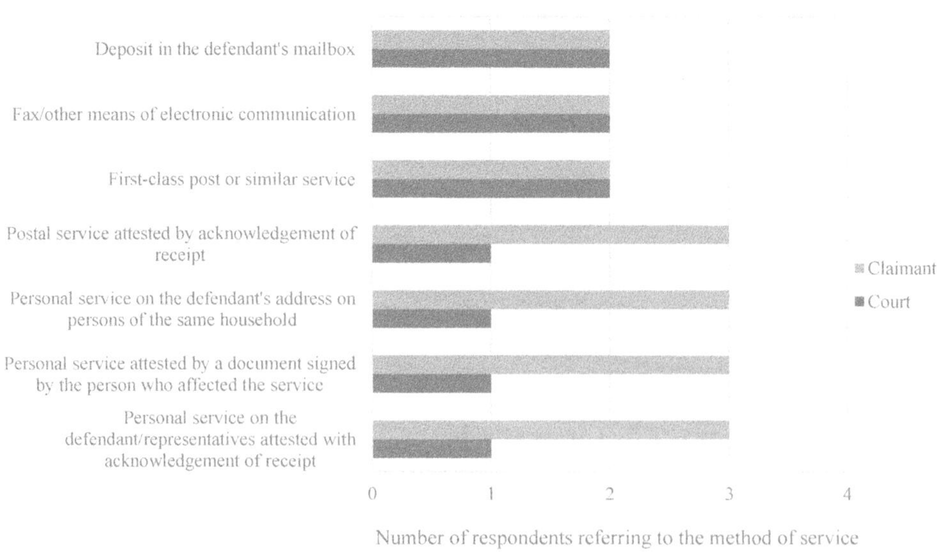

Fig. 3.9. Methods used to serve the EOP on the defendant by the court or the claimant

On the basis of available data and the e-Codex WP7 Study on service of the EOP, the postal service with its acknowledgement of receipt appears to be the prevalent method employed. Service by post or signed-for courier in the framework of the Service Regulation are indicated as a means to solve service difficulties. Nevertheless, obtaining an acknowledgement of receipt might prove difficult in practice. Respondents indicate that service is one of the problematic aspects of the EOP procedure when this has to be carried out abroad. Together with the difficulty in obtaining the acknowledgement of receipt, the claimant or his representative may sometimes have a problem determining what legal means are accepted as valid service within the Member State where this has to be carried out. Information on the European websites is not always updated and not immediately available in all official languages. These long transition periods can easily result in additional procedural delays and in more efforts by the interested party to find the necessary information.[630]

As regards time necessary to carry out the service, the survey respondents indicated that in practice it may take more than 4 weeks. The duration is influenced by service-related difficulties. Another aspect hinted at by the surveys – and confirmed by additional information gathered from correspondence with legal practitioners and other European studies (i.e. the e-Codex WP7 Report and the UK Country Report on Mutual Trust and Free Circulation of Judgments)[631] – is that the court is formally responsible for service of the EOP. However, in practice, some local courts request the claimant to carry out the service, or the party prefers to take care of it in order to speed up the process.

For the ESCP, service also appears to be problematic, especially in relation to cross-border cases. The difficulties are related to the language in which these documents are served, and in obtaining the acknowledgement of service. To mitigate this second identified problem and to speed up the process, one respondent indicated he had started to use the provisions of Article 14 Service Regulation. He requests the Royal Court of Justice 'to put together a formal pack (as they would do if serving through diplomatic channels/ Hague Convention etc.), and to then send that sealed bundle' back to him. The solicitor then uses courier providers (for example DHL, UPS, or other available providers) to serve a 'signed for' package that will reach the defendant within days. In such cases, the claim form and related documents are served on the defendant within an average of 2 weeks compared to periods ranging from 2 to 6 months when carried out by the national transmitting and receiving agency in accordance with the Service Regulation. However, the respondent emphasises that transmitting the documents by post is not enough to ensure '*good* service', but this has to be in line with the Service Regulation; hence, it has to include a signed delivery option and a confirmation of receipt, and the originating Member States have to be involved in the process through their authorities.

For enforcement, the EOP and ESCP judgments do not need to be served on the debtor in order for the claimant to proceed to the execution stage, but a registration of the judgment is necessary for this purpose.

630 Velicogna, Lupo & Onțanu (2015), Section 4.

631 EX725 Her Majesty's Court Service, *Making a cross border claim in the EU*, at 5; Velicogna, Lupo & Mellone (2016), at 12; Hess (2017).

Hearings
The available empirical data give no indication as to the holding of court hearings.

Challenging Mechanisms (Opposition, Appeal, Review)
Based on the responses provided by practitioners, no generalisation can be made in relation to these aspects of the European instruments. Only one solicitor provided information regarding the use of opposition in the EOP procedure. According to this respondent, the defendants challenged the orders within 25–50% of the cases he had handled in the period 2008–2013.[632] In two claims, the defendant had opposed the EOP following the lapse of the 30-day period established by the Regulation.

On the topic of the ESCP, none of the practitioners mentioned being aware of or having had information about appeal proceedings being initiated in relation to this procedure. However, one respondent indicated that the expected time necessary for an ESCP appeal was somewhere between 3 and 6 months.

Data on the use of the review in EOP and ESCP procedures are not conclusive. One of the survey respondents indicated the review had been used in an EOP case, while two other respondents stated that they were either not aware of any requests or they did not know. In the event the defendant sought to obtain an annulment of the EOP, the reasons given were that the English court lacked jurisdiction and that the period for appeal under the national legislation had not lapsed. The English judge rejected the request. In relation to the ESCP, one respondent indicated he did not know, and the second said that the review had not been used. There is no indication of hearings being held in EOP or ESCP review requests in accordance with Part 23 CPR.[633] The only general hint these few replies can give is that the review mechanism appears to be seldom used.

Representation
Even though representation seems to be used to some extent both in EOP and ESCP cases, the fact that only two respondents provided information in relation to the EOP and one in relation to the ESCP prevents any generalisation of the results. In EOP claims, the rate of representation appears to be high (in more than 75% of the cases) for claimants and lower for defendants (between 25% and 50% of the cases). For ESCP claims, the results revert. Claimants seem to appear more often in person in the procedure (representation in less than 25% of the cases), while defendants seem more likely to use legal representation (in more than 75% of the cases). However, there is no explanation for such results.

Procedural Timeframe
Based on the survey answers, there is no conclusive information on whether the EOP is issued within a period of 30 days from the registration of the application. Of the three respondents providing information on this aspect of the procedure, one mentioned that

632 The solicitor had followed a total number of 14 cases between 2008–2013. In 2015, the solicitor mentioned having regularly handled around 2–3 EOP claims a year.

633 For the EOP, CPR Rule 78.8 in conjunction with PD 78.6.1 and 2 and Part 23.8 CPR. For the ESCP, Part 78.19 in conjunction with ESCP and PD 78.18.1–18 and Part 23.8 CPR.

the orders were to be issued within a period of 30 days, another considered the courts did not comply with this timeframe, and the third said he did not know. However, in terms of average time necessary to obtain the order, one respondent indicated it takes more than 9 months. Another practitioner sitting in an interview also indicated it takes a long time for a claim to be handled by the English County Court in this area. The court repeatedly refused to register the claim and referred the plaintiff to the domestic Money Claim Online procedure. As regards the ESCP, the only respondent providing information indicated that the handling of the claim from registration to the court issuing the judgment takes between 3 to 6 months on average. According to the practitioner, the same period is to be expected in the event of an appeal. The longer periods needed to obtain an order or a judgment may well be influenced by the time necessary to serve the order or documents of the proceedings on the defendant.

Costs, Interests, Penalties

According to the EX50 on Civil and Family Court Fees list, the EOP- and ESCP-related court fees applied are variable and depend on the amount of the actual claim. As to the possibility of paying the court fees, especially for claimants resident in other Member State, some difficulties might be encountered in practice. Although according to English practitioners the courts are set to be increasingly equipped to receive payments by bank transfer, the smaller county court premises might only be able to receive payments by physical deposit with the court or by cheques issued in pounds sterling.

Another aspect regarding costs of proceedings, especially in relation to the ESCP, is that these can easily reach values higher than the actual claim. Additionally, there is a significant chance the claimant will not be able to recover all the costs, and the court will proceed to assess the needed character of the costs and their proportionality in relation to national practice and case law.

3.7.3.5. Enforcement

Information on execution of the EOP and the ESCP in England is limited. This is in part due to the fact that only a small number of practitioners replied to the questionnaires, while only a few provided feedback on their experience or lack of experience with these European procedures. Only one enforcement officer replied to the EOP survey, while others indicated they had not yet had the opportunity to enforce any European uniform procedures. Therefore, the amount of data available can offer only a limited insight into the practice in English courts.

All four practitioners providing information on EOP enforcement in England mentioned that difficulties were encountered at this stage. Two respondents confirmed a problematic enforcement also in relation to the ESCP. Among the most frequent difficulties creditors encounter are: (1) obtaining information with regard to the debtor's assets and financial situation; (2) selecting the method of enforcement; (3) the high costs of enforcement; (4) needing to provide translations of the EOP/Declaration of enforceability (in relation to the EOP); and (5) finding the competent authority (in relation to the ESCP). ECC UK emphasises the difficulties encountered by consumers who do not employ the services of a legal practitioner after obtaining the judgment.

According to the organisation, consumers become stranded because they do not know how to enforce the judgment, and it considers that the court should provide the necessary information. This might be an indication that more easily accessible or direct information should be offered to parties, especially when they handle their claim in person. Further, most respondents perceive enforcement difficulties to be similar to the ones parties might experience within a purely domestic case. In practice, once the judgment is registered, the enforcement officer or agent will follow the same execution process as with any decision issued under domestic law.

Abandoning enforcement appears to be relatively common with regard to the EOP and the ESCP, especially for the latter. Respondents point to percentages ranging from 10 to 30% in relation to the EOP and 75% of the cases for the ESCP. The reasons behind this are the lack of assets, the high costs of enforcement, and time issues. In EOP claims, the enforcement was abandoned owing to striking-off procedures initiated by the English companies involved.

As regards the enforcement timeframe, the actual registration of the judgment appears to be swift. A former barrister indicated that the paper request transmitted to the High Court Master may take 7–10 days, while in situations justifying urgent treatment the title may be requested in person. In terms of length of execution, this depends on the type of enforcement method. A warrant for amounts of £5,000-£10,000 may take between 1.5–2 months to execute, while enforcement involving immovable property will require more time and procedural stages. In relation to an ESCP judgment, a solicitor indicated that enforcement took more than 4 months, and the plaintiff decided to discontinue the procedure due to cost and time issues. Prolonged proceedings in smaller value claims and the prospect of limited enforcement possibilities could have a deterring effect on parties deciding whether to initiate court proceedings.

The refusal and the limitation or stay of enforcement mechanisms do not appear to have been used so far. Practitioners providing feedback were not aware of such situations.

There are indications that the registered judgment is sometimes subject to an appeal procedure in accordance with national procedural rules, a situation that may significantly delay the execution. According to a respondent, this can take around 18 months to resolve.

As regards execution of the EOP and ESCP decision issued by English courts abroad, some respondents were able to provide information. When the creditor is represented, the English solicitor will collaborate with a local lawyer in securing execution of the decision. Enforcement in some Member States appears to work more smoothly (Germany, Spain), while in others delays can appear (Italy), along with limitations regarding the object of enforcement (cost-related orders might not be executed in Greece).

3.7.3.6. Practitioners' Assessment

Practitioners' views diverge as to the efficiency of the EOP and the ESCP in terms of 'speediness, affordability and protection of parties' rights' in comparison to national procedures available for uncontested and small value claims. For the EOP, two of the three respondents agree on its efficiency. They welcome the procedure, and consider it to be highly effective in terms of speed and affordability in enforcing cross-border litigation.

The downsides referred to remain the costs of enforcement and of lawyers in other Member States. For the ESCP, the reactions were more of disenchantment as to its efficiency, though it was still seen as a valid instrument. Its efficiency is affected by the need to provide further training to court staff, by the low threshold, by the service issues, and by the high costs of enforcement. As regards the value limit, Regulation 2015/2421 amending the ESCP Regulation mitigates this downside by increasing the threshold to €5,000. In view of the process of the UK leaving the EU, however, this increase is not likely to have much influence on the future of English court proceedings. As regards practitioners' perspectives as to the effectiveness of the European uniform procedures, the division between the EOP and the ESCP is maintained. While the EOP is seen mostly as an effective procedure – although difficulties and sometimes limited familiarity affect its outcome – the ESCP is considered not to be feasible or worth the effort in view of the low threshold and the disproportionate costs it entails in England. The increase in the ESCP threshold from 2017 could improve this situation for English claimants and consumers until the UK leaves the EU. Overall, practitioners indicated that a significant number of EOP- and ESCP-related obstacles remain: namely, (1) the limited familiarity of parties and practitioners with the procedure; (2) the limited number of cases that do not allow practitioners to set a practice; (3) problematic service; (4) difficult enforcement and lack of information about this stage of the proceedings; (5) the level of court fees; and (6) the low threshold of the ESCP.

To improve the way the EOP and the ESCP function, respondents consider there is a need for more information on the various stages of the proceedings, for the training of practitioners and courts, and possibly for the creation of a step-by-step guide for practitioners that have only occasional opportunities to apply these procedures. Further actions concern the possibility of using registered e-mail addresses to serve the documents of the proceedings or the order issued, increasing the ESCP threshold, and reviewing the enforcement process. Regulation 2015/2421 amending the ESCP already addresses some of these aspects, raising the procedure threshold and establishing electronic service at the same level as postal service as a primary means of communicating documents of the proceedings. It remains to be seen whether these amendments will contribute successfully to a better functioning of the ESCP, but the situation in England gives rise to certain reservations.

3.7.4. *Overall Assessment*

The EOP and the ESCP seem to be only moderately known in England, with very few practitioners appearing to have a solid knowledge and understanding of them. There is a certain level of general awareness as to their existence, but according to statistics their use remains modest. The adoption of CPR 78 rules accommodating the EOP and the ESCP within the national legislation does not seem to have contributed extensively to creating a general level of familiarity and confidence in choosing these procedures in cross-border litigation over other domestic instruments. Nevertheless, the CPR rules help create a certain visibility of the instruments for judges and practitioners.

As case law involving European uniform procedures is rare, practitioners have no indication as to how courts would interpret and apply certain provisions. This maintains a degree of uncertainty with regard to well-known domestic procedures. However, one aspect that can be noted throughout the analysis is the tendency of the English judge to interpret the Regulations within the light of familiar domestic procedures and practice. Their application is sometimes complemented by national requirements that are not actually compatible with the aims of the European instruments (i.e. requesting the submission of evidence in the EOP, translation of all evidence documents not in English for the ESCP). In addition, the fact that in some cases the parties had their EOP or ESCP claim refused several times by a court unaware of the procedures did not encourage potential users to file other claims in accordance with the European uniform procedures. In these circumstances, it becomes cheaper and less time consuming for a claimant to file a request according to a domestic procedure with which the court staff and judges are familiar. The rejection of EOP and ESCP claims because of the court's unfamiliarity with them limits the parties' right of access to justice, and can even lead to tragic outcomes if no assets remain available by the time an enforcement title is obtained.

Practitioners seem to be more enthusiastic about and familiar with the EOP than with the ESCP. It would have been good to raise awareness and provide more information tailored to the needs of the parties and practitioners. This could have been addressed at the national as well as the European level in order to facilitate and encourage the use of these instruments in cross-border litigation. However, the UK's departure from the EU makes it scarcely possible to provide additional measures to improve the functioning of these European uniform procedures, as other activities have taken priority.

Chapter 4

FRANCE

4.1. Introduction

The French legal system is one of 'civil law', a 'European-continental law' jurisdiction, relying mainly on codified law.[634] The precedent does not constitute a source of law,[635] but *Conseil constitutionnel* and *Cour de cassation* case law have significant authority in the interpretation of legal texts by French judges.[636] Court proceedings in civil and commercial matters in France are carried out according to provisions of the Code of Civil Procedure (*Code de procedure civile – CPC*)[637] and of the Code of Judiciary Organisation (*Code de l'organisation judiciaire – COJ*).[638]

This chapter considers the procedural choices creditors have in order to recover debts before French courts, focusing on the special available procedures. The EOP and the ESCP are added to these domestic instruments in cross-border litigation. Section 4.2 offers an overview of the national ordinary procedure and its characteristics, followed in Section 4.3 by a functional analysis of the national special procedures available for the purpose of debt recovery. The characteristics of these national tailored solutions are analysed in comparison to the EOP and the ESCP. Section 4.4 examines the positions of French stakeholders with regard to EOP and ESCP Regulations. Section 4.5 scrutinises the incorporation of EOP and ESCP procedures into the national legislation. The analysis in Section 4.6 focuses on enforcement in France in general and on the execution of EOP and ESCP decisions. Finally, Section 4.7 analyses the functioning in practice of the EOP and the ESCP in accordance with available statistics, published national case law, and the outcome of the empirical research results.

634 Fauvarque-Cosson & Fournier (2012), at 344; Steiner (2010), at 37, 63, and subsequent.

635 Steiner (2010), at 85.

636 Fauvarque-Cosson & Fournier (2012), at 346; Guinchard, Chainais & Ferrand (2012), at 49–50, 78–79.

637 The New Code of Civil Procedure is the result of a substantive and successive reform of the 1806 Napoleonic Code of Civil Procedure. The New Code of Civil Procedure was renamed Code of Civil Procedure by Law No. 2007–1787 of 20 December 2007, when the old code of civil procedure was abrogated (*Art 26-II L. n°2007-1787 du 20 déc. 2007*). See further, Després (2012), at 1; Cadiet (2011), at 338–351; Cadiet & Amrani-Mekki (2008), at 314–315; Cadiet (2005), at 49–68.

638 The Code de l'organisation judiciaire (Ordonnance No. 2006–673 of 8 June 2006, Law No. 2008–526 of 12 May 2009 and Decree No. 2008–522 of June 2, 2008) contains provisions regarding the courts, the functioning, and the competence of jurisdictions.

4.2. The French Legal System: An Overview

4.2.1. *General Aspects*

The first instance jurisdiction of civil courts is divided between the main civil court, *Tribunal de grande instance* (TGI), which is the general first instance court,[639] and the special jurisdiction courts: namely,[640] the *Tribunal d'instance* (TI), which is competent to hear cases up to a value of €10,000;[641] the *jurisdiction de proximité* (JP) for small claims up to a level of €4,000;[642] the *Tribunal de commerce* (TC), criminal courts that trial commercial cases,[643] and the *Conseil des Prud'hommes*, which handles labour law cases.[644] The JP disappeared as of 1 July 2017.[645] Jurisdiction regarding EOP and ESCP cases in France is shared between the TI and the TC in accordance with the civil or commercial nature of the filed claim.[646] TI and TGI cases are handled by professional judges, while TC cases are decided by judges who are specialists in their field.[647]

639 Article L.211-3 and R.211-3-4 COJ. See Guinchard, Chainais & Ferrand (2012), at 990–991; Cadiet (2011), at 335.

640 Guinchard, Chainais & Ferrand (2012), at 1008–1009; Hérons & Le Bars (2012), at 507–533; Couchez & Lagarde (2011), at 328–329; Cadiet (2011), at 335–336.

641 Article L.221-4 COJ. Guinchard, Chainais & Ferrand (2012), at 1009–1018; Douchy-Oudot (2012); Cadiet (2011), at 336.

642 *On jurisdiction de proximité*, see further Caubet (2013) at 51–58.

643 Article L.721-1 to L.721-7 Commercial Code (*Code de commerce* – C.com.). See also Guez (2012); Cadiet (2011), at 336; Cadiet & Amrani-Mekki (2008), at 311.

644 Cadiet (2011), at 336; Cadiet & Amrani-Mekki (2008), at 311–312, de Roo & Jagtenberg (1994), at 132–151.

645 By Law No. 2011-1862 of 13 December 2011 on the division of cases between courts and the relief of the courts on certain judicial procedures (*Loi relative à la répartition des contentieux et à l'allégement de certaines procedures juridictionnelles*), as of 1 January 2013 the *jurisdictions de proximité* were supposed to disappear, and their competence transfer to TI. Law No. 2012-1441 of 24 December 2012, and then Law No. 2014-1654 of 29 December 2014 and Law No. 2016-1547 of 18 November 2016 regarding the modernisation of XXI-century justice repeatedly postponed the entering into force until 1 July 2017 (www.justice.gouv.fr/organisation-de-la-justice-10031/lordre-judiciaire-10033/juridiction-de-proximite-19668.html).

646 On the EOP, see Articles L.221-7 of the Code of Judicial Organisation (*Code de l'organisation judiciaire*) and L.722-3-1 of the Commercial Code (*Code de commerce*), Point 3.1. Juridictions matériellement compétentes pour connaître de la demande, Circulaire de la DACS C3 06-09 du 26 mai 2009 relative à l'application du règlement (CE) n° 1896/2006 du Parlement européen et du Conseil du 12 décembre 2006 instituant une procédure européenne d'injonction de payer, Justice 2004/4, 30 août 2009, 16/51, and Information communicated by Member States in accordance with Article 29 of Regulation (EC) No 1896/2006 of the European Parliament and the Council of 12 December 2006 creating a European order for payment procedure available at https://e-justice.europa.eu/content_european_payment_order-353-fr-en.do?member=1. On the ESCP, see Articles L.221-4-1 of the Code of Judicial Organisation and L.721-3-1 of the Commercial Code, Point 3.1. Juridictions matériellement compétentes pour connaître de la demande, Circulaire de la DACS C3 07-09 du 26 mai 2009 relative à l'application du règlement (CE) n° 861/2007 du Parlement européen et du Conseil du 11 juillet 2007 instituant une procédure européenne de règlement des petits litiges, Justice 2004/4, 30 août 2009, 17/51, and Information communicated by Member States in accordance with Article 25 of Regulation (EC) No 861/2007 of the European Parliament and the Council of 11 July 2007 establishing a European Small Claims Procedure, available at https://e-justice.europa.eu/content_small_claims-354-fr-en.do?member=1.

647 Article L.721-1 C. com., Article L.722-6 C. com., Article L.723-1 C. com. See also Guez (2012); Perrot (2006), at 92–221.

In handling the case and issuing a judgment, the French judge is bound to adhere to the subject matter of the dispute in accordance with the limits established by the parties' claims.[648] However, the judge does not have a passive role – the CPC grants him significant prerogatives in shaping the trial.[649]

Representation by a lawyer is compulsory before the TGI,[650] but optional for the TI and the TC. Parties may defend themselves in TI or TC cases, or can choose to be represented or assisted by lawyers or other persons in accordance with CPC provisions.[651]

4.2.2. *The Ordinary National Procedure*

A claim is initiated by the parties presenting themselves voluntarily before the judge (*présentation volontaire des parties devant le juge*); by the claimant summoning the defendant to appear before the judge (*assignation*); by filing a common request with the court's secretarial office (*remise d'une requête conjointe au secrétariat de la juridiction*); or by request or a declaration filed with the secretarial office (*requête ou déclaration au secrétariat de la juridiction*).[652] In the case of debt recovery claims, the summoning of the defendant through a bailiff is the most likely means to initiate a court claim. For claims up to €4,000, there is a simpler way: a declaration before the clerk's office (*déclaration au greffe*).[653] Subsequently, the clerk will summon the defendant to a hearing.[654]

Following registration of the case on the court's docket (*rôle*), and the establishment of a procedural *dossier* for the case, the TGI president forwards the case to the competent chamber, and sets a date for a preliminary hearing (*audience d'appel*).[655] During this stage, a decision is issued on the circuit to which the case is allocated. Simple cases in a state of adjudication are sent directly to trial (short circuit – *circuit court*).[656] In most claims, the president finds the case is not in a state of being trialed, and directs it to the middle circuit (*circuit moyen*), a sort of fast track,[657] or to the long circuit (*circuit long*) for complex cases.[658] Cases in these two circuits undergo a preparatory stage in which parties exchange documents and conclusions under the supervision of a judge (*juge de mise en état*).[659] In addition to the traditional means of service or exchange of documents,

648 Articles 4 and 5 CPC.
649 Articles 7(2), 8, 10, 11(2), 12(2)-(3), and 13 CPC.
650 Articles 751 and 755 CPC.
651 See Articles 827 and 853(1) CPC on the option parties have in appearing in person before the TI and the TC, and Articles 828 and 853(2) et (3) CPC regarding representation of parties and the persons or professionals by whom they can be assisted.
652 Article 54 CPC.
653 Article 843 CPC.
654 Article 844 CPC.
655 Articles 758 and 759 CPC.
656 Article 760 CPC. This is rarely the case in practice. See Guinchard, Chainais & Ferrand (2012), at 1187–1188.
657 Article 761 CPC.
658 Article 762 CPC.
659 Articles 764–770 CPC. The *juge de mise en état* exercises his powers in different directions: he attempts to conciliate the parties, controls the development of the case, and examines the exceptions and incidental demands invoked by the parties.

French law allows the use of electronic means of communication, provided the defendant has expressly consented to their use.[660] If the case reaches trial, a hearing is established. In practice, however, before the TGI, the written preparatory stage of the case becomes increasingly important, while the oral debate tends to lose central place.[661] Although the parties' right to an oral hearing is recognised, it is not considered to be 'a prerequisite for adversarial proceeding'.[662] The oral phase retains its importance before the TI and the TC, where direct contact between the parties and the judge is favoured.[663] The debates are closed as soon as the court considers it has been sufficiently informed about the case. In exceptional circumstances, during the deliberation the court can ask the parties to submit written briefs (*notes en délibéré*) in support of their position.[664]

Conciliation during court proceedings is available for a wide range of matters, and is based either on compulsory legal provisions[665] or on the judge's or parties' initiative. This practice is encouraged especially for proceedings before the TI or the JP.[666] An attempt to encourage the parties to reach an agreement can be carried out by the judge or by a legal conciliator (*conciliateur de justice*).[667] Mediation may also be used for the same purpose (Article 130–1 CPC).[668] If no agreement is reached, the case proceeds to judgment.

A judgment is issued following adversarial proceedings (*jugement conradictoire*),[669] in proceedings deemed to have been adversarial (*jugement réputé contradictoire*),[670] or by default.[671] Appeals are usually possible, except for claims below €4,000,[672] and are generally open to the parties as a guarantee of justice (principle of double degree of jurisdiction).[673] The period during which the parties can bring an appeal has a

660 Article 748–1 in conjunction with Article 748–2 CPC regarding this use of communication between legal professionals. See Guinchard, Chainais & Ferrand (2012), at 626–627.

661 Articles 779(3) and 786 CPC establish situations for which pleadings are either renounced or carried out before the *juge de mise en état*, who will make a report for the other members of the court for the decision to be taken according to the requirements of a collective decision. See further, Cadiet & Amrani-Mekki (2008), at 321; Guinchard, Chainais & Ferrand (2012), at 1217–1220.

662 Cadiet (2011), at 357–358.

663 See Cadiet (2011), at 351–352; Guinchard, Chainais & Ferrand (2012), at 1217–1220; Ferrand (2010), at 57.

664 Article 445 CPC.

665 Article 845 CPC establishes at the beginning of the court proceedings before the TI that an attempt at a conciliation of the parties by the judge is compulsory. See also Article 4 of Law No 2016–1547 modernising the Justice of the 21st Century (*Loi n° 2016–1547 du 18 novembre 2016 de modernisation de la justice du XXIe siècle*).

666 Ferrand (2010), at 61.

667 Article 21 CPC in conjunction with Article 768(1) CPC, Article 834(1) CPC and Article 860–2 CPC. Douchy-Odot (2013), Section 1, para. 21–54; D'Ambra (2009), at 673–689.

668 Douchy-Odot (2013), Section 1, para. 43–48.

669 Article 467 in conjunction with Article 14 CPC.

670 Article 473(2) CPC. See Douchy-Odot (2013a), para. 73–80.

671 Article 471 CPC.

672 Article R.221–4(2) COJ. On judgments that are subject to appeal and restrictions to appeal, see further Juilon (2009), at 1175–1185.

673 Article 543 in conjunction with Article 546 CPC. See Guinchard, Chainais & Ferrand (2012), at 829–832.

suspensive effect on execution of the judgment (Article 539 CPC), unless a provisional enforcement is ordered by the judge.[674] This suspensive effect is prolonged if an appeal is lodged. The appeal is meant to provide a re-adjudication of the case by another court on the points criticised by the parties (*effet dévolutif de l'appel*).[675] A special means of appeal, *opposition*, is available for setting aside default judgments or judgments deemed to have been adversarial. This allows the party to request that the case be re-examined by the same judge who issued the ruling in his absence.[676] Special means of review are available for appeal judgments or first court judgments not subject to appeal. The most frequently used is the appeal before the Supreme Court (*pourvoi en cassation*), which challenges the compliance of the judgment with the rules of law.[677] Other means are the judicial review (*recours en revision*) for judgments obtained through fraud based on erroneous facts findings,[678] and the third party opposition (*tierce opposition*) in order for third parties to avoid the adverse consequences of a judgment they were not party to and that harms their interests.[679] In principle, these means also do not suspend execution of the judgment.[680] Under French law, a judgment acquires *res judicata* once it is no longer subject to an appeal or to review (Article 501 CPC). From this moment, the creditor can proceed to enforce the judgment according to applicable legal provisions.

4.2.3. Costs of Ordinary Court Proceedings

No court fee is applicable in the case of filing a claim with the civil court, but there are a number of other costs that the parties need to pay, a list of which is provided in Article 695 CPC. The losing party is responsible for these costs, excluding the lawyer's fees. However, the judge may decide on an equity basis to grant higher costs than those in the list. The amount granted in such cases varies significantly, and does not correspond to the real expenses of the party with legal representation. The lawyer's fees can be fixed or based on an hourly rate that can vary between €100 and €1,000.[681]

674 Article 515 CPC. On provisional enforcement, see Guinchard, Chainais & Ferrand (2012), at 834–839 and 921–938. Défossez (2006), para. 15, 36. Article 526 CPC on provisional executions ordered by the court of first instance aims to reinforce the effectiveness of judgments of first instance and to avoid the dilatory appeal tactic. However, this provision is subject to criticism due to the limitation it imposes on the principle regarding the double degree of jurisdiction.

675 Article 561 CPC. See Guinchard, Chainais & Ferrand (2012), at 858–859; Juilon (2009a), at 1277–1284.

676 Articles 571–578 and 540 CPC. See Guinchard, Chainais & Ferrand (2012), at 823–829; Douchy-Odot (2013a), para. 109–187; Boursier (2010).

677 Articles 604–639 CPC. On *pourvoi en cassation*, see Guinchard, Chainais & Ferrand (2012), at 888–910; Fattaccini (2009), at 1320–1377; Vuitton & Vuitton (2013a); Vuitton & Vuitton (2013); Boucard (2009).

678 This involves a retraction of the judgment having *res judicata* and a re-adjudication of the case. Articles 593–603 CPC. See Guinchard, Chainais & Ferrand (2012), at 883–888; Marchand (2011).

679 Articles 582–592 CPC. See Guinchard, Chainais & Ferrand (2012), at 874–883.

680 Article 579 CPC.

681 See www.service-public.fr/particuliers/vosdroits/F1816; Decree No. 72–784 of 25 August 1972 and Decree No. 75–785 of 21 August 1975; Decree No. 80–608 of 30 July 1980.

Bailiff's fees for the writ (*assignation*) and notification of judgment to the debtor add to the costs of the procedure.[682] Together with the fixed rate established by Administrative Order of 26 February 2016, a variable part of the fees may be added, together with the costs related to travelling, reimbursement of costs advanced by the notary, and a fee for handling the file.[683]

Translation fees might be added to the costs of the proceedings if documents are drafted in a language other than French. Article 23 CPC leaves this to the appreciation of the judge if he is able to understand the language of the parties and to read the documents provided.[684]

4.3. National Tailored Solutions for the Recovery of Monetary Claims

As well as the ordinary national procedure, French law offers a number of special processes that facilitate the recovery of money claims. Claims with a value up to €10,000 in civil and commercial cases are in the competence of the TI (and the JP)[685] or the TC. The CPC facilitates the submission of cases below €4,000 to courts through a simplified method of registering the claim, the *déclaration au greffe* (declaration registered with the clerk's office).[686] The EOP has a direct national equivalent in the *injonction de payer*, and certain functional similarities to the *référé* and the *injonction de faire*. The procedures can be initiated by using a standard form that – like the European uniform procedures – can be filled in online. They are all accelerated and, except for the *injonction de faire*, provide the party with enforceable titles that can be executed immediately. For this reason, in practice, the *injonction de payer* and the *référé* are preferred to the *injonction de faire*. The ESCP does not have a national court equivalent. In 2016, a new electronic simplified procedure to handle small value claims was established.[687] This present section analyses the national special procedures for parties seeking to recover their cross-border debt, looking at their characteristics, features, and use in practice.

682 Article 2 Administrative Order (*Arrêté*) of 26 February 2016 establishing the regulated fees of bailiffs, NOR: EINC1605791A, Official Journal of the French Republic n° 0050 of 28 February 2016 texte n° 38 (available at www.legifrance.gouv.fr/affichTexte.do?cidTexte=JORFTEXT000032115547&categorieLien=id). This administrative order establishes the bailiff fees for a transitory period until 28 February 2018 following a repeal of the Decree No. 96-1080.

683 www.service-public.fr/particuliers/vosdroits/F2158.

684 The judge can also reject an evidence document if translation is required and this is not submitted by the party, C.Com, 27 Nov. 2012, n°11-17.185, ECLI:FR:CCASS:2012:CO01177.

685 The JP disappeared as of 1 July 2017 (www.justice.gouv.fr/organisation-de-la-justice-10031/lordre-judiciaire-10033/juridiction-de-proximite-19668.html). Law No. 2016-1547 of 18 November 2016 regarding the modernisation of the XXI century justice. Véricel (2013), at 230.

686 Article 843 CPC. This is the most frequent means used for submitting a claim to the TI or the JP when the party is not represented by a lawyer or a legal councillor. The declaration may be written or verbal, and it does not require the claimant to first notify the defendant. Ferrand (2010), at 54–55. For information regarding the initial claim forms and their submission to the court, see Guinchard, Chainais & Ferrand (2012), at 582–588; Vuitton (2013), para. 7–21; Douchy-Oudot (2012a), para. 54–88; Lebeau (2012), para. 16–39.

687 Decree No. 2016-285 of 9 March 2016 regarding a simplified procedure for the recovery of small claims, Official Journal of the French Republic n° 60 of 11 March 2016.

4.3.1. *Injonction de Payer*

4.3.1.1. General Aspects

The national order for payment procedure *(injonction de payer)* was introduced in 1937 to facilitate the recovery of small commercial debts.[688] In 1957, the procedure was extended to civil claims.[689]

Articles 1405–1425 CPC regulate the procedure for both civil and commercial cases. The simplified procedure is an alternative to the ordinary court proceedings for (1) the recovery of determined debts resulting from contracts or statutory acts; (2) amounts arising from the acceptance or drawing of a bill of exchange, a promissory note, or the endorsement of one of these titles; (3) the assignment of professional debt claims (*cession de créance professionelle par bordereau Dailly*); or (4) damages resulting from a crime that the offender had committed himself to pay, in accordance with an alternative measure established by the public prosecutor (*composition pénale*, Article 41–2 of the Code of criminal procedure).[690] To use the procedure, the debt has to be certain, determined, and to have fallen due. There is no threshold limiting use of the procedure. The *injonction de payer* is designed as a single-sided procedure until issuance of the order by the court. These characteristics are also common to the EOP. In contrast to the *injonction de payer*, however, the judge retains a more administrative role.[691]

Jurisdiction over national order for payments is divided between the TGI (for claims above €10,000), the TI, the JP, and the TC.[692] The CPC does not contain any limitation regarding use of the *injonction de payer* only for national claims, but, in practice, this requirement seems to subsist in demanding the debtor be domiciled in France or have some connection with the French territory (e.g. an office, an apartment in France).[693]

688 Decree-Law No. of 25 August 1937 regarding simplified recovering of small commercial debt, Official Journal of the French Republic of 27 August 1937. Charlet (2013), at 39; Chainais (2010), at 623; Ferrand (2001), at 131.

689 Miguet (2012), para. 4.

690 Article 1405 CPC. Moreover, the procedure may also be used in additional areas, such as the recovery of joint ownership expenses (Article 60 Decree No. 67–223 of 17 March 1967 on the status of joint ownership), the recovery of professional contributions regarding the dairy products by an inter-professional organisation (Article D. 632–10 Rural and Maritime Fishing Code), and for the recovery of unemployment benefits contributions by the organisation paying these (Article R.1235–1 and subsequent Labour Code).

691 Guinchard, Chainais & Ferrand (2012), at 1408–1409.

692 Article 1406 CPC as amended by Article 2 Decree No. 2012–1515 of 28 December 2012. Since 1 January 2013, requests for an *injonction de payer* can also be registered with the president of the TGI.

693 Miguet (2012), points 50–51; Guinchard, Chainais & Ferrand (2012), at 1413; Dossier: L'injonction de payer, une procédure de recouvrement de créances, partie 1 by Infogreffe, available at www.infogreffe.fr/societes/informations-et-dossiers-entreprises/dossiers-thematiques/procedures-judiciaires/dossier-injonction-de-payer.html.

4.3.1.2. The Procedure

The claimant has to submit a request (personally or by proxy) with the registry of the competent court or to send it by post.[694] As with the EOP, representation of the parties during proceedings is not mandatory, including before the TGI.[695] The claim can be submitted by way of special available standard forms[696] that are available electronically.[697] An entirely electronic procedure of filing an order for payment is available for cases when the TC, the TI, and the JC have jurisdiction, and the IP WEB portal allows the electronic handling of the order for payment claims submitted by bailiffs.[698] Guidelines are available to assist claimants in filling in the standard forms.[699] The form is available only in French, and requires the party to complete all the information in French, but their purpose is similar to that indicated in the EOP Regulations. As well as the standard form, the claimant using the *injonction de payer* is required to attach to his claim all the

694 Article 1407(1) CPC.

695 Article 4-III of Law No. 2011-1862 of 13 December 2011. See Lauvergnat (2013), at 35; Guinchard, Chainais & Ferrand (2012), at 1412.

696 The standard forms are: Form Cerfa No. 14896 for the TGI, Form Cerfa No. 12948*01 for the TI, Form Cerfa No. 12947*01 for the JP and Form Cerfa No. 12946*01 for the TC. See http://vosdroits.service-public.fr/particuliers/F1746.xhtml.

697 www.service-public.fr/particuliers/recherche?keyword=injonction%20de%20payer&rubricFilter=serviceEnLigne&rubricTypeFilter=formulaire after the creation of a personal account or through www2.infogreffe.fr/infogreffe/jsp/ip/fonctionnementIP.jsp for commercial claims. The second website gives the claimant the choice of proceeding with an electronic submission and the court's treatment of the claim.

698 On the electronic communication in the order for payment procedures before the TI and the JP, see Articles 748-1 - 748-6 CPC, Order of 24 December 2012, and Order of 3 March 2011 creating the IP WEB. The electronic service of filing an electronic claim for an order for payment is available at www2.infogreffe.fr/infogreffe/jsp/ip/fonctionnementIP.jsp (TC) or through an individual account at https://service-public.fr/portail/. Following completion of the electronic form, the claimant will be asked whether he will opt for an electronic submission of the claim, provided he has the required certification, or whether he will make an ordinary request and send it to the court by post. For valid electronic submission the forms and supporting documents need to have an electronic signature attached (Certigreffe, Digigreffe, available at www.certigreffe.fr/, or www.eurodigigreffe.fr/); Dossier: *L'injonction de payer, une procédure de recouvrement de créances*, partie 2 by Infogreffe, available at www.infogreffe.fr/societes/informations-et-dossiers-entreprises/dossiers-thematiques/procedures-judiciaires/dossier-injonction-de-payer.html. Guidelines on preparing the electronic submission of an *injonction de payer* are also available on the website of the Paris TC, www.greffe-tc-paris.fr/fr/fond-referes-requetes/injonction_payer.html. On the success of the IP WEB pilots, see the speech of Thierry Ghera, President of the Valence TGI, at the reunion launching the IP WEB at Lyon Court of Appeal, 3 June 2014, available at www.ca-lyon.justice.fr/images/stories/ipweb/intervention_de_t._ghera_prsident_du_tgi_de_valence.pdf. On the use of electronic communication, see Caprioli (2013), Commentaires, 37; Bauvin, Ghera & Mecarelli (2012), at 224–226; Ghera (2012), at 284; Chainais & Tapie (2009), at 860; Coze (2006), comm. 185.

699 The guidelines available online contain information on the type of disputes for which the procedure can be used; on the courts having jurisdiction; on how to make a claim and the documents that should be attached to it; on the means of registering the claim with the court and the steps following registration of the claim; on the development of the procedure subsequent to an opposition; and on the means of obtaining an enforceable decision. The guidelines are available at www.formulaires.modernisation.gouv.fr/gf/getNotice.do?cerfaNotice=51156&cerfaFormulaire=12948.

documents supporting it.[700] Thus, in contrast to the EOP, the judge bases his decision not only on the information contained by the standard form but also on the evidence filed by the party.[701]

The judge will issue an order for payment (*ordonnance d'injonction de payer*) for the whole or part of the claim, or will reject it when this does not appear to be justified on the basis of the form and evidence submitted by the claimant.[702] The claimant cannot appeal the decision, but may revert to ordinary proceedings in the event of a rejection.[703] In issuing the order, the judge decides on the principle amount as well as on penalties, interest, and costs. This is similar to the EOP.[704] When the order is issued for part of the claim, the debtor has the choice of following ordinary court proceedings or of giving notification of the *ordonnance d'injonction de payer* to the debtor. When the *ordonnance* has been served, the claimant cannot initiate a new procedure for the remaining amount.[705] This limitation applies also to EOP cases based on restrictions established by the national applicable law[706] – an aspect subject to different solutions within the EU.

Like the EOP, the *injonction de payer* is a one-step procedure, about which the defendant is only subsequently informed. The claimant has 6 months to serve the *injonction de payer* on the debtor together with the claim form.[707] Until service of the order, the *injonction de payer* does not interrupt prescription.[708] According to the requirements of Article 1413 CPC, the service is carried out by a bailiff who informs the debtor of the consequences of the order: namely, (1) he has to pay the amount mentioned in the order or make an opposition; (2) he has a delay period in which to oppose the order and the court before which the opposition has to be registered;[709] and (3) if he files no opposition during the set timeframe, no other appeal is possible, and the creditor will be able to take enforcement measures.[710] The order for payment becomes void if is not served within 6 months of being issued. Following the moment of notification, the defendant has a month in which to oppose the claim.[711] In contrast to the EOP, the defendant has to indicate in the opposition the reasons he is opposing the *injonction de payer.*

In both national and European procedures, the opposition determines the transfer of the case to ordinary court procedures where the claimant needs to prove his claims in

700 Article 1407(2) and (3) CPC.

701 Chainais (2010), at 628–631; Chainais & Tapie (2009), at 860.

702 Article 1409 (1) and (2) CPC.

703 Ferrand (2001), at 136–137.

704 See Annex V - Form E of the EOP.

705 Article 1409(3) CPC.

706 See Annex III - Form C of the EOP.

707 Article 1411 CPC.

708 Miguet (2012), para. 69 and 89. This choice by the French legislator has been criticised by legal scholars. Guinchard, Chainais & Ferrand (2012), at 1414; Chainais (2010), at 638–641.

709 According to Article 1415 CPC the competent court to file an opposition with is the court that issued the order for payment – thus, the TGI, TI, JP, or TC.

710 Article 1416(1) CPC. If the debtor is not served in person, or the bailiff does not find a person on whom to serve the order, the one-month delay for opposition will run from the moment of the first act of execution, freezing totally or partly the debtor assets (Article 1416(2) CPC).

711 Article 1416(1) CPC. A standard opposition form is available, Cerfa n° 15602*01 (www.service-public.fr/particuliers/vosdroits/R10223).

adversarial proceedings. If the parties fail to appear before the judge in the ordinary procedure, the claim will be dismissed and *the ordonnance d'injonction de payer* will be void.[712] By way of Decree No. 2008–1346, the French legislator adopted provisions similar to the national procedure for the Regulation, thus transferring national approaches to the EOP. If following opposition the parties fail to appear before the judge on the set date for the hearing, the EOP will be void.[713] In practice, only around 5%-7% of the *ordonnances d'injonction de payer* are opposed.[714] Consumers in particular tend not to oppose the *ordonnance* against legal entities. According to the literature, defendants are deterred from acting because they are unaware of applicable legal provisions and of possible additional costs that such an action would imply. Chainais considers that – upon the court's decision – an information notice regarding opposition should be handed to the debtor. This would make the party aware of the effects of his action, and secure his access to justice.[715]

If the order for payment is not opposed, or if the defendant opposing the order decides to withdraw the act, the claimant has a month to request the court to attach the executory formula to the order; otherwise it becomes void.[716] In practice, for this reason the creditor may request the executory formula in advance.[717] The order acquires *res judicata* following the lapse of time for the opposition.[718] After this moment, an appeal before the Supreme Court (*pourvoi en cassation*) is admissible for limited reasons, such as for compliance of the order with form requirements (e.g. if the executory formula was attached to the order in error).[719]

The recognition and enforcement abroad of a French order for payment under the Brussels I*bis* Regulation does not seem to pose any problems.[720]

4.3.1.3. Costs of Proceedings

Costs of judicial proceedings vary between civil and commercial courts. While no court fee is required for filing an *injonction de payer* with the civil court, a fee of €39 (€38.87) has to be paid by the claimant for the commercial courts,[721] and, in the event of opposition, a subsequent fee of €97.35.[722] This can be paid by cheque or bankcard. Bailiff's fees for the writ (*assignation*), notification of judgment to the debtor, and enforcement

712 Article 1419 CPC.

713 Article 1424–11 CPC.

714 Charlet (2013), at 39–40; Guinchard, Chainais & Ferrand (2012), at 1420; Chainais (2010), at 621–650; Chainais & Tapie (2009), at 860.

715 Chainais (2010), at 647.

716 Articles 1422(1) and 1423 CPC.

717 This practice was also validated by Supreme Court case-law (Cass. 2e civ., 23 January 1991, No. 89–18747). Miguet (2012), para. 97–98.

718 Article 1422(2) CPC.

719 Guinchard, Chainais & Ferrand (2012), at 1418–1419; Miguet (2012), para. 108–116; Cadiet (2009), Comments to Article 1422, at 850; Perrot (1991), at 411.

720 Miguet (2012), para. 51.

721 See information available at www2.infogreffe.fr/infogreffe/jsp/ip/fonctionnementIP.jsp#, and http://vosdroits.service-public.fr/particuliers/F1746.xhtml.

722 On the procedure by the Paris TC, see information available at www.greffe-tc-paris.fr/fr/fond-referes-requetes/injonction_payer.html.

add to the costs of the procedure.[723] Lawyers' fees need to be added as well if the parties decide to be represented.

4.3.1.4. Use in Practice

The *injonction de payer* procedure is a popular approach for creditors seeking to recover their debt or to persuade the debtor to pay. Its success is due to its simplicity, low cost, and short period within which the court issues the order.[724] For example, according to the French Ministry of Justice statistics, in 2014, a total of 541,278 orders for payment were filed with the TIs and the TGIs, compared to 325,171 ordinary procedures for debt recovery and 232,015 *référé*.[725] Of the total number of 541,278 orders, only 21,588 were opposed: namely, 3.98% of the orders. The *injonction de payer* is the instrument chosen most often by the claimant in seeking to obtain the payment of debts in France.

4.3.2. Ordonnance de Référé

4.3.2.1. General Aspects

The *ordonnance de référé* (interim order) is a provisional measure issued after an adversarial procedure when urgent judicial reaction is necessary.[726] It aims to provide an effective accelerated procedure for situations requiring immediate intervention by the judge to prevent illicit acts from being undertaken or damages from incurring.[727] The general provisions are contained in Articles 484 – 492–1 CPC. The *référé* is employed in a wide range of civil and commercial matters where such intervention is required,[728] in obtaining execution of an obligation whose existence cannot be seriously denied, or in receiving reimbursement of part of the debt held by the creditor against the debtor if this cannot be seriously contested (*référé provision*).[729]

Apart from the general *référé*, autonomous special forms of *référé* have also been developed.[730] This is the case for the *référé-injonction de faire*, *référé provision,* and procedures '*en la forme des référé*'. In the event of a *référé-injonction de faire,*[731] the judge is able to order the execution of a duty. This is possible with regard to obtaining the

723 Article 2 Administrative Order (*Arrêté*) of 26 February 2016 establishing the regulated fees of bailiffs, NOR: EINC1605791A, Official Journal of the French Republic n°0050 of 28 February 2016 texte n° 38 (available at www.legifrance.gouv.fr/affichTexte.do?cidTexte=JORFTEXT000032115547&categorieLien=id).

724 Lauvergnat (2013), at 35.

725 www.justice.gouv.fr/statistiques-10054/.

726 Article 484 CPC.

727 Cadiet & Jeuland (2013), at 510–511.

728 On the interpretation of the notion of 'urgent', see Cayrol (2013), para. 363–365.

729 Articles 808 and 809(2) CPC for the TGI, Articles 848 and 849 CPC for the TI, and Articles 872 – 873 CPC. See further Desprès (2012).

730 Cadiet & Jeuland (2013), at 510.

731 Introduced by Decree No. 85–1330 of 17 December 1985 modifying certain provisions of the New Code of Civil Procedure, Official Journal of the French Republic of 18 December 1985, p. 14723.

payment of small claims, especially for consumer-related cases, on the delivery of goods, the restitution of things, or the provision of services.[732] Its use is closer to the objective of the ESCP than of the EOP. However, this form of *référé* is less used, owing to other forms of *référé* and with the *injonction de faire* procedure.[733] The *référé provision* appears to be a success regarding debts that cannot be contested seriously by the defendant (urgency is not a requirement for this type of *référé*), providing a mechanism that prevents the debtor from using the judicial system in order to delay payment.[734] It often concerns debts that have already fallen due at the time of the application, as is the case for EOP debts.[735] In practice, it is also a way for parties to reach an agreement and to close the dispute without the claim reaching trial, thus contributing to the clearing of overcrowded court dockets.[736] The procedure '*en forme de référé*' is a hybrid one.[737] The practice developments were codified in Article 492–1 CPC.[738] The procedure '*en forme de référé*' follows the procedural steps of the *référé*, but unlike this provisional order, it is actually a decision on the merits.[739] The decision has *res judicata*, despite the fact of being enforceable on a provisional basis unless the judge decides the opposite.[740] In contrast to this form of *référé*, the EOP is an enforceable decision after the period of opposition for the debtor has lapsed (Article 18 EOP).

4.3.2.2. The Procedure

Generally, the procedure begins with the claimant filing a writ (*assignation*) by bailiff, summoning the defendant to appear before the court.[741] Subject to nullity, the writ has to include a description of the claim, the evidence, and the legal provisions relied on by the claimant.[742] To speed up the procedure, the parties are not required to draft and submit an extensive volume of documents and evidence in support of their claim. Like the EOP and the ESCP, the *référé* is designed as an accelerated procedure subject to simplified procedural requirements (e.g. non-mandatory representation) to facilitate its application. As opposed to the ESCP, the *référé* is not a judgment on the merits of the claim, though it is designed as an adversarial procedure. The defendant is notified in

[732] Article 809(2) final thesis CPC, Article 849(2) final thesis CPC and Article 873(2) final thesis CPC.

[733] See Guinchard, Chainais & Ferrand (2012), at 1381–1382; Vuitton (2011a), para. 100; Jeuland & Manin (2004), at 8–9. For the *injonction de faire*, see Section 4.3.3.

[734] Articles 809(2) 849(2) and Article 873(2) CPC. Vuitton (2011a), para. 75–77 and 83–84.

[735] In certain situations, if the amount owed appeared to be incontestable, a *référé provision* was also awarded by the judge for obligations that had not yet fallen due. See Vuitton (2011a), para. 83.

[736] Vuitton (2011a), para. 72.

[737] Guinchard, Chainais & Ferrand (2012), at 1351.

[738] Article 4 establishing Article 492–1 CPC, Decree No. 2011–1043 of 1 September 2011, Official Journal of the French Republic n° 0203 of 2 September 2011, at 14884, text n° 5 (available at www.legifrance.gouv.fr/affichTexte.do;jsessionid=621EE5D7B75738D919B8D155D36AC922.tpdjo15v_2?cidTexte=JORFTEXT000024529472&dateTexte=20110902). Foulon & Strickler (2011), at 2668–2672; Fricero (2012), at 251.

[739] Foulon & Strickler (2011), at 2693–2696.

[740] Article 492–1(3) CPC.

[741] Article 485(1) CPC; Vuitton (2011), para. 64.

[742] Article 56 CPC. See also Cayrol (2013), para. 478–480; Lacabarats (2009), at 65.

order to allow him to prepare his defence and to appear before the court.[743] This distinguishes it also from the EOP, where the defendant is notified of the order only after its issuance by the judge.

The hearing occupies a central part of *référé* proceedings.[744] Similar to the EOP and the ESCP, parties are dispensed from mandatory representation.[745] If the defendant does not attend the hearing, the judge may issue a default order or an order deemed to be the result of adversarial proceedings.[746] The judge (*juge de référé*) may request any investigation measure he deems appropriate to clarify the situation within which he needs to decide (e.g. inquiry, expert investigation measure, personal verifications, summoning of the parties).[747] This characteristic of the *ordonnance de référé* is shared by the ESCP.[748]

The *référé* judge issues an order for the debtor to make an advanced payment (*provision*) for an amount that appears to be incontestable according to the evidence.[749] The *référé* order is subject to general methods of appeal,[750] although this does not suspend its execution, apart from limited situations expressly established by law.[751] Similarly, the ESCP judgment subject to appeal does not automatically suspend its execution.[752] When the *référé* is issued as default judgment, the interim order can be opposed (*opposition*),[753] which is different from the EOP opposition mechanism. In order to guarantee an accelerated procedure, the appeal and opposition timeframe are reduced to 15 days from the date of service of the *référé* order on the defendant.[754] Special means of review such as third-party opposition (*tierce opposition*) or an appeal before the Supreme Court (*pourvoi en cassation*) are possible.[755]

The order is enforceable on an interim basis (*exécutoire de plein droit à titre provisoire*) from the moment of service on the defendant (*signification*).[756] The execution may be subject to security to cover possible damages the order can cause to the debtor.[757] The judge can impose a fine (*astreinte*) on the debtor in seeking to ensure execution of the *référé* order or to accelerate the enforcement by declaring the judgment enforceable on

743 Articles 484 – 486 CPC in conjunction with Article 653 CPC.
744 Cayrol (2013), para. 514–515; Lacabarats (2009), at 656–657.
745 Article 828 CPC for the TI, Article 853 CPC for the TC and Article 751(1) in conjunction with 1418(8) CPC for the TGI.
746 Guinchard, Chainais & Ferrand (2012), at 1347.
747 *Ibidem*, at 1348.
748 Article 7(1) ESCP.
749 This may represent part of the debt or the debt in its entire amount. Cadiet & Jeuland (2013), at 512–513; Vuitton (2011a), para. 80–81 and 86–87.
750 Article 490(1) CPC. See also Lacabarats (2009), at 662–665.
751 Article 524 CPC.
752 Article 15(1) ESCP.
753 Article 490(2) CPC. On opposition, see also Section 4.2.2 above.
754 Article 490(3) CPC.
755 Vuitton (2011a), para. 32–33.
756 Article 489 CPC. The order is served on the defendant in accordance with the general provisions regarding notification of judgments (Articles 675–682 CPC). See Paris, 23 mars 1984, *Recueil Dalloz*, 1984, Information rapides, at 248. Comment 1 to Article 489 in Després (2012), at 438; Vuitton (2011a), para. 17–18.
757 Article 489 CPC in conjunction with Articles 517–522 CPC.

presentation of the decision.[758] He is also able to rule on the costs of the procedure.[759] The immediate enforceability is deemed to secure the effectiveness of the protection measure. The *ordonnance de référé* does not have *res judicata*,[760] but it retains a certain degree of authority. It cannot be subject to modification or to another *référé* unless new circumstances justify it.[761] In practice, when the interim measure satisfies the beneficiary, and the defendant is convinced of the legitimacy of the ordinance, the parties do not consider it necessary to commence ordinary proceedings. Thus, the interim measure becomes *de facto* final and binding.[762] This is usually the case for *référé provision* situations when creditors are awarded an interim payment.[763] No legal provision obliges parties of a *référé* order to start another court action.[764]

4.3.2.3. Costs of Proceedings

Costs of *référé* differ between civil and commercial courts. There is no fee for filing a request for *référé* with the civil courts. If the TC is competent, court fees vary between €45.06 and €209.28.[765] The amount is to be paid by cheque drawn up to the benefit of the court's clerk (*Greffe du TC*).[766] A bailiff's fees for the writ (*assignation*), notification of judgment to the debtor, and enforcement add to the costs of the procedure.[767] If the parties decide to be represented, lawyer's fees will be added.

4.3.2.4. Use in Practice

The *référé* is a relatively popular means of recovering monetary debts,[768] and may be employed successfully by parties also in cross-border litigation provided the debtor has assets in France or is established in France (Article 31 Brussels I Regulation).[769] The reduced timeframe for obtaining an enforceable decision and executing it (sometimes in

758 Article 491(1) CPC in conjunction with Article L.131-1 CPC ex. On *astreinte* ordered in a *référé* procedure, see further Cayrol (2013), para. 674–679; Vuitton (2011a), para. 49–50. On *exécution sur présentation de la minute* (Article 489(2) CPC), see Cadiet & Jeuland (2013), at 515.

759 Article 491(2) CPC.

760 The judge competent to hear the case on merits will not be bound by the interim order, and can always issue a judgment completely different from the *référé*. On the absence of *res judicata* for an interim order, see Civ. 2e, 10 February 2011, case note by Bugada (2011).

761 Article 488 CPC. On the provisional *res judicata* (*autorité de la chose jugée au provisoire*), see Cadiet & Jeuland (2013), at 514–515; Guinchard, Chainais & Ferrand (2012), at 1386–1387; Lacabarats (2009), at 660.

762 Guinchard, Chainais & Ferrand (2012), at 1380–1381; Vuitton (2011a), para. 15.

763 Article 809(2) CPC, Article 849(2) CPC, and Article 873(2) CPC. See Cayrol (2013), para. 564–571; Guinchard, Chainais & Ferrand (2012), at 1380–1381; Vuitton (2011a), para. 72.

764 Guinchard, Chainais & Ferrand (2012), at 1336.

765 www.greffe-tc-paris.fr/fr/pages/prise_date_refere_ligne.html and www.infogreffe.fr/referes-requetes/tarif-ordonnance-refere.html.

766 See www.greffes.com/fr/formalites/guide-des-formalites/fond_referes_requetes/tarifs/ordonnances_de_refere/145-448.html.

767 See Section 4.2.3.

768 Cayrol (2013), para. 6.

769 On the interpretation of the provisions of the Brussels I Regulation, and the developments of the case law, see Cayrol (2013), para. 264–270; Gruau (2013).

a timeframe of 2 to 4 weeks) makes this interim order a popular mean of recovering debts, being much faster than the ordinary procedure and the *injonction de payer*, and as efficient as a trial on merits.[770] In 2014, 232,015 demands for *référé* were filed with the TGI and the TI, with an additional 18,138 cases filed with the TC (in total 250,153 *référés*).[771] However, the *injonction de payer* appears to be the national instrument favoured by creditors willing to obtain a final court judgment on the merits.[772]

4.3.3. *Injonction de Faire*

4.3.3.1. General Aspects

The *injonction de faire* procedure was introduced in 1988,[773] and the provisions regulating it are Articles 1425–1 to 1425–9 CPC. Although the procedure is part of the same chapter as the *injonction de payer*, and certain common features can be identified between these two instruments, the *injonction de faire* has a different purpose. It offers the claimant a simplified, faster, and cheaper procedure for small claims whose value does not exceed €10,000.

The procedure is designed as a tool for consumers to use against professional entities such as commercial companies, service providers, or any other persons with whom they have concluded a contract, to persuade them to fulfill their obligation.[774] Some of its characteristics (e.g. the threshold, consumer focus) brings this national procedure closer to the purpose of the ESCP, while the aim of providing a simplified, speedier, and cheaper procedure is shared by all three instruments (European and domestic procedures).

In most cases, if the claimant opts to make use of the *injonction de faire*, he may choose to submit his claim to the court at the domicile of the defendant, or to the court where execution of the obligation is to take place.[775] Further, based on the value of the claim, jurisdiction is shared between the TI and the JP.[776]

4.3.3.2. The Procedure

The procedure is designed in two phases. As with the EOP, the first phase of the *injonction de faire* is one-sided, leading to delivery of the order. The second phase follows non-execution of the obligation (partly or entirely), and is adversarial.

770 Guinchard, Chainais & Ferrand (2012), at 1380; Gruau (2013).

771 Justice statistics available at www.justice.gouv.fr/statistiques-10054/.

772 See Section 4.3.1.4. Chainais & Tapie (2009), at 860.

773 Decree No. 88–209 of 4 March 1988, Official Journal of the French Republic of 5 March 1988, p. 3008. The procedure was intended to improve justice regarding day to day claims (*pour ameliorer la justice du quotidien*). See Miguet (2012), para. 2.

774 Article 1425–1 CPC. This procedure is not intended to secure the execution of an obligation of delivery of goods or provision of services. If the claimant seeks to make a money claim in accordance with French law, he can initiate an order for payment procedure. See further Miguet (2012a), para. 12–22.

775 Article 1425–2 CPC.

776 Article 1425–1 CPC in conjunction with Article L.221–4 and Article L.231–3 COJ. For certain cases (e.g. a dispute between the person renting an apartment and the owner regarding rent, consumer's credit, funeral expenses) the TI has exclusive jurisdiction regardless of the value of the claim (Art. R.221–4 – R.221–22–1 COJ).

The creditor is required to submit a request (personally or by proxy) with the registry of the competent court or to send it by post.[777] As with the *injonction de payer* and the European procedures, this can be done by way of standard forms available online,[778] and can also be filled in electronically.[779] However, the submission of the claim cannot be filed electronically. Form guidelines are available for the parties.[780] In contrast to EOP and ESCP standard forms and guidance, the information is available only in French. Together with the standard form, the claimant has to submit the evidence on which he relies.[781] Similar to the ESCP procedure, the judge bases his decision on his appreciation of the evidence submitted to him and on information contained in the standard claim form. If the request to issue an *injonction de faire* is rejected, the claimant may choose to start an ordinary procedure against his debtor.[782] This is not the case for the ESCP judgment, which has *res judicata*. In this respect, the *injonction de faire* resembles more closely the EOP, which allows the claimant to start ordinary court proceedings in the event the request is rejected by the court.[783] If the judge appreciates the claim to be founded, he will issue an *ordonnance injonction de faire*. Nonetheless, the order does not have *res judicata*, and thus is not subject to appeal.[784] The order sets the period within which the debtor has to fulfill his duty and the conditions according to which this has to be executed.[785] As with the ESCP, the court serves the parties with notice of the order by postal service accompanied by an acknowledgement of receipt.[786] Additionally, a second simple notification by post of the *injonction de faire* is sent on the same day. Unlike the *injonction de payer* and the European procedures, the *ordonnance injonction de faire* is not an immediately enforceable title, and the debtor cannot be constrained to execute the order. For this reason, the judge will set a hearing date following issuance of the *ordonnance* if the creditor does not notify the court that the debtor has executed his duty.[787] This is also the case for a partially executed *injonction de faire*.[788] At this stage, the procedure enters a second phase, which is adversarial and is conducted according to the provisions of the national ordinary procedure.[789] A settlement must be attempted by the judge before issuing a judgment on the merits, a characteristic that is common to the ESCP.[790] If issued by default, the judgment is subject to appeal or opposition, and has *res judicata*.[791]

777 Article 1425-3(1) CPC.
778 Available at http://vosdroits.service-public.fr/particuliers/F1787.xhtml.
779 The claimant has to register at https://service-public.fr/portail/ in order to access the electronic form, otherwise the forms are available in pdf format, and can be filled in and signed before submisssion to the court or delivery by post.
780 See www.formulaires.modernisation.gouv.fr/gf/getNotice.do?cerfaNotice=50801&cerfaFormulaire=12288.
781 Article 1425-3(3) CPC.
782 Article 1425-9 CPC.
783 Article 11(3) EOP Regulation and Article 1409(2) CPC.
784 Article 1425-4(1) and Article 1425-9 CPC. See also Guinchard, Chainais & Ferrand (2012), at 1431.
785 Article 1425-4(1) and (2) CPC.
786 Article 7(2) final thesis in conjunction with Article 13(1) ESCP Regulation and Article 1425-5 CPC.
787 Article 1425-4(3) and Article 1425-7(1) CPC.
788 Article 1425-8(1) CPC.
789 See Guinchard, Chainais & Ferrand (2012), at 1430-1431.
790 Article 12(3) ESCP Regulation and Article 1425-8(1) CPC.
791 Articles 1425-8 and Article 1425-9 CPC. See Miguet (2012a), para. 80-83; Picod & Davo (2010), at 375.

Should the claimant not appear in court for the hearing, the claim lapses, unless the claimant can provide the court with serious reasons for not attending.[792] This is not the case with the ESCP, where the court has to issue the judgment based on the claim or counterclaim.[793]

4.3.3.3. Costs of Proceedings

As with the *injonction de payer* and the *référé*, the claimant does not need to pay any court fees for making use of this procedure.[794] Costs that are incurred may be related to lawyers' fees or to the judgment following the ordinary procedure.

4.3.3.4. Use in Practice

In practice, the success of the *injonction de faire* is limited.[795] According to the literature, the procedure was doomed from the beginning to be of limited use, due to reforms introducing the *référé* as a means of securing the performance of a duty or service.[796] If the claim cannot be contested seriously by the debtor, the *référé-injonction de faire* can be used successfully for the same purpose as the *injonction de faire*.[797] The advantages are that this is faster than the *injonction de faire*, it includes an adversarial phase before delivery of the order, and it can be executed on an interim basis.[798]

4.3.4. *Plateforme de Traitement des Petites Créances*

4.3.4.1. General Aspects

Since June 2016, a new extrajudicial procedure for the recovery of claims up to a value of €4,000 is available.[799] This includes the principle as well as interest.[800] The procedure is regulated mainly by the Code of Civil Enforcement procedure Articles L.125 and R.125–1–125–8. This simplified procedure can be used for debts resulting from a contract (e.g. sale-purchase agreements concluded with commercial entities, loan agreements) or from a statutory obligation (e.g. unpaid invoices, credit, rent, bank overdraft), bill of exchange, promissory note, and acceptance of assignment of professional debt claims (*cession de créance professionelle par bordereau Dailly*).

792 Article 1425–7(2) and (3) CPC.
793 Article 7 ESCP Regulation.
794 On the *injonction de faire*, see information available at http://vosdroits.service-public.fr/particuliers/F1787.xhtml.
795 The procedure is used in around 1% of cases. See Charlet (2013), at 36; Véricel (2008), at 14.
796 Guinchard, Chainais & Ferrand (2012), at 1430.
797 Jeuland & Manin (2004), at 8.
798 Miguet (2012a), para. 86–87. See also Section 4.3.2 on *référé*.
799 Article 1244–4 Civil code (now repealed), Decree No. 2016–285 of 9 March 2016 regarding the simplified procedure of recovering small claims, NOR: JUSC1527481D, Official Journal of the French Republic n° 60 of 11 March 2016; Chapter V, Title II, Code of civil enforcement procedure.
800 Article R.125–1(2) CPC ex.

The procedures are handled on paper or electronically by bailiffs through a dedicated website: petitescreances.fr.[801] Since 1 January 2017, the competence rests with bailiffs from the territorial jurisdiction of the court of appeal where the debtor is domiciled.[802] Thus, it appears the procedure is limited to being used against French debtors. It is not immediately clear from the platform information whether this limitation also applies to the creditor.

4.3.4.2. The Procedure

Following registration, the creditor can initiate the procedure directly using the electronic platform.[803] All the information and forms are available in French, and the procedure is conducted in French. For the bailiff to proceed, the claimant has to provide information about the debtor's identity, evidence of the debt (e.g. invoices, loan agreement, lease agreement), and the margin of negotiation he is prepared to leave to the bailiff for recovery of the debt. On receiving the necessary information, the bailiff will prepare and send a registered letter with acknowledgement of receipt to the debtor, inviting him to take part in this simplified procedure for small value claims.[804] A standard letter format is available online.[805] Similar to the ESCP procedure, the debtor has a month to reply by making use of a standard form. The reply can be sent electronically through the dedicated online platform following registration, or by sending the form to the bailiff.

The debtor can agree to take part in the procedure and pay the debt.[806] In this case, a negotiation between the parties is carried out by the bailiff. This appears to be similar to the ESCP court settlement procedure reached by the parties or through court intervention. The bailiff who receives both parties' agreement with regard to the amount of debt settlement and the means of payment will issue an enforceable title without further formalities.[807] A copy of the agreement is communicated to the parties by the bailiff.[808]

If the debtor refuses expressly or implicitly to take part in the procedure, does not respond within a month of the moment of service,[809] or cannot come to an agreement, the creditor can register a claim with the court having jurisdiction in order to obtain an enforceable title.[810]

To avoid possible conflicts of interest, the bailiff in charge of handling the simplified procedure cannot proceed to execution of the enforceable debt.[811]

801 www.petitescreances.fr. The platform has been developed and is managed by the French Association of Bailiffs.

802 Article 4 Decree No. 2016-285.

803 A registration for an online account allowing acccess to the online platform is available at www.idcert.fr/?t=1&fs=5729fd23b9361012b41d8db3&f=0&m=0&ad=1.

804 Article R.125-2 CPC ex.

805 www.service-public.fr/particuliers/vosdroits/R44053.

806 A model reply is available at www.service-public.fr/particuliers/vosdroits/R44057.

807 Article R.125-4 CPC ex.

808 Article R.125-6 CPC ex.

809 A model reply is available at www.service-public.fr/particuliers/vosdroits/R44058.

810 Article R.125-2(III) CPC ex.

811 Article R.125-8 CPC ex.

4.3.4.3. Cost of Proceedings

All procedural costs are the responsibility of the creditor. These concern registration of the claim with the bailiff (€9.92), issuance of the enforceable title by the bailiff (€30),[812] and enforcement costs based on the amount of debt recovered. The bailiff costs for the execution are fixed to €21.45 for a debt recovered up to a value of €188. For amounts above €188, the cost varies for the difference between 11.70% for amounts up to €125, and 3.90% for amounts between €1,525.01 and €4,000.[813]

4.3.4.4. Use in Practice

The simplified online procedure is still young, however, and no clear indication as to its success is available at the moment.

4.4. National Attitudes towards EOP and ESCP Regulations

France's initial position on the establishing of the European uniform procedures was reserved. It questioned the coherence and usefulness of developing a multitude of instruments seeking to facilitate the recovery of uncontested and small monetary claims in cross-border cases. Legal scholars were more positive, however, considering the limitation of national procedures in cross-border litigation. The following pages provide an overview of the main opinions expressed by the French legislator, stakeholders, and legal scholars.

4.4.1. The EOP

In 2000, French authorities instigated discussions on the establishment of a new procedure for the recovery of cross-border debt that would match the domestic *injonction de payer*. This initial concept materialised in a different instrument, the European Enforcement Order (EEO),[814] followed in 2004 by the European Commission proposal for a uniform European payment order.[815]

Parliamentary discussions in France on the EOP procedure were limited, focusing on its limitation to cross-border cases and on the observance of principles of proportionality and subsidiarity.[816] In accordance with the principle of subsidiarity, a European order for

[812] See Decree No. 2016-230 of 26 February 2016.

[813] See www.service-public.fr/particuliers/vosdroits/F1746.

[814] Correa Delcasso (2005), at 146-147.

[815] Proposal for a Regulation of the European Parliament and of the Council creating a European order for payment procedure, COM(2004) 173 final.

[816] Document E 2179 Livre vert sur une procédure européenne d'injonction de payer et sur des mesures visant à simplifier et à accélérer le règlement des litiges portant sur des montants de faible importance, 17 December 2003, updated 12 December 2009 (available at www.assemblee-nationale.fr/europe/dossiers_e/e2179.asp); Document E 2553 Proposition de Règlement du Parlement européenne et du conseil instituant une procédure européenne d'injonction de payer, Rapport d'information, Délégation

payment should only concern cases having a cross-border dimension.[817] The basis of the Commission's competence in seeking to establish a uniform procedure applying to both national and cross-border claims – Article 65 EC Treaty – was questioned by French authorities and stakeholders (e.g. *Chambre de Commerce et d'Industrie de Paris*).

The French Government's reply to the 2002 Green Paper[818] was constrained, questioning the architecture of the projects put forward in the area of civil justice,[819] and the paper's relevance when the EEO was being negotiated. A multitude of instruments were seen as a source of confusion rather than serving the purpose for which they had been adopted.[820] Scholars pointed also to a lack of vision in the construction of the civil justice area. They considered the EOP to be the result of a 'chaotic' legislative process,[821] the construction of which 'did not yet reach sufficient solidity',[822] being a 'sort of fusion between existing models, secured by the adaptation of the minimal standards already put in place by the EEO'.[823] Others were more positive about the EOP.[824]

Stakeholders were in favour of an 'evidence' model for the EOP, similar to the *injonction de payer* procedure.[825] This would allow the judge to conduct a thorough examination of the claim, which was seen as a guarantee of the quality of justice, discouraging abusive claims and contributing to a lower number of oppositions to the EOP.[826]

The celerity of the procedure is considered to be its major asset.[827] Furthermore, the use of standard forms, and their availability online in all official languages of the Member States, was considered to contribute to the accessibility of the procedure.[828] Nevertheless,

de l'Assemblée Nationale pour l'Union européenne, N° 2369, 9 juin 2005, at 36 (available at www.assemblee-nationale.fr/12/europe/rap-per/p2369.asp#TopOfPage).

817 Réponse des autorités françaises au Livre Vert sur une procédure européenne d'injonction de payer et sur des mesures visant à accélérer le règlement des litiges portant sur des montants de faible importance, at 1 ('Réponse des autorités françaises au Livre Vert'); Rapport par M. Philippe Solignac au nom de la Commission juridique, *Vers des procédures européennes de recouvrement des créances. Réactions de la CCIP au Livre vert de la Commission européenne*, adopté à l'Assemblée générale du 22 mai 2003, at 8–9 ('Rapport Solignac 2003').

818 Green Paper on a European Order for Payment Procedure and on Measures to Simplify and Speed up Small Claims Litigation, COM(2002) 746 final.

819 Réponse des autorités françaises au Livre Vert, at 2.

820 Réponse des autorités françaises au Livre Vert, at 2. Perrot (2004), at 375; Lopez de Tejada & d'Avout (2007), at 717.

821 Nourissat (2007), at 5–6.

822 Amrani-Mekki (2011), at 252.

823 Beraudo & Beraudo (2011), para. 121.

824 Beraudo & Beraudo (2011), para. 24–25; Guinchard (2010), at 46–47; Guinchard (2008), at 465; Douchy-Odot (2008), at 16.

825 Réponse des autorités françaises au Livre Vert, at 9; Document E 2179 Livre vert sur une procédure européenne d'injonction de payer et sur des mesures visant à simplifier et à accélérer le règlement des litiges portant sur des montants de faible importance, 17 December 2003, updated 12 December 2009 (available at www.assemblee-nationale.fr/europe/dossiers_e/e2179.asp); Rapport Solignac 2003, at 20–22, 25. Legros (2007), at 10.

826 Réponse des autorités françaises au Livre Vert, at 9. Legros (2007), at 10.

827 Guinchard, Chainais & Ferrand (2012), at 1423.

828 Réponse des autorités françaises au Livre Vert, at 8; Rapport Solignac 2003, at 22–24.

some scholars doubted the progress they achieved, and questioned their judicial status and their compulsory nature, as well as the use of electronic means to submit applications to the court.[829] On the one hand, the standard form format and the limited open boxes were points of criticism;[830] on the other hand, the standardisation was seen as 'a facility offered to the parties' by the Regulation that 'guarantees the good circulation of documents regardless of the language used', and favouring an electronic treatment of the claim.[831]

The definition of cross-border cases was criticised for being too narrow.[832] Additionally, the provision regarding jurisdiction was also subject to criticism, due to its limiting the jurisdiction to the defendant's court of domicile only for consumers. French scholars consider that this places the defendant at a disadvantage, and hinders protection of his procedural rights.[833] Particular worries also concerned the service of documents and the information with which the defendant should be provided for guaranteeing his procedural rights.[834] A number of scholars addressed the issue of service of the EOP on the defendant.[835] The serving of procedural documents is a sensitive area and a crucial element for guaranteeing the defendants' procedural rights in French law, and the Regulation does not set a uniform rule in this regard. It establishes only minimum standards regarding methods of notification, allowing the use of means that give little certainty as to whether the defendant is actually aware of the order issued against him.[836] The text is criticised for focusing too much on the 'swiftness of the procedure' and for not sufficiently protecting the defendant's interests.[837] According to Guinchard, the security of service on the defendant himself when carried out by a bailiff or similar professional would have a better result in protecting procedural rights as guaranteed by Article 6 ECHR than the additional appeals available with the Regulation.[838]

As regards the phase of examination of the claim, scholars express a wide range of opinions. These include criticism that examination is limited to the formal regularity of the EOP forms; that the judges are not provided with the actual conditions to allow even a summary examination of the grounds of the claims;[839] and concerning the flexibility

829 Nourissat (2007), at 7; Lopez de Tejada & D'Avout (2007), at 732–737.

830 Beraudo & Beraudo (2011), para. 50.

831 Amrani-Mekki (2011), at 258–259.

832 Lopez de Tejada & D'Avout (2007), at 738–743; Guinchard (2008), at 468; Nourissat, (2007), at 5.

833 Guinchard (2008), at 477–478; Guinchard (2006), at 16–18; Niboyet (2008), at 104.

834 The French Government favoured in-person service on the defendant, and stressed the importance of making a distinction with regard to the method of serviced used. See Réponse des autorités françaises au Livre Vert, at 11–12. The Paris Chamber of Commerce favoured service by bailiff, pointing to the significance of this stage of the proceedings in guaranteeing the defendant's procedural rights. See Rapport Solignac 2003, at 30–31.

835 Payan (2012), at 531–534; Guinchard (2010), at 50; Jeuland (2007), at 27; Ferrand (2005), at 335–336; Legros (2007), at 14; Niboyet (2008), at 104; Miguet (2012), para. 18.

836 Jeuland (2007), at 27; Ferrand (2005), at 335–336; Legros (2007), at 14; Niboyet (2008), at 104; Miguet (2012) point 18.

837 Guinchard (2010), at 50; Lopez de Tejada & D'Avout (2007), at 723 and 726; Legros (2007), at 14; Ferrand (2005), at 335–336; Ferrand (2005a), at 194–195.

838 Guinchard (2008), at 481–482; Guinchard (2006), at 18.

839 Amrani-Mekki (2011), at 261–262; Lopez de Tejada & D'Avout (2007), at 729–730; Nourissat (2005), at 612.

the Regulation offers by facilitating a certain dialogue between the judge and the claimant, who can complete, modify, and rectify his request when considered necessary.[840]

The opposition system and the transfer to the ordinary national procedure are perceived as important elements for the EOP's success, and are essential aspects to be considered when choosing the jurisdiction competent to issue the order.[841]

As regards the EOP's overall achievementse, some authors consider that, although the EOP has had the perspective of becoming an effective means for creditors to use, it has only achieved an 'embryo' harmonisation of procedural rules, and it still relies too extensively on national procedural rules.[842] Other scholars view the EOP as an instrument that has the potential to be more successful than other European instruments.[843] It can be more easily assimilated in the national practice due to its use in practice and to existing national order for payments in most Member States.[844] Nevertheless, as some authors point out, the use in practice of the EOP has not yet reached the level of its theoretical importance within the European construction.[845] Member States were not too hasty to implement the new procedure, and the information they communicated to the Commission on competent jurisdictions is in certain instances not accurate.[846]

4.4.2. The ESCP

Overall, the French Government and stakeholders were positive about establishment of the ESCP procedure, seeing it as big step forward in the construction of EU law, even if certain 'weaknesses' were subsequently identified.[847]

In consideration of the national threshold for claims filed with the *juge de proximite*, €4,000, stakeholders were in favour of a higher ESCP threshold.[848] Regulation 2015/2421 addressed this aspect in amending the ESCP.

As with the EOP previously, the definition of cross-border cases was criticised for being too narrow.[849] This limitation is regarded as contributing to its low level of success

840 Nourissat (2007), at 7.

841 Guinchard (2010), at 49; Nourissat (2007), at 8.

842 Legros (2007), at 15; Lopez de Tejada & D'Avout (2007), at 724–726, 728–729.

843 Guinchard (2008), at 470–471; Guinchard, Chainais &Ferrand (2012), at 1429.

844 Jeuland (2007), at 27.

845 Guinchard (2010), at 46–47; Guinchard (2007), at 8.

846 Beraudo & Beraudo (2011), para. 121.

847 Beraudo & Beraudo (2011), para. 121; Piedelièvre (2007), at 53; Guinchard (2008), at 465–472; Guinchard (2013), at 65–79; Niboyet (2008), at 104–105.

848 Council of the European Union, French Delegation, Interinstitutional File 2013/0403 (COD), 8530/14, ADD3, Brussels, 4 April 2014, at 2; Réponse des autorités françaises au Livre Vert, at 18; Rapport Solignac 2003, at 45; Rapport de Francine Orsal, *Proposition de Règlement instituant une procédure européenne pour les demandes de faible importance. Réactions de la CCIP* présenté au nom de la Commission du droit de l'entreprise et adopté à l'Assemblée générale, 9 mars 2006, at 16–18 ('Rapport Orsal 2006'). Guinchard (2013), at 69–70. Replies by French stakeholders (i.e. Trans Europe Experts, CCI Lorraine, ECC France, Carrefour, individual practitioners) to the European Commission 2013 Consultation on the ESCP Regulation and proposal to amend the procedure.

849 Guinchard (2008), at 468–469.

in practice.[850] Additionally, the reliance on national rules for many aspects of the Regulation that leads to extensive variations between Member States is seen as a weakening element.[851]

The use of standard forms was seen as an asset that facilitates the establishment of a written procedure,[852] although opinions were varied as to the appropriateness of an oral or written procedure.[853] The oral hearing is an important characteristic of the French judicial system, and later reports commissioned by the European Commission point to a likely frequent use of oral hearings in the ESCP, contrary to its design.[854] In the 2013 Commission consultation, stakeholders favoured limiting the use of oral hearings to situations when this is necessary to decide the case (i.e. Trans Europe Experts, CCI Lorraine and Picardie, ECC France).[855] With Regulation 2015/2421, the French Government favoured an approach that gives the judge the possibility of appreciating whether a hearing is necessary.[856] Furthermore, French authorities backed an optional use of videoconferencing for hearings and the taking of evidence. This was due to technical and economic constraints a compulsory provision would involve considering the high number of domestic competent courts (over 400) and the limited number of annual claims.[857]

The judge is required to play a more active and reinforced role in managing the ESCP compared to other national procedures.[858] French authorities and scholars expressed their concern about requiring judges to provide assistance to parties.[859] The application of Article 10 ESCP can create difficulties and touch upon the principle of impartiality of the judge,[860] which in practice can be problematic. The task of offering information when parties request pertains to clerks,[861] but according to the initial text of the ESCP they seemed to have to take on the role of advising parties, an activity normally carried out by lawyers and legal counsellors in domestic procedures.[862] In view of the clarifications of Regulation 2015/2421, the French authorities are not opposed to giving practical assistance to potential claimants, in which instance related costs and possible arrangements need to be evaluated.[863]

850 Guinchard (2013), at 68–69; Nioche (2011), at 279.
851 Guinchard (2008), at 471; Guinchard (2013), at 71–79; Nourissat (2009), at 17.
852 Réponse des autorités françaises au Livre Vert, at 19; Rapport Solignac 2003, at 47–48; Rapport Orsal 2006, at 21–22.
853 Réponse des autorités françaises au Livre Vert, at 21; Rapport Solignac 2003, at 52.
854 Deloitte Report, Final Report, Part I, 2013, at 78.
855 Documents on file with the researcher.
856 Council of the European Union, French Delegation, Interinstitutional File 2013/0403 (COD), 8530/14, ADD3, Brussels, 4 April 2014, at 4.
857 *Ibidem*, at 4–5.
858 Piedelièvre (2007), at 53; Niboyet (2008), at 105–106; Nourissat (2009), at 17; Ferrand (2010), at 58–61.
859 On non-mandatory representation as a benefit of the ESCP, see Douchy-Odot (2008), at 18. For the critics of Article 10 ESCP, see Piedelièvre (2007), at 53.
860 Réponse des autorités françaises au Livre Vert, at 20–21.
861 *Ibidem*, at 20.
862 Piedelièvre (2007), at 53; Guinchard (2008), at 472.
863 Council of the European Union, French Delegation, Interinstitutional File 2013/0403 (COD), 8530/14, ADD3, Brussels, 4 April 2014, at 5.

As regards the service of ESCP documents, French stakeholders welcomed simplifying the Regulation by way of having a main service method, by post with an acknowledgement of receipt.[864] The French Government also supported the option introduced by Regulation 2015/2421 of service by electronic means and maintaining a choice between electronic and postal service as main service methods.[865]

As regards the execution of ESCP judgments, suppression of the exequatur is seen as one of the key developments.[866] Ferrand points to the fact the European legislature was in favour of making the judgment efficient immediately in opting for a model in which the judgment becomes enforceable notwithstanding the possibility of an appeal (Article 15 ESCP). This reinforces the effectiveness of the judicial decision against a possible increased protection of the right of defence.[867] The speediness of the procedure, however, should not be the instrument's only objective, and should not undermine the principle of fair trial as guaranteed by Article 6 ECHR. Within this framework, the scholar welcomes the review procedure as 'an equilibrium between efficiency and justice'.[868] However, the text provides no indications as to the means of review; there is no specific form for this purpose, and no specific conditions or a specific timeframe.[869] This leads to different national interpretations and solutions.

As with the EOP, scholars underline the importance of the approach of the national legislator in facilitating application of the ESCP, and signal the fact that inaccurate information is sometimes communicated to the Commission on the application of the instrument. This leads them to question the understanding of the national legislator regarding the economic implications of an efficient civil justice system that relies extensively on the elimination of obstacles to the enforcement of decisions.[870]

4.5. Implementation of the EOP and the ESCP in National Practice

General Provisions

The EOP and ESCP Regulations were incorporated by amendment into the CPC. Decree No. 2008-1346 of 17 December 2008 was published some days after the date of the EOP procedure became applicable.[871] The provisions rule on certain aspects related to application of the European uniform procedures. A new chapter, Chapter 1, was added to the Title IV (Obligations and Contracts) of Book III of the CPC for the ESCP. This corresponds to Articles 1382–1390 CPC. For the EOP, a new section – Section II – was added to the chapter dedicated to the national *injonction de payer*, Chapter 2 of Title IV

[864] Rapport Orsal 2006, at 23-24.

[865] Council of the European Union, French Delegation, Interinstitutional File 2013/0403 (COD), 8530/14, ADD3, Brussels, 4 April 2014, at 6.

[866] Niboyet (2008), at 105; Ferrand (2010), at 64.

[867] Ferrand (2010), at 63 and 66.

[868] *Ibidem.*

[869] Nioche (2011), at 288.

[870] Beraudo & Beraudo (2011), para. 121.

[871] Decree No. 2008-1346, 17 December 2008, Official Journal of the French Republic of 19 December 2008.

concerning Articles 1424-1–1424-15 CPC. Section III of the same chapter rules on court fees for the EOP procedure (Article 1425 CPC).

The choice of incorporating the rules on EOP and ESCP application into the French CPC can contribute to the visibility of these European procedures for the national practitioners and parties. Additionally, they provide support and certainty on certain matters for which the Regulations need to rely on national legislation for their application.[872] In addition to Decree No. 2008-1346, the Ministry of Justice issued two Guidelines regarding application of the EOP and the ESCP.[873] These documents seek to clarify certain aspects related to the French courts' application of the Regulations, such as the scope of the instruments, the conditions regarding the handling of the claims, the appeals and the execution of the EOP and the ESCP in France, and whether for particular circumstances specific articles of the CPC should be applied.

The French Government notified the European Commission that the district courts (*tribunaux d'instance*, TI) and the commercial courts (*tribunaux de commerce*, TC) have jurisdiction to handle EOP and ESCP claims.[874] However, the Guidelines point to the lower courts, *jurisdictions de proximité*, as being competent.[875] Law No. 2011-1862 on the assignment of cases to courts and the alleviation of certain judicial proceedings[876]

872 Such as, for example: territorial competence of courts if this is not specifically identified by the Brussels *Ibis* Regulation (Article 1382(2) CPC for the ESCP and Article 1424-1(2) CPC for the EOP); the way to submit the application form to the court (Article 1383 CPC for the ESCP and Article 1424-2 CPC for the EOP); notification and communication (Articles 1387 and 1389 CPC for the ESCP and Articles 1424-5 – 1424-7 CPC for the EOP); the organisation of hearings (Article 1388 CPC for the ESCP and Articles 1424-10 – 1424-11 CPC following the opposition for the EOP); certification of the decision (Article 1390 CPC) or of the EOP (Article 1424-14 CPC); and the review (Article 1391 CPC for the ESCP and Article 1425-15 CPC for the EOP).

873 Circulaire de la DACS C3 06-09 du 26 mai 2009 relative à l'application du règlement (CE) n° 1896/2006 du Parlement européen et du Conseil du 12 décembre 2006 instituant une procédure européenne d'injonction de payer, Official Gazette of the Ministry of Justice, 2009/4, 30 August 2009, Texte 16/51; Circulaire de la DACS C3 07-09 du 26 mai 2009 relative à l'application du règlement (CE) n° 861/2007 du Parlement européen et du Conseil du 12 décembre 2006 instituant une procédure européenne de règlement des petits litiges, Official Gazette of the Ministry of Justice, 2009/4, 30 August 2009, Texte 17/51 (available at www.textes.justice.gouv.fr/art_pix/1_boj_20090004_0000_p000.pdf).

874 Information communicated by Member States in accordance with Article 29 of Regulation (EC) No. 1896/2006 of the European Parliament and the Council of 12 December 2006 creating a European order for payment procedure available at https://e-justice.europa.eu/content_european_payment_order-353-fr-en.do?member=1; Information communicated by Member States in accordance with Article 25 of Regulation (EC) No. 861/2007 of the European Parliament and the Council of 11 July 2007 establishing a European Small Claims Procedure, available at https://e-justice.europa.eu/content_small_claims-354-fr-en.do?member=1.

875 Point 3.1 Juridictions matériellement compétentes pour connaitre de la demande, Circulaire de la DACS C3 06-09 du 26 mai 2009 relative à l'application du règlement (CE) n° 1896/2006; Point 3.1. Juridictions matériellement compétentes pour connaitre de la demande, Circulaire de la DACS C3 07-09 du 26 mai 2009 relative à l'application du règlement (CE) n° 861/2007. See also Section 4.7.2.

876 Law No. 2011-1862 of 13 December 2011 on the assignment of cases to courts and the alleviation of certain judicial proceedings (*Loi n°2011-1862 relative à la répartition des contentieux et à l'allègement de certaines procédures juridictionnelles*), Official Journal of the French Republic of 14 December 2011. On this inconsistency, see also Oudin (2009), at 17 and 27 (available at www.acj.si/en/project-results); Beraudo & Beraudo (2011), para. 41.

clarified this situation by amending the French Code of Judicial Organisation (COJ) and the Commercial Code (C.com.). Articles 221-4-1 and 221-7 COJ established that ESCP and EOP cases are to be handled by the TI, while commercial cases are the competence of the president of the TC for the EOPs and of the judges of the TC for ESCP claims.[877] The territorial competence of a particular French court is to be further determined according to the provisions of Articles 1382(2) and 1424-1(2) CPC read in conjunction with the provisions of Article 42 CPC. The claim may be submitted personally to the court in both procedures, or sent by post[878] or by electronic means.[879] However, submitting an EOP or ESCP claim by electronic means appears to be technically impossible at the moment.[880]

Information regarding the EOP procedure and the forms to be used for initiating a cross-border claim are available online using the website of the TC Paris,[881] Infogreffe (Clerk Offices for Commercial Courts),[882] Service Public,[883] and the website of the Ministry of Justice.[884] Similarly, information regarding the ESCP is available on the website of the Ministry of Justice and Service Public,[885] as well as on the ECC France website.[886]

EOP Provisions

The Ministry of Justice Guidelines establish that EOP standard forms have to be completed in French, but competent courts can accept them in a different language, provided the information is completed in French.[887]

877 The French legislator chose to derogate from the usual rules of competence in the COJ regarding the threshold of the claim and to establish the competence of 'professional' judges to handle EOPs and ESCPs. See Ferrand (2010), at 54-55.

878 Article 1383 CPC regarding the ESCP and Article 1424-2 CPC regarding the EOP.

879 Article 748-1 CPC. See also Deloitte Report, Final Report, Part II, 2013, at 45.

880 For the national *injonction de payer*, an electronic request can be filed by a French bailiff, IP WEB procedure. See Exécution judiciaire en Europe, 'La procédure européenne d'injonction de payer en France', at 4 (available at www.europe-eje.eu/sites/default/files/pj/dossiers/ipe_france_fr.pdf).

881 More information regarding the EOP and the forms to be used is available on the website of the TC, www.greffe-tc-paris.fr/fr/fond-referes-requetes/injonction_payer_europeenne.html. However, this website gives inaccurate information as to the languages the claimant can submit the forms, as it creates the impression the applications can be filed in languages other than French.

882 www.infogreffe.fr/societes/referes-requetes/litiges-transfrontaliers-injonction-payer.html.

883 www.service-public.fr/professionnels-entreprises/vosdroits/F32082.

884 The Ministry of Justice website giving information on the Decree incorporating the EOP within the national procedural system provides also links to the forms available on the Judicial Atlas: www.justice.gouv.fr/europe-et-international-10045/textes-et-reformes-10314/decret-relatif-a-la-procedure-europeenne-dinjonction-de-payer-17324.html.

885 www.service-public.fr/professionnels-entreprises/vosdroits/F32084.

886 www.europe-consommateurs.eu/fr/resoudre-votre-probleme/autres-alternatives/procedures-judicaires-europeennes-simplifiees/.

887 Point 3.2. Circulaire de la DACS C3 06-09 du 26 mai 2009 relative à l'application du règlement (CE) n° 1896/2006 du Parlement européen et du Conseil du 12 décembre 2006 instituant une procédure européenne d'injonction de payer, Official Gazette of the Ministry of Justice, 2009/4, 30 August 2009, Texte 16/51 and Point 3.2.5.

The rules incorporating the EOP into the national procedural system provide claimants with the possibility of desisting from proceedings if the court proposes that the claimant modify the claim, and issues an order only for that part of the claim that would preclude further action regarding the remaining amount.[888]

The CPC establishes a duty on the claimant to serve the EOP on the defendant by a bailiff[889] if this is to be carried out in France, or according to the provisions of the Service Regulation if the defendant is domiciled in a different Member State.[890] Service through electronic means can be used, provided the CPC provisions are observed.[891]

In accordance with the CPC, an opposition to the EOP can be made by a declaration with the court's clerk, who subsequently delivers a proof of receipt, either by letter with acknowledgement of receipt or by electronic means.[892] For the security of the legal circuit, the French CPC sets an additional time limit of 10 days following the lapse of the opposition delay, in order to allow Form F – if used – to reach the court.[893] In the event of an opposition, the CPC sets the rules regarding transfer to the national procedure, including the summoning of parties to a court hearing, the closing of the case if the parties do not appear in court, and the subsequent judgment to replace the EOP.[894] In the review procedure, the French legislator opted to apply the EOP mechanism as a national opposition procedure (Articles 1424-8 – 1424-13 CPC).[895] Furthermore, if the claim exceeds the threshold for which the TI is competent (€10,000), the review procedure will be handled by the TGI, before which representation by a lawyer is compulsory.[896]

If the EOP is not opposed, the court's clerk declares the EOP enforceable (Form G), and sets the enforcement formula on Form E.[897] He then notifies the claimant.[898]

888 Article 1424-3 CPC. Similar to the national order for payment, if the claimant desists from serving the EOP on the defendant, he may initiate a new ordinary procedure for the entire debt. See Amrani-Mekki (2011), at 262-263.

889 The CPC sets the requirements the bailiff needs to observe when informing the defendant of his procedural rights, the court handling the case, and the timeframe within which the party has to respond to the EOP (Articles 1424-5(2)-(3) – 1424-6 CPC).

890 Article 1424-5 CPC.

891 Articles 748-1 – 748-6 CPC. Information communicated by Member States in accordance with Article 29 of Regulation (EC) No. 1896/2006 of the European Parliament and the Council of 12 December 2006 creating a European order for payment procedure (https://e-justice.europa.eu/content_european_payment_order-353-fr-en.do?member=1). See also, Beraudo & Beraudo (2011), para. 58, 60.

892 Article 1424-8 CPC and Articles 748-1 – 748-6 CPC on the use of electronic means of communication. See information provided by Exécution judiciaire en Europe, 'La procédure européenne d'injonction de payer en France', at 8, available at www.europe-eje.eu/sites/default/files/pj/dossiers/ipe_france_fr.pdf.

893 Article 1424-14 CPC.

894 Articles 1424-9 – 1424-13 CPC. Under national procedure, legal representation before the TI or the TC is not mandatory. However, if the value of the claim exceeds the limit of the competence of the TI (€10,000), the ordinary procedure will be handled by the TGI before which legal representation is mandatory.

895 Based on Article 1424-15 CPC, the review will be treated as an opposition.

896 Information provided by Exécution judiciaire en Europe, 'La procédure européenne d'injonction de payer en France', at 9, available at www.europe-eje.eu/sites/default/files/pj/dossiers/ipe_france_fr.pdf.

897 Article 1424-14 CPC.

898 If the claimant resides in France, the clerk notifies him of the EOP becoming enforceable by registered letter with an acknowledgement of receipt (*letter recommandée avec avis de reception*). If the claimant resides abroad, he will be notified according to the provisions of Regulation 1393/2007.

ESCP Provisions
As with the EOP, Ministry of Justice Guidelines establish that ESCP forms have to be completed in French, but competent courts can accept standard forms in other languages if the information is completed in French.[899]

The French courts have to provide information, usually given by their clerks, but this is not meant to be 'a substitute to legal advice provided by lawyers'.[900]

Similar to the EOP, rules accommodating the ESCP within the national procedural system offer claimants the possibility of desisting from proceedings if the claim or counterclaim is considered by the court to fall outside the scope of the Regulation. Otherwise the application is handled according to the ordinary national procedure.[901]

The CPC establishes that the court is to employ a bailiff to notify the defendant if service by post does not result in receiving an acknowledgement of receipt signed by the defendant, or when he is domiciled abroad.[902] In this latter situation, the Service Regulation provisions apply. Further, the court is required to notify parties of the ESCP judgment by registered letter with acknowledgement of receipt.[903] Service of documents through electronic means can be used, provided the provisions on electronic service are observed.[904]

In accordance with Article 1388 CPC, the court may decide to hold a hearing.[905] If this is the case, it will be organised according to the rules applicable for procedures on the merits.

Should the French court reject the application for an ESCP due to the claim appearing to be clearly unfounded or inadmissible, or fail to complete or rectify the standard claim form, the judgment cannot be appealed, but the claimant may seek further to recover his claim through ordinary national proceedings.[906]

899 Point 3.2.5. Circulaire de la DACS C3 07–09 du 26 mai 2009 relative à l'application du règlement (CE) n° 861/2007 du Parlement européen et du Conseil du 11 juillet 2007 instituant une procédure européenne de règlement des petits litiges, Justice 2004/4, 30 août 2009, 17/51.

900 Point 3.2.2. Circulaire de la DACS C3 07–09 du 26 mai 2009 relative à l'application du règlement (CE) n° 861/2007 du Parlement européen et du Conseil du 11 juillet 2007 instituant une procédure européenne de règlement des petits litiges, Justice 2004/4, 30 août 2009, 17/51.

901 Article 1384 and Article 1386 CPC. Article 1386 CPC regarding the treatment of counterclaims not falling within the object of the Regulation gives a wider interpretation to Article 5(7) ESCP Regulation, which considers only cases in which the counterclaims exceeds €2,000. See Nioche (2011), at 285.

902 Article 1387 CPC. See further the Exécution judiciaire en Europe, 'La procédure européenne de règlement des petits litiges en France', at 7, available at www.europe-eje.eu/sites/default/files/pj/dossiers/france_petit_litige_fr.pdf.

903 Article 1389 CPC.

904 Articles 748-1 – 748-6 CPC. Information communicated by Member States in accordance with Article 25 of Regulation (EC) No. 861/2007 of the European Parliament and the Council of 11 July 2007 establishing a European Small Claims Procedure (https://e-justice.europa.eu/content_small_claims-354-fr-en.do?member=1). See also Beraudo & Beraudo (2011), para 76.

905 In accordance with information provided by France to the Report drafted by Deloitte to the European Commission, oral hearings are 'an important element of their judicial system'. Being a core aspect of their judicial system, therefore, it is more likely that oral hearings are held more often. The Deloitte Report, Final Report, Part I, 2013, at 78.

906 Article 1385 CPC.

The parties may appeal an ESCP judgment according to the French national opposition procedure,[907] or file for an extraordinary appeal if the judgment is not or is no longer challengeable by appeal with the Court of Appeals (*pourvoi en cassation*) or a judicial review (*recours en revision*).[908] The same provisions regarding the opposition (or similar procedural rules) apply if the review procedure is initiated.[909]

As with the EOP, the court's clerk declares the ESCP judgment enforceable by issuing the certificate (Form D).[910] He will also arrange for the claimant to be notified of the ESCP becoming enforceable.[911]

Costs

EOP and ESCP court fees are paid by the claimant only in commercial cases if the TC is the competent jurisdiction to handle the application, with additional fees being required in the event of an opposition to an EOP and its transfer to the ordinary national procedure.[912] The claimant needs to pay the court fee within 15 days of the application or from the moment the court notified the opposition. In accordance with the information provided by Infogreffe and the Paris TC on EOP claims, the court fee for initiating this procedure amounts to €37.07, and should be paid by cheque addressed to the Clerk's Office of the Commercial Court (e.g. *Greffe du Tribunal de Commerce de Paris*), or by online payment by bankcard.[913] Prior to 2011, the court fees could be paid only by cheque or in cash at the court clerk's office.[914]

The costs of service of the EOP by bailiff in France varies based on the value of the debt notified. For example, for a debt of €5,000 the bailiff may charge a fee of around €80. If the service is cross-border, the costs will be of €43.50 if the French bailiff is acting as transmitting agency and €50 if he is the receiving agency requested to carry out the service in France.[915] For the ESCP, the costs of service are advanced by the Public Treasury.[916]

[907] Articles 571–578 CPC. The legislator extended application of the CPC rules o on appeal for ESCP claims. However, in purely national cases the judgments cannot be appealed if their value is below €4,000.

[908] Information communicated by Member States in accordance with Article 25 of Regulation (EC) No 861/2007 available at https://e-justice.europa.eu/content_small_claims-354-fr-en.do?member=1.

[909] Article 1391 CPC. On the review procedures, see Beraudo & Beraudo (2011), para. 103–105; Nioche (2011), at 287–289.

[910] Article 1390 CPC.

[911] If the claimant resides in France, the clerk notifies him of the ESCP becoming enforceable by registered letter with an acknowledgement of receipt (*letter recommandée avec avis de reception*) (Article 1389 CPC). If the claimant resides abroad, he will be notified according to the provisions of Regulation (EC) No 1393/2007.

[912] Article 1425 CPC.

[913] The court fees applicable since 1st January 2014 for the TC Paris are available on the court's website: www.greffe-tc-paris.fr/fr/fond-referes-requetes/tarifs_fond.html, and on Infogreffe at www.infogreffe.fr/societes/referes-requetes/litiges-transfrontaliers-injonction-payer.html, www2.infogreffe.fr/infogreffe/jsp/ip/fonctionnementIP.jsp#.

[914] Deloitte Report, Final Report, Part I, 2013, at 91–92.

[915] See information provided by Exécution judiciaire en Europe, 'La procédure européenne d'injonction de payer en France', at 6 (available at www.europe-eje.eu/sites/default/files/pj/dossiers/ipe_france_fr.pdf).

[916] Article 1397 CPC. The service costs are to be borne by the French Treasury in accordance with the provisions of the French CPC (Article 670–3(3) CPC).

When parties are represented, lawyers' fees are freely negotiated, and vary according to diverse aspects of the case as well as depending on the individual lawyer, but the average hourly fees before tax are between €250 and €499.[917] Enforcement costs can be added if execution measures are necessary.

4.6. Enforcement in France: From National to European Judgments

Enforcement rules in France are contained in various laws. This section seeks to give an overview of the main characteristics of the French enforcement system, the rules that regulate this area, the professionals involved in securing the execution, and the costs of enforcement. The second part of this section will focus on how EOP and ESCP judgments are enforced in France, and on specific aspects of the procedure.

4.6.1. Main Aspects regarding the Execution of Judicial Decisions

Enforcement rules in France are not part of the CPC. A Code of civil enforcement procedures (*Code des procédures civiles d'exécution – CPC ex.*)[918] was adopted in two steps: first the legislative part in 2011,[919] and then one year later, in 2012, a regulatory framework.[920] The CPC ex. is the main text ruling on execution proceedings.[921] Specific provisions regarding enforcement measures remain subject to other laws (e.g. Code of Judicial Organisation on the function and competence of the judge of execution, Labour Code on employees' attachment of earnings, Transport Code on attachment of movable properties such as ships, and Commercial Code on the judicial selling of commercial assets).[922]

Bailiffs (*huissiers de justice*) carry out the enforcement of judgments in France.[923] Their territorial competence is related to that of the TGI within the jurisdiction in which they have their headquarters.[924] In their capacity as public and ministry officers, the French bailiffs secure the lawfulness of the enforcement proceedings (i.e. the grounds and forms of execution, and the type, structure, and means chosen by the creditor for attachment). The bailiffs can also request police participation in entering

917 Tinel (2007), at 17 (available at https://e-justice.europa.eu/content_costs_of_proceedings-37-fr-en.do).

918 Ordinance No. 2011–1895 of 19 December 2011 on the legislative part of the *Code des procédures civiles d'exécution*, Official Journal of the French Republic of 20 December 2011, Supplemented with the Decree No. 2012–783 of 30 May 2012 concerning implementation of the Code (*partie réglementaire*), Official Journal of the French Republic of 31 May 2012.

919 Ordinance No. 2011–1895. The legislative part comprises 167 Articles divided into six books.

920 Decree No. 2012–783 of 30 May 2012 (*Décret n° 2012–783 du 30 mai 2012*), Official Journal of the French Republic of 31 May 2012. The regulatory part groups 491 Articles divided into six books as the legislative part.

921 Vinckel (2013), para. 23.

922 Vinckel (2013), para. 23–25.

923 Article L.122–1 - 122–2 CPC ex.

924 Article 2 Decree No. 2007–813 of 11 May 2007 (*Décret n° 2007–813 du 11 mai 2007 modifiant Décret n° 69–1274 du 31 décembre 1969 pris pour l'application à la profession d'huissier de justice de la loi n° 66–879 du 29 novembre 1966 sur les sociétés civiles professionnelles*).

premises if the debtor resists enforcement measures,[925] or ask the enforcement judge or the prosecutor to issue necessary authorisations or decide upon required measures related to execution.[926]

Additional steps are required in order to execute a judgment.[927] A warrant of execution (*titre exécutoire*) must be delivered in the name of the State in order to empower the creditor to obtain enforcement. The copy of the decision has to include the standard enforcing formula (*formule exécutoire*),[928] and notification has to be given beforehand to the party against which execution measures will be carried out.[929] The use of electronic communication means is allowed if the defendant has expressly consented to this.[930]

The creditor will give a mandate to a bailiff to initiate enforcement proceedings.[931] He can choose the execution methods that he considers appropriate to secure the enforcement or the conservation of his claim.[932] The rules governing the execution of money judgments depend on the method of enforcement chosen. These include:

- attachment of the debtor's assets (*saisie des meubles*);[933]
- attachment of intangible assets (*saisie des droits incorporels*);[934]
- attachment of the debtor's real estate property (*saisie immonilière*);[935]
- attachment of earnings (*saisie des rémunérations du travail*);[936]
- attachment of bank accounts (*saisie-attribution d'un compte bancaire*);[937] and
- amounts owed by third parties (*saisie-attribution*).[938]

However, the choice must be in line with the principle of proportionality, and, in certain cases, the freedom of choice may be subject to limitation and to a particular hierarchy of the means of execution.[939] For example, in the case of *saisie immobilière* for real estate property and the credit corresponding to such assets, a certain order

925 Article L.122-1 CPC ex., Article L.153-1 - 153-2 CPC ex.

926 Article L. 213-6 COJ, Article L.122-2 CPC ex, and Article R.151-1 - 151-4 CPC ex. The president of the TGI fulfills the duties of the enforcement judge, but he may delegate these tasks to other judge(s) (Article L.213-5 COJ). Normand (2013), points 1-2, 11-12, 14-24; Casal (2013), para. 41. As regards the prosecutor's activities related to enforcement, see Articles L.121-5 - 121-6 CPC ex.; Casal (2013), para. 47-48; Hoonakker (2012), at 66-68.

927 Article 500 CPC gives a definition of a final judgment having *res judicata*.

928 Article 502 CPC. An omission or inexact enforcing formula results in the nullity of the execution acts. Défossez (2006), points 46-48.

929 Article 503(1) CPC.

930 Article 748-1 CPC in conjunction with Article 748-2 CPC. See further Vinckel (2013), para. 40.

931 Article L.111-1 - L.111-4 CPC ex.

932 Article L.111-7 CPC ex. On the principle of freedom of choice of means of execution, see Vinckel (2013), para. 106.

933 Book II, Title II of the Legislative part and Book II, Title II of the Regulatory part of the CPC ex.

934 Book II, Title III of the Legislative part and Book II, Title III of the Regulatory part of the CPC ex.

935 Book III of the Legislative part and Book III of the Regulatory part of the CPC ex.

936 Article L.211-1 and Article L.212-1 in conjunction with Article R.212-1 CPC ex. and Articles L.3252-1 - 3252-13, and R.3252-1 - 3252-49 Labour Code. For more details on attachment of earnings, see also Hoonakker (2012), at 184-199.

937 Article L.162-1 and Article L.211-1 - 211-2 together with R.162-1 and R.211-18 - 211-23 CPC ex.

938 Article Article L.211-1 - 211-5 together with and R.211-1 - 211-17 CPC ex. For more details, see Hoonakker (2012), at 155-184.

939 See Vinckel (2013), para. 8, 106, and 108-110; Payan (2012), at 148-150.

concerning means of execution needs to be observed in order to protect the debtor's home.[940] Furthermore, certain assets of the debtor may escape enforcement measures in accordance with law (e.g. assets necessary for the debtor's professional activity and for his family life, maintenance obligations).[941]

The enforcement judge becomes involved only in particular situations, such as in the case of attachments of earnings or for particular difficulties. Any problems related to the writs of execution, protective measures, damages, periods of grace, or possible controversies arising from the execution process are to be handled by an enforcement judge (*juge de l'exécution*).[942] The decisions are subject to appeal, but this does not suspend the execution process.[943]

In French law, the debtor is not compelled to communicate information regarding his assets. Most of the information necessary for the execution is protected.[944] The CPC ex. allows the bailiff to obtain certain information directly: namely, the address of the debtor, the identity and address of his employer or any third party owing money to or holding it for the debtor (financial status of the debtor), and his properties.[945] In accordance with the law, public bodies as well as credit institutions have a duty to provide information to a bailiff having an enforceable title against a debtor.[946] In practice, bailiffs have access to information contained in the National Database for Bank Accounts (*Fichier national des comptes bancaires et assimilés*, FICOBA) in which all the bank accounts or similar accounts are registered in France,[947] the System for the Registration of Vehicles (*Système d'immatriculation des véhicules*, SIV),[948] and the Professional Database of the Land Registry (*Serveur Professionnel de Données Cadastrales*, SPDC).

Furthermore, in order to persuade the debtor to collaborate for the purpose of a speedier enforcement, the judge may use incentive measures, such as the award of a penalty (*astreinte*). The *astreinte* is independent of the awarded damages, and – in the event of non-voluntary payment of the award by the debtor – is payable up until the moment of execution of the judgment.[949] However, if the penalty is to be enforced in a

940 See for example Articles L.311-5, L.311-8, L.212-2 CPC ex.

941 Article L.112-2 CPC ex. See Payan (2012), at 159–161.

942 Article L.213-6 COJ, Articles L.121-1 – L.121-3 CPC ex, and Article R. 121-1 CPC ex. On conservative measures, see Article R.511-1 – R.511-6 CPC ex. See du Rusquec (2014).

943 Article R.121-19 – 121-21 CPC ex. For detailed information regarding the appeal procedure, admissibility of the appeal and its effects, see Normand (2013), para. 30–71.

944 Vinckel (2013), para. 7; Hoonakker (2012), at 87–94.

945 Articles L.152-1 to L.152-3 CPC ex. Vinckel (2013), para. 107; Casal (2013), para. 40; Hoonakker (2012), at 87–94; Payan (2012), at 229–234.

946 Articles L.152-1 to L.152-3 CPC ex. The bailiff can use the information obtained only for the execution of the enforceable title for which this was requested, and cannot be communicated to third parties or used to create a nominal data base. Such activities are incriminated by the law (Article 226-21 Criminal Code).

947 On FICOBA, see www.cnil.fr/documentation/fichiers-en-fiche/fichier/article/ficoba-fichier-national-des-comptes-bancaires-et-assimiles/. Casal (2013), para. 40; Cuniberti, Normand & Cornette (2011), at 196–197.

948 On SIV, see www.cnil.fr/documentation/fichiers-en-fiche/fichier/article/siv-systeme-dimmatriculation-des-vehicules/.

949 Articles L.131-1 – 131-4 CPC ex. Guinchard, Chainais & Ferrand 2012, at 355–358 and 918; Vinckel (2013), para. 115–117; Cuniberti, Normand & Cornette (2011), at 259–272.

different Member State, the amount of the payment needs to have been finally determined by the court of origin, otherwise it cannot proceed to the imposing and execution of the penalty.[950] For similar aims in money judgments, an increase in the interest rate can be set if the debtor does not pay the amount awarded by the judgment within two months of the moment of notification regarding the enforceable title.[951]

The costs of enforcement in France vary according to the type of measure chosen and the activities the bailiff needs to undertake. Information regarding bailiff fees, charges, and reimbursements is detailed in a temporary Administrative order following the repeal of Decree No. 96–1080 of 12 December 1996.[952] Further, Article L.111–8 CPC ex. establishes a difference between costs of enforcement (*execution forcée*) and those for the voluntary recovery of a debt (*recouvrement amiable*). The costs of the latter are borne by the creditor.[953] The enforcement costs are mainly the responsibility the defendant. In the case of a bad faith debtor, the creditor who justifies the necessary character of the measures taken to secure recovery of his debt may request the enforcement judge to place responsibility for all or part of the expenses incurred on the debtor (Article 111–8(3) CPC ex.).

No overall national information is available on the length of the enforcement proceedings. The 2013 World Bank Institute Report indicates that the enforcement of a contract takes an average of 390 days and costs the party around 17.2% of the value of the claim.[954]

4.6.2. *Executing EOP and ESCP Judgments*

In addition to the special provisions on delivery of the enforcement certificate by the court clerk's office (Article 1390 and Article 1424–14 CPC), and the Regulations' provisions on enforcement (Articles 18 and 21–23 EOP and Articles 20–23 ESCP), execution of the EOPs and ESCPs follows the national procedural rules, in keeping with any enforceable decision issued by a French court.[955]

No additional fees are charged by the court for the delivery of Form G for the EOP or of Form D for the ESCP. In France, the enforcement character of the document is given by the enforcing formula (*formule exécutoire*), which the clerk can attach to the EOP (Form E) or ESCP judgment, or to the additional required certificates, Form G or Form

[950] Article 55 Brussels *Ibis*. For a criticism of this provision, see Payan (2012), at 172–184.

[951] Article L.313–3 Code monétaire et financière. See Article 1153(3) Code civil regarding the moment from which the two months delay is calculated. Guinchard, Chainais & Ferrand 2012, at 917.

[952] Administrative Order (*Arrêté*) of 26 February 2016 establishing the regulated fees of bailiffs, NOR: EINC1605791A, Official Journal of the French Republic n° 0050 of 28 February 2016, texte n° 38 (available at www.legifrance.gouv.fr/affichTexte.do?cidTexte=JORFTEXT000032115547&categorieLien=id). For additional information on the level of bailiffs' fees, see Fiche 2 – Agents d'exécution, available at www.europe-eje.eu/fiche-thematique/fiche-2-agents-execution-3.

[953] Article 111–8(2) CPC ex. This concerns a means of voluntary recovery of debt that does not rely on an enforcement title.

[954] International Bank for Reconstruction and Development / The World Bank, *Doing Business in Italy 2013, Smart Regulations for Small and Medium-Size Enterprises* (available at www.doingbusiness.org/~/media/WBG/DoingBusiness/Documents/Subnational-Reports/DB13-Italy.pdf).

[955] Article 21(1) EOP, Article 21(1) ESCP.

D. As regards authenticity, the orders or judgment issued by a French court must include the seal (*sceau*) and signature (*paraphe*) of the clerk.[956]

The formalities regarding enforcement of EOP and ESCP titles are minimal. The creditor has to provide the French bailiff with a copy of the EOP or ESCP judgment declared enforceable and satisfying the conditions necessary to establish its authenticity (Article 21(2)(a) EOP and Article 21(2)(a) ESCP). If necessary, a translation of these documents must be added (Article 21(2)(b) EOP and Article 21(2)(b) ESCP). The translations have to be certified by a qualified person in one of the Member States, and will be necessary for decisions issued in a language other than French, English, German, Spanish, and Italian.[957]

Additionally, according to the CPC provisions, the EOP or ESCP judgment needs to be served on the defendant before execution.[958] In contrast to judgments issued according to national procedures, an appeal against an ESCP judgment or the EOP/ESCP review procedures does not automatically suspend execution.[959] In the event of a review or appeal request, or when an appeal is still possible, the judge, upon the defendant's request, can limit the enforcement to protective measures, make execution conditional on the provision of a security, or, in exceptional instances, stay the enforcement proceedings.[960] According to Nioche, in an application to review an ESCP, the court with which the request is lodged can withdraw its judgment insofar as it orders a provisional enforcement or stays the enforcement proceedings before re-examining the merits of the claim.[961] In any case, the judge (*juge de référé*), in emergency situations, or the enforcement judge, following the service of the decision on the defendant, can order a stay of enforcement by granting a period of grace.[962] The stay and limitation of enforcement applies also when the small claims judgment is executed in the Member State of the court that issued the decision.[963] According to the literature, the same applies to EOPs, even if not expressly stated in the Regulation text.

[956] Beraudo & Beraudo (2011), para. 108.

[957] Information communicated by Member States in accordance with Article 29 of Regulation (EC) No 1896/2006 of the European Parliament and the Council of 12 December 2006 creating a European order for payment procedure available at https://e-justice.europa.eu/content_european_payment_order-353-fr-en.do?member=1; Information communicated by Member States in accordance with Article 25 of Regulation (EC) No 861/2007 of the European Parliament and the Council of 11 July 2007 establishing a European Small Claims Procedure (https://e-justice.europa.eu/content_small_claims-354-fr-en.do?member=1).

[958] Article 503 and 675 CPC. Cuniberti, Normand & Cornette (2011), at 115–116 and 130–131.

[959] Article 15(1) ESCP and point 4.1 of the Circulaire de la DACS C3 07–09 du 26 mai 2009 relative à l'application du règlement (CE) n° 861/2007 du Parlement européen et du Conseil du 11 juillet 2007 instituant une procédure européenne de règlement des petits litiges, Justice 2004/4, 30 août 2009, 17/51, and point 4.4. Circulaire de la DACS C3 06–09 du 26 mai 2009 relative à l'application du règlement (CE) n° 1896/2006 du Parlement européen et du Conseil du 12 décembre 2006 instituant une procédure européenne d'injonction de payer, Justice 2004/4, 30 août 2009, 16/51.

[960] Article 23 EOP, Article 23 ESCP.

[961] Nioche (2011), at 291.

[962] Article 510 CPC. Nioche (2011), at 291; Cuniberti, Normand & Cornette (2011), at 131–132.

[963] Article 15(2) ESCP.

A diverse handling between the execution of an EOP in a different Member State and in the Member State of origin would not be justified.[964]

Under no circumstance may the French judge or the enforcement judge review the enforceable judgment as to its substance.[965] Their competence is limited to deciding upon matters regarding execution of the EOP or the ESCP decision by the bailiff.

The costs of executing EOPs or ESCP judgments in France are generally identical to those that the parties would incur in a purely national enforcement procedure. In certain cases the application of fixed fees for cross-border service carried out by bailiff, and the need to use translation services for the EOP and the ESCP, can add to the enforcement costs.[966] The translation costs are based on the fees, which are on average €15 per hour for accredited translators in France,[967] or on average €20 per page according to the Deloitte Report.[968]

4.7. The EOP and the ESCP in Practice

This section analyses the way in which the EOP and the ESCP function in France. The first part is dedicated to the available statistics on the use of the European uniform procedures. The second part then focuses on data provided by the identified national case law. The last part of the analysis concentrates on the empirical findings and a triangulation of the results with case law and statistical data.

4.7.1. *Available Statistical Data*

The French Ministry of Justice publishes annual statistics on the activity of the civil courts, including procedures for the recovery of money claims (i.e. *injonction de payer, référé*), as well as special reports on particular procedures (e.g *injonction de faire*).[969] Additional reports are available on the proceedings handled by the commercial courts (TC) and the commercial chambers of the TGI. Although no statistical data on the EOP and ESCP procedure has been published so far in the annual reports, the French Ministry of Justice has been gathering data on the application of EOP and the ESCP by civil courts since 2009. These statistics were provided by the Ministry upon request, and cover the period 2009–2014. Table 4.1 below presents the number of EOP and ESCP cases handled by French civil courts since the Regulations became applicable.

964 Beraudo & Beraudo (2011), para. 110.

965 Article 22(3) EOP, Article 22(2) ESCP.

966 For example, the cost of servicing a document cross-border is €43.50 if the French bailiff is acting as transmitting agency, and €50 if he is the receiving agency requested to carry out the service in France. See information provided by Exécution judiciaire en Europe, 'La procédure européenne d'injonction de payer en France', at 6 (available at www.europe-eje.eu/sites/default/files/pj/dossiers/ipe_france_fr.pdf). See Section 4.5.

967 Tinel (2007), at 72 (available at https://e-justice.europa.eu/content_costs_of_proceedings-37-fr-en.do).

968 Deloitte Report, Final Report, Part I, 2013, at 84.

969 Munoz-Perez & Sommer (2013).

	2009		2010		2011		2012		2013		2014	
Applications for	TI	JP	TI	JP	TI	JP	TI	JP	TI	JP	TI	JP
EOP[970]	893	-	1093	-	960	-	343	-	n/a	-	n/a	-
ESCP	n/a	n/a	14	7	19	29	25	48	42	27	46	62

Table 4.1. Number of EOP and ESCP claims received by French civil courts *(Tribunal d'instance* - TI and *Juge de proximité* - JP) according to the Ministry of Justice statistics[971]

On an annual basis, the information presented above can be read as follows:

Applications for	2009	2010	2011	2012	2013	2014
EOP	893	1093	960	343	n/a	n/a
ESCP	n/a	21	48	73	69	108

Table 4.2. Consolidated annual data on the number of EOP and ESCP claims received by French civil courts according to the Ministry of Justice statistics

EOP Regulation

From the annual aggregated data on the number of EOP claims submitted to the French courts (Table 4.2), it can be seen that the number of applications is generally increasing (Fig. 4.1). The 2012 statistical data shows a huge decrease in the number of cases in comparison to 2011. This raises some doubts as to the soundness of the data. Even though the causes for this outcome are not clear, the switch of the court registration system in the national *injonction de payer* procedures may have contributed. The new application, IPWEB, does not allow registration of the EOP in the system, which has led to difficulties in keeping statistics on EOP requests. The clerks have to continue to keep separate registries.[972] Further, the number of applications for the same period (2012) in the European Commission Report regarding the EOP Regulation is different from that in the Ministry of Justice statistics.[973] The European report indicates of 335 applications compared to 343 in the Ministry statistics for the same period (Table 4.2). The reason for this difference is not clear.

970 As indicated in the clarifications provided by the Ministry of Justice, no exhaustive data with regard to application of the EOP is available for the period 2013–2014. This situation is related to the fact that national courts are using an electronic application, IPWEB, for the registration of domestic orders for payment, and it does not allow EOP cases to be registered separately.

971 The number of cases also includes the number of review requests filed in EOP and ESCP procedures.

972 One clerk participating in an interview for this research pointed to this difficulty in the registration of EOP cases. Based on the information communicated to the court, new European software that was being piloted should have been in place during 2013 for registration of the European procedures. In 2014, as a temporariy solution, the courts were still registering EOP applications manually in separate registries.

973 Commission EOP Report, Annex, at 13.

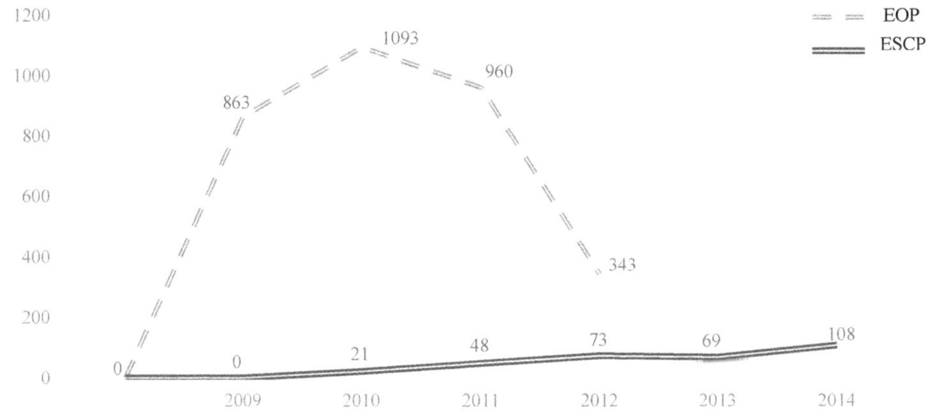

Fig. 4.1. Evolution of the number of EOP and ESCP applications during 2009–2014

The European Commission Report as well as the national data provide information as to the various outcomes of EOP applications, such as requests for the completion or correction of standard Form A, or to the oppositions and the timeframe necessary for the issuance of an order (Tables 4.3 and 4.4). According to statistics provided by the Ministry of Justice, most EOP applications are fully or partially awarded by the judges. The rate of awards in the number of decisions is above 70% for all 4 years (2009–2012).[974] However, according to the European Commission Report, the EOP was issued by the courts in 91% of the applications filed in 2012. The reason for this difference and sudden increase in the rate of success between the two sets of data is not clear. As no statistics are available for 2013 and 2014, no further verifications are possible.

Similar to the *injonction de payer*, the rate of EOP oppositions remains low, with an average of 15.9% of the EOPs issued for the period 2009–2011.[975] This outcome is in line with results presented by the Commission EOP Report, where the opposition rate affected around 16% of the EOPs issued in 2012. Further, the number of applications in which the French courts declared not having jurisdiction is below 2%, which appears to indicate that application of the jurisdiction rules creates no major difficulties for the claimants filing EOP applications in France. Further, the Report shows that in 2012, of a total of number of 335, 118 applications were returned by the court to the claimant for completion or rectification purposes. This concerns over 35% of the cases filed, and indicates a certain difficulty in correctly filling in all the necessary details of the standard form in order for the court to be able to proceed immediately to an assessment of the claim and to the issuance of the EOP.

974 The level of EOPs awarded in the total number of decisions issued within the EOP procedure was 71.7% in 2009, 74.0% in 2010, 74.9% in 2011, and 71.1% in 2012.

975 In the national *injonction de payer*, the rate of opposition is around 5%. See Section 4.3.1.

Based on Ministry of Justice statistics, the review mechanism was seldom used in the period for which data is available. Only one case was registered in 2010. Although no further information is available for the period 2012–2014, it is highly likely that the number of review requests has remained low over the years. The number of rejected EOP claims remained below the 30% threshold for the entire period. However, the reasons that the courts rejected the applications are not provided. The data is not detailed on the basis of the criteria set by Article 11(1) EOP, nor is it clear whether applications were also rejected for other reasons. The Ministry of Justice statistics show that the average time necessary for the issuance of an EOP (Form E) was around 1.25 months for the period 2009–2011. The procedural timeframe was slightly longer for claims where the court issued a partial awarded (almost 1.5 months). During the same period, the average time for a judge to reject an application was 1.3 months. If the court was considered not to be competent, the judge on average issued a decision in less than 1 month. Thus, for the period 2009–2011, regardless of the applications outcome, the average duration of an EOP case in France was less than 1.5 months. These results come close to the time goal set by Article 12 EOP, according to which the order should be issued as soon as possible and normally within a period of 30 days from the date the application was lodged. According to the Commission EOP Report, the length of the EOP proceedings in 2012 was 2 months. The report does not make the same detailed differentiation regarding EOP applications that the Ministry of Justice makes per type of decisions issued by the courts. However, it is remarkable that the duration of the proceedings increased in comparison with previous years, although the time necessary to obtain a decision often displayed a stable or a decreasing trend (see Table 4.3).

As regards the experience of the commercial courts (TC) with the EOP, the Ministry of Justice was unable to provide any data. The special status of these courts and their activities appears to limit the possibility of the Ministry to obtain sound data. According to information presented by the president of the National Council of the Clerks of Commercial Courts (*Conseil National des Greffiers des Tribunaux de Commerce*) during a conference organised by the Trans Europe Experts in 2013, the French TCs registered 321 EOP cases in 2012.[976] Upon request, the National Council of the Clerks of the Commercial Courts agreed to invite all TCs to share their EOP-related experiences by making these research surveys available to the courts.

[976] According to Mr. Barbin, President of the Conseil National des Greffiers des Tribunaux de commerce, at the workshop on procedures for the recovery of money claims in Europe; Conference organised by Trans Europe Experts on 22 March 2013 in Paris. The data regarded cases handled by 108 out of 134 TCs requested to provide data. See also Guinchard (2013a), at 335.

	2009			2010			2011			2012		
Results	No.	%	Length procedure (months)	No.	%	Length procedure (months)	No.	%	Length procedure (months)	No.	%	Length procedure (months)
Total no. EOP issued	824	100.0	1.3	1062	100.0	1.4	946	100.0	1.3	435	100.0	n/a
Withdrawal of the application from the roll	4	0.5	1.7	0	0.0	0.0	7	0.7	1.7	2	0.5	n/a
Court not competent	15	1.8	1.0	17	1.6	1.4	8	0.8	0.7	5	1.1	n/a
Rejection of the claim	214	26.0	1.1	249	23.4	1.3	223	23.6	1.5	119	27.4	n/a
Full award	202	24.5	1.2	227	21.4	1.1	224	23.7	0.8	96	22.1	n/a
Partial award	389	47.2	1.4	569	53.6	1.5	484	51.2	1.5	213	49.0	n/a
Opposition	94	15.9	n/a	129	16.2	n/a	112	15.8	n/a	n/a	n/a	n/a
Review	0	0.0	n/a	1[977]	n/a	n/a	0	0.0	n/a	n/a	n/a	n/a

Table 4.3. Quantitative data on EOP procedures and the outcome of the claims according to Ministry of Justice statistics

	No. applications	EOPs for enforcement	Applications returned for completion/ rectification	Modification of application	No. oppositions	No. EOPs issued	Length of proceedings
EOP	335	n/a	118	n/a	+/-16%	305	2 months

Table 4.4. Statistical data on use of the EOP in France in 2012 according to the Commission EOP Report, COM(2015) 495 final

977 The request for review was filed in 2010, and the case was closed in 2011, with a partial acceptance of the claim.

	2008			2009			2010			2011			2012			2013			2014		
	No. cases	No. reject	No. oppos	No. cases	No. reject	No. oppos	No. cases	No. reject	No. oppos	No. cases	No. reject	No. oppos	No. cases	No. reject	No. oppos	No. cases	No. reject	No. oppos	No. cases	No. reject	No. oppos
TC Agen	2 cases handled																				
TC Auxerre	0	0	0	0	0	0	0	0	0	0	0	0	0	0	0	0	0	0	0	0	0
TC Aubenas	0	0	0	0	0	0	0	0	0	0	0	0	0	0	0	0	0	0	0	0	0
TC Avignon	Almost non-existent																				
TC Bobigny	n/a	n/a	n/a	n/a	n/a	n/a	n/a	n/a	n/a	n/a	n/a	n/a	n/a	n/a	n/a	11	n/a	n/a	2[978]	n/a	n/a
TC Cahors	0	0	0	0	0	0	0	0	0	0	0	0	0	0	0	0	0	0	0	0	0
TC Chaon sur Saone	0	0		0	0		0	0	0	3	0	0	1	0	0	0	0		0	0	0
TC Compiegne	n/a	n/a	n/a	n/a	n/a	n/a	n/a	n/a	n/a	n/a	n/a	n/a	2	0	2	1	0	1	0	0	0
TC Coutances	0	0	0	0	0	0	0	0	0	0	0	0	0	0	0	0	0	0	0	0	0
TC Draguignan	1 case handled – application rejected																				
TC Lorient[979]	0	0	0	0	0	0	0	0	0	1	0	n/a	1	0	n/a	1	0	n/a	0	0	0
TC Manosque	0	0	0	0	0	0	0	0	0	0	0	0	0	0	0	0	0	0	0	0	0
TC Paris	n/a	n/a	n/a	47	4	4	66	13	4	56	4	14	65	9	5	n/a	n/a	n/a	n/a	n/a	n/a
TC Poitiers	0	0	0	0	0	0	1	0	n/a	2	0	n/a	2	0	n/a	0	0		0	0	0
TC Vannes[980]	0	0	0	0	0	0	2	0	n/a	1	1	0	0	0	0	1	0	n/a	0	0	0

Table 4.5. Statistical data on the handling of EOP cases from some of the commercial courts in France. The information was gathered with the assistance of the National Council of the Commercial Courts Clerks and the Paris Commercial Court *(Tribunal de commerce de Paris)*

978 Until 22 May 2014.

979 According to information provided by the TC Lorient, less than 25% of the cases handled were subsequently opposed by the defendant.

980 In two of the 4 EOP cases handled by the TC Vannes, the defendant opposed the EOP. However, the information is not available on a yearly basis.

In addition to this, the TC Paris provided its own statistics for the period 2009–2012. The data that became available concerns 15 of a total of 136 commercial courts (TC)[981] (Table 4.5). The 14 TCs that replied have generally handled a limited number of EOPs, except for TC Paris, which has had extensive experience with this European procedure. From information that is available, the number of applications rejected is seen to be very low. Similarly, the opposition statistics point to a low level of use of this mechanism. However, not all commercial courts that handled claims were able to provide information on whether the EOP was opposed. Two courts registered outcomes that are more particular. With one court, all the EOP issued were opposed (TC Compiegne 2012–2013, Table 4.5), while in the other case, half of the EOPs were opposed by the defendant (2 of 4 cases, TC Vannes). For TC Paris, and with the court having handled most EOP cases in absolute terms from the sample, the average opposition level is situated at 13.15% of the EOP issued. Although this information cannot be generalised for all commercial courts in France, the result is in line with statistics provided by the Ministry of Justice and the Commission EOP Report on the activity of the civil courts.

Statistics compiled by TC Paris indicate the extent to which additional steps need to be taken by the creditor for the recovery of monies owed to him. In this particular type of instance, for more than half of the EOPs issued (on average 61% of the EOPs) the claimants had to request delivery of a Declaration of enforceability in order to proceed to execution.

ESCP Regulation

The number of ESCP applications registered by French civil courts has been steadily increasing (Fig. 4.1). These cases are registered using the CITI software application, and makes the retrieval of statistical data at the national level easier for the civil courts. Tables 4.1 and 4.2 above present aggregated data as well as information per type of competent court (TI or JP) on the ESCP applications received during the period 2009–2014. Similar to the EOP situation, national statistical data on the number of ESCP applications do not fully match information published in the Report prepared by Deloitte for the European Commission on the ESCP (Table 4.6).[982] The reason for these differences for the period 2010–2011 is not clear.

ESCP	2009	2010	2011	2012	2013	2014
Ministry of Justice statistics	3	21	48	73	69	108
European Commission Final Report[983]	3	27	49	54[984]	n/a	n/a

Table 4.6. Quantitative data on the ESCP applications received by the French civil courts according to the Ministry of Justice statistics in comparison with the data published in the Final Report drafted by Deloitte for the European Commission for the assessment of the ESCP

981 See www.justice.gouv.fr/budget-et-statistiques-10054/chiffres-cles-de-la-justice-10303/.

982 Deloitte Report, Final Report, COM(2013) 495 final, Brussels, 19.07.2013.

983 Deloitte Report, Final Repor, Part I, COM(2013) 495 final, Brussels, 19.07.2013, at 63.

984 Statistical data is only partial for 2012.

The Deloitte Report presents data only on the numbers of cases for which the civil courts granted a partial or full award of the claim. Information with regard to other types of outcomes are available in the Ministry of Justice statistics (rejected claims, settlements) (see Table 4.7). In accordance with the Deloitte Report, the data presented concern applications of the European procedure handled by the district courts (TI) and the courts of commerce (TC).[985] However, it is remarkable to observe that the data match almost exactly the values provided by the Ministry of Justice on the number of awards issued by the civil courts – hence, not including commercial court statistics. The data regarding application of the ESCP before the commercial courts are surprisingly scanty in comparison to those of the civil courts for the same period. As to the EOP, the reason might be linked to the difficulty the Ministry has in obtaining statistics from TCs.

ESCP (Tribunal de commerce-TC)	2011	2012	2013
Ministry of Justice statistics	4	1	1

Table 4.7. Quantitative data on the number of ESCP claims handled by commercial courts

Similar to the EOP, the available data appear to indicate that the application of jurisdiction rules does not create significant difficulties in practice for the parties. Information available indicates that courts at times declined their jurisdiction on ESCP applications.

For the period 2010–2014, this concerns an average of around 5.64% of the total number of ESCP judgments issued. Additionally, during the 5-year period analysed, the court declared itself not competent to handle the application in 3.1% of the decisions issued. The level of settled claims is very low considering the provisions of Article 12(3) ESCP Regulation, which recommends that the courts seek to facilitate settlement whenever appropriate. Only two such cases were registered: one in 2011 and another in 2014.

The level of rejected applications is below 10% (approx. 9.6%) for the period analysed. Regrettably, the data do not reveal the reasons for rejection.

As regards the procedural timeframe, the Ministry of Justice statistics show a significant increase in the time required for handling an application, from an average of 2.8 months in 2010 to 4.6 months in 2011 and 2012. The statistics offer no explanation for these results. Additionally, the time necessary has also risen exponentially for struck off cases and rejected applications. Nonetheless, the ESCP claims are generally handled within the 6-month period the European Commission initially aimed to establish.

The data gathered by the National Council of the Commercial Courts on the ESCP cases handled by TCs confirm a very low number of applications. Between 2009–2014, almost none of the respondent courts (14) received an ESCP application.

985 Table 19, Deloitte Report, Final Report, Part I, COM(2013) 495 final, Brussels, 19.07.2013, at 63.

Results	2010			2011			2012			2013			2014		
	No.	%	Length procedure (months)	No.	%	Length procedure (months)	No.	%	Length procedure (months)[986]	No.	%	Length procedure (months)	No.	%	Length procedure (months)
Total no. ESCP decisions issued	15	100.0	2.8	47	100.0	4.6	51	100.0	4.6	68	100.0	n/a	87	100.0	n/a
Withdrawal of the application	0	0.0	–	0	0.0	–	0	0.0	–	0	0.0	n/a	1	1.1	n/a
Struck off the roll	3	20.0	2.1	2	4.3	4.5	5	9.8	8.1	5	7.4	n/a	4	4.6	n/a
Voluntary renunciation	1	6.7	1.0	8	17.0	6.6	5	9.8	3.9	11	16.2	n/a	8	9.2	n/a
Void application	0	0.0	–	1	2.1	5.4	0	0.0	–	0	0.0	–	1	1.1	n/a
Settlement	0	0.0	–	1	2.1	9.0	0	0.0	–	0	0.0	–	1	1.1	n/a
Declined jurisdiction in favour of another court	2	13.3	1.0	1	2.1	0.3	1	2.0	0.0	5	7.4	n/a	3	3.4	n/a
Other reason to decline competence	0	0.0	–	0	0.0	–	2	3.9	0.9	3	4.4	n/a	2	2.3	n/a
Inadmissibility	1	6.7	11.2	5	10.6	1.3	11	21.6	2.5	7	10.3	n/a	5	5.7	n/a
Court not competent	1	6.7	5.4	0	0.0	–	2	3.9	0.1	1	1.5	n/a	3	3.4	n/a
Rejection of the claim	2	13.3	4.2	3	6.4	3.7	5	9.8	6.1	1	1.5	n/a	15	17.2	n/a
Full award	4	26.7	2.0	19	40.4	4.5	12	23.5	4.3	30	44.1	n/a	38	43.7	n/a
Partial award	1	6.7	2.4	7	14.9	6.1	8	15.7	7.6	5	7.4	n/a	6	6.9	n/a

Table 4.8. Quantitative data on ESCP procedures and the outcome of claims according to Ministry of Justice statistics

986 Based on calculations performed on partial data for 2012 provided by the French Ministry of Justice.

4.7.2. *Case Law*

4.7.2.1. Quantitative Data regarding Case Law

In France, court decisions are not automatically published on the national portal, *Legifrance*, which permits access to legal texts, judgments, and other legal information.[987] Only decisions considered to be of significance for the interpretation of a specific legal matter are published on this website.[988] As well as the decision published on the *Legifrance* portal, private legal databases (such as *Dalloz, LexisNexis, Lexbase,* or *Lamy*) publish various other cases considered relevant for scholars and practitioners. Of the 21 published cases identified, only one involved an EOP claim, and it concerned the enforcement in France of an EOP issued by an Italian court, *Tribunale ordinario di Brescia*. The judgment was an appeal to the Supreme Court (*pourvoi en cassation*) initiated by legal representatives of the French company in a reorganisation procedure, requesting the court to stop and to revert the execution process of an enforceable EOP.[989] Eight of the 20 EOP cases analysed were published on the *Dalloz* and *LexisNexis* databases.[990] In addition, information on a number of EOP and ESCP cases was provided by ECC France, by legal scholars, and by practitioners. The remaining 13 cases were collected with the help of practitioners.[991] Four additional cases concern domestic orders for payment procedures and not EOPs.[992]

987 www.legifrance.gouv.fr.

988 The Documentation and Study Service of the Court of Cassation carries out the selection (Article R433-3 in conjunction with Article R433-4 Code de l'organisation judiciaire). The presidents of the Court of Appeal, and the presidents or the judges of the other courts of first instance can also communicate to this service the decisions they consider of particular interest (Article R433-3 Code de l'organisation judiciaire).

989 Cour de cassation, Chambre commerciale, 28 janvier 2014, N° de pourvoi 112-25008, ECLI:FR:CCASS: 2014: CO00116, Bulletin 2014, IV, n° 26.

990 CA Versailles, Chambre 14, 31 mars 2010, N° 09/01176; CA Grenoble, Chambre commerciale, 30 juin 2011, N° 11/01943; CA Riom, Chambre des référes, 19 septembre 2013, N° 13/00025; CA Douai, Chambre 02, Section 02, 14 mai 2013, N° 12/02093; CA Douai Chambre 02, Section 02, 14 mars 2013, N° 12/02210; CA Nîmes, 10 mai 2012, N° 11/01267.

991 CA Colmar, Chambre 3 civile, Section A, 16 décembre 2013, N° 3 A 12/00029; CA Dijon, 1re Chambre civile, 9 juin 2015, N° 14/01155; CA Riom, 1re Chambre civile, 7 avril 2014; N° 13/01233; CA Versailles, Chambre 12, 9 décembre 2014, N° 13/01145; CA Douai, Chambre 2, Section 2, Arrêt du 14 mars 2013, N° 2011/00619; TC Créteil, Chambre 2, 18 mars 2013, N° 2012F00900; TC Créteil, 1re Chambre, 28 janvier 2013, N° 2012F00683; TC Créteil, 1re Chambre, 11 février 2014, N° 2012F00518; TC Nanterre, Chambre 6, 9 novembre 2011, N° 201 1F00195; TC Nanterre, Chambre 4, 10 avril 2015, N° 2013F03851; TC Nanterre, Chambre 4, 19 décembre 2012, N° 2010F03902; TC Nanterre, Chambre 2, 23 février 2011, N° 2010F04309; TC Lille, 23 février 2012, N° 2011/00619.

992 The Paris Court of Appeal cases contain a wrongful reference to Articles 1424-4 – 1424-5 CPC. The cases concern two orders for payment issued by a Portuguese court, enforcement of which was brought in France on the provisions of the Brussels I Regulation. See CA Paris, Pôle 1, Chambre 1, 26 mai 2011, N° 10/18208; CA Paris, Pôle 1, Chambre 1, 26 mai 2011, N° 10/18209. In the case handled by the Créteil Commercial Court (TC Créteil, Chambre 2, 8 mars 2011, N° 2010F00947), the claimant chose to file the claim in accordance with the *injonction de payer* procedure instead of the EOP. The claimant company based its choice on the fact the European procedure is not mandatory. The forth case (CA Poitiers,

In a fifth case, the appeal referred not only to the domestic *injonction de payer* but also to an EOP awarded for part of the claim.[993]

As regards ESCP cases, one was included in a training module created by the Academy of European Law on behalf of DG Justice of the European Commission.[994] This was a judgment issued by JP Angers in 2010, where a consumer sought to recover money he had paid for an electrical bicycle purchased online, and which was delivered in a damaged state.[995] The other three cases were followed by ECC France, which provided assistance to consumers.

As Table 4.9 reveals, the number of EOP cases published or identified was higher than for the ESCP. This was confirmed by the available statistical data that show a higher use of the first European uniform procedure.

	2009	2010	2011	2012	2013	2014	2015
EOP decisions	–	1	3	1	5	2	1
EOP enforcement	–	1	1	1	2	2[996]	1
ESCP decisions	–	2	–	–	–	2	–
ESCP enforcement	–	–	–	–	–	–	–

Table 4.9. EOP and ESCP cases handled by French courts and identified by the researcher from various databases and sources

The EOPs represent a mix of decisions on the merits, on opposition procedures handled according to the national procedure, on enforcement activities, on the execution of EOPs within insolvency proceedings, and on requests for review. The ESCPs are all judgments on the merits. Information on the execution of two of the four ESCPs is available and will be discussed in Section 4.7.2.7.

Chambre 2 Civile, 23 février 2010, N° 08/01986) concerns an enforcement procedure initiated by a German company against a French private party. The procedure was based on an order for payment issued in Germany, which the company sought to execute in France on the basis of the EEO Regulation. Remarkably, the defendant stated in his defence that the German court was wrong in applying the national order for payment. Instead, it should have applied the EOP, which provides higher procedural guarantees for the party. However, the EOP procedure was not applicable when proceedings were initiated against the French citizen, and the defendant was served with the order in accordance with the applicable rules.

993 CA Versailles, Chambre 14, 31 mars 2010, N° 09/01176.

994 Academy of European Law, *Training module on the European Small Claims Procedure. Guide to the training module*, No. JUST/2012/JCIV/FW/0163/A4 implementing Framework Contract JUST/2010/JCIV/PR/0016/A4, at 139 (available at www.era-comm.eu/EU_Civil_Justice_Training_Modules/kiosk/pdf/EN_small.pdf).

995 Juridiction de proximité Angers, 6 Décembre 2010 N° 91.10–438, Vielle Société By Lifestyle 4 U Gmbh (not published).

996 One of the decisions is a second appeal, *pourvoi*, on a Court of appeal decision related to enforcement of a debt in an insolvency procedure.

4.7.2.2. Case Classification

EOP cases are commercial ones handled by the TCs, or are appeals trialed by the Courts of Appeal, following a transfer of the claim to the national ordinary procedure or challenges of enforcement activities. With one exception, they are all B2B cases.[997] The exception is a B2C case involving the execution in France of an EOP issued by a German court.[998] In one of the B2B cases, a French professional mentions seeking to obtain an EOP, while at the same time pursuing a *référé* to recover fees related to services carried out for the debtor.[999] In another case, the French Court of Appeal decided to stay proceedings due to the close link between a *référé* and an opposed EOP continuing in accordance with the Italian ordinary procedure.[1000] Some cases have repeated players (3 cases). One of these cases regards enforcement activities to be undertaken in France on the basis of an EOP issued by a German court.[1001] There are also cases in which the creditor is a repeated player (a French creditor seeking to obtain payment of his debt from a German and a Belgium company, both of which opposed the EOPs). In most B2B cases, the French companies are debtors of foreign legal entities (i.e. Belgium, Germany, Italy, Poland, Spain, and the United Kingdom). The creditors decided to file EOP claims to recover their debt.

ESCPs were handled by the TI or the JP,[1002] and were all C2B claims. In all but one case, the consumers were French consumers who had ordered a product on the internet from a seller in a neighbouring Member State (i.e. Germany, Belgium). In one case, the claimant was a Belgian consumer who had ordered fishing products from the website of a French company.

As regards the type of cases, the EOP has been used for the recovery of debts resulting from unpaid invoices for services agreements (6 cases),[1003] sale-purchase agreements (3 cases), a distribution agreement (1 case), and a rental agreement (1 case). In addition to these, there are situations in which the agreement included the combination of a sale-purchase agreement and another agreement: namely, maintenance services (2 cases) or a lease agreement (1 case). As to the ESCP, all claims regarded sale-purchase agreements

997 CA Dijon, 1re Chambre civile, 9 juin 2015, N° 14/01155; CA Riom, 1re Chambre civile, 7 avril 2014; N° 13/01233; CA Versailles, Chambre 12, 9 décembre 2014, N° 13/01145; CA Douai Chambre 02, Section 02, 14 mars 2013, N° 12/02210; CA Douai, Chambre 02, Section 02, 14 mai 2013, N° 12/02093; CA Grenoble, Chambre commerciale, 30 juin 2011, N° 11/01943; CA Nîmes, 10 mai 2012, N° 11/01267; CA Riom, Chambre des référes, 19 septembre 2013, N° 13/00025; CA Versailles, Chambre 14, 31 mars 2010, N° 09/01176; TC Créteil, Chambre 2, 18 mars 2013, N° 2012F00900; TC Créteil, 1re Chambre, 28 janvier 2013, N° 2012F00683; TC Créteil, 1re Chambre, 11 février 2014, N° 2012F00518; TC Nanterre, Chambre 6, 9 novembre 2011, N° 201 1F00195; TC Nanterre, Chambre 4, 10 avril 2015, N° 2013F03851; TC Nanterre, Chambre 4, 19 décembre 2012, N° 2010F03902; TC Nanterre, Chambre 2, 23 février 2011, N° 2010F04309.

998 CA Colmar, Chambre 3 civile, Section A, 16 décembre 2013, N° 3 A 12/00029.

999 CA Versailles, Chambre 14, 31 mars 2010, N° 09/01176.

1000 CA Grenoble, Chambre commerciale, 30 juin 2011, N° 11/01943.

1001 CA Riom, 1re Chambre civile, 7 avril 2014.

1002 The activity of the *Juridictions de proximité* has been prolonged by Article 99 Law No. 2014–1654 of 29 December 2014 until 1 January 2017.

1003 Including invoices for legal services.

concluded on the internet (4 cases), where the products were not delivered (1 case) or partially not delivered (1 case), were delivered in a damaged state (1 case), or were a combination of missing, damaged, and different products the consumer did not order (1 case).

4.7.2.3. Conduct of Proceedings

All EOPs analysed were proceedings following opposition or actions contesting enforcement activities, while the ESCP cases were all decisions on the merits. In one ESCP case, the judge issued the judgment only on the basis of the evidence and allegation provided by the claimant. The defendant failed to reply to the court, not sending back the Form C that had been sent to him, or giving any other type of answer.

Complete information on the length of the proceedings is available in only four cases. According to this, the period necessary for the delivery of an EOP (Form E) varies between 21 days and 2 months and 8 days following registration of the application (Form A), with an average duration of approx. 1.5 months. This is in line with statistical data from the Ministry of Justice (Table 4.3). As regards the ESCP, information on the duration of court proceedings is available in only one of the four cases. The court took 2 months and 12 days to deliver a judgment. The result matches data in the national statistics for the same period, 2010 (Table 4.8). For both European procedures, available case law shows a speedy treatment of the applications by French courts.

In none of the analysed cases has the judge rejected an application for an EOP or an ESCP. However, in one case the TC judge appears to have rejected the opposition filed against an EOP as being ill-founded (*mal fondé*).[1004] The reasons for this peculiar decision are not clear, but it certainly shows some deficiencies in the judge's understanding and application of the European procedure. Subsequently, the Court of Appeal upheld the first judgment, as the defendant was not contesting existence of the debt.

The EOP cases provide no information as to the use of EOP Forms B or C. Of the eight EOP issued by the French TCs only one was not opposed. The defendant usually filed the opposition within a short period after being served with the EOP. It is presumed Form F of the Regulation was used for this purpose, but the decisions do not always contain specific information in this regard. Following opposition, the clerk proceeded to summon the parties to a hearing, and the case continued in accordance with the national ordinary procedure. In three of the nine opposed EOP cases, the defendant did not take part in the proceedings, nor did he submit a written statement to the court. The judge proceeded to issue a judgment on the basis of the submissions and evidence put forward by the claimant and his representative.[1005]

[1004] CA Douai, Chambre 02, Section 02, 14 mai 2013, N° 12/02093.

[1005] TC Nanterre, Chambre 2, 23 février 2011, N° 2010F04309; TC Nanterre, Chambre 6, 9 novembre 2011, N° 2011F00195; TC Crétail, Chambre 1, 28 janvier 2013, N° 2012F00683.

EOP	No. of cases identified in the found case law
EOP issued (Form E)	9
Opposition and passage to the ordinary procedure	8
Contesting execution EOP	4
Seeking execution of EOP in insolvency proceedings	4
Review	2
National order for payment instead of EOP	5
ESCP	
ESCP judgment	3
ESCP treated as a national procedure	1
Enforcement ESCP	2[1006]

Table 4.10. Information on the EOP and ESCP awards and their execution according to case law

Following opposition or challenging of an enforcement, the proceedings involved a court hearing or a debate before a judge who was preparing the case for the deliberation phase.[1007] This was carried out in accordance with the CPC rules regarding application of the European uniform procedures and the supplementing domestic rules. French proceedings rely to a large extent on oral hearings and debates between the parties. In one ESCP case, the *juge de proximité* decided to hold a hearing, and summoned the Belgian consumer to court. However, the party had not requested it, and the court offered no explanation as to why a hearing was considered necessary. The judge actually treated the ESCP application as a national *déclaration au greffe*,[1008] revealing a certain lack of understanding and familiarity with the ESCP, and a tendency to transplant characteristics of a well-known domestic proceeding to the European procedure.

A review was requested in two EOP cases. In one situation, the review was invoked in a subsidiary motion to an opposition that the clerk had not properly registered. The opposition was rejected by the court, and the clerk wrongly issued Form G, declaring the EOP enforceable.[1009] In appeal, the court put aside the first judgment. The judge did not address the review request, but proceeded from the perspective of the opposition, which had been submitted previously to the lower court. The case gives no indication as to the legal basis for requesting the court to review the EOP, or the reasoning of the first instance judge on rejecting the opposition. The Court of Appeal approach and interpretation of the national legislation is in line with the CJEU in the *eco cosmetics* interpretation: namely, that a national mechanism should allow the defendant to raise the irregularity

1006 Information on the execution activities undertaken for ESCP judgments was provided by the ECC for 2 cases it had followed.

1007 For the issuance of the EOP (Form E) by the French courts, there is no indication that hearings are generally organised for this purpose.

1008 On the *déclaration au greffe*, see Sections 4.2 and 4.3 above.

1009 CA Douai Chambre 02, Section 02, 14 mars 2013, N° 12/02210.

of the title if the EOP does not provide a tool for putting aside a wrongly issued Form G. The second case represents an interesting application of the review mechanism. The defendant based his request on the fact that he had never undertaken commercial transactions with the creditor company.[1010] As in the first situation, the case provides no information regarding the legal grounds the party relied on for the judge to accept the request, nor the provisions on which the court based its reasoning in declaring the EOP null and void. The case highlights some flaws in the way the review mechanism was understood by the court. This could be the result of confusion between the review mechanism set by the EOP and the domestic review mechanism, as the term used for both institutions is the same: '*réexamen*'. The parties did not make use of the review in any of the ESCP cases analysed.

Information on the issuance of Form G by French courts concerns only the two EOP cases that were subject to a review request. In all the other circumstances, Form G was issued by courts in other Member States, and was used for the execution of EOPs in France. For the ESCP, the data available suggest that form D was delivered to the creditor in two of the four cases.

The EOP as well as the ESCP cases give no indication of particular difficulties regarding the filling in of the claim form or the need for translation. For the EOP, the general use of legal representation by the parties may have contributed to this outcome. As regards the ESCP, ECC France offered assistance to consumers and helped them communicate constructively with courts when these parties were less familiar with the procedure.

In some cases, the French courts proceeded to particular awards. This was the case of a French Court of Appeal that declared the EOP issued by the commercial court (TC) null on the basis of the provisions of the CPC.[1011] Another EOP application was filed by a company in liquidation proceedings. According to the law, it no longer had the capacity to appear in court. Instead, the officer who was nominated to liquidate the legal entity within the insolvency proceedings could have initiated the claim. Because the regularisation by the liquidator was not sufficient to cover the invoked nullity, the EOP was declared null in an appeal proceeding, due to non-compliance with the provisions of French law. The court did not include any reference to the EOP Regulation in its reasoning, or to its requirements. An opposition should have been sufficient to prevent the title from becoming enforceable, but instead the EOP was handled as a domestic award to be challenged by appeal. This indicates a limited understanding and familiarity with the EOP by some courts and practitioners alike, even several years after the Regulation's entrance into force.

4.7.2.4. Representation of the Parties

In the cases analysed, parties in the EOP proceedings were usually represented by a lawyer, while in the ESCP claims they appeared in person. Although representation was not

[1010] TC Créteil, Chambre 2, 18 mars 2013, N° 2012F00900.
[1011] CA Versailles, Chambre 12, 9 décembre 2014, N° 13/01145.

compulsory, this choice could have been influenced by various characteristics of the cases, such as the type of parties (i.e. mostly legal entities), the stage of the proceedings (i.e. transfer of the proceedings to the national ordinary procedure following opposition, appellate proceedings, contesting execution measures), and the court handling the case.[1012]

Additionally, using the services of a local lawyer appears to have been the easiest choice for legal entities, especially as some were registered in other Member States, and were probably not very familiar with the French legal system. With few exceptions, all EOP parties were legal entities undertaking commercial activities with French counterparties. In the EOPs analysed, a non-represented party coincided with the party not actually participating in the proceedings following an opposition or review request.

Representation	No. of EOP cases	No. of ESCP cases
Creditor	2	–
Debtor	1	–
Both parties	13	–
Represented by lawyers in various jurisdictions	2	–
Representation only by a lawyer from a foreign jurisdiction	1	–
Lawyers as creditors	1	–

Table 4.11. Representation of the parties by lawyers in EOP and ESCP cases

In a few cases, representatives of the parties were repeated players, but this was often related to the fact they were representing a repeated player they had assisted in previous disputes.

4.7.2.5. Amounts and Costs Claimed

The EOP claims varied from €971.04 to €188,866.57, excluding costs. In most cases, interest was also awarded from a specific date until repayment of the debt. However, the amount of interest was not always expressly stated, as the amount depends on the period of time the interest continues to accumulate until payment of the principle has been completed. Costs of the legal proceedings were in most cases awarded by the French courts, including expenses incurred by the parties for the case, and they varied from the fees due for registration of a claim with a commercial court (€38.87) to other accessory expenses and costs (up to €3,500). In two cases, the award contained contractual penalties (€145.65 and €3,421.28).[1013]

1012 Representation is compulsory before the Court of Appeal, but optional before the TI and TC.

1013 TC Nanterre, Chambre 6, 9 novembre 2011, N° 201 1F00195; TC Nanterre, Chambre 2, 23 février 2011, N° 2010F04309.

The ESCP claims varied from €35€ to €1,800. In one case, the court awarded the consumer not only the principle amount (€469) but also ordered the company to pay legal interest and to bear the costs of the proceedings.

4.7.2.6. Service and Language Aspects

Service carried out in the EOP procedure concerned communication of the order to the defendant or of the enforceable title prior to initiating execution proceedings. In most circumstances, when service was carried out in France, the services of a bailiff were employed, which is in line with the national service practice. The EOP was served on the defendant himself or on his legal representative. Service by registered letter was occasionally used as well. In two cases it is not clear which service methods provided by the EOP Regulation were actually used. The judicial decision only mentions that the EOP was served by depositing it at the office of the company (e.g. *acte d'huissier de justice déposé à l'étude* or *signifiée par dépôt en l'étude*). It is possible the bailiff left a notification requesting the defendant to collect the documents from his office. Further, it is not clear what information was provided to the defendant in the notification or whether the method can be considered an equivalent to any of the ten means provided by the Regulation.[1014]

The use of translated documents for service is seldom mentioned in EOP cases. In one instance, it is mentioned that the EOP was served in German in France, and the defendant signed the documents in German, attesting that he had received them. It appears the party was familiar with the language and aware of the documents he had been served with. Furthermore, for enforcement purposes, France had notified the European Commission that it would accept Form G in German. In another case, however, the opposition form sent in a different language created serious problems for the defendant. The court did not register the opposition (Form F) sent in German.[1015] The outcome is even more staggering, as the court issued Form G declaring the EOP enforceable. The French clerk did not seem to recognise Form F or to consider it sufficient proof of the intention of the defendant. The use of a standard form, and especially of Form F, which contains only standard text, should not impede a local judge or clerk from registering an opposition, as a parallel reading of the forms in the two languages would be possible without much difficulty. In a final case containing information on language matters, translated documents were used for serving the EOP in France and, subsequently, for enforcement purposes.

One ESCP case offers information on the language and translation aspects. The consumer had to provide the bailiff in Germany with a translation of Form D in German in order to proceed to execution of the judgment and to inform the defendant of the enforceable title issued against him.[1016] For this purpose, the bailiff informed the consumer that he could himself contact an official translator or, alternatively, the bailiff could take care of it for an additional fee of €300. The amount claimed by the professional

1014 Such as for example Article 14(1)(d) EOP.

1015 TC Lille, 23 février 2012, N° 2011/00619.

1016 Article 21(2)(b) ESCP.

almost matched the value of the debt the consumer sought to recover (€367), and was highly disproportionate in relation to the claim.

In general, the EOPs analysed contain a reference as to how the order was served, or indicate that the court had checked the information related to service. This is of particular importance as well for safeguarding parties' procedural rights. A remarkable interpretation was offered by an enforcement judge in a claim related to the enforcement in France of an EOP issued by a court in a different Member State. The judge proceeded to analyse the way in which the EOP had previously been served on the defendant, the information the defendant had received, and whether the provisions of Articles 1424–5 and 1424–6 CPC on requirements for the service of the EOP in France had been complied with.[1017] Further, the interpretation underlines the fact that the defendant had not been informed of the court having competence to receive the opposition in the event he should decide to oppose the order. The court proceeded by declaring the service null, due to the fact that the bailiff had not provided the defendant with the information set by Article 1424–6 CPC. It is worth emphasising that the court did not refer at any point to the requirements set by Articles 12(3) and 16 EOP, but only tested the service against the national rules adopted for the Regulation's application. The court concluded that the lack of information resulted in damages to the debtor, which should allow the party to request a review with the court of the Member State of origin. Although protective of the defendant's procedural rights, the action of the French court is surprising, as it proceeds to analyse matters the debtor should have raised before the court of origin, as well as reviewing the decision of a court in another Member State, an action prohibited under Article 22(3) EOP. Moreover, the French judge cannot instruct a court in a different Member State on a possible review action to be filed with the latter. The Court of Appeal rightfully rejected this interpretation,[1018] as the safeguard of procedural rights should not be based on actions breaching express legal provisions and legal security.

4.7.2.7. Enforcement

All eight cases on involving enforcement of EOP decisions in France are actions that oppose execution of the title. The creditors sought to attach their debtors' accounts or movable assets in order to recover their debt. In response, the debtors tried to contest (1) the validity of the EOP title; (2) the competence of the court involved in the execution procedure; (3) the nullity of the execution measures; or (4) sought to obtain suspension of the execution. The courts rejected the debtor defence in three of the seven cases. In one case, the enforcement judge proceeded to review the EOP decision of the court in a different Member State.[1019]

In three cases, execution took place within the debtors' insolvency and reorganisation proceedings. In two of these three cases, the same entities were involved and the action concerned the same enforceable EOP. In each situation, the creditors had not registered as such in the insolvency proceedings of the French legal entity. Hence, the French court

[1017] TI de Chalon sur Saône, G 1ère instance 11 13–868, 10 juin 2014.

[1018] CA Dijon, 1re Chambre civile, 9 juin 2015, N° 14/01155.

[1019] TI de Chalon sur Saône, G 1ère instance 11 13–868, 10 juin 2014. See also Section 4.7.2.6 above.

could not validate attachment of the debtor's accounts in one case, while in the other case the creditor was requested to return the amount he had been paid in breach of rules regarding reorganisation proceedings.

Information as to the enforcement of ESCP judgments is available for two cases. In one case, the creditor was able to partially recover the award due from an insolvent debtor company, while for the other case, the enforcement activities were still ongoing. The consumer had to translate Form D in order to be able to initiate execution of the French judgment in another Member State.

4.7.2.8. Influence of the National Procedure

As the analyses of European uniform procedures have revealed, some courts have the tendency to interpret them from the perspective of a national procedure. They either test compliance with the requirements of the procedure against the provisions of the CPC or exchange them for national ones, or even possibly swap European procedure mechanisms for familiar domestic ones.

The number of cases is not extensive, and is limited to a certain typology. This narrows the conclusions that can be drawn in relation to the practice of French courts and practitioners. Nonetheless, valuable insights have been gained into application of the European procedures in France. The courts of appeal proved to have a better understanding of the EOP procedure, rightfully overturning decisions of the commercial courts.

Finally, the outcome of some EOP and ESCP cases shows there is a great need to provide information and training to the judiciary and legal practitioners. The European procedures are not always well known and understood, even several years after their entry into force.

4.7.3. EOP and ESCP Procedures: Empirical Findings

4.7.3.1. Preliminary Aspects regarding Data Collection

The data analysed in this section were collected through surveys, interviews, and correspondence with French practitioners and the ECC France office. Together with this, the findings of the study carried out by the ECC office were included in the analysis as part of that organisation's views.[1020] The study was carried out between September 2010 and April 2011, and concerns 18 consumers the organisation followed and assisted in their use of the EOP or the ESCP for recovering their cross-border claims.

In order to conduct the research with French courts and practitioners, several requests for assistance were sent first to national branches of professional organisations. These included the National School for the Judiciary (*École Nationale de la Magistrature, ENM*), the National Association of Small Claim Judges (*Association Nationale des Juges*

[1020] Centre Européen de la Consommation, Zentrum für Europäischen Verbraucherschutz e.V., Procédure de règlement des petits litiges et injonction de payer européenne. Des procédures simplifiées pas si simples dans la pratique, July 2011 (available at www.cec-zev.eu/fileadmin/user_upload/cec-zev/PDF/documentation/etudes/Procedure_reglement_petits_litiges.pdf).

de Proximité), the National Association of District Court Judges (*Association Nationale des Juges d'Instance*), the National Council of Commercial Courts Clerks (*Conseil National des Greffiers des Tribunaux de Commerce*), the National Council of Bar Associations (*Conseil National des Barreaux, CNB*), the Delegation of French Bar Associations (*Délégation des Barreaux de France, DBF*), the Association of Lawyers specialising in Procedure and Enforcement (*Association des Avocats Praticiens des Procedures et de l'Exécution, AAPPE*), and the National Chamber of Bailiffs (*Chambre Nationale des Huissiers de Justice*). The *Conseil National des Greffiers des Tribunaux de Commerce* and the *Délégation des Barreaux de France* agreed to make the research visible to their members.[1021] The *Conseil National des Greffiers des Tribunaux de Commerce* forwarded to the researcher the replies and the feedback it received.[1022] The *Association des Avocats Praticiens des Procedures et de l'Exécution*, while positive about the possibility of informing its members of the research being conducted, did not provide any follow-up information on the communication to its members or on replies. As well as national professional organisations, a number of courts, bar associations, and orders of bailiffs were subsequently contacted regarding assistance and making the research visible to their members.[1023] For courts, the selection included courts in large cities that are important commercial centres or popular tourist destinations, or are situated in the proximity of border regions.[1024] When contacted, courts situated near central inland administrative units often declared they had not received any or only a few EOP or ESCP requests. Additional responses by French judges and clerks were collected at a training conference on civil and commercial judicial cooperation organised by the Romanian National Institute for Magistracy.[1025] An invitation was also sent to 47 Bar Associations.[1026] In addition to this, individual requests were sent to 47 lawyers that had represented parties in EOP cases handled by French courts.[1027] Three legal officers from the Chamber of Commerce and Industry (*Chambre de Commerce et Industrie, CCI*) were also invited to share their experiences.[1028] Invitations to participate in the research were sent by

[1021] For this purpose the *Délégation des Barreaux de France* published a notice on its Weekly Newsletter, inviting French lawyers who applied the EOP and/or the ESCP to share their experiences and views on the instruments. *L'Europe en Bref*, Lettre hebdomadaire d'informations juridiques de la Délégation des Barreaux de France, No. 754/8–22 October 2015, at 13.

[1022] Fifteen TC clerks replied (8 replies to the EOP survey, 2 replies to the ESCP survey, and 7 brief comments regarding the TCs lack of or limited experience with the European uniform procedures).

[1023] A number of 57 *Tribunaux d'instances*, 47 *Tribunaux de commerce* and 3 *Tribunaux de grande instance* were contacted by telephone and in writing in order to request their participation in the researchs.

[1024] This resulted in 10 EOP surveys replies, 7 ESCP survey replies, and 1 interview. Several invitees declined to participate in the research, or to provide written feedback on the lack of or limited experience with the European procedures.

[1025] Four EOP survey replies and 3 ESCP survey replies. *Practical exercises in implementing the judicial cooperation instruments in civil and commercial matters*, Final Conference, 20–21 November 2014, Bucharest, Romania.

[1026] 6–12 February 2015.

[1027] This resulted in an overall number of 5 EOP survey replies, 1 ESCP survey reply, 1 lawyer taking part in an interview, and several others sharing their opinions in writing.

[1028] Two replied to the EOP survey, 1 to the ESCP survey, and one of them agreed to be interviewed regarding the EOP procedure.

email to the presidents of seven Regional Chambers of Bailiffs (*Chambres Régionales des Huissiers de Justice*), and 21 County Chambers (*Chambres Départementales*) for which the contact details were available online.[1029] Further individual requests were sent to seven bailiffs' offices, one of which forwarded the invitation to another 111 bailiffs.[1030, 1031] To increase the study's visibility and to reach other practitioners, a request for assistance was sent to five university professors who had expertise in this area or had previously conducted research with French practitioners. Finally, an invitation to take part in this research was published on a dedicated private international law website.[1032]

This resulted in an overall number of 33 EOP survey responses,[1033] 16 ESCP survey responses,[1034] three interviews[1035] and a significant volume of punctual feedback and correspondence from French practitioners.[1036]

4.7.3.2. Familiarity with European Procedures and Handling Practices

The survey results show a significant difference in familiarity regarding the two European procedures. More than 70% of the EOP respondents rate their familiarity above level 3 (Fig. 4.2), while only 38% of the ESCP respondents have the same perception (Fig. 4.3). The ESCP respondents appear to be less familiar with the procedure. This is possibly because it is rarely used, as revealed by official statistics and survey data. Limited use of the ESCP was also mentioned in an earlier study carried out by the Trans European Expert Association.[1037] The high rate of respondents declaring themselves to be unaware of the ESCP procedure (31%) should be an alarm signal for professional organisations, and lead to activities and training to familiarise them with the instrument they are called to apply. This is confirmed also by an earlier study by the Trans European Expert Association.[1038] Practitioners will not be able to properly apply a procedure of which they have little knowledge, let alone apply it in view of the objectives it aims to achieve. Potential ESCP users are also not highly aware of its existence, as was revealed by an Eurobarometer study involving 87% of the respondents.[1039]

1029 During April and May 2014.
1030 During September and October 2014.
1031 This resulted in 3 EOP survey responses, 2 ESCP survey responses, and some additional feedback by other bailiffs on their lack of or limited experience.
1032 On 19 July 2015. See http://conflictoflaws.net/2015/surveys-on-european-order-for-payment-and-small-claims-procedures/.
1033 Survey responses were provided from 22 judges and clerks, 5 lawyers, 2 legal advisers, and 3 bailiffs.
1034 Survey responses were provided by 12 judges and clerks, 1 lawyer, 1 legal adviser, and 2 bailiffs.
1035 Interviews were conducted with 1 court, 1 lawyer, and 1 legal adviser who agreed to a discussion on the European procedures.
1036 A significant number of contacted courts, lawyers, and bailiffs declined to take part in the study due to their lack of experience, or because they considered they could not make a significant contribution due to limited practical experience.
1037 In fact, the French experts consider the ESCP, as well as the EOP, to comprise 5% of the court claims, though the EOP appears to be much better known and applied. Fauvarque-Cosson & Behar-Touchais (2012), at 154 and 166–167.
1038 Fauvarque-Cosson & Behar-Touchais, (2012), at 349–350.
1039 Special Eurobarometer 395, *European Small Claims Procedure*, 2013, at 69.

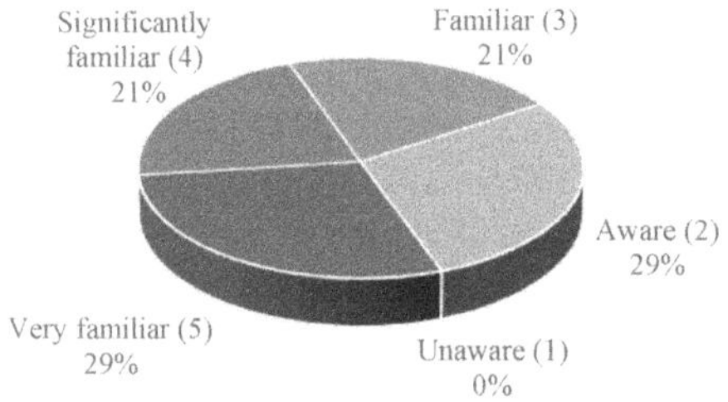

Fig. 4.2. Professionals' perception of their familiarity with the EOP (26 responses)

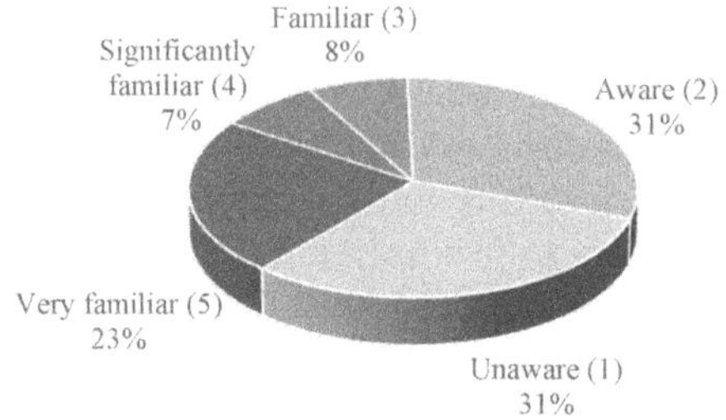

Fig. 4.3. Professionals' perception of their familiarity with the ESCP (13 responses)

In general, EOP and ESCP respondents who rate their knowledge at about level 3 have applied the procedure at least once.[1040] Only in a few situations did repeated users rate their knowledge at awareness level 2, owing to having had the opportunity to apply the procedures several times.[1041] The reasons for this difference are not completely clear. No significant difference with regard to the level of declared personal knowledge is registered among the various professions groups. The high level of familiarity is not necessarily due to training sessions, although professionals who attended training programmes were more likely to reply that they were 'Very familiar' with the instruments (75% of EOP respondents and 100% of ESCP respondents who indicated they had participated in a dedicated training course, workshops, or information session).[1042] For respondents who had never attended a training or information session, their practical experience contributed to their familiarity with the European uniform procedures. This appears to be more often the case in relation to the ESCP, while for the EOP the relation is less clear. A limited number of respondents indicated they had never had the opportunity to apply either of the procedures.[1043] This does appear to be connected to a lower level of familiarity with them. Additional research would be necessary to better understand the link between practical experience and a higher perception of familiarity, as well as the influence the experience has on the perception.

As regards perception of general awareness of the procedures, the results point in general to a lower level of familiarity in comparison to respondents' own personal knowledge (Figs. 4.4–4.5). In only a few cases did respondents rate their own personal knowledge below that of the general awareness level.[1044] The reasons for this are not clear, nor can it be linked to a lack of practical experience, as the majority of the practitioners had the opportunity to apply the procedures several times. The perception of the general level of awareness is to some extent higher for the EOP. Only 3% of the

1040 The number of cases handled is significantly higher for the EOP procedure.
1041 This is the case for 3 EOP survey respondents and 1 ESCP survey respondent.
1042 Six of 8 EOP survey respondents indicated they had followed some form of training; two ESCP survey respondents.
1043 One EOP survey respondent and 3 ESCP survey respondents.
1044 There are 4 EOP survey respondents and 3 ESCP survey respondents in this situation.

respondents consider other practitioners to be 'Unaware' of the EOP, while for the ESCP the percentage is eight times higher. ECC France pointed also to certain deficiencies in the potential users' awareness of the procedures and to the limited knowledge that courts have at times regarding how the Regulations' provisions should be applied. These aspects were confirmed by subsequent findings of the Trans European Expert Group study.[1045] Along with the possible personal knowledge factor, the more limited use of the ESCP in practice certainly contributes to this outcome.

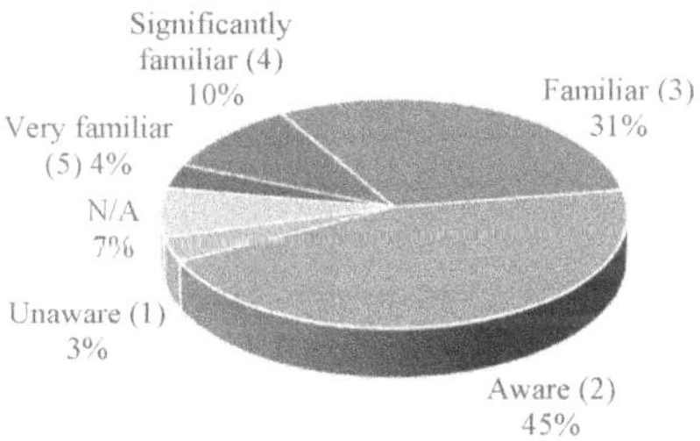

Fig. 4.4. Professionals' perception of general EOP awareness (29 responses)

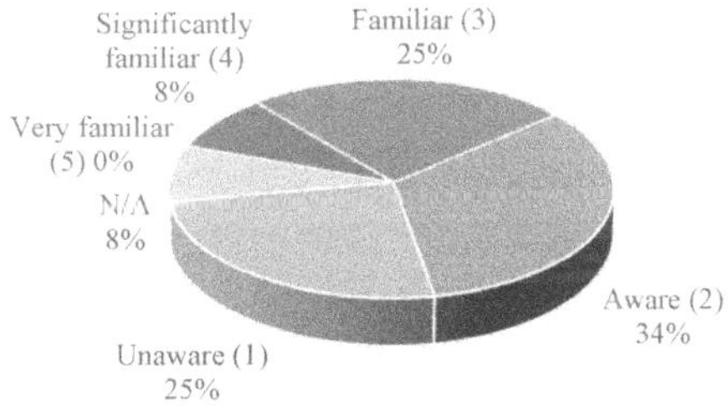

Fig. 4.5. Professionals' perception of general ESCP awareness (12 responses)

Practitioners' limited knowledge can also be due to inadequate training or a complete lack of training. Further, this influences the way in which EOP and ESCP claims are handled, and might in part explain the additional requirements some judges set in relation to these instruments. In such cases, the European procedures are handled in a manner that is similar to domestic ordinary or special procedures (*injonction de payer* or *déclaration au greffe*).[1046] French courts and practitioners are aware that the EOP and the ESCP exist, but the manner in which they should be applied is not always clear, or it is influenced by requirements relating to more familiar procedures.

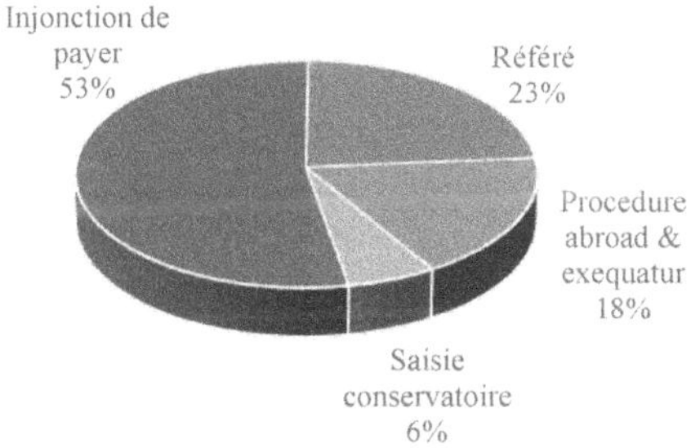

Fig. 4.6. National procedures chosen over the EOP (11 responses)

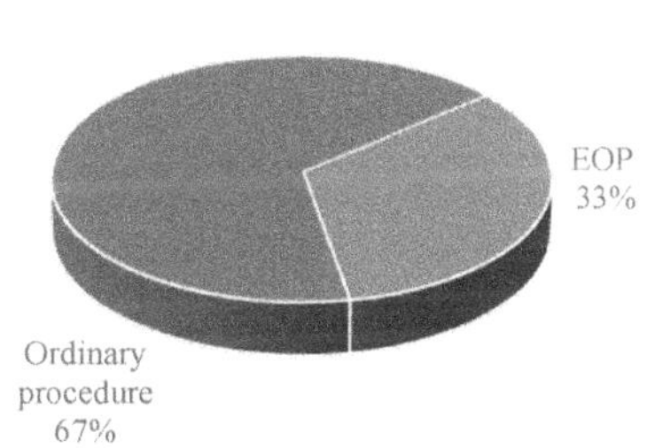

Fig. 4.7. National procedures chosen over the ESCP (3 responses)

1045 Fauvarque-Cosson & Behar-Touchais (2012), at 438 and 455–456.

1046 See further Section 4.7.3.4.

Some of the practitioners responding to the EOP survey (39.28%) and to a lesser extent the ESCP survey (27.27%) indicated that certain national procedures are preferred by parties in seeking to recover cross-border debts (Figs. 4.6–4.7).[1047] The *injonction de payer* and the *référé* appear in particular to be preferred over the EOP, while the ordinary national procedure before the *juge de proximité* is most often used in the case of small value claims, due to its simplified submission procedure (*déclaration au greffe*). According to respondents, the reasons for this are the greater familiarity with these domestic instruments or the fact that interested parties ignore the existence of the EOP and/or ESCP. Additionally, in relation to the EOP, some respondents indicated that foreign lawyers prefer to employ the services of a French lawyer or bailiff to initiate a domestic procedure in France, rather than make use of the EOP even though this would involve fewer costs in a cross-border dispute. Although general information regarding the European procedures is made available by national administration service[1048] and by some courts' websites (e.g. Tribunal de commerce Paris),[1049] it is available only in French. Hence, foreign parties who do not understand French would have difficulty in finding and using the information. Additionally, some of the information can be to a certain extent deceiving, such as indicating that French courts receive claim forms or other forms in languages other than French, the language of the proceedings.[1050] Case law and empirical findings show that forms sent in other languages might have 'fatal' consequences for the defendant.[1051] For the future, the information offered to potential users should be considered more carefully and fully mirror the reality of French practice. This has the potential of encouraging parties to make use of these instruments in cross-border litigation.

Finally, better training of the courts and practitioners would be highly beneficial, and improve the way EOP and ESCP claims are handled.

4.7.3.3. Case Classification

The information available is limited, and prevents a generalisation of the results. However, according to respondents' replies, the EOP is usually employed in B2B cases

1047 Of the respondents, 7.14% indicated there is no other national alternative procedure preferred over the EOP, while 53.57% declared they did not know. For the ESCP, 72.72% of the respondents replied they did not know whether a national procedure is preferred.

1048 See for example for the EOP, the information available at www.service-public.fr/professionnels-entreprises/vosdroits/F32082.

1049 See www.greffe-tc-paris.fr/fr/fond-referes-requetes/injonction_payer_europeenne.html.

1050 For example, information on the website of the TC Paris mentions that Form A can be submitted in any of the languages that French authorities communicated the European Commission it accepts for enforcement purposes: 'Vous souhaitez engager une procédure d'IPE devant le tribunal de commerce de Paris
I. Demande
1° Remplir le formulaire A de demande (les langues acceptées sont le français, l'anglais, l'allemand, l'italien, l'espagnol).' However, the case law analysed does not provide an indication of French courts treating applications received in languages other than French (on the consequences of using a foreign language, see Section 4.7.2.6).

1051 CA Douai Chambre 02, Section 02, 14 mars 2013, N° 12/02210. See Sections 4.7.2.6 and 4.7.3.4.

and, occasionally, in B2C or C2B cases, while the ESCP appears to be most often used in C2B cases. The data available show that EOP claims often involve a foreign entity from a neighbouring Member State, and occasionally a repeat player seeking to obtain payment for his services. For the ESCP, it is often the case of a French consumer seeking to obtain reimbursement from a company in a different Member State. As indicated in available case law, the transactions are often concluded online by the parties, and involve the transmission of defective goods.

According to respondents, the amounts that creditors seek to recuperate are not very high. The EOP is usually used in claims amounting to thousands of euros,[1052] while the ESCP concerns debts involving hundreds.

As regards the type of contractual relationship upon which the claims are based, the surveys and additional data provide a broader perspective and confirm the results of the case law analysis. Both the EOP and the ESCP are most often used for claims related to sale-purchase or service agreements. Additionally, the EOP also concerns loan agreements, tenancy agreements, and financial contract claims, while the ESCP is occasionally used in lease agreement (i.e. cars) claims.

4.7.3.4 Conduct of Proceedings and Encountered Difficulties

Handling of Cases

The empirical data point to the very active involvement of court clerks in the handling of EOP and ESCP cases (Fig. 4.8). However, both clerks and judges providing feedback on the division of tasks have a tendency to point to a more active role having been played by members of their own profession. Lawyers and legal advisers appreciate the clerks' more active role in handling the forms (levels 2 and 3). This might be because clerks are in charge of administrative tasks (registering tasks, verifying whether the application contains all the necessary information, releasing the forms, contacting the representatives for communication purposes or for additional information). Following registration, the clerk transfers the case file to the judge, provides him with the necessary forms, signs the forms together with the judge, and receives the opposition. Additionally, some respondents indicated that clerks are responsible for filling in the forms, which they subsequently submit for validation to the judge handling the case. The judge then proceeds to assess the merits of the application and to issue the decision.

Further, TC clerks appear to have a more active involvement in the handling of EOP forms, which might be related to the way TC activity is organised in France. The clerks seem to take care of all aspects of the procedure, and only require validation of the order by the judge in charge or by the president of the court. In relation to EOP handling, two respondents remarked that this is done in a manner similar to the domestic *injonction de payer*. During an interview with court clerks, it became clear that allocation of the

[1052] The most detailed information was provided by the TC Paris, which registered claims ranging from €391 to €399.661 (with an average of €38.265). All other respondents indicated lower maximum limits for the claims they had handled.

European uniform procedures to judges is not necessarily subject to a predetermined internal rotation system or limited to particular designated judges. The European procedures claims are allocated to judges who, based on their work charges, are able to handle the case in accordance with the procedural timeframe set by the Regulation. Although it could not be verified whether other French courts have the same internal mechanism of case allocation, such a system could create an opportunity for judges to handle a higher number of EOPs and/or ESCPs. Moreover, the clerks handling the domestic order for payments would most likely be in charge of the European instruments. This provides the possibility of maintaining efficient registration of the cases they receive and of establishing a working practice when it comes to administrative and notification tasks.

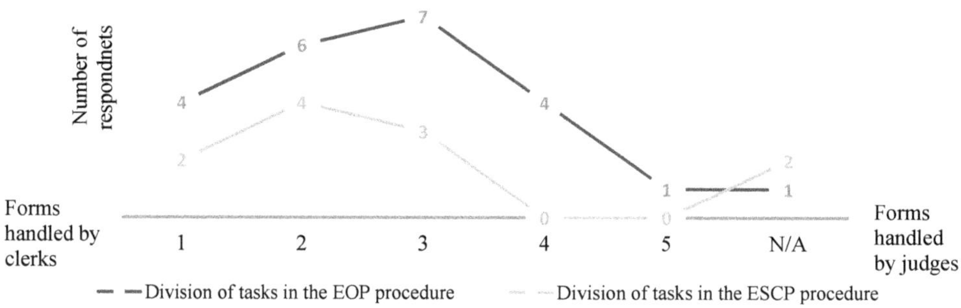

Fig. 4.8. Division of tasks between judges and clerks in the handling of EOP and ESCP forms (survey results)

As regards possible tensions at the level of coordination between French procedural rules and the European uniform procedures, a significant number of respondents indicated that they had encountered no difficulties or problematic aspects affecting application (Figs. 4.9–4.10). This might be a consequence of the provisions added to the CPC on application of the EOP and the ESCP and the dedicated guidelines. The two most problematic aspects perceived by the respondents in practice are (1) the rules on the competence of the courts in accordance with Brussels I, now Brussels I*bis* Regulation; and (2) the relation between the EOP and the ESCP service of documents rules and the domestic rules on service by a bailiff. Respondents indicated that the clerks are sometimes not well informed with regard to the jurisdiction rules of the Brussels I*bis* Regulation, and have a tendency to apply French rules regarding competence. This confirms an active involvement of clerks in the earlier stages of EOP and ESCP case handling. Further, for the EOP, it appears judges have difficulties in assessing the case based only on the information contained in Form A. They prefer to consider the application on the basis of the actual evidence indicated by the creditor. This leads to a handling of the EOP in a manner similar to the domestic procedures, such as *injonction de payer*, where the judge assesses the claim and issues the order on what appears to be the merits in accordance with submitted written evidence. This prolongs the procedural timeframe for issuance of the EOP if the claimant has not submitted the evidence upfront, or if the documents have not been drafted in French.

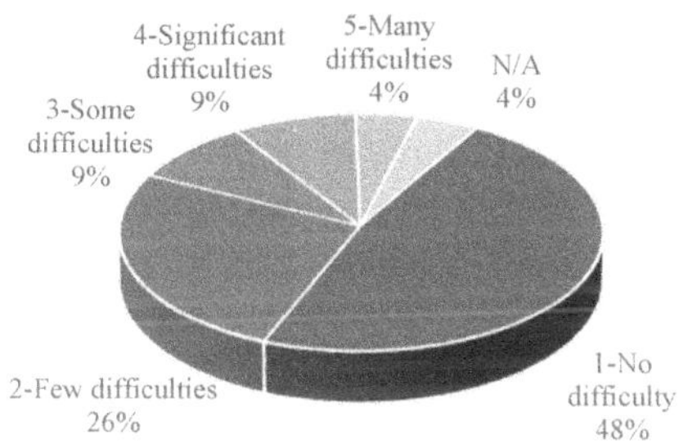

Fig. 4.9. National procedural rules create difficulties in the handling of EOP claims (23 responses)

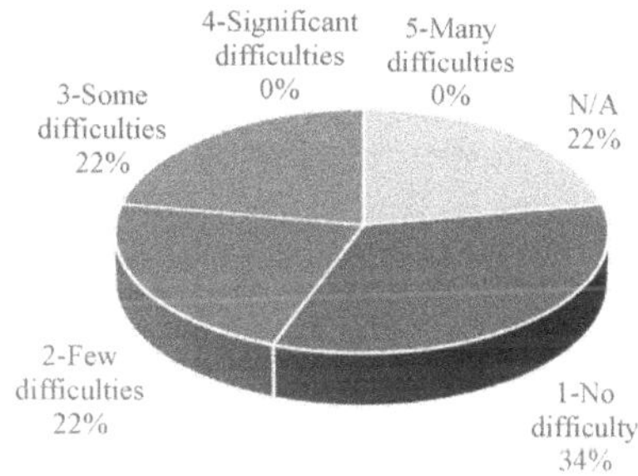

Fig. 4.10. National procedural rules create difficulties in the handling of ESCP claims (9 responses)

For documents submitted together with the ESCP claim form, the automatic translation requirement is problematic. The Regulation does not make this a mandatory requirement, leaving it to the appreciation of the judge if it 'appears to be necessary for giving the judgment' (Article 6(1)-(2) ESCP); in practice, however, the claimant has to provide translation for all documents. These difficulties can be addressed through dedicated training programmes for court clerks and judges as well as for other practitioners. As regards the methods used to serve EOPs to French defendants by courts in other Member States, better information and coordination at the European level with regard to necessary details for the application of the procedure should be made available, such as on the dedicated e-Justice Portal.

Forms

The use of standard forms is challenging in practice, though most of the respondents indicated they had not encountered difficulties in using them. Lay parties appear to have problems most often, while courts also find it difficult to deal with the forms on occasion. Respondents reported situations when the court (1) requested the claimant to re-send the application, as it considered the online printed form looked slightly different from the one in the Regulation; (2) did not issue the correct standard form to the party; or (3) decided to issue the rejection decision in accordance with the domestic format, ignoring the dedicated form. One practitioner pointed to a lack of practical experience with the procedures as the reason for these difficulties.

Parties need assistance in properly filling in the standard forms, as they sometimes cannot fully complete the application. This is due to incomplete information on the debtor, the address of the court not always being updated on the Judicial Atlas, and the language barriers preventing claimants from briefly describing the claim in the language of the proceedings (Fig. 4.11).[1053] The lack of legal knowledge is a significant barrier for lay users, especially non-repetitive players, as information available on dedicated websites is often too general and sometimes not available in all EU official languages. The request to determine the basis for the court jurisdiction as well as the actual individualisation of the competent court is challenging when the Judicial Atlas reveals more courts having jurisdiction for the same area. These are common difficulties for EOP and ESCP users. However, statistical data show that in practice only a small number of EOP cases were rejected due to lack of jurisdiction of the French court. The ECC considers that cross-border litigation 'involves complex legal reasoning, in particular with regard to jurisdiction, and because each litigation is a particular case, it is very complicated to propose a general information source (e.g. internet site) that is sufficient for the general public to use'. In trying to overcome these hurdles, claimants might rely on legal representation services or seek advice from the ECC (i.e. consumers) or the Enterprise Europe Network (i.e. small and medium-size businesses). Furthermore, parties find the language used in Form A to be too complex and technical. Lay users have difficulty understanding the provisions of the form; thus, they need to request additional information and explanations in order to be able to properly fill it in. Interest is also difficult to calculate, as well as determining the additional costs that can be claimed for possible legal services involving lawyers and bailiffs. ECC France even commented that consumers prefer to choose the ESCP over the EOP, as ESCP application forms seem less complicated and easier to use.

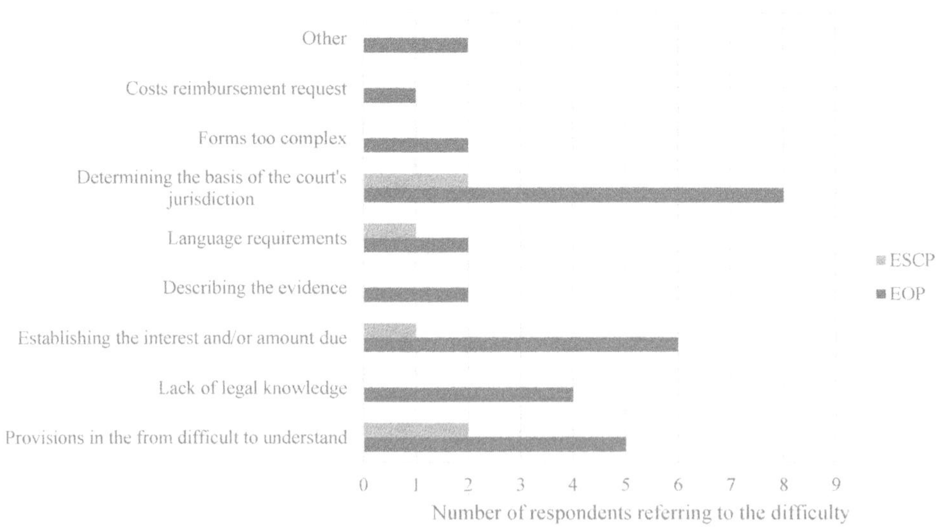

Fig. 4.11. The most common difficulties encountered by the parties using the EOP and/or the ESCP

[1053] ECC France mentioned having occasionally assisted French claimants to translate into German the short description of the claim in Form A.

If standard Form A is not complete or not properly filled in, the court will send the claimant Form B, requesting that he complete or rectify Form A. Based on the survey and interview responses, 44% of the EOP respondents indicate that Form B had been used by the courts, while only 12.5% of the ESCP respondents referred to a similar request being received by the ESCP claimant.[1054] The data available shows a limited use of Form B in the total volume of applications (less than 25% of the cases filed).[1055] The use of the services of a lawyer or legal adviser might result in a low need for the court to use Form B. The number of replies is overall modest, especially in relation to the ESCP, and can only hint at the national situation. Figure 4.12 provides an overview of the reasons for which claimants were requested to rectify and/or complete Form A.

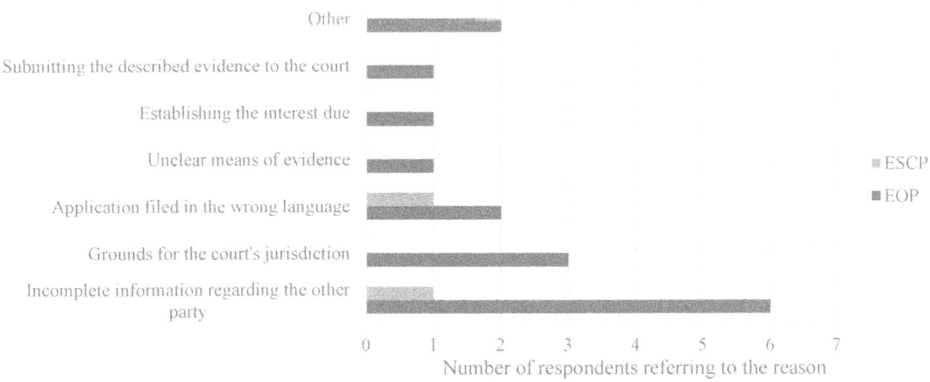

Fig. 4.12. Reasons for most requests for rectification and/or completion of the application form

These difficulties are closely related to the problems parties have in using the European uniform procedures. This is particularly visible for the EOP, as more respondents provided input on this instrument. Among the related identified difficulties are (1) the grounds on the basis of which the jurisdiction is retained; (2) the language in which the application has to be filed; (3) establishing the interest due; and (4) describing the elements of evidence the claimant intends to use in support of his claim. Other reasons for using Form B are related to national procedural rules and the interpretation of the Regulation in accordance with familiar practices, due to an overly formalistic attitude of the courts or an incorrect understanding of the Regulation's provisions. For example, the requirement to submit the evidence documents to the court together with the application, or requesting the claimant to resubmit the application form because the one used looks

1054 Twelve of 27 EOP respondents and 1 of 8 ESCP respondents. The European Commission Report confirms a significant rate of requests to complete or rectify EOP Form A. See also Section 4.7.1 above.

1055 Eleven of 20 EOP survey respondents (55%) indicated the use of Form B in less than 25% of the cases, and 8 of 20 respondents (40%) replied that they were not able to say. Four of 7 ESCP survey respondents (57.14%) indicated the use of Form B in less than 25% of the cases, and the remaining respondents were not able to say.

slightly different from the regulation annex even though it contains all the necessary information.[1056] Supplementing the EOP requirements with additional national provisions creates unnecessary delays for the claimant, and highlights deficiencies in the way the European procedure is understood and applied by French courts. Furthermore, such practices do not comply with the interpretation of the CJEU *Szyrocka* ruling that confirms the exclusive nature of the requirements set by Article 7 EOP, and with which an application should comply.

According to respondents, no requests to complete or rectify the ESCP answer form (Form C) were sent by the French courts. Further, marginal information became available in relation to EOP Forms C, D, and F. In one circumstance, the judge appears to have made use of Form B instead of Form C to propose a modification of the EOP application. The judges of another court participating in the research seemed reluctant to use the codes set by Form D to bring about rejection of the application. Instead, they preferred to motivate the decision in accordance with national procedural rules. This limits the possibility of a foreign claimant understanding immediately the reasons for rejection, and enhances the need to make use of translation services.

It seems that some courts rarely receive Form F, as defendants prefer to oppose the EOP order in accordance with the national format. This makes the task of the clerks more difficult in practice. As they only occasionally receive Form F, they might not immediately recognise it, particularly if it is sent in a language different than that of the proceedings. Thus, a standard form that can seem clear at first will be easily ignored or put aside, leading to serious consequences for the rights of the defendant. Better practical training for the clerks with regard to use of the standard forms would certainly have a positive impact on the efficient functioning of the European procedures, and for the protection of parties' rights.

If the debtor does not oppose the EOP within the set timeframe, Form G will be issued by the court. The practice of the French courts appears to be divided, with 57.14% of the respondents indicating that the court proceeds to issue the declaration upon request of the claimant.[1057] The remaining respondents mentioned that the clerk proceeds on his own initiative to send Form G to the claimant. For this purpose, prior to issuing the Declaration of enforceability, the court proceeds to verify the way the EOP was served on the defendant. In practice, there have been situations in which the court refused to issue the Declaration of enforceability because the service of the EOP on the defendant had not been carried out in an appropriate manner. This verification is essential for guaranteeing the defendant's access to justice. As regards ESCP Form D, the ECC remarked that French courts do not proceed to an automatic release of the certificate to the party. The creditor has to file a request with the court for this purpose. In practice, situations were reported in which consumers could not proceed to execute EOPs or ESCPs in other Member States because the courts did not immediately issue the forms required for enforcement purposes.

1056 The claimant printed the online form in order to fill it in, and the website version appeared to him to look as if it were different than Annex I of the EOP Regulation.

1057 Twelve of 21 EOP survey and interview respondents.

Finally, with regard to the availability of standard forms, some courts do provide access to the forms on their websites or refer parties to European portals. Greater availability of the standard forms with all courts would improve awareness with regard to the European uniform procedures, as well as contribute to the court staff and judges becoming more familiar with their content.

Language

According to the empirical data collected, language problems are not extensive. Almost 11% of the EOP respondents and 25% of the ESCP respondents indicated that parties or courts have encountered difficulties with regard to the language in which the forms have to be filled in, drafted, or actually submitted.[1058] Respondents mention that the forms and evidence are usually filed in French. In one case, the ESCP application was sent in German, and the court requested the party to provide a translation of Form A into French. In relation to both procedures, ECC France reports that consumers encounter difficulties in filling in the application form in a foreign language. In a few EOP and ESCP cases, the organisation provided French consumers with assistance in translating into German the descriptive part of the form, as the German court had jurisdiction, and the consumers were not fluent in German. Subsequently, this created difficulties for the claimants in communicating with the courts. Language is a serious barrier for parties that do not speak the language of the proceedings, or have limited competence in this regard. When a foreign court or a French court sends Form B to the claimant, it often communicates it in the language of the proceedings. This creates problems of understanding for the party that does not speak the language; hence, assistance from dedicated organisations or from legal practitioners is necessary. Legal terminology can pose difficulties for native speakers, but also for courts in the case of translation from other languages. The clerks of one court remarked that although foreign parties do make the effort to translate EOP application into French, the legal terminology does not necessarily match that used for the institutions they refer to, and this can pose a problem. For the above-mentioned reasons, more information and assistance in using the European uniform procedures is necessary. To help resolve the problem, the creation of a legal terminology glossary across the Member States could be considered.

The language in which a form is submitted to the court has proven to be crucial, as there is a chance the French court will not take into account a form (i.e. an opposition form) submitted in a foreign language. Although EOP Form F is considered to be straightforward, the clerk receiving it might not be able to read or recognise it.[1059] Practitioners also pointed to situations in which the court rejected EOP applications, and the reasons were provided only in French in a domestic format; hence, the foreign claimant is likely forced to make use of translation services in order to understand the decision. This has a serious impact on protection of the party's access to justice, the costs of the proceedings, and the implied timeframe. Furthermore, EOP Forms E and G and

1058 Three of 25 EOP respondents and 2 of 8 respondents provided feedback or replied regarding language-related aspects.

1059 See also Section 4.7.2.3.

the ESCP judgment and Form D are always issued in French by the French courts. They do not seem to provide the parties with any translation. The claimant who has to arrange for service of the EOP has to assess whether a translation is necessary for this purpose. Respondents did not indicate that they had encountered service difficulties for language reasons, even when the forms were communicated in a different language (i.e. German). Regarding the service of forms from other Member States, one lawyer remarked that German courts serving EOPs on French parties often include a translation of the documents for the purpose of guaranteeing a defendant's procedural rights. In relation to notification for enforcement purposes, a lawyer indicated that he proceeds to a communication of the EOP title as issued by the foreign court. To this he attaches the corresponding standard forms in French. He also mentioned including an explanation of the implications of the title and the consequences of not complying with the order of the court. However, he did not provide an actual translation of Forms A, E, and G for this purpose. According to the respondent, this allows the defendant to immediately understand what type of title has been issued against him. What remains questionable is whether this can be considered sufficient guarantee for the protection of the defendant's procedural rights, especially when consumers are involved.

When enforcement needs to be carried out abroad, the creditor will probably need to provide translated forms to the foreign enforcement authority. This increases the costs the creditor has to advance for execution purposes. For titles issued by courts in other Member States, although France indicated it can accept documents drafted in English, German, Italian, and Spanish, in practice it is not always clear whether the bailiff will understand the language and be willing to enforce an EOP or an ESCP in a foreign language. A translation might well be requested. In this respect, ECC France considers that a clearer information list regarding all Member States should be made available so that parties know with certainty whether translation will be necessary. Related costs might be significant, especially in relation to ESCPs. In addressing these aspects, Regulation 2015/2421 sought to limit translation costs in the ESCP procedure. As of July 2017, upon request, the court in the Member State of origin is required to issue Form D in a language other than its own. The free text fields will remain nevertheless in the language of the proceeding, but the translation costs will be limited to this part of the title, reducing translation costs for the creditor seeking enforcement of his title in another Member State. Unfortunately, no similar amendment has yet been introduced in relation to the EOP. Further, as regards an EOP enforcement, a respondent commented that foreign lawyers prefer to contact a French colleague immediately if execution has to be carried out in France. Language proficiency is likely to limit their activities, and finding a bailiff who can speak the language in which the title is issued might also be a challenging task, even if it is a language that France has indicated it accepts for enforcement purposes.

Service

Service of the EOP on the defendant is carried out in France in accordance with various methods (Fig. 4.13).

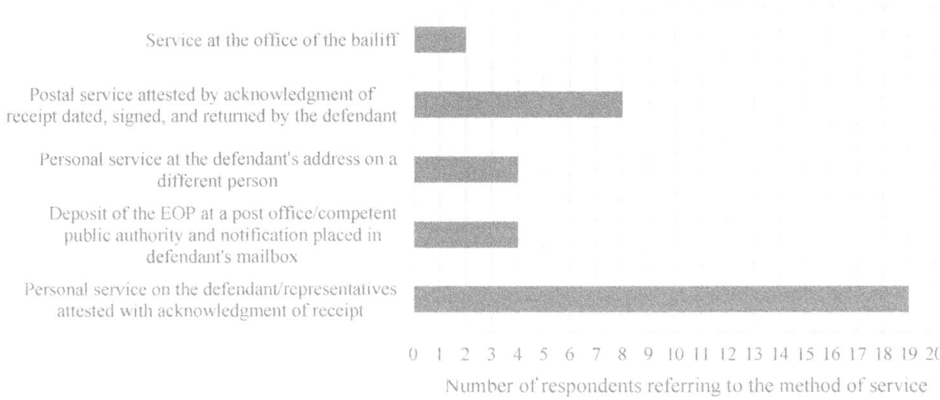

Fig. 4.13. Methods used to serve the EOP on the defendant

In general, the claimant is responsible for service of the EOP, and will have to advance the costs. He will request a bailiff to proceed to a communication of the order on the defendant in accordance with Article 1424-5 CPC. The court is not directly involved in the process, and will only subsequently proceed to verify the way service was carried out. For this reason, clerks and judges made only minor remarks on this aspect. When service complies with the provisions of the Regulation and with national rules on service, and the EOP is not opposed, the court issues Form G declaring the order enforceable. According to a respondent, in a case he had handled, the French court refused to issue the Declaration of enforceability, as the bailiff in Luxemburg had not served the EOP correctly on the defendant. The order had to be served again in order to guarantee the debtor's procedural rights. Further, respondents indicated that the EOP is most often served directly on the defendant, or on a person in the same household accepting receipt of the document, or on an employee of the company, in the case of a legal entity. These methods are deemed to guarantee a high level of certainty that the defendant is aware of the procedure. Alternatively, when the bailiff does not find the person he has to serve, he leaves a notification for the debtor to collect the documents from the bailiff's office. However, this method does not seem to directly fit within the service methods set by Article 14(d) EOP, unless the bailiff can be considered to be a 'competent public authority'.

Additionally, there are indications that sometimes the EOP is served by post accompanied by acknowledgement of receipt at the request of the clerk's office. In one situation, postal service with acknowledgement of receipt was carried out by a German court on a French debtor. The EOP was declared enforceable in Germany, and a French lawyer contacted a local bailiff to proceed to execution of the title in France. The debtor denied having received the EOP, and was threatening to contest execution. The bailiff requested proof of service in order to continue his activity.[1060] In serving the EOP, the German court proceeded in accordance with its national procedural rules and the methods set by the Regulation, but not in consideration of the service requirements in place in the Member State where service had to be carried out (France). This raised questions with regard to the validity of the Declaration of enforceability, to the soundness of the verification the court of origin conducted prior to issuing Form G, and to the protection of the debtor's right to a fair trial. By not opposing the EOP and having a passive attitude, the debtor had no remedies under the provisions of the European regulation other than to challenge the order, and this was eventually enforced. In the light of the *eco cosmetics* case, a national mechanism to challenge the EOP title when certain aspects of the procedure have not been complied with should be made available in the Member State of origin.

On ESCP postal service with acknowledgement of receipt, little information is available. Normally, the court should take care of the communication,[1061] but in practice there can be situations in which the claimant is requested to serve the documents. This appears to be related to the limited familiarity and experience of the judges (*juge de proximité*) with the procedure.

A small percentage of respondents experienced difficulties with the service of EOP or ESCP documents. Over 78% of the EOP respondents mentioned not having encountered difficulties or not being aware of such situations.[1062] A similar experience was reported by over 77% of the ESCP respondents.[1063] If difficulties were indeed encountered, these related to (1) the difficulty of obtaining an acknowledgement of receipt; (2) using an incorrect address for the defendant; (3) the language in which the service was carried out; and (4) the validity in France of service by registered post with acknowledgement of receipt when carried out on a French defendant, as domestic law requires service to be carried out by a bailiff.[1064] The difficulties mentioned concern not only service of the European uniform procedures in France but also abroad to other Member States. In order to overcome the aforementioned difficulties, additional research is usually undertaken or assistance is requested from related professional organisations.

The time necessary to serve, in a valid manner, the EOP or the ESCP-related documents and forms on the defendant appears to be on average above 2 weeks (Fig. 4.14).

[1060] The German court provided a copy of the acknowledgement of receipt it had received.

[1061] See also the European Commission, *Practice Guide for the application of the European Small Claims Procedure under Regulation (EC) No 861/2007 of the European Parliament and the Council of 11 July 2007 establishing a European Small Claims Procedure*, 2013, at 38.

[1062] Twenty-two of 28 EOP respondents.

[1063] Seven of 9 ESCP respondents.

[1064] In addition to these difficulties, practitioners are occasionally faced with (1) situations when the defendant claims he never received the ESCP documents or the EOP; (2) problems in identifying the method of service to use and the professional that should be contacted for this purpose in another Member State; (3) the foreign defendant never collecting the postal communication in the ESCP procedure; or (4) requirements in other Member States to serve the documents through a local bailiff.

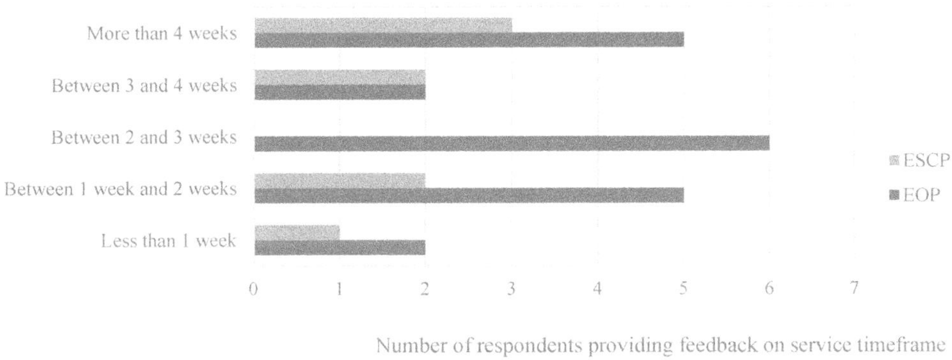

Fig. 4.14. Timeframe necessary to serve the EOP or ESCP claim on the defendant

Most respondents indicated that the longer period needed to serve the order or documents was related to reported difficulties. However, occasionally this might also have had to do with longer notification periods set by legislation in the other Member States.

In relation to the EOP, as previously mentioned, the court will proceed to a verification of the manner in which service was carried out, as well as of its validity prior to declaring the order enforceable in order to secure the defendant's procedural rights and access to justice.

Hearings

Data are limited with respect to the holding of hearings in the ESCP procedure or to the review proceedings. Most respondents indicated they were not aware of hearings being held for this purpose. Only the ECC reported hearings that had been held in an ESCP procedure. The court had summoned the parties for a hearing, not because it considered it to be necessary for the conduct of the proceedings but due to some confusion as to the national *déclaration au greffe* proceeding for smaller value claims. Fortunately, according to the ECC, such situations are rare in practice. For the rest, the parties do not seem interested in requesting the holding of a hearing, nor are the courts eager to propose them *ex officio*, although hearings play a significant role in domestic proceedings. One of the respondents remarked that an oral hearing by way of video conference is a technique rarely used by French courts, though this is possible in accordance with the provisions of the ESCP Regulation. This is possibly triggered also by the level of dedicated technology available to the courts. The handling of the ESCP primarily in writing is in line with the European legislator's aim, as well as contributing to a speedier and less costly treatment.

As regards hearings being organised in EOP and ESCP review proceedings, as implemented in the CPC, most respondents stated they were not aware of such hearings taking place in practice. Only two respondents referred to a summons of the parties by the clerk in EOP review proceedings. These were claims handled by commercial courts (TC), but no further details became available.

Challenging Mechanisms (Opposition, Appeal, Review)
According to the data available, the EOP opposition mechanism is not used extensively in practice. Fifty percent of the EOP respondents considered the opposition was rarely made use of,[1065] a result in line with statistics provided by the Ministry of Justice.[1066] As regards the time limit during which to lodge an opposition, the defendants appear to generally comply with this requirement. Only one respondent mentioned that oppositions had been filed after the 30-day period had lapsed. This had to do with three EOPs handled by a commercial court, but no further information was provided. As the rate of opposition was low, research respondents could provide only scant information on the transfer of the EOP claim to the ordinary procedure.

Data on appeals filed against ESCP judgments were also limited. Of the practitioners, 55.55% reported that no appeal procedures had been lodged, while the remaining 44.45% mentioned that they were not aware of the mechanism having been activated by the parties. This might be due to the fact that amounts disputed were quite small, and parties might have had no desire to continue the procedure or possibly did not consider it worth the effort, time, and costs involved. No information is available with regard to the procedural timeframe necessary to deal with an appeal. One respondent considered it to be between 6–9 months, but this information must be viewed cautiously, as the practitioner himself had not handled any appeal request in practice. Further, the statistical data available do not contain any relevant information on this aspect, nor does the available case law; hence, no triangulation is possible in order to verify the soundness of this information.

The review mechanism has rarely been used in practice, and remains an uncommon means to challenge EOP or ESCP decisions. None of the ESCP respondents had experience with this mechanism. The ECC even remarked that none of the cases it followed or assisted consumers with had reached that far. Of the EOP respondents, 11.11% indicated that a review had been requested.[1067] In accordance with the Ministry of Justice statistics, the mechanism was used only once, and in 2010. However, one of the respondents reported two requests for an EOP review in 2010. Some confusion might have occurred during registration of the cases, or between the review mechanism set by the EOP Regulation and the domestic review procedure. In both cases, the same terminology is used – '*réexamen*' – but the mechanisms are different, which may have led to confusion. In one case, the practitioner mentioned that the review had been requested by the defendant and accepted by the court, due to a limited understanding of the procedure. The mechanism was not actually made use of for one of the reasons set by Article 20 EOP. Another practitioner mentioned that a hearing had been organised by the TC in the review proceeding,[1068] but no further information was provided as to the outcome.

1065 Twelve of 24 EOP respondents estimated the opposition rate to be below 25%. Further, 8.33% of practitioners (2 respondents) estimated the opposition rate to be between 25–50% of the EOP cases, 4.16% of practitioners (1 respondent) to be above 75%, and 37.5% of practitioners (9 respondents) did not know.

1066 According to which the opposition concerns around 16% of the EOP cases. See Section 4.7.1.

1067 Three of 27 EOP respondents.

1068 Article 1424–10 in conjunction with Article 1424–15 CPC.

Representation

Representation appears to be commonly used in France in relation to the European uniform procedures, although this is not mandatory. This is especially the case for the EOP, as has also been confirmed by case law data. Further, EOP claimants appear to make use of legal representation more often in comparison to defendants. Over 43% of the respondents consider that claimants are represented in more than half of the EOP cases.[1069] According to 29.16% of the EOP respondents, defendants are represented in less than a quarter of the EOP cases.[1070] The lower representation rate of defendants might be related to the infrequent use of the opposition mechanism. Unless the defendant opposes the EOP or contests enforcement actions, the courts or other practitioners cannot easily be aware of whether the defendant is making use of legal representation. Additionally, some lawyers participating in the research indicated they had only represented claimants in EOP proceedings.

In the ESCP procedure, most respondents indicated a rate of representation as being below 25% of the cases. In consideration of the difficulties encountered by consumers, the ECC remarked that the assistance of a legal adviser familiar with these procedures is 'often much needed in practice'. Therefore, consumers look for the assistance of consumer organisations, while companies more often opt for the services of a local lawyer or the assistance of commercial associations that can provide advice.

Procedural Timeframe

Based on the empirical data available, the EOP generally appears to be issued within the 30-day period recommended by the Regulation (Fig. 4.15). These results are in line with earlier national statistical data (2009–2011) provided by the Ministry of Justice, which indicates a timeframe of over a month to handle the claim.[1071]

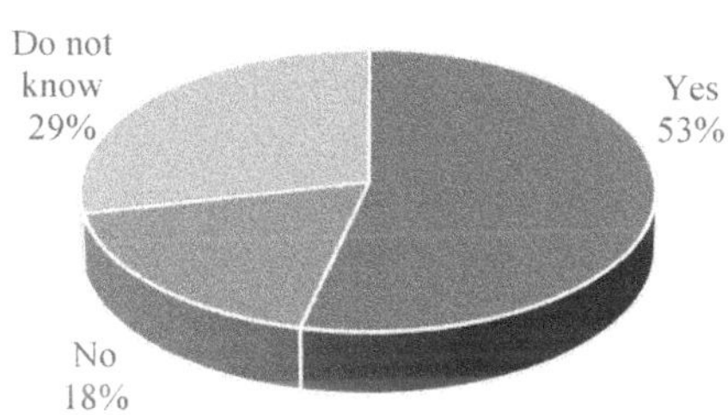

Fig. 4.15. EOP issued within 30 days (28 respondents)

1069 Ten of 23 EOP respondents. Further, 35% of the respondents (8 out of 23 respondents) consider that claimant representation concerns less than 25% of the cases they had handled.

1070 Seven of 24 EOP respondents. Of the EOP respondents (11 of 24), 45.83% indicated that they were not aware to what extent defendants make use of the services of a lawyer or legal adviser.

1071 See Section 4.7.1.

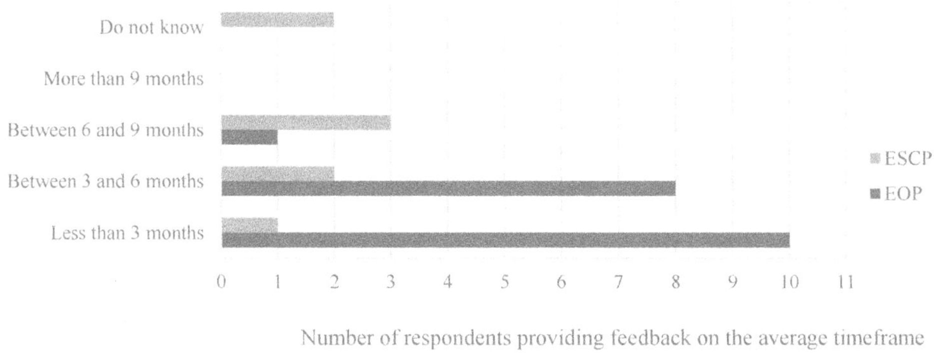

Fig. 4.16. Average timeframe necessary to conclude an EOP or ESCP procedure

According to some respondents, issuing of the EOP is delayed owing to matters related to the organisation of the courts (e.g. limited judicial staff, work overload). Figure 4.16 offers an overview of respondents' opinions as to the average timeframe necessary to obtain an enforceable EOP or ESCP (from lodging the standard Form A to delivery of the declaration or certification of enforceability). According to most respondents, a claimant will most probably obtain a Declaration of enforceability (Form G) within a period of 3 months from submitting an EOP request. However, a significant number of respondents reported that it can take the claimant between 3 to 6 months to obtain an enforceable EOP.

This increase in the length of proceedings is due to a series of concurrent elements such as (1) the extra time the court needs in issuing the EOP; (2) hindrances in serving the order or arranging for the service of the EOP on the defendant; (3) language difficulties; and (4) the competent court's lack of or limited knowledge of the procedure. For the ESCP, most respondents estimate the period necessary to obtain a judgment to be between 3 to 9 months. This result comes to a certain extent within the average length revealed by statistics provided by the Ministry of Justice. The reasons for prolonging ESCP cases beyond 6 months are not clear, as respondents were not able to provide additional information on this aspect. Practitioners participating in this research often had very limited experience with the ESCP, and were not able to provide extensive details. However, according to ECC France, the length of the ESCP procedure has decreased in the last few years, and it takes the claimant no more than 3 months to obtain a judgment. No information is available as to the timeframe for an appellate proceeding, however, as none of the respondents had dealt with this situation in practice.[1072]

Costs, interest, penalties

Very little information has become available on the costs of the proceedings, and on the interest and penalties claimants requested in relation to the European uniform

[1072] For an estimate of the timeframe regarding ESCP appellate proceedings, see sub-section *Challenging mechanisms* above.

procedures. Generally, claimants are required to pay court fees only in commercial claims. This is a flat fee of €37.07. Based on the empirical data gathered, users have no difficulty in this respect. As regards proceedings, the losing party generally has to pay the costs, including all costs related to the procedure apart from those the law declares unrecoverable.[1073] The translation fee and bailiff costs and fees are recoverable, but they have to be advanced by the claimant. It is the same with service costs. When service has to be carried out cross-border in France in accordance with the Service Regulation, the foreign claimant is required to pay a fixed fee of €50 for the services of the bailiff. However, according to ECC France, in practice there are cases in which bailiffs have requested significantly higher fees. In relation to the recovery of a lawyer's fee, another respondent remarked that the courts seldom award it to the claimant; thus, he has to bear the costs of his own lawyer.

As regards the interest claimed, some details were provided in relation to the EOP, but the outcome cannot be generalised. According to this information, there are courts that do not take interest requests into account, but the reason for this is unknown.

4.7.3.5. Enforcement

Enforcement information is limited, as not all survey respondents were able to provide feedback on all dedicated questions; hence, results should be viewed with caution. Additionally, a significant number of practitioners indicated that they had no practical knowledge regarding various enforcement matters. This was also because few bailiffs had provided feedback on their own execution-related experiences. Further, most respondents (judges, clerks, lawyers, and legal advisers) who provided information on this stage of the proceedings were not always directly involved in the execution. Over 54% of the EOP and ESCP respondents indicated that they did not know whether or not claimants experienced difficulties in the execution of the acquired title (Figs. 4.17–4.18).

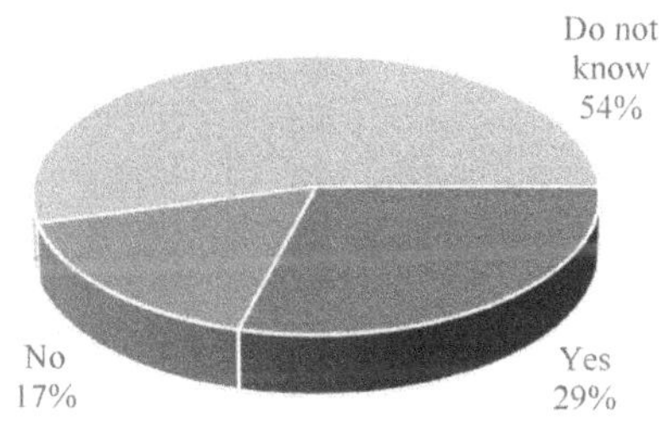

Fig. 4.17. Claimants experiencing difficulties in the EOP enforcement following delivery of Form G (24 respondents)

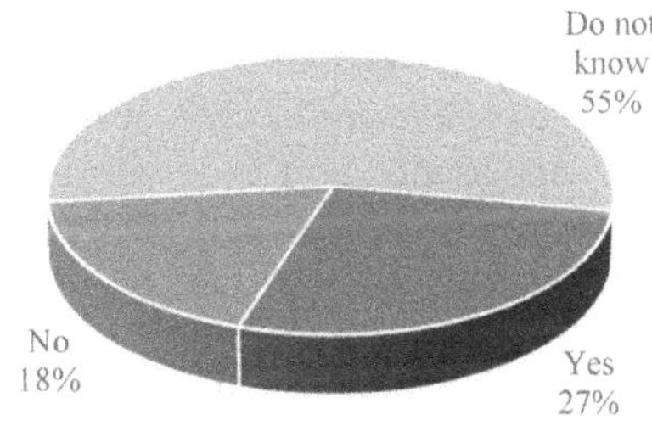

Fig. 4.18. Claimants experiencing difficulties in the ESCP enforcement following delivery of Form D (11 respondents)

1073 In accordance with Article 700 CPC.

Figure 4.19 provides an overview of the difficulties reported in connection with EOP or ESCP enforcement

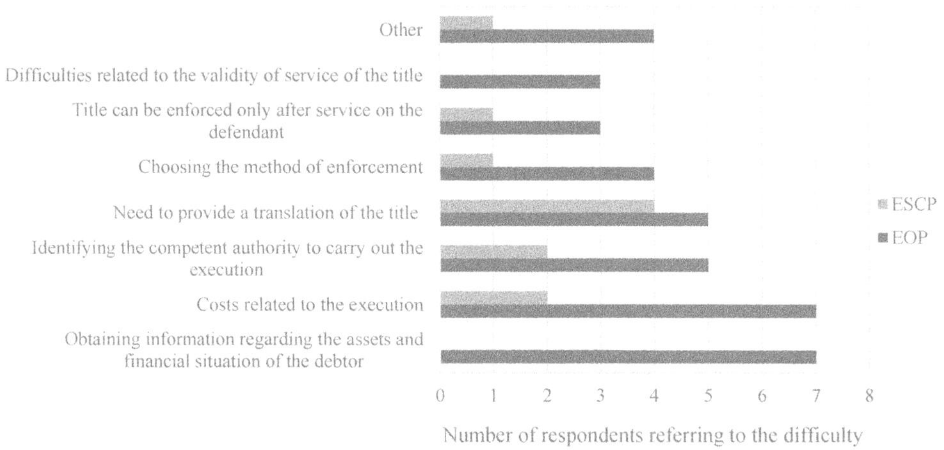

Fig. 4.19. Difficulties related to the enforcement of EOP and ESCP judgments

Some of these difficulties have to do with the fact that the available enforcement information is often general and theoretical. Parties, especially unrepresented creditors, find themselves in doubt as to whether translation is needed,[1074] which is the competent authority they should contact in the Member State of enforcement, and what are the actual costs they should expect to advance for this last stage of the procedure, or whether the bailiff will recover it from the debtor. These factors can easily prolong the time necessary to initiate the execution, and will involve additional costs (e.g. for translation of the certificate and the decision, for the services of the bailiff). According to one respondent, bailiffs sometimes also have limited knowledge of the European procedures or no actual practical experience. There have been situations in which a French bailiff refused to take up the case, or the EOP execution took a significantly longer period, due to inexperience and requests for additional information on the way the European procedure had previously been handled by the court. In view of the bailiffs' territorial competence, this can lead to situations in which the creditor is trapped, having no alternative in terms of which bailiff on whom to rely. In an opposing perspective, if the bailiff is familiar with the European procedure, execution is reported to be fast and less cumbersome for the creditor. Additionally, respondents also mentioned cases in which the debtors repaid the debt once they were served with the enforceable title.[1075] This appears to be linked to small or modest cross-border debts.

[1074] On this argument, see also Section 4.7.3.4.

[1075] One court assumed the debtors paid in the EOP cases it had handled, as creditors did not subsequently file any requests related to execution.

Some respondents perceive enforcement of the European uniform procedures to be similar to the enforcement of domestic titles (Figs. 4.20–4.21).[1076] More extensive participation and feedback from French bailiffs would have provided a clearer picture in this regard.

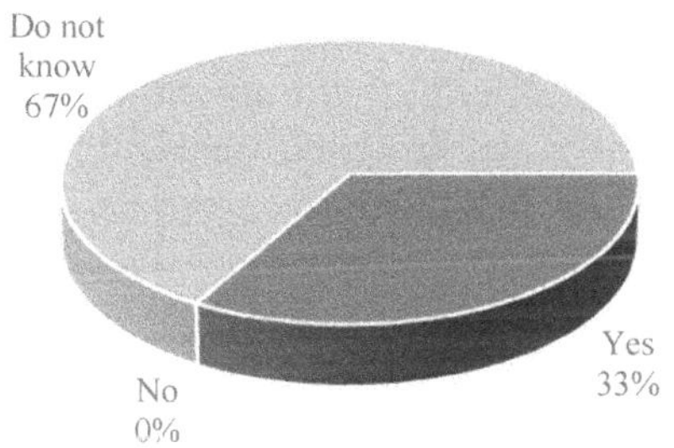

Fig. 4.20. EOP enforcement difficulties are similar to those experienced in the domestic procedures (17 respondents)

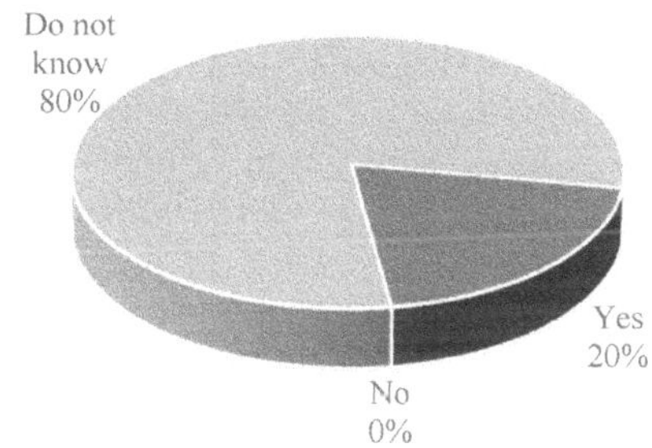

Fig. 4.21. ESCP enforcement difficulties are similar to those experienced in domestic procedures (7 respondents)

One particular situation was reported by a French lawyer who experienced enforcement difficulties with an EOP issued in Germany due to the method of service used.[1077] The bailiff sought additional information from the creditor in order to proceed with the execution. Although the title was eventually enforced, the process took additional time and raised important questions with regard to safeguarding the debtor's procedural rights.

Based on available data, creditors do not often appear to desist from enforcement proceedings, although it happens occasionally with EOP titles (Figs. 4.22–4.23). This might be triggered by the high costs of enforcement the creditor has to bear upfront compared to the value of the debt, as well as by the insolvency status of the debtor. One lawyer commented that the costs of execution are too high in France; hence, the creditor will sometimes simply decide not to pursue the execution.

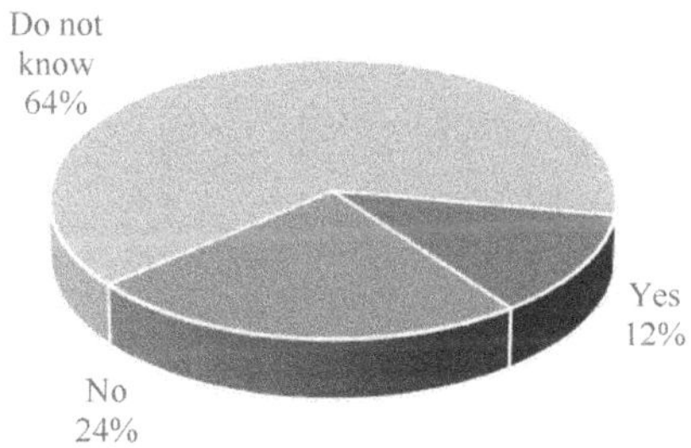

Fig. 4.22. Creditor decided not to pursue the EOP enforcement procedure (25 respondents)

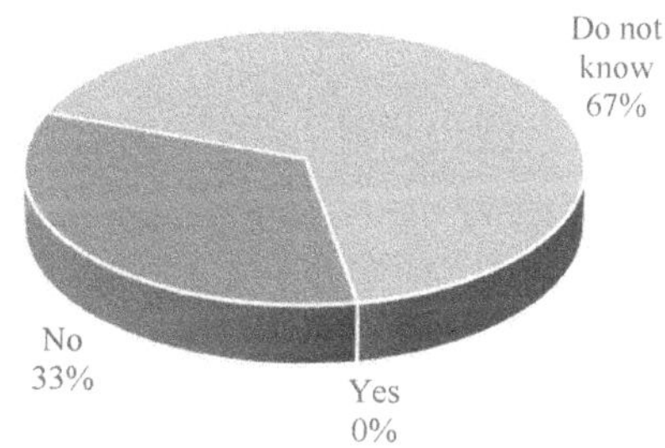

Fig. 4.23. Creditor decided not to pursue the ESCP enforcement procedure (8 respondents)

1076 Unfortunately, a significant number of respondents had no experience with this stage of the proceedings.

1077 On this case, see Section 4.7.3.4.

None of the respondents reported encountering requests for a refusal of enforcement or for a limitation or stay of enforcement. The majority of practitioners were unable to provide any information in this respect.

As regards the time necessary to execute an EOP or an ESCP in France, most respondents were not able to estimate what this might be (46.66% EOP respondents and 60% ESCP respondents).[1078] The other respondents indicated either that execution takes less than a month for EOP titles, or between 3 to 4 months for both European uniform procedures. When enforcement requires a longer timeframe, this is due in part to the time necessary to serve the enforceable title on the debtor. Another factor is possibly the limited familiarity with the European procedures on the part of professionals that have to carry out the execution-related tasks. Other reasons could also contribute to longer execution periods, but no additional information became available. Further studies regarding this stage of the procedures are necessary to better understand this process, as lengthy execution stages might have a negative influence on the use of these instruments.

Data regarding the enforcement of French EOP and ESCP titles in other Member States was also scarce. Respondents generally indicated that they were not aware of enforcement proceedings undertaken abroad (92% of EOP respondents and 100% of ESCP respondents).[1079] The only information EOP respondents could offer was that these usually involved neighbouring Member States (Germany, and Luxembourg in particular).

4.7.3.6. Practitioners' Assessment

Practitioners have divergent views with regard to the efficiency of the EOP and the ESCP in terms of 'speediness, affordability and protection of parties' rights' compared to national procedures available for the recovery of uncontested or small value claims (Figs. 4.24–4.25).

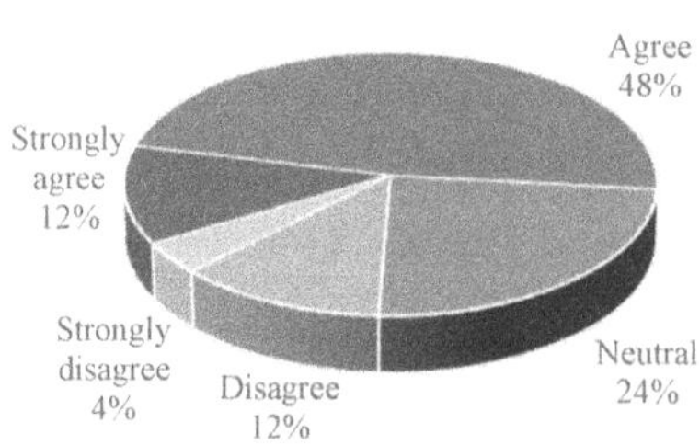

Fig. 4.24. Respondents consider EOP an overall efficient solution (25 respondents)

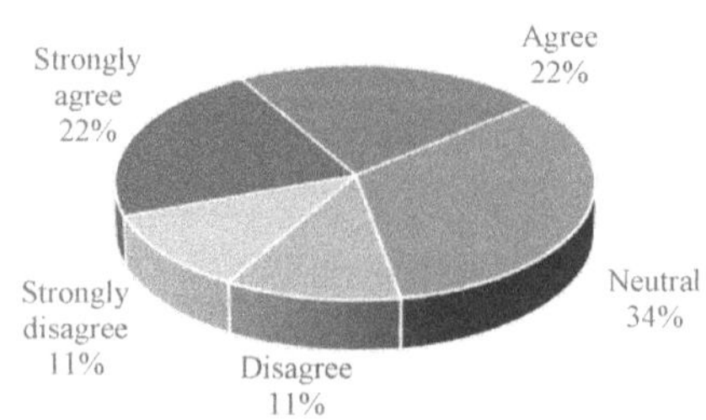

Fig. 4.25. Respondents consider ESCP an overall efficient solution (9 respondents)

[1078] Seven of 15 EOP respondents and 3 of 5 ESCP respondents.

[1079] Twenty-three of 15 EOP respondents and 7 ESCP respondents.

However, the overall impression is more positive in relation to the EOP. Sixty percent of the respondents consider the EOP to be a speedy and affordable procedure that provides protection for parties' rights. This has to do with (1) the perceived reasonable delay set by the Regulation for obtaining an enforceable title; (2) removal of the exequatur; (3) harmonisation of the procedural rules; and (4) the use of forms and their availability in all official languages. These elements are considered to contribute to a speedier handling of the claim and to diminish procedural costs. One respondent remarked that the EOP can be an efficient procedure, 'subject to the way it is applied'. Respondents who considered that the EOP does not achieve the 'speediness, affordability and protection of parties' rights' it aims for link this to the complexity of the procedure, the limited familiarity of practitioners with the instrument, the language problems it raises, and the lack of clarity of the forms. The perceived complexity of the procedure and the forms' lack of clarity may well be related to the limited knowledge and familiarity of some practitioners with the EOP. Some practitioners actually remarked that limited knowledge on the functioning of the European procedures can slow down the handling of the claim and the execution stage, and for this reason professionals should follow an appropriate training programme. In relation to the ESCP, practitioners are appreciative of the procedural timeframe set by the Regulation, allowing the creditor to obtain a judgment more quickly than in a national procedure. Furthermore, the judge can decide whether a hearing is necessary, and the ESCP is less costly than a domestic proceeding. In contrast, some practitioners consider the ESCP to be too complex for its low threshold. It is hoped that an increase to €5,000 will change this view.

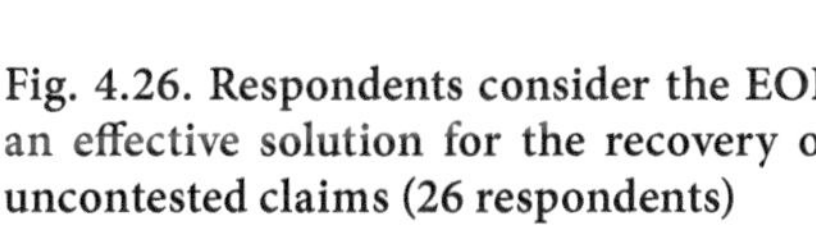

Fig. 4.26. Respondents consider the EOP an effective solution for the recovery of uncontested claims (26 respondents)

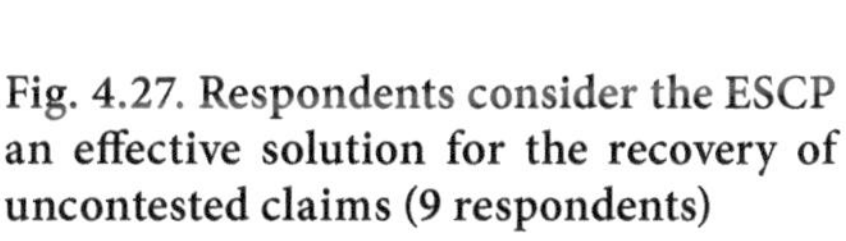

Fig. 4.27. Respondents consider the ESCP an effective solution for the recovery of uncontested claims (9 respondents)

As regards the effectiveness of the European uniform procedures in the recovery of cross-border debts, practitioners often have either an optimistic or a neutral approach (Figs. 4.26–4.27). The positive perception is linked to the actual recovery of the debt, while the neutral view is related to the lack of information and experience with the enforcement stage of the procedures. Another aspect that contributes to the neutral perception appears to be the limited knowledge that potential parties and professionals have of the existence of this instrument. At the other end of the appreciation spectrum, one judge remarked that the existence of the EOP had been ignored at his court until as late as 2014; hence, he could provide little in the way of information.

Although application of the EOP and the ESCP has improved over the years, some obstacles remain. Over 55% of the EOP respondents[1080] and more than 66% of the ESCP respondents[1081] 'strongly agree' or 'agree' that certain elements hinder application of the procedures. The most important of these obstacles are (1) the lack of familiarity and experience of all legal professions, as well as potential users; (2) the need for additional training for courts and practitioners; (3) the difficulties in finding information or sufficiently detailed information with regard to a number of aspects (i.e. the fees to be paid and the means available for payment,[1082] the competent courts and their contact details); (4) the language barriers; (5) the forms being too complicated for lay users; (6) the coordination between national rules regarding service and the methods set by the regulations; and (7) the way the creditors should proceed to enforce the title abroad and who they should contact for this purpose (the court or a bailiff). Some of these obstacles could be addressed at the national level by the French authorities or professional bodies (e.g. dedicated training sessions for courts and professionals, offering more detailed and practical information on domestic rules and practices for potential users on national or European portals).[1083] In view of the small number of cases, the concentration of competence should be considered. This would maximise the use of resources and might improve the manner in which the European uniform procedures are applied. Practitioners and the ECC agree on the need for more dedicated training for judges, clerks, lawyers, and bailiffs across France. Furthermore, training should include practical aspects on application of the procedures.

The use of the EOP and the ESCP should be promoted to practitioners and to possible interested parties, along with national information points. According to the ECC, this should cover three levels: legal (explanations regarding the procedure, the estimated costs, jurisdiction, procedural timeframe, translation requirements), technical (assistance in filling in the application forms, finding contact details of the court and/or bailiff), and linguistic (assistance in understanding the communications and documents sent by a foreign court, small translations for filling in the forms).[1084] Further, practitioners consider it would be useful to create a detailed guide per Member State containing information on national practical aspects (e.g. valid service methods that should be used; party or entity in charge of service and costs; court fees and means of payment available; enforcement and entity in charge of the process; language and translation requirements). It would be desirable for potential parties to have access to precise information on the functioning of the European uniform procedures prior to initiating a court proceeding. Moreover, in relation to the EOP, one respondent was of the opinion that unified service methods are fundamental for eliminating the difficulties posed by identifying the means that should be used in each Member State.

1080 Fifteen of 27 EOP respondents.

1081 Six of 9 ESCP respondents.

1082 Payment of fees related to the procedures is particularly problematic for claimants who reside outside the euro zone.

1083 Such as the service-public.fr and/or e-Justice portal.

1084 Centre Européen de la Consommation, Zentrum für Europäischen Verbraucherschutz e.V., Procédure de règlement des petits litiges et injonction de payer européenne. Des procédures simplifiées pas si simples dans la pratique, July 2011, at 9 (available at www.cec-zev.eu/fileadmin/user_upload/cec-zev/PDF/documentation/etudes/Procedure_reglement_petits_litiges.pdf).

4.7.4. *Overall Assessment*

French courts and practitioners are generally aware of EOP and ESCP procedures, but seem to be more familiar with the EOP, which is used more often. The way the procedures are applied is sometimes influenced significantly by domestic procedures. This results, for example, in supplementing requirements set by the EOP Regulation for the issuance of the title with those of familiar national procedures. The judges remain keen on assessing the referred evidence in the EOP procedure.

The coordination between the Regulations' provisions and domestic rules might not always be straightforward, such as with regard to the valid methods to be used to serve defendants in France. However, the implementation of specific provisions for application of the European uniform procedures in the CPC as well as the publication of dedicated guidelines for each instrument facilitate the handling of the EOP and the ESCP. This contributes to create a legal certainty with regard to various procedural aspects for the parties as well as for courts and practitioners.

The clerks are particularly active in the handling of EOP and ESCP claims, supporting the decisional process of the judge. Hence, dedicated training for clerks as well as for judges should be considered in order to properly familiarise them with the practical aspects of the procedures, especially concerning forms and related requirements. This could be coupled with a concentration of jurisdiction in a smaller number of courts to maximise the use of expertise and to minimise the costs of training.

Users – lay users in particular – encounter difficulties in filling in the forms, and assistance for consumer or business organisations in making use of the procedures should be better organised and promoted. It remains to be seen whether Regulation 2015/2421 will succeed in securing better assistance for parties in the ESCP procedure. Representation by a legal professional remains high for procedures for which representation is not mandatory. Legal entities are more likely to employ the services of a lawyer, especially for the EOP procedure. The domestic procedures continue to be preferred by parties and practitioners as better known instruments. Raising awareness of the existence of the EOP and the ESCP for the recovery of cross-border claims should be one of the first steps to improve their use.

The claimant retains an active role in the service of the EOP on the defendant. This is sometimes the case also in the ESCP procedure, although the court should communicate the documents. Personal service on the defendant or on a member of his household or his employee is a favoured method of communication as a guarantee of observing the party's procedural rights. Courts will pay significant attention to verifying the method used prior to issuing the Declaration of enforceability. Further, the procedural timeframe set by both Regulations is seen as an aspect that encourages speedier treatment of the claim in comparison to national procedures.

Information with regard to language aspects can be confusing at times, especially with respect to the language in which forms are accepted by French courts. It is not always clear whether the professionals would be able to manage with forms in the four languages agreed upon by French authorities. Furthermore, specific information on various procedural aspects relevant for application of the instruments are available only in French at the national level. A party or professional not speaking French would have significant difficulty in finding and using the information. Domestic procedural aspects necessary for using the European uniform procedures should be better addressed and more transparent, especially for foreign users.

In practice, practitioners and parties seem interested in applying the European uniform procedures, and particularly the EOP. Statistical data show an increase in their use and an improvement in the speed with which claims are treated. Raising awareness and providing parties and practitioners with more detailed information and national guidelines would most certainly encourage and facilitate the use of the EOP and the ESCP in cross-border claims.

Chapter 5

ITALY

5.1. Introduction

The Italian legal system is one of civil law.[1085] Judicial decisions do not have a binding authority in proceedings other than those in which they are rendered, which include decisions of the Supreme Court (*Corte di cassazione*).[1086] The Italian civil procedure rules are contained mainly in the 1940 Code of Civil Procedure (CPC).[1087] Some procedural rules are also contained in the Italian Constitution,[1088] the Civil Code (e.g. evidence provisions, enforcement),[1089] and special legal acts (e.g. *processo telematico*).[1090] The CPC has been the object of continuous reform and modification since the 1990s in an attempt to deal with the increasing crisis involving civil justice and a backlog of

1085 After unification in 1861, the first Italian codes were 'modelled on the French Napoleonic Codes', but in the 1940s there was a shift towards the German approach and methodology. This had a significant impact on the Italian process and procedural law. Lupoi (2012), at 16; Pozzo (2012), at 453 and 455–457; Glyn Watkin (1997), at 41; Zweigert & Kötz (1998), at 104–105.

1086 Up until the 2006 reform, single sections of the Supreme Court could disagree with decisions issued by the full chamber. In the years following, reforms have tried to render case law more predictable and coherent in order to give the court the possibility of making a stronger contribution to the interpretation of legal provisions. Lupoi (2014), at 19–20.

1087 The code was inspired by three basic principles of procedure: orality, concentration, and immediacy. However, this innovative system was not met with a positive response. By 1950, under pressure from the lawyers, the code was reformed, eliminating the preclusions. This change has led to many negative side-effects, including the present chronic backlog facing Italian courts. See Lupoi (2014), at 28–30.

1088 The Italian Constitution establishes fundamental procedural rights and guarantees. They represent minimum standards to which the procedure has to adhere, and play an important role in the way civil procedural rules are interpreted and applied. See Articles 3, 24, 101, 104(1), 108(2), 111, 113. Silvestri (2014), at 81; Cappelletti, Merryman & Perillo (1967), at 118–120.

1089 The substantive provisions regarding admissibility and the effects of the different means of taking evidence are contained in the Civil Code (Articles 2697–2739), while the Code of Civil Procedure sets the rules governing their admission in the course of civil proceedings (Articles 191–266).

1090 Ministry Decree No. 44/21 February 2011, Official Gazette, General Series No. 89/18 April 2011 (*Regolamento concernente le regole techniche per l'adozione nel processo civile e nel processo penale, delle technologie dell'informazione e della comunicazione, in attuazione dei principi previsti dal decreto legislative 7 marzo 2005, n. 82, e successive modificazioni, ai sensi dell'articolo 4, commi 1 e 2, del decreto legge 29 dicembre 2009, n.193, convertito nella legge 22 febbraio 2010, n.24*).

cases.[1091] The reforms of November 2014 proposed a series of measures aimed at improving the efficiency of civil proceedings and discouraging excessive litigation.[1092] This ongoing reform is partly a response to reforms already undertaken that have not succeeded in reducing the backlog and the duration of proceedings. The situation hampers access to justice, and is a serious drawback for economic activities. Furthermore, civil proceedings in Italy are subject to the law in force at the time that the claim is registered with the court. The increased number of civil rule amendments has led to different sets of provisions applying at the same time, which has added to the complexity of the proceedings.

This chapter discusses from which proceedings creditors may choose in order to seek recovery of their debts before Italian courts. Section 5.2 provides an overview of the national ordinary procedure and its characteristics. In addition to the ordinary procedure, which often proves very lengthy, the CPC offers alternative instruments for dealing with uncontested and small value claims. These are examined in Section 5.3 and compared to the European uniform procedures. Section 5.4 analyses the position of Italian stakeholders with regard to the EOP and the ESCP. Section 5.5 focuses on implementation of the European uniform procedures in the national procedural system and practice. Section 5.6 examines the domestic execution process and the enforcement of EOPs and ESCPs in Italy. Section 5.7 looks at the functioning of the EOP and the ESCP in practice on the basis of available statistics, published case law, and the results of the empirical research.

5.2. The Italian Legal System: An Overview

5.2.1. General Aspects

The CPC contains very detailed rules on the actual ordinary procedure before the court of first instance (*Tribunale*), the jurisdiction of which is generally shared between the *Tribunale* and the Justice of the Peace (*Giudice di pace*), based on the type of matters and the value of the claim.[1093] The Justice of the Peace is competent for cases up to a value of €5,000,[1094] while the *Tribunale* handles all disputes exceeding this amount and claims

[1091] The successive rounds of civil justice reforms failed to improve the functioning of the Italian system. The temporary solutions ('patchwork approach') are inefficient or ineffective, the caseload of civil courts continues to be very high, and the duration of court proceedings is unacceptably long. Silvestri (2014), at 80–86; Lupoi (2014), at 31–33; Lupoi (2012a), at 25–26.

[1092] Decree-Law No. 132/12 September 2014 regarding urgent means for the alternative handling of cases outside the courts, and other interventions involving the backlog in the area of civil proceedings (*Misure urgenti di degiurisdizionalizzazione ed altri interventi per la definizione dell'arretrato in materia di processo civile*), Official Gazette No. 212/12 September 2014 and the conversion act Law No. 162/10 November 2014, Official Gazette No. 261/10 November 2014.

[1093] Article 7 CPC; Article 9 CPC. For a detailed presentation of the structure of the judiciary, see Di Frederico (2012); Nicolì (2012), at 1–120.

[1094] Article 7(1) CPC. The Justice of the Peace was established by Law No. 374 of 21 November 1991. See Lupoi (2014), at 64. Following reorganisation of the judicial circumscriptions, 474 offices of the Justice of the Peace were closed. At present, there are 372 offices. Legislative-Decree No. 156/7 September 2012

whose value might not be determined.[1095] Justice of the Peace proceedings are mostly oral, but can also include the submission of written defences. The trial is meant to be quick; hence, the Justice of Peace will seek to achieve a conciliation of the parties from the first hearing.[1096] The Court of Appeal is the first instance court in exceptional cases (e.g. recognition and enforcement of foreign judgments), while jurisdiction in EOP and ESCP cases is shared between Justice of the Peace offices, *Tribunali*, and Courts of Appeal.[1097]

Civil proceedings in Italy have an adversarial character. The parties have control over the dispute and the evidence on which claims will be adjudicated (*principio dispositivo* – principle of party control over proceedings), but in certain situations the judge can put forward additional evidence or facts.[1098] The Italian judge must individualise and apply the appropriate legal rules to the claim (*principio iura novit curia*) and adjudicate only on the facts, the claims, and the evidence at hand.[1099]

Generally, the parties have to be represented in court by a lawyer, though in exceptional circumstances a party may litigate in person for claims not higher than €1,100.[1100] The court proceedings are set to be carried out in Italian, and all documents in a foreign language need to be translated.[1101]

5.2.2. The Ordinary National Procedure

The claimant initiates ordinary court proceedings by requesting a bailiff (*ufficiale giudiziario*) to serve a summons on the defendant, who is instructed to appear before the judge on a specific date (*citazione in giudizio*).[1102] The document has to be served

on the review of the judicial circumscriptions – offices of the Justice of the Peace (*Revisione delle circoscrizioni giudizi – uffici giudici di pace*).

1095 Article 9 CPC.

1096 Article 320(1)-(3) CPC.

1097 For the EOP, see the Information communicated by Member States in accordance with Article 29 of Regulation (EC) No 1896/2006 of the European Parliament and the Council of 12 December 2006 creating a European order for payment procedure, available at https://e-justice.europa.eu/content_european_payment_order-353-it-en.do?member=1. For the ESCP, see the Information communicated by Member States in accordance with Article 25 of Regulation (EC) No 861/2007 of the European Parliament and the Council of 11 July 2007 establishing a European Small Claims Procedure, available at https://e-justice.europa.eu/content_small_claims-354-it-en.do?clang=it.

1098 Article 115 CPC. Comite & Liguori (2014), at 135. For example, the judge can decide *ex officio* to hear the testimony of a person to whom the parties made reference (Article 281*ter* CPC). This does not override the parties' burden of proof. See Comite & Liguori (2014), at 258; Lupoi (2014), at 41–42.

1099 Article 112, Article 113(1) and Article 116 CPC. Comite & Liguori (2014), at 133–134 and 136–137; Lupoi (2014), at 40–42.

1100 Article 82(1) CPC.

1101 Article 122–123 CPC. Regions with significant linguistic minorities allow proceedings to be conducted in other languages (e.g. German in Alto Adige).

1102 Article 163 CPC. Article 137 and subsequent CPC provide the rules in accordance with which service by the bailiff is carried out. Following Law No. 53/1994, lawyers may be authorised by the Bar Association to directly serve certain procedural documents on their counterparts, usually by post (Article 1 Law No. 53/1994) or by electronic means (*notificazione con modalita telematica*) (Article 3*bis* Law No. 53/1994). This form of service is especially popular with bigger and more congested courts. See Lupoi (2014), at 119–122.

within a specific timeframe before the hearing (i.e. at least 90 days before if the defendant resides in Italy or 150 days if he resides abroad).[1103] The bailiff can also arrange service by registered mail or through certified email (PEC).[1104] The *citazione* contains information concerning the court before which the claim is made, the details of the parties and their representatives, the claim and the evidence that the claimant intends to use, and the date of the first hearing (*udienza di comparizione*).[1105] The claimant has to submit the *citazione* including proof of service, evidence of having paid the court fees, and all documents relevant for registration of the case (*iscrizione della causa a ruolo*).[1106] Since 30 June 2014, *Tribunale* submission of documents has been done electronically.[1107] The instruction judge (*giudice istruttore*) confirms the date of the first hearing or postpones it, depending upon his schedule and workload.[1108] In practice, the hearing is often postponed.

The defendant becomes party to the proceedings immediately after being served with the claim, and needs to appoint a lawyer and file a response to the claim (*comparsa di risposta*),[1109] and formally present the defence to the court (*costituzione in giudizio*).[1110] If no response or defence is filed, the judge will issue a default judgment. If defence is filed, the judge verifies at the first hearing (*udienza di trattazione*) whether the procedural acts performed are valid or need amendment,[1111] and whether the parties are duly represented. He also requests clarifications if necessary, and raises the issues he can point out *ex officio*.[1112] If the claim is subject to pre-trial compulsory mediation proceedings or assisted dispute resolution, the judge on his own initiative or upon the

[1103] Article 163*bis*(1) CPC. The service is carried out on the person of the defendant (Article 138 CPC), or on someone at the address of residence or his workplace (Articles 139–140 CPC). In this second instance, the bailiff sends the defendant a warning by registered post with acknowledgement of receipt. Rules regarding service on legal entities are contained in Article 145 CPC. If no one is available or willing to receive the document, the bailiff leaves a notice on the door of the defendant and deposits the documents with the local city or town hall. If service has to be carried out in a different Member State, the Service Regulation provisions apply (see also Law No. 160/2000). If the *Legge annuale per il mercato e la concorrenza* (Article 25 Legislative Proposal No. 2085 of 2015) is adopted by the Chamber of Deputes (Italian Parliament), the Poste Italiene will no longer have a monopoly on the service of documents from 17 September 2017. This might see other entities undertaking postal services directly involved in the communication of judicial documents in Italy as well as abroad to other Member States.

[1104] Article 1 Law No. 890/20. November 1982; Article 149 and Article 149*bis* CPC. If the certified email address was indicated in the summons documents.

[1105] Article 163 CPC. The defendant is also informed that he must present his defence formally 20 days prior to the date of the hearing, or 10 days before if the periods of time were abridged.

[1106] Article 165 CPC.

[1107] Article 16*bis*(1) Decree-Law No. 179/2012.

[1108] Article 168*bis*(5) CPC. See Lupoi (2014), at 124.

[1109] Article 166 CPC. Twenty-two days before the hearing or 10 days before if the periods of time were abridged.

[1110] Articles 166–167 CPC.

[1111] If the court declares a procedural act or activity to be null and void, it will order the party to renew it, except when this is no longer possible. Hence, the case will go back to the stage of the invalid act. Lupoi (2014), at 111.

[1112] Article 182 and Article 183(1) CPC.

defendant's objection will verify the fulfillment of this requirement.[1113] The parties can make a joint request for the instruction judge to attempt a settlement (*conciliazione*).[1114] Until the evidence-gathering phase has been finalised, the judge may formulate a proposal of transaction or settlement for the parties. Similar to the ESCP provision, the judge is expected to proceed in this manner if a settlement appears possible.[1115]

In practice, this first hearing is often only a formality, as – due to an excessive caseload – the judge generally does not have the time to study the case in detail.[1116] At this stage, considering the complexity of the case and the evidentiary means, the judge may order the case to be shifted to a summary procedure (*procedimento sommario di cognizione*).[1117] However, in a court system labouring under a backlog, it seems unlikely that the judge will be able to proceed in this manner.

After the hearing, the parties submit and exchange written briefs (*memorie*). Three parallel memoranda sessions are submitted to the instruction judge,[1118] meaning that within a period of 80 days the parties have a final opportunity to modify and complete their claims, counter-claims, and defences.[1119] This written part of the proceedings is crucial for the parties and for subsequent developments in the case. Following the lapse of this period, no further factual or evidentiary issues can be brought before the judge. In theory, these strict, relatively short periods for the parties to put forward their claims, defences, and evidence – that are to a certain extent also common to the EOP and ESCP[1120] should contribute to making the general national procedure speedier and more efficient. However, in practice, in order to bypass the rigidity of the terms and the fact that the next hearing will take place many months after the *udienza di trattazione*, the judge states that the deadlines for filing the memoranda will start to run from a future date, instead of at the moment of the first hearing.[1121] After the 80 days, if the claim can be decided on the basis of documentary evidence already submitted, the judge or the panel of judges proceed to render a judgment.[1122] Otherwise, at a second hearing, the

1113 Since 21 March 2011, mediation has been a compulsory pre-trial step for certain types of disputes (e.g. insurance contracts, financial and banking contracts, lease agreements). See Article 5 Decree-Law No. 28/4 March 2010. The parties may choose to appear voluntarily before the Justice of the Peace seeking to settle their dispute (Article 320 CPC). On Assisted Dispute Resolution prior to court proceedings for claims below €50,000, see Article 3(1) Decree-Law No. 132/12 September 2014 as approved by Law No. 162/10 November 2014. On pre-trial assisted dispute resolution by lawyer(s), see Article 3(2) in conjunction with Article 2(3) and Article 2(2) letter a) Decree-Law No. 132/12 September 2014 as approved by Law No. 162/10 November 2014.

1114 Article 185 in conjunction with Article 186 and Article 18(3) CPC.

1115 Article 12(3) ESCP and Article 185*bis* CPC.

1116 Lupoi (2014), at 126.

1117 Article 183*bis* CPC introduced by Article 14 Decree-Law No. 132/12 September 2014 as approved by Law No. 162/10 November 2014. This Article has applied since 10 December 2014. On the *procedimento sommario di congnizione*, see Section 5.3.3.

1118 Article 183 CPC.

1119 Article 183(6) CPC.

1120 For example, in the EOP procedure there is a strict period of 30 days for the defendant to oppose the order (Article 12(2)(b)). In the ESCP, the defendant has 30 days to respond to the claim, and the claimant has 30 days to respond to counterclaims (Article 5(3) and (6)).

1121 Lupoi (2014), at 127.

1122 Article 187(1) CPC. This is rarely the case in practice.

case should be ready to enter the investigation stage (*fase istruttoria*).[1123] The evidence-gathering phase involves a hearing (*udienza di assunzione dei mezzi di prova*),[1124] during which the instruction judge proceeds to take the evidence admitted.[1125] This phase is closed if all the evidence has been acquired or if further proof is considered unnecessary.[1126] The case then proceeds to the decision stage.[1127] The complexity of rules and stages makes it impossible for a private party to follow a trial without the assistance of a lawyer.

Before the case is deliberated, parties and their representatives are required to present their conclusion (*precisazione delle conclusioni*). This can be done in three ways: writing, mixed, or orally.[1128] In practice, the written method is the most frequently used. The parties deposit their final written defences (*comparse conclusionali*), and then proceed to reply to the other parties' written defence (*memorie di replica*).[1129] Once the replies have also been submitted, the judge has 30 days to issue his decision.[1130] This procedural timeframe is identical to the one set by EOP and ESCP Regulations. The judge decides the case at his own discretion based on the evidence.[1131]

Once the decision has been published, the court communicates the enacting terms of the judgment (*dispositivo*) to the parties, but in order to obtain a copy of the decision the parties need to pay a fee, which is often a percentage of the value of the decision.[1132] A copy may be requested before payment if the party is bringing an appeal or initiating enforcement proceedings. The first instance judgment is provisionally enforceable.[1133]

Appeal proceedings are subject to two different deadlines: a 6-month period from the date of publication of the judgment[1134] and a 30-day period if the winning party has served a copy of the decision on the debtor.[1135] In appeal, a higher court will re-adjudicate the claims.[1136] The appellant will serve a *citazione* on the other party and, subsequently, submit it to the court. The proceedings will follow the same course as the first instance proceedings.[1137] Since 30 June 2015, it has been possible to file appeal documents

1123 In practice, it may happen that several months or sometimes years pass between the various hearings, especially with the larger courts. See Silvestri (2014), at 81–84.

1124 Article 183(7) in conjunction with Article 184 CPC. The date of the taking of evidence hearing is communicated to the parties by the clerk.

1125 If this is not possible within the same hearing, the judge will establish other hearings for this purpose (Article 202 CPC). Moreover, the judge can always re-open the evidence-gathering phase.

1126 Article 209 CPC.

1127 Article 188 CPC.

1128 Article 281*quinquies* and Article 281*sexies* CPC.

1129 Article 281*quinquies*(1) in conjunction with Article 190(1) CPC.

1130 Article 281*quinquies*(1) CPC.

1131 Article 116(1) CPC.

1132 See Section 5.2.3.

1133 Article 282 CPC. The provisional enforceability of the first instance decision seeks to mitigate the incentive of filing an appeal in order to delay the civil process and compel the parties to comply with the decision. See Comite & Liguori (2014), at 262.

1134 Article 327(1) CPC.

1135 Article 325(1) CPC. See Lupoi (2014), at 135–136.

1136 The parties cannot introduce new claims, exceptions, or defences at this stage (Article 345 CPC). In appeal, the higher court revises the proceedings that took place before the first instance and the decision.

1137 Article 359 CPC. Following the reform introduced by Decree-Law No. 83/22 June 2012 implemented by Law No. 134/7 August 2012, appeal requests are filtered at the first hearing (Article 348*bis* CPC). See further Lupoi (2014), at 145–149.

electronically.[1138] The execution of the decision during appeal proceedings is suspended upon request, and the judge may impose the payment of a security for this purpose.[1139] The right to bring a second appeal (*ricorso per cassazione*) is set by the Constitution.[1140] Even if the grounds are limited to the legitimacy of the decision and procedural acts, and to the interpretation of legal provisions, this means of appeal is very often implemented.[1141] In practice, most requests for a *ricorso per cassazione* are based on the provisions of Article 360(5) CPC, which require the Supreme Court to check the legal reasoning of the lower court for an omission of a fact that is in dispute and is fundamental for the decision.[1142] Like the appeal, the *ricorso* is subject in Italy to two procedural deadlines: a 6-month period from the date of publication of the judgment[1143] and a 60-day period if the winning party has served a copy of the decision on the debtor.[1144] In addition to the strict formal requirements, the parties must be represented by a lawyer who is allowed to represent clients at this stage (*avvocato cassazionista*).[1145] A decision issued by the *Cassazione* is final. The judgment becomes *res judicata* once it cannot be subject to ordinary appeals (*appello, ricorso in Cassazione, revocazione ordinaria*). Extraordinary means of appeals are also available: namely, revision of the judgment (*revocazione*) and opposition of a third party (*opposizione di terzo*).[1146]

The duration of ordinary court proceedings is notorious for being very long, although it has decreased over the years. Down from 423 days in 2013, it reached an average duration of 375 days before a *Tribunale* in 2016.[1147] As regards the Justice of the Peace, the average duration in 2013 was 345 days.[1148] The average duration of an appeal procedure in 2013 was 1,061 days, with a period of 1,428 days for an ordinary procedure

[1138] Technical Communication on the Computerization of the Judicial System (*Relazione tecnica sull'informatizzazione della giustizia*), 29 July 2014 (available online at www.giustizia.it/giustizia/it/contentview.wp?previsiousPage=mg_2_7_5&contentId=ART1051146).

[1139] Article 283(1) CPC.

[1140] Article 111 Constitution.

[1141] Article 360(1) CPC. The parties may agree to use the *ricorso in cassazione* directly and to skip the appeal before the Court of Appeal (Article 360(2) CPC. See on this Lupoi (2014), at 150.

[1142] This request is to a certain extent controversial because it implies that the *Corte di Cassazione* has to examine the merits of the dispute, at the risk of going beyond its role. See Lupoi (2014), at 152–153.

[1143] Article 327(1) CPC.

[1144] Article 325(2) CPC.

[1145] See Mandrioli & Carratta (2014), Volume II, at 539–626.

[1146] Article 395–403 CPC and Article 404–408 CPC. See further Mandrioli & Carratta (2014), Volume II, at 640–667.

[1147] *Sintesi della Relazione del Ministro sull'amministrazione della giustizia per l'anno 2016, ai sensi dell'art. 86*, R.D. 30 gennaio 1941, n.12, *Inaugurazione Anno Giudiziario 2017*, 18 January 2017 (available at www.giustizia.it/giustizia/it/mg_2_15_7.page). The actual duration in 2016 was 981 days. See *Andamento della durata media degli affari del civile - anno 2016*, 16 marzo 2017 (available at www.giustizia.it/giustizia/it/mg_1_14_1.page;jsessionid=-KFtZEjdzZDOzC4vDicwumij?facetNode_1=4_26&facetNode_2=1_5_33&contentId=SST1263302&previsiousPage=mg_1_14).

[1148] *Durata media dei procedimenti civili suddivisione per ufficio e material*, Direzione Generale di Statistica, Ministero della Giustizia, 2013. For the same period, the average period invovlving *Tribunale* cases was 423 days (available at https://reportistica.dgstat.giustizia.it/VisualizzatoreReport.Aspx?Report=/Pubblica/Statistiche%20della%20DGSTAT/Materia%20Civile/2.%20Durata%20dei%20Procedimenti%20(fino%20al%202013)/1.%20Totale%20nazionale).

case. This situation hampers parties' access to justice and also hinders economic activity. The judges and clerks are under severe pressure, and work hard to reduce the backlog, but even though these legal professionals are among the most productive in Europe in terms of issuing decisions, the situation has still not been resolved.[1149]

5.2.3. Costs of Ordinary Court Proceedings

The party initiating court proceedings is required to pay the court fees. This includes the unified contribution (*contributo unificato*), an advanced flat fee owed by private parties to the Treasury in civil litigation (*anticipazioni forfettarie dai private all'erario nel processo civile*),[1150] and the registration fee involving the judgment (*tassa di registro*).[1151] The present costs of court proceedings are based on the levels set by Law Decree No. 90/24 June 2014.[1152] The *contributo unificato* and the *tassa di registro* vary in accordance with the value of the dispute. Following the last increase, the *contributto unificato* in ordinary proceedings ranges from €43 for claims up to €1,100 and €1,686 for claims above €520,000.[1153] These fees are increased by 50% if the lawyer fails to indicate his certified email address and fax number or if the party omits to provide his tax code in the claim.[1154] With regard to appeals, the value of the *contributo unificato* increases by 50%, thus ranging between €64.50 and €2,529.[1155] Payment of the *contributo* is a highly problematic aspect of cross-border claims, including the European uniform procedures, due to the methods available. These comprise payment by stamp (*bollo*);[1156] through payment institutions (e.g. banks, *Poste Italiane*, collection agents) by using Form F23;[1157] through any office of the Italian Post (*Poste Italiane*) by filling in a special form (*bollettino*

1149 The clearance rate data concerns litigious and non-litigious cases handled between 2010–2015. European Commission, *The 2017 EU Justice Scoreboard*, 2017, at 9.

1150 Article 30 Decree of the President of the Republic No. 115/30 May 2002.

1151 Article 37 Decree of the President of the Republic No. 131/26 April 1986 regarding the consolidated text on the registration fee (*testo unico delle disposizioni concernenti l'imposta di registro*), Official Gazette No. 99/30 April 1986.

1152 Decree-Law No. 90/24 June 2014 regarding urgent measures for administrative simplification and transparency and for the efficiency of the judicial offices (*Misure urgenti per la semplificazione e la trasparenza amministrativa e per l'efficienza degli uffici giudiziari*), Official Gazette No. 144/24 June 2014, converted and amended by Law No. 114/11 August 2014, Official Gazette No. 190/18 August 2014.

1153 Article 13(1) Decree of the President of the Republic No. 115/30 May 2002.

1154 Article 13(3)*bis* Decree of the President of the Republic No. 115/30 May 2002.

1155 Article 13(1)*bis* Decree of the President of the Republic No. 115/30 May 2002.

1156 Article 192(1) letter c) Decree of the President of the Republic No. 115/30 May 2002. The *bollo* can be purchased from tobacco shops (*tabaccherie*) and collection agents (Equitalia Group). The stamp needs to be accompanied by a statement of payment form signed by the vendor. The form is available online on the website of the Tax Authority www.agenziaentrate.gov.it/wps/wcm/connect/27143b80426a6edd9e959fc065cef0e8/Comunicazione+di+Vesamento+del+Contributo+Unificato.pdf?MOD=AJPERES&CACHEID=27143b80426a6edd9e959fc065cef0e8.

1157 Article 192(1) letter a) Decree of the President of the Republic No. 115/30 May 2002. Information regarding Form F23 and the way it should be filled in are available in Italian on the website of the Tax Authority www.agenziaentrate.gov.it/wps/content/Nsilib/Nsi/Home/CosaDeviFare/Versare/F23/Modello+F23/. Additionally, the form may be filled in online (available at www.agenziaentrate.gov.it/wps/content/Nsilib/Nsi/Home/CosaDeviFare/Versare/F23/Programma+di+compilazione+F23/).

di conto corrente postale);[1158] or by electronic means (*pagamento telematico*).[1159] Electronic payment is limited to persons who are specially registered, such as lawyers. Following payment, an electronic receipt is received. This can be uploaded electronically in the court file or deposited in paper format at the clerk's office.[1160] In order to use any of these means, the party needs to be physically present or to delegate a lawyer to carry out payment in his name. Thus, a party resident abroad will most probably need the services of an Italian lawyer for this purpose. In addition to these methods of payment, the Tax Authority has established an e-payment service, @e.bollo,[1161] but for the moment it appears to be available only to Italian residents.

The *anticipazioni forfettarie dai privati all'erario nel processo civile* is a flat fee of €27 that is paid at the beginning of the trial as the *contributo unificato*.[1162] This flat fee is also charged for appeals.

The *tassa di reggistro* for judgments regarding money claims amounts to 3% of the value of the award,[1163] and this fee is payable to the Tax Authority (*Agenzia delle Entrate*). In accordance with Article 57(1) Decree No. 131/1986, the parties are jointly and severally liable for its payment. In practice, the text is not uniformly interpreted, although the Court of Cassation issued decisions on the matter in accordance with which the losing party bears these costs,[1164] which can be paid by using the previously mentioned Form F23. Additionally, the parties need to pay a fee when requesting copies of the case documents or certified copies.[1165] If the court fees are not paid, the clerks will seek to collect them from the party responsible through a publicly owed entity, Equitalia Giustizia SpA.[1166] As of 1 July 2017, the preparatory acts related to recovery continue to be carried out by Equitalia Giustizia, while the collection tasks have been taken over by

1158 Article 192(1) letter b) Decree of the President of the Republic No. 115/30 May 2002. The form of the bolletino is available online on the website of the Tax Authority, www.agenziaentrate.gov.it/wps/wcm/connect/08577a00426a6ec89e819fc065cef0e8/boll_cc.pdf?MOD=AJPERES&CACHEID=08577a00426a6ec89e819fc065cef0e8. The number of the bank account into which the *contributo unificato* is to be paid is 57152043 in the name of the *Tresoreria provinciale dello Stato*.

1159 Article 30 Ministry Decree No. 44/21 February 2011, Official Gazette, General Series, No. 89/18 April 2011.

1160 For more information regarding this method of payment, see https://pst.giustizia.it/PST/it/pst_1_0.wp?tab=tab_scheda&contentId=SPR382&previousPage=pst_1_8.

1161 In the first phase of implementation of the service, this will be available on the intranet of public institutions that are members of the Nodo of Payment Services (Agenzia per l'Italia Digitale). Public institutions that provide or issue electronic documents will activate this payment service. In the second stage, the stamp will be made available for citizens to purchase from the public institutions upon request. See further information available on www.agenziaentrate.gov.it/wps/content/Nsilib/Nsi/Documentazione/Servizio+e.bollo/.

1162 Article 30 Decree of the President of the Republic No. 115/30 May 2002.

1163 Tariffs Parte 1 Article 8 point 1 letter b) Decree of the President of the Republic No. 131/1986.

1164 *Inter alia* Cass. Sent. n. 11149/2006.

1165 Article 196 in conjunction with Articles 267–270 and Annexes 6–8 Decree of the President of the Republic No. 115/30 May 2002. For example, based on the number of pages a certified copy of a judgment of no more than 4 pages amounts to €7.37 (€8.60 for decisions up to 10 pages).

1166 Management of the justice debt was assigned to Equitalia Giustizia S.p.a. (Article 1(367), and subsequently Law No. 244/2007), and the services it carries out are based on a convention signed together with the Ministry of Justice on 10 September 2010.

the Agenzia delle Entrate-Riscossione.[1167] Along with procedural fees, the parties are also liable for lawyer's fees, which differ per county and per professional.

In general, the losing party will bear the cost of the judicial proceedings, but there are certain limitations.[1168] The judge can sanction vexatious litigation based on the provisions of Article 96 CPC.[1169] Because the law does not set any limitation on the amount, the court has complete discretion in setting the punitive award.[1170]

5.3. National Tailored Solutions for the Recovery of Monetary Claims

Several national simplified procedures are available in Italy for the recovery of money claims. The *procedimento per ingiunzione (ingiunzione di pagamento)* is the most successful in practice, being favoured by parties and lawyers over other proceedings. This special procedure is a direct national equivalent to the EOP procedure.[1171] The ESCP does not have a direct correspondent in domestic procedures. Proceedings before the Justice of the Peace are set to handle small value claims, but this has not led to the establishment of a distinct special procedure.[1172] This section analyses the national special procedures that parties can use in seeking to recover their debt, looking at their characteristics and use in practice.

5.3.1. Procedimento per Ingiunzione

5.3.1.1. General Aspects

The *procedimento per ingiunzione* regulated by Articles 633–656 CPC was introduced in 1922,[1173] and is applicable in purely national money claims as well as in cross-border

1167 Article 1(1) and (11) Decree-Law No. 193/2016, Official Gazette No. 249/24 June 2016. Reply from the Director of Equitalia Giustizia SpA to a request for information (*Regolamento CE 1896/2006 – attribuzioni Agenzia delle riscossione – Riscontro*), 18 May 2017, Prot. N. 2017-EQUIGIU-0061112 (document on file with the researcher).

1168 Article 91(1)-(2) CPC. Following the Justice (Mini)Reform in November 2014, when deciding upon the costs of the proceedings, the judge is supposed to take into consideration whether the winning party refused an invitation from the other party to reach a settlement in claims below €50,000 or did not reply to the invitation within a period of 30 days. See Article 4 Decree-Law No. 132/2014 as approved by Law No. 162/10 November 2014. See Biavati (2013), at 271–274; Lupoi (2012a), at 32–33. On the recovery of lawyer's fees, see https://e-justice.europa.eu/content_costs_of_proceedings-37-it-en.do?clang=it.

1169 Article 96 CPC. According to Article 96(1) CPC, upon the winning party's request, the court may order the losing party to pay not only the legal costs of the proceedings but also the damages the party can prove he has suffered. In practice, this is not often used because it is difficult for the winning party to prove that he has suffered additional damages as a consequence of the proceedings. See Lupoi (2012a), at 31.

1170 See Lupoi (2012), at 103–104; Lupoi (2012a), at 31–32.

1171 Castellaneta (2009), at 7; Fauvarque-Cosson & Behar-Touchais (2012), at 119.

1172 Fauvarque-Cosson & Behar-Touchais (2012), at 120.

1173 According to Cappelletti, the procedure is 'the most important summary proceeding'; Cappelletti, Merryman & Perillo (1967), at 122–123. See also, Balena (2012), Volume III, at 195.

disputes.[1174] It can also be used in the recovery of professional debts resulting from services provided by lawyers, clerks, bailiffs, or any legal professional providing specific services concerning claims submitted to the court.[1175] Additionally, the order may be issued for rights subject to condition or counter performance if the claimant offers proof establishing the presumption that these acts will be fulfilled.[1176] Compared to the EOP, the national order for payment has a broader application. It concerns not only the collection of determined or determinable pecuniary claims that have fallen due but is also available for claims regarding the delivery of goods or fungible assets (*cose fungibili*).[1177] This characteristic of the *procedimento per ingiunzione* is common to the ESCP, which allows the petitioner to have claims other than money.[1178] As with the EOP, the national order for payment is not subject to any set threshold.

Jurisdiction over the national order for payments is divided between the Justice of the Peace and the *Tribunale*, in keeping with the same criteria applicable to the ordinary national procedures.[1179] If the defendant opposes the order, the same judge that issued the order will handle the ordinary procedure.[1180] In contrast to the EOP, representation by a lawyer is compulsory for claims above €1,100.[1181]

5.3.1.2. The Procedure

The procedure is initiated by a special means called *ricorso*.[1182] Up until 30 June 2014, the claimant or his representative submitted the claim directly to the court's clerk for registration, or, alternatively, where available through the Trial On-Line system (*Processo Civile Telematico-PCT*).[1183] Since the above date, however, all claims and documents have to be filed electronically with the court.[1184]

1174 The provisions of Article 633(3) CPC that limited the use of the *ingiunzione di pagamento* to purely national cases was abrogated by Article 9 c.1. Decree-Law No. 231/9 October 2002. In addition, the provisions of Article 641(2) and Article 644 CPC now set longer periods for action if the debtor is resident abroad. See also Cataldi (2009), at 98–103.

1175 Article 633(1) point 2) CPC.

1176 Article 633(2) CPC. See here also Article 664 CPC regarding the payment of administrative/service fees (*canoni*). Cataldi (2009), at 83–84.

1177 Article 633(1) CPC. In this case, the claimant has to declare the amount of money that he is willing to accept if the specific performance is not complied with (Article 639 CPC). This is not an alternative duty for the debtor to choose, but an equivalent payment in case he does not comply with the order to deliver the goods. Comite & Liguori (2014), at 532; Graziosi (2011), at 231–322.

1178 See Annex I ESCP, Form A Claim Form Section 7 – About your claim.

1179 Article 637 CPC.

1180 Article 645(1) CPC. On the judge competent to handle the opposition trial, see further Tedoldi & Merlo (2009), at 468–496.

1181 Article 82(1) CPC. See also Section 5.2.1.

1182 Article 638 CPC.

1183 Carnevali & Resca (2014), at 161–184; Carnevali & Resca (2013), at 273–314.

1184 Article 16*bis*(4) Decree-Law No. 179/2012. Points 1 and 8 of Circular of 28 October 2014 on the implementation by the clerks' office following the entrance into force of the provisions established by Article 16*bis* and subsequent. of the Decree-Law 179/2012 and 90/2014 (*Circolare 28 ottobre 2014-Adempimenti di cancelleria conseguenti all'entrata in vigore degli obblighi di cui agli art. 16 bis e*

In contrast to the EOP, the claim must be proven by written evidence.[1185] Together with the *ricorso*, the claimant has to include the power of attorney and a declaration of residence or election of domicile within the administrative territory of the court, otherwise he will be served documents of the proceedings at the clerk's office.[1186] The rules on evidence are less restrictive than those governing written evidence in the ordinary national procedure.[1187] As well as general information regarding the parties, their representatives, and the claim, the application has to contain particular details that are required for its validity. These details are (1) the claimant's fiscal code (*codice fiscal*) as well as that of his legal representative and of the defendant, and (2) the lawyer's certified e-mail address (*indirizzo di posta elettronica certificata-PEC*) and his fax number. If this information is missing, the claimant is required to pay higher court fees.[1188]

The judge will decide on the basis of the documents submitted. The application will be rejected if the amount is not due or determined, if the court does not have jurisdiction, if the claim is lacking legal grounds, or if the proof provided is considered insufficient and the claimant does not proceed to the submission of additional evidence (*integrazione*) within the period set by the judge, or if he does not withdraw the claim.[1189] Similar to the EOP, rejection of the application or a partial award does not preclude the applicant from initiating a new, similar procedure or making use of other proceedings available in accordance with national law.[1190] Based on what appears to be justified on the basis of the submitted evidence, the judge may partially or entirely admit the claim and award the costs of proceedings.[1191] Similar to the EOP, the judge has to issue the decree within a period of 30 days from the moment of registration of the application.[1192] The national order is issued in an electronic format, and is made available to legal representatives in the case's electronic file.[1193]

sgg. d.l. 179/2012 e 90/2014) (available online at www.giustizia.it/giustizia/it/mg_1_8_1.wp?previousPage=mg_1_8_1&contentId=SDC1076955).

1185 Article 633(1) point 1) in conjunction with Article 634 CPC.

1186 Article 638(1)-(2).

1187 Article 634–635 CPC. Simple invoices provided by a commercial entity are considered to be acceptable means of proof in this procedure. For a professional debt, if the claim is based on costs and fees for which the law establishes only a minimum and a maximum, the proof submitted to the court has to include the opinion of the member of the professional order regarding the claimed expenses (Article 636 CPC). In the event of an opposition, the general rules regarding written evidence apply. See Lupoi (2014), at 209–210. On the type of written evidence that is considered sufficient, see Balena (2012), at 197–199; Comite & Liguori (2014), at 529; Verde (2009), at 125–190.

1188 Article 638(1) in conjunction with Article 125(1) CPC. See Article 13 Decree of the President of the Republic No. 115/2002 and Section 5.2.3.

1189 Article 640(1)-(2) CPC. See further Storto (2009), at 319–320.

1190 Article 640(3) CPC and Article 11(3) EOP. See Balena (2012), at 201 and 217; Verde (2009), at 117–118; Carratta (2007), at 1529.

1191 In Italy, the costs of proceedings (*spese*) include not only the court fees but also the lawyer's fees. Storto (2009), at 354–355.

1192 Article 641(1) CPC and Article 12(1) EOP.

1193 Point 8 Circular of 28 October 2014 (available online at www.giustizia.it/giustizia/it/mg_1_8_1.wp?previsiousPage=mg_1_8_1&contentId=SDC1076955).

The claimant has to serve the authenticated copy of the order on the debtor.[1194] Similar to the EOP, the debtor is informed of his options and the effects of failing to oppose the order. He is ordered to pay or deliver the goods, or to oppose the order within a set period. This is longer than the EOP opposition period: namely, 40 days from the date of service if the defendant is resident in Italy,[1195] and 50 days if he resides in another Member State.[1196] The service is carried out by bailiff (*ufficiale giudiziario*) upon the claimant's request.[1197] The national order for payment (*decreto*) needs to be served on the debtor within a set period, otherwise it will be void. This is 60 days if the debtor is resident in Italy or 90 days from the time the court issued the decree if the debtor is resident abroad.[1198] This should not be the case for the EOP;[1199] if the order is declared void, the claimant may always refile the claim.[1200]

In practice, only a small number of orders for payment issued are opposed.[1201] If the debtor decides to oppose the *ingiunzione di pagamento* within the set period, he will have to approach the bailiff's office at the court that issued the order and initiate proceedings. The bailiff serves a summons on the claimant, as in the ordinary court proceedings, requesting him to appear in court on a date set by the debtor (*atto di citazione*). Subsequently, he communicates the notice of opposition to the clerk.[1202] The task of initiating court proceedings following the opposition rests with the defendant. This is different from the EOP, and has consequences for the European procedure.[1203] The defendant cannot simply state that he opposes the order, as is done in the EOP procedure.[1204] Unlike the EOP, the opposition may also include a counterclaim, provided

1194 Article 643(2) CPC.

1195 Article 641(1) CPC. In accordance with Article 641(2), the judge may reduce the term to 10 days or increase it to 60 days for justified reasons (*giusti motivi*). See further Storto (2009), at 350–351.

1196 Article 641(2) CPC. If the debtors are resident in another Member State, the period for payment of the debt or opposition to the decree can be reduced for justified reasons (*giusti motivi*) to 20 days, while for debtors who are resident in other countries, this cannot be reduced to less than 30 days or increased to more than 120 days.

1197 Article 643(2) in conjunction with Article 137 CPC. If the claimant has a legal representative, it is the lawyer's task to submit this request to the court's bailiff's office. See further also Valle (2009), at 435–462.

1198 Article 644 CPC. The dominant opinion within the legal literature is that the *ingiunzione di pagamento* would be invalidated only if it were not served. If the service were carried out outside the established period, the debtor would not suffer any prejudice. The period for him to oppose the order would begin to run only from the moment he received the copy. Alternatively, the debtor may raise the issue of the *ingiunzione*'s ineffectiveness. See Cassazione 2 aprile 2010, n. 8126. Balena (2012), at 202; Valle (2009), at 444–448, 452–453.

1199 See further Section 5.5.

1200 Article 644 CPC.

1201 Around 20–30% of the number of orders issued by the court. Question 3 of the *Osservazioni sul Libro Verde sul Procedimento europea d'ingiunzione di pagamento-COM(2002) 746 del 20/12/2002 presentate dalla Presidenza dell'E.U.R. -Unione Europea dei Funzionari Giudiziari*, Padova, 30 May 2003, at 2. Biavati (2013), at 578.

1202 Article 645(1) CPC.

1203 See Section 5.7.

1204 Article 645(2) CPC and Article 17(1) EOP. The tasks that the defendant needs to fulfill are aimed at reducing oppositions for dilatory purposes. Lupoi (2014), at 210; Balena (2012), at 217.

the necessary links exist between the claims.[1205] The summons will put forward the arguments and evidence giving rise to the opposition. The passage to the national procedure and the opposition judgment have certain particularities: for example, the reversed position of parties (the creditor being the defendant within this procedure), the creditor bearing the burden of proof in most situations, and the application of more restrictive rules relating to evidence.[1206] The parties are summonsed to appear before the judge, as in the ordinary procedure, but this has to take place within an expressly established maximum period.[1207] Like the EOP, after the opposition the procedure continues in accordance with the ordinary national procedure.

The *ingiunzione* also provides for a late opposition in specific circumstances.[1208] This is an exceptional remedy available to the defendant if he proves that he was not immediately aware of the order due to the irregularity of service, to unforeseeable circumstance (*caso fortuito*), or to force majeure.[1209] The reasons for which the debtor is allowed to proceed to lodging a late opposition somewhat resemble the EOP review criteria, although the two mechanisms are not identical.[1210] Additionally, a late opposition is possible only within a limit of 10 days from the first act of execution. After this the court will reject it, and no other means of objection are available.[1211] The nullity of the service becomes irrelevant in such circumstances; the order is considered valid and effective.[1212] Nonetheless, if the order was not opposed, the judge will verify whether service was properly carried out. If there are doubts as to the debtor being aware of the proceedings, the judge will order the claimant to proceed to a renewal of service. If the service was carried out in a valid manner upon the claimant's request, the judge declares the order enforceable once the opposition period lapses, or if following the opposition the defendant did not formally present the defence to the court (*costituzione in giudizio*).[1213] The order acquires in this case the effects of a judgment on the merits.[1214] It also acquires *res judicata* in the event that the opposition was rejected by the judge.[1215]

1205 Article 36 CPC. See Tedoldi & Merlo (2009), at 529–530.

1206 See Balena (2012), at 204–206, 208–210; Lupoi (2012), at 209; Cataldi (2009), at 76; Verde (2009), at 116.

1207 Article 645(3) in conjunction with Article 163*bis*(1) and (3) CPC. This amounts to 120 days (90 days + 30 days) if the debtor is resident in Italy and to 180 days (150 days + 30 days) if he is resident abroad.

1208 Article 650(1) CPC.

1209 This provision was criticised in the literature because on the one hand it requests a burdensome proof from the defendant opposing the order, and on the other hand it is applicable in situations where service is null, which would be in contradiction to the principle of nullity (*quod nullum est nullum producit effectum*). Balena (2012), at 204. Regarding force majeure, see Corte Costituzionale, Sentenza n. 120, 20 maggio 1976.

1210 Article 20(1) EOP. For an analysis on this aspect, see Picciotto & Carlisi (2010), at 327–329.

1211 Article 650(3) CPC. On the interpretation that there is still the possibility of opposing the *ingiunzione* on the basis of the provisions of Article 650(1) CPC if the defendant was not immediately aware (*tempestiva conoscenza*) of the order, see Tedoldi & Merlo (2009), at 501–504.

1212 Comite & Liguori (2014), at 540.

1213 Article 647(1) CPC. The request may also be made orally before the judge.

1214 This is the dominant opinion expressed in the legal literature. See *inter alia* Balena (2012), at 214; Comite & Liguori (2014), at 543.

1215 Article 653(1) CPC.

The *ingiunzione di pagamento* become enforceable titles once the judge attaches the declaration of enforceability to the original title.[1216] At the request of the interested party, the clerk provides an authenticated copy of the order for payment.[1217] For execution purposes, the order for payment does not have to be served subsequently.[1218] Upon request, the judge may also declare the *ingiunzione di pagamento* enforceable from the moment of its issuance, without the creditor needing to wait the minimum time set by law for the debtor to comply with the order (*precetto*). This is possible in cases in which (1) the debt is based on a promissory note, a bank or cashier cheque (*assegno bancario* and *assegno circolare*), a stock exchange credit certificate (*certificato di liquidazione di borsa*), or a document issued by a public notary or another authorised public official; (2) there is a danger of serious prejudice if there is a delay of execution; or (3) the claimant produces a document signed by the debtor attesting the right claimed.[1219] In the two latter situations, the judge has power of discretion, and may award enforcement on the condition that the security fee be paid by the claimant. For serious reasons (*motivi gravi*), the defendant may request the instruction judge to suspend the provisional execution awarded.[1220] During the opposition trial, the instruction judge may decide to award provisional enforcement of the order. This will concern the part of the debt that is uncontested, unless the opposition concerns procedural exceptions.[1221] Finally, the court may award provisional enforcement if the claimant offers a security, covering a possible reimbursement of the debt claimed, the expenses, and the damages that can arise from a provisional execution.[1222] Thus, in contrast to the EOP, the national procedure also provides for provisional enforcement measures in various situations.

During the opposition trial, the parties may reach a settlement. Based on the agreement reached by the parties, the instruction judge confirms enforcement of the order already awarded or, alternatively, reduces the amount accordingly.[1223] In such circumstances, the *ingiunzione* continues to generate its effects as if it were never opposed. Alternatively, if the settlement led to an agreement on the non-existence of the debt, the claimant has to expressly renounce the order.[1224] If the opposition is considered to be partially founded, the judgment will be the enforceable title, and the provisional executed debts will remain in place up to the limit of the new decision.[1225]

1216 Article 654(1) CPC.

1217 Point 17 Circular of 28 October 2014 (available online at www.giustizia.it/giustizia/it/mg_1_8_1.wp?previsiousPage=mg_1_8_1&contentId=SDC1076955).

1218 Article 654(2) CPC.

1219 Article 642 CPC. For a more detailed analysis of situations in which the judge may award a provisional execution of the *ingiunzione di pagamento*, see Zucconi Galli Fonseca (2009), at 177–194.

1220 Article 649 CPC. This choice of the legislator to suspend the provisional execution following Article 642 CPC and not to annul it was criticised because it continues to maintain the effects of the enforcement acts already in place up until finalisation of the opposition trial. See Balena (2012), at 2010–211.

1221 Article 648(1) CPC. Zucconi Galli Fonseca (2009), at 198–201.

1222 Article 648(2) CPC. The judge retains the power of discretion in granting provisional enforcement; see Balena (2012), at 211–212; Zucconi Galli Fonseca (2009), at 194–197.

1223 Article 652 CPC. Biavati (2013), at 587.

1224 Comite & Liguori (2014), at 541.

1225 Article 653 CPC.

5.3.1.3. Costs of Proceedings

Similar to the ordinary procedure, the costs of court proceedings include the *contributo unificato*, the advanced flat fee (*anticipazioni forfettarie*), and the *tassa di registro* for registration of the order. Likewise, the claimant needs to pay the advance flat fee of €27.[1226] In contrast to the ordinary procedure, however, the value of the *contributo unificato* is reduced by 50 percent.[1227] This reduced court fee applies also in the case of an opposition by the debtor. The *tassa di registro* for the enforceable order for payment amounts to 3% of the value of the award.[1228] Additionally, as in the ordinary procedure, parties are required to pay additional fees if they request copies of documents or certified copies.[1229]

5.3.1.4. Use in Practice

The statistics published by the Italian Ministry of Justice contain no specific data as to the number of orders for payment issued each year by the courts. The only specific reference to this national procedure appears with regard to the Justice of the Peace. The latest Ministry of Justice report on the civil electronic trial (PCT) indicates 436,518 requests for *decreti ingiuntivi* filed between April 2016-March 2017.[1230]

With regard to the timeframe necessary to handle a national order for payment request, the literature points to a significant drop since the introduction of electronic filing. At *Tribunale di Milano*, an electronic *ingiunzione di pagamento* can be obtained in 15 days compared to 60 days in the paper-based procedure.[1231] Other Ministry of Justice statistics on PCT show average results for a number of courts in November 2016 varying from 16 (Ancona) to 36 days (Catania).[1232]

5.3.2. Provvedimenti Anticipatori di Condanna

The *provvedimenti anticipatori* regulated by Articles 186*bis*-186*quater* CPC are simplified procedures that can be issued during the petition phase (*fase di trattazione*) of the ordinary procedure. They are interim orders that are immediately or provisionally

[1226] Article 30 Decree of the President of the Republic No. 115/30 May 2002.

[1227] Article 13(3) Decree of the President of the Republic No. 115/30 May 2002.

[1228] Tariffs Parte 1 Article 8 point 1 letter b) Decree of the President of the Republic No. 131/1986.

[1229] Article 196 in conjunction with Articles 267–270 and Annexes 6–8 Decree of the President of the Republic No. 115/30 May 2002.

[1230] Ministero della Giustizia, *Processo civile telematico. Stato dell'arte*, 31 March 2017, at 2 (available at http://pst.giustizia.it/PST/resources/cms/documents/PCT_Stato_arte_sintetico_31_03_2017.pdf).

[1231] Carnevali & Resca (2013), at 312. See data available also in Silvestri (2009), at 6 (available at www.acj.si/en/project-results). According to data provided by the *Tribunale di Milano* regarding the *Processo telematico* (electronic filing) for the period 1 January 2007 – 31 December 2010, around 50% of the 59,178 *decreti ingiuntivi telematici* registered were handled within a period of 2 weeks, while the paper files – around 85% of the 103,705 *decreti ingiuntivi* – needed more than 5 weeks for the judge to issue the order (*decreto*).

[1232] Ministero della Giustizia, *Processo civile telematico. Stato dell'arte*, 31 March 2017, at 9.

enforceable, and have the potential to become *res judicata* or to be subsequently confirmed by a judicial decision. Furthermore, they also maintain their effects if the main proceedings within which they were rendered are discontinued.[1233] The orders are issued within a shorter period, and involves parties renouncing a full scrutiny of the case.

There are three type of interim orders (1) the ordinance to pay uncontested amounts (*ordinanza di pagamento di somme non contestate*),[1234] (2) the injunction-ordinance (*ordinanza-ingiunzione*),[1235] and (3) the ordinance following preliminary investigation (*ordinanza post-istruttoria*).[1236] The law does not set any limitation as to their use in cross-border claims.

5.3.2.1. Ordinanza di Pagamento di Somme Non Contestate

This interim instrument is available for cases involving the payment of money claims.[1237] It is not a default proceeding, and the defendant participates in the trial.[1238] This feature is closer to the ESCP than to the EOP. The defendant only partially contests the claim, however, and on application of the claimant, the judge issues an ordinance regarding payment of that part of the claim that is uncontested. The debtor's silence regarding the claim is not considered to be acceptance.[1239] The claimant may request an *ordinanza* up until the final hearing, when the parties submit the conclusions (*udienza di precisazione delle conclusioni*).[1240] In practice, the judge usually deals with this request at the first hearing.[1241] If the request was not submitted in a public hearing, the judge summons the parties for a hearing,[1242] which, according to Didone, is a means of guaranteeing the adversarial character of the procedure.[1243] Compared to the EOP and the ESCP, the holding of a hearing is compulsory. For the remaining part of the claim, the case continues in accordance with the ordinary procedure.

The ordinance is not a full judgment on the merits of the claim. The purpose of this proceeding is to accelerate the handling of claims, providing an immediately enforceable title and discouraging the initiation of litigation only for dilatory purposes.[1244] Like the EOP and the ESCP, the *ordinanza di pagamento di somme non contestate* is an enforceable

1233 See Biavati (2013), at 396.

1234 Article 186*bis* CPC.

1235 Article 186*ter* CPC.

1236 Article 186*quarter* CPC.

1237 Article 186*bis* CPC was introduced by Article 20 Law No. 353/26 November 1990 and became applicable from 1 January 1993. This instrument was inspired by the order for payment procedure applying in labour cases (Article 423 (1) *Ordinanze per il pagamento di somme* CPC).

1238 Non-contestation of the claim must be certain, and must come from parties participating in the trial. Article 186*bis* CPC cannot be applied in default proceedings. See Salvati (2014), at 74; Didone (2010), at 22.

1239 Salvati (2014), at 72; Didone (2010), at 19–21.

1240 Article 186*bis*(1) CPC.

1241 Salvati (2014), at 71.

1242 Article 186*bis*(1) CPC. See Negri (2012), at 405–407.

1243 Didone (2010), at 7.

1244 Comite & Liguori (2014), at 199; Didone (2010), at 386.

title. The order is subject to revision, revocation, and amendments as a result of the judgment in the ordinary proceedings.[1245]

In practice, the procedure is not highly successful, and is seldom used. This is partly because the defendant often contests the entire claim.[1246] The *proceso cosi detto sommario* and its efficiency in practice has the potential to further impair implementation of the procedure.[1247]

5.3.2.2. Ordinanza-Ingiunzione

Introduced at the same time as the *ordinanza di pagamento di somme non contestate*,[1248] the *ordinanza-ingiunzione* is available for the recovery of money claims as well as to request the delivery of goods. The order may be requested during ordinary court proceedings up until the final hearing for the submission of conclusions. Any parties can request it if the prerequisites for delivery of an order for payment (*decreto ingiuntivo*) are met.[1249] According to Salvati, this procedure is 'a transposition of the national order for payment procedure into the ordinary court proceedings'.[1250] The request can be made during a hearing or by submission to the court's clerk, and in practice it appears that if it is raised at the first hearing, the instruction judge will deal with it immediately. Compared to the EOP and the ESCP, the summonsing of the parties before the instruction judge for a public hearing is a compulsory element of the proceedings. Similar to the ESCP, the defendant is aware of the request, and he participates. Written evidence of the debt is necessary,[1251] and the judge proceeds to examine it to establish existence of the creditor's right. If the debtor does not take part in the hearing and the order was issued in default, the *ordinanza-ingiunzione* has to be notified. However, in contrast to the EOP and the ESCP, the national order becomes void if it is not served within a set period.[1252] Similar to the European uniform procedures, the debtor is informed that he has a set timeframe within which to oppose the order, otherwise the title becomes enforceable and may be executed.[1253] In contrast to the European procedures, this order is not always immediately enforceable, an aspect that was criticised and about which doubts were expressed regarding its usefulness.[1254] The party obtaining it can ask the judge to grant provisional

[1245] Article 186*bis*(3) in conjunction with Article 177(1)-(2) and Article 178(1) CPC. See Cassazione 25 maggio 2005, n. 11023 in Didone (2010), at 237; Biavati (2013), at 397; Negri (2012), at 415–416.

[1246] Biavati (2013), at 396; Negri (2012), at 388–389.

[1247] Negri (2012), at 422–423.

[1248] Article 20 Law No. 353/26 October 1990.

[1249] Article 186*ter*(1) CPC. See Salvati (2014), at 75. On doctrinal interpretations of this aspect, see Didone (2010), at 62–63.

[1250] Salvati (2014), at 75–78.

[1251] Article 186*ter*(1) in conjunction with Article 633(1) point 1) and Article 634(2) CPC. The fees owed by debtors to legal professionals for the legal services they provided are not subject to this procedure. Any document can constitute written evidence. Salvati (2014), at 75 and 79–80; Didone (2010), at 54–61.

[1252] Article 186*ter*(5) in conjunction with Article 644 CPC.

[1253] Article 186*ter*(5) in conjunction with Article 647 CPC. If the defendant does not appear (default proceeding), the order acquires the enforceability of an order for payment that was not opposed. Didone (2010), at 64.

[1254] Negri (2012a), at 428–429.

enforcement if the debtor's defences are not based on written proof or if they cannot be immediately decided upon.[1255] The provisional title may be used to start enforcement while the final judgment is still pending in the ordinary proceedings. The *ordinanza-ingiunzione* is subject to revocation.[1256] In practice, this instrument is rarely used because claimants prefer the order for payment (*decreto ingiuntivo*).[1257]

5.3.2.3. Ordinanza Post-Istruttoria

This proceeding was introduced in 1995,[1258] and in contrast to the first two interim orders, it was issued not during but at the end of the investigation phase (*fase istruttoria*).[1259] The *ordinanza* is available for money claims and for requesting the delivery of goods or the release of assets.[1260] The instruction judge issues the order upon the party's oral or written request,[1261] and it concerns the part of the claim that is considered to be already proven by the evidence submitted to the court. Unlike the EOP, the judge bases his decision on an analysis of the evidence. The procedure is constructed on the idea that during the investigation phase the judge is able to reach a conclusion regarding at least part of the claim. Hence, for practical and time reasons the judge is able to split the claim and issue a separate ordinance for the benefit of the claimant.[1262] The order may also be issued in default procedures.[1263] In theory, the order can be revoked by the judge,[1264] but in practice it will usually be confirmed because the judge will use the same evidence to render the final decision.[1265] The case may continue for the rest of the claim. Additionally, the debtor may by *ricorso* notify the creditor and the court that he wants the judge to issue a decision within a period of 30 days from moment the order was awarded, or from the moment he received it. If no such request is made, the provisional order automatically obtains the full effects of a judgment.[1266] Similar to the ESCP, the decision is subject to appeal.[1267]

Despite the *ordinanza post-istruttoria* being an enforceable title, the instrument did not achieve the success it was expected to have, and it is seldom used in practice. This appears to be a consequence of the fact that the order 'effectively anticipates the

1255 Article 186*ter*(2) in conjunction with Article 648(1) CPC. The provisional execution of the order will not be granted if the defendant does not recognise the private deed (*scrittura private*) produced against him, or has requested the initiation of an action for forgery of a public document (*querela di falso*). See Biavati (2013), at 398.

1256 Article 186*ter*((3) in conjunction with Article 177 and Article 178(1) CPC.

1257 Biavati (2013), at 397; Negri (2012a), at 429; Didone (2010), at 53–54.

1258 Decree-Law No. 432/18 October 1995.

1259 Article 186*quater*(1) CPC. Didone (2010), at 88–92.

1260 Article 186*quarter*(1) CPC.

1261 Didone (2010), at 100.

1262 Biavati (2013), at 399.

1263 Didone (2010), at 102–104.

1264 Article 186*quater*(2) CPC.

1265 Lupoi (2012), at 139–140; Negri (2012a), at 492–493.

1266 In the case of Article 186*ter*(4) CPC, some consider that the claimant may also require the court to pronounce a decision on the merits. See Biavati (2013), at 399.

1267 Article 186*quater*(3)-(4) CPC. Didone (2010), at 133–136.

judgment'.[1268] Thus, the judge needs to examine the entire case file when writing the *ordinanza*, but without having a final judgment and with the parties retaining the possibility of requesting it at a later stage.[1269] If they do so, the judge will have to re-examine the file and write the decision for the entire case, which appears counter-productive in a system seriously affected by backlog.

5.3.3. *Procedimento Sommario di Cognizione*

5.3.3.1. General Aspects

The *procedimento sommario di cognizione* regulated by Articles 702*bis*-702*quater* CPC is another simplified procedure that can be used in less complex cases as an alternative to the ordinary proceedings.[1270]

Introduced in 2009 as part of a reform to rationalise the judicial system,[1271] this instrument is available for cases in which the *Tribunale* has jurisdiction,[1272] and includes monetary claims. The *procedimento sommario di cognizione* is not a proper summary procedure. Scholars consider it to be 'hybrid' proceeding that has certain summary characteristics (i.e. a summary evidentiary gathering phase), or a simplified version of the ordinary procedure.[1273] Its application is not limited to purely national cases.[1274]

1268 Lupoi (2012), at 140. See also Salvati (2014), at 81.

1269 Biavati (2013), at 399–400.

1270 On the discussion regarding the meaning of 'simple' case, see Salvati (2014), at 12; Lupoi (2014), at 194; Bove (2010), para. 4 (available at www.judicium.it/admin/saggi/36/bove%20%20procedimento%20sommario%20cognizione.pdf). *Osservatorio Valore Prassi di Verona. Protocollo sul procedimento sommario di cognizione*, at 4 (available at www.valoreprassi.it/administrator/download/prot_proc_sommario.pdf). On the criteria that should determine the handling of the case according to the *procedimento sommario*, see Tribunale di Mondovì, Order of 10 November 2009, *Giuda al Diritto, Il Sole-24 Ore*, 16(2009)50, at 50–51. Order of 5 November 2009, Tribunale di Mondovì; Order of 18 November 2009, Tribunale di Varese in Didone (2010), at 331–341.

1271 Law No. 69/2009 on provisions for the economic development, simplification, and competitiveness in the area of civil trial (*Disposizioni per lo sviluppo economico, la semplificazione, la competitivita' nonche' in materia di processo civile*), Official Gazette, General Series No. 140/ 19 June 2009, Ordinary Supplement No. 95 that introduced a new heading to Title I of the CPC, Heading III-bis, 'Del processo sommario di cognizione'. The procedure was inspired by another instrument available for commercial claims, established by Article 19, Decree-Law No. 5/2003 abrogated by Article 54 Law No. 69/2009. See Didone (2010), at 303.

1272 Article 702*bis*(1) CPC. See Osservatorio Valore Prassi di Verona, *Protocollo sul procedimento sommario di cognizione*, points 2–4 (available at www.valoreprassi.it/administrator/download/prot_proc_sommario.pdf); Osservatorio sulla giustizia civile del Tribunale di Roma, *Protocollo sul procedimento sommario di cognizione*, Part A, published in *Il Foro Italiano*, 2010, part V, at 195–196 (available at www.osservatorigiustiziacivile.it/link/RomaProtocolloCivileNuovo2010.pdf).

1273 Salvati (2014), at 12–13. Bove (2010), para. 1 and 5 (available at www.judicium.it/admin/saggi/36/bove%20%20procedimento%20sommario%20cognizione.pdf). Didone (2010), at 335–341.

1274 See Osservatorio Valore Prassi di Verona, *Protocollo sul procedimento sommario di cognizione*', para. 6. Didone (2010), at 305–308.

5.3.3.2. The Procedure

The claimant has to file the claim by the special means of *ricorso*,[1275] but the requirements make it almost identical to the *atto di citazione* used to initiate ordinary procedures.[1276] In contrast to the European uniform procedures, representation is mandatory. Furthermore, a hearing is a compulsory element, and, similar to the EOP and the ESCP, short procedural timeframes are included. The claimant serves documents of the proceeding on the defendant at least 30 days before the hearing.[1277] The defendant is expected to file a defence at the latest 10 days prior to the hearing.[1278] Unlike the EOP and the ESCP, the judge can switch the case to the ordinary national procedure if the claim appears complex.[1279] He will decide at the first hearing whether to leave the case to proceed in accordance with the *procedimento sommario* or to continue in accordance with the national ordinary procedure.[1280] This creates uncertainty as to the development of the case, an aspect that has a negative influence on the use of the procedure.[1281] If the defendant submits a counterclaim that requires an extensive instruction phase for the purpose of gathering evidence, the judge can split the case, and handle the counterclaim in accordance with the ordinary procedure, while the claim will continue in the summary proceeding.[1282] This is in contrast to the solution offered by the ESCP Regulation, where a counterclaim exceeding a €2,000 threshold will result in the entire case being dealt with in accordance with the relevant national procedural law.[1283]

1275 Article 702*bis*(1) CPC.

1276 Apart from the requirements of Article 125 CPC, the *ricorso* also has to contain all the elements established by Article 163 CPC for the *citazione* in the ordinary procedure. See Salvati (2014), at 10–11; Lupoi (2014), at 198; Lupoi (2010d), para. 3 (available at www.judicium.it/wp-content/uploads/saggi/106/Lupoi.pdf).

1277 Didone (2010), at 310; Bove (2010), point 3.

1278 Article 702*bis*(3) CPC. See Didone (2010), at 311–312.

1279 On the power of the judge to switch the case to the ordinary procedure, see Silvestri (2014a), at 254; Lupoi (2014), at 197–198.

1280 This possibility is perceived as a limitation of the summary procedure. Caponi (2009), at 54. The literature points to the danger of abusive use by the defendant, who can propose complex evidentiary activities when these are not necessary or relevant for the case, but that result in the judge's decision to send the claim to be trialled according to the ordinary procedure. See Lupoi (2010d), point 1. There are no Ministry guidelines or fixed standards to help guide the judge's decision on this matter. In order to provide 'operative guidelines', some *Tribunali* have established guidelines (*protocolli*) for their local practice. See for example Osservatorio Valore Prassi di Verona, *Protocollo sul procedimento sommario di cognizione*; Osservatorio sulla giustizia civile del Tribunale di Roma, *Protocollo sul procedimento sommario di cognizione*, Part A, published in *Il Foro Italiano*, 2010, part V, at 195–196; Osservatorio sulla giustizia civile del Tribunale di Bologna, *Protocollo sul procedimento sommario di cognizione*, (available at www.osservatorigiustiziacivile.it/link/BolognaProtocolloProcedimentoSommarioCognizione08Giu2010.pdf). Lupoi (2014), at 197–198.

1281 See Gerardo & Mutarelli (2011), at 6 (available at www.judicium.it/wp-content/uploads/saggi/201/Gerardo-Mutarelli.pdf); Lupoi (2010d), para. 1.

1282 Article 702*ter*(4) CPC. On the interpretation of this provision and the severability of the case, see Bove (2010), para. 4; Lupoi (2010d), para. 6; Didone (2010), at 317–318.

1283 Article 5(7) ESCP.

During the first hearing, the judge proceeds to take evidence by the means he considers most appropriate,[1284] an aspect more closely approaching that of the ESCP. Further, with respect to gathering evidence, the judge is not bound to follow the strict rules applicable in the ordinary procedure, and any formality not essential to the adversarial nature of the proceeding will be set aside.[1285] In contrast to the European procedures, in the *procedimento sommario* orality plays an important role, but the parties can be invited to file written briefs.[1286]

The order is 'the functional equivalent of a full judgment', and is provisionally enforceable.[1287] The order is subject to appeal,[1288] which must be lodged within a period of 30 days from the moment the order is communicated to the parties.[1289] The appeal period is identical to the one communicated by the Italian Government for the ESCP.[1290] The appellate proceedings are the same as in the ordinary procedure, the difference being that the rules regarding evidence are less restrictive. New types of evidence and documents are admitted by the court if the judge considers them essential for adjudication of the case, or if the party proves that it was impossible to produce the proof previously without any fault on his part.[1291] If the order is not appealed, it acquires *res judicata*.[1292]

5.3.3.3. Costs of Proceedings

Similar to the ordinary procedure, the costs of court proceedings for the *procedimento sommario di cognizione* include the *contributo unificato*, the advanced flat fee (*anticipazioni forfettarie*), and the *tassa di registro* for registration of the summary judgment. The advanced flat fee is €27.[1293] As for the national order for payment, the *contributo unificato* is reduced by 50% compared to the value applicable for the ordinary procedure.[1294] If the instruction judge decides that the case is not suitable for a summary

1284 Article 702*ter*(5) CPC. See Gerardo & Mutarelli (2011), at 1–2; Lupoi (2010d), para. 6.

1285 The judge has discretionary powers as regards setting aside the formalistic level of the activities related to the evidentiary phase and allowing the use of 'atypical' proof. However, this power has some limitations (the principle of party control over the evidence – *principio dispositivo* – and the principle of adversarial procedures). Salvati (2014), at 15–18; Bove (2010), para. 5; Tiscini (2010), para. 9 (available at www.judicium.it/wp-content/uploads/saggi/48/tiscini%20I.pdf). See Order 5 November 2009, Tribunale di Mondovì; Order, 18 November 2009, Tribunale di Varese in Didone (2010), at 331–341. On the order being applied following a single hearing, see Order 6 November 2009, Tribunale di Cagliari in Didone (2010), at 341–345.

1286 Lupoi (2014), at 199; Didone (2010), at 320.

1287 Article 702*ter*(6) CPC.

1288 Article 702*quater* CPC.

1289 Article 702*quater* CPC.

1290 Information communicated by the Member States in accordance with Article 25 of Regulation (EC) No 861/2007 of the European Parliament and the Council of 11 July 2007 establishing a European Small Claims Procedure, available at https://e-justice.europa.eu/content_small_claims-354-it-en.do?clang=it#a_25.

1291 Article 702*quater* CPC. See Didone (2010), at 324–325.

1292 Article 702*quater* in conjunction with Article 2909 CPC.

1293 Article 30 Decree of the President of the Republic No. 115/30 May 2002.

1294 Article 13(3) Decree of the President of the Republic No. 115/30 May 2002.

proceeding, and that it needs to proceed in accordance with the national ordinary procedure, the claimant is required to supplement the court fee (the remaining 50%).[1295] The *tassa di registro* for the summary judgment is set to 3% of the value of the award.[1296] Moreover, the parties need to pay additional fees when requesting copies of documents or certified copies.[1297]

5.3.3.4. Use in Practice

The adoption of this procedure by the Italian legislator was received positively by scholars, especially as the first published decisions making use of this instrument were granted within only a few months. However, it soon became clear that the courts were less open to its use.[1298] A study published in 2011 by Gerardo and Mutarelli shows a low rate of use of the *procedimento sommario* in the chosen courts compared to the ordinary national procedure, although a certain growth trend was identified.[1299] Based on the information gathered, the summary procedures initiated by the courts amounted to only 1.29% of the cases handled in accordance with the ordinary procedure.[1300] Furthermore, according to the the Ministry of Justice report on civil cases handled by the Italian courts, a total of 12,760 were trialled by the *Tribunali* in accordance with the *procedimento sommario di cognizione* in 2012, in comparison to 391,909 claims handled by the same courts within the ordinary procedure. This represents barely 3.25% of the number of ordinary procedure claims.

In practice, it appears that requests filed in accordance with the summary procedure are often switched to the ordinary procedure due to the backlog of cases facing judges.[1301]

5.4. National Attitudes towards EOP and ESCP Regulations

The EOP and the ESCP generated considerable debate among Italian scholars and stakeholders who analysed in detail all the provisions of the European procedures. While some were more sceptical about the success of the procedures in practice, others welcomed the establishing of uniform procedures in cross-border cases, although regretted the exclusion of national cases from the scope of the procedures. The Government and stakeholders were also actively involved in consultations initiated by

1295 See the Guidance published by the Ministry of Justice 4.8.2009 (*Circolare 4.8.2009 del Ministero della Giustizia*) (available at www.diritto.it/archivio/1/28636.pdf). Tiscini (2010), para. 9.

1296 Tariffs Parte 1 Article 8 point 1 letter b) Decree of the President of the Republic No. 131/1986.

1297 Article 196 in conjunction with Articles 267–270 and Annexes 6–8 Decree of the President of the Republic No. 115/30 May 2002.

1298 Lupoi (2014), at 196; Silvestri (2014a), at 254; Gerardo & Mutarelli (2011), at 4; Silvestri (2009), at 4; Lupoi (2010d), para. 1.

1299 Gerardo & Mutarelli (2011), at 3.

1300 The reseach involving courts shows very small deviations; at *Tribunale di Trani*, for example, the summary proceedings represented 1.91% of the ordinary proceedings. See Laboragine (2011), c. 59; Silvestri (2014a), at 254.

1301 Lupoi (2014), at 198. On an analysis of the possible causes that contributed to the limited success of this alternative procedure, see Gerardo & Mutarelli (2011), at 5–8.

the European Commission and in the negotiation of the Regulations' text. The following pages present an overview of the main opinions expressed by the Italian legislator, stakeholders, and legal scholars.

5.4.1. *The EOP*

The Italian Government did not reply to the European Commission consultation on the 2002 Green Paper.[1302] However, the Commission received replies from Italian stakeholders who were in favour of an EOP[1303] as an alternative to national procedures and applicable not only in cross-border cases.[1304]

The text and negotiations involving the EOP were not subject to particular parliamentary debates, with only one Italian Parliament member requesting information on the state of the discussion during negotiations.[1305]

Scholars' reactions were mixed. Some considered the EOP an important step in the construction and consolidation of the European judicial area, and an essential stage for decisively overcoming the intermediary procedures of recognition in cross-border litigation.[1306] A cheaper and faster proceeding was expected to have a deterrent effect on unfair conduct.[1307] The Regulation was also considered to be a 'logical development' of the European Enforcement Order (EEO), and a 'typified and special model' of it.[1308] In contrast, some scholars saw the EOP as a fragile instrument due to its simple opposition mechanism.[1309] Many authors underlined the EOP's hybrid nature, and the compromise format that sought to combine the simplicity and efficiency already in the existing domestic models.[1310] The articulated and complex nature of a procedure that is

1302 COM(2002)746. Letter from the European Commission in reply to the researcher's request for information, DG JUST/A1/JG/Is Ares(2014) 4654593, 22 December 2014, Brussels (document on file with the researcher).

1303 This included the European Union of Rechtspfleger (E.U.R) (www.rechtspfleger.org/en/), a group of professors (Antonio Carratta, Augusto Chizzi, Claudio Consolo, and Marco De Cristofaro) connected with an Italian review dedicated to international procedural law (Gruppo della Rivista di Diritto processuale civile internazionale: INT'L LIS), and a Milan-based Italian lawyer (documents on file with the researcher).

1304 Osservazioni sul Libro Verde sul Procedimento europeo d'ingiunzione di pagamento – COM(2002) 746 del 20/12/2002 presentate dalla Presidenza dell'E.U.R. – Unione europea dei funzionari giudiziari, at 1–2; Gruppo della Rivista di Diritto processuale civile internazionale: INT'L LIS, at 1; *Libro Verde sul Procedimento Europeo di ingiunzione di pagamento sulle misure atte a semplificare ed accelerare il contenzioso in materia di controversie di modesta entità*, Avv. Antonio Ferraguto, Sciume Zaccheo & Associati, Milano, at 5–6.

1305 Interogazione a risposta scritta: 4/13250 presentata da Delmastro Delle Vedove Sandro il 01/03/2005 nella seduta numero 594, Legislatura 14, Atto Camera, Camera dei Deputati.

1306 Carratta (2007a), at 37; Carratta (2007), at 1539; Porchia (2009), at 56; Finocchiaro (2009), at 21; Porcelli (2007), at 101 and 111; Fradeani (2007), at 124; Di Cola (2007), at 241; Cultrera (2008), at 716–717; Bastianon (2008), at 2871; Mellone (2014a), at 273–274.

1307 Porchia (2009), at 71.

1308 Lupoi (2008), at 174, 185; Porchia (2009), at 69; Porcelli (2007), at 101; Porcelli (2006), at 1262.

1309 Campeis & De Pauli (2007), at 356.

1310 Porcelli (2013), at 146; Graziosi (2011), at 230; Milan (2009), at 302–303; Finocchiaro (2009), at 36; Lupoi (2008), at 205; Porcelli (2006), at 1277–1278; Guzzi (2006), at 148. Bertoli criticises the inadequate hybrid model. See Bertoli (2008), at 411–412.

complemented by the provisions of the national law was also commented upon.[1311] The EOP's frequent referral to the national law was criticised, as it was seen to lead to the possibility of a contrary effect on simplification and to varied applications of the same procedure.[1312]

The EOP's optional nature was considered a weakening element that would discourage its use, also because international trade actors were not accustomed to EU law remedies.[1313] During negotiations, the Government favoured an instrument that would harmonise existing national orders for payment procedures, and would apply to national and cross-border cases.[1314] This view was shared by scholars.[1315]

The definition of cross-border cases raised a number of concerns,[1316] among which was the fact the EOP could be used for purely internal cases based on a choice of jurisdiction clause involving the court of another Member State.[1317] However, such a practice could not be identified in the available case law or empirical findings.

With regard to the model of procedure, stakeholders favoured a document-based model for the EOP, such as the national *decreto ingiuntivo*, which has a positive outcome in practice.[1318] Graziosi criticises the EOP model as an unbalanced compromise between existing national models of order for payment and the possibility of proceeding to an automatic evaluation procedure.[1319] According to Graziosi, the judge's evaluation as to whether the EOP application appears to be founded does not even reach the level of a

1311 However, the judge should not be tempted to relate this instrument to the national order for payment procedure. Picciotto & Carlisi (2010), at 308.

1312 Mellone (2014), at 85–86; Porcelli (2011), at 263–264; Graziosi (2011), at 229; Marinelli (2009), at 582; Lupoi (2008), at 206; Cultrera (2008), at 716–717; Porcelli (2006), at 1285–1286.

1313 Note Italian Delegation, Proposal for a Regulation of the European Parliament and of the Council creating a European order for payment procedure, 14656/04 ADD2, JUSTCIV 173 CODEC 1233, Interinstitutional File: 2004/0055 (COD), Brussels, 19 November 2004, at 3; Mellone (2014), at 85; Lupoi (2008), at 206; Seatzu (2008), at 1621.

1314 Note Italian Delegation, Proposal for a Regulation of the European Parliament and of the Council creating a European order for payment procedure – Direction of future work, 12052/04 ADD 12, JUSTCIV 116 CODEC 965, Interinstitutional File 2004/0055 (COD), Brussels, 9 September 2004, at 1–2; Note Italian Delegation, Proposal for a Regulation of the European Parliament and of the Council creating a European order for payment procedure, 14656/04 ADD2, JUSTCIV 173 CODEC 1233, Interinstitutional File: 2004/0055 (COD), Brussels, 19 November 2004, at 1–3.

1315 Farina (2012), at 216–217; Porcelli (2011), at 256–263; Biavati (2010), at 392–393; Mondini (2009), at 41; Romano (2009), at 63; Finocchiaro (2009), at 30; Lupoi (2008), at 176; Bertoli (2008), at 405–407; Seatzu (2008), at 1615–1616; Porcelli (2007), at 112–113 and 115–118; Porcelli (2006), at 1267–1269; Fradeani (2007), at 165–166; Bonato (2007), at 183–184 and 189.

1316 Picciotto & Carlisi (2010), at 308–311; Romano (2009), at 64–66; Mondini (2009), at 41; Bonato (2007), at 196 and 210–2014.

1317 Farina (2012), at 218–220; Lupoi (2010), at 402–403; Bonato (2007), at 210–212.

1318 Gruppo della Rivista di Diritto processuale civile internazionale: INT'L LIS, at 13; 'Libro Verde sul Procedimento Europeo di ingiunzione di pagamento sulle misure atte a semplificare ed accelerare il contenzioso in materia di controversie di modesta entità', Avv. Antonio Ferraguto, Sciume Zaccheo & Associati, Milano, at 9–14. For the E.U.R the simple, straightforward cases should be handled by clerks and only the more 'difficult' cases be sent to the judge to decide on. Osservazioni sul Libro Verde sul Procedimento europeo d'ingiunzione di pagamento – COM(2002) 746 del 20/12/2002 presentate dalla Presidenza dell'E.U.R. – Unione europea dei funzionari giudiziari, at 7–8.

1319 Graziosi (2011), at 237–238.

summary assessment of the claim.[1320] The description of evidence approach is seen by Milan as a decrease in the level of the EOP's rigour compared to the *ingiunzione di pagamento*.[1321] From an opposite perspective, Porcelli sees the description as securing 'procedural fair play' and adversarial proceedings, placing the defendant in a position of knowing the arguments put forward against him if he decides to oppose the order, and allowing him to prepare his defence.[1322]

Further, the claimant's possibility of refusing the court's proposal to issue an EOP for part of the claim does not resonate with the Italian procedural system. It is perceived as an element that prolongs the procedure and wastes the judge's time. Thus, it would have been preferable to establish a uniform rule that would not preclude the claimant from initiating judicial proceedings for that part of the claim not awarded by the court.[1323] The referral to national legislation as to how the remaining claim should be treated creates disparities and places creditors at a disadvantage in systems that preclude additional proceedings.[1324]

The Italian Government's decision not to mention the possibility of submitting the EOP claim by electronic means was criticised by Farina, as the means are available in domestic proceedings.[1325] The use of electronic means can potentially contribute to the efficient functioning of the EOP, and would allow parties residing abroad to file a claim easily.[1326] However, up until now the use of electronic communication has not played a significant role in application of the EOP in Italy, owing to technical and interoperability constraints.[1327] Some steps have been taken in this regard in the eCodex pilot carried out with *Tribunale di Milano*, which enabled the court to receive EOP applications electronically from other Member States involved in the project. However, the domestic electronic process (*processo telematico*) is not designed to automatically include the treatment of EOP cases[1328] or the identification of non-national users.[1329]

The use of standard forms in the procedure was a welcome element, although legal practitioners favoured a free format containing standard compulsory information.[1330]

1320 *Ibidem*.

1321 Milan (2009), at 302.

1322 Porcelli (2013), at 146; Porcelli (2006), at 1284–1285. On a negative impact of the provision, see Finocchiaro (2009), at 54; Porchia (2009), at 72; Lupoi (2008), at 199.

1323 Note Italian Delegation, Proposal for a Regulation of the European Parliament and of the Council creating a European order for payment procedure, 14656/04 ADD2, JUSTCIV 173 CODEC 1233, Interinstitutional File: 2004/0055 (COD), Brussels, 19 November 2004, at 5; Graziosi (2011), at 239–240. On the provision of Article 10(2) referring to the national procedural law for the remaining part of the inital claim, see also Marinelli (2009), at 592–593.

1324 Romano (2009), at 118.

1325 Farina (2012), footnote 432, at 247–248.

1326 Mellone (2012), at 15 (available at www.irsig.cnr.it/BIEPCO/documents/case_studies/EuropeanSmallClaim_Mellone.pdf).

1327 Velicogna, Lupo & Onţanu (2017); Mellone (2014), at 90.

1328 See further on this Section 5.5.

1329 Mellone (2012), at 16.

1330 Osservazioni sul Libro Verde sul Procedimento europeo d'ingiunzione di pagamento – COM(2002) 746 del 20/12/2002 presentate dalla Presidenza dell'E.U.R. – Unione europea dei funzionari giudiziari, at 7; Note Italian Delegation, Proposal for a Regulation of the European Parliament and of the Council

The forms were even considered to be an aspect that could be translated to the *procedimento per ingiunzione*. It was initially expected that the forms would encourage parties to prefer the European procedure;[1331] this did not happen in practice, however, as parties and practitioners much prefer the domestic order for payment. While some scholars considered that standard forms facilitated submission of the claim, as well as the possibility of judges' assessing and understanding the forms irrespective of the language,[1332] others pointed to the rigidity of the contents that allow only 'minimum' freedom in the compilation of the application.[1333] Another criticism concerns the complexity of the application form and the difficulties a claimant – especially a layperson – might encounter in filling in the information (e.g. jurisdiction, principal amount, quantification of interest, penalties, costs of the proceedings, description of evidence).[1334] Italy does not have a system of providing information and assistance to citizens on how to fill in the standard forms.[1335] However, as rightfully indicated by Mellone, the '(correct) use' of the standard forms is of core importance for securing a good and well-functioning dialogue between the parties and the court.[1336]

Another important point made by various groups of stakeholders concerns the service of documents and the need to arrive at a uniform means of notification, which would provide at least a minimum guarantee that the debtor was aware of the order.[1337] In this context, service by registered post with acknowledgement of receipt appears to be a method appropriate for wide use.[1338] The EOP Regulation seeks to secure the outcomes of service, but the number of methods raises difficulties and uncertainties in the process of verifying the conditions established for the means of notification chosen by the creditor, especially those provided for in Article 14 EOP (e.g. deposit of the order in the defendant's mail box).[1339] Furthermore, not all means specified in this article are actually applicable in Italy, due to the higher guarantees set by the national system.[1340] The Regulation does not establish any foreclosure period within which the debtor must be

creating a European order for payment procedure – Direction of future work, 12052/04 ADD 12, JUSTCIV 116 CODEC 965, Interinstitutional File 2004/0055 (COD), Brussels, 9 September 2004, at 3; Gruppo della Rivista di Diritto processuale civile internazionale: INT'L LIS, at 15, 20, 25; Libro Verde sul Procedimento Europeo di ingiunzione di pagamento sulle misure atte a semplificare ed accelerare il contenzioso in materia di controversie di modesta entità, Avv. Antonio Ferraguto, Sciume Zaccheo & Associati, Milano, at 15–16.

1331 Lupoi (2008), at 175; Di Cola (2007), at 280.

1332 Di Cola (2007), at 280. Picciotto & Carlisi (2010), at 319.

1333 Picciotto & Carlisi (2010), at 317.

1334 Mellone (2014), at 87; Mellone (2012), at 13; Picciotto & Carlisi (2010), at 318–322; Romano (2009), at 82.

1335 Mellone (2012), at 14.

1336 *Ibidem*, at 7.

1337 Gruppo della Rivista di Diritto processuale civile internazionale: INT'L LIS, at 21–24; Libro Verde sul Procedimento Europeo di ingiunzione di pagamento sulle misure atte a semplificare ed accelerare il contenzioso in materia di controversie di modesta entità, Avv. Antonio Ferraguto, Sciume Zaccheo & Associati, Milano, at 8.

1338 Gruppo della Rivista di Diritto processuale civile internazionale: INT'L LIS, at 24.

1339 Picciotto & Carlisi (2010), at 323–324; Porchia (2009), at 66; Seatzu (2008), at 1613–1614; Fradeani (2007), at 132–143.

1340 Campeis & De Pauli (2007), at 367–368.

informed of the EOP. Based on the practice of the Italian bailiffs' offices and on studies undertaken under the eCodex project, there is a danger that the provisions of Article 644 CPC setting procedural deadlines for service on the defendant (60 days if the debtor is domiciled in Italy and 90 days if he is domiciled abroad) will be applied by analogy to the EOP.[1341] Following this date, the order will be considered ineffective. Such an interpretation seems not to match the *ratio* for which the European procedure was enacted, and will create additional requirements as well as making the order inefficient.[1342] Further, the provision of Article 12(5) EOP establishes a duty on the court to 'ensure that the order is served on the defendant in accordance with the national law'. This requires the court to verify compliance with the minimum standards set by the EOP and the domestic rules of service carried out by the claimant.[1343] According to Finocchiaro, a simpler solution would have been to make the court responsible for service of the order on the defendant.[1344]

The fact that the debtor can oppose the EOP without needing to provide a reason does not contribute to the procedure's popularity with Italian creditors.[1345] The procedure is seen to be 'heavily unbalanced' in favour of the debtor, thereby giving creditors little incentive to choose it.[1346] Furthermore, this phase of the EOP raises sensitive procedural questions with regard to its coordination with and integration into the national law.[1347]

Passage to the national ordinary procedure was flagged from the beginning as problematic and requiring some coordination between the European and national provisions.[1348] Domestic rules provide for a multitude of solutions,[1349] and opinions are varied. These range from the adaptation of special national procedural mechanisms (e.g. opposition to the national order for payment, special labour procedure, ordinary procedure trial following an opposition to execution proceedings) to specific actions to be undertaken by the judge and/or the parties. Scholars have different views as to the tasks of the judge, clerk, and parties following opposition and the transfer to ordinary proceedings.[1350] For example, some scholars consider that, following an opposition, the judge should limit

1341 Campeis & De Pauli (2007); Mellone (2014a), at 283; Velicogna, Lupo & Mellone (2016).

1342 See *inter alia* Carpi, Colesanti & Taruffo (2015), at 3538; Velicogna, Lupo & Onţanu (2015), at 18–19; Graziosi (2011), at 244; Romano (2009), at 128–129.

1343 Mellone (2014a), at 281–283; Romano (2009), at 127–128.

1344 Finocchiaro (2009)1, at 53.

1345 Lupoi (2014), at 210; D'Alessandro (2011), at 733.

1346 D'Alessandro (2011), at 726 and 737–738; Porchia (2009), at 72; Lupoi (2014), at 210; Seatzu (2008), at 1615.

1347 Romano (2009), at 151–152. See also Sections 5.7.2 and 5.7.3.

1348 Caglioti (2014), at 4 (available at www.filodiritto.com/articoli/2014/02/regolamento-ce-18962006-procedimento-europeo-di-ingiunzione-di-pagamento-e-relativa-opposizione-regime-fiscale/); Lupoi (2014), at 210; Silvestri (2009), at 11–12 (available at www.acj.si/en/project-results); Cataldi (2011), at 1133–1134; D'Alessandro (2011), at 726 and 728; Graziosi (2011), at 247–248; Picciotto & Carlisi (2010), at 324–327; Porchia (2009), at 72; Marinelli (2009), at 596–599; Romano (2009), at 153–154; Finocchiaro (2009), at 57; Cultrera (2008), at 716–717; Carratta (2007), at 1533; Guzzi (2006), at 148–149.

1349 Porcelli (2013), at 148–149; Farina (2012), at 249–258; Graziosi (2011), at 247–250; Porchia (2009), at 67–68; Marinelli (2009), at 598–599; Milan (2006), at 165–167. See also Section 5.7.2.

1350 Farina (2012), at 254–255; Picciotto & Carlisi (2010), at 327; D'Alessandro (2011), at 729–730 and 732; Finocchiaro (2009), at 57; Lupoi (2008), at 200–201; Carratta (2007), at 1533–1534. See further Section 5.7.2.

himself to acknowledging it, and the clerk should make note of it on the EOP. The initiation of adversarial proceedings (*giudizio di opposizione*) would remain at the discretion of the defendant, as in the *ingiunzione di pagamento*. Other scholars consider that the *ingiunzione di pagamento* mechanism does not apply to the EOP.[1351] Opposition to the EOP cannot be considered as an application to initiate adversarial proceedings, since the forms do not contain the reasons for opposition.[1352] Thus, the use of national provisions following the decision of the creditor to initiate court proceedings becomes necessary.[1353] The payment of court fees following the debtor's opposition leads to additional difficulties of interpretation, owing to the lack of specific applicable national provisions and the substantial differences that exist in comparison to the *ingiunzione di pagamento*.[1354]

The non-compulsory representation rule in EOP proceedings produced mixed responses. On the one hand, the non-mandatory legal representation for filing an EOP claim or an opposition was expected to raise a problem of coherence or adjustment and coordination with the Italian system, where representation is largely compulsory in court proceedings.[1355] On the other hand, it was agreed that the choice was appropriate, and undoubtedly has practical advantages such as reducing the costs of the proceeding and falling into line with the opposition form, which can easily be employed by a layperson.[1356]

With regard to enforcement of the EOP, various aspects were discussed, such as the lack of an immediate[1357] or provisional enforcement rule,[1358] enforceability during opposition,[1359] *res judicata*,[1360] and issuance of the Declaration of enforceability.[1361] The situation in which an opposition is received by the court after the issuance of Form G if the debtor responded within the timeframe stipulated in Article 16(2) EOP was addressed by several scholars.[1362] Graziosi favoured adaptation of the opposition to execution in the national procedure (Article 615 CPC) as a way to address this matter.[1363] In contrast,

1351 D'Alessandro (2011), at 729–730, 732; Finocchiaro (2009), at 57; Lupoi (2008), at 200–201; Carratta (2007), at 1533–1534.

1352 See further Section 5.7.2.

1353 D'Alessandro (2011), at 729–730 and 732; Lupoi (2008), at 200–201; Porcelli (2006), at 1281; Guzzi (2006), at 150–151.

1354 Caglioti (2014), at 2.

1355 Porchia (2009), at 64 and 67. In practice, lawyers continue to represent parties in most EOP cases, see Sections 5.7.2 and 5.7.3.

1356 Fradeani (2007), at 148–149.

1357 Mellone (2014), at 85; Graziosi (2011), at 231.

1358 Bertoli (2008), at 414–415.

1359 Such as Article 642 CPC on provisional execution in the national order for payment procedure; Porcelli (2013), at 143; Porcelli (2006), at 1281–1282.

1360 D'Alessandro (2010), at 45; Porchia (2009), at 69; Romano (2009), at 161–162 Finocchiaro (2009)1, at 60–61; Lupoi (2010a), at 456–458; Carratta (2007a), at 27–29; Di Cola (2007), at 283.

1361 Carratta (2007), at 1535. The wording of Article 18(1) EOP seems to indicate that the court has to declare the EOP enforceable without the creditor having to request it. A different interpretation would mean that the claimant residing abroad would have to name a legal representative in Italy to request the enforceable title, a situation that would be in opposition to the *ratio* of the European instrument. Mellone (2014a), at 284.

1362 David (2009), at 408; Bastianon (2008), at 2881.

1363 Graziosi (2011), at 242–243.

Romano considered that if the Declaration of enforceability is wrongly issued, the review set by Article 20 should apply, while material errors or omissions relating to Form G should be rectified according to the rules of the Member State of origin.[1364] Regarding an interpretation by analogy of the reasoning of the CJEU in the *eco cosmetics* case, this review-based solution is not in line with the reasoning of the court, which preferred a strict reading of the provisions of Article 20 EOP.[1365]

The review in exceptional cases (Article 20 EOP) has no match in the Italian civil procedure, although its characteristics have certain similarities to two national mechanisms: late opposition (*opposizione tardiva* in the *ingiunzione di pagamento* procedure)[1366] and revision (*revocazione*).[1367] As the Regulation does not establish any special form in which the review should be carried out, the literature offers various interpretations: namely, requesting it when initiating an ordinary national procedure, for an opposition, or as the procedures in chambers (*rito camerale*).[1368] With regard to the meaning of 'extraordinary circumstances', the interpretation by Italian scholars is divided. Marinelli considers they concern the situation that might justify a revision, such as the 'pathological faults' that interfere in the process of issuing the order (e.g. fraudulent misrepresentation, obtaining documents that were previously hidden by the other party, false documents).[1369] According to Lupoi, practice should provide a restrictive interpretation of the notion in order to avoid transforming it into an 'extraordinary' opposition.[1370] In contrast, Romano is of the opinion that the review provision is drafted widely enough to include any situation in which omission of the opposition is for excusable/justified reasons (*ragioni scusabili*).[1371]

As to whether the grounds of refusal of enforcement in the EOP are exclusive, D'Alessandro considers they are mandatory because 'they cast an exceptional rule in comparison with the national procedural law'.[1372] Further, according to the same scholar, Article 22 EOP concerns enforcement in terms of a broader understanding; thus, it involves not only the ground of refusal of enforcement but should also be seen as grounds of non-recognition.[1373]

[1364] Romano (2009), at 169.

[1365] Joined Cases C-119/13 to C-120/13, *eco cosmetics GmbH & Co. KG v Virginie Laetitia Barbara Dupuy, Raiffeisenbank St. Georgen reg. Gen. mbH v. Tetyana Bonchyk*, 4 September 2014, ECLI:EU:C:2014:2144, points 45 and 49.

[1366] Article 650 CPC. Referring to the first two situations in Article 20(1)(a) EOP.

[1367] Article 656 in conjunction with Article 395(1)-(2) and (5)-(6) and Article 404(2) CPC. Referring to the situations in Article 20(2) EOP, see also Picciotto & Carlisi (2010), at 327–329; Porcelli (2013), at 149–150; Finocchiaro (2009), at 64; Lombardini (2008), at 24.

[1368] Porcelli (2013), at 150; Picciotto & Carlisi (2010), at 329; Marinelli (2009), at 605–606; Romano (2009), at 185–186; Lupoi (2008), at 202; Porcelli (2006), at 1282.

[1369] Marinelli (2009), at 605.

[1370] Lupoi (2008), at 202. On the restrictive interpretation of cases in which a review under Article 20(3) can be applied, see also Farina (2012), at 263.

[1371] Romano (2009), at 191.

[1372] D'Alessandro (2010), at 48. The interpretation of this article should also be viewed from the perspective of the interpretation of Article 41(2) Brussels *Ibis* and the recognition of the national grounds of refusal alongside those laid down by the Regulation. See commentaries to Articles 39–44 Brussels *Ibis* Regulation by Kramer (2015), at 417–420; Commentaries to Article 41 by Cuniberti & Rueda (2016), at 840–843.

[1373] D'Alessandro (2010), at 48–49.

The wording of Article 23 EOP is expected to give rise as well to different problems of interpretation. The text does not establish any criteria that would 'direct the court' in choosing between the limitation or stay of enforcement, and making it conditional on provision of security.[1374] Finally, the meaning of the limitation of enforcement proceedings to protective measures is left to the interpretation of the national law of the place of enforcement. However, there are Member States, such as Italy, where the national procedural law does not provide for any kind of limitation of enforcement proceedings to protective measures.[1375] According to some scholars, this grants the judge the power to stay enforcement after the attachment of assets (*pignoramento*).[1376] This solution is criticised, as it can lead to the same result as that for letter c) of Article 23 concerning stay of enforcement.[1377]

5.4.2. *The ESCP*

Like the EOP, the ESCP is depicted in the literature as being a fundamental stage in the 'communitarisation' of the rules of private international and procedural law.[1378] The parliamentary debate on the initial proposal and the amendment of the Regulation was limited, and restricted to information on the developments of the negotiations.[1379] Nonetheless, the Italian Ministry of Justice had an active role in the negotiations.[1380]

According to Milan, the procedure has the merit of establishing a unitary approach to small claims and of facilitating access to justice.[1381] The fact that the ESCP applies to monetary as well as non-monetary claims was considered to be a strong asset.[1382] However, some scholars pointed out that the ESCP achieves only part of its objective of simplifying cross-border litigation and reducing costs.[1383] The European procedure mitigates part of these costs but does not eliminate them.[1384]

1374 *Ibidem*, at 50.
1375 *Ibidem*.
1376 Romano (2009), at 189, note 116.
1377 D'Alessandro (2010), at 50.
1378 Bastianon (2008), at 2871–2872.
1379 Interogazione a risposta scritta: 4/13250 presentata da Delmastro Delle Vedove Sandro il 01/03/2005 nella seduta numero 594, Legislatura 14, Atto Camera, Camera dei Deputati; See *Audizione del Ministro della giustizia, Andrea Orlando, sul Consiglio Giustizia e affari interni del 4 e 5 dicembre 2014*, Documentazione per le Commisioni, Audizioni e Incontri in ambito UE n. 15, Camera dei Deputati, Legislatura 17, 15 December 2014, at 4; *Intervento del guardasigili Andrea Orlando sull'amministrazione della giustizia nel 2014*, Chamber of Deputies, Monday 19 January 2015, at 14.
1380 However, the Italian Delegation also considered it interesting to explore the possibility of adopting a directive that would harmonise certain particular aspects of the national procedures regarding small claims, and would be followed by an amendment of the Regulation (EC) No 44/2001 that eliminated the exequatur for small claims judgments. Resoconto riunione 4–5 Luglio 2005, Riunione del Comitato sulle Questioni di Diritto Civile, Controversie di modesta entità, at 2 (document on file with the researcher); Note of the Italian Delegation, Proposal for a Regulation establishing a European Small Claims Procedure, 7388/1/05 JUSTCIV 54, CODEC 177, Interinstitutional File 2005/0020 (COD), Brussels, 19 July 2005, at 2.
1381 Milan (2009a), at 327.
1382 Pozzi (2008), at 613.
1383 The costs of representation and the translation of documents are unlikely to result in being proportional to a claim below €2,000. See Mellone & Pancaldi (2008), at 314–315.
1384 Mellone & Pancaldi (2008), at 315; Pozzi (2008), at 614–615.

The alternative nature of the procedure was seen as a drawback and as an element that would not encourage parties to choose it over national procedures.[1385] Additionally, the low efficiency of the courts and the significant delays in proceedings were expected to affect the procedure's decision-issuing phase.[1386] In the 2013 European Commission consultation on the ESCP, ECC Italy and IRSIG-CNR called for a concentration of the courts having jurisdiction in handling ESCP cases to allow better training and the specialisation of judges, and to increase their capacity to handle the complexities associated with harmonised cross-border procedures. This would help centralise the know-how, the linguistic skills, and the technology in fewer locations, so that a standardised practice could be developed.[1387]

As with the EOP, some scholars favoured applying the ESCP to internal litigation as well,[1388] an approach backed initially by the Ministry of Justice in negotiations concerning the text.[1389] The limitation of the ESCP to cross-border cases was criticised for leading to reverse discrimination with respect to purely internal claims.[1390] In addition, the fact that the ESCP does not provide an escape clause for highly complex cases is perceived as being a missing element.[1391]

The referral to the national provisions for various procedural aspects was seen as leading to a contrary effect regarding simplification and various applications of a uniform procedure.[1392] Additionally, in the recent literature, and similar to the EOP, it was pointed out that the application of these procedures lacks 'a common system of legal interoperability' between the Member States that would speed up its functioning.[1393]

Italy supported the establishment of a fixed threshold for the procedure covering monetary as well as non-monetary claims.[1394] The €2,000 limit was an acceptable compromise, but stakeholders criticised it for being too low.[1395] In comparison to national rules, the value of the ESCP claim does not include interest, damages, or other costs that are already due at the time of submission of the claim.[1396] To the European Commission's proposal of increasing the procedure's threshold, the Italian Government

1385 Della Pietra (2011), at 311–316; Castellaneta (2009), at 66.

1386 Asprella (2008), at 35; Pozzi (2008), at 624–625.

1387 Responses submitted by IRSiG-CNR and ECC Italy (document on file with the researcher).

1388 Porcelli (2011), at 256–263; della Pietra (2011), at 317–318; Leandro (2009), at 90.

1389 Document provided by the Ministry of Justice, Department of Judicial Affairs, Office II, on the meeting of 16 March 2004 regarding the Small Claims Procedure, at 1 (document on file with the researcher).

1390 See Milan (2009a), at 329; Leandro (2009), at 99; Castellaneta (2009b), at 96; Pozzi (2008), at 617.

1391 Pozzi (2008), at 621.

1392 Porcelli (2011), at 263–264; Castellaneta (2009), at 66; Mellone & Pancaldi (2008), at 293–294. In comparison with the EOP, see Milan (2009a), at 326.

1393 Mellone (2012), at 2.

1394 *Proposta di regolamento del Parlamento europeo e del Consiglio che istituisce un procedimento europeo per controversie di modesta entità* ('small claims'), Ministero della Giustizia, Dipartimento per gli Affari di Giustizia, Direzione Generale della Giustizia Civile, Ufficio II, FASC. 020.004.006-4, Prot.2005.m_dg DAG. 25899, 14/10/2005, at 3–4 (document on file with the researcher).

1395 Response of IRSIG-CNR to the 2013 European Commission consultation on the ESCP amendment (document on file with the researcher).

1396 Article 10 CPC vs. Article 2(1) and Recital 10 ESCP. See Bina (2008), at 1633.

and most Italian stakeholders replied positively, favouring a threshold that matched the €5,000 set by Regulation 2015/2421.[1397]

If the claim falls outside the scope of the Regulation and is not withdrawn by the claimant, there is a problem in individualising the internal procedural norms that will allow the transfer,[1398] and in whether – considering the small value of the claim – the special provisions regarding the Justice of the Peace should apply.[1399]

The use of standard forms responds to the need for uniformity and simplification,[1400] using to the largest extent possible a non-technical vocabulary.[1401] Nonetheless, certain elements – such as the connection element for determining the jurisdiction of the court under Brussels I (now Brussels I*bis*) and the terminology – are not easy for a layperson to understand.[1402] In addition, it was pointed out that some formulations and definitions may pose problems even to a trained person, because they are not always perfectly compatible with domestic procedural mechanisms.[1403] Certain aspects regarding the format and content of the forms were also criticised.[1404] Although a welcome element,[1405] the guidelines are not exhaustive.[1406] The fact that Form A favours the attachment of well-detailed and comprehensive documents is seen as a guarantee that the judge – from the initial phase of the trial – has a complete overview of all elements of the case.[1407]

1397 The CSM and one of the lawyers were the only respondents opposing an increase in the threshold amount for claims. See response of the CSM (*Consiglio Superiore della Magistratura* – CSM), at 7 (document on file with the researcher). For a proposed upper threshold, see ECC Rome (at 4) and IRSiG-CNR (at 6) (documents on file with the researcher). Council of the European Union, Italian Delegation, Interinstitutional File 2013/0403 (COD), 8530/14, ST 8530 2014 INIT, Brussels, 3 April 2014 (available at http://data.consilium.europa.eu/doc/document/ST-8530–2014-INIT/en/pdf).

1398 Bina (2008), at 1638.

1399 Article 316 and subsequent CPC or those regarding the ordinary procedure. See also Caglioti (2015) (available at www.filodiritto.com/articoli/2015/06/criticit-relative-alla-trasmissione-della-domanda-in-formato-telematico-notifiche-e-comunicazione-atti-e-mutamento-di.html).

1400 Salomone (2013), at 202; Mellone & Pancaldi (2008), at 305.

1401 Noviello (2011), at 331.

1402 Mellone & Pancaldi (2008), at 306; Pozzi (2008), at 618; Noviello (2011), at 331 and 333–334; Mellone (2012), at 13. Responses of ECC Bolzano and Rome Offices to 2013 European Commission consultation on the ESCP (documents on file with the researcher).

1403 Noviello (2011), at 331; Asprella (2008), at 37.

1404 See further della Pietra (2011), at 321; Noviello (2011), at 335.

1405 Della Pietra (2011), at 320–321.

1406 Mellone & Pancaldi (2008), at 306.

1407 Mellone & Pancaldi (2008), at 304. For a criticism of and dangers relating to the format chosen by the European legislator, see Pozzi (2008), at 618. Note of the Italian Delegation, Proposal for a Regulation establishing a European Small Claims Procedure, 7388/1/05 JUSTCIV 54, CODEX 177, Interinstitutional File 2005/0020 (COD), Brussels, 19 July 2005, at 3; Meeting Document, Proposal for a Regulation of the European Parliament and of the Council establishing a European Small Claims Procedure – Observations by delegations, 7388/1/05, JUSTCIV 54, CODEC 177+ADD1 and 2, Interinstitutional File: 2005/0020 (COD), Brussels, 6 October 2005, at 63; *Proposta di regolamento del Parlamento europeo e del Consiglio che istituisce un procedimento europeo per controversie di modesta entità* ('small claims'), Bruxelles, 16 e 17 novembre 2015, Ministero della Giustizia, Dipartimento per gli Affari di Giustizia, Direzione Generale della Giustizia Civile, Ufficio II, FASC. 020.004.006–4, Prot.2005.m_dg DAG. 41186, 22/11/2005, at 3; *Proposta di regolamento del Parlamento europeo e del Consiglio che istituisce un procedimento europeo per controversie di modesta entità* ('small claims'), Bruxelles, 9 febbraio 2006,

The language problem only appears to have been resolved, with the ESCP staying within the lines of the principles set by the Service Regulation. Nevertheless, the language and translation requirements can create difficulties for the parties and the court,[1408] considering the short timeframe the Regulation sets for particular stages of the procedure,[1409] and can increase the costs.[1410] The ESCP contains no specific uniform provision on the consequences of a claimant's failure to provide the necessary translated documents for service on the defendant.[1411]

Scholars emphasise that further simplification of the means of service of documents would be beneficial, such as allowing the use of fax or emails as means of communication if available in the Member State where proceedings are initiated.[1412] Regulation 2015/2421 reinforces the possibility of using electronic means of service and communication (e.g. hearings, taking of evidence). However, the government has not extended the use of electronic means to include the submission of the claim, the filing of a response, or the serving of ESCP documents, although reforms have been carried out at the national level (i.e. *processo telematico*). If service by post is not possible, it is considered that prevalence should be given to Article 13(1) EEO ('Service with proof of receipt by the defendant'), even though the ESCP is silent on the matter.[1413] Pozzi criticises the fact that the Regulation does not set any criteria for less secure alternative methods of service.[1414] The Regulation opens the door to an application of the provisions of Article 14 EEO ('Service without proof of receipt by the defendant'), which is deplored because it provides fewer guarantees for the defendant.[1415]

The provision establishing a duty to provide assistance to the parties is not welcome, as it raises practical problems as well as ones of interpretation.[1416] Thus, in Italy no institutionalised assistance is provided to the parties, an aspect that was also emphasised in responses to the European Commission consultations in 2013.[1417]

Ministero della Giustizia, Dipartimento per gli Affari di Giustizia, Direzione Generale della Giustizia Civile, Ufficio II, FASC. 020.004.006-4, Prot.2005.m_dg DAG. 19284, 15/02/2006, at 6.

1408 Responses of ECC Bolzano and Rome Offices to the 2013 European Commission consultation on the ESCP (documents on file with the researcher).

1409 Mellone & Pancaldi (2008), at 307–309; Pozzi (2008), at 624.

1410 Mellone (2012), at 19–21.

1411 Leandro (2009), at 79–80.

1412 Della Pietra (2011), at 322; Mellone & Pancaldi (2008), at 307; Asprella (2008), at 36–37.

1413 Pozzi (2008), at 622.

1414 *Ibidem.*

1415 *Ibidem.*

1416 Note of the Italian Delegation, Proposal for a Regulation establishing a European Small Claims Procedure, 7388/1/05 JUSTCIV 54, CODEX 177, Interinstitutional File 2005/0020 (COD), Brussels, 19 July 2005, at 4; Meeting Document, Proposal for a Regulation of the European Parliament and of the Council establishing a European Small Claims Procedure – Observations by delegations, 7388/1/05, JUSTCIV 54, CODEC 177+ADD1 and 2, Interinstitutional File: 2005/0020 (COD), Brussels, 6 October 2005, at 64; *Proposta di regolamento del Parlamento europeo e del Consiglio che istituisce un procedimento europeo per controversie di modesta entità* ('small claims'), Ministero della Giustizia, Dipartimento per gli Affari di Giustizia, Direzione Generale della Giustizia Civile, Ufficio II, FASC. 020.004.006-4, Prot.2005.m_dg DAG. 25899, 14/10/2005, at 9.

1417 Response of ECC, Bolzano Office (document on file with the researcher).

Italian authorities and stakeholders back the use of videoconferencing if the technology is available.[1418] According to Milan, the choice of making certain requirements less rigid (e.g. taking of evidence) or giving the judge discretionary power in relation to certain procedural decisions (e.g. holding an oral hearing) in order to simplify and speed up ESCP proceedings does not touch on the right to a fair trial, considering the possibility of appeal and the non-compulsory nature of the procedure.[1419] The possibility of taking evidence through written statements or by making use of a videoconference or other communication technology can give rise to coordination problems with national rules, as parties are generally summoned to court.[1420] The judge's power of discretion as to the holding of an oral hearing and the need to justify the rejection are considered reasonable legislative solutions that are in line with the requirements of Article 6 ECHR.[1421] According to D'Alessandro, the duty of the court to seek a settlement between the parties is possible only if there is an oral hearing,[1422] the possibility of which was an amendment backed by the Italian Government in the negotiation of Regulation 2015/2421.[1423]

The procedural timeframe is articulated in a manner that achieves an acceleration of the proceedings, but set periods might pose difficulties in practice.[1424] Article 14(2) ESCP allowing courts to extend time limits for the issuance of a judgment created concerns that extensions would hamper the objective of the Regulation, in view of the lengthy proceedings and the dysfunctionalities of the Italian judicial system.[1425] For others, this is seen as an element of flexibility.[1426]

Article 7(3) ESCP is criticised for its neutral and incomplete formulation of the rule on default judgments, leaving many aspects to the national procedural rules rather than

1418 Note of the Italian Delegation, Proposal for a Regulation establishing a European Small Claims Procedure, 7388/1/05 JUSTCIV 54, CODEX 177, Interinstitutional File 2005/0020 (COD), Brussels, 19 July 2005, at 6; *Proposta di regolamento del Parlamento europeo e del Consiglio che istituisce un procedimento europeo per controversie di modesta entità* ('small claims'), Bruxelles, 16 e 17 novembre 2005, Ministero della Giustizia, Dipartimento per gli Affari di Giustizia, Direzione Generale della Giustizia Civile, Ufficio II, FASC. 020.004.006–4, Prot.2005.m_dg DAG. 41186, 22/11/2005, at 2; *Proposta di regolamento del Parlamento europeo e del Consiglio che istituisce un procedimento europeo per controversie di modesta entità* ('small claims') Bruxelles, 9 febbraio 2006, Ministero della Giustizia, Dipartimento per gli Affari di Giustizia, Direzione Generale della Giustizia Civile, Ufficio II, FASC. 020.004.006–4, Prot.2005.m_dg DAG. 19284, 15/02/2006, at 8. See replies from the European Consumer Centre – Rome and Bolzano Offices, Cofconsumatori, the Superior Council of the Judiciary (*CSM*), a research organisation (Research Institute on Judicial Systems, Italian National Research Council – IRSiG-CNR), as well as two lawyers to the 2013 European Commission consultation on the ESCP (documents on file with the researcher).

1419 Milan (2009a), at 335.

1420 Mellone & Pancaldi (2008), at 311–312.

1421 *Ibidem*.

1422 Article 12(3) ESCP. See D'Alessandro (2008), at 88.

1423 Council of the European Union, Italian Delegation, Interinstitutional File 2013/0403 (COD), 8530/14, ST 8530 2014 INIT, Brussels, 3 April 2014 (available at http://data.consilium.europa.eu/doc/document/ST-8530-2014-INIT/en/pdf).

1424 Leandro (2009), at 71; Mellone & Pancaldi (2008), at 309–310.

1425 D'Alessandro (2008), at 88–89.

1426 Salomone (2013), at 205.

adopting uniform provisions that, according to Pozzi, would have been more appropriate.[1427]

The option of leaving the choice of appeal to national law was criticised in the Italian literature.[1428] In Italy, the law does not exclude the possibility of a second appeal, *ricorso per cassazione*,[1429] which can affect the celerity of the ESCP procedure, and could have been limited.[1430] Another aspect that is not clear, based on the national procedural rules, is whether the non-mandatory representation provision in Article 10 ESCP applies to appeals. According to D'Alessandro, it seems reasonable that the appeals should be regulated in analogy with the first instance proceedings.[1431] Further, the ESCP review mechanism is not common to the Italian procedural rules, and may pose interpretation problems.[1432]

Responses to the 2013 Commission consultation on the ESCP pointed to the need for Member States to provide structured and updated information on national enforcement procedures. In practice, the stakeholders recognise this procedural step as an element that created significant difficulties for the party seeking execution of the ESCP. As well as step-by-step detailed information, it was considered that an effective cooperation mechanism between national enforcement authorities offering assistance in cross-border litigation could provide the actual support that the parties need.[1433]

As to whether the ESCP's grounds of refusal of enforcement are exclusive, D'Alessandro is of the opinion that they are mandatory because 'they cast an exceptional rule in comparison with the national procedural law'.[1434] In accordance with the same scholar's opinion, Article 22 ESCP concerns enforcement in a broader understanding, these being not only grounds of refusal of enforcement but also grounds of non-recognition.[1435]

1427 Pozzi (2008), at 620–621.

1428 Milan (2009a), at 337; D'Alessandro (2008), at 94–96; Asprella (2008), at 41–42.

1429 Article 111(7) Italian Constitution guarantees the right to a second appeal (*ricorso per Cassazione*). Note from the Italian Delegation, Proposal for a Regulation establishing a European Small Claims Procedure, 7388/1/05 JUSTCIV 54, CODEX 177, Interinstitutional File 2005/0020 (COD), Brussels, 19 July 2005, at 10; Meeting Document, Proposal for a Regulation of the European Parliament and of the Council establishing a European Small Claims Procedure – Observations by delegations, 7388/1/05, JUSTCIV 54, CODEC 177+ADD1 and 2, Interinstitutional File: 2005/0020 (COD), Brussels, 6 October 2005, at 157; *Proposta di regolamento del Parlamento europeo e del Consiglio che istituisce un procedimento europeo per controversie di modesta entità* ('small claims') Bruxelles, 7 dicembre 2005, Ministero della Giustizia, Dipartimento per gli Affari di Giustizia, Direzione Generale della Giustizia Civile, Ufficio II, FASC. 020.004.006-4, Prot.2005.m_dg DAG. 55675i, at 9. D'Alessandro (2009), at 84.

1430 D'Alessandro (2008), at 95–96; Milan (2009), at 3.

1431 D'Alessandro (2009), at 84.

1432 In the national law, the principle of conversion of the reasons of nullity into reasons of appeal applies (Article 161(1) CPC). See Leandro (2009), at 88–89; Asprella (2008), at 41–42. Other scholars consider the review to be a safeguard, a remedy with regard to exceptional circumstances; see Bertoli (2008), at 423–424.

1433 Responses submitted by IRSIG-CNR and ECC Italy (documents on file with the researcher). A unified enforcement system proposed by ECC Italy, Rome Office, and one of the lawyers does not currently appear to be an achievable development with EU legislation.

1434 D'Alessandro (2010), at 48. On this argument, see also Leandro (2009), at 75. For a discussion on this argument regarding the EOP, see also Section 5.4.1.

1435 D'Alessandro (2010), at 48–49.

Similar to Article 23 EOP, Article 23 ESCP can give rise to problems of interpretation.[1436] Scholars criticised these provisions for not being clear about the conditions in which a stay or limitation of enforcement should be granted, and about the criteria that should guide the judge when deciding upon such applications.[1437] The ESCP's extensive reliance on national rules in the execution phase and on the limited provisions of the Regulation is lamented in the literature.[1438]

5.5. Implementation of the EOP and the ESCP in National Practice

General Provisions

Italy has not adopted any statute or legislation to coordinate application of the EOP and the ESCP with national procedural rules.[1439] Scholarly works and the practice of the courts were attempts to fill the gaps, and interpretations of how the national procedural rules should complement the provisions of the European procedures were proposed.[1440] The Ministry of Justice issued a note to clarify certain aspects of the coordination between provisions of the EOP Regulation and the national legislation on registration, notification of claims, and applicable court fees.[1441] In addition, the Ministry replied to questions raised on a case-by-case basis by its various legal departments and by courts on aspects regarding application of the European uniform procedures. This concerned, for example, the provisions applicable on the *contributo unificato* and the proof of payment,[1442] the party responsible for serving the EOP on the defendant,[1443] and the question of whether the EOP should be filed electronically following the entrance into force of provisions on electronic applications for national orders for payment.[1444] This resulted in diverse court solutions.[1445]

1436 D'Alessandro (2010), at 50; Romano (2009), at 189, note 116. See also Section 5.4.1 on the EOP.

1437 Carpi, Colesanti & Taruffo (2015), at 3266.

1438 Milan (2009a), at 342–343.

1439 Italy has mainly relied on the direct effect of the EOP and the ESCP Regulations.

1440 Silvestri (2009), at 9 (available at www.acj.si/en/project-results); Biavati (2011), at 273. See further also Sections 5.6.2 and 5.7.

1441 Nota 1° settembre 2010 – Regolamento CE 1896/2006.

1442 Circolare riguardante l'applicazione in Italia del Regolamento (CE) n.1896/2006 del Parlamento europeo e del Consiglio del 12 dicembre 2006, che istituisce un procemendimento europeo di ingiunzione di pagamento, Direzione Generale della Giustizia Civile, Ufficio II all' Ufficio I, Roma, 22/12/2009, m_dgDAG 164532 (document on file with the researcher).

1443 Reply from the Director of the Ufficio II, Direzione Generale della Giustizia Civile to a request for clarification regarding application of the EOP in one of the first cases handled by the Italian courts, m_dg.DAG 15/04/2009.0052844.U (document on file with the researcher).

1444 Reply of the Ministry of Justice to a question from the Chief Clerk of the Court of Appeal of Catanzaro (prot. N. 4810 del 13 aprile 2015) regarding the way a claim based on Regulation (CE) n. 1896/2006 should be submitted and the national provisions regarding the electronic process (*Circolare riguardante la modalità di presentazione di domanda ai sensi del Regolamento (CE) n.1896/06 e normativa interna sul processo civile telematico, Quesito del Dirigente Amministrativo della Corte d'Appello di Catanzaro, prot. N.4810 del 13 aprile 2015*), Dipartimento per gli Affari di Giustizia, Direzione Generale della Giustizia Civile, Ufficio II, Fasc. 0220.004.002–64 (document on file with the researcher).

1445 See further Sections 5.4.2 and 5.7.

The Italian Government notified the European Commission that courts having jurisdiction for handling these claims and the review proceedings are the *Giudice di pace*, the *Tribunale*, and the Court of Appeal.[1446] The Justice of the Peace hears claims involving (1) movable property up to a maximum of €5,000; (2) damages caused by vehicles and boats up to €20,000; (3) the relationships between the owners or the holders of residential property on the emission of smoke or heat, noise, vibrations (*scuotimenti*), and similar phenomena that are above the normal level of tolerance; and (4) interest and incidental charges for the late payment of social security or welfare contributions. The *Tribunale* has jurisdiction over claims regarding (1) real estate leases and tenants of companies' premises; (2) agricultural contracts; (3) matters in the area of company, banking, and financial law, and loans for public works; (4) patents and trademarks; and (5) shipping law. Finally, for claims involving damages arising out of practices restricting competition and the abuse of dominant position, the Court of Appeal retains competence.[1447]

The application forms can be submitted to the courts only in paper form,[1448] and in person or by a legal representative with the clerk's office, or sent by registered post.[1449] The forms need to be completed in Italian, otherwise the court will request a translation or demand that the party submit the forms again but drafted in Italian.[1450] Additionally, on the claimant's declaration that the information provided is true to the best of his knowledge and is given in good faith in standard Form A, the only applicable national provision appears to be Article 96 CPC on aggravated responsibility. The judge will be able to award damages to the defendant if the claimant acts in bad faith or with gross negligence.[1451]

General information on the European procedures is available nationally on the ECC Italy website.[1452] The Ministry of Justice does not maintain a file of extensive information for litigating parties; apart from the EOP Guidelines, the institution limits itself to notifications on political developments but neglects the practical aspects and clarifications that could assist parties seeking to employ one of the European procedures.

1446 As provided by Article 7(3) CPC where falling within the scope of Article 2(2)(d)(i) EOP.

1447 Information communicated by Member States in accordance with Article 29 of Regulation (EC) No 1896/2006 of the European Parliament and the Council of 12 December 2006 creating a European order for payment procedure, available at https://e-justice.europa.eu/content_european_payment_order-353-it-en.do?member=1; Information communicated by Member States in accordance with Article 25 of Regulation (EC) No 861/2007 of the European Parliament and the Council of 11 July 2007 establishing a European Small Claims Procedure, available at https://e-justice.europa.eu/content_small_claims-354-it-en.do?clang=it. See also Leandro (2009), at 83–84; D'Alessandro (2009), at 79.

1448 Silvestri (2009), at 10 (available at www.acj.si/en/project-results); Finocchiaro (2009), at 21–64; Bastianon (2008), at 2880.

1449 According to the literature, submission by way of the clerk's office is the method most often used if the party is represented by a lawyer. See Biavati (2011), at 274; Rota (2011), at 295.

1450 Article 122 CPC. According to D'Alessandro, in the light of Article 152(2) CPC, the judge will need to accept the translations of documents of the proceedings even if the party deposits these after the established time has lapsed. D'Alessandro (2008), at 16 and 85.

1451 Graziosi (2011), at 232–234.

1452 Information on the ESCP in English available at www.ecc-net.it/service.php?s=Il%20Procedimento%20Europeo%20per%20le%20controversie%20di%20modesta%20entit%C3%A0&lang=en. General information on the uniform European procedures is available at www.ecc-net.it/service.php?s=Altre%20procedure%20giudiziarie%20transfrontaliere&lang=it.

EOP Aspects
Electronic filing of the EOP is not yet available at the national level, although the electronic process (*processo telematico*) is compulsory for a number of procedural stages and for the domestic order for payment procedure.[1453] According to the Ministry of Justice, the compulsory use of electronic means for submitting EOP claims in accordance with the national provisions would preclude the parties and their legal representatives resident in other Member States from filing cases with Italian courts as well as from receiving communications from the court.[1454] This is due to technical and registration requirements that cannot be fulfilled easily by foreign users.

Standard Form A must be submitted in duplicate, as the second copy is for service on the debtor.[1455] Once the EOP is issued, the clerk informs the claimant by *biglietto di cancelleria*.[1456] Subsequently, the claimant is required to pay a registration fee (*imposta di registro*) and to obtain the EOP (Form E) to serve on the debtor.[1457]

Because a claimant residing abroad is not able to personally undertake serving the EOP on the defendant, he needs to designate an Italian lawyer to carry out the required procedural steps on his behalf.[1458] However, the opinion also exists that the court should serve the EOP.[1459] The judge retains only a supervisory role in order to make sure the EOP has been served on the defendant.[1460] The Guidelines also clarify that the clerk's office will ensure that the acceptance or rejection of the claim is communicated to the claimant.[1461] However, courts do not always follow this line of interpretation in practice.[1462] The Regulation does not provide for a preclusion period within which service of the EOP has to take place. Based on the outcome of a survey carried out under the e-Codex project, it appears that service of the EOP on the debtor could be subject in practice to a preclusion period of 60 days in accordance with the provisions of Article 644

1453 Reply of the Ministry of Justice to a question from the Chief Clerk of the Court of Appeal of Catanzaro (prot. N. 4810 del 13 aprile 2015), Dipartimento per gli Affari di Giustizia, Direzione Generale della Giustizia Civile, Ufficio II, Fasc. 020.004.002–64, m_dg.DAG. 22/04/2015.0064544.U (document on file with the researcher). In Italy, the only court authorised to receive EOP claims filed electronically is the *Tribunale di Milano* wihin the e-Codex pilot project.

1454 *Ibidem*. Subsequently, this was included in a Guideline sent to all Italian courts on the Requirements to be observed by clerks' offices with regard to the electronic civil process (*Adempimenti di cancelleria relativi al Processo Civile Telematico*), Circolare dg_DAG.23/10/2015.0159552.U, point 8.1 (document on file with the researcher).

1455 By analogy with the ESCP, EOP Form A should be submitted to the court in duplicate. See della Pietra (2011), at 322.

1456 Article 133(2) CPC. On a different interpretation, see Finocchiaro (2009), at 48.

1457 Article 12(5) EOP in conjunction with the Guideline of the Ministry of Justice of 1 September 2010 (*Nota del Ministero della Gisutizia del 1 settembre 2010 – Regolamento CE 1896/2006 – Procedimento di ingiunzione di pagamento*) (available at www.giustizia.it/giustizia/it/mg_1_8_1.wp?facetNode_1=0_0&facetNode_2=4_32&previsiousPage=mg_1_8&contentId=SDC391384). Graziosi (2011), at 243–244.

1458 Mellone (2014a), at 283.

1459 In practice, a problem arises when the service needs to be undertaken abroad by an Italian bailiff. Caglioti (2015).

1460 Marinelli (2009), at 594–595.

1461 Nota 1° settembre 2010– Regolamento CE 1896/2006.

1462 See further Section 5.7.2.

CPC.[1463] In the literature, this interpretation of the national provisions is criticised for the differences in application that it might entail at the national level.[1464]

The way in which transfer should be carried out following opposition is not subject to a unitary interpretation and application.[1465]

No direct equivalent for the EOP review exists within the national procedural rules, although the Italian Government makes a distinction between Article 20(1) and 20(2) EOP.[1466] The review under Article 20(1) EOP must be lodged with the same court that issued the EOP, and handled according to Article 650 CPC following late opposition to an *ingiunzione di pagamento*. As regards Article 20(2) EOP, the feasible solution is to make use of the summons (*citazione*) in the ordinary national procedure and to submit it to the court that issued the order. As rightfully pointed out by scholars, the review is not a parallel mechanism to Article 650 CPC on late opposition, and it has certain elements that are also contained in various CPC institutions.[1467] The review decision is subject to appeal.[1468]

Following a lapse of the period to oppose the EOP, the decision becomes enforceable. The judge checks the formal requirements, and if these have been complied with he issues Form G.[1469]

ESCP Aspects

Standard Form A along with the evidence must be submitted in duplicate. The second copy is used for service on the debtor.[1470]

If it is necessary to obtain written evidence, the literature points to the application of Article 257*bis* CPC on written statements from a witness.[1471] In practice, a similar reference appears less likely if the claimant is not represented. In keeping with national procedural rules, oral hearings by means of videoconference or other communication technology are not possible.[1472]

As to the means of communication accepted, Italy expressly mentions only postal service.[1473] With the ESCP, the notifications and service of documents appear to be a

1463 Velicogna, Lupo & Mellone (2016), at 14 and 33–34.

1464 See criticism of this interpretation in Section 5.4.1 above. See also comments to Article 12 EOP Regulation in Carpi, Colesanti & Taruffo (2015), at 3538; Velicogna, Lupo & Onţanu (2017); Graziosi (2011), at 244.

1465 See further Sections 5.4.1 and 5.7.2–3. Silvestri (2009), at 11–12; Biavati (2011), at 274–275.

1466 Information communicated by Member States in accordance with Article 29 of Regulation (EC) No 1896/2006 of the European Parliament and the Council of 12 December 2006 creating a European order for payment procedure, available at https://e-justice.europa.eu/content_european_payment_order-353-it-en.do?member=1.

1467 Graziosi (2011), at 246; Picciotto & Carlisi (2010), at 327–329. On the matter, see also Section 5.4.2.

1468 Campeis & De Pauli (2007), at 376–377.

1469 *Ibidem*, at 372–373 and 376.

1470 Della Pietra 2011, at 322.

1471 See also the Decree of the Ministry of 17 February 2010, Official Gazette No. 49/11 March 2010 regarding the forms used for witnesses' written statements, and the respective guidelines for filling them in. Rota (2011), at 296.

1472 D'Alessandro (2009a), at 82.

1473 For the ESCP, the use of fax or electronic means of service is not possible. See Rota (2011), at. 295.

duty of the court.[1474] Upon request of the court, the bailiff proceeds to notify the parties. For parties resident abroad, the provisions of the Service Regulation and of Article 142 CPC on notification on persons not resident in Italy should apply.[1475] In practice, service abroad seems to create difficulties, because for national procedures the service is the responsibility of the claimant, who requests the bailiff's service and bears the costs.[1476]

Similar to the EOP, the clerk informs the claimant of the judgment by *biglietto di cancelleria*, and a registration fee (*imposta di registro*) must be paid for the judgment.[1477]

For the ESCP, following issuance of the judgment and its communication, the defendant may lodge an appeal within a period of 30 days. This is filed before the *Tribunale* if the decision was issued by the Justice of the Peace, or with the court of appeal if the first court competent was the *Tribunale*.[1478] In addition, a second appeal may be lodged before the Supreme Court within a period of 60 days from the moment the appeal decision was communicated.[1479]

As to review, according to one interpretation, the means that the Italian Government intended to apply would be an appeal (*impugnazione*) submitted with the court that issued the judgment.[1480] Another author considers that the provisions of Article 327(2) CPC apply. These allow an opposition irrespective of the lapse of time for appeals if the defendant is not aware that proceedings have been submitted against him.[1481]

Following a lapse of the appeal period, the decision becomes enforceable. The judge then determines whether the formal requirements have been complied with in order to issue Form D.[1482]

Costs

After registration of the claim, the party submitting it will have to pay court fees. The Ministry of Justice Guidelines on the EOP establish that the court applies the fees in accordance with national legislation.[1483] This includes the court's unified fee (*contributo unificato*), the registration fee (*imposta di registro*), and the advanced flat fee owed by private parties to the Treasury in civil litigation (*anticipazioni forfettarie dai private all'erario nel processo civile*).[1484] Just as for the national *ingiunzione di pagamento*, the unified contribution is reduced by 50% for the EOP. In ESCP claims, the general court fees apply, since no express exemptions were established by the Italian legislator.[1485] This includes the *contributo unificato*, the *anticipazioni forfettarie dai private all'erario nel*

1474 Article 5 ESCP. Caglioti (2015).
1475 See Caglioti (2015).
1476 See further also Section 5.7.3.
1477 Pozzi (2008), at 625–626.
1478 Article 325(1) in conjunction with Article 326(1) CPC.
1479 Article 325(2) in conjunction with Article 326(1) CPC.
1480 Leandro (2009), at 89. Hess (2017), Chapter 5 para. 896.
1481 Rota (2011), at 297.
1482 Mellone & Pancaldi (2008), at 313–314.
1483 According to provisions of the Decree of the President of the Republic No. 115/30 May 2002.
1484 Nota 1° settembre 2010 – Regolamento CE 1896/2006. D'Alessandro (2011), at 722; Caglioti (2014), at 3.
1485 See Caglioti (2015); Caglioti (2014a), at 1 (available at www.filodiritto.com/articoli/2014/07/gratuito-patrocinio-controversie-di-modesta-entit-regolamento-ce-8612007-aspetti-fiscali.html).

processo civile, and the *imposta di registro*.[1486] For claims up to €1,033, if the claim is handled by the Justice of the Peace, the EOP or the ESCP claimant will pay only the *contributo unificato*.[1487] In light of the applicable legal norms in cross-border claims up to a value of €5,000, the level of court fees is lower for EOP claims than for ESCP procedures. Nevertheless, according to the literature, even if the claimant does not pay the required court fees, the Italian judge still needs to render his judgment in EOP and ESCP cases. Failure to pay court fees is not mentioned among the reasons for which the court may reject the application.[1488] In practice, situations vary.[1489] The Italian Government provides information on the e-Justice Portal as to the applicable legal provisions regarding the costs of judicial proceedings. However, the exact level of court fees is not expressly individualised, and for a long period the information has been available only in Italian.[1490] Further, according to the e-Justice Portal, the *contributo unificato* for the EOP and the ESCP can be paid by making use of methods available within the domestic procedures.[1491] The particularity of the payment means that the parties or their representatives are required to be physically present in Italy.[1492] The website provides neither information on the additional method provided by the Ministry of Justice nor the IBAN details available for the payment of contributions in the EOP procedure as mentioned by the Ministry of Justice.[1493] Although wire transfer set up for the EOP procedure is a significant step forward in facilitating a claimant's tasks, the language difficulty remains. It is not clear whether the Italian Government also intended to use the same account for the ESCP, as no further reference is made to this procedure. A study carried out for the 'Building Interoperability for European Proceedings Online' project in Italy revealed the possibility of paying the court contribution online into an account held by the Provincial Tax Authority of Viterbo (*Tresoreria Provinciale di Viterbo*).[1494] As discovered, the payment can be made only through the postal service, or any office of the Italian Post (*Poste Italiane*), by using a special form (*bollettino di conto corrente postale*).[1495] This requires online registration and a mobile phone number for

1486 See Section 5.2.3 above. e-Justice website provides information on the type of court fees that need to be paid in EOP and ESCP claims (https://e-justice.europa.eu/content_court_fees_concerning_european_payment_order_procedure-305-it-en.do?clang=it and https://e-justice.europa.eu/content_court_fees_concerning_small_claims_procedure-306-it-en.do?clang=it). See further Caglioti (2014a), at 2.

1487 Nota 1° settembre 2010 – Regolamento CE 1896/2006 in conjunction with Article 13(3) Decree of the President of the Republic No. 115/30 May 2002 establishing a unified contribution (*contributo unificato*) and Article 46 Law No. 374/ 21 November 1991, Official Gazette No. 278/27 November 1991. See Caglioti (2014), at 3 and footnote 20; Finocchiaro (2009), at 35.

1488 Caglioti (2015). Article 285 Testo Unico (Decree No. 131/26 April 1986) does not apply.

1489 See Sections 5.7.2 and 5.7.3.

1490 On the EOP, https://e-justice.europa.eu/content_court_fees_concerning_european_payment_order_procedure-305-it-en.do?clang=it. On the ESCP, https://e-justice.europa.eu/content_court_fees_concerning_small_claims_procedure-306-it-en.do?clang=it.

1491 See Section 5.2.3.

1492 See also Hess (2017), Chapter 5 para. 903.

1493 Details are available at www.giustizia.it/resources/cms/documents/fac_simile_invito_al_pagamento_Reg_CE_18962006.pdf.

1494 This current postal account number – 57152043 – is in the name of *Tesoreria provinciale dello Stato di Viterbo*. (information available at www.contributounificato.it/esenzioni.html). See also Ng (2012), at 8 (available at www.irsig.cnr.it/BIEPCO/documents/case_studies/EPO_Simulation_Gar_Yein.pdf).

1495 For futher details regarding the means of payment, see Section 5.2.3.

receiving an SMS with the activation code. Again, all the information is available only in Italian, and the registration can be problematic for a non-speaker of the language.[1496] This path is more complicated than the EOP-dedicated method. The Ministry of Justice Guidelines provide a standard communication form that the court can use to request payment of the fee, but details are available only in Italian. The claimant is informed of the need to pay the *contributo unificato* and/or the *anticipazioni forfettarie* for the service of documents; he is also instructed to specifiy the means that can be used for such a purpose, and requested to submit proof of payment within the 10 days following payment. In addition, the party is warned that he will face enforcement activities if he fails to pay the court fees.[1497] A similar warning is published on the e-Justice Portal for both European procedures. The recovery activity is undertaken by Equitalia Giustizia SpA at the request of the judicial office involved.[1498] Since 1 July 2017, this task has been shared between Equitalia Giustizia SpA and Agenzia delle Entrate-Riscossione.[1499]

As to the various court fees that need to be paid in the European procedures, the *anticipazioni forfettarie dai private all'erario nel processo civile* is a flat fee of €27, identical to the one applying in other national procedures. This applies also to appeals in the ESCP procedure. The *tassa di registro* amounts to 3% of the value of the award, and is to be paid to the Tax Authority (*Agenzia delle Entrate*).[1500] This last fee is not mentioned in the Ministry of Justice EOP Guidelines, and thus should be paid in accordance with the national provisions applicable.[1501] Additionally, and as in other national procedures, the parties are required to pay additional fees if they request copies of the documents or certified copies.

5.6. Enforcement in Italy: From National to European Judgments

Enforcement of judicial decisions in Italy is carried out in accordance with various laws and regulations. This section presents an overview of the main characteristics of the proceedings, considering the applicable rules, the professionals involved in the process, and the costs entailed for the parties. The second part focuses on the execution of the EOP and the ESCP, examining specific aspects.

1496 Ng (2012), at 8.

1497 The fees are also subject to interest for the corresponding period up until recovery of the due amounts, and until the debt is registered as paid in the national 3SG Registry. Recovery under Title VII of the Unified text on judicial costs. See Caglioti (2015).

1498 On the EOP, https://e-justice.europa.eu/content_court_fees_concerning_european_payment_order_procedure-305-it-en.do?clang=it. On the ESCP, https://e-justice.europa.eu/content_court_fees_concerning_ small_claims_procedure-306-it-en.do?clang=it.

1499 Reply by the Director of Equitalia Giustizia SpA to a request for information (*Regolamento CE 1896/2006 – attribuzioni Agenzia delle riscossione – Riscontro*), 18 May 2017, Prot. N. 2017-EQUIGIU-0061112 (document on file with the researcher).

1500 Tariffs Parte 1 Article 8 point 1 letter b) and Article 16 Decree of the President of the Republic No. 131/1986. Nota 1° settembre 2010. For the interpretation regarding the application of this fee to the ESCP, see Caglioti (2014a), at 2; Caglioti (2015).

1501 The parties are jointly and severally liable for its payment. In practice, the interpretation of the text on which party has a duty to pay it is not uniform. The payment can be made by using Form F23, but this would require the party's presence or that of his representative.

5.6.1. *Main Aspects regarding the Execution of Judicial Decisions*

The enforcement rules are part of several legislative acts, with the procedures known to be 'over-regulated' and abundant in 'minutely-detailed rules', and 'complex technicalities and formalism'.[1502] The main provisions regarding enforcement of judicial decisions are part of the Third Book (*Terzo Libro*) of the CPC. Additional rules and fundamental principles are contained in the Civil Code (e.g. extension of attachments, repayment of a credit subject to attachment, the principle that the creditors have the right to satisfy their claims on the debtor's property),[1503] in special enforcement procedures (e.g. tax collection, the garnishment of salaries earned by publish servants, attachment of assets owned by the State or public entities, attachment of ships and aircrafts), and in legislation regarding the activity carried out by the *ufficiali giudiziari*.[1504] The CPC contains rules on (1) the enforceable title; (2) compulsory expropriation (*espropriazione forzata*); (3) the execution by delivery or release; (4) the compulsory execution of duties to be carried out or not; (5) opposition to enforcement; and (6) the suspension and termination of enforcement.[1505]

Execution activity is carried out by the *ufficiali giudiziari* (bailiffs) and clerks,[1506] while the enforcement judge (*giudice dell'esecuzione*) controls, directs, and supervises enforcement activity.[1507] The courts competent to handle enforcement matters are the *Tribunale,* within whose jurisdiction the debtor's assets are situated in the case of movable or immovable property, or of the place of residence or domicile/headquarters if the execution concerns vehicles.[1508] Similarly, the *ufficiale giudiziario* is competent to perform activities within the circumscription of the office to which he belongs.[1509]

A judicial decision does not need to have *res judicata* in order to be enforceable. However, if the judgment is reversed in appeal, the enforcement activities initiated need to be stayed, the assets returned, and incurred damages covered.[1510]

To proceed to the execution,[1511] the creditor needs to obtain an authentic copy of the enforceable title containing the enforcement writ (*formula esecutiva*).[1512] The court provides it to the winning party.[1513] The creditor is required to register the title with the

1502 Silvestri (2010), at 207–211.

1503 Articles 2910 - 2933 (Title IV Chapter II on Enforcement - *Dell'esecuzione forzata*) Civil Code.

1504 Decree of the President of the Republic No. 1229/15 December 1959 on the organisation of enforcement officers and their assistants, Official Gazette No. 26/1 February 1960.

1505 Articles 474–632 CPC.

1506 Both of them are public servants. Public notaries, lawyers, and accountants registered in a special court record can be entrusted with the task of liquidating the debtor's attached property or assets. Their activity is also under the surveillance of the enforcement judge. See Silvestri (2010), at 209.

1507 Mandrioli & Carratta (2015), Volume IV, at 27; Lupoi (2014), at 221; Lupoi (2011), at 90; Silvestri (2010), at 209.

1508 Article 26 CPC. Mandrioli & Carratta (2015), Volume IV, at 33; Soldi (2014), at 204–208.

1509 Article 106(1) Decree of the President of the Republic No. 1229/15 December 1959 on the organisation of enforcement officers and their assistants, Official Gazette No. 26/1 February 1960.

1510 Lupoi (2014), at 223.

1511 This concerns not only a judgment; decrees (*decreti*) and orders (*ordinanze*) may also be used to enforce claims.

1512 Article 475(1) CPC.

1513 Article 475(2) CPC. The court issues one valid copy for enforcement purposes. No other copies of the enforceable decision are sent without due cause (Article 476(1) CPC). See Mandrioli & Carratta (2015), Volume IV, at 46–47.

local tax agency (*Agenzia delle Entrate*). Subsequently, and by bailiff, the creditor has to serve the copy of the decision on the defendant together with a request to pay the amount due or perform the duty established within a set period of time, but not less than 10 days (*precetto*).[1514] The creditor needs to include in the notice a declaration of residence or an election of domicile within the jurisdiction of the court of enforcement.[1515]

The Italian system offers two forms of enforcement: namely, generic enforcement for money claims (*esecuzione per espropriazione*)[1516] and specific enforcement (*esecuzione in forma specifica*). Specific enforcement has to do the delivery of specific movable assets (*esecuzione per consegna*) or immovable property (*esecuzione per rilascio*), or involves a specific action (*esecuzione degli obblighi di fare o di non fare*).[1517]

The creditor has 90 days to initiate the execution (*esecuzione per espropriazione*), otherwise the notice of performance (*precetto*) becomes ineffective, and the attachment is struck off.[1518] The bailiff will proceed to a preliminary attachment of the debtor's assets, *pignoramento*.[1519] Methods that the creditor can employ include (1) the attachment of movables (*espropriazione mobiliare*);[1520] (2) the attachment of immovables (*espropriazione immobiliare*);[1521]and (3) the attachment of amounts owed to the debtor by third parties (*esprorpiazione presso terzi*).[1522] The bailiff acts with regard to assets that he considers to be easily and immediately ready to be attached. If they are available, he should give priority to attaching sums of money, available credits, or financial assets.[1523] The general rule is that the creditor may cumulatively file several attachment petitions regarding the debtor's assets, or choose a particular type of execution method.[1524] Certain kinds of assets and sources of income may not be subject to execution measures.[1525]

One of the problems related to enforcement activies in Italy concerns access to information about the debtor's assets.[1526] There is no general rule that imposes on the debtor a duty to disclose these details, although the bailiff may request it.[1527] Although

1514 Article 479(1) CPC in conjunction with Article 482 CPC. See Lupoi (2014), at 223.

1515 Article 480(3) CPC. See further Soldi (2014), at 167–169.

1516 Lupoi (2014), at 223.

1517 Articles 605–611 CPC *on esecuzione per consegna o rilascio* and Articles 612–614*bis* CPC *on esecuzione degli obblighi di fare e di non fare*. See Lupoi (2014), at 223; Mandrioli & Carratta (2015), Volume IV, at 183–201.

1518 Article 481 CPC.

1519 Article 491 CPC. The form of the *pignoramento* consists of an injunction or order the enforcement officer carries out on the debtor, requesting him to refrain from any direct act that would diminish the gurantee of the creditor on the expressely individualised assets and their fruits (Article 492(1) CPC).

1520 Articles 513 – 542 CPC. For further analysis, see Mandrioli & Carratta (2015), Volume IV, at 111–127.

1521 Articles 555 – 598 CPC. The attachment and sale of immovable property is longer, costlier, and more complex. Lupoi (2011), at 97–98. For further analysis, see Mandrioli & Carratta (2015), Volume IV, at 146–176.

1522 Articles 543 – 554 CPC. This is often considered to be the most efficient procedure, and usually concerns the debtor's wages and bank accounts. Lupoi (2011), at 96–97. For further analysis, see Mandrioli & Carratta (2015), Volume IV, at 128–145.

1523 Article 517 CPC. Carpi, Colesanti & Taruffo (2015), at 1972–1973.

1524 Article 483 CPC. Lupoi (2014), at 225; Mandrioli & Carratta (2015), Volume IV, at 65–66.

1525 Articles 514–515 in conjunction with Article 545 CPC. Lupoi (2011), at 96–97.

1526 Lupoi (2011), at 93; Silvestri (2010), at 211.

1527 Carpi, Colesanti & Taruffo (2015), at 1963–1968.

determining whether the debtor has property (immovable or movable registered assets) or is a shareholder in a company does not pose particular problems, an investigation into whether he is employed or involved in an income-generating activity is more complicated and costly.[1528] According to the literature, information regarding a debtor's bank accounts, financial investments, and savings are the most difficult to obtain.[1529] This situation is likely to change with the establishment of the Agenzia delle Entrate-Riscossione, which is authorised to access all databases, as well as to acquire information from the National Social Security Institute (*Istituto Nazionale della Previdenza Sociale*, INPS) with regard to labour and collaboration activities.[1530]

Execution proceedings are subject to opposition by the debtor or by third parties.[1531] If enforcement involves decisions not having *res judicata*, the debtor may only lodge an appeal and request the stay of enforcement during the appeal.[1532] This type of opposition is not always granted.[1533] Alternatively, the debtor can oppose certain procedural acts (*opposizione agli atti esecutivi*), contesting their validity.[1534] This kind of opposition may be raised before the enforcement judge within a period of 20 days from the service of the enforceable title (*precetto*), or from the date of initiation of the execution.[1535] This action may concern, for example, procedural errors or faults in the proceedings, and can result in a renewal of the procedural steps. The opposition trial is conducted in two stages. The first takes place in chambers before the enforcement judge, and the second follows the rules of ordinary court proceedings.[1536] The decision issued is subject to a second appeal before the Cassazione.[1537] Third parties affected by the execution may also oppose it (e.g. the attachment concerns assets that are the property of a third party).[1538] Proceedings before the execution judge are along the same line as the debtor's opposition to the acts of execution.[1539]

The costs of enforcement are borne by the debtor,[1540] and include expenses relating to notification of the enforceable decision on the debtor and to notice of performance

1528 Article 492*bis* CPC. The bailiff's access to the database is defined as not requiring the payment of any fee. However, for procedures submitted from 11 December 2014 a unified contribution of €43 applies with regard to submitting a request to the *Tribunale*, and to the bailiff if he has individualised assets on which enforcement can be carried out (Article 19 Decree-Law No. 132/14 converted in Law No. 162/14). See Di Giacomo (2015), at 119–121; Carpi, Colesanti & Taruffo (2015), at 1900–1902; Lupoi (2014), at 225; Lupoi (2011), at 93–94.

1529 Lupoi (2014), at 225–226.

1530 Article 3 Decree-Law 193/2016.

1531 Articles 615 – 618 CPC on the debtor's opposition to enforcement acts, and Articles 619 – 622 CPC on third parties' opposition to enforcement acts.

1532 Articles 615 - 616 CPC.

1533 Lupoi (2014), at 231–232.

1534 Articles 617 – 618 CPC. Mandrioli & Carratta (2015), Volume IV, at 22–231.

1535 Article 617 CPC. Mandrioli & Carratta (2015), Volume IV, at 228–231.

1536 *Ibidem*, at 233–234.

1537 *Ibidem*, at 234–235.

1538 Article 619(1) CPC.

1539 Mandrioli & Carratta (2015), Volume IV, at 242.

1540 Article 95 in conjunction with Article 492(3) CPC. When proceeding to the attachment of assets or money, the bailiff will consider the amount of the principle as well as the interest and costs, including costs corresponding to the enforcement proceedings.

(*precetto*). The lawyer's fees and the fee owed for the electronic research regarding the debtor's assets are also borne by the debtor. The claimant needs to advance upfront a contribution of €43 for the *ufficiale giudiziario* to search for this information.[1541]

The unified execution contribution ranges from €278 for the enforcement of immovable property to €139 for any other means the interested party decides to use.[1542] If the execution procedure regards movable assets for the amount of or with a value below €2,500, the contribution is unified: €43.[1543] For opposing execution acts, the debtor or an interested third party has to pay a unified contribution of €168.[1544]

No overall national information is available on the length of the enforcement proceedings. Based on a study carried out involving a sample of courts in different important Italian cities, the 2013 World Bank Institute Report indicates that the enforcement of a contract takes an average of 1400 days and costs the party around 26.2% of the value of the claim.[1545]

5.6.2. *Executing EOP and ESCP Judgments*

The CPC contains no express provisions regarding the execution of EOP and/or ESCP decisions. The courts need to proceed to an interpretation of the Regulations and the national legislation in a way that secures their effective application.

EOP Form G and ESCP Form D are issued upon request by the interested party. If the EOP or the ESCP is issued by an Italian court, a creditor resident in a different Member State might encounter difficulties in obtaining the enforceable copy, and need to request the services of an Italian lawyer. This is because the party or his representative needs to pay the *imposta di registro* for the decision with the *Agenzia delle Entrate*, and subsequently to pick up the authenticated copy issued from the court.[1546]

If the EOP or the ESCP is issued by an Italian court, the preliminary activities set by the national law prior to initiation of the execution proceedings – such as the attachment of a writ of execution to the title (*l'apposizione della formula esecutiva sul titolo*),[1547]

1541 Article 13(1 *quinquies*) Decree of the President of the Republic No. 115/30 May 2002, as amended and supplemented. Di Giacomo (2015), at 122.

1542 Article 13(2) Decree of the President of the Republic No. 115/30 May 2002.

1543 *Ibidem*.

1544 *Ibidem*.

1545 International Bank for Reconstruction and Development / The World Bank, *Doing Business in Italy 2013, Smart Regulations for Small and Medium-Size Enterprises*, at 37 (available at www.doingbusiness.org/~/media/WBG/DoingBusiness/Documents/Subnational-Reports/DB13-Italy.pdf). In France, the same process takes 390 days and the costs 17.2% of the value of the claim. See Section 4.6.1.

1546 For further information on the means available for the payment of the *imposta/tassa di registro*, see Section 5.2.3 above.

1547 With regard to the need to attach a writ of execution (*formula esecutiva*) to the copy of the EOP, opinions are divided. Most scholars seem to favour the interpretation that no writ of execution needs to be attached to the title. See on this Romano (2009), at 197; Campeis & De Pauli (2007), at 372–373; Lupoi (2010a), at 457; Bertoli (2008), at 417. On an opposing opinion, see Carratta (2007a), at 30–32; Farina (2012), at 274–275. On the titles issued in other Member States if this is a formal requirement of the national law, see Farina (2012), at 271–272 and 274–275. Carpi, Colesanti & Taruffo (2015), at 3549; Romano (2009), at 917. On the need to attach a writ of execution to the ESCP, see Ng (2012), at 13. On

service of the title, and the notice of performance (*precetto*) to the debtor[1548] – are set to apply also to European procedures enforced in Italy. In practice, it appears that the bailiff is not going to start the execution without attaching a writ of execution from the court (*formula esecutiva*).[1549] Considering the particularities and complexity of the procedure, it is highly probable that the party residing abroad or a layperson needs to rely on the services of a local lawyer.[1550] The notification of the enforceable title must be carried out by a bailiff, and includes the copy of the decision satisfying the conditions for its authenticity (certified copy),[1551] a translation of the forms by an authorised translator (Form A, E, and G for the EOP and Form D for the ESCP) if these were not drafted in Italian,[1552] and a notice of performance informing the debtor that he is required to pay within a specific timeframe.[1553] If service of the EOP or the ESCP needs to be carried out in another Member State, the provisions of the Service Regulation apply. If the debtor does not comply willingly with the award, the creditor through his legal representative will file a request with the head of the *Ufficio Notificazioni Esecuzioni e Protesti* competent to handle the enforcement proceedings, requesting initiation of the execution against the debtor. The bailiffs competent to conduct enforcement of the European uniform procedures are those who are legally qualified to undertake execution activities within the requested area.[1554] Following registration of the request, the *ufficiale giudiziario* proceeds to attach the debtor's assets. However, the execution cannot be initiated prior to the lapse of the period set in the *precetto*, within which the debtor must comply.[1555]

On the basis of the aims of the two Regulations, the claimants should not be required to have a postal address in the Member State of enforcement or an authorised representative other than a bailiff competent to pursue the execution activities. However, it is only the ESCP that contains an express provision in this regard,[1556] and it is in conflict with the national provision in Article 480(3) CPC that requires the creditor to include in the *precetto* a declaration of residence or election of domicile in Italy.[1557] As the provisions of the Regulations are directly applicable and should have prevalence, it is assumed that the election of domicile is not necessary, and thus neither are the consequences set out in the same paragraph. The claimant resident abroad will be by law

an opposing opinion in accordance with which this is not necessary for the ESCP judgment, see Bina (2008), at 1642. On the titles issued in other Member States, see Farina (2012), at 271–272.

1548 Article 479(2) CPC in conjunction with Article 137 CPC. Farina (2012), at 266–267.

1549 Ng (2012), at 13.

1550 *Ibidem*.

1551 See Farina (2012), at 272.

1552 *Ibidem* at 268–269. Carpi, Colesanti & Taruffo (2015), at 3265; Lupoi (2010a), at 458; D'Alessandro (2010), at 46–47; Romano (2009), at 198–199.

1553 On the service of the notice of performance and its particularities, see Soldi (2014), at 179–182. According to Lupoi, the debtor should only be notified of the *precetto*. Lupoi (2010a), at 457.

1554 Article 106(1) Decree of the President of the Republic No. 1229/15 December 1959 on the organisation of enforcement officers and their assistants, Official Gazette No. 26/1 February 1960.

1555 Article 482 CPC. If there is a danger the creditor will not be able to fulfill this debt following the lapse of the established period, the judge can authorise immediate execution following payment of the security fee. Farina (2012), at 267.

1556 Article 21(3) ESCP. D'Alessandro (2010), at 47.

1557 See Section 5.6.1. Farina (2012), at 276–278.

considered to be 'domiciled' with the clerk's office of the execution judge.[1558] Further, according to Farina, in initiating the execution on the debtor's assets, the creditor in any case will need to rely on a legal representative. If the creditor is still able to proceed personally to a direct attachment of the debtor's movable assets simply by registering a request with the competent bailiff, representation by a lawyer becomes necessary regarding the attachment of assets or sums with third parties or the attachment of immovable property, thereby resolving the problem of domicile.[1559]

With regard to the refusal of enforcement and the stay or limitation of enforcement, the competence belongs to the *Tribunale* as with the other aspects related to execution.[1560] Coordination with the national procedural mechanisms appears difficult, however, as more solutions have been proposed by the literature. The debtor needs to submit a request to the execution judge if a situation justifies a refusal of enforcement.[1561] The action must be filed by *atto di citazione* as in the ordinary national procedure, and the judge should issue a decision on the matter (or an order if the summary procedure under Article 702*bis* CPC is used).[1562] Another opinion is that the request can be handled by the court in accordance with the provisions of Article 615 CPC on the opposition to execution activities.[1563] The debtor should not be able to invoke before the execution judge a reason he could have raised before the judge in the Member State of origin, but he did not, in order to obtain a refusal of enforcement.[1564] The same applies if he could have opposed the order or requested a review.[1565] However, he should be able to invoke exceptions on the merits of the claim, which he could not have raised before the court of origin, and which are subsequent to the issuance of the title (e.g. facts that modified the right or led to extinction of the right).[1566] The stay or limitation of enforcement presupposes that a review request or an appeal with regard to an ESCP was filed in the Member State of origin. The judge can limit or stay enforcement, but this is left to his discretion.[1567] As no specific domestic provision was established on how the stay or limitation should be handled, there is some difficulty in interpreting whether the execution judge should apply only the provisions of the Regulations or in coordination with Article 624*bis* CPC on suspending the execution upon the parties' request.[1568] Another aspect that is not

1558 This can create additional difficulties with regard to determining the court before which the debtor can proceed to initiate an opposition to execution. Generally, this is the court within whose jurisdiction the creditor has declared his domicile or elected his residence. The provisions of Article 27 CPC can offer a possible practical solution in the court having jurisdiction for the area where the third party is situated (if execution is undertaken for assets or amounts available with a third party) or in the place where the assets are located. Farina (2012), at 277–278.

1559 Farina (2012), at 276–277.

1560 See information available on the e-Justice Portal https://e-justice.europa.eu/content_european_payment_order-353-it-en.do?member=1); Rota (2011), at 298; Farina (2012), at 295–296.

1561 Campeis & De Pauli (2007), at 373–374; Picciotto & Carlisi (2010), at 331.

1562 Picciotto & Carlisi (2010), at 331.

1563 Carpi, Colesanti & Taruffo (2015), at 3550; Farina (2012), at 308; Biavati (2011), at 275; Lupoi (2010b), at 461; Marinelli (2009), at 601; Lupoi (2008), at 204; Bertoli (2008), at 418.

1564 Carpi, Colesanti & Taruffo (2015), at 3550; D'Alessandro (2010)1, at 48.

1565 Romano (2009), at 199.

1566 Carpi, Colesanti & Taruffo (2015), at 3550; Romano (2009), at 200 and 206–209.

1567 Carpi, Colesanti & Taruffo (2015), at 3266.

1568 Rota (2011), at 298; Carratta (2007), at 1538.

easily applicable in light of the existing national procedural rules is the limiting of enforcement proceedings to protective measures. Italian law does not provide for such specific means within the execution procedure.[1569] According to Farina, a stay or a limitation of enforcement of an EOP or an ESCP cannot be requested in advance of an action already being initiated.[1570] In contrast, Lupoi considers that for Article 23(a)-(b) EOP, the debtor can request a limitation of enforcement proceedings prior to a concrete execution activity. This can be handled in accordance with the protective interim procedure provided by Articles 669*bis* and subsequently by the CPC.[1571] By analogy, the solution can also apply to the ESCP. The request can be introduced by *citazione* if the execution has not yet been initiated or by *ricorso* in the opposite situation.[1572] A stay of EOP or ESCP enforcement proceedings can be carried out in Italy in accordance with the provisions of Article 700 CPC regarding urgent measures in interim proceedings.[1573] Another possible interpretation proposed by Lupoi and Carratta is using Article 487 CPC in conjunction with Article 617 CPC and subsequent Articles.[1574] An intervention by the Italian legislator would rightfully contribute to a unitary interpretation of the national provisions that should be applied in coordination with Article 23 EOP and ESCP.

The opposition to execution by the debtor or interested third parties in accordance with Articles 617–619 CPC, or for formal reasons regarding the title under Article 615 CPC, does not create significant problems within the process of executing EOP and ESCP decisions.[1575] Under Article 615 CPC, the debtor is able to invoke not only opposition reasons related to the form of the title but also the inexistence of the right of the creditor as established by the enforceable title.[1576]

With regard to the costs of executing EOP and ESCP decisions, the national enforcement fees and costs apply.[1577]

5.7. The EOP and the ESCP in Practice

This section analyses the way the EOP and the ESCP function in Italy. The first part is dedicated to the available statistics on the use of the European uniform procedures, while the second part focuses on the analysis of data provided by the national case law. Finally, the analysis concentrates on the empirical findings and a triangulation of the results with case law and statistical data.

1569 Article 23(a) EOP and Article 23(a) ESCP. See Rota (2011), at 298. The author refers to Article 686 CPC on conversion of the protective seizure ordered before the issuance of a decision in an attachment measure at the moment of obtaining an enforceable judgment. This might be seen as a possible national provision that could match the scope of the European rules.

1570 Farina (2012), at 291–292.

1571 Lupoi (2010c), at 462; Carpi, Colesanti & Taruffo (2015), at 3551.

1572 Carpi, Colesanti & Taruffo (2015), at 3551.

1573 Farina (2012), at 293–294.

1574 Lupoi (2010c), at 263; Carratta (2007), at 1538.

1575 Farina (2012), at 309–310. For opposition to enforcement for reasons of form against an EOP, see Romano (2009), at 212–213; Porcelli (2013), at 151; Carratta (2007a), at 36.

1576 Such as, for example, when the debtor has already paid the amount awarded (Article 22(2) EOP). Farina (2012), at 310–311 and 313.

1577 See Section 5.6.1 above.

5.7.1. *Available statistical data*

The annual reports regarding the activity of Italian courts published by the Directorate General of Statistics of the Ministry of Justice (*Direzione generale di Statistica Ministero della Giustizia*) contain no information on EOP and ESCP cases. The only data available at the national level were collected by the Office II – Department of Justice Affairs (*Ufficio II – Dipartimento per gli Affari di Giustizia*) of the Ministry of Justice on the basis of a questionnaire drafted by the European Judicial Network concerning the EOP. The questionnaire was transmitted to the Italian Courts of Appeal in 2009 and 2011 in order to gather data on the functioning and application of this European procedure.[1578] The Courts of Appeal were requested to collect the information from the *Tribunali*, Officies of the Justice of the Peace, and the Bar Association conducting activities within their territorial jurisdiction. The information gathered on both occasions is not exhaustive, and was not provided by all the Italian courts. With regard to the soundness of the information delivered by the respondent courts, two factors influenced the results. The first was the wording of the relevant question in the questionnaire. In fact, it contained two questions as to (1) whether the procedure was 'often used' and (2) whether the respondent institution could indicate the number of cases it had registered. Some of the respondent courts only commented that the procedure was not often used. It was not clear whether 'not often used' could also have indicated that the procedure had never been applied by the court. The respondents did not indicate the element of comparison they had employed in assessing the use of the EOP. The second aspect contributing to this state of affairs is the lack of a special registration code in the SICID Registry regarding the EOP procedure. Hence, as indicated in a protocol issued by the Department of Justice Affairs of the Ministry of Justice in 2011, the clerks are obliged to register this type of claim in the same manner as the national *decreti ingiuntivi*.[1579] This makes it impossible to differentiate between the procedures and to provide sound data to the Ministry. The situation has changed somewhat in the last few years, however, according to the results of discussions with court members. The SICID system now allows EOP cases registered under the *decreti ingiuntivi* code to be flagged. However, the problem remains because not all clerks activate flagging from the beginning, with the result that a subsequent modification of the registration no longer appears possible.

The Department of Justice Affairs, Directorate-General of Civil Justice, recommended the creation of a registration system that would differentiate and automatically classify the European uniform procedures.[1580] However, the situation has not yet changed in practice. In the future, it would be desirable to establish specific registration codes for the

1578 According to documents transmitted by the Ministry of Justice, Department of Justice Affairs, Directorate-General of Civil Justice to the Presidents of the Courts of Appeal in 2009 (DAG 12/10/2009.0124551.0) and 2011 (DAG 20/01/2011.0007385.0), the European Judicial Network was seeking to obtain data on how the EOP was applied by judicial bodies, and on the efficiency of the provisions of the Regulation in practice, in order to prepare a practical guideline for the application of the European procedure (documents on file with the researcher).

1579 Protocol of the Department of Justice Affairs, Directorate-General of Civil Justice of the Ministry of Justice following up on the Note from the same Directorate of 1.7.2010 prot. 91275U, prot. DAG 13/04/2011.0052337.U. (document on file with the researcher).

1580 *Ibidem*.

European procedures in order to differentiate them from national procedures, thus allowing the Ministry to gather sound data and analyse developments relating to practice in this area of law.

EOP Regulation

The existing data seems to indicate that the filed applications concern mostly claims submitted to the Italian courts for the issuance of an EOP and, occasionally, for execution requests. Table 5.1 below presents the information available on EOP cases handled by the Italian courts during 2009–2010. The data should be viewed with caution, however, as not all courts replied to the questionnaires.

<table>
<tr><th>Court of Appeal</th><th>Ordinary court of first instance</th><th>2009</th><th>2010</th></tr>
<tr><td rowspan="2">Ancona Court of Appeal</td><td>Tribunale di Ancona</td><td>0</td><td>No data provided</td></tr>
<tr><td>Tribunale di Pesaro</td><td>0</td><td>No data provided</td></tr>
<tr><td rowspan="3">Aquila Court of Appeal</td><td>Tribunale di L'Aquila</td><td>1</td><td>0</td></tr>
<tr><td>Tribunale di Avezzano</td><td>0</td><td>1</td></tr>
<tr><td>Tribunale di Chieti</td><td colspan="2">2</td></tr>
<tr><td>Bari Court of Appeal</td><td></td><td colspan="2">3</td></tr>
<tr><td rowspan="8">Bologna Court of Appeal</td><td>Tribunale di Bologna</td><td>5</td><td>Not often used</td></tr>
<tr><td>Tribunale di Ferrara</td><td>0</td><td>6</td></tr>
<tr><td>Tribunale di Modena</td><td>No data provided</td><td>Not often used</td></tr>
<tr><td>Tribunale di Parma</td><td>0</td><td>No data provided</td></tr>
<tr><td>Tribunale di Piacenza</td><td colspan="2">4</td></tr>
<tr><td>Tribunale di Ravenna</td><td>No data provided</td><td>Not often used</td></tr>
<tr><td>Tribunale di Reggio Emilia</td><td>No data provided</td><td>Not often used</td></tr>
<tr><td>Tribunale di Rimini</td><td>2</td><td>12</td></tr>
<tr><td>Brescia Court of Appeal</td><td>Tribunale di Mantova</td><td>1</td><td>No data provided</td></tr>
<tr><td rowspan="5">Cagliari Court of Appeal</td><td>Tribunale di Cagliari</td><td>2[1581]</td><td>0</td></tr>
<tr><td>Tribunale di Lanusei</td><td colspan="2">1</td></tr>
<tr><td>Tribunale di Nuoro</td><td>0</td><td>No data provided</td></tr>
<tr><td>Tribunale di Oristano</td><td>1</td><td>No data provided</td></tr>
<tr><td>Tribunale di Sassari</td><td colspan="2">1</td></tr>
<tr><td rowspan="4">Caltanissetta Court of Appeal</td><td>Tribunale di Caltanissetta</td><td>0</td><td>0</td></tr>
<tr><td>Tribunale di Enna</td><td>0</td><td>0</td></tr>
<tr><td>Tribunale di Gela</td><td>1</td><td>0</td></tr>
<tr><td>Tribunale di Nicosia</td><td>0</td><td>0</td></tr>
</table>

1581 In its response to the 2011 Questionnaire, the same *Tribunale* reported that it had handled only one EOP claim in 2009.

<table>
<tr><th>Court of Appeal</th><th>Ordinary court of first instance</th><th>2009</th><th>2010</th></tr>
<tr><td rowspan="3">Campobasso Court of Appeal</td><td>Tribunale di Campobasso</td><td>0</td><td>0[1582]</td></tr>
<tr><td>Tribunale di Isernia</td><td>0</td><td>Not often used</td></tr>
<tr><td>Tribunale di Larino</td><td>0</td><td>0</td></tr>
<tr><td rowspan="5">Catania Court of Appeal</td><td>Tribunale di Caltagirone</td><td>0</td><td>0</td></tr>
<tr><td>Tribunale di Catania</td><td>0</td><td>1</td></tr>
<tr><td>Tribunale di Modica</td><td>0</td><td>0</td></tr>
<tr><td>Tribunale di Ragusa</td><td>0 (Procedure not known)</td><td>2</td></tr>
<tr><td>Tribunale di Siracusa</td><td>0</td><td>No data provided</td></tr>
<tr><td rowspan="4">Catanzaro Court of Appeal</td><td>Tribunale di Catanzaro</td><td>0</td><td></td></tr>
<tr><td>Tribunale di Crotone</td><td>0</td><td>0</td></tr>
<tr><td>Tribunale di Rossano</td><td>0</td><td>0</td></tr>
<tr><td>Tribunale di Vibo Valentia</td><td colspan="2">1[1583]</td></tr>
<tr><td rowspan="10">Firenze Court of Appeal</td><td>Tribunale di Arezzo</td><td>4–5</td><td>4–5[1584]</td></tr>
<tr><td>Tribunale di Firenze</td><td colspan="2">Not often used</td></tr>
<tr><td>Tribunale di Grosseto</td><td colspan="2">2</td></tr>
<tr><td>Tribunale di Livorno</td><td>0</td><td>1</td></tr>
<tr><td>Tribunale di Lucca</td><td>0</td><td>0</td></tr>
<tr><td>Tribunale di Montepulciano</td><td colspan="2">3</td></tr>
<tr><td>Tribunale di Pisa</td><td colspan="2">Not often used</td></tr>
<tr><td>Tribunale di Pistoia</td><td colspan="2">5</td></tr>
<tr><td>Tribunale di Prato</td><td>5</td><td>5[1585]</td></tr>
<tr><td>Tribunale di Siena</td><td colspan="2">2</td></tr>
</table>

1582 A Note was made in the response that it was impossible for the *Tribunale di Campobasso* to retrieve the requested data from the SICID Electronic Registry. They did a manual research by sample, but the result was negative. They did not find any EOP cases.

1583 The response registered DAG 16/03/2011.0037891.E from 8 February 2011 from the *Tribunale di Vibo Valentia* is in conflict with the one registered by DAG 16/02/2011.0021238. E from 3 February 2011, which mentioned 0 (zero) EOP cases registered.

1584 The *Tribunale di Arezzo* together with the detached units of Montevarchi and Sansepolcro replied that they had handled an average of 4–5 cases per year.

1585 EOP cases represent 0.15% of the total number of *ingiunzioni di pagamento* registered with the *Tribunale di Prato*.

Court of Appeal	Ordinary court of first instance	2009	2010
Genova Court of Appeal	*Tribunale di Chiavari*	0	0
Lecce Court of Appeal	*Tribunale di Lecce*	0	No data provided
	Tribunale di Brindisi	0	No data provided
	Tribunale di Taranto	0	1
	Tribunale di Ascoli Piceno	0	No data provided
	Tribunale di Camerino	2	No data provided
	Tribunale di Macerata	0	No data provided
Milan Court of Appeal	*Tribunale di Busto Arsizio (and detached units of Gallarate and Saronno)*	6	Not often used
	Tribunale di Como	1	2
	Tribunale di Lecco	No data provided	6[1586]
	Tribunale di Lodi	Not often used	
	Tribunale di Milano	17	15–20
	Tribunale di Monza	7	Not able to provide data[1587]
	Tribunale di Pavia	0	3[1588]
	Tribunale di Sondrio	0	0
	Tribunale di Varese	Not often used	
	Tribunale di Vigevano	0	1
	Tribunale di Voghera	0	Not often used

1586 In comparison to 1,868 *ingiunzioni di pagamento* registered in 2010. Thus, EOP claims account for 0.32% of the national order for payments handled by this court.

1587 The *Tribunale di Monza* indicated that the registration of EOP cases was identical to the claims submitted under the *ingiunzione di pagamento*. Hence, they were unable to retrieve relevant data in order to answer the questionnaire.

1588 Two of the 3 cases were rejected by the court.

Court of Appeal	Ordinary court of first instance	2009	2010
Napoli Court of Appeal	*Tribunale di Ariano Irpino*	0	0
	Tribunale di Napoli	2	1
	Tribunale di Nola	3–4	
	Tribunale di S. Angelo dei Lombardi	0	0
	Tribunale di S. Maria Capua Vetere	0	1
	Tribunale di Torre Annunziata	2[1589]	0
Palermo Court of Appeal	*Tribunale di Agrigento*	1	No data provided
	Tribunale di Marsala	0	No data provided
	Tribunale di Palermo	0	No data provided
	Tribunale di Termini Imerese	0	No data provided
	Tribunale di Trapani	0	No data provided
	Tribunale di Sciacca	0	No data provided
Peruggia Court of Appeal	*Tribunale di Spoleto*	0	No data provided
Potenza Court of Appeal	*Tribunale di Melfi*	0	No data provided
Reggio Calabria Court of Appeal	*Tribunale di Locri*	0	No data provided
Roma Court of Appeal	*Tribunale di Cassino*	2	0
	Tribunale di Frosinone	0	0
	Tribunale di Latina	1	1
	Tribunale Ordinario di Roma	Not often used	
	Tribunale di Roma-Section VI Civil	8	No data provided
	Tribunale di Roma-Section VII Civil	8	Not often used
	Tribunale di Roma-Section 4bis Mobiliare	0	No data provided
	Tribunale di Teramo	0	0[1590]

1589 In the 2009 questionnaire, the same court declared that it had handled 0 (zero) EOP cases.
1590 The response is the result of research carried out in the SICID Electronic Registry.

Court of Appeal	Ordinary court of first instance	2009	2010
Torino Court of Appeal	*Tribunale di Acqui Terme*	0	No data provided
	Tribunale di Alba	2–3	
	Tribunale di Alessandria	0	No data provided
	Tribunale di Asti	0	0
	Tribunale di Biella	Not often used	No data provided
	Tribunale di Cuneo	1	1
	Tribunale di Ivrea	1	No data provided
	Tribunale di Casale Monferrato	8	
	Tribunale di Mondovì	1	No data provided
	Tribunale di Novara	5	No data provided
	Tribunale di Pinerolo	2	No data provided
	Tribunale di Saluzzo	0	1
	Tribunale di Torino	2	Not often used[1591]
	Tribunale di Tortona	0	0
	Tribunale di Verbania	2	Not often used
	Tribunale di Vercelli	2	0
Trento Court of Appeal[1592]	*Tribunale di Bolzano*	4	20
	Ufficio del Giudice di Pace di Bressanone	6	
	Ufficio del Giudice di Pace di Egna	0	2[1593]
	Ufficio del Giudice di Pace Merano	4[1594]	1[1595]
	Ufficio del Giudice di Pace Silandro	4[1596]	1[1597]
	Tribunale di Trento	1	3

1591 The EOP procedure was not often used in comparison to the number of *ingiunzioni di pagamento* filed with the *Tribunale di Torino.*

1592 According to the report sent by the Trento Court of Appeal following the 2011 Questionnaire, a total of 47 EOP cases had been registered with all the *Tribunali* and *Uffici del Giudice di Pace* since the Regulation's entrance into force.

1593 In one case, the claimant was resident abroad; in the other, he was in Italy. Neither of the parties was a consumer.

1594 In comparison to 588 *ingiunzioni di pagamento* registered in 2009 by the same Justice of the Peace office.

1595 In comparison to 543 *ingiunzioni di pagamento* registered in 2010 by the same Justice of the Peace office.

1596 In comparison to 98 *ingiunzioni di pagamento* registered in 2009 by the same Justice of the Peace office.

1597 In comparison to 84 *ingiunzioni di pagamento* registered in 2010 by the same Justice of the Peace office.

Court of Appeal	Ordinary court of first instance	2009	2010
Trieste Court of Appeal	*Tribunale di Gorizia*	No data provided	Not often used
	Tribunale di Pordenone	No data provided	4
	Tribunale di Tolmezzo	1	0
	Tribunale di Trieste	11	17
	Tribunale di Udine	4	8
Salerno Court of Appeal	*Tribunale di Vallo Della Lucania*	0	0
Venezia Court of Appeal	*Ufficio del Gudice di Pace di Legnago-Verona (suppressed)*	1	No data provided
	Judice di Pace di Verona	4	No data provided
	Tribunale di Verona	3–4	No data provided

Table 5.1. Number of EOP cases handled by Italian courts according to data collected by the Department of Justice Affairs, Directorate-General of Civil Justice, Ministry of Justice in 2009 and 2011 on the basis of the European Judicial Network EOP Questionnaire

ESCP Regulation

To date, no statistics have been collected for the ESCP in Italy.[1598] This may be partly because, like the EOP, the SICID system does not provide a specific registration code.[1599] As indicated in one published ESCP case, the clerk registered the European procedure under the code of an ordinary national procedure,[1600] making it subsequently impossible to differentiate between the two procedures.

1598 A reply was provided by the Italian Ministry of Justice to the MS questionnaire on the ESCP on the European Commission Assessment of the socio-economic impacts of the policy options for the future of the European Small Claims Regulation, Final Report, RTD-L05–2010, Deloitte, 19 July 2013. However, it was unable to provide any data on the number of ESCP application received by the 846 offices of the Justice of the Peace. Review of the operation of Regulation (EC) No 1896/2006 and Regulation (EC) No 861/2007, Questionnaire Part II, Regulation 861/2007 establishing the European Small Claims Procedure, m-dg. DAG.01/07/2013.0086502. E (document on file with the researcher).

1599 Protocol of the Department of Justice Affairs, Directorate-General of Civil Justice of the Ministry of Justice following up on the Note from the same Directorate of 1.7.2010 prot. 91275U, DAG 13/04/2011.0052337.U. (document on file with the researcher).

1600 See Ufficio Giudice di Pace di Parma, Sezione 1, Procedimento No. 7667/2013, Sentenza No. 347/2014 di 6/02/2014 (available at https://aldricus.files.wordpress.com/2015/09/2015-06-30-ester.pdf).

5.7.2. *Case Law*

5.7.2.1. Quantitative Data regarding Case Law

Information on cases handled by the Italian courts is generally not available to the public. Decisions that are considered to be of particular significance in a certain legal matter are published by various legal databases, law reviews, or legal blogs such as Il Foro Italiano, Guida al diritto, Il corriere giuridico, INT'L Lis, Giuffrè, Giuraemilia, Altalex, and Aldricus. The 22 EOP cases were identified using these sources. In addition, information on 16 other EOPs was obtained from the Ministry of Justice files, and from judges and clerks who had applied the procedure. The information regards particular standard forms used in EOP proceedings and court decisions following oppositions, raising to 38 the total number of EOP cases analysed. One ESCP case has been identified so far.[1601] Additionally, five cases were identified, in which one of the party's legal representatives asked the court to interpret the national provisions in line with the text of the ESCP Regulation. In all cases, reference to the European procedure was made in relation to the court's interpretation regarding the extent of the costs that should be awarded.[1602] In considering the published cases, it appears that the EOP is a better known procedure, and in practice is used more often than the ESCP. An alternative explanation may be that EOP cases seem to generate more difficulties, especially in relation to the transfer to the ordinary procedure following opposition.

The majority of EOP claims or oppositions were handled by the *Tribunale*, with one case being trialled by a Justice of the Peace. There was also a special appeal request against a review decision declaring an issued order null, as well as a review handled by the Supreme Court.

The distribution of published and traced EOP and ESCP cases is shown below.

	2008	2009	2010	2011	2012	2013	2014	2015	2016
EOP	0	13	4	3	6	5	2	4	1
ESCP	n/a	0	0	0	0	0	1	0	0

Table 5.2. Annual distribution of EOP and ESCP cases identified

The EOP cases represent a mixture of EOP awards: opposition procedures, requests for additional information from the court (Form B), proposals to modify the application for an EOP (Form C), declarations of enforceability (Form G), and a special appeal against a review procedure that declared an EOP null. The ESCP was a judgment in an aviation

1601 Ufficio Giudice di Pace di Parma, Sezione 1, Case No. 7667/2013, Decision No. 347/2014.

1602 Corte Costituzionale, Sentenza n. 157, 4 June 2014; Tribunale di Roma, Sezione XII, Case No. 23097/18 November 2013; Tribunale di Roma, Sezione XII, Case No. 35042/13 March 2013; Tribunale di Roma, Sezione XII, Decision of 12 September 2012; Tribunale di Roma, Sezione XII, Decision of 17 May 2012.

case for reimbursement and compensation for denied boarding, in accordance with Regulation 261/2004.[1603]

As regards the courts that handled the identified EOPs, the majority were *Tribunali* from the north of Italy,[1604] and only two from the south, *Tribunali di Napoli* and *Taranto*.[1605]

5.7.2.2. Case Classification

As to the typology of the EOP cases, most of the applications were B2B (32). There were also an apparent C2B[1606] and two B2C cases. Of the published cases, no C2C case could be individualised. All B2C cases were actions initiated by foreign companies against Italian parties. The C2B appears to have been between an Italian consumer and a company with headquarters in Germany.

The ESCP case was a C2B, with three consumers filing a claim against an English airline company.

Information on the type of contractual relationship on which the EOP claim arose was seldom mentioned explicitly. On the basis of the data available, the EOP had been used to recover money claims resulting from sale-purchase agreements.

The ESCP case was based on a service contract between the consumers and the airline company.

1603 Regulation (EC) No 261/2004 of the European Parliament and of the Council of 11 February 2004 establishing common rules on compensation and assistance to passengers in the event of boarding being denied, and of cancellation or long delays involving flights, and repealing Regulation (EC) No 295/91, O.J. 2004 L46/1.

1604 Corte di Appello di Trieste, Sezione 1 Civil, Case No. 189/2013, decision issued on 13 May 2014; Ufficio del Giudice di Pace di Trieste, Decision No. 4710/10 January 2015; Tribunale di Trieste, Case No. 565/23 February 2009; Tribunale di Trieste 29 March 2009; Tribunale di Trieste, Case No. 3/17 April 2009; Tribunale di Trieste, Decision No. 3617/15 December 2009; Tribunale di Trieste, Case No. 4/5 June 2009; Tribunale di Trieste, Case No. 5/5 June 2009; Tribunale di Trieste, Case No. 6/5 June 2009; Tribunale di Trieste 15 June 2009; Tribunale di Trieste, Case No. 9/17 June 2009; Tribunale di Trieste Case No. 9/2009; Tribunale di Trieste, Case No. 10/2009; Tribunale di Trieste, Case No. 1819/ 3 June 2010; Tribunale di Trieste, Case No. 3294/29 October 2012; Tribunale di Trieste, Case No. 6617/26 August 2015; Tribunale di Genova, 28 January 2014; Tribunale di Varese 12 November 2010; Tribunale di Milano 18 July 2011; Tribunale di Milano 28 October 2010; Tribunale di Milano, Case No. 76746/2013; Tribunale di Milano, Case No. 10488/8 April 2015; Tribunale di Mantova 7 July 2011, Case No. 1964/11; Tribunale di Mantova 14 July 2011; Tribunale di Verona, Case No. 7443/26 May 2012; Tribunale di Piacenza 18 September 2010; Tribunale di Forli, Case No. 2192/2011, Decision issued 22 Janaury 2013; Tribunale di Forli, Case No. 45/24 January 2013; Tribunale di Forli, Case No. 450/2012, Decision issued 17 June 2013; Tribunale di Firenze, 25 November 2009; Tribunale di Firenze, Sezione 3, Decision No. 1734/2013; Tribunale di Rovereto, Decision No. 688/2012; Tribunale di Rovereto, Decision No. 511/2012.

1605 Tribunale di Napoli, 4 December 2009; Tribunale di Taranto, Sezione II, Decision No. 5949/15 September 2016.

1606 The identity of the parties was anonymous. However, based on the format used to refer to each of the parties in two different publications, it seems that the claimant was a consumer and the defendant a legal entity with headquarters in a different Member State.

5.7.2.3. Conduct of Proceedings

The vast majority of published or traced cases did not contain a direct indication as to how the EOP or ESCP claim had been filed. However, as a result of an amendment of the national law on the electronic filing of domestic orders for payment, some confusion arose as to whether the EOPs had to be filed in a similar manner. The *Tribunale di Milano* had to address this issue before the Ministry of Justice was required to provide clarification.[1607] Rightfully, the Italian judge interpreted the Regulation's provisions as being autonomous from the interpretation given by national rules, and thus their application preceded them. Extending the national electronic filing requirements to the EOP was equivalent to imposing subsequent formal requirements, which the CJEU had ruled out in a previous case.[1608] Hence, the domestic electronic filing requirements are not intended to rule on the submission of EOP application forms.

The published EOP cases indicated that the orders were issued by judges on the basis of the forms submitted to him. There was no indication that public hearings had been organised.

As regards the length of the EOP procedure, only two cases provided relevant information concerning the timeframe from the moment a claim was submitted to the court (Form A) up until the actual issue of the order (Form E).[1609] In these instances, the EOP was issued in 23 and 14 days, respectively. This is in line with the national practice regarding the *ingiunzione di pagamento*, where the orders are issued much faster than in other national procedures. The ESCP decision was issued within a period of 3 months and 8 days from the moment the claim form (Form A) was submitted.

Because none of the 38 EOP cases referred to a rejection of an application for an order, no data was available in relation to the use of Form D.

The Italian judges on several occasions used Form B requesting additional information or clarification they deemed necessary to decide EOP claims. This concerned 11 cases; hence, almost 30% of the total number of cases. The clarification or information had to do with (1) the interest claimed and, occasionally, the period for which the interest rates should be applied; (2) the type of costs claimed; (3) whether penalties were claimed; (4) the evidence the party intended to use; (5) the grounds of jurisdiction for the court to retain competence; and (6) the use of standard Form A and the signature of the applicant. On one occasion, the court sent Form C proposing that the claimant modify the application. The amendment concerned the amount of costs claimed. The judge proposed reducing the amount in accordance with documents submitted to the court.[1610]

1607 Tribunale di Milano, Case No. 10488/8 April 2015. Subsequently, the Ministry of Justice issued a Ministry Guideline specifying that the *processo telematico* requirements did not apply to the filing of EOP procedures, as this requirement would prevent foreign parties not represented by a lawyer from submitting a request to the Italian courts in accordance with the provisions of Article 24 EOP. See Circolare dg_DAG.23/10/2015.0159552.U, Adempimenti di cancelleria relativi al Processo Civile Telematico (reference on file with the researcher).

1608 See Case C-215/11 *Iwona Szyrocka v SiGer Technologie GMH*, ECLI: EU:C:2012:794.

1609 Tribunale di Milano, Case No. 10488/8 April 2015 and Ufficio del Giudice di Pace di Trieste, Decision No. 4710/10 January 2015.

1610 Tribunale di Trieste, Case No. 3/17 April 2009 (Form C issued on 28 April 2009).

Unfortunately, there was no information as to whether the party accepted the court's proposal. Additionally, there were no details as to the type of documents the claimants usually attached to Form A. The EOP was issued by the Italian judge in 34 cases, and one case concerned the enforcement in Italy of an order issued in a different Member State. The Declaration of enforceability was awarded in two of the EOP claims. When issued correctly, Form G was granted by the court after a period of 4 months and 20 days from the moment the court delivered the EOP (Form E).[1611] No information was provided as to whether Form G had been issued upon a registered request by the claimant or whether the court had proceeded automatically after the time to oppose had lapsed. In one of the published cases, Form G was incorrectly issued because the defendant had opposed the order. The court was unable to understand the documents it received, as the translation into Italian accompanying the document was unintelligible.[1612] Form G was requested in two additional cases, but the judge rejected both applications due to oppositions filed within the 30-day limit set by the Regulation.[1613]

The ESCP case does not indicate whether the defendant replied to the court within the 30-day period set by Article 5(3) ESCP. The court did not hold a hearing, and the claimants did not request it. The judgment was issued only on the basis of the documents and the standard claim form. However, in their application the claimants requested the court to issue a Declaration of enforceability (Form D), and the judgment was issued only within the form usually used for domestic claims. This is counter to the aim of the Regulation, which standardises this aspect of the procedure.[1614]

The EOP order was opposed in 17 cases: namely, 44.73% of them. In all but one case the proceeding was transferred to the national ordinary procedure. In this instance, the court declared the EOP enforceable, and the defendant sought to file a review on the basis of Article 20 EOP. The high number of opposed EOP cases available could be due to the problematic interpretation of this stage of the proceedings. Various interpretations exist regarding the sequence of procedural steps or paths the file should follow; hence, the cases are of particular interest to practitioners and courts. Of the total number of oppositions, information on the use of Form F was provided in three cases. In a fourth case, the foreign defendant sent the form as well as a letter in German, but the translation of the letter proved unintelligible for the Italian judge.[1615] For the remaining ten cases, it can be presumed the defendant made use of the standard form, or sent some other written document in which his intention to oppose the EOP was clearly stated. With regard to transfer to the ordinary procedure, the practice of the Italian courts is not

1611 Tribunale di Trieste, Case No. 3617/15 December 2009. According to information provided on Form G, Form E was issued on 25 July 2009, and it was served on 23 July 2009. This prior notification raises some questions on the manner in which the defendant was notified of the existence of the order or of possible errors.

1612 Tribunale di Mantova, 7 July 2010.

1613 Tribunale di Milano, 18 July 2011; Tribunale di Torino, 31 August 2012.

1614 See also di Napoli (2015) (available at http://aldricus.com/2015/09/18/una-concreta-applicazione-fra-le-poche-note-del-procedimento-europeo-sulle-controversie-di-modesta-entita/).

1615 As seen in the data results in the decision issued by *Tribunale di Mantova*, 7 July 2010, both the letter and the form were in German. The letter was accompanied by an unintelligible translation in which the word 'opposition' did not appear.

unitary. Seven interpretations can be identified among the decisions: five are variations in the transfer in accordance with the provisions of the ordinary procedure; one is a reinstatement in accordance with the ordinary procedure; and one adopts a solution that mirrors the internal *procedimento per ingiunzione*. According to one interpretation,[1616] following the opposition, upon the judge's request the clerk notified the claimant of the action of the defendant and of the hearing established by the judge in accordance with Article 183 and Article 163*bis* CPC. The creditor was required to pay the necessary unified court fees, and to notify the defendant of the date of the hearing. The first stage of the ordinary procedure was not considered necessary; hence, the defendant needed to appoint a lawyer and to file a response to the claim (*comparsa di risposta*) 20 days before the hearing, and to formally present his defence to the court (*costituzione in giudizio*).[1617] The court in Napoli took a slightly different approach.[1618] Similar to the previous interpretation, the judge requested the clerk to inform the claimant of the opposition and to set a date for the hearing in accordance with the ordinary procedure. However, in accordance with this court, the claimant had to serve on the defendant a summons (*atto di citazione*) as provided by Article 163 CPC as the first procedural step in initiating ordinary proceedings. Along the same lines,[1619] following the judge's request to the clerk's office for notification, and after establishing a date for the hearing in accordance with Article 183 CPC, the creditor was required to serve a summons on the debtor (*atto di citazione*),[1620] as in the ordinary court proceedings, requesting him to appear in court on the set date. This was to allow the debtor to present a defence to the court (*costituzione in giudizio*).[1621] The *Tribunale di Milano* chose a different path.[1622] The court held the creditor responsible for initiating the transfer to the ordinary procedure. He was to act in accordance with Article 163 CPC, by serving an *atto di citazione* on the defendant. Another interpretation of the national rules regarding transfer set a duty on the judge to initiate it.[1623] The judge had to request the clerk's office to notify the creditor of the opposition and to establish a date for the hearing (Article 183 CPC). The hearing would have to observe the time requirements set by Article 163*bis* CPC. Following this step, the creditor was to integrate the application by submitting additional information about the claim and the means of evidence (*integrazione*).[1624] Subsequently, the defendant had the option (*facolta*) of filing his response and presenting a defence to the court at least 20 days before the hearing.[1625] The *Tribunale di Taranto* proposed a different approach,

1616 Tribunale di Firenze, 25 September 2009.

1617 Article 166–167 CPC.

1618 Tribunale di Napoli, 4 December 2009.

1619 Tribunale di Piacenza, 18 September 2010; Tribunale di Milano, 18 July 2011; Tribunale di Forli, Case No. 2192/2011.

1620 Artcile 163 CPC.

1621 Article 166–167 CPC.

1622 Tribunale di Milano, 28 October 2010. Tribunale di Rovereto, Decision No. 511/2012 and Decision No. 668/2012. For a similar interpretation within the Justice of the Peace procedure, see Ufficio del Giudice di Pace di Trieste, Case No. 4710/2014.

1623 Tribunale di Varese, 12 November 2010; Tribunale di Verona, 26 Ma 2012; Tribunale di Forli, Case No. 40/2012; Tribunale di Firenze, Sezione 3, Decision No. 1734/2013.

1624 Article 163 CPC.

1625 Article 166–167 CPC.

which sought to reconcile the EOP provisions with the uncertainty as to which national provisions applied in the event of transfer to the ordinary procedure.[1626] The court made use of the reinstatement mechanism as if the case had been stayed. The creditor was to resume proceedings and complete the claim to be communicated to the defendant in accordance with Article 125 CPC in order for it to be served on the defendant.

Although in most cases the court itself or the claimant was expected to initiate the trial following opposition, the *Tribunale di Genova* had an opposite view.[1627] According to the judge, it was the defendant's duty to inform the claimant of the opposition and of the decree issued by the judge to set the date of the hearing. Additionally, he was required to present his defence to the court at least 20 days before the hearing.[1628] The most different approach regarding the provisions that should rule the transfer was adopted by the *Tribunale di Mantova*. This court considered that the transfer following opposition to the EOP should follow the path of the national *procedimento per ingiunzione* as set by Article 645 CPC.[1629] This last interpretation seems the most unfortunate, as it departed from the provisions of Article 17 EOP, which establish that 'the proceedings shall continue before the competent courts [...] in accordance with the rules of ordinary civil procedure'.

The interpretations by which the Italian courts sought to fill the legislative gap do not create a unitary approach. This leads to confusion not only for a foreign party but also for local practitioners. The present situation can easily result in additional delays, more costs, and possibly the renewal of some of the procedural actions or documents that should be submitted to the court.

In one of the cases, the Italian court proceeded to issue the Declaration of enforceability of an EOP that had been opposed.[1630] The claimant sought to execute the EOP in Germany. In order to prevent execution, the defendant opposed proceedings in Germany and then initiated a court proceeding in Italy for an interim measure under Article 700 CPC. The result was that the Italian court did not take into consideration the opposition already filed by the defendant resident abroad, since a standard form in a language different than that of the proceedings was used, accompanied by a letter that had been translated unintelligibly into Italian. According to the court, the transfer to the ordinary procedure following an opposition (Article 17 EOP) should be handled in accordance with Article 645 CPC. Thus, the defendant was responsible for initiating the proceedings following the opposition, an action that he did not undertake. This interpretation sets additional requirements for the defendant in comparison to the provision of Article 12(3)(b) in conjunction with Article 12(4)(c) EOP. According to the Regulation, the defendant is required to lodge a statement of opposition only if he intends to oppose the order. The wording of the text does not hint at any additional steps for the validity of the opposition. This interpretation by the court is in contrast to the aim of the Regulation, which seeks to establish a uniform procedure. Further, the judge

[1626] Tribunale di Taranto, Sezione II, Decision No. 5949/15 September 2016.
[1627] Tribunale di Genova, 28 January 2014.
[1628] Article 166–167 CPC.
[1629] For characteristics of an opposition to a national order for payment regarding proceedings, see Section 5.3.1.2.
[1630] Tribunale di Mantova, Case No. 1964/7 July 2011.

proceeded to examine the possibility of using the review mechanism, but concluded that none of the criteria for its application had been fulfilled. The question that arises is whether the court could have interpreted the Declaration of enforceability that was incorrectly issued as 'other exceptional circumstances' in accordance with Article 20(2) EOP, or whether an effective solution should be made available in the national law for debtors encountering such situations, in keeping with the reasoning of the CJEU in the *eco cosmetics* case.[1631]

The review of an EOP was requested in one case.[1632] The debtor sought to use Article 20 EOP to prevent enforcement when he was served the notice of performance (*precetto*). The debtor argued that the *Tribunale di Bergamo* was in error in issuing the EOP, as it lacked jurisdiction. The *Tribunale* declared the EOP null on the reasoning that Article 20 may be used to raise any error with regard to the requirements that need to be fulfilled in order to issue the order. The Court of Appeal in Brescia upheld the reasoning. The Supreme Court in consideration of Recital 25 EOP proceeded to a strict interpretation of the provisions of Article 20, upholding a line of interpretation followed by the CJEU: namely, that the review is an exceptional means, and does not give the defendant a second opportunity to oppose the claim. Thus, it cannot be used by the defendant to raise matters that he could have presented through an opposition (Article 16 EOP).[1633]

5.7.2.4. Representation of the Parties

In an analysis of the identified cases, it emerges that the parties were often represented by a lawyer. And from the available information, it appears that at least one of the parties was represented in 20 EOP cases.

Representation in the application procedure	**Number of EOP cases**
Creditor	12
Debtor	1
Both parties are represented	7
Representation in the execution process	
Creditor	1
Debtor	–
Both parties are represented	–

Table 5.3. Representation of parties by a lawyer in the EOP procedure

1631 Joined Cases C-119/13 to C-120/13, para. 51 last section.

1632 Corte di Cassazione, Sezioni unite, Decision No. 10799/26 May 2015.

1633 According to the court, the circumstances that could justify use of the review are similar to those that justify an exceptional review (*revocazione straordinaria*) on the basis of Article 656 CPC.

Some of the parties were occasionally repeated players. In two situations, both parties were repeated players as well as being legal entities. In addition to this, two different claimants repeatedly used the EOP procedure in three different cases filed with the same court.

In the ESCP case, claimants were represented by a lawyer who actually filled in their claim form.

5.7.2.5. Amounts and Costs Claimed

Not all the EOP cases provided information on the amount of debt claimed, but some gave an indication. The amount of the principle varied from €2,256,848.86 to €412.28, with most of claimants requesting reimbursements for amounts of tens of thousands of euros. Interest and costs were added to some of the claims. Costs were requested less often than interest, and sometimes the judge only mentioned them in the decisions, but without specifying the exact amount awarded. In one EOP case, the costs awarded were revealed, and amounted to €178.

The payment of court fees in the EOP cases did not seem to be problematic. Nonetheless, this could also be because the claimant in a significant number of cases was represented by a lawyer. With regard to penalties, these were not requested in any of the identified cases. It is not clear whether penalties were never or rarely requested by the claimant or whether it was only the case in the documents in question.

In the ESCP case, the principle amounted to €927 including the price of the ticket paid and the compensation applicable in accordance with Regulation 261/2004. In addition, the claimants requested costs of €500 plus TVA (hence, €300 for legal assistance, plus additional costs), as well as legal interest from the moment the parties were prevented from boarding the plane. The court awarded the amount requested, including interest (hence, €1,861.40, of which €634.40 was the cost of the proceedings). The case does not provide detailed information on the court fees paid. However, the documents do show that for enforcing purposes in relation to obtaining the enforceable title, the claimants had to pay the Italian tax authority (*Agenzia delle Entrate*) a €200 fee for registering the judgment.

5.7.2.6. Service and Language Aspects

Information regarding the service of an EOP on a defendant was often not available. Due to the many opposition proceedings, more details exist regarding notification of the creditor that the EOP had been opposed. This was usually undertaken by the clerk's office upon the judge's request. As to service of the EOP on the defendant, it was not clear whether this was generally communicated together with the copy of Form A and Form F. In one case, it was mentioned expressly that Form F was not served together with the order. In three of four cases that contained information regarding service, it was mentioned that the judge had verified the date of the service prior to issuing the Declaration of enforceability (Form G).

Details regarding the language in which the EOP was served or Form F was sent to the court were rarely available or mentioned. It can be presumed that the language was either that of the court or one that the party understood. In one instance, Form F was submitted to the Italian court in German.[1634] From the case description, it does not appear that the court requested the defendant to re-send the form in Italian, the language of the proceedings. The letter accompanying the standard form was also in German, and its translation was not of a standard sufficient for the judge to understand its message. The opposition was not taken into consideration. In this case, the language in which the form had been filed had serious implications for the outcome of the case.

In the ESCP case, the documents available show that the bailiff at the request of the clerk's office proceeded to send, by registered mail, standard Forms A (official copy) and C as well as the documents that were attached to the claim form. However, it is not clear whether these were sent to the English defendant in English or in Italian, or whether translation services were used or requested.

5.7.2.7. Enforcement

Two EOP cases provide information on enforcement of the order. In one case regarding an EOP declared enforceable by the court of another Member State, the judge of execution recognised the same effects as those involving a national *ingiunzione di pagamento*, basing his argument on the reasoning of the CJEU in the *Szyrocka* case.[1635] Hence, in order for the EOP to be an effective choice for interested parties, claimants should be able to make use of the same rights as when choosing national instruments. The judge allowed the registration of a judicial hypothec (*ipoteca giudiziale*) against an Italian private party for an amount of €25,000. The other case concerns an EOP that was wrongly declared enforceable in Italy.[1636] The creditor sought to execute the order in Germany, where the defendant opposed the execution and succeeded in staying enforcement until the validity of the title was decided in Italy. He then initiated a court proceeding in Italy for an interim measure under Article 700 CPC, seeking to obtain a revocation or suspension of the enforcement title in accordance with Article 20 EOP. The first instance court ruled that Article 700 CPC could not be used to oppose an enforceable title issued by the judge by decree. The judge ruled that this could be carried out only on the basis of Article 17 EOP, where the judge has the same powers as those provided by Article 645 CPC within the *ingiunzione di pagamento* procedure, or by an opposition to enforcement in accordance with Article 615 CPC. The first solution was no longer available, as the opposition period had lapsed. With regard to the second option, it was clear that Article 615 CPC was not applicable because the execution had been carried out in Germany. In response to this, the defendant filed a *reclamo* against the interim measures.[1637] The panel upheld the reasoning of the first judge that Article 700 CPC could not be used for the purpose of revoking or suspending the enforceable title.

1634 Tribunale di Mantova, Case No. 1964/7 July 2011.

1635 Tribunale di Trieste, Case No. 6617/2015, Decreto 26 August 2015; Case C-215/11.

1636 Tribunale di Mantova, Case No. 1964/7 July 2011.

1637 Article 669*terdecies* CPC.

5.7.2.8. Influence of the National Procedure

As seen from the EOP case law under study, particular national procedures, such as the *ingiunzione di pagamento*, can strongly influence the way transfer following opposition is carried out. This is also a significant aspect regarding the activities each party is expected to undertake, and can have strong implications for their rights, especially as the practice of the courts is not unitary or well defined at the national level.

Another aspect noticed almost immediately is that representation was often used. In more than half of the EOPs at least one of the parties was represented (57.57% of cases).[1638] Representation is compulsory in the majority of court cases in Italy, and this national characteristic was dominant in the application of the European procedures, even though it is not a mandatory requirement. An additional factor that possibly encourages parties to choose legal representation is the complexity of the procedural steps they are expected to undertake. Furthermore, the party is expected to be present in court (i.e. acquiring the Declaration of enforceability) for particular stages of the proceedings, and this would be too burdensome for a party residing abroad; hence, the services of a lawyer turn out to be necessary, and less costly and time consuming for the claimant than undertaking the activity in person.

5.7.3. EOP and ESCP Procedures: Empirical Findings

5.7.3.1. Preliminary Aspects regarding Data Collection

The data analysed in this section were collected through surveys, interviews, and correspondence with Italian practitioners and ECC Italy. In addition, earlier data collected by the Italian Ministry of Justice and the ECC Italy investigation on the functioning of the ESCP for the period 2009–2011[1639] were used to triangulate the validity of the present research findings. In order to conduct research with Italian courts and judges, several requests were sent to the Director of the Office II – International Relations, General Directorate for Civil Justice, Department of Justice Affairs (*Ufficio II – Relazioni Internazionali, Direzione Generale della Giustizia Civile-Dipartimento per gli Affari di Giustizia*) of the Ministry of Justice, and the High School of Magistracy (*Scuola Superiore della Magistratura*). The request for support included the dissemination of the EOP and ESCP surveys to judges, an invitation to take part in interviews regarding application of the European procedures, and assistance in identifying courts having the most experience in this area of law. No direct support was provided by the Ministry or the School in this respect. However, for research purposes, the Director of the Office II agreed to provide access to responses sent by the Italian

[1638] Not in all identified cases is information expressely provided regarding representation of the parties. The percentage is based on the number of cases that refer specifically to the representation of parties by a lawyer.

[1639] Centro Europeo Consumatori Italia, *Il Procedimento Europeo per le Controversie di Modesta Entità. Un indagine del Centro Consumatori Italia e Adiconsum sull'implementazione del Reg CE 861/2007 sul funzionamanto della procedura a livello UE* (periodo 2009–2011).

courts following the 2009 and 2011 surveys.[1640] The Ministry also provided a copy of the replies it had sent to the 2013 European Commission Review of the operation of Regulation (EC) No 1896/2006 and Regulation (EC) No 861/2007.[1641] The EOP data set is not complete, however, as not all the courts replied to the 2009 and 2011 surveys.[1642] After 2011, considering the limited experience indicated in the surveys by Italian courts, the collaborator of the Director of the Office II did not request that the courts provide subsequent data or information on the EOP. The same decision was made with regard to the ESCP in view of the high number of Justice of the Peace offices (846) in 2013. Further, specific courts, judges, and clerks across the country were contacted directly with the support of an IRSiG-CNR researcher working with Italian courts and providing training for the Italian judiciary and clerks.[1643] This included *Tribunali* and *Giudici di Pace*. Twelve courts and a Justice of the Peace agreed to take part in the research by replying to one or both surveys, participating in interviews and/or sending case law on the EOP as well as additional feedback on the European uniform procedures that they considered relevant for their experience. Additional survey responses from the Italian judiciary were collected at a training conference on civil and commercial judicial cooperation organised by the Romanian National Institute of Magistracy in 2014.[1644] Following the conference, additional requests were sent to Italian judges, and resulted in a couple of interviews.[1645]

An invitation to participate in the research was sent to 152 Italian Bar Associations, requesting their assistance in making the project known to their members as well as in making it possible for interested lawyers to have access to the EOP and ESCP online surveys.[1646] Additionally, direct requests were sent to lawyers who had representated parties in EOP and/or ESCP cases that had been traced and/or published.[1647]

Invitations were also sent to bailiffs' offices (*Uffici Notificazioni, Esecuzioni e Protesti – UNEP*) of 26 Courts of Appeal, as well as to the bailiff in charge of the Department of Foreign Documents of the Rome Court of Appeal, the Italian Association of Bailiffs in Europe (*Associazione Ufficiali Giudiziari in Europa – AUGE*), and UIL.P.A. Giustizia.

1640 The EOP surveys were based on questionnaires drafted by the European Judicial Network.

1641 *Review of the operation of Regulation (EC) No 1896/2006 and Regulation (EC) No 861/2007 on the ESCP*, m_dg.DAG. 01/07/2013.0086502.E (document on file with the researcher).

1642 See Section 5.7.1.

1643 A total of 28 requests were sent to courts and Justices of the Peace, and 12 agreed to take part in the research.

1644 This included three replies to the EOP survey and two to the ESCP survey. *Practical exercises in implementing the judicial cooperation instruments in civil and commercial matters*, Final Conference, 20–21 November 2014, Bucharest, Romania.

1645 Seven requests were sent to participating judges, two of whom agreed to an interview to discuss their experiences. Overall, 6 judges, 3 Justices of the Peace, and 1 clerk replied to the EOP survey, and 3 judges and 2 clerks agreed to participate in an in-depth interview. Three judges and 3 Justices of the Peace replied to the ESCP survey.

1646 During June 2014.

1647 Sixteen direct requests were sent to lawyers. Overall, 16 lawyers replied to the EOP survey and 18 to the ESCP.

One bailiff in charge of the Department of Foreign Documents with the Court of Appeal in Rome replied to the EOP survey.[1648]

In order to increase the study's visibility for local practitioners, four (associate) professors were requested to assist in distributing the EOP and ESCP surveys to practitioners within their network or to professional associations of which they were a member. An invitation to take part in the research was also placed on dedicated private international law websites.[1649]

To complete the professionals' framework, ECC Italy (Rome and Bolzano Offices) directors were invited to share their association's experience with the European procedures from a consumer perspective. Further, the director of ECC Rome agreed to take part in an interview discussing further aspects related to application of the procedures in Italy.

This resulted in an overall number of 30 EOP survey responses,[1650] 27 ESCP survey responses,[1651] 6 interviews[1652] and a significant amount of timely feedback and correspondence with Italian practitioners.

5.7.3.2. Familiarity with European Procedures and Handling Practices

The survey results show that respondents generally have a high perception of their knowledge of the EOP and the ESCP (Figs. 5.1–5.2), with more than 50% of the respondents rating their familiarity with the procedure above level 3.

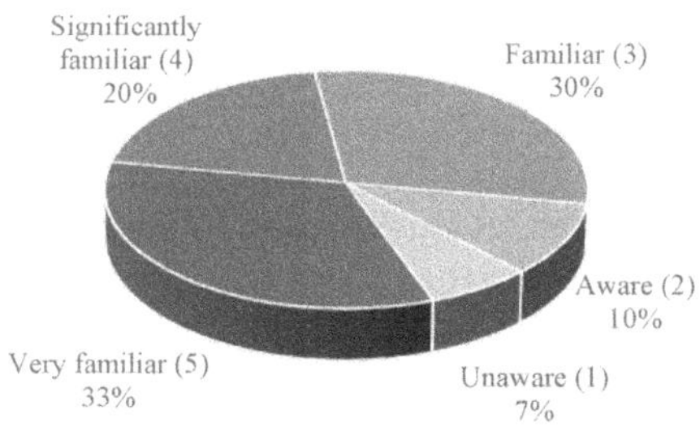

Fig. 5.1. Professionals' perception of their familiarity with the EOP (30 responses)

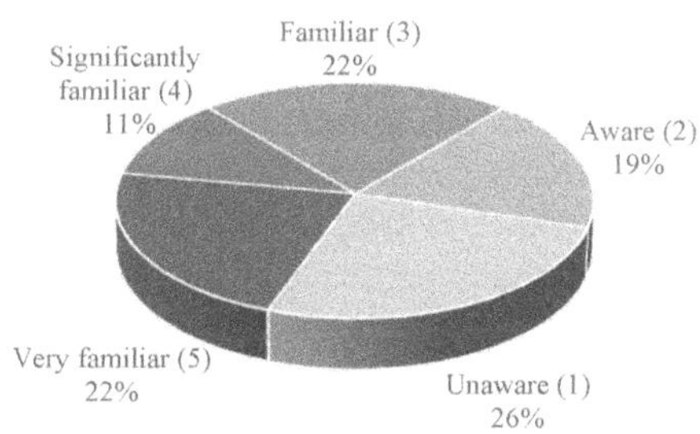

Fig. 5.2. Professionals' perception of their familiarity with the ESCP (27 responses)

1648 Another bailiff declined to participate in the research because he applies national provisions to the execution of enforceable EOPs and ESCPs.

1649 See Aldricus on 13 November 2014 (https://aldricus.com/2014/11/13/due-questionari-per-raccogliere-lesperienza-dei-pratici-sullingiunzione-di-pagamento-europea-e-il-procedimento-europeo-per-le-controversie-di-modesta-entita/) and on 19 July 2015 on Conflicts of laws (http://conflictoflaws.net/2015/surveys-on-european-order-for-payment-and-small-claims-procedures/).

1650 6 judges, 3 Justices of the Peace, 1 clerk, 16 lawyers, 1 bailiff, 1 professor, and 2 ECCs replied to the EOP survey.

1651 3 judges, 4 Justices of the Peace, 18 lawyers, 1 professor, and the ECCs replied to the ESCP survey.

1652 Interviews were conducted with 3 judges, 2 clerks, 1 bailiff, and 1 ECC.

The level of knowledge is particularly high (83% of respondents) in relation to the EOP, which may be due to the more frequent use of the EOP than the ESCP by courts and practitioners, as seen from the data, statistics, and case law.[1653] Most of the EOP respondents have applied the procedure several times. In contrast, the ESCP appears to have been less often applied by the practitioners participating in this study.[1654] Some respondents expressly indicated they had never had the opportunity to handle an ESCP claim (6 of 27), although they were aware of the procedure and its characteristics. In practice, it appears that there are only limited opportunities for a practitioner to apply the ESCP, due to the small number of cases registered. This was also mentioned in an earlier study carried out by the Trans Europe Experts Association.[1655] The high level of familiarity indicated by respondents might also have been influenced by their participation in dedicated professional training. Practitioners who indicated that they had followed some form of training (almost 30% of the EOP survey respondents and 16% of the ESCP survey respondents) considered themselves to be 'significantly or very familiar' (scale level 4 and 5) with the European uniform procedures.

Further, some respondents pointed to a need for more dedicated training by professional associations as well as to adequate preparation by the clerks who receive applications. More practical information on the European procedures could contribute to increasing familiarity with them. For the ESCP, practitioners who had never received an application generally indicated that they were unaware of the procedure.[1656] A subsequent study carried out in coordination with the Max Planck Institute confirmed that insufficient familiarity with the ESCP was considered by practitioners to be one of the main impediments to its application.[1657]

The respondents' perception of others' general awareness of the European procedures was lower in comparison to their own (Figs. 5.3–5.4). None of the respondents considered other professionals to be 'very familiar' with the European procedures. Further, the level of familiarity and awareness was rated to be higher for the EOP than for the ESCP. As well as the knowledge factor, the results might have been influenced by the frequency with which the procedures were used in practice and the experience that practitioners had when seeking to apply them. A significant percentage of the respondents pointed to practitioners and courts not being generally aware of the EOP and the ESCP. Especially regarding the ESCP, the lack of awareness was mentioned in more than 50% of the answers. Additionally, limited familiarity and unawareness of the European uniform procedures on the part of Italian consumers and businesses was

1653 Some court respondents indicated there had been more than 50 EOP cases in a year; or where the annual average was around 10 cases a year or fewer; or where barely 1 EOP claim had been received annually.

1654 Respondents who had handled ESCP applications mentioned receiving between 1 and 4 cases. One respondent, a Justice of the Peace, indicated having handled 20 cases since January 2009 (July 2014).

1655 Not many claims below €2,000 were registered at the national level, and thus there were few opportunities to make use of the European procedure; see Fauvarque-Cosson & Behar-Touchais (2012), at 151.

1656 One Justice of the Peace indicated that he was familiar with the ESCP procedure, and advised colleagues on applying it in the claims they received, although he had never had an ESCP case of his own.

1657 Hess (2017), Chapter 5 para. 900.

revealed by earlier studies (e.g. 80% of ESCP respondents in Italy had not heard of the procedure).[1658]

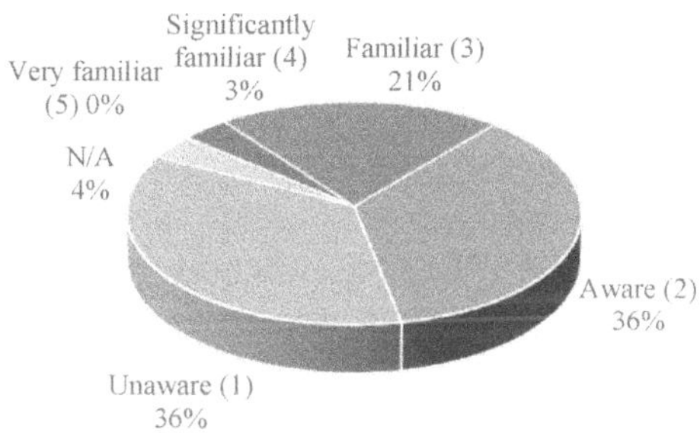

Fig. 5.3. Professionals' perception of general EOP awareness (30 responses)

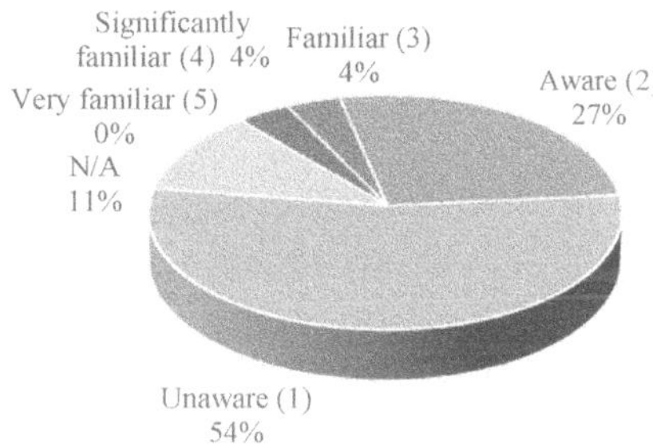

Fig. 5.4. Professionals' perception of general ESCP awareness (26 responses)

The Italian procedural system underwent numerous reforms over the years in order to improve its functioning and to provide speedier and simplified procedures for parties. However, these have not proven successful. Practitioners and courts prefer to use the procedures they know best, rather than take chances that their claim might be rejected due to the court's limited awareness, or to having to comply with particular additional requirements because of the court's uncertainites on how to proceed with the request. Therefore, most respondents indicate a certain preference for the use of national procedures instead of the EOP or the ESCP (76.66% of the EOP respondents and 70.37% of the ESCP respondents). Figures 5.5 and 5.6 provide an indication of the preferred alternative procedures. The most popular of these are the *ingiunzione di pagamento* and the ordinary proceedings undertaken before a Justice of the Peace for small value claims. These particular preferences were also mentioned in an earlier study.[1659]

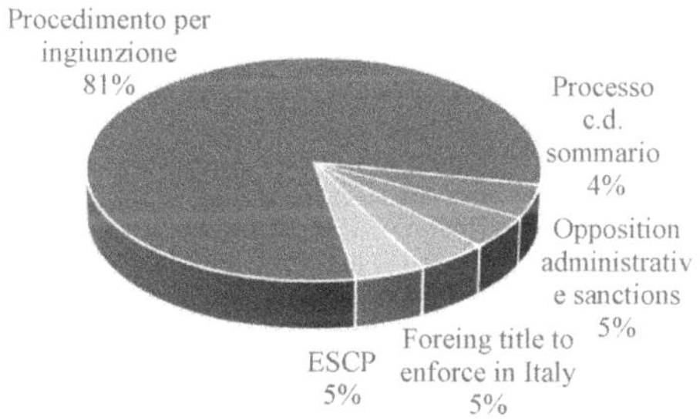

Fig. 5.5. National procedures chosen over the EOP (29 responses)

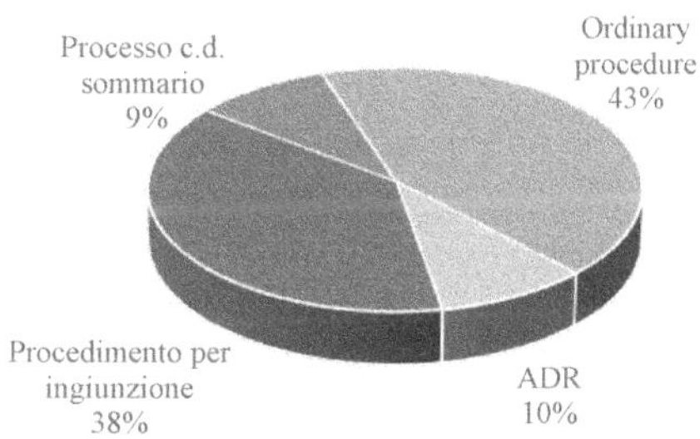

Fig. 5.6. National procedures chosen over the ESCP (27 responses)

1658 Special Eurobarometer 395, *European Small Claims Procedure*, 2013, at 69; Fauvarque-Cosson & Behar-Touchais (2012), at 475.

1659 Fauvarque-Cosson & Behar-Touchais (2012), at 155 and 167.

The reasons that parties and practitioners continue to prefer domestic procedures might be related to a series of aspects indicated by the respondents. Limited knowledge or unawareness of the European procedures is one of the reasons most often highlighted. Other reasons are (1) the legislative lacuna or non-unitary practice of the courts (EOP); (2) fear of the order being opposed (EOP); (3) no clear indication of how the court will deal with the procedure following opposition (EOP); (4) the perception that the European procedure does not offer the same guarantees as the national procedure (EOP); (5) the possibility of requesting a provisional attachment of assets (*sequestro conservativo*) in an *ingiunzione* claim (EOP); (6) the possibility of filing a national order for payment (*procedimento per ingiunzione*) electronically and to obtain it in less than two weeks (EOP); and (7) the low threshold of the procedure (ESCP). Practitioners and potential users seeking to apply the Regulations would certainly benefit from better training for professionals and courts, and from a heightened awareness with regard to the European uniform procedures and their functioning, as well as from clarification of the aspects that create difficulties at the level of coordination between national and European provisions.

5.7.3.3. Case Classification

According to the collected data, the EOP procedure is most often used in B2B claims and occasionally in B2C or C2B cases. From the more limited information available on the ESCP, the procedures appear to be used primarily in C2B cases and seldom in B2B and C2C claims.

With regard to the type of contractual relationship, the EOP is most often used in sale-purchase agreements, service agreements, and loan agreement claims, and occasionally in relation to immovable property purchase agreements, administration contracts, and procurement contacts. ESCP claims are often related to sale-purchase agreements, service agreements, holiday package deals, and aviation cases concluded by consumers. These results are in line with the EOP and ESCP case law analysed in the present study.

5.7.3.4. Conduct of Proceedings and Encountered Difficulties

Handling of Cases

The EOP and ESCP survey respondents had divergent views as to the division of tasks between judges and clerks in handling European procedures claims (Fig. 5.7). The judges and clerks considered the judge to be more involved in the handling of EOP and ESCP forms, while lawyers perceived clerks as playing a more active role. A possible explanation for this result could be related to clerks being the ones who came into contact first with the parties or their representatives. They registered the applications, proceeded to verify that the forms complied with requirements set by the Regulations, and that the court fees (*contributo unificato* and *anticipazioni forfettarie*) had been paid. Furthermore, they communicated with the parties, notified claimants or their representative of the issuance of orders or of judgments, and published the judge's decision. In addition, some respondents indicated that the standard forms were prepared and sent to the judge by the clerks.

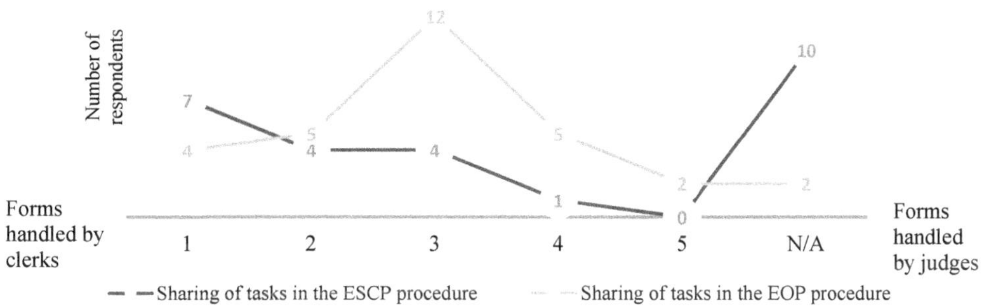

Fig. 5.7. Division of tasks between judges and clerks in the handling of EOP and ESCP forms (survey results)

The task of the judge was mainly to assess the merits of the claims. Where necessary, he could request the completion or rectification of the application (Form B), propose a modification of the claim (Form C for the EOP), issue the order (Form E for the EOP) or the ESCP judgment, and declare the EOP enforceable (Form G) or certify the ESCP (Form D). The judges were allocated cases on the basis of a rotation system; hence, their chances of receiving a significant number of EOP and/or ESCP cases annually were to a certain extent limited, considering the modest number of cases registered in comparison to other domestic procedures such as *ingiunzione di pagamento*. Clerks had a greater possibility of dealing with a higher number of cases due to their registration and administrative tasks being carried out by the same person(s). Thus, it was more likely for them to establish some handling practice in relation to the formal verification of the forms, service, and communications with the parties. Moreover, the clerks in charge of these claims were the ones handling the domestic order for payments cases, and were used to the speedier treatment of the claim, giving them priority over other cases. Overall, the EOP and the ESCP were to a certain extent handled like national procedures, but practices might have varied on the basis of the courts' own internal arrangements. In relation to the ESCP, a significant number of respondents, mostly lawyers, were not able to provide any feedback on the division of tasks at court level, probably due to the infrequent use and application of the procedure.

With regard to possible tensions at the level of coordination between the national procedural rules and provisions of the European uniform procedures, a significant percentage of the respondents perceived some aspects to be problematic (Figs. 5.8–5.9). These were mostly related to the lack of specific domestic rules or guidelines to clarify and coordinate the way in which provisions of the Regulations needed to be applied or supplemented by national rules. Respondents also complained about the limited dissemination of information regarding the EOP and the enforcement stage to be carried out in Italy. This raised doubts regarding how EOP requests needed be processed and how certain stages of the procedure had to be handled. As the ESCP procedure was seldom used, parties and practitioners were sometimes not aware of its existence or of how to use its forms.

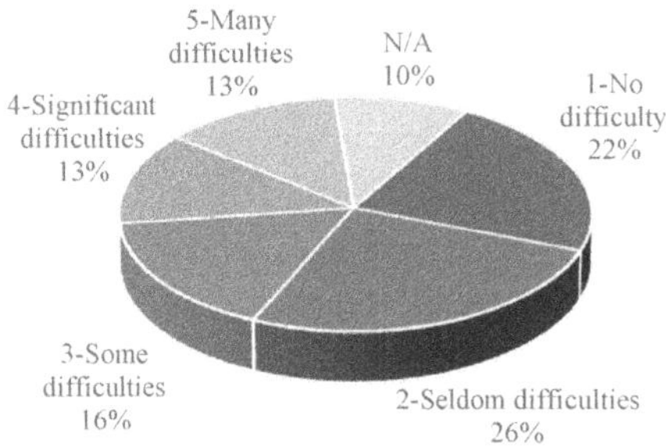

Fig. 5.8. National procedural rules create difficulties in the handling of EOP claims (31 responses)

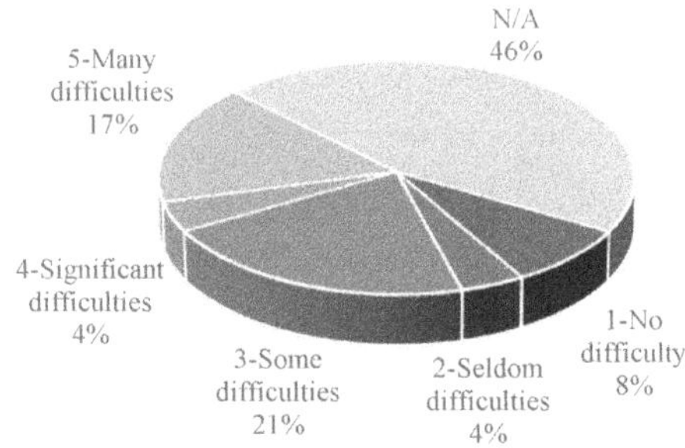

Fig. 5.9. National procedural rules create difficulties in the handling of ESCP claims (24 responses)

The courts' practices in handling EOPs were divergent. This was particularly the case with regard to the effects of the opposition, service, and duties that parties has in the proceedings. The way the EOP was applied was influenced by the domestic order for payment procedure. For example, in the *ingiunzione di pagamento,* the role of the parties following opposition was reversed, requesting the debtor opposing the procedure to take active steps in continuing the procedure. In relation to the EOP, not all courts proceeded to an automatic transfer of the case to the ordinary procedure, but waited for the claimant to file a new request or for the defendant to continue proceedings.[1660] A foreign party not using the services of an Italian lawyer is very unlikely to be aware of the actions expected of him in order for the proceeding to continue. This prolongs proceedings and involves additional costs for the party. Furthermore, some lawyers and judges submitted or requested the submission of evidence documents, as in the domestic *ingiunzione*. The court fees and their payment also raised difficulties. At first this was because no wire payment from abroad was possible for the EOP, and then because following an opposition the claimant was expected to initiate a new procedure, thus paying a new *contributo unificato,* while for the *ingiunzione di pagamento* only the difference in fees was charged. For the ESCP, the payment of court fees remained problematic, as thus far the Ministry of Justice has made no special arrangements to facilitate it.[1661] It is hoped this will change with the application of Article 15a Regulation 2015/2421. The introduction of compulsory electronic filing and handling of the *procedimento per ingiunzione* in 2014 affected the registration of EOP applications for a brief period. National legislation did not address the way the EOP could be received after June 2014, and courts were not sure how to proceed. For this reason, some courts rejected claims filed by foreign claimants because they were not filed electronically. However, following a demand for clarification from the *Tribunale di Lamenzia Terme,*

1660 See Section 5.7.2.3.

1661 The e-Justice Portal refers to wire transfers being possible in order to pay the court fees, but does not provide concrete details regarding the account to which payment should be made (available at https://e-justice.europa.eu/content_court_fees_concerning_small_claims_procedure-306-it-en.do?clang=it).

the Ministry of Justice issued an interpretation notice explaining why paper submissions have been maintained in relation to the EOP while the national procedure has been switched to an electronic format.[1662]

Other difficulties indicated by respondents relate to the enforcement stage, the inability of Equitalia Giustizia to recover court fees owed by parties not having a tax residence in Italy,[1663] the cumbersome court proceedings in Italy, and the determining of the court competent to issue the order. With regard to the ESCP, the appeal governed by national law provisions may significantly prolong proceedings that are intended to be fast,[1664] and the procedural timeframe set by the European uniform procedures is difficult to achieve in consideration of the application of domestic rules. Furthermore, judges and clerks were sometimes unaware that they did not have to automatically set a date for a hearing and that service of the forms had to be carried out by the court and not by the claimant as in domestic procedures. Another difficulty facing the courts with regard to communicating ESCP procedural forms and copies was the fact that the clerk was unable to arrange for the service of procedural documents to a defendant in another Member State.[1665] A solution needs to be found, considering the 14-day period within which the court is required to dispatch to the other party documents it has received.

Identifying the difficulties is a first step towards finding appropriate solutions to facilitate and encourage the use of the EOP and the ESCP, considering the particularity of the national procedural system, the need for further coordination between the applicable rules, the aims of the European procedures, and practitioners' training and demands for information.

1662 Reply of the Ministry of Justice to a question from the Chief Clerk of the Court of Appeal of Catanzaro (prot. N. 4810 del 13 aprile 2015) regarding the way a claim based on Regulation (CE) n. 1896/2006 should be submitted, and national provisions regarding the electronic process, Dipartimento per gli Affari di Giustizia, Direzione Generale della Giustizia Civile, Ufficio II, Fasc. 020.004.002–64, m_dg.DAG. 22/04/2015.0064544.U (document on file with the researcher). Circolare 23 ottobre 2015 – Adempimenti di cancelleria relativi al Processo Civile Telematico, Ministry of Justice, Department for Legal Affairs, Directorate-General for Civil Justice, 23 October 2015, point 8.1 (available at www.giustizia.it/giustizia/it/mg_1_8_1.wp?previsiousPage=mg_14_7&contentId=SDC1187890). At the national level in Italy, the only court authorised to receive EOP claims filed electronically is the *Tribunale di Milano* within the e-Codex pilot project.

1663 This could change with the establishment of the Agenzia delle Entrate-Riscosioni, which might be able to conclude agreements with similar institutions in other Member States. This would facilitate the recovery of public debts resulting from court actions, but the prepatory activities will continue to be carried out by Equitalia Giustizia. See also Section 5.5.

1664 A respondent indicated this might take a few years. Furthermore, the Ministry of Justice considered that no ESCP procedural deadline should apply for the appeal, as the national procedure is likely to take longer due to the re-examination process; *Review of the operation of Regulation (EC) No 1896/2006 and Regulation (EC) No 861/2007 on the ESCP* (m_dg.DAG. 01/07/2013.0086502.E) (document on file with the researcher).

1665 It is hoped that the approval of the Project of Law No. 2085 of 2015 (DDL concorrenza 2015) can in practice facilitate the service abroad of procedural documents by opening up the market to service providers other than Poste Italiane S.p.A.

Forms

The use of standard forms is not common in court proceedings in Italy. Most respondents indicated that the use of forms was problematic for parties and sometimes for their representatives.[1666] Apart from the assistance ECC Italy offers consumers and, occasionally, a court clerk providing information to a party on the EOP or the ESCP, there is no body in charge of providing information or advice. Based on the EOP and ESCP surveys and the additional data gathered, Fig. 5.10 provides an overview of the difficulties encountered in completing the application form.[1667]

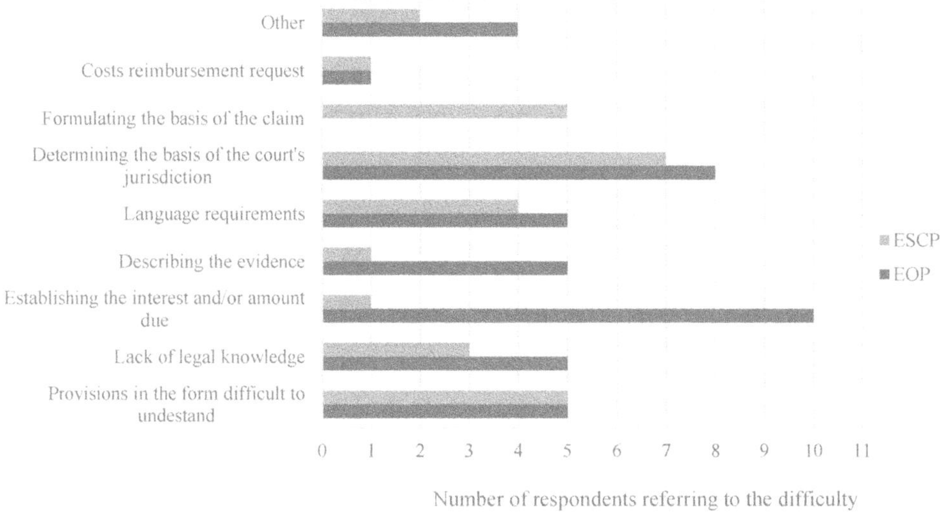

Fig. 5.10. Most common difficulties encountered by parties using the EOP and/or the ESCP

Indicating the basis of the court's jurisdiction constitutes one of the biggest difficulties. Limited knowledge – especially legal knowledge – as well as the way in which the provisions in the forms are drafted create significant problems for unrepresented parties. Other significant problems relate to language requirements, the formulation of the basis of the claim in the ESCP application, the description of the means of evidence in the EOP, and establishing the amount of interest requested and calculating the amount due.

Of the respondents, 42.30% mentioned that courts used Form B to request completion and/or rectification of the EOP application form.[1668] As indicated in the 2009 and 2011 Ministry of Justice EOP surveys, 24.32%[1669] and 45.9%, respectively,[1670] of the courts

1666 This is 64% for the EOP (16 of 25 respondents) and 83% for the ESCP (10 of 12 respondents).

1667 The 'Other' type of difficulties concern disinformation, the confusion between representation carried out by a lawyer and the legal representative of an entity, and difficulty in filling in the standard forms.

1668 Eleven of 26 EOP respondents.

1669 From a total of 35 courts that indicated they had received EOP applications in 2009, 9 have sent a Form B to the parties, requesting a completion and/or correction of Form A.

1670 Of a total of 61 courts that indicated they had received EOP applications in 2010, 28 mentioned that they have made use of Form B to a certain extent to request a completion and/or correction of Form A.

indicated that they had requested claimants to complete and/or to rectify the claim form. These findings confirm the difficulties claimants have had in filling out Form A correctly. With regard to the usage rate of Form B, all sources indicated scant usage. Of the survey and interview respondents, 62.5% indicated the use of Form B for less than 25% of the cases.[1671] This finding is confirmed also by the opionion provided by Italian courts responding to the Ministry of Justice surveys. They also pointed to a small number of cases (e.g. 30% or between 20–30%).

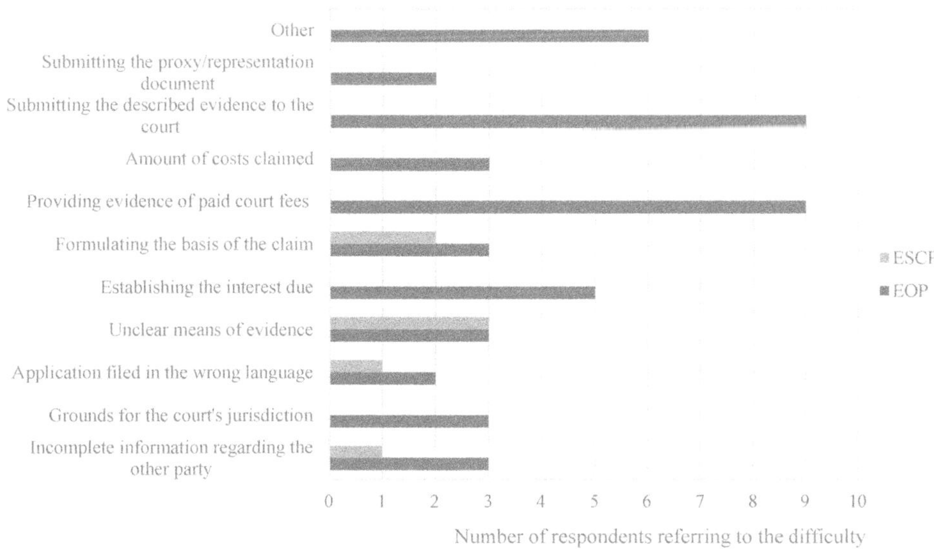

Fig. 5.11. Reasons for most requests for correction and/or completion of the application form

The use of Form B in the ESCP procedure appears to be more modest, with 28.57% of the survey and interview respondents referring to its use, and in such cases it is often for less than 25% of the claims.[1672] This is in line with the EOP findings. Figure 5.11 offers some insight into why judges make use of Form B.[1673]

A number of the identified reasons are closely linked to the difficulties parties experience in using the EOP and/or the ESCP (Fig. 5.10) (i.e. indication of the means of evidence, formulating the basis of the claim, establishing the basis of the court's jurisdiction, determining interest, observing language requirements). Additional reasons have to do

1671 Ten of 16 respondents chose an answer indicating less than 25% of the cases, while 3 of 16 (18.75%) respondents replied that they were not able to say.

1672 Four of 14 ESCP respondents.

1673 The 'Other' reasons for requesting an amendment of the EOP application refer to confusion between Code 3 and 5 with regard to indicating the quality of representation; errors in establishing the type of contractual relationship and the amount of costs to be reimbursed; forms filled in by hand; requesting the claimant to submit a filled in copy of Form E for the court to issue the order; and advising the claimant to modify the application form.

with national procedural rules (i.e. submitting documents proving the representative standing and the payment of the court fee, interpretation of the provision of the Regulation in line with well-known domestic procedures, and requesting the submission of evidence documents).[1674] If the court decides to supplement the EOP application with additional requirements in accordance with domestic procedures, this results in an unnecessary delay in the proceedings and demonstrates the court's lack of a solid understanding of the European procedure. The success of the *ingiunzione di pagamento* and the lack of clear EOP provisions lead to a reverse transfer of requirements from the domestic procedure closest to the European instrument. This might also discourage parties or their representatives from choosing to use the European procedure again.

The survey responses indicated that Italian judges occasionally requested that Form C ESCP be corrected.[1675] One respondent indicated that Form C was filed after the 30-day period set by Article 5(3) ESCP had lapsed. No further information was provided on the outcome or consequences of the late submission.

With regard to the use of EOP Forms C, D, and F, the respondents did not provide particular relevant data. Following issuance of the EOP (Form E), the court proceeded to issue Form G and to declare the EOP enforceable upon the claimant's request. Of the respondents, 95.65% indicated the court proceeded to issue the declaration following an oral or written request from the party or his representative.[1676] In one of the interviews, a judge explained that Form G had been issued at the parties' request because the files do not remain with the judge following delivery of the order. Upon the claimant's request, the clerk forwards the file to the judge to verify whether service has been properly carried out and the opposition period has lapsed. An additional aspect that might prevent the judge from automatically issuing Form G is that he might not know the date when the claimant served the EOP on the defendant and whether the EOP can be still opposed.[1677] Therefore, upon request of Form G, the claimant or his lawyer also have to prove when the service took place and that this was carried out in accordance with the applicable rules.

Finally, from discussions with practitioners it emerged that the forms were not generally available at the courts or on the courts' portals. In an ESCP report for the European Commission, the Ministry of Justice referred to having sent all the standard forms to the courts, as well as European Judicial Atlas links and the European Judicial Network contact to the judges. In practice, one clerk mentioned that he referred parties to the European dedicated portals, while a judge remarked that the standard EOP and ESCP forms were not available at the courts or the clerks' office because parties had not requested them, otherwise they would have become available. Another explanation is

1674 Aspect confirmed also by the Ministry of Justice 2011 research. Ricognizione dell'utilizzo del procedimento europeo di ingiunzione di pagamento in Italia (Regolamento CE. 1896/2006) – risultati del questionario diffuso presso le Corti d'Appello, Fasc. 020.004.002–26, 04/04/2011.m_dgDAG.48060, at 2 (document on file with the researcher).

1675 Two of 14 respondents. This was to obtain clarification on the means of evidence the defendant intended to use.

1676 Twenty-three of the 24 respondents to EOP surveys, interviews, and other communication exchanges.

1677 This aspect is also referred to in the Ministry of Justice Report drafted on the basis of the EOP 2011 survey. Ricognizione dell'utilizzo del procedimento europeo di ingiunzione di pagamento in Italia (Regolamento CE. 1896/2006) – risultati del questionario diffuso presso le Corti d'Appello, Fasc. 020.004.002–26, 04/04/2011.m_dgDAG.48060, at 6 (document on file with the researcher).

that parties continue to rely significantly on the services of lawyers who most likely know where to find the EOP or ESCP standard forms. However, having the forms directly available from courts or on their portals or that of the Ministry of Justice would certainly increase their visibility and possibly encourage their use.

Language

Based on the empirical data, 91.66% of the respondents indicated that parties and practitioners seldom encountered language or translation-related difficulties in the EOP procedure. An explanation might be that the claimants are often Italian parties or are represented by an Italian lawyer. Language problems and translation difficulties are often related to foreign claimants, as also indicated in data from the 2009 and 2011 Ministry of Justice EOP surveys.[1678] Some of the judges and clerks participating in the research mentioned that in most cases the forms were submitted in Italian. Occasionally, the claimants sought to submit standard Form A with additional explanations and information written in a different language. In those circumstances, the clerk asked the party to file a new application in Italian or to provide a translation. The judges were generally not willing to accept the forms or their content written in a different language.[1679] Thus, a foreign claimant is most likely to need to advance the translation costs or to employ a local lawyer. Respondents indicated that in some circumstances language requirements for service resulted in the claimant needing to arrange for translation, which prolonged the procedural timeframe. The 2009 and 2011 EOP surveys confirm that translation is required and made use of by the claimant for service and enforcement purposes. Additionally, standard forms in the language of the proceedings and the language of the defendant are used in parallel for service purposes. One judge indicated that Form F had been sent to defendants in Italian. This type of situation might create difficulties for a foreign party who is not familiar with the language. Furthermore, the Italian authorities indicated that they accepted documents only in Italian for enforcement purposes;[1680] hence, titles issued by courts in other Member States have to be translated. One respondent indicated that in a B2B case in Italy the foreign claimant sought to enforce an EOP issued by a German Court in German, and the party was not able to provide translations to the enforcement judge. This resulted in procedural difficulties, as the enforceable title had to be served on the debtor in Italy in accordance with domestic provisions.

Similar to the EOP, 83% of the ESCP survey respondents indicated that they had not encountered language or translation-related difficulties. A translation appears to have been requested each time the application was sent in a language other than Italian, and this also included additional evidence documents.

The ECC Italy offices indicated that there were certain difficulties for non-Italian consumers in filling in the standard forms in the language of the proceedings and

1678 See Ricognizione dell'utilizzo del procedimento europeo di ingiunzione di pagamento in Italia (Regolamento CE. 1896/2006) – risultati del questionario diffuso presso le Corti d'Appello, Fasc. 020.004.002–26, 04/04/2011.m_dgDAG.48060, at 2 and 6 (document on file with the researcher).

1679 One respondent indicated that the Justice of the Peace issued the EOP without requesting a translation of the documents provided in Spanish, because he could understand the language.

1680 https://e-justice.europa.eu/content_european_payment_order-353-it-en.do?clang=it#a_22. See further Section 5.7.3.5.

describing the facts. Occasionally, other ECC offices provided support in completing the claim form in the necessary language. Nevertheless, ECC Italy stressed that for consumers, the need for translation is most often related to enforcement, as they tend to file the claim with their national courts to obtain the ESCP judgment and then seek recognition in Italy. The translation difficulties are mostly economical, as the costs might easily be higher than the actual value of the claim. Respondents gave no indication of language requirements involving service, or difficulties in relation to the ESCP.

Service

Service of the EOP on the defendant was carried out by a variety of means, and often required claimants to be actively involved (Fig. 5.12). The service activities are undertaken by the bailiff (*ufficiale giudiziario*) upon the party's request or by his lawyer through electronic service by certified email (P.E.C.). Service of the EOP on the defendant by bailiff is also referred to in the e-Codex WP7 Study on the service of EOP documents.[1681] Occasionally, it is possible that the clerk requests the bailiff to serve the EOP on the defendant, an aspect confirmed by the Ministry of Justice surveys. Additionally, there is an indication that some Justice of the Peace offices might be willing to take the necessary steps to serve the EOP on the defendant if the claimant is not represented or resident in Italy. This is also the case for the ESCP. The clerk requests the bailiff to proceed to serve the documents, often by making use of the postal service with an acknowledgement of receipt to be signed by the party. However, there seems to be some difficult legislative correlation between the internal provisions and the possibility for the clerk to initiate service on a defendant outside Italy, as the costs are the responsibility of the claimant.[1682]

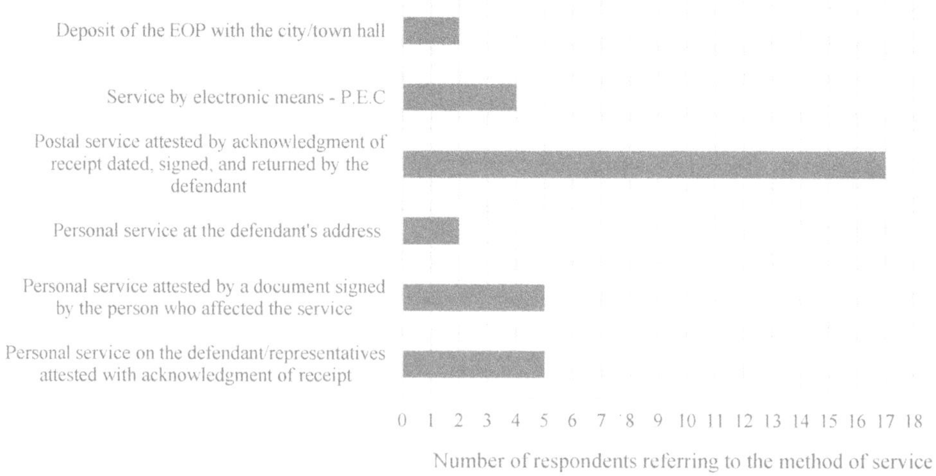

Fig. 5.12. Methods of service used to serve the EOP on the defendant

1681 Velicogna, Lupo & Mellone (2016).

1682 Article 1(97) Law No. 190/2014 regarding Article 46(1bis) Law No. 374/21 November 1991.

After opposition, the court might notify the foreign claimant of the opposition. The 2011 Ministry of Justice report shows the non-unitary practice of the courts with regard to information sent to claimants on the issuance of the EOP or an opposition. If the party is represented by an Italian lawyer, there is a greater chance the clerk will notify him by email of the issuance of the order.[1683]

Based on the empirical data gathered, postal service attested by acknowledgement of receipt dated, signed, and returned by the defendant is the method used most often in the EOP procedure. Other methods involve a personal service on the defendant or at his domicile or headquarters' address, and rely on an acknowledgement of receipt to be signed by the party or the bailiff carrying out the service. These methods are set to guarantee a high degree of certainty that the defendant has actually received the documents. Following legislative reforms, practitioners are encouraged to use modern communication means extensively in domestic court proceedings for the submission and communication of documents. This is also reflected in the EOP service methods and the modest use of registered email addresses (P.E.C.) to communicate the order on defendants in Italy. For cross-border service, the provisions of the Service Regulation apply.

More than 77% of the EOP respondents mentioned that they had not encountered service difficulties nor were they aware of such aspects.[1684] Similarly, 83.33% of the ESCP respondents declared that they had not encountered or not been aware of difficulties in relation to service by post with acknowledgement of receipt.[1685] Practitioners who indicated having experienced or being aware of difficulties related this to (1) the use of an incorrect address of the defendant; (2) difficulty in obtaining an acknowledgement of receipt; or (3) being uncertain about whether the acknowledgement of receipt had been signed by the defendant (the document of proof was not properly filled in). The available information related to service was limited because Italian judges and clerks are not often involved in the service of judicial documents, and only one bailiff was able to share his experience with the EOP and ESCP. One respondent in particular pointed to the difficulty in receiving the acknowledgement of receipt when postal service involved a common law country. Nonetheless, service in Italy can also be problematic. According to practitioners, a foreign consumer in an ESCP procedure cannot access from abroad the services of Italian bailiffs (*UNEP*), and the bailiffs have little experience in handling these European procedures. In trying to mitigate these difficulties, the bailiff or the court clerk may try to use the national postal service with acknowledgement of receipt. However, this can be very slow and problematic.

1683 Ricognizione dell'utilizzo del procedimento europeo di ingiunzione di pagamento in Italia (Regolamento CE. 1896/2006) – risultati del questionario diffuso presso le Corti d'Appello, Fasc. 020.004.002–26, 04/04/2011.m_dgDAG.48060, at 3 (document on file with the researcher).

1684 Nineteen of 25 respondents to the EOP survey.

1685 Ten of 12 respondents to the ESCP survey.

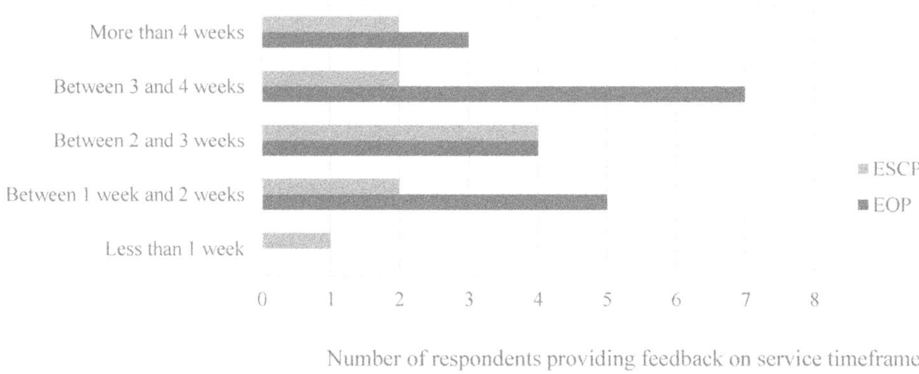

Fig. 5.13. Timeframe necessary to serve the EOP or the ESCP claim on the defendant

Further, in accordance with the empirical data available, the period of time necessary to serve the EOP or ESCP claim on the defendant is most likely to be above two weeks (Fig. 5.13). Respondents indicate that in most circumstances this was a consequence of the above-mentioned service difficulties. In relation to the EOP, one respondent also linked this result to the fact that the period necessary to serve the order on the defendant increased if the communication needed to be carried out by the claimant. The party first had to request that the necessary certified copies be issued by the court. Only then was he able to file a request with the bailiff's office (UNEP).

The judge verifies whether the EOP service is in compliance with the provisions of the Regulation and the national rules if there is an opposition or a request for the issuance of Form G. He also verifies the proof of service issued by the bailiff, the postal acknowledgement signed by the party, or the proof submitted by the lawyer. If the service is carried out at the claimant's request, he must submit proof of communication to the court. This is particularly important for guaranteeing the defendant's procedural rights and completion of the required procedural steps to inform the party of the procedure undertaken against him.

Hearings

Scant data are available regarding ESCP hearings. Most respondents indicated that they did not know whether hearings had been held. Apparently they were held occasionally, however, for example following a request from the claimant or as part of the court's investigation activities in accordance with the national procedure. One lawyer remarked that sometimes clerks and judges did not understand that they did not have to automatically set a first hearing (*udienza di comparizione*). This is most likely due to the limited experience many courts have had with the EOP; hence, they sought to apply the instrument in a manner with which they were familiar in domestic procedures. Nonetheless, there have also been cases in which the judge refused the request because he deemed it unnecessary for the handling of the case.

Challenging Mechanisms (Opposition, Appeal, Review)

It appears that debtors do not often oppose EOPs, though case law points in the opposite direction. According to 60% of the respondents, this concerned less than 25% of the orders.[1686] Further, 15% of the respondents mentioned that more than 75% of the EOPs were opposed, while 25% indicated they did not know how often they had been opposed. This is in line with the results of the 2009 and 2011 Ministry of Justice surveys, in which most courts reported very limited or no use of the opposition. With regard to the time limitation for submission of an opposition, the defendant generally appeared to comply with it, although Form F was not always used. Only one respondent referred to an opposition being filed after the 30-day limitation period. In this particular case, the defendant also raised an exception with regard to the nullity of the service. The transfer procedure following opposition appears problematic, as there is no national legal provision or guideline to secure a uniform interpretation, and the courts have to find their own way of dealing with the process.[1687] Additionally, the automatic transfer to the ordinary national procedure does not fit within the familiar domestic approach of the *ingiunzione di pagamento*, where there is a reversed duty for the defendant contesting the order to continue the court proceedings. Due to this different approach, the claimant is expected by some courts to file a new case (*iscrizione della causa a ruolo*). Therefore, once an opposition is received by the court, the clerk proceeds to register it, but no further action is taken unless the claimant decides to file a new claim or contest that the opposition was sent within the 30-day limitation period. In these circumstances, the claimant is generally likely to abandon the procedure following opposition. Other courts proceed to set a date for a hearing (*fissazione dell'udienza di comparizione*) and inform the defendant that he has a duty to submit a statement of defence and to indicate the evidence he intends to use in accordance with Article 167 CPC, or alternatively for the claimant to file a claim in accordance with Article 163 CPC. Another problematic aspect is that the clerk or the judge cannot automatically verify whether the opposition was filed within the required 30-day time limit when service of the EOP was arranged by the claimant. The court notifies the claimant of the received opposition, and then the party has to take the necessary steps to verify and to act if he considers it necessary. There has been some discussion over a possible interpretation in accordance with which the defendant should notify the claimant of the opposition. This interpretation has its origin in the national rules, but the approach has not been widely embraced by practitioners. The difficulties related to the opposition, the lack of automatic transfer to an ordinary procedure, and the absence of legislative provisions to clarify some aspects of the EOP that require coordination with national rules seem to influence the choices made by lawyers and parties. They continue to have a large preference for the domestic order for payment, as it does not pose these problems. Moreover, opposition to an EOP

1686 Twelve of 20 respondents indicated that the EOP opposition rate was less than 25% in their cases; some also mentioned that they had not encountered any oppositions in the cases they had handled.

1687 See Section 5.7.2.3 and Ricognizione dell'utilizzo del procedimento europeo di ingiunzione di pagamento in Italia (Regolamento CE. 1896/2006) – risultati del questionario diffuso presso le Corti d'Appello, Fasc. 020.004.002–26, 04/04/2011.m_dgDAG.48060, at 3–4 (document on file with the researcher).

automatically prevents the order from becoming enforceable, which is not the case with the *ingiunzione di pagamento*, which retains provisional enforcement.

Information on appeals against ESCP judgments is very limited, and is probably related to the modest use of the procedure. Only one respondent indicated that appeals had been filed against ESCP judgments, but no further details as to the number of requests or the outcome were offered. Other respondents indicated that they were not aware of such proceedings taking place (56.25%)[1688] or that an appeal mechanism was never made use of in the cases they knew of (31.25%).[1689] The fact that the appeal is disciplined by the national procedural law was indicated as problematic by one of the respondents because of the way domestic proceedings function. An appeal is expected to prolong the ESCP proceedings by some years, a situation that simply does not match a procedure aiming to provide a speedy resolution.[1690] Unfortunately, the data available give no indication as to the type of appeal used. Obtaining information on this aspect of the ESCP procedure would be desirable for future research projects, as it could significantly affect the instrument's effectiveness.

The EOP and ESCP review mechanisms do not appear to be employed often. Most EOP respondents replied that the review had never been applied (62.96%), or that they were not aware of its use (25.92%).[1691] Only 11.11% of the respondents indicated that there had been some review requests against EOPs.[1692] The reasons invoked were not actually related to the ones contained in Article 20 EOP. Instead, they concerned (1) the manner in which the interest had been calculated; (2) non-submission of the evidence; or (3) the defendant not receiving the documents served.[1693] Of the review requests (5 cases), only one was accepted by the court. The reason for the review was the wrongful calculation of the awarded interest. This outcome indicates a certain lack of understanding of the nature of the review procedure on the part of the national judge. The results of the 2009 and 2011 Ministry of Justice surveys confirm the very limited use of the EOP review mechanism; only 6.25% of the responding courts in 2009 and 5.08% of the courts in 2010 registered a request for review.[1694] However, the survey provides no information on the success rate or the reasons behind the review request. In the vast majority of cases, the courts had not received such requests. This was the case for 84.37% of the responding

1688 Nine of 16 respondents providing information about their experience with the ESCP.

1689 Five of 16 respondents providing information about their experience with the ESCP.

1690 An aspect also singled out in the reply of the Ministry of Justice to the European Commission Review of the operation of Regulation (EC) No 1896/2006 and Regulation (EC) No 861/2007 on the ESCP. Italian authorities were of the opinion that ESCP procedural deadlines should not concern the appeal as well, because this might require a longer time for re-examination, 2013, m_dg. DAG. 01/07/2013.0086502.E (document on file with the researcher).

1691 Seventeen of 27 respondents providing feedback on the EOP and, respectively, seven of the 27 respondents providing feedback on the ESCP.

1692 Three of 27 respondents providing information about their experiences with the EOP.

1693 For this third reason, the judge rejected the requests on the basis that the review was not the appropriate means to challenge a lack of service or a faultier service. This interpretation of the national judge is in line with the CJEU *eco cosmetics* case it predates.

1694 Two of 32 courts providing information on the review mechanism in the 2009 survey, and, respectively, three of 59 courts for 2010.

courts in 2009 and 93.22% of the responding courts in 2010. With regard to the ESCP, the data available do not indicate any use of the review mechanism. Most ESCP survey respondents indicated they had not been aware of the mechanism (64.28%) or that the review had never been employed (37.72%).[1695]

Representation

Representation is commonly used in relation to the European uniform procedures, an aspect that was also confirmed by the analysed case law and the Ministry of Justice EOP surveys.[1696] The empirical data available show a particularly steady use of lawyers by claimants filing EOP requests, even if this is not mandatory in accordance with the Regulation. Over 83% percent of the respondents indicated that claimants had made use of a lawyer's services in the EOP procedure.[1697] The practice might also have been influenced by the mandatory nature of representation in domestic proceedings, as well as by the limited information available and the need for the claimant to play an active role in the proceedings. All of this makes representation necessary. Defendants also make use of legal representation services, but perhaps to a lesser extent than claimants. Of the respondents, 18.75% indicated this had been the case in less than 25% of the EOP cases. Twenty-five percent of the respondents mentioned that representation services had been used by defendants in more than 75% of the EOP cases they knew of, and 50% of the respondents were not able to provide any information. The Ministry of Justice in its 2009 and 2011 EOP surveys indicated a significant use of lawyers' services for filing the claims and following the procedure through various stages. In some surveys, the use of lawyers was linked to the foreign claimant having no alternative means to pay the court fees (*contributo unificato*), to collect the certified EOP to be served on the defendant, or to file an opposition and pursue the claim in accordance with the ordinary procedure. Further, according to the results of the 2011 survey, filling in forms without the assistance of a lawyer did not appear to be particularly problematic.

With regard to the ESCP procedure, claimants and defendants employed the services of a lawyer, although this is not mandatory. However, the empirical data is extremely limited, as respondents were often not able to assess the extent to which legal services had been used by parties. Respondents who were able to offer information always indicated that the claimant or both parties had been represented. The use of a lawyer is also confirmed by available ESCP case law. However, the infrequent use of the ESCP and the limited number of practitioners with experience in applying this instrument make it more difficult to gain a broader picture of the actual situation.

The Ministry of Justice surveys as well as some of the empirical data gathered indicate that foreign claimants were accustomed to sending EOP applications by postal service

1695 Response provided by 9 of 14 ESCP survey respondents and, respectively, 5 of 14 ESCP respondents.

1696 See Section 5.7.2.4 above. Ricognizione dell'utilizzo del procedimento europeo di ingiunzione di pagamento in Italia (Regolamento CE. 1896/2006) – risultati del questionario diffuso presso le Corti d'Appello, Fasc. 020.004.002–26, 04/04/2011.m_dgDAG.48060, at 5 (document on file with the researcher).

1697 Fifteen of 18 respondents providing input on this aspect of the procedure in EOP surveys.

without employing the services of a local lawyer. A clerk remarked that over the years there has been an increase in the number of EOP applications submitted by Italian lawyers in comparison to earlier periods, when the small number of applications were sent by foreign claimants by postal service. To sum up, the extensive use of lawyers' services in EOP and ESCP procedures increases the costs of litigation. These costs might not always be awarded by the court to the winning party, which could have a negative impact on the use of the procedures, especially as in some circumstances a lawyer's services become indispensable for a foreign party, and in domestic procedures the recovery of representation costs does not create difficulties.

Procedural Timeframe

Based on the empirical data gathered, EOP decisions are issued within the 30-day period recommended by the Regulation. This outcome is confirmed by the available case law, as well as the Ministry of Justice 2011 survey. Figures 5.14 and 5.15 present an overview of the results.

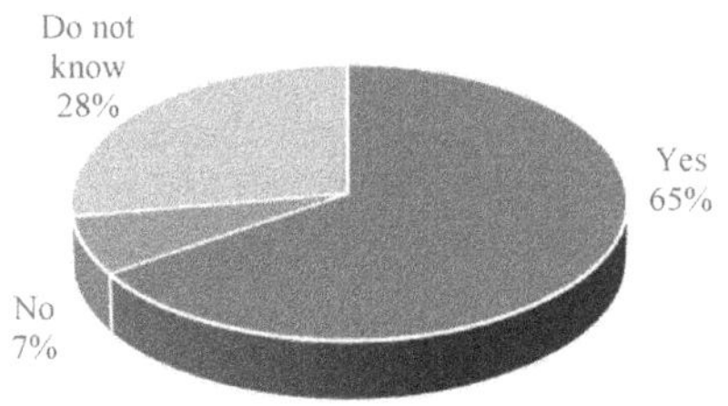

Fig. 5.14. EOP issued within 30 days (survey results, 29 respondents)

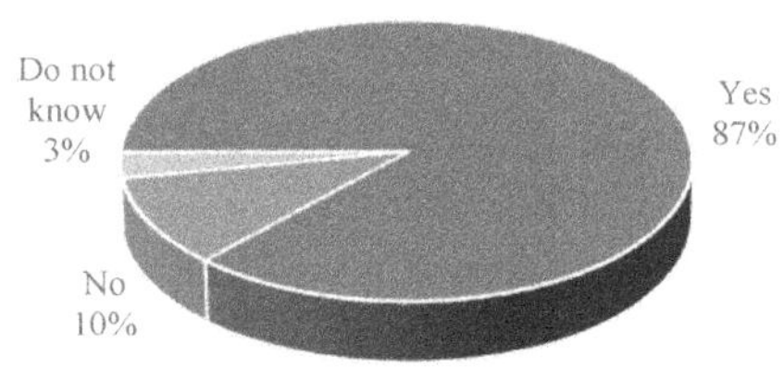

Fig. 5.15. EOP issued within 30 days (Ministry of Justice 2011 Survey, 68 respondents)

However, following domestic reforms allowing electronic submission and treatment, the *ingiunzione di pagamento* is issued within an even shorter timeframe than the EOP. Judges and clerks are used to handling the domestic and European order for payment with priority, issuing them in a period ranging from a few days to several weeks. Some respondents indicated that prior to the 2014 electronic filing reform, issuance of the EOPs took a bit longer than 30 days because they had been assigned to judges receiving paper-based *ingiunzioni di pagamento*. These judges were a bit slower than their colleagues who were handling online cases. If the issuance of the EOP took longer than the recommended 30 days, respondents attributed this to the court's considerable workload. Nevertheless, in accordance with available information, in such circumstances the EOP would be issued within a period of 45–47 days. With regard to the average period of time necessary from the lodging of Form A to the moment of receiving Form G in the EOP procedure, the following results emerge:

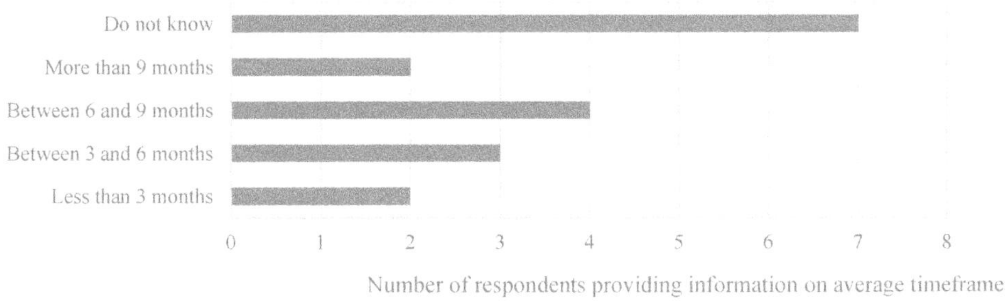

Fig. 5.16. Average time necessary to conclude an EOP procedure

The timeframe for the entire EOP procedure up until the moment the claimant actually manages to obtain the Declaration of enforceability (Form G) is likely to be above 3 months, even if the court is generally successful in issuing the order within the 30-day period. The reasons behind this have to do with (1) service issues (i.e. the time necessary to serve the EOP on the defendant, service difficulties, obtaining the acknowledgement of receipt in order to be able to request the issuance of Form G); (2) slowness of the court proceedings or of the clerks' office; (3) overload of courts; and (4) suspension of proceedings during the judicial holiday period.

With regard to the ESCP, only a handful of respondents were able to provide information on the timeframe for concluding the procedure, so the information is not conclusive. Two respondents mentioned that the average time necessary to obtain an ESCP judgment was less than or around 6 months from the moment the request was filed.[1698] The other two respondents were not able to provide input on this aspect of the European procedure. In triangulating this information with the only published ESCP case handled by an Italian court, the average time to obtain the judgment was just above 3 months.[1699] No information is available as to the time necessary for an appeal, or whether this would be in any way shorter than in any domestic proceedings.

Costs, Interest, Penalties

The court fees applicable to the European uniform procedures are flat court fees (*contributo unificato*), together with an additional fee for the notifications to be carried out by the court (*anticipazioni forfettarie*), as well as the fee for the issuance of copies of the decisions to be served.[1700] Some courts replying to the 2009 Ministry of Justice survey were in favour of making the information on court fees available on the Judicial Atlas. Although the e-Justice Portal mentions the possibility of making electronic

1698 One respondent indicated that proceedings had taken between 3 and 6 months, while another one mentioned that it had been less than 3 months. A lawyer complained that the court had not respected the Regulation procedural timeframe, and that he had been forced to follow the proceeding on a step-by-step basis.

1699 See also Section 5.7.2.3.

1700 With regard to the need to also pay the fee for issuance of the copy, some courts replying to the 2009 Ministry of Justice survey expressed doubts as to whether this had to be paid for in the EOP procedure.

payments, it does not provide the practical information necessary to carry out the payment, to say nothing of the longer period of time during which the information was available only in Italian. Respondents did remark that claimants sending an application by postal service from another Member State often did not include proof of payment of the court fee, and that there had been difficulties related to the payment. In 2014, a clerk in charge of order for payment claims did not even seem to be aware of the 2010 Ministry of Justice Note in order to be able to inform foreign parties of the existing means of payment allowing them to carry out payment of the EOP court fee from abroad. This influenced the number of EOP applications received by the court. Interested foreign parties requesting information on how to make the payment were referred to other payment means that required a physical presence in Italy or relied on a local legal practitioner to carry out the payment; hence, the parties declined to make use of the procedure. Fortunately, other respondents referred to this same problem for the period prior to publication of the 2010 Note. Clerks who registered the cases took notice of the missing court fee payment and requested the claimant to pay it and send proof to the court. Prior to 2010, in order to facilitate the payment a couple of general courts provided the foreign party with details of the local tax authority's bank account used for the recovery of amounts owed to the public administration.[1701] Such a pragmatic approach by the courts facilitated application of the EOP and secured its effective implementation. In relation to the payment of court fees, some judges issue Form B requesting the party to submit proof of the court fee payment within a set period of time. If the party does not comply with the request, the case is closed. This is a loophole that courts may employ in order to make sure the *contributo unificato* is paid. Payment of the court fee in the ESCP procedure appears to be less problematic, as local consumers are aware of the means of payment available. On a general basis, if – following a notification sent by the clerk – the party does not pay, the case cannot be struck off.[1702] The claim is analysed and the judge issues a decision. However, documents concerning the court fees owing are forwarded to Equitalia Giustizia, which is expected to recover them from the claimant. In practice, it appears that Equitalia Giustizia is not actually able to collect the amount due as *contributo unificato* from persons that are not registered in Italy for tax purposes.[1703] There are no cross-border instruments they can use to pursue collection of the debt; nevertheless, once notified, the claimant can pay the court fee voluntarily. This problem was also singled out by some courts in the Ministry of Justice 2009 and 2011 surveys. If the court fees cannot be collected, after a number of years they are written off, and the court is notified that the debt could not be recovered.

With regard to the costs of EOP proceedings, the general rule is that the losing party is responsible for them. One judge mentioned that he systematically does not award the

1701 As resulting from the Ministry of Justice 2009 and 2011 surveys.

1702 Article 285 Testo Unico (Decree No. 131/26 April 1986) does not apply. The opinion is that such action would not be compatible with the provisions of the EOP Regulation. For this reason, the court has to proceed to recovery of the debt corresponding to the court fee – until July 2017 through Equitalia Giustizia and afterwards through Equitalia Giustizia and the Agenzia delle Entrate-Riscossione (Decree-Law No. 193/2016).

1703 See Section 5.5.

lawyer fees incurred by the claimant in the EOP procedure. The reason behind this is an interpretation of Article 25 EOP in conjunction with Recital 26. However, this interpretation might be criticised as not being in line with Point 9 of the Form A Guidelines, which refers to these kinds of costs in the examples for 'Other' costs (Code 02).

With regard to interest claimed and its calculation, one judge remarked that the EOP is problematic because the judge does not usually make the calculation in other domestic procedures (e.g. *ingiunzione di pagamento*). In the EOP procedure, the claimant or his lawyer often only provide information related to the principle and the interest rate applicable, leaving the calculation to the judge. The amount of interest requested is to be calculated up until the moment of submission of the claim. Afterwards, legal interest is due up until the total repayment of the debt. The Ministry of Justice 2009 EOP survey confirms that the courts recognise and award interest in accordance with the provisions of national law or the law applicable to the contract. In the ESCP procedure, a prior research carried out by ECC Italy revealed a problem for the claimant in calculating the interest he seeks to be awarded.

5.7.3.5. Enforcement

Information is scarce regarding the execution of enforceable EOPs and ESCPs in Italy, and is provided mainly by the courts, lawyers, and ECC Italy. Only one bailiff was available to provide feedback on the EOP procedure. Another bailiff limited himself to commenting that the enforcement had been carried out in accordance with national legislation. The information available is fragmented, and more than 50% of the respondents indicated that they did not have relevant information related to this stage of the proceedings. As Figures 5.17 and 5.18 show, a number of respondents did identify certain difficulties related to the enforcement process.

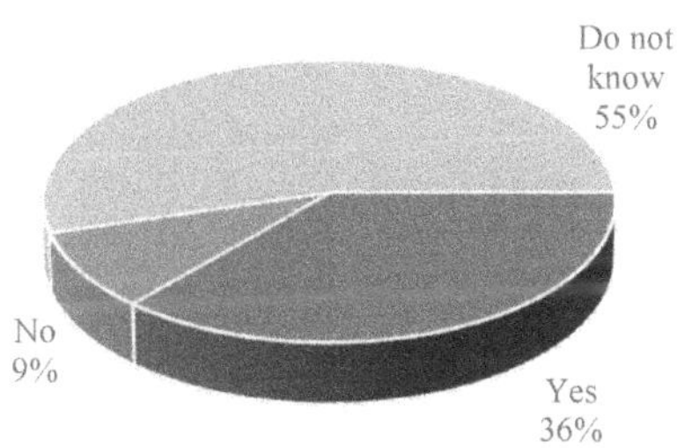

Fig. 5.17. Claimants experiencing difficulties with EOP enforcement following the delivery of Form G (22 respondents)

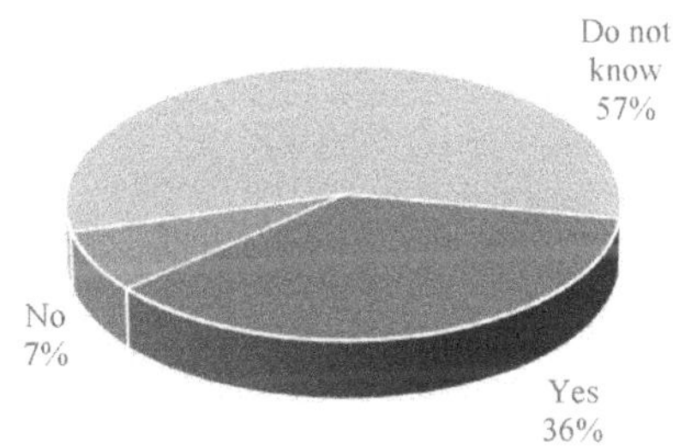

Fig. 5.18. Claimants experiencing difficulties with ESCP enforcement following the delivery of Form D (14 respondents)

Nevertheless, the results should be viewed with caution, as most of the respondents who provided information on possible execution difficulties following the delivery of enforcement certification had handled only a very limited number of cases. Among the most frequent difficulties reported in enforcing the EOP or the ESCP were (1) obtaining information on the debtor's assets and financial situation (EOP); (2) costs related to the execution (EOP, ESCP); (3) identifying the competent national authority (EOP, ESCP); (4) choosing the method of enforcement (EOP, ESCP); (5) the need to request and obtain the Declaration of enforceability and to provide a translation (EOP, ESCP); and (6) the order or the judgment can be enforced only after the title is served on the defendant (EOP, ESCP). Some of these difficulties seem to be more common with lay claimants or for enforcement proceedings that have to be carried out abroad. The 2009 Ministry of Justice EOP survey also revealed a need for more information concerning the competent authorities and the manner in which the enforcement can be pursued in other Member States. Most of the courts participating in the survey did not consider themselves to be sufficiently prepared to advise parties on enforcement or on information available online for this purpose. Now, several years later, research confirms that practitioners do not consider the information available to be sufficient for the purpose of facilitating cross-border enforcement. Therefore, more practical information that can be used for enforcement purposes by parties or practitioners from other Member States should be made available at the national and European level in all the official languages of the European Union.

Some respondents remarked that the enforcement proceedings are very different across Member States, and some users consider they are too complex and should be simplified, particularly when it comes to small value claims. The limited information available and the complexity of proceedings in Italy require a significant number of actions from the creditor (i.e. collecting the copies to be served on the debtor, registering a request with the court's bailiff office, paying enforcement fees). This might be facilitated by using the service of a local lawyer, while making practical information available for enforcement purposes may facilitate the execution and encourage the use or re-use of EOP and/or ESCP procedures without needing to incur the costs of employing the services of various lawyers in different Member States.

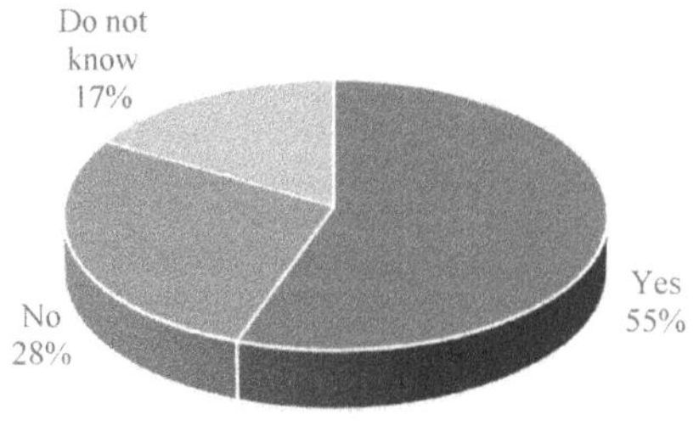

Fig. 5.19. EOP enforcement difficulties are similar to those experienced in domestic procedures (18 respondents)

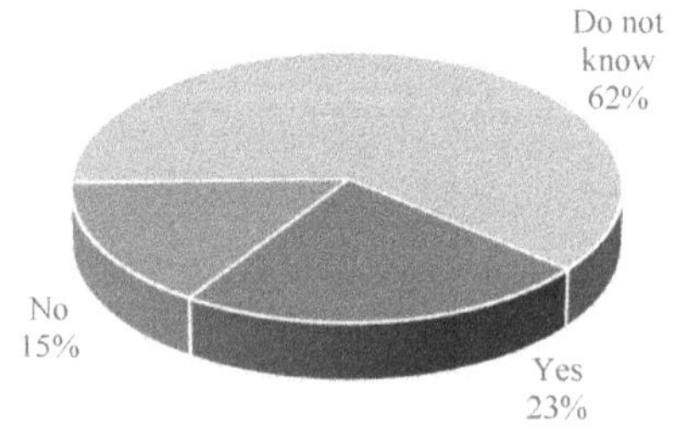

Fig. 5.20. ESCP enforcement difficulties are similar to those experienced in domestic procedures (13 respondents)

With regard to similarities between difficulties encountered in the execution of domestic proceedings and the execution of EOP and/or ESCP titles, respondents' opinions were very much divided (Figs. 5.19–5.20). Some considered enforcement to be quite similar, but involving higher costs due to cross-border situations. A more limited group of respondents saw it as involving difficulties other than purely domestic titles. In order to better understand the situation and the perception that bailiffs have on this matter, it would have been useful if more members of this group of legal professionals had participated.

Very little information is available on the procedural timeframe necessary to enforce an EOP or an ESCP in Italy. In most cases, respondents were unable to make a global estimate of the time needed for the successful completion of this last procedural stage (61.11% of EOP survey respondents and 100% of ESCP survey respondents).[1704] The length of the process was influenced by a number of practical aspects such as (1) the time necessary to notify the debtor of the title; (2) obtaining the necessary translations of the titles for enforcement purposes; (3) the time required to employ a certain enforcement mechanism (for example, auctioning the debtor's immovable property requires more time than attachment of the party's bank account). Further, some respondents remarked that the execution process was slow and highly similar to purely domestic enforceable titles, an aspect that can result in annulling any advantages of the European procedures in cross-border litigation. In relation to the EOP procedure, most respondents indicated that the execution stage took somewhere between 3 to 4 months (22.22%).[1705] This final stage of the European uniform procedures should be investigated further in future studies, as its outcome might well influence the extent to which these instruments are used.

It appears that creditors choose not to pursue an enforcement much more often in relation to the EOP than to the ESCP (Figs. 5.21–5.22), but this might be influenced by the extent to which each of these two procedures is actually used. The ESCP seems to be less used than the EOP. Among the reasons that creditors do not pursue the execution were (1) practical difficulties (e.g. language, difficulties in obtaining information on the debtor's assets, selecting the enforcement method); (2) complexity of the enforcement procedure; (3) costs of enforcement; and (4) the solvability of the debtor and the risk of spending additional money that cannot be recovered.

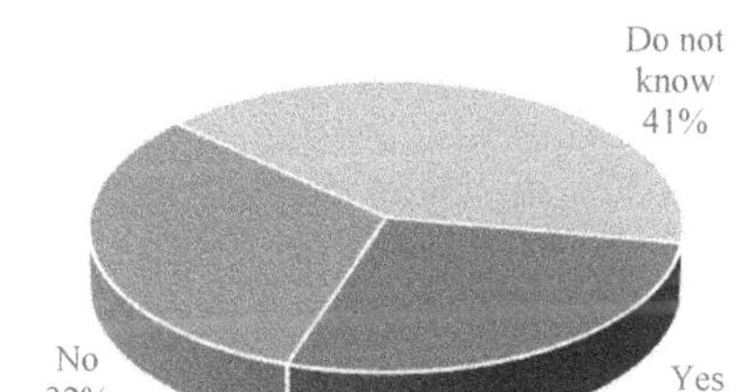

Fig. 5.21. Creditor decided not to pursue the EOP enforcement procedure (22 respondents)

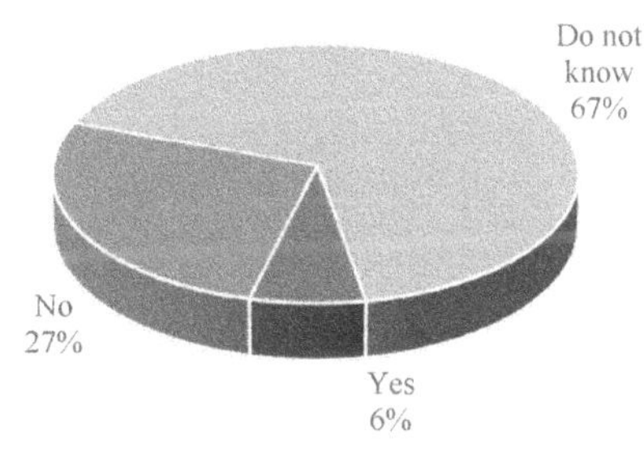

Fig. 5.22. Creditor decided not to pursue the ESCP enforcement procedure (15 respondents)

1704 Eleven of 18 EOP survey respondents and 2 ESCP survey respondents.

1705 Four of 18 EOP survey respondents. Further, 2 respondents indicated that the enforcement stage had taken longer than 4 months, and 1 said that it had required between 2 and 3 months.

The limited participation of bailiffs in this study prevented a more extensive analysis of the possible outcome. Furthermore, a significant number of the respondents were not aware of whether or not enforcement proceedings had been abandoned.

Thus far, the refusal and the limitation or stay of enforcement proceedings do not appear to have been used often. The only bailiff responding to the EOP survey indicated that the enforcement of EOP titles issued by courts in other Member States was sometimes refused in Italy. Reasons determining the refusals included the scant knowledge of the European procedure and of its standard forms. However, the extent to which refusal of enforcement affects the execution process is not clear.

With regard to the execution of EOP and ESCP decisions issued by Italian courts in other Member States, most respondents were not able to provide any input (80.95% EOP survey respondents and 100% of the ESCP survey respondents).[1706] Respondents who provided information with regard to the enforcement of European titles noted that the titles whose execution was sought had been related to sale-purchase agreements and concerned neighbouring Member States (Austria, Spain). Furthermore, one of the respondents remarked that the creditors experienced difficulties in finding a local lawyer to represent their interests in the execution process.

5.7.3.6. Practitioners' Assessment

In terms of 'speediness, affordability and protection of parties' rights', most practitioners considered the EOP and the ESCP to be efficient procedures for the recovery of uncontested monetary and small value claims in cross-border litigation (Figs. 5.23–5.24).

These European procedures were perceived to be simpler than national alternatives, as they are less costly for the parties (i.e. translation costs) and tend to be faster in comparison with other instruments. They can be further improved if the electronic submission and treatment of the claims in e-Codex continues to develop. Moreover, with the EOP, practitioners were very positive about the avoidance of an adversarial procedure for an uncontested claim and the uniformity of the instrument's civil procedure rules.

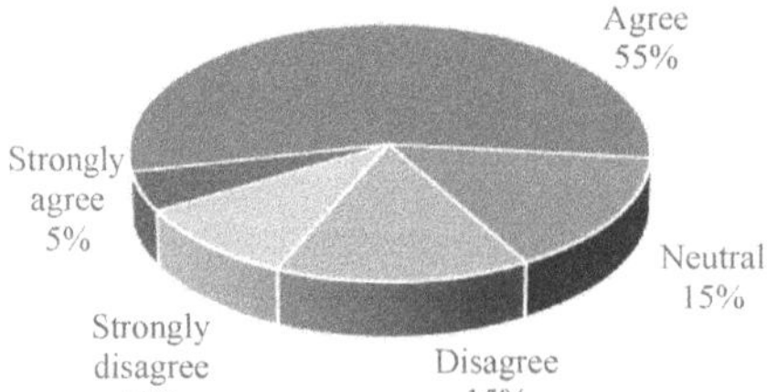

Fig. 5.23. Respondents consider EOP an overall efficient solution (20 respondents)

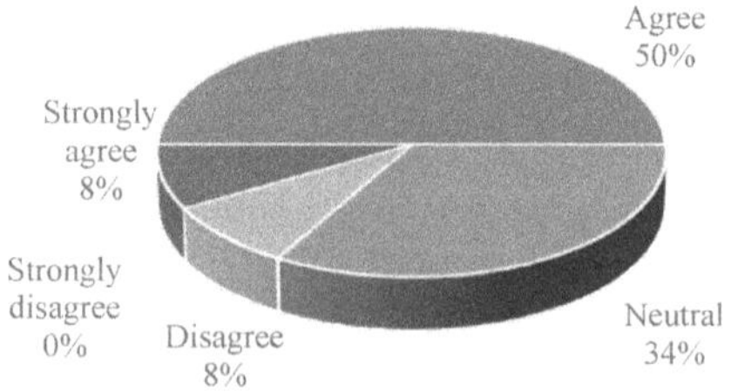

Fig. 5.24. Respondents consider ESCP an overall efficient solution (12 respondents)

[1706] Seventeen of 21 EOP survey respondents and 12 ESCP survey respondents.

The drawbacks identified in the EOP and the ESCP are partly related to the practitioners' limited knowledge and experience, and to the infrequent use of the procedures. Additional aspects that make the procedures less appealing to potential users are (1) the fact the EOP is applied like an *ingiunzione di pagamento*; (2) the procedural threshold of the ESCP being too low;[1707] (3) the opposition mechanisms that prevent the order from becoming enforceable; and (4) the execution being similar to that of any national procedure.

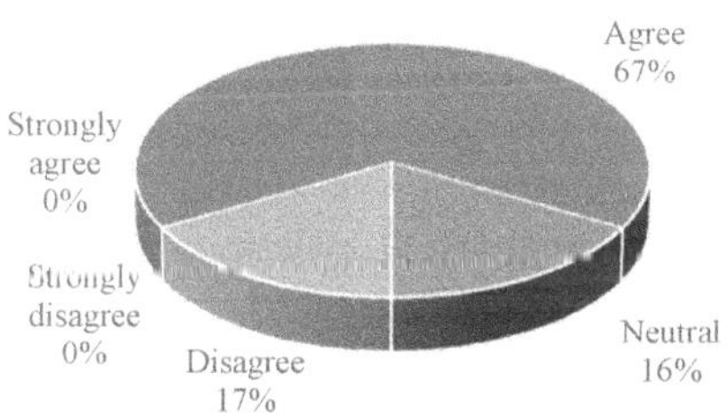

Fig. 5.25. Respondents consider the EOP an effective solution for the recovery of uncontested claims (18 respondents)

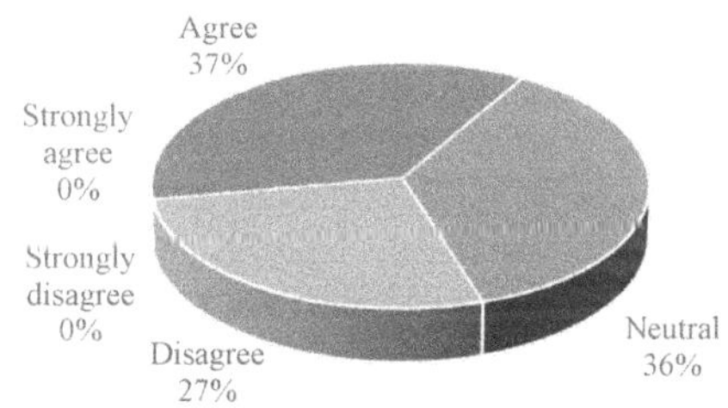

Fig. 5.26. Respondents consider the ESCP an effective solution for the recovery of small claims (10 respondents)

Further, practitioners' views on the effectiveness of the European uniform procedures are mostly positive, especially for the EOP (Figs. 5.25–5.26). The limited experience in practice with the procedures circumscribes some of the respondents' ability to assess their effectiveness. In relation to the EOP, one practitioner remarked that the more the procedure is not contested the more effective it is. Regardless of the relatively positive perception concerning the efficiency and effectiveness of the EOP and the ESCP, the existence of obstacles to their successful application is acknowledged by courts and practitioners (70.58% of the EOP survey respondents and 80% of the ESCP survey respondents).[1708]

The obstacles most often referred to are (1) the extent to which the European procedures are known to parties, practitioners, and courts; (2) the lack of national legislation clarifying certain aspects of the EOP and the ESCP that require the application of national provisions (i.e. the way in which an opposed EOP is transferred to the national ordinary procedure; the payment of ESCP court fees); (3) the limited practical experience of some courts and practitioners; (5) the lack of unitary court practices in relation to the EOP and the ESCP; (6) courts or offices are not used to working with forms, and unrepresented parties encounter difficulties in filling them in; (7) sometimes the use of a lawyer's services becomes unavoidable due to the particularities of the domestic procedural rules (i.e. execution process, collecting copies to be served or titles for

1707 This aspect of the ESCP procedure was addressed by Regulation 2015/2421, which raised the threshold to €5,000 for claims filed after 14 July 2017.

1708 Twelve of 17 EOP survey respondents and 8 of 10 ESCP survey respondents who provided feedback on this aspect.

enforcement purposes); (8) information with regard to the European uniform procedures and their application is not easily accessible, and no institutionalised assistance is provided in the ESCP; and (9) the recovery of court fees owed by parties resident in other Member States. In 2010 and 2015, the Ministry of Justice made certain moves to clarify particular EOP procedural steps.[1709] These concerned the possibility of paying the due court fees and notification fee by bank transfer, the duty of the claimant to serve the order on the defendant, and the obligation of the courts to register paper-based EOP applications. The Ministry of Justice 2009 and 2011 EOP surveys and the 2011 ECC Italy ESCP study[1710] also confirmed these existing obstacles, as well as the practitioners providing additional feedback or participating in interviews for this research. To date, a few obstacles have been addressed by the Italian authorities, and this has sometimes been the result of courts' requests for clarification, as they do not know whether certain national provisions should apply in interaction with the EOP Regulation. A more coherent and dedicated approach addressing the obstacles that continue to exist should be adopted at the national level.

To improve the way the EOP and the ESCP are applied, some of the respondents consider there is a need for more information, especially of a practical nature, for practitioners as well as for the parties. The Ministry of Justice EOP surveys also revealed that practitioners wish to have more access to information on national and European websites. A better presentation of the domestic applicable provisions with regard to the payment of court fees, service of documents, and the enforcement stage was considered desirable. In addition, more publicity should be given to the European uniform instruments, including by the professional legal orders. Additional training on the functioning and application of these instruments would be welcomed by all legal professional categories, including court clerks. Furthermore, national practice guides on how to apply the EOP and the ESCP in Italy would be welcome, especially because for some courts a significant period of time might pass before they receive another EOP or ESCP request, or the judge might be allocated a new case based on the rotation system of assigning registered claims. Long periods between EOP or ESCP applications may well lead to a decrease in the professional's expertise and prolong the time necessary to handle the procedure. The 2011 Ministry of Justice EOP survey revealed that some courts consider it useful to have a more centralised system at the level of the courts in order to coordinate the assignment of EOP applications to judges. The courts are favourable to the creation of a specific registration code for the EOP procedure to distinguish it from domestic orders for payment. One lawyer suggested that a set of common best practices should be established, which would facilitate and encourage uniform application of the instruments. This could be doubled by a concentration of competences of the courts. Furthermore, certain aspects of the way the EOP and the ESCP are applied should be

[1709] Nota 1° settembre 2010 – Regolamento CE 1896/2006; *Adempimenti di cancelleria relativi al Processo Civile Telematico*), Circolare dg_DAG.23/10/2015.0159552.U, point 8.1 (document on file with the researcher).

[1710] Centro Europeo Consumatori Italia, *Il Procedimento Europeo per le Controversie di Modesta Entità. Un indagine del Centro Consumatori Italia e Adiconsum sull'implementazione del Reg CE 861/2007 sul funzionamento della procedura a livello UE* (periodo 2009–2011).

better clarified to secure a uniform interpretation of the provisions of the Regulations and of the tasks the parties and/or the professionals are required to accomplish. One respondent remarked that it should be made clear that the EOP is not the same as the *ingiunzione di pagamento* and that they are not connected to each other.

For the ESCP, assistance should be provided free of charge in accordance with the provisions of the Regulation, and information about this should be easily accessible to interested parties. An increase in the ESCP threshold to at least €5,000 as carried out by Regulation 2015/2421 is considered to be a desirable step. It remains to be seen whether after July 2017 this increase will favour more active use of the ESCP. Other practitioners recommended establishing a system that allows the electronic filing of ESCP claims as well as sets up a mechanism (electronic tool) to assist parties in translating the procedures' standard text.

The execution stage should also be improved by facilitating uniformity in the enforcement legislation as well as simplifying this part of the procedure. Some of the practitioners' EOP and ESCP recommendations are achievable at the national level: for instance, increasing the extent to which dedicated information is made available for parties and practitioners, and offering more training and dedicated events to legal professionals. Moreover, better coordination between the national and European provisions, and clarification as to which rules should complement the Regulations, would make court's tasks easier and enable the European procedures to be applied in a coherent and unitary manner.

5.7.4. *Overall Assessment*

The European procedures are instruments known to Italian courts and practitioners. This is especially the case for the EOP, which is used more often than the ESCP. However, the way the European uniform procedures are applied and their coordination with national rules is sometimes problematic. Judges are given the difficult task of filling the legislative gaps in order to secure an effective application of the European procedures in Italy. This leads to particular national procedures having a strong influence, because they are considered to be similar to the European ones (i.e. the EOP and the *ingiunzione di pagamento*), in terms of how the latter are applied and their rules supplemented in practice. The intervention of the Italian legislator and of the Ministry of Justice in an attempt to facilitate application of the European procedures has thus far been minimal, and has temporarily resolved or clarified only certain procedural issues. The need to complement the Regulations' provisions with national rules when the Regulations do not contain specific provisions has led to a non-unitary national practice. One of the most striking examples is the continuation of the procedure following the lodging of an opposition to an EOP. Case law has revealed numerous judicial interpretations in this regard. The lack of clarity as to which national procedural rules should apply in connection with the European procedures creates uncertainty, which places parties and their representatives at a disadvantage, or discourages them from making use of these instruments. Familiar national procedures continue to be preferred in practice. Furthermore, some national rules are not compatible with the aim of the Regulations, and require the claimant's physical presence to carry out procedural activities. This is particularly problematic for foreign parties, and is possibly one of the reasons that the legal representation rate is still significantly high, even though some judges may not award representation fees. Access to practical information for parties and practitioners is limited, and a layperson can hardly find his way around the domestic procedural rules and practices related to application of the European uniform procedures. Moreover, the language barrier adds to the difficulties, as information is available only in Italian. Additional steps should be taken in this regard, with more detailed practical information being made available on the e-Justice Portal.

As seen in case law and in the empirical data available, the EOP and the ESCP facilitate the process of obtaining a decision in a short period of time within a system renowned for its particularly lengthy proceedings. Nonetheless, the service of documents remains to a certain extent problematic and slow, and requires the claimant's active involvement. The enforcement process remains too complex even though the exequatur was abolished. This situation does not seem highly likely to change in the near future, although a significant number of reforms have been passed in order to improve the performance of the Italian justice system.

In summary, the EOP and the ESCP in Italy would benefit from a clearer legislative framework aimed at eliminating uncertainties as to how the European procedures should be applied. This would unify existing practices and interpretations, and facilitate their application. Additionally, more dedicated professional training for each legal profession that is called to apply the EOP and the ESCP would contribute to a greater degree of familiarity and to an improved implementation of the European instruments.

Chapter 6

ROMANIA

6.1. Introduction

The Romanian legal system is a civil law system, relying generally on codified law. The precedent is not considered a source of law, but the decisions of the Constitutional Court and of the High Court for Cassation and Justice (*Înalta Curte de Casaţie şi Justiţie*) have significant authority, and are followed by the other Romanian courts.[1711]

Court proceedings in Romania are carried out in accordance with the provisions of the Code of Civil Procedure,[1712] the special laws regarding organisation of the judiciary[1713] and the applicable court fees.[1714] A new Code of Civil Procedure (*Noul Cod de procedură civilă* – NCPC) was adopted on 15 July 2010,[1715] and the law for its entry into force amended part of the NCPC text in 2012.[1716] The present code is the materialisation of a need to establish a legislative framework that complies with the requirements of a modern justice system. The text seeks to simplify and accelerate the judicial proceedings (including the execution phase), to secure the predictability of judicial proceedings, and to facilitate direct application of the EU procedural

1711 Article 146 letter (d) and Article 126(3) Constitution in conjunction with Article 23 and 24 Law No. 304/2004 regarding the organisation of the judiciary (*Legea nr. 304/2004 privind organizarea judiciară*), republished in Official Gazette of Romania No. 827/13 September 2005, and Articles 514–518 NCPC. See Leş (2014), Volume I, at 34–36.

1712 This is the main piece of legislation on civil procedure. Spinei (2012), at 365–367.

1713 Law No. 303/2004 regarding status of the judiciary and public prosecutors, Official Gazette of Romania No. 826 from 13 September 2005; Law No. 304/2004; the Regulation for interior organisation of the courts approved by Decision No. 387/2005 of the Plenary of the Superior Council of the Magistracy, and the Regulation regarding the organisation and administrative functioning of the High Court of Cassation and Justice.

1714 Government Emergency Ordinance No. 80/2013 regarding the judiciary stamp fees (*Ordonanţa de urgenţă nr. 80/2013 privind taxele judiciare de timbru*), Official Gazette of Romania No. 392/29 June 2013.

1715 Law No. 134/2010 regarding the Code of Civil Procedure, Official Gazette of Romania No. 485/15 July 2010 and republished following Law No. 76/2012 in the Official Gazette of Romania No. 365/30 May 2012.

1716 Law No. 76/2012 for the application of Law No.134/2010 regarding the Code of Civil Procedure (*Legea nr. 76/2012 pentru punerea în aplicare a Legii nr. 134/2010 privind Codul de procedură civilă*), Official Gazette No. 365/30 May 2012.

instruments.[1717] To draft the new Code of Civil Procedure, the commission in charge took into consideration different European and international sources of procedural law.[1718] Since its coming into force on 15 February 2013,[1719] the NCPC has been amended several times, the last being in March 2017.[1720] A significant number of amendments concern the execution phase, the competence of bailiffs in the execution process, and their access to information.[1721] This continuous process of amendments shows that Romanian civil procedure is still developing and adjusting to the needs of modern judicial practice, seeking solutions aimed at securing optimal access to justice for the parties, and facilitating the activities of courts and practitioners.

This chapter considers the procedural choices available to creditors to recover debts before Romanian courts. Along with the ordinary national procedure, the Romanian NCPC offers two special alternative proceedings to which the EOP and the ESCP are added in cross-border litigation. Section 6.2 presents an overview of the national ordinary procedure and its characteristics, followed by a functional analysis of the national special procedures in Section 6.3. The characteristics of these national tailored solutions are also considered in comparison to the EOP and the ESCP. Section 6.4 examines the positions of Romanian stakeholders with regard to EOP and ESCP Regulations, while Section 6.5 scrutinises accommodation of the EOP and the ESCP within the national legislation. The analysis in Section 6.6 focuses on the main theoretical aspects regarding the execution of judgments and the enforcement of EOPs and ESCP decisions. Finally, Section 6.7 analyses the functioning in practice of the EOP and the ESCP in accordance with available statistics, published national case law, and the outcome of the empirical research.

1717 The Reasons for the project of a Law regarding the Code of Civil Procedure, PL-x No. 413/2009 available at www.cdep.ro/pls/proiecte/upl_pck.proiect?cam=2&idp=10395.

1718 For the elaboration of the NCPC the working commission considered a number of national legislations and international instruments, such as the previous Romanian 1940 Code of Civil Procedure, the Codes of Civil Procedure of a number of countries (Quebec – Canada, France (including its 1991 Law on enforcement), Italy, Switzerland, Germany, Finland, the Netherlands), the Enforcement Code of the Republic of Moldova, the European Convention of Human Rights, a number of European Regulations and Directives (Directive 2000/35 on combatting late payment in commercial transactions, Brussels I Regulation, European Enforcement Order Regulation, EOP Regulation, ESCP Regulation), the Storme Commission's work on drafting a European Judicial Code, the Model Code of Civil Procedure for South America elaborated by the Ibero-American Institute of Civil Procedure, and the ALI/UNIDROIT Principles and Rules of Transnational Civil Procedure.

1719 The Government Emergency Ordinance No. 4/2013 for the amendment of Law No. 76/2012 for the application of Law No. 134/2010 regarding the Code of Civil Procedure, as well as for the amendment and supplement of certain connected normative acts, Official Gazette of Romania No. 68 of 31 January 2013. This act delayed the entrance into force of the NCPC until 15 February 2013. The Ordinance was later approved with modification by Law No. 214/2013, Official Gazette of Romania No. 388 of 28 June 2013.

1720 Law No. 138/2014 amending and supplementing Law No. 134/2010 regarding the Code of Civil Procedure, as well as amending and supplementing certain related normative acts, Official Gazette of Romania No. 753/16 October 2014; Law No. 17/2017 approving the Government Emergency Ordinance No. 1/2016 for the modification of Law No. 134/2010 regarding the Code of Civil Procedure, as well as other connected legal acts, Official Gazette of Romania No. 196 of 21 March 2017.

1721 Reasons for the project of Law for the amendment and supplement of Law No. 134/2010 regarding the Code of civil procedure, as well as for the amendment and supplement of other connected normative acts, PL-x No. 437/2014, available at www.cdep.ro/pls/proiecte/upl_pck.proiect?cam=2&idp=14358.

6.2. The Romanian Legal System: An Overview

6.2.1. *General Aspects*

Jurisdiction of first instance courts is divided between the District Courts (*judecătorii*) and Higher General Courts (*tribunale*). The District Courts are competent to hear cases up to a value of RON200,000 (approx. €44,500), as well as matters in a number of expressly established domains.[1722] The Higher General Courts are competent to handle all other claims above the RON200,000 threshold and those that the law sets exclusively in their competence.[1723] The Higher General Courts also handle appeals registered against decisions issued by the District Courts.[1724] Similar to national procedures, the jurisdiction of Romanian courts in European procedures depends on the subject matter and the value of the claim. Thus, ESCP claims fall within the exclusive jurisdiction of the *judecătorii*, while for the EOP the competence is divided between the *judecătorii* and the *tribunale*.[1725]

In handling the case and awarding a judgment, the Romanian judge is bound to adhere to the scope and particulars of the dispute established by the parties.[1726] However, he is not generally hindered by legal qualifications made by the parties regarding the acts and the facts that are the subject of the dispute. The judge is expected to play an active role in truth-finding (e.g. requesting additional explanations [orally or in writing] and evidence; proceeding to a legal re-qualification of the claim).[1727] As indicated in Article 80(1) NCPC, the parties may exercise their procedural rights in person or by way of a representative. Representation is not compulsory,[1728] but it is always possible and is often used in practice.[1729]

1722 Article 94(1) NCPC.

1723 Article 95 points 1 and 4 NCPC.

1724 Article 95 point 2 NCPC.

1725 Information communicated by Member States in accordance with Article 29 of Regulation (EC) No 1896/2006 of the European Parliament and the Council of 12 December 2006 creating a European order for payment procedure, available at https://e-justice.europa.eu/content_european_payment_order-353-ro-en.do?member=1; Information communicated by Member States in accordance with Article 25 of Regulation (EC) No 861/2007 of the European Parliament and the Council of 11 July 2007 establishing a European Small Claims Procedure, available at https://e-justice.europa.eu/content_small_claims-354-ro-en.do?member=1.

1726 Article 22(6) and Article 397(1) NCPC. See Leş (2014), Volume I, at 60–61 and 598; Tăbârcă (2013), Volume I, at 72–76.

1727 Article 22 NCPC. See also Văcărelu & Ognean (2014), at 299.

1728 The Constitutional Court declared unconstitutional the NCPC provision imposing mandatory representation by a lawyer in the event of a second appeal (recurs). The relation between the aim the legislator sought to achieve (procedural discipline) and the limitation of the fundamental right of access to justice (Article 21 Constitution) was considered by the court to be disproportionate. Decision No. 462/17 September 2014 and Decision No. 485/23 June 2015. The rule on compulsory representation by lawyer in the event of a second appeal was harshly criticised as a limitation of the right of access to justice, also in light of the sanction applied – nullity of the procedural act. See Deleanu (2013), Volume I, at 385.

1729 Leş (2014), Volume I, at 205–208; Titirigă (2014), at 223–224; Leş (2009a), at 129.

According to the provisions of the NCPC and of the Constitution, legal proceedings before Romanian courts must be conducted in Romanian.[1730]

6.2.2. The Ordinary National Procedure

The NCPC offers claimants a plethora of means to choose from when submitting a claim. This can be registered either in person by the party or his representative, or, alternatively, filed by post or by courier services, faxed, scanned and sent by email, or sent in an electronic format.[1731] The application registered by the clerk is randomly assigned to one of the court's panels[1732] for verification as to whether the application fulfils all the requirements set by the NCPC.[1733] If the application does not comply with them, the court notifies the applicant of the deficiencies and sets a period for the party to make the necessary amendments.[1734] The completion or the rectification of the claim within a set period is a common aspect also provided by EOP and ESCP procedures.[1735] Subsequent to submission of the statement of defence and of the answers to the statement of defence, the court *ex officio*[1736] will summon the parties to a first hearing.[1737] The trial stage before the first instance court is divided into two subparts consisting of (1) the investigation parte (*cercetarea procesului*) that is a preparatory phase, and (2) the debate in a public hearing of the parties' claims and defences.[1738] The investigation is set to take place in chambers (*camera de consiliu*),[1739] and the parties are summonsed to

1730 Article 18 NCPC and Article 128 of the Constitution. Non-observance of this principle results in the nullity of the judicial decision. Article 18(4) NCPC establishes that all 'requests and procedural acts have to be drawn up only in Romanian'. See Leş (2014), Volume I, at 74–76.

1731 Article 199(1) NCPC.

1732 Article 199(2) NCPC. The assignment of cases to the court's panels is carried out automatically through an informatics system, ECRIS, in which all the information regarding the cases is registered (Article 95(2) Regulation regarding the internal organisation of the courts). See Leş (2014), Volume I, at 611–612.

1733 Article 200(1) NCPC. On aspects verified by the panel, see Articles 194–197 NCPC.

1734 Article 200(3) NCPC. See Zidaru (2013), at 151–160.

1735 Article 9 EOP and Article 4(4) ESCP.

1736 Article 154 NCPC. The summons and service of documents of the proceedings are carried out by the court through its procedural agents (seldom used because it had not yet been put into place as a court service), by postal service with declared content and acknowledgement of receipt (by the Romanian Post; the usual means used in practice), by bailiff or courier upon the interested party's request (newly introduced means of serving procedural acts and summons that are carried out at the expense of the party requesting it), or by modern means of communication (fax, email, or other means that ensure transmission of the text of the document and confirmation of it being received by the addressee). If the parties live in another Member State, the summons are served according to the provisions of the Service Regulation. See Leş (2014), Volume I, at 456–460.

1737 Article 201 NCPC. The first hearing is set by the judge within a maximum period of 60 days from the time the court receives an answer to the statement of defence. Alternatively, the parties may expressly request the case to be trialled only on the basis of the documents submitted to the court (Article 15 NCPC).

1738 Article 237 and Article 244 NCPC. See Tăbârcă (2013a), Volume II, at 33–35.

1739 Article 213 and Article 240(1) NCPC. In the future, the proceedings in chambers may gain a significant place in the handling of a case. The adversarial debates in chambers has been postponed until 1 January

participate.[1740] When all aspects of the claim have been clarified, a date for a public debate is set.[1741] At least five days prior to the hearing, the parties have to submit written notes regarding their claims and defences.[1742] The parties may agree to the debate on the merits taking place in chambers, or in a party's absence.[1743] Nevertheless, in practice, the public hearing continues to retain its central role in court proceedings. Once the debates are closed, the judge can request the parties to submit a supplement to the notes (*completări la note*) previously filed.[1744] Non-submission is not sanctioned. The judge decides the case based on the evidence, the oral claims, and the applicable legal provisions.

During the entire phase of the court proceedings, the judge may try to conciliate the parties, giving them the necessary indications and summoning them to appear in person, even if they are represented.[1745] If it appears possible, he may recommend that the parties use mediation to settle their dispute.[1746] This characteristic of national proceeding has a certain resemblance to the duty of the judge in the ESCP (i.e. facilitating the process of parties reaching a settlement when this appears appropriate).[1747]

2019. Previously, the pre-trial phase was organised during the court's public hearings. See Article XII Law No. 2/2013 regarding certain measures for the relief of courts and for preparing the application of Law No. 134/2010 regarding the Code of Civil Procedure, Official Gazette of Romania No. 89/12 February 2013 and Government Emergency Ordinance No. 62/2015 prolonging certain procedural timeframes established by Law No. 2/2013, Official Gazette of Romania No. 964/24 December 2015.

1740 Article 237 NCPC. The parties are summoned to each of the chamber hearings and are served documents (Article 240(1) NCPC). In accordance with Article 241(3) NCPC, when the court has the relevant contact details, for speeding up this stage of proceedings, the parties may be notified of the date of the next hearing or be notified of documents by telephone, wire, fax, e-mail, or any other means of communication. The parties or their lawyers must confirm receipt of the documents or the notification. This mechanism is meant to guarantee the effectiveness of the notification within a short time during the preparatory stage of the trial. See also Leş (2014) Volume I, at 686–690 and 692–693; Tăbârcă (2013a), Volume II, at 49–50.

1741 Article 244(1) NCPC.

1742 Article 244(2) NCPC. According to Tăbârcă, submission of the written notes is necessary for parties to benefit from a better presentation of their claims and defences, and offers the court the information that allows it to issue a correct judgment. Tăbârcă (2013a), Volume II, at 527. According to some scholars, non-submission of the notes does not affect the parties' right to formulate oral conclusions or prevent the court from continuing the discussion on the merits of the claim or from issuing the judgment. See Leş (2014) Volume I, at 695; Dănăilă (2016), at 644–646.

1743 Article 244(3) and (4) NCPC.

1744 Article 394(2) NCPC. This provision has been criticised by legal scholars and practitioners for breaching the principles of adversarial proceedings, the right of defence and a fair trial. See Leş (2014) Volume I, at 695; Larionescu & Trantea (2009), at 692–699.

1745 Article 21(2) in conjunction with Article 227(1) NCPC. When offering indications to the parties, the judge has a duty to remain impartial. See Leş (2014) Volume I, at 669–670; Tăbârcă (2013), Volume I, at 137–140; Theohari & Eftimie (2016), at 60–63, Theohari (2016), at 619–620.

1746 Article 21(1) in conjunction with Article 227(2)-(4) NCPC. Parties refusing to participate in an information session on the advantages of the mediation may be sanctioned with a judicial fine between RON100 – 1,000 (approx. €20 – 200) (Article 187(1) point 1 f) NCPC). See Leş (2014) Volume I, at 671–674; Tăbârcă (2013), Volume I, at 137–140; Theohari & Eftimie (2016), at 60–63; Theohari (2016), at 619–620.

1747 Article 12(3) ESCP.

The judgment is rendered in a public hearing,[1748] and the court communicates *ex officio* the judgment to each party.[1749] On 15 January 2015, in an attempt to improve and facilitate the judicial services, the Ministry of Justice issued a public statement according to which parties and their lawyers may request that judgments be communicated to them by email, or in an electronic format, as soon as these become available in ECRIS, the courts' file registration system.[1750] In practice, although the system is not yet fully operational at the national level, it appears that some courts make successful use of this tool.[1751] Upon the party's request or that of his representative, the court sends the credentials that will allow the file's documents to be viewed electronically.

A judgment acquires *res judicata* from the moment the judge renders it in the public hearing,[1752] and it is provisional until the judgment becomes final and binding.[1753] A first instance judgment is generally subject to appeal,[1754] which can be filed within a period of 30 days from the date the decision was communicated.[1755] In contrast to the EOP and the ESCP, in the national procedure the execution is suspended automatically if the judgment is challenged. However, the judge can order a provisional enforcement.[1756] The appeal provides a re-adjudication of the case by a higher court on the criticised points.[1757] A second appeal (*recurs*) can be brought against appeal decisions, judgments that are not subject to appeal, or certain decisions established by law.[1758] A higher court verifies whether the decision rendered complies with the applicable legal provisions. In this case, enforcement of the decision is suspended only upon the appellant's request.[1759] Other special means of challenging judicial decisions are the request for annulment (*contestația*

1748 The motivation for the judgment has to be written within 30 days (Article 426(5) NCPC).

1749 Article 427 NCPC and Article 110(3) of the Regulation regarding the organisation and functioning of the courts.

1750 Press Communication of the Ministry of Justice regarding the possibility of sending the closing minutes and the judgments to the parties and other participants in an electronic format, 15 January 2015 (available at www.juridice.ro/wp-content/uploads/2015/01/Comunicat-de-pres%C4%83-referitor-la-posibilitatea-de-a-transmite-p%C4%83r%C8%9Bilor-%C8%99i-participan%C8%9Bilor-la-un-proces-%C3%AEncheierile-de-%C8%99edin%C8%9B%C4%83-%C8%99i-hot%C4%83r%C3%A2rile-%C3%AEn-format-electronic.pdf).

1751 For example, the courts in Bucharest, Timişoara, Cluj-Napoca.

1752 Article 430(1) NCPC.

1753 Article 430(4) NCPC. See Leş (2014) Volume I, at 931–932.

1754 Article 466(1) NCPC. Sometimes the law expressly provides that the decision can be subject only to appeal (e.g. objection to a writ of execution, decision issued by a District Court in a small value claim) or that no appeal is available (e.g. rejection by the court of the debtor's request to annul an order for payment, the decision issued following acknowledgement of the claim). See Negrilă (2016), at 36–37.

1755 Article 468(1) NCPC.

1756 Article 468(5) NCPC. For the provisional enforcement measures, see Article 448 and Article 449 NCPC. On suspension of provisional enforcement, see Article 450 NCPC.

1757 Article 476, Article 477, and Article 479(1) NCPC.

1758 Article 483 NCPC. Claims below RON500,000 (approx. €113,112) are not subject to a second appeal. This limitation applies from 1 January 2017. A transition period was established for the application of this provision. Article XVIII of Law No. 2/2013 regarding the Code of Civil Procedure, Official Gazette of Romania No. 89/12 February 2013, prolonged by Government Emergency Ordinance No. 62/2015. See further Spineanu-Matei (2016), at 121–128.

1759 Article 484(2) NCPC.

în anulare) and the motion for revision (*revizuirea*). These means have limited grounds of application,[1760] and the execution is suspended only upon the party's request and on condition of a security deposit.[1761]

Due to the characteristics of the process described, the issuance of a judgment in the national ordinary procedure may easily take longer than the established EOP and ESCP timeframes. Romanian judges and courts are under considerable pressure to handle cases within a short period in order to comply with the requirements set by Article 6(1) ECHR and Article 21(3) of the Constitution. As seen in official statistics, the courts are overloaded, and face increasing numbers of filed cases. Unfortunately, the statistics are not detailed enough to provide specific details on debt recovery claims involving the ordinary procedure.

6.2.3. *Costs of Ordinary Court Proceedings*

The costs of judicial proceedings in accordance with Article 451(1) NCPC include (1) court fees and judiciary stamps; (2) lawyers, experts, and specialists' fees; (3) monies due to witnesses for their travelling expenses and any loss incurred as a result of attending the trial; (4) costs of travelling and accommodation if necessary; and (5) any other expenses incurred for the efficient organisation of the trial. Court fees for judicial services are paid in advance by the user, except under certain circumstances established by law.[1762] The level of court fees for monetary claims varies between RON20 (approx. €4.52) for claims up to RON500 (approx. €113) and RON6,105 (approx. €1,381), plus 1% for amounts above the RON250,000 for claims higher than RON250,000 (approx. €56,561).[1763] Upon request of the interested party, the losing party bears the costs of judicial proceedings.[1764] The court can make certain exceptions, allowing reductions, rescheduling, or a moratorium on the payment of court fees.[1765] If the party does not pay the court fees, or not in the amount established by the court within the set period, and does not deposit proof of payment, the claim will be annulled by the judge.[1766] Appellate

1760 Article 503 and Article 509 NCPC.

1761 Article 507 NCPC for the request for annulment; see Article 512 NCPC for the motion for revision.

1762 Article 33 Government Emergency Ordinance No. 80/2013. The Government Emergency Ordinance No. 80/2013 repealed the Government Ordinance No. 32/1995 on judiciary stamps required for court claims.

1763 Article 3(1) Government Emergency Ordinance No. 80/2013. Doctrine perceives the level of court fees to be excessive, and the system of legal aid is not actually functional. See Leş (2014) Volume I, at 563; Deleanu (2013), Volume I, at 893. The ECtHR condemned Romania for excessive court fees that can hinder access to justice; nonetheless, the system of court fees was also subsequently extended to other proceedings that were not previously subject to fees. ECtHR, *Weissman and others v. Romania*, 63945/00, ECHR 2006-VII; ECtHR, *Notar v. Romania*, 42860/98, ECHR 2004-II.

1764 Article 453(1) NCPC. An exception to this principle is established by Article 454 NCPC if the defendant admits the claims before the first hearing, and he was not previously served with a notice of delay, or not considered to be in default by law. Leş (2014) Volume I, at 559–560 and 576–586.

1765 Article 42 Government Emergency Ordinance No. 80/2013. See further on this matter Leş (2014) Volume I, at 567–569.

1766 Article 197 in conjunction with Article 200(3) NCPC. On the annulment of the claim due to non-payment or partial payment of the court fees, see Leş (2014) Volume I, at 570–571; Zidaru (2013), at 167–168.

proceedings are also subject to court fees. Appeal fees for money claims are 50% of the amount applicable to the contested claim, but not less than RON20 (approx. €4.52).[1767] On the basis of the grounds invoked for the action, the court fees for second appeals range from RON100 (approx. €22.62) to 50% of the fee due for the contested money claim, but not less than RON100.[1768] In addition to this, parties are required to pay a fee of RON5 (approx. €1.13) per certified copy of judgment that attests the decision is final and binding.[1769]

6.3. National Tailored Solutions for the Recovery of Monetary Claims

The Romanian legislator opted in the NCPC for the establishment of two special procedures to facilitate the recovery of money claims. These are the *procedura ordonanţei de plată* (order for payment procedure) and the *procedura cu privire la cererile de valoare redusă* (small value claims procedure). Here the EOP and the ESCP find a direct national equivalent. The national instruments are accelerated procedures that offer parties an immediately enforceable title. This section analyses these procedures, examining their features and use in civil and commercial litigation.

6.3.1. *Procedura Ordonanţei de Plată*

6.3.1.1. General Aspects

Procedura ordonanţei de plată regulated in Articles 1014–1025 NCPC has its origin in two former procedures established in 2001 and 2007.[1770] The *ordonanţa de plată* is to a significant extent a synthesis of the former procedures' provisions to which new legislative solutions were added.[1771] The order for payment is a simplified procedure, and is an alternative instrument available for the recovery of pecuniary claims for a specific amount that has fallen due (*creanţă certă, lichidă şi exigibilă*).[1772] These characteristics are shared by the EOP, but in contrast to the latter, the national procedure does not

1767 Article 23(1) Government Emergency Ordinance No. 80/2013.

1768 Article 24(1) and (2) Government Emergency Ordinance No. 80/2013.

1769 Article 9 letter (l) Government Emergency Ordinance No. 80/2013. This needs to be arranged by the party after receiving a copy of the judgment. The copy communicated by the court does not contain the certification required for enforcement purposes.

1770 These are the writ of payment (*somaţia de plată*) and the payment order (*ordonanţa de plată*). They were established by Government Ordinance No. 5/2001 regarding the writ of payment (Official Gazette of Romania No. 422/30 July 2001), and the Government Emergency Ordinance No. 119/2007 on measures for combatting delays in execution of payment obligations resulting from contracts concluded between professionals (Official Gazette No. 738/31 October 2007). Both procedures were repealed by Law No. 76/2012 for the application of Law No. 134/2010 regarding the Code of Civil Procedure. See also, Boroi & Stancu (2015), at 853.

1771 See on this Bozeşan (2014), at 1–2 and 4–6; Dinu (2013), at 7–13; Fodor & Popa (2013), at 84. On the imperative need for the NCPC to establish a national procedure for the recovery of a money claim following the EOP Regulation, see Leş (2015), at 1413.

1772 Article 1014(1) NCPC.

require that the debt be uncontested;[1773] thus, the creditor may choose to use this accelerated procedure also if he expects the debtor to contest the claim.[1774] The claim should result from a contract,[1775] and have its origin in a regulation (e.g. statutes of an association) or another written document (e.g. letter, invoice, e-mail) signed by the parties or undertaken by any other means established by law.[1776] Similar to the EOP, the procedure establishes no threshold for its application. Further, the *ordonanţa de plată* cannot be used for the recovery of debts related to insolvency proceedings,[1777] for debts resulting from labour agreements or the payment of social security rights,[1778] for the enforcement of administrative, fiscal, or customs acts, for criminal actions, or for the restitution of executed performances.[1779]

Jurisdiction is divided between the District Courts (*judecătorii*) and the Higher General Courts (*tribunale*), based on their material competence.[1780] The NCPC provisions contain no limitation regarding application of the *ordonanţa de plată* only to national claims. Hence, parties can make use of this special procedure in cross-border situations. However, opinions in the legal literature are divided. Some scholars consider that the *ordonanţa de plată* applies only for domestic litigation, while cross-border cases should be handled in accordance with the EOP Regulation.[1781] These views are reflected in the practice of some Romanian courts that rejected applications made under the national procedure, because they considered that the EOP should be used instead for cross-border cases.[1782] Other scholars rightfully oppose this interpretation, as *ordonanţa de plată* provisions contain no such limitations.[1783]

Similar to the EOP, the representation of parties during the proceedings is not mandatory.[1784]

1773 On a criticisable contrary interpretation, see Judecătoria Botoşani, Decision No. 96/16 January 2014 that considers that the procedure is applicable only for uncontested claims. Barbu (2014), at 282–283.

1774 Article 1019(3) in conjunction with Article 1021(1) NCPC.

1775 This concerns civil contracts concluded between natural persons, consumers and professionals, between professionals, or between professionals and authorities. See further Constanda (2013), at 604–607; Frenţiu & Băldean (2013), at 1418–1420; Deleanu (2013), Volume II, at 670–671.

1776 Article 1014(1) NCPC. See also discussion on the types of written documents in Fodor & Popa (2013), at 96–97; Bozeşan (2014), at 49–52.

1777 Article 1014(2) NCPC.

1778 Article 119(2) Law No. 76/2002 regarding the social security system and encouraging of working relations. See on this also Tăbârcă (2013a), Volume II, at 781.

1779 Bozeşan (2014), at 29–30, 35–43, and 52–53; Deleanu (2013), Volume II, at 670–671; Tăbârcă (2013a), Volume II, at 781.

1780 For claims above RON200,000 (approximately €44,500), excluding interest, expenses, and disbursements or other amounts falling due after registration of the claim, the Higher General Courts have jurisdiction (Article 94 point 1 letter k) in conjunction with Article 95 point 2 and Article 98(1)-(2) NCPC. For claims below RON200,000, the competence belongs to the District Courts.

1781 Tăbârcă (2013a), Volume II, at 779; Dinu (2013), at 42.

1782 See for this purpose Judecătoria Oradea, Civil Section, Civil Judgment No. 3164/2011, (available online at http://portal.just.ro/271/Lists/Jurisprudenta/DispForm.aspx?ID=31).

1783 Bozeşan (2014), at 17–18; Constanda (2016), at 897–899.

1784 Article 83 and Article 84 NCPC.

6.3.1.2. The Procedure

An application can be filed by using one of the means available under the general rules of the ordinary procedure. In contrast to the European procedures, the national proceedings include a compulsory pre-trial phase.[1785] Thus, prior to initiating court proceedings, the creditor is required to send a payment notice (*somaţie*) requesting the debtor to pay off the debt within a period of 15 days of notification.[1786] Notification is carried out by a bailiff or sent by registered post with declared content and acknowledgement of receipt.[1787] If the debtor does not pay within the set period, the creditor can initiate court proceedings. The application can also be filed electronically, a means of communiation also allowed by the EOP (Article 7(5) EOP).[1788] However, unlike the European procedures, the use of standard forms is not a common feature in national proceedings.[1789] Article 1017 NCPC establishes a list of elements that the application needs to contain (e.g. identification details of the parties, details of the claim, the amount of the debt, the interest, or damages). In addition, the creditor must submit the documents attesting the amount of the debt claimed, as well as any other element he intends to use as evidence, along with proof that the debtor has already received a notice of payment.[1790] The application is rejected as inadmissible if no proof of payment is provided.[1791]

As well as the principle amount, the claimant can request interest[1792] and additional damages for expenses incurred in recovering the debt.[1793] Similar to the EOP procedure, the claimant has the opportunity to correct or complete his application if elements of the request are missing.[1794] However, in contrast to the European procedure, the judge in charge of the case will always summon the parties to appear before him for explanations and clarifications.[1795] The public hearing plays a central role in the national procedures,

1785 On the compulsory nature of the pre-trial procedure, see Bozeşan (2014), at 60; Dinu (2013), at 43–44.

1786 Article 1015(1) NCPC.

1787 In practice, this requirement has been applied strictly by the courts. Judecătoria Sectorului 6 Bucureşti, s. civ., încheiere din 13.05.2013, not published. See Bozeşan (2014), at 58.

1788 Article 148(2) NCPC. For the EOP, Romania informed the European Commission that the means of communication accepted are post and fax. These remain the only acceptable means for the EOP, though the NCPC allows the use of other modern means of communication (see https://e-justice.europa.eu/content_european_payment_order-353-ro-en.do?member=1).

1789 Only one Romanian procedure uses standard forms for its application. See further on this Section 6.3.2.

1790 Article 1017(2) NCPC.

1791 In practice, the courts apply this provision differently. See on this Bozeşan (2014), at 63–66.

1792 If interest was not determined by the parties' agreement, legal interest applies. Article 1018(1) NCPC and Government Ordinance No. 13/2011 on the legal interest and penalties for monetary duties (*Ordonanţa Guvernului nr. 13/2011 privind dobânda legală remuneratorie şi penalizatoare pentru obligaţiile băneşti*), Official Gazette of Romania No. 607/29 August 2011. On the level of legal interest between professionals, see discussion by Constanda (2016b), at 907–909; Bozeşan (2014), at 229–244.

1793 Article 1018(2) NCPC.

1794 Article 200(3) in conjunction with Article 1017(1) – (3) and Article 1023 NCPC. See Boroi & Stancu (2015), at 860–861; Bozeşan (2014), at 108–119; Frenţiu & Băldean (2013), at 1423.

1795 Article XII (1)-(2) Law No. 2/2013 in conjunction with Government Emergency Ordinance No. 95/2016. As of 1 January 2019, the analysis of the merits of the case will take place in chambers with the parties being summonsed, and the adversarial debate will be held in public. However, based on the provisions

and is extensively used. Ten days before the oral hearing, a notice is served on the parties.[1796] In contrast to the EOP, the national order for payment procedure is an adversarial proceeding. The defendant has to submit a statement of defence at least 3 days prior to the hearing,[1797] and in issuing its decision the court takes into account the arguments and evidence of both parties.[1798] Based on the facts, failure to file a statement of defence may be interpreted as an acknowledgement of the claims.[1799] Subsequently, the defendant will not be able to propose evidence and raise exceptions unless they concern public policy, but can only provide explanations and clarifications regarding the allegations.[1800] The order is awarded based on the evaluation of evidence submitted to the court and on compliance of the claim with the requirements set by Article 1014(1) NCPC.[1801]

In contrast to the EOP opposition, in the national procedure the party is not notified as to whether the defendant had submitted a statement of defence or communicated a copy of the document. It is the claimant's duty to actively follow the case and to request information from the court.[1802] However, this hinders the claimant's possibilities of being well informed of the statement of opposition, especially if he appears in person in court, and the defendant had deposited his documents 3 days before the hearing. In practice, the possibility of the claimant being able to consult the statement of defence before the hearing is almost non-existent, since the file is no longer available in the archive 3 to 5 days prior to the date of the hearing, but is with the judge. Hence, it is very likely that the claimant or his lawyer will have access to the statement of opposition only on the day of the hearing.[1803] This situation interferes with the claimant's possibility of defending himself efficiently, thereby affecting his right of access to justice and a fair trial.

During the hearing, the judge seeks to persuade the debtor to pay the debt, or to encourage the parties to reach a settlement on the means of payment.[1804] If the parties reach an agreement, the court acknowledges the settlement, and issues an enforceable

of Article 244(3) NCPC, parties may also agree to the debate taking place in chambers. See Bozeşan (2014), at 126–127.

1796 Article 1019(1) NCPC. According to doctrine, this concerns only the summons of the debtor for the first hearing. For the following public hearings the general rules regarding the summons will apply. See Boroi & Stancu (2015), at 861–862; Loznean (2015), at 388–389; Tăbârcă (2013a), Volume II, at 785.

1797 Article 1019(3) NCPC.

1798 Bozeşan (2014), at 22–25; Dinu (2013), at 30.

1799 Article 1019(3) NCPC. This aspect of the national procedure was criticised by scholars. See Deleanu (2013), Volume II, at 673. On the presumption of recognition and the duty of the court to corroborate non-submission of the statement of defence with the actual 'circumstances of the case', see Tăbârcă (2013a), Volume II, at 786; Fodor & Popa (2013), at 94.

1800 Article 208(2) NCPC. See Constanda (2016c); Dinu (2013), at 57–58; Fodor & Popa (2013), at 94.

1801 Bozeşan (2014), at 128–132.

1802 Article 1019(4) NCPC.

1803 Scholars have criticised this choice on the part of the legislator. Gheorghe (2013), at 41; Fodor & Popa (2013), at 94; Bozeşan (2014), at 128.

1804 Article 1019(1) NCPC.

decision.[1805] If the claimant declares in court that he has received the payment, the judge will close the case.[1806]

Similar to the EOP, the judge issues the *ordonanţa de plată* for the entire amount of the claim or part of it based on what appears to be founded on the basis of the documents submitted, and on the explanations and clarifications provided by the parties.[1807] If the order was issued for only part of the claim, the creditor may initiate ordinary court proceedings for the remaining part.[1808] In contrast to the EOP, the court also sets the period within which the debtor has to pay the amount awarded by order (i.e. no less than 10 days and not longer than 30 days from the date of communication of the order).[1809]

If the debtor contests the claim, the judge proceeds to determine whether the opposition is founded. If the defence is found to be justified, or the use of means of evidence other than written ones is necessary, the court rejects the claim.[1810] The claimant may file a new claim in accordance with the ordinary proceedings.[1811]

Similar to the EOP, for the *ordonanţa de plată* the court has to issue the order within a brief period of time, within 45 days from the moment the claim was registered.[1812] This does not take into account the period necessary for communication of the documents of the proceedings, and the completion and correction of the application.

A remarkable characteristic of the national procedure is the fact that both the defendant and the claimant may file a request for an annulment of the order issued by the court.[1813] The reasons for this are limited, and are expressly provided by the text (i.e. the non-fulfilment of all requirements necessary for issuance of the order, payment of the debt before issuance of the order).[1814] In the context of the EOP, the first means resembles one of the review reasons in the European procedure,[1815] while the second means is a reason for refusing enforcement of the EOP.[1816] The application is handled by the same court that issued the *ordonanţa de plată*, but involves a panel of two judges.[1817]

1805 Article 1020(2) NCPC. See Tăbârcă (2013a), Volume II, at 788; Loznean (2015), at 390; Leş (2015), at 1421.

1806 Article 1020(1) NCPC. No proof is required as to whether the debtor has paid the debt. See Tăbârcă (2013a), Volume II, at 787; Loznean (2015), at 390.

1807 Article 1022(1) and (2) NCPC.

1808 Article 1022(2) NCPC.

1809 Article 1022(3) NCPC. Upon the parties' agreement, the judge may set a different timeframe. See Dinu (2013), at 67. A longer period can also be set in the context of Article 1022(4) NCPC (payment of the usual expenses for the association of owners or the maintenance payments).

1810 Article 1021 (1)-(2) NCPC. Judecătoria Botoşani, Decision No. 96/2014, Barbu (2014), at 282–283; Leş (2015), at 1421. For a discussion on this aspect, see Dinu (2013), at 62–65; Bozeşan (2014), at 155–157.

1811 Article 1021(3) NCPC.

1812 Article 1023(1) NCPC.

1813 Article 1024(1) and (2) NCPC.

1814 Article 1024(3) NCPC. Tăbârcă (2013a), Volume II, at 792. Criticism was expressed in the literature on the limitation of the request for annulment to these reasons, see Dinu (2013), at 69–71.

1815 Article 20(2) EOP.

1816 Article 22(2) EOP.

1817 Article 1024(4) NCPC. For an analysis of the evidence to be used for requesting the annulment and the period within which the arguments must be raised, see Tăbârcă (2013a), Volume II, at 793–794.

The *ordonanța de plată* has provisional *res judicata* and is enforceable from the moment of its issuance.[1818] As with the EOP, the execution is not automatically suspended if the national order is challenged. The debtor has to request it and pay a security for this purpose.[1819] If the order is subject to the special review procedure, execution is carried out at the creditor's risk.[1820] Following the court's decision on the request for annulment, the judgment becomes final and can no longer be subject to a second appeal.[1821]

6.3.1.3. Costs of Proceedings

The court fees for filing a claim in accordance with the *ordonanța de plată* procedure are fixed at RON200 (approx. €45.25).[1822] If annulment of the order is requested, the interested party has to pay an additional court fee of RON100 (approx. €22.62).[1823] Additional costs may be added, such as for the translation of documents if requested; the lawyer's fees; the fee for bringing a request for annulment of the order; or the execution fees.

6.3.1.4. Use in Practice

Statistics provided by the Supreme Council of Magistracy regarding use of the national procedure show that the order for payment is a well-known instrument, and is often used by parties. Prior to the coming into force of the NCPC, a significant number of files were handled each year. From 4.01% of *ordonanțe de plată* in the total number of cases filed with the competent courts in 2011 and 4.11% in 2012, this decreased to 1.04% in 2013 and to 0.10% in 2014.

1818 Article 1025(1) NCPC.

1819 Article 1024(5) in conjunction with Article 1025(1) NCPC.

1820 He will need to reimburse the debtor if the decision is overturned (Article 1025(1) in conjunction with Article 637 NCPC).

1821 Article 1024(6) – (8) NCPC.

1822 Article 6(2) Government Emergency Ordinance No. 80/2013. The ordinance increased the level of court fees. Before 29 June 2013, the court fee for the issuance of an *ordonanța de plată* was RON150 (approx. €33.94) (Article 2(1^3) Law No. 146/2007 regarding judiciary stamp fees) together with a judiciary stamp based on the value of the claim varying from RON0.30 to RON5 (approx. €0.07 to €1.31)(Article 3(1)-(2) Government Ordinance No. 32/1995 regarding the judiciary stamp). Prior to 15 February 2013, the payment order and the writ of payment court fee was RON39 (approx. €8.82) to which a judiciary stamp of RON0.30 (approx. €0.07) applied. If the application for the issuance of an order for payment is made by a claimant who is exempted from paying the court fee (e.g. associations of owners for the recovery of costs of utilities), he is also not required to pay this fixed fee. Boroi & Stancu (2015), at 861.

1823 This applies to claims registered after 29 June 2013. The Government Emergency Ordinance No. 80/2013 contains no specific text regarding the request of annulment of an order for payment. By way of interpretation scholars are of the opinion that the fee applicable in this case is 50% of the fee applicable for the claim, as for an appeal. See on this Constanda (2013d), at 620; Deleanu (2013), Volume II, at 916; Frențiu & Băldean (2013), at 1438; Bozeşan (2014), at 254–255; Deleanu (2013a), at 45–64. On the succession of laws regarding the court fees and the moment according to which they are calculated, see Bozeşan (2014), at 255–257; Theohari, Ilie, Bîrlog & Cristea (2012), at 351–352.

	2011	2012	2013	2014
Ordonanţe de plată	77,438	80,944	18,200	1,794
Civil Cases registered with District and General courts	1,928,771	1,967,267	1,739,765	1,784,282

Table 6.1. Number of new cases registered on an annual basis by District Courts and High General Courts in Romania[1824]

The average time necessary for a District Court to handle an *ordonanţe de plată* claim is around 4 months. However, there has been a slight increase, with 117 days (3.9 months) in 2013 and 125 days (4.16 months) in 2014.[1825] The changes introduced by the NCPC may require more time for parties to re-accustom themselves to the characteristics of the proceeding. Additionally, the establishment of a new alternative procedure regarding national small claims may also have contributed to this result.[1826] Prior to the coming into force of the new code, there were no alternatives to the two order for payment procedures.

6.3.2. *Procedura cu privire la Cererile de Valoare Redusă*

6.3.2.1. General Aspects

Procedura cu privire la cererile de valoare redusă is a new special procedure introduced by the NCPC (Articles 1026–1033 NCPC). The ESCP was a significant source of inspiration for the Romanian legislator,[1827] and therefore important similarities exist between the two instruments. The national procedure applies for claims not exceeding RON10,000 (approx. €2,262.44).[1828] Thus, the threshold was very close to the one established by the initial ESCP Regulation: €2,000. As to the ESCP, this amount excludes interest, court fees, or other accessory disbursements.[1829] Furthermore, the national

1824 The information regarding the national order for payment (*ordonanţa de plată*) was provided by the Superior Council of Magistracy. See further Section 6.7.1. The total number of cases registered by District Courts and High General Courts includes all the areas of law for which these courts are competent (except criminal cases), as seen in Reports regarding the State of Justice 2011–2014 published by the Superior Council of Magistracy (available at www.csm1909.ro/csm/index.php?cmd=24).

1825 Superior Council of Magistracy, *Report regarding the State of the Justice System 2014*, at 80.

1826 In accordance with the *Report regarding the State of Justice System 2014* (Superior Council of Magistracy), there was an increase in the activity of the District Courts (*judecătorii*) partly due to the high number of claims filed on the basis of the national small claims procedure (at 24).

1827 Loznean (2015a), at 394; Bozeşan (2014), at 286; Dănăilă (2016c), at 919; Măstăcăneanu (2012) (available online on www.juridice.ro), Tabacu (2009), at 238.

1828 The procedure is available not only for money claims but also for claims regarding the provision of services or the handover of a movable asset whose value is not above the threshold. Opinions regarding application of this procedure in relation to property ownership rights (*drepturi reale*) are divided. See Bozeşan (2014), at 286–287; Tăbârcă (2013a), Volume II, at 796; Măstăcăneanu (2012); Leş (2015), at 1316–1317; Dinu (2011), at 71.

1829 Article 1026(1) NCPC.

procedure mirrors the limitations of the ESCP's scope.[1830] Similar to the European procedure, the domestic small claims procedure relies on the use of standard forms for submission of the claim and for conducting the proceedings.

In accordance with the NCPC, the national small claims procedure is an alternative to the ordinary procedure. The claimant is free to choose between the two procedures when filing a claim with the competent District Court in Romania.[1831] If the initial claim is filed in accordance with the ordinary procedure, the applicant may choose to revert to using the simplified small claims procedure by making an express request in this regard, up until the date of the first hearing.[1832] In addition, the claimant may even choose to use the *ordonanţa de plată* procedure if its requirements are fulfilled. NCPC provisions do not contain any limitations regarding it being applied only to domestic claims; thus, parties can also use the procedure in cross-border litigation.[1833] Similar to the ESCP, if the court considers that the application cannot be handled according to the procedure, it informs the claimant, who is then able to withdraw the claim. Otherwise, the court proceeds according to the ordinary procedure.[1834] The representation of parties during the proceedings is not mandatory.[1835]

6.3.2.2. The Procedure

The procedure is initiated by the claimant filling in the standard application form and submitting it to the court together with the evidence he intends to use.[1836] The submission can be carried out by any of the means available within the ordinary procedure. The national small claims procedure standard forms are very similar to the ESCP ones, using a system of boxes to be ticked or filled in. Three standard forms were adopted: an application form, a completion and/or rectification of the claim form, and an answer form.[1837] Similar to the ESCP, the claim and the answer forms include guidelines. As with the ESCP, if the information provided by the claimant is not sufficiently clear or is inadequate, or the claim form is not filled in correctly, the claimant is offered the possibility of completing or rectifying the standard form, or providing additional information or documents within a period set by the court.[1838] The judge requests this by

1830 Article 1026(2)-(3) NCPC and Article 2(1)-(2) ESCP.

1831 Article 1027(1) NCPC. The choice of using this special procedure must be express; it cannot be presumed. Dănăilă (2016a), at 923. On jurisdiction, see Article 1028 NCPC.

1832 Article 1027(2) NCPC.

1833 Some scholars consider that the national special procedure applies for internal claims, while the Regulations concern cross-border litigation. Dinu (2011), at 69.

1834 Article 1027(3) NCPC.

1835 Article 83 and Article 84 NCPC.

1836 Article 1029(1) and (3) NCPC.

1837 Order of the Minister of Justice No. 359/C/2013 for the approval of the forms used in the *procedura cu privire la cererile de valoare redusă* established by Articles 1025–1032 of Law No. 134/2010 regarding the Code of Civil Procedure, Official Gazette of Romania No. 69/ 1 February 2013.

1838 In accordance with Article 1030 (11) NCPC, the court informs the claimant of the consequences of failing to comply with the request to complete, rectify, or provide additional information or documents.

using the dedicated standard form.[1839] If the claimant fails to comply with the court's requirements, his application is annulled.[1840]

The entire procedure is written, and is set to take place in chambers; similar to the ESCP, however, the court may summon the parties for a hearing if necessary or at the request of one of the parties.[1841] The court may also reject this request. The national procedure does not allow the use of videoconference or teleconference for the oral hearings. This also impedes the use of such means within the ESCP. After receiving the claim form, or the rectification and completion form, the court immediately serves it on the defendant together with the answer form, a copy of the claim form, and the submitted documents.[1842] In contrast to the ESCP, Romanian legislation does not establish a specific timeframe for the court to serve the defendant with the documents, but requests that it acts immediately. However, identical to the ESCP, the defendant has to submit his response within 30 days of service. The use of the form, however, is not compulsory. Together with the form, the defendant has to attach copies of the evidence documents he intends to use.[1843] Upon receiving the answer, the court must act immediately and dispatch to the claimant a copy of the answer form, the documents, and, if necessary, the counterclaim.[1844] Again, the national rules do not provide for a specific timeframe. If the defendant filed a counterclaim resulting from the same legal relationship or in connection with it, the answer form has to be accompanied by an additional claim form.[1845] The text of the ESCP Regulation is more restrictive in this respect, limiting the formulation of a counterclaim to the 'same contract or fact on which the original [ESCP] claim was based'.[1846] The claimant has 30 days from the moment of service to respond.[1847] As with the ESCP, the national procedure contains no specific provision requiring the claimant to file a response to the answer submitted by the defendant. In practice, it may be the case that a second round of arguments or additional information is necessary for the judge to

1839 Article 1029(4) NCPC in conjunction with Annex No. 2 Order of the Minister of Justice No. 359/C/2013.

1840 Article 1029(5) NCPC. In accordance with Article 200 NCPC, the decision of annulment may be subject to a request for review (*cerere de reexaminare*) within a period of 15 days from its communication.

1841 Article 1030(1)-(2) NCPC. Even if the hearing is set to take place in chambers, in practice, there were cases in which the court heard the parties in a public hearing instead. This was also related to the legal provision that established hearings would take place in chambers from 1 January 2019 (Article XII(2) Law No. 2/2013 prolonged by Government Emergency Ordinance No. 95/2016). See Bozeşan (2014), at 297; Dănăilă (2016b), at 631–632. For a contrary opinion see Dinu (2011), at 73; Tabacu (2009), at 239.

1842 Article 1030(3) NCPC.

1843 Article 1030(4) NCPC in conjunction with Annex 3 Order of the Minister of Justice No. 359/C/2013. The defendant is also informed of the consequences of not replying to the court; hence, losing the right of proposing evidence and of raising exceptions (apart from public order exceptions). Article 1029(11) NCPC in conjunction with Article 208(2) NCPC.

1844 Article 1030(5) NCPC.

1845 Unlike the ESCP Regulation (Article 5(7) ESCP), NCPC provisions contain no express reference as to the manner in which the counterclaim should be filed. Scholars' opinions are divided. According to some, the counterclaim could be made in the usual format of the ordinary procedure, see Bozeşan (2014), at 293–294; Dinu (2011), at 76. Others consider that the counterclaim should be filed by using the standard claim form, see Măstăcăneanu (2012).

1846 Recital 16 ESCP. Dinu (2011), at 76.

1847 Article 1030(6) NCPC.

be able to decide the case. Additionally, the court may also admit evidence other than written documents; nonetheless, the expenses incurred involving their administration should not be disproportionate in relation to the value of the claim or counterclaim.[1848] If the counterclaim cannot be handled in accordance with the *procedura cu privire la cererile de valoare redusă* because of non-compliance with Article 1026 NCPC, the court splits the case and decides separately on the counterclaim in the ordinary procedure.[1849] Some scholars consider this solution more rational than the one offered by the ESCP, which opts for the entire case to be handled in the ordinary procedure.[1850] However, this is not without risk, as in practice it may lead to inconsistent awards.

In contrast to the ESCP, the NCPC text does not contain any special provision related to the judge's duty to try to encourage parties to reach a settlement. The court renders a written decision within a 30-day period from the moment it receives all the necessary information, or from the date of the oral hearing if this is the case.[1851] This characteristic is shared by the ESCP. If the defendant does not reply to the court, the judge issues a judgment on the basis of the documents available to him.[1852] Furthermore, like the ESCP judgment, the national decision is immediately enforceable,[1853] and, similar to the ESCP, it is subject to appeal within a period of 30 days from the time it is communicated.[1854] The ordinary rules on appeal procedure apply.[1855] The appeal judgment is final, and the court communicates it to the parties.[1856] For serious reasons, the court may suspend enforcement during the appeal proceedings, but only following payment of a security deposit representing 10% of the contested value.[1857] However, the text does not define what these 'serious reasons' (*motive temeinice)* might be.

Identical to the ESCP provisions, the national small claims procedure applies the loser-party-pays rules regarding the costs of the proceedings; nevertheless, the court will not grant the winner expenses that were not necessary or that were disproportionate in comparison to the value of the claim.[1858]

6.3.2.3. Costs of Proceedings

The court fees for filing a claim in accordance with this national procedure are fixed at RON50 if the value of the claim is not above RON2,000 (approx. €452.49), and RON200

1848 Article 1030(9) NCPC.
1849 Article 1030(7) NCPC. See on this argument also Bozeşan (2014), at 294–297; Leş (2015), at 1436.
1850 Article 5(7) ESCP. Leş (2009a), at 125–126.
1851 Article 1031(1) NCPC.
1852 Article 1031(2) NCPC.
1853 Article 1031(3) NCPC.
1854 Article 1033(1) NCPC. For ESCP, see further Section 6.5.
1855 Article 468(5) in conjunction with Article 1032(2) NCPC.
1856 See Section 6.2 above.
1857 Article 1033(2) NCPC.
1858 Article 1032 NCPC. On the interpretation of the national provision in line with Article 16 and Recital 29 ESCP due to their identical wording, see Boroi & Stancu (2015), at 874. Further, the legal literature suggests that the court should draw the parties' attention to the fact that they may request reimbursement of the costs of proceedings. Frenţiu & Băldean (2013), at 1449.

(approx. €45.25) for claims whose value is higher than RON2,000.[1859] Additional costs, such as fees for the translation of documents, lawyer's fees, and execution fees, may be added.

6.3.2.4. Use in Practice

Following the entry into force of the NCPC, since the first year of its application, a significant number of cases have been registered with the courts.[1860] This rose from 27,488 claims in 2013 to almost double in 2014, with 50,465 files. The procedure was used 28 times more often than the *ordonanţa de plată*, which registered only 1,794 cases for the same period.

6.4. National Attitude towards EOP and ESCP Regulations

During the initial consultations and the negotiation process, Romania was not a Member State, and thus could not be actively involved in the legislative process.[1861] Nonetheless, following accession to the European Union, the Romanian legislator did not initiate any internal discussions on application of the procedures, or participate in the consultation on the ESCP opened by the European Commission in 2013.[1862] The Regulations had a significant influence on the provisions of the new Civil Procedural Code regarding the *ordonanţa de plată* and the *procedura cu privire la cererile de valoare redusă*, especially on the latter, which mirrors the ESCP in domestic legislation. The EOP and the ESCP are nominated among the sources of legislation that were taken into consideration when the provisions of the present Code of Civil Procedure were drafted, but the law contains no explicit reference or specific provisions facilitating application of the Regulations within the national procedural system. Legal scholars in Romania were mostly positive regarding the usefulness of such procedures, although certain concerns were raised. The following pages describe the attitudes and the positions held by the Romanian legislator, stakeholders, and legal scholars.

6.4.1. *The EOP*

Scholars' opinions regarding the EOP are divided. Some see it as a useful tool, a step forward in establishing a space of freedom and justice within the EU,[1863] while others

[1859] Article 6(1) Government Emergency Ordinance No. 80/2013.

[1860] The *Report regarding the State of Justice 2014* (Superior Council of Magistracy) points to an increase in the number of cases handled by District Courts, which is partly due to the high number of claims filed on the basis of the national small claims procedure (at 24).

[1861] COM(2002)746. Letter from the European Commission in reply to a request for information by the researcher, DG JUST/A1/JG/Is Ares(2014) 4654593, 22 December 2014, Brussels (document on file with the researcher).

[1862] Official reply letter no. 2465/A/10.02.2015 sent by the Office of Public Relations of the Senate, Parliament of Romania, following a request for information sent by the researcher. Official Reply no. 6b/20E/20.01.2015 sent by the Public Information Office, Chamber of Deputies, Parliament of Romania, following a request for information sent by the researcher (documents on file with the researcher).

[1863] Deleanu (2013), Volume II, at 687; Cupşan-Morar (2010), at 165; Leş (2009), at 27; Moţiu (2009), at 18; Savu (2007), at 76–77.

view it as a limited solution for speeding up access to justice due to its scope, and to the risk of transfer to the national ordinary procedure.[1864] Leş refers to the EOP as a very advanced legal rule and highly efficient in initiating court proceedings. According to Leş, these provisions could be developed and adapted into a regulation on a common content of applications in all sorts of cross-border disputes.[1865]

The interpretation of the phrase 'specific amounts that have fallen due at the time of the application' raised concerns[1866] because it could lead to different interpretations in several Member States with regard to the level of interest and penalties. It might also generate concern as to whether these amounts have to be precise and expressly determined at the moment of application or can they be determined by the court at the time the EOP is issued.[1867]

The use of forms for initiating court procedures is considered to be an element that facilitates access to justice.[1868] Leş remarked that the content of the information in the application form was rigorously established even though it was to be filed by using a standard form.[1869] Furthermore, the Regulation as well as the national legislation do not provide a definition of what constitutes a 'clearly unfounded' or 'inadmissible' application, leaving this to doctrinal interpretation,[1870] and thus to a possible different interpretation and application of a uniform procedure.

The non-evidence model chosen for the EOP procedure was a point of concern. The issuance of an EOP only on the information contained in the application form 'appears to be difficult to accept' when the parallel national procedure is an evidence-based proceeding.[1871] With regard to observance of the debtor's procedural rights, the literature has rightfully pointed to possible difficulties for the judge in verifying the compliance of EOP service with the provisions of the national rules and the standards set by the Regulation.[1872] On the costs of legal representation, Moţiu opines that these should be borne by the defendant based on the content of Form A. The Form A guidelines clarify the claimant's possibility of also claiming other costs related to the procedure as well as court fees (e.g. representative's fees or pre-litigations costs).[1873]

The non-compulsory nature of the representation of parties is perceived as contributing to the speeding up of EOP proceedings, thereby leading to a more efficient handling of the cases.[1874] This perception may be influenced by the non-mandatory nature of representation in national proceedings.

1864 Deleanu (2013), Volume II, at 687; Leş (2009), at 27.
1865 Leş (2009), at 27.
1866 Article 4 EOP.
1867 Moţiu (2009), at 22–23. See here also the *Szyrocka* case (C-215/11, para. 42–48 and 52–53).
1868 Leş (2009), at 25; Moţiu (2009b), at 73.
1869 Leş (2009), at 25; Leş (2009a), at 126.
1870 Leş (2009), at 26; Leş (2009a), at 127.
1871 Moţiu (2009), at 26. See further Sections 6.7.2 and 6.7.3.
1872 Article 12(5) EOP. See A. Circa in Leş (2015), at 975.
1873 Moţiu (2009), at 28. On a further nuanced interpretation, see Popovici (2015), at 268.
1874 Leş (2009a), at 129; Moţiu (2009), at 28.

Deleanu was very reserved about the EOP because of the manner in which the defendant is able to oppose it without providing reasons for doing so.[1875] However, in practice, only 6.8% of the identified EOP cases were opposed.[1876] Further, the scholar voiced concerns that the review can be requested for extraordinary circumstances, other than *force majeure*, and these 'extraordinary circumstances' cannot be interpreted other than in a subjective manner.[1877] In such circumstances, the procedure would not actually achieve its goals of simplifying and speeding up litigation.[1878] Thus, there was an expectation that the use of the special national procedures would continue to prevail in practice.[1879]

Moţiu sees the opposition and review mechanisms as a guarantee of the defendant's procedural rights, because the EOP is issued only on the basis of information provided by the claimant.[1880] The first statement from the Ministry of Justice regarding mechanisms by which the review requests would be analysed by Romanian courts raised criticism. The *contestaţia la executare* (contesting enforcement proceeding) mechanism in the special national order for payment procedure (Article 10 Government Ordinance No. 5/2001) is a different mechanism than the EOP review. This internal mechanism has another nature, and its legal grounds and purpose are different than those of the European procedure.[1881] First, the internal order for payment procedure was – and is – based on a evidence model. Second, it allows any interested person, including a third party, to contest the enforcement, which is not the case with the EOP procedure. Third, the request is handled by the court where enforcement takes place, and not the court of origin. Fourth, the contestation concerns only the execution measures; thus, it does not lead to a nullity of the order/decision previously issued. Hence, the review needs to be carried out in keeping with the provisions of Article 20 EOP and not the national *contestaţia la executare*.[1882] With the NCPC, the Ministry of Justice chose to adopt a different approach.[1883]

Finally, Romanian scholars consider the immediate enforceability of the EOP and the abolition of the exequatur to be the procedure's most significant achievements,[1884] although it was remarked that the procedure is not well known, and parties and their lawyers are reluctant to use it.[1885]

1875 Deleanu (2013), Volume II, at 687.
1876 See Section 6.7.2.
1877 Deleanu (2013), Volume II, at 687.
1878 Deleanu (2013), Volume II, at 687; Pîrvu (2009), at 151.
1879 Referring to the applicable writ of payment (*somaţia de plată*) and the payment order (*ordonanţa de plată*). Pîrvu (2009), at 151–152.
1880 Moţiu (2009a), at 73–74.
1881 Moţiu (2009a), at 77–78; Cupşan-Morar (2010), at 165.
1882 Moţiu (2009a), at 78–80; Popovici (2015), at 266.
1883 See further on the argument Section 6.5.
1884 Leş (2009a), at 131; Pîrvu (2009), at 151; Savu (2007), at 85.
1885 Duagi (2013), at 62.

6.4.2. *The ESCP*

The ESCP is perceived mostly as a useful procedure for small claims,[1886] 'accessible and easy to start', and 'positively influencing' the development of the national small claims procedure,[1887] although the €2,000 threshold was considered by some to be a little too low.[1888] In the consultation regarding the ESCP opened by the European Commission in 2013, a Romanian lawyer underlined the fact that the ESCP was a useful tool for cross-border disputes, but he favoured increasing the procedure's threshold.[1889] This has now been achieved by Regulation 2015/2421. Some also consider the ESCP to be more complicated and difficult than the ordinary procedure, and – due to the limited scope of the Regulation – not an efficient solution for speeding up judicial proceedings.[1890]

Deleanu expressed concerns about the multiplication of EU directives and regulations establishing procedures for money claims within the same area of law, and which are parallel to general or special internal proceedings applicable for the same type of disputes. According to Deleanu, this can lead to confusion rather than to simplification. In such circumstances, it would have been preferable to have one single regulation that was clear and coherent, with the necessary particularisations, instead of several instruments. Furthermore, he considers the procedure to be useless for situations in which the judgment is declared null and void following a review for extraordinary circumstances that, as pointed out for the EOP, cannot be appreciated other than in a subjective manner.[1891]

The use of standard forms emerges as an element that facilitates access to justice.[1892] According to Leş, a more rigorous provision regarding information that the claim form should provide would have been an asset.[1893] The claimant's possibility of rectifying or completing the claim form was welcomed as being a positive aspect of the procedure,[1894] as it is in line with national practices. Further, as previously pointed out for the EOP, the notions of 'clearly unfounded' or 'inadmissible' are not defined, and the national rules do not contain a clarification of their meaning.[1895] Transferring the ESCP claim to the national ordinary procedure when the counterclaim submitted by the defendant exceeded €2,000 was criticised by Romanian scholars, although the solution was perceived to be rational. The criticisms were linked to the possibility the provision leaves open to abuse by the defendant, who could expressly quantify the claim above the Regulation threshold.[1896] Additionally, a point was made that the means chosen for submitting the ESCP claim form to the court are less formal than the ones established,

1886 Titirigă (2014), at 229; Tabacu (2009), at 239.
1887 Titirigă (2014), at 224.
1888 Leş (2009a), at 124.
1889 Document on file with the researcher.
1890 Deleanu (2013), Volume II, at 687.
1891 *Ibidem*.
1892 Leş (2009), at 25; Leş (2009a), at 126.
1893 *Ibidem*.
1894 Leş (2009a), at 127.
1895 *Ibidem*, at 127–128.
1896 Article 5(6)-(7) ESCP. Leş (2009a), at 125.

for example, by the Service Regulation, allowing the application to be sent also by e-mail or fax.[1897]

Tabacu expressed her disagreement with the provisions of the Regulation limiting the request of translation by the court to documents that 'appear to be necessary for giving the judgment'.[1898] This author considers that the Member State has a right to draft documents in its official language, and the provisions of the national legislation request court proceedings to take place in Romanian. Thus, she considers that in all instances a translation is necessary, as the language of the court is the language in which the procedure has to take place.[1899] This indicates that there is some confusion in understanding the meaning of the ESCP provision. Using evidence submitted in a different language would not automatically imply that the proceedings are taking place in a different language or that the court is supposed to issue its judgment in a language other than Romanian. The court would conduct its proceedings in Romanian, but have the freedom to base part of its judgment or the entire judgment on a document drafted in a foreign language. Another misunderstanding appears to be related to the language in which ESCP documents are served. One scholar considers that a party is not entitled to request translations of the documents communicated if these are drafted in the language of the proceedings.[1900]

Assistance to the parties in filling in the forms is considered to be useful, in view of the differences in legal institutions and terminology that could be involved when litigation takes place in a different state.[1901] This view may be influenced by the non-mandatory nature of representation in national proceedings. In the 2013 ESCP consultation initiated by the European Commission, one lawyer highlighted the lack of free assistance for parties filing an application form in Romania. Further, he considered that the legal aid Directive could perhaps establish a more 'generous regime for cross-border cases' in covering court fees. The lawyer advocated for a non-limitation of the courts' possibility of holding oral hearings, but rather facilitating the use of electronic means of communication in ESCP proceedings,[1902] though such means are not available within the national procedures. The respondent pointed to the requisite of the Member States to provide more information regarding enforcement and the costs of proceedings. Finally, he emphasised the need to advertise the ESCP widely, to provide explanations, and to make legal help available for cross-border disputes. In Romania, the non-compulsory nature of representation is seen as a means of speeding up proceedings and as a more efficient manner of resolving the cases.[1903]

In the process of amending ESCP Regulations,[1904] the Senate was not able to comply with the 8-week-period established by the Treaty for discussing the text and replying to

1897 Leş (2009), at 25.

1898 Article 6(2) ESCP.

1899 Tabacu (2009), at 243.

1900 Article 6(3) ESCP. Popovici (2015), at 280.

1901 Tabacu (2009), at 243–244.

1902 Especially when these means of communication were used previously, and the sellers or service providers have been issuing their own documents in this format.

1903 Leş (2009a), at 129.

1904 Proposal for a Regulation of the European Parliament and of the Council amending Regulation (EC) No 861/2007 of the European Parliament and the Council of 11 July 2007 establishing a European Small

the notification.[1905] During the negotiation process, the main points raised by the Romanian delegation had to do with the use of distance means of communication technology for the purpose of holding oral hearings. The Romanian Government backed a text that resembles a solution adopted by Article 8 Regulation 2015/2421: namely, favour the use of communication technology when 'such tools are available' with the courts, and allow parties to request to be heard in person.[1906] Furthermore, the Government stressed that the ESCP article on the taking of evidence should be in line with Regulation (EC) No. 1206/2001 on cooperation between the courts of Member States in the taking of evidence in civil and commercial matters.

Finally, the abolition of the exequatur by the ESCP and the immediate enforceability of the judgment are considered revolutionary solutions with regard to the cross-border execution of judgments.[1907]

6.5. Implementation of the EOP and the ESCP in National Practice

General Provisions

The EOP and ESCP Regulations became applicable following the accession of Romania to the EU in 2007. To date, Romania has not adopted any express provisions (legislation or guidelines) dedicated to application of the European uniform procedures.[1908] The NCPC contains no specific provisions in this regard.[1909] The only article in the code making implicit reference to the European procedures is Article 636 NCPC, and the provision concerns European enforceable titles for which the exequatur procedure was not required. In this case, the NCPC establishes that they are immediately enforceable in Romania without any preliminary formality.[1910]

In accordance with the requirements of Article 29 EOP and Article 25 ESCP, the Romanian Government notified the European Commission regarding the courts that have jurisdiction for handling these types of claims and for review proceedings; the means of communication available; the languages accepted; the authorities that are competent for enforcement purposes; and the availability of an appeal for ESCP

Claims Procedure and Regulation (EC) No 1896/2006 of the European Parliament and of the Council of 12 December 2006 creating a European order for payment procedure, COM (2013)794 final.

1905 The European Commission notified the national Parliament on 13 December 2013, while the chamber resumed its activities on 1 February 2014. Official reply letter no. 2465/A/10.02.2015 sent by the Office of Public Relations of the Senate, Parliament of Romania, following a request for information sent by the researcher (document on file with the researcher).

1906 Council of the European Union, Romanian Delegation, Interinstitutional File 2013/0403 (COD), 9995/14 INIT, Brussels, 19 May 2014 (available at http://data.consilium.europa.eu/doc/document/ST-9995-2014-INIT/en/pdf).

1907 Leş (2009a), at 131.

1908 On the usefulness of adopting internal legislation to facilitate application of the European procedures, see Popovici (2015), at 274; Florescu (2013), at 27 (available at www.euroquod.ro/ue/files/pubs/somatie2013.pdf).

1909 See also Titirigă (2014), at 217–218; Moţiu (2009a), at 80; Pîrvu (2009), at 152–153.

1910 On the application of this provision of the NCPC to the EOP and ESCP, see Boroi & Stancu (2015), at 968, 973 and 977; Leş (2015), at 992–993.

judgments. The EOP communication used to make references by analogy to the provisions of a previous national order for payment procedure, Government Ordinance No. 5/2001.[1911] According to this, the courts competent to receive EOP claims are the District Courts (*judecătorii*) or the Higher General Courts (*tribunale*), based on the value of the application. The new provisions maintain the same competence rules.[1912] On the ESCP, the Romanian authorities indicated that the bodies competent to issue a decision in ESCP claims are the District Courts (*judecătoriile*).[1913] If translation is necessary for serving the order or the forms and documents on the defendant, the court informs the claimant, requesting him to provide the necessary documents. The court itself does not translate the forms or documents.

The means of communication accepted in EOP and ESCP proceedings have been modified over the years. At first only postal service and fax communication were accepted,[1914] but with the application of the NCPC, the means broadened and now a claim can also be filed by way of an email containing a scan of the claim form or by an electronic document.[1915] In accordance with the national procedural and constitutional rules, the court proceedings need to take place in Romanian.[1916] Based on the provisions of Article 154(6) NCPC, in communicating procedural acts the court is able to use not only postal service and fax but also other means of communication such as e-mail or any other method that would allow transmission of the text and a confirmation of its receipt.[1917]

For a period, some information on the abolition of the exequatur and on the text of the EOP and ESCP Regulations was available on the Ministry of Justice website. Following an update of the website, however, the information is no longer available, nor are details regarding these instruments and their application in Romania. The only reference to the EOP and the ESCP is part of a handbook that appears more appropriate

1911 Government Ordinance No. 5/2001 was repealed by Law No. 76/2012 for the application of Law No. 134/2010 regarding the Code of Civil Procedure from the moment of entrance into force of the new code, 15 February 2013.

1912 Article 94(1) letter k) and Article 95 (1) NCPC. Information on the e-Justice Portal referring to 'letter j' is not correct (https://e-justice.europa.eu/content_european_payment_order-353-ro-en.do?member=1). For payment orders, see Article 1015 NCPC. The District Courts or the Higher General Courts have jurisdiction in EOP cases base on the value of the claim. See Section 6.2.1.

1913 Article 94 point 1 letter k) NCPC. Information on the e-Justice Portal referring to 'letter j' is not correct (https://e-justice.europa.eu/content_small_claims-354-ro-en.do?member=1). See also Section 6.2.1.; Titirigă (2014), at 219.

1914 At the time of notification, Article 82 of old Code of Civil Procedure was interpreted in a broad way. The provision 'any request sent to the courts must be in writing…' did not impose or restrict this to post; hence, fax could also fall within the interpretation of written request. Romania indicated then that the means of communication allowed for the EOP (and later for the ESCP) are mailing and faxing. See Titirigă (2014), at 222–223.

1915 See information communicated to the European Commission available at https://e-justice.europa.eu/content_european_payment_order-353-ro-en.do?member=1 and https://e-justice.europa.eu/content_small_claims-354-ro-en.do?member=1.

1916 Information communicated by Member States in accordance with Article 29 of Regulation (EC) No 1896/2006 of the European Parliament and the Council of 12 December 2006 creating a European order for payment procedure, Consolidated Version, Updated 11.07.2014, at 30 in conjunction with Article 18(1) and (4) NCPC, and Article 128 Constitution.

1917 Popovici (2015), at 278.

for professionals than for laypersons.[1918] General information on the EOP and the ESCP can be found on the ECC Romania website. The existing brochures explain the circumstances in which parties can choose to use these procedures, and they also provide links to the electronic forms of the EOP and the ESCP.[1919] Importantly, most of the information is available in Romanian. For a period of time, detailed brochures on the ESCP and one guide on the European procedures were also available in English.

EOP Aspects

In accordance with the main line of interpretation offered by the legal literature, following an opposition the court establishes a date for the creditor to submit a claim in accordance with the ordinary procedure.[1920] Subsequently, in response, the defendant files a statement of defence.[1921] In accordance with EOP case law, the court informs the claimant of the opposition and of the possibility of submitting a new claim in keeping with the national ordinary procedure,[1922] or requests both parties to deposit written conclusions.[1923]

The review procedure as such is not available in the national legislation. At first, the Ministry of Justice stated that in the event of a request for review of the EOP, the defendant is able to apply for an extension of time needed to lodge an opposition if the reasons leading to this situation are justified.[1924] This can be done by way of *contestaţie la executare* (objection to enforcement proceeding), by which the defendant is able to invoke substantive arguments against the enforcement order, in this case an EOP. Consequently, the court was able to re-examine the EOP for purposes laid down by Article 20 EOP (Review in exceptional cases).[1925] This interpretation extending to the EOP the provision applicable to a national order for payment procedure (in accordance with Government Ordinance No. 5/2001) gave the Romanian judge the power to review the EOP issued by another court during enforcement proceedings. However, this does

1918 'Practical Handbook on European Private International Law', prepared by Kunda & Gonçalvse de Melo Marinho (2010).

1919 On the EOP, see www.eccromania.ro/teme-ecc/proceduri-judiciare-speciale-europene/#1483016720322–5baa27c3–7d68. On the ESCP, see www.eccromania.ro/teme-ecc/proceduri-judiciare-speciale-europene/. ECC Romania also created brochures with general information regarding the EOP and ESCP, see www.eccromania.ro/media/pdf/Somatia_europeana_de_plata.pdf, www.eccromania.ro/media/pdf/procedura_europeana_cereri_valoare_redusa_ro.pdf and www.eccromania.ro/media/pdf/01.Procedura_europeana_privind_cererile_cu_valoare_redusa.pdf.

1920 In accordance with the present Article 194 NCPC, previously Article 112 old Code of Civil Procedure. See Pîrvu (2009), at 155; Cupşan-Morar (2010), at 163. On a contrary interpretation, see Popovici (2015), at 258.

1921 See Section 6.2 on the ordinary court proceedings in Romania.

1922 Judecătoria Sector 3, Bucureşti, Files No. 11606/301/2012, 42193/301/2012; Judecătoria Sector 6, Bucureşti, Files No. 15073/303/2012, 3183/303/2014; Tribunalul Ilfov, File No. 649/93/2013; Tribunalul Comercial Mureş, File No. 509/1371/2012. See also Section 6.7.2.3.

1923 Judecătoria Ploieşti, File No. 34172/281/2012.

1924 Now Article 186 NCPC, previously Article 103 old Code of Civil Procedure.

1925 Information communicated by Member States in accordance with Article 29 of Regulation (EC) No 1896/2006 of the European Parliament and the Council of 12 December 2006 creating a European order for payment procedure, Consolidated Version, Updated 11.07.2014, at 29 (available at http://ec.europa.eu/justice_home/judicialatlascivil/html/pdf/vers_consolide_en_1896.pdf).

not correspond to the aims of the European Regulation or to the purpose of Article 20 EOP.[1926] At present, on the basis of Article 713(1) NCPC, the debtor is no longer able to use *contestaţie la executare* in order to raise substantive or factual arguments that he could previously have invoked by means of opposition or appeal in objecting to a judicial decision subject to enforcement.[1927] The Romanian Government has proceeded to announce new domestic means by which the review can be requested. These are the exceptional appeal methods of *contestaţia în anulare* (the request for annulment) and *revizuirea* (the motion for revision) provided for by the NCPC.[1928] In addition to this, the national order for payment request for annulment of the order is indicated as an applicable means.[1929] However, these means are broader than the scope of the review. As a result, it is considered by some that the only applicable proceeding for handling a request for review involves the provisions of Article 20 EOP supplemented with the rules of the ordinary national procedure provided for by the NCPC.[1930]

ESCP Aspects

During the first years of the ESCP's application, Romania informed the European Commission that a special appeal (*recurs*) could be lodged in accordance with Article 17 ESCP within a period of 15 days from the moment the judgment was communicated to the defendant.[1931] Following the entrance into force of the NCPC (15 February 2013), the present means of challenging the judgment is an appeal (*apel*), and not the previously announced *recurs*.[1932] Thus, on the basis of the NCPC the general appeal proceeding for claims up to a value of RON200,000 (approx. €44,500) is an *apel*.[1933] The appeal can be lodged within a period of 30 days from the date the party received notification of the decision.[1934] The court competent to deal with the request is the High General Court (*tribunal*).[1935] If the claimant is a consumer filing a claim against a legal entity that has breached the consumer's legal rights and interests, no court fees are charged for the handling of the case.[1936]

1926 See also Section 7.4.2. related to the EOP Regulation. Cupşan-Morar (2010), at 165.

1927 This provision is applicable to claims filed after 15 February 2013. See also Gavriş (2013b), at 201–202.

1928 Articles 503–508 NCPC for *contestaţia în anulare* and Articles 509–512 NCDP for *revizuirea*. See also Pîrvu (2009), at 158–159; Popovici (2015), at 263.

1929 Articles 1021–1024 NCPC. The indication of the number of NCPC texts on the e-Justice Portal has not been updated for some time (https://e-justice.europa.eu/content_european_payment_order-353-ro-en.do?member=1).

1930 On a similar interpretation, see Popovici (2015), at 265–266; Pîrvu (2009), at 160.

1931 Previous Article 282^1 Code of Civil Procedure. Information communicated by Member States in accordance with Article 25 of Regulation (EC) No 861/2007 of the European Parliament and the Council of 11 July 2007 establishing a European Small Claims Procedure, Consolidated Version, Updated 08.10.2013, at 40 (available at http://ec.europa.eu/justice_home/judicialatlascivil/html/pdf/vers_consolide_en_861.pdf).

1932 See information on the e-Justice Portal, https://e-justice.europa.eu/content_small_claims-354-ro-en.do?member=1. Titirigă (2014), at 225; Tabacu (2009), at 244.

1933 Article 483(2) final NCPC. Frenţiu (2014), at 22.

1934 Article 468(1)-(2) NCPC.

1935 Article 95 point 3 NCPC. See also Titirigă (2014), at 226.

1936 Article 29(1) letter f) Government Emergency Ordinance No. 80/2013.

As to the review procedure, the same mechanism announced for the EOP should by analogy apply to the ESCP.[1937]

Costs

With regard to court fees applicable for the EOP and the ESCP, the information provided by Romanian authorities on the e-Justice website was for a long period available only in Romanian. The website refers the parties to the general provisions on monetary claims in the Government Emergency Ordinance 80/2013. In accordance with this communication, the level of court fees vary from RON20 (approx. €4.52) for claims with a value up to RON500 (approx. €113) to RON6,105 (approx. €1,381), plus 1% of the amount above the RON250,000 threshold for claims above RON250,000 (approx. €56,561).[1938] In practice, fees that the courts appear to apply to EOP claims mostly mirror the fees established by law for the matching national procedure (the *ordonanța de plată*).[1939] These are a fixed amount, and from 2013 they were increased to RON200 (approx. €45.25).[1940] For the ESCP cases, the court fees range from RON20 (approx. €4.52) for claims up to RON500 (approx. €113) to a maximum of RON1,230 (approx. €273.33) for a claim of €5,000. In the event of an appeal to an ESCP judgment, the court fee is 50% of the fee owed for the contested amount, but not less than RON20 (approx. €4.52).[1941]

The fees can be paid in cash at the Tax Authority Office in the place of domicile or residence of the natural person, at the headquarters of the legal person, or by wire transfer into a special account called *Taxe judiciare de timbre și alte taxe de timbru* (in English: Judiciary stamp fees and other stamp fees)[1942] belonging to the territorial administration. If the party is resident in another country, he needs to make the payment into the account corresponding to the administrative territorial unit where the court is situated.[1943] However, this is only a partial solution to the problem for a claimant resident abroad. The

1937 See Hess (2017), Chapter 5 para. 896.

1938 Article 3(1) Government Emergency Ordinance No. 80/2013. Doctrine perceives the court fees level to be rather excessive. Information on EOP court fees in Romania is available at https://e-justice.europa.eu/content_court_fees_concerning_european_payment_order_procedure-305-ro-en.do?clang=ro. Information regarding court fees for ESCP in Romania are available at https://e-justice.europa.eu/content_court_fees_concerning_small_claims_procedure-306-ro-en.do?clang=ro.

1939 Some authors favour this interpretation, considering the fact that the national legislation has not established an express level of court fees for the EOP and the ESCP. See Pîrvu (2009), at 155; Popovici (2015), at 268. For the practice approach, see Sections 6.7.2.5 and 6.7.3.4.

1940 Article 6(2) Government Emergency Ordinance No. 80/2013.

1941 Article 23(1) letter (b) in conjunction with Article 3(1) Government Emergency Ordinance No. 80/2013.

1942 Article 40(1) Government Emergency Ordinance No. 80/2013. The information was made available by Romania also on the e-Justice Portal for the EOP and ESCP. However, it is only available in Romanian at the moment: https://e-justice.europa.eu/content_court_fees_concerning_european_payment_order_procedure-305-ro-ro.do?member=1 and https://e-justice.europa.eu/content_court_fees_concerning_small_claims_procedure-306-ro-ro.do?member=1. Details of the relevant accounts are available on the portal dedicated to courts http://portal.just.ro/SitePages/acasa.aspx. Choose the court that will receive the claim in the EOP or the ESCP proceedings, and then go to the '*Bine de știut*' or '*Informații de interes public*' sections, where the relevant information is provided for parties. However, in this case as well, the information is available only in Romanian.

1943 Article 40(2) Government Emergency Ordinance No. 80/2013.

party still needs to identify the appropriate payment details corresponding to the court having jurisdiction. This might be difficult for a party not speaking Romanian, as the information on a court's portal is only available in Romanian. And although web pages dedicated to the courts have the same format and section names, they are not consistent when it comes to publishing the information in the same sections.[1944] Furthermore, although the law allows the electronic payment of court fees, the system is not yet operational. Once it is functioning, however, it will simplify the process of court payments significantly for non-resident parties.

6.6. Enforcement in Romania: From National to European Judgments

The enforcement of judicial decisions in Romania is carried out in accordance with the provisions of the NCPC and the laws and regulations regarding bailiffs. This section provides an overview of the main characteristics of these enforcement proceedings, considering the applicable rules, the professionals involved in the process, and the costs entailed for the parties. The second part focuses on execution of the EOP and the ESCP, examining specific aspects of their execution and amendments introduced by Law No. 138/2014, Government Emergency Ordinance No. 1/2016, and Law No. 17/2017.

6.6.1. Main Aspects regarding the Execution of Judicial Decisions

Provisions regarding the enforcement of judicial decisions are part of Book V of the NCPC. The rules regard the enforceable title; the initiation of execution proceedings if the debtor does not voluntarily comply with the judgment or order issued by the court; the suspension, the limitation, and the termination of enforcement; and the means of enforcement the creditor may choose for this purpose.[1945] The laws and regulations concerning the activity of bailiffs complete the legal framework. They focus on the bailiffs' competence in execution proceedings, on the organising of their professional activity, their rights, their duties and responsibilities, and on the minimum and maximum level of fees that bailiffs can request for their services.[1946]

Enforcement proceedings are carried out at the place where the debtor obtains revenues or the place where the revenues or the assets subject to execution are situated.[1947] This may be accomplished by any of the means provided for by law, simultaneously or in a successive manner, until collection of the entire debt, due interest, penalties or other amounts awarded, including the costs of the execution has been completed.[1948] These means include:

1944 Sometimes information regarding the corresponding Tax Authority Account is provided in the section 'Information of Public Interest' (*Informații de interes public*) or in the 'Good to Know' section (*Bine de știut*) on the http://portal.just.ro/SitePages/acasa.aspx. See also Hess (2017), Chapter 5 para. 903.

1945 Articles 622–914 NCPC.

1946 Law No. 188/2000 regarding bailiffs, republished, Official Gazette of Romania No. 738/20 October 2011, further supplemented and amended. Regulation for the application of Law No. 188/2000 regarding bailiffs.

1947 Article 683 NCPC.

1948 Article 622(3) NCPC.

- seizure of the debtor's assets (*sechestrarea bunurilor mobile*);[1949]
- attachment of the debtor's real estate property (*urmărirea silită a bunurilor imobile*);[1950]
- garnishment of earnings, of bank accounts, of intangible assets, and of amounts owed by third parties (*poprire*);[1951] and
- attachment of immovable assets (*urmărirea silită a fructelor și a veniturilor imobilelor*).[1952]

The creditor may decide on the means of execution to use based on the information he has or has obtained from the bailiff on the debtor's assets. In certain circumstances, the means chosen may be subject to limitations by law (e.g. the extent of the income that can be subject to enforcement, commonly owned assets).[1953]

The bailiffs have exclusive competence for all execution activities.[1954] In accordance with Article 627 NCPC, they must play an active role in the execution process, persevering through all available legal means in order to obtain speedy and full payment of the debt. For this purpose, bailiffs can request the debtor in writing to provide clarifications regarding his income and assets. They can also seek to persuade him to execute the judgment voluntarily by pointing to the consequences of a forced execution procedure and the estimated costs it would imply. The unjustified refusal of the debtor to provide the necessary or requested clarifications, or the provision in bad faith of incomplete information, can be sanctioned with a judiciary fine between RON100 and RON1,000 (approx. €22.62 to 226.24).[1955] Furthermore, the state through its agents (i.e. Public Ministry, police) has a duty to ensure an effective and swift execution of the judicial decision.[1956]

The bailiff has the right to request and obtain data and information regarding the debtor and his assets from public institutions, credit institutions and any other natural or legal person, including tax authorities.[1957] If the parties have no knowledge of the assets, or refuse to cooperate, the public prosecutor, upon the bailiff's request, takes the steps necessary to obtain information related to bank accounts, deposits, financial

1949 Articles 731–752 NCPC on the seizure of assets, and Articles 753–780 NCPC on the selling of assets and subsequently obtaining payment of the debt.

1950 Articles 813–863 NCPC.

1951 Articles 781–794 NCPC. *Poprirea* is carried out by the bailiff without a notice of performance (*somație*) being sent prior to enforcement. See further Dinu & Stanciu (2015), at 278–301.

1952 This type of attachment concerns the unpicked fruits and harvest of crops (Articles 795–799 NCPC), and the income generated by immovables owned by the debtor (Articles 800–812 NCPC). See further Dinu & Stanciu (2015), at 301–317.

1953 Article 629 in conjunction with Article 727 (assets that cannot be subject to enforcement), Article 728 (assets that can be subject to execution only for particular debts), Article 729 (the limits of garnishing income), and Article 813–818 (immovable property) NCPC.

1954 Article 623 NCPC.

1955 Article 627(3) in conjunction with Article 188(2) NCPC. The fine is established by the president of the court of enforcement upon the bailiff's request.

1956 Article 626 in conjunction with Article 658 and Article 659 NCPC. See also Gavriş (2016), at 355–356; Dinu & Stanciu (2015), at 88–89 and 92–94. On the participation of the agents of the state upon the bailiff's request in case of an opposition to execution, see Article 682 NCPC.

1957 Article 660(1)-(2) NCPC. See Dinu & Stanciu (2015), at 61–63.

instruments, or other property that might be subject to execution.[1958] For enforcement purposes, the bailiffs have free access to data registered in the land registry, the commercial registry, and other public registries.[1959]

If the exact amount of interest, penalties, or other amounts is not mentioned expressly in the enforcement title, the bailiff calculates it.[1960] Additionally, upon the creditor's request the bailiff may update the value of the principal according to the criteria contained in the enforcement title, or in accordance with the rate of inflation at the moment the judgment became enforceable if the title does not provide for such criteria.[1961] During the execution proceedings, the creditor and the debtor may agree, under supervision of the bailiff, to the enforcement being carried out, entirely or partly, on the income of the debtor or any other of his assets, or that the selling of immovables is to be done by common agreement (*bună învoială*) of the parties.[1962]

To initiate enforcement proceedings, the interested party must obtain a certified copy of the judgment, which is issued by the court's clerk within a maximum period of three days from the moment it is requested.[1963] A decision that is an enforceable title, but that might still be challenged through an appeal or a second appeal, can be executed at the risk of the creditor, who is held liable for damages. The bailiff receiving the request has three days to demand the enforcement court to issue a writ of execution (*încuviințarea executării silite*). The court is required to issue it within a period of seven days and to communicate it *ex officio* to the bailiff.[1964] The bailiff serves the writ of execution on the debtor together with the enforceable title and a notice of performance (*somație*).[1965] The execution is initiated only after the period set in the notice of performance has lapsed.[1966]

The court competent to decide upon matters related to the execution process (e.g. to receive objection to enforcement – *contestație la executare*)[1967] is the one located where the debtor has his domicile or premises. If these are situated abroad, the competent court is the one within the jurisdiction where the creditor has his domicile or headquarters,

1958 Article 660(3) NCPC. This is no longer possible because the provision was declared unconstitutional. Constitutional Court, Decision No. 473/2013.

1959 Article 660(4) NCPC. The information obtained may be used only for the procedure for which it was requested. See also Dinu & Stanciu (2015), at 63.

1960 Article 628(2) NCPC. Dinu & Stanciu (2015), at 13.

1961 Article 628(3) NCPC. The reason for this update is to maintain the value of the award. The update of the principal can be made by the bailiff irrespective of the existence in the award of a due amount of interest, penalties, or other similar sums. See Boroi & Theohari (2014), at XXI; Dinu & Stanciu (2015), at 13–14.

1962 Article 630 NCPC.

1963 See Theohari, Ilie, Bîrlog & Cristea (2012), at 260–261.

1964 Article 666(1)-(2) NCPC. The need to obtain a writ of execution for proceeding to enforcement has been amended several times. During 2014–2016, no court decision regarding the issuance of a writ of execution was necessary (Law No. 138/2014 amending and supplementing Law No. 134/2010 regarding the Code of Civil Procedure, as well as the amendment and supplementing of certain connected normative acts, Official Gazette of Romania No. 753/16 October 2014). This was reintroduced by Government Emergency Ordinance No. 1/2016 for the amendment of Law No. 134/2010 regarding the Code of Civil Procedure, as well as other connected legislative acts (Official Gazette of Romania No. 85/4 February 2016).

1965 Article 667 and Article 668 NCPC.

1966 Article 673 NCPC.

1967 For further details, see Lucaciuc (2014).

unless he is also situated abroad. In this case, the competence is retained by the court within the jurisdiction where the office of the bailiff is situated.[1968]

The costs of enforcement are established by the bailiff and are incumbent upon the debtor.[1969] However, the party requesting the enforcement acts or activities has a duty to advance the necessary expenses.[1970] The costs of enforcement proceedings vary, based on the level of fees set by each bailiff and the amount of the debt. However, their maximum level is established by law. For example, for money claims below RON50,000 (approx. €11,312.22) subject to enforcement proceedings, the fees are a maximum of 10% of the value of the debt, thus maximum RON5,000 (approx. €1,131.22). For debts above RON100,000 (approx. €22,624.43), the maximum enforcement fees the bailiff can charge are RON6,300 (approx. €1,425.34) plus 1% of the amount above the RON100,000 threshold.[1971] Furthermore, the NCPC provides a list of enforcement expenses. In accordance with Article 670(3) NCPC, these include (1) the stamp fees requested for initiating the enforcement proceedings; (2) the bailiff's fees; (3) the lawyer's fees related to enforcement; (4) the expert's, the translator's, and the interpreter's fees; (5) the expenses related to the publicity of the execution procedure and the carrying out of enforcement acts; (6) the transport costs; and (7) other expenses established by law or necessary for carrying out the enforcement. If an objection to enforcement (*contestație la executare*) is filed, the party filing it needs to pay a court fee that is calculated on the basis of the value of the assets whose execution is contested, or the value of the debt if this is lower than the value of the assets. However, it cannot be higher than RON1,000 (approx. €226.24).[1972]

6.6.2. *Executing EOP and ESCP Judgments*

In executing EOP and/or ESCP decisions issued by courts of other Member States, minimum formalities are necessary in Romania. If the EOP or the ESCP is issued by a Romanian court, the claimant needs to request the court to issue a certified copy of the order or of the judgment in order to proceed to enforcement. For this purpose, the interested party needs to pay a fee of RON5 (approx. €1.31), and submit proof of payment.[1973] The clerk's office issues the certified copy within three working days.[1974] If

1968 Article 651 NCPC. The courts are not all competent at the same time, and there is no right of free choice for the creditor. He has to follow the order of competence established by Article 651. See Boroi & Theohari (2014), at XXVI-XXVII; Dinu & Stanciu (2015), at 63–65.

1969 Article 670(2) NCPC. If the bailiff cannot recover the costs of enforcement from the debtor due to his financial status and lack of assets subject to enforcement, the creditor will bear them (excluding the bailiff fees). The creditor will be able to recover them when the financial status of the debtor allows it, within the prescribed period (Article 670(5) NCPC). In accordance with Article 39(3) of Law No. 188/2000, the bailiff cannot execute a decision on the condition of an anticipated payment of his fees. See also Gavriș (2016a), at 438–439; Dinu & Stanciu (2015), at 111–115.

1970 Article 670(1) NCPC.

1971 Article 39(1) Government Emergency Ordinance No. 80/2013.

1972 Article 10(2) Government Emergency Ordinance No. 80/2013. If the challenge concerns aspects that cannot be ascribed a value, the court fee will be RON100 (€22.62).

1973 Article 9 letter (l) Government Emergency Ordinance No. 80/2013.

1974 See Theohari, Ilie, Bîrlog & Cristea (2012), at 260–261.

the party is not resident or domiciled in Romania, or has no representative there, this may lead to difficulties, as the document needs to be picked up from the Court' Archive Office.

The creditor has to file a request with the bailiff (*executor judecătoresc*), who acts within the jurisdiction of the court where the execution measures are to be carried out,[1975] and the request must include all the relevant documents that justify it. For the EOP, these are a certified copy of Form E and the Declaration of enforceability (Form G), together with a certified translation of the EOP in Romanian if necessary;[1976] and for the ESCP, a certified copy of the judgment and the Certificate concerning judgment in the ESCP (Form D), together with a certified translation in Romanian if necessary.[1977] Moreover, the NCPC establishes that the request has to contain information on the identity and domicile or headquarters of the debtor and creditor, the goods or type of performance due, and the means of execution the creditor wishes to use.[1978] The bailiff authorised to conduct execution proceedings of an EOP or an ESCP may be a different one, depending upn the type of assets on which enforcement will be carried out and the domicile or headquarters of the debtor.[1979]

As soon as he receives the request for enforcement, the bailiff registers it and proceeds to request the court to issue a writ of execution (*încuviințarea executării silite*).[1980] This allows the creditor to request the competent bailiff to use – simultaneously or successively – all the enforcement methods available until the debt has been paid in full, including the costs of enforcement.[1981] The bailiff communicates a copy of the resolution to the

1975 For the means by which the request can be submitted, see Article 664(1)-(2) NCPC. Dinu & Stanciu (2015), at 98–99.

1976 Article 21(1) and (2) EOP in conjunction with Article 664(4) NCPC.

1977 Article 21(1) and (2) ESCP in conjunction with Article 664(4) NCPC.

1978 Article 664(3) NCPC.

1979 Article 652 in conjunction with Article 653(4) NCPC. The bailiff competent to carry out enforcement activities is the one whose offices are within the jurisdiction of the Court of Appeal where the domicile or headquarters of the debtor are, or where the assets are, if the execution assets are movables. The law establishes an alternative competence, and the creditor has the possibility of choosing. If the debtor is domiciled or has his headquarters abroad, this no longer constitutes a difficulty for the (foreign) creditor, as any Romanian bailiff is competent to initiate enforcement proceedings upon his request. The bailiff competent to handle the request is the one located within the jurisdiction of the Court of Appeal where the immovables are situated if the execution concerns immovable assets. The bailiff in charge of the execution proceedings retains competence if the domicile of the debtor or its headquarters changes. Neveretheless, if the bailiff handling the execution comes to the conclusion that there are no assets (movable or immovable) within the territory on which he can exercise his powers, the creditor may submit a request to the judge of execution demanding the file be transferred to another bailiff who can continue the execution.

1980 Article 665 and Article 666 NCPC.

1981 Article 666(4) NCPC. For example, if the garnishment of a debtor's bank account (*poprire*) does not produce sufficient funds to cover the EOP or the ESCP debt, the bailiff may subsequently seize one of the party's assets (*sechestrarea bunurilor mobile*), such as a car. Following the selling procedure, if the amounts due are fully recovered, the enforcement ends and the remaining amount is transferred by the bailiff to the debtor. If the sum obtained is still not sufficient to cover the debt, the bailiff can successively proceed with another means of enforcement. Alternatively, the bailiff may proceed from the beginning to use various methods simultaneously: for example, attaching the real estate assets of the company subject to enforcement together with the garnishment of the bank accounts of the legal entity and the amounts owed by third parties. If the amounts owed by third parties are sufficient to cover the amount

defendant, together with a certified copy of the enforceable EOP or ESCP and a notice of performance (*somaţie*).[1982] If the debtor is not served with the title and the notice of performance, the execution is null.[1983] Execution proceedings are initiated only after the notice period has lapsed[1984] if the debtor did not pay the debt voluntarily.[1985] As previously mentioned, if the creditor does not have exact information on the financial situation of the debtor, the bailiff needs to obtain it in order to proceed to enforcement.[1986]

According to Romanian law, the parties may challenge EOP or ESCP enforcement proceedings (*contestaţie la executare*) with the enforcement court.[1987] This may concern the execution process itself, any act of execution, the conclusions of the enforcement judge, the refusal of the bailiff to enforce or carry out an enforcement act, and, if necessary, clarifications regarding the meaning, extent, and application of the enforceable title.[1988] The procedure may be filed within a period of 15 days from the moment the person contesting it became aware of the execution act, the interested party was served with the attachment order, or the debtor received the conclusions approving the enforcement or the notice of performance. The procedure is handled in accordance with the rules applicable to the ordinary procedure,[1989] and it is subject to appeal,[1990] during which the court may stay the execution. The court competent to stay or limit execution in Romania is the one within the jurisdiction where the enforcement measures are undertaken.[1991] Generally, a stay of execution of the EOP or the ESCP by the court upon the party's request is conditional on the provision of a security deposit,[1992] which is calculated based on the value of the debt challenged or subject to review. The security

due, the attachment will be lifted for the rest of the assets; if not, the execution will continue on the other property. The Declaration of enforceability may be subject to control by *contestaţie la executare* (objection to enforcement) submitted to the enforcement court (Article 666(6) NCPC). On costs of enforcement provisions and the means of execution that can be chosen, see Section 6.6.1.

1982 Article 667(1) NCPC. Article 675(1) establishes that the debtor can not benefit from a notice of performance if (1) he fails to comply with his duties resulting from the enforcement proceedings; (2) he scatters his wealth to keep it hidden; (3) he is in a state of insolvency or he diminishes the guarantees given to his creditor; or (4) he is subject to enforcement proceedings from other creditors.

1983 Article 667(2) NCPC.

1984 If the execution is carried out by means of garnishment of earnings, of bank accounts, of intangible assets, and of amounts owed by third parties (*poprire*), the debtor will only subsequently receive a copy of the garnishment order, the approval of enforcement measures, and the enforcement title (Article 783(1) NCPC).

1985 Article 673 NCPC.

1986 See Section 6.6.1.

1987 Article 714 NCPC.

1988 Article 712(1)-(2) NCPC. The court competent to issue clarifications regarding the enforceable title is the court that issues it if this is a Romanian court (Article 713(3) NCPC). See further Dinu & Stanciu (2015), at 176–186; Popovici (2015), at 269–273.

1989 Article 717 NCPC.

1990 Article 718 NCPC.

1991 Article 651 and Article 652 NCPC corresponding to previous Article 373 Code of Civil Procedure, as notified by the Romanian authorities. Information available at https://e-justice.europa.eu/content_small_claims-354-ro-en.do?member=1.

1992 According to an opinion in the literature, this duty is not applicable if stay or limitation is requested in exceptional circumstances (Article 23 c) EOP). See Popovici (2015), at 274.

ranges between 10% of the value of the claim if this is below RON10,000 (approx. €2,262.44) and RON14,500 (approx. €3,280.54) plus 0.1% for the amount that is above the RON1,000,000 threshold (approx. €226,244.34).[1993] Thus, in the event of a stay of enforcement proceedings in ESCP cases, the maximum amount of security will be approx. RON1,625 (about €361), an amount that appears reasonable. Together with the security deposit, a court fee of RON50 (€11.31) is required to be paid.[1994] Furthermore, the enforcement acts and the measures of preservation of the assets, incomes, and bank accounts undertaken or carried out prior to a contestation are maintained, unless otherwise decided.[1995] This provision appears to have broader implications than Article 23(a) EOP and Article 23(a) ESCP, which set that the enforcement proceedings are limited to 'protective measures', although the court of enforcement has the freedom to consider and to dispose accordingly on the measures to be maintained.

EOP or ESCP enforcement costs are influenced by the number of services or notifications the bailiff is required to carry out during the proceedings, and the type of execution means applied, but their minimum and maximum levels are, as previously mentioned, set by law.[1996]

6.7. The EOP and the ESCP in Practice

This section analyses the way in which the EOP and the ESCP function in Romania. The first part is dedicated to the statistics available on the use of the European uniform procedures, while the second part focuses on an analysis of the data provided by identified national case law. The last part of the analysis concentrates on the empirical findings, and triangulates results with data from the first two parts if these are available.

6.7.1. Available Statistical Data

The annual statistics reports concerning the activity of the judiciary in Romania published by the Ministry of Justice in Romania contain no information on application of the EOP and the ESCP. The International Law and Treaties Direction of the Ministry of Justice did not respond to requests for information regarding the use of these two European procedures.[1997] The data analysed in this section were provided by the Statistics Office of the Superior Council of Magistracy (*Consiliul Superior al Magistraturii*), and the information concerns only EOP cases. This partial data became available because this European procedure was allocated a special code in the courts' registration system, ECRIS, which made EOP cases easier to trace for the period 2011–2014.

1993 Article 719(2) NCPC.

1994 Article 10(1) letter b) Government Emergency Ordinance No. 80/2013.

1995 Article 701(3) NCPC. Acts of execution undertaken the same day that the request for stay of enforcement is decided upon by the court are invalidated (*desființate de drept*), based on the provisions of Article 701(4) NCPC.

1996 Order of the Ministry of Justice No. 2550/C/2006 published in the Official Gazette of Romania No. 936/20 November 2006. For the minimum and maximum level of fees, see the Annex of the Order.

1997 The researcher contacted the Director of the International Law and Treaties Direction by email on 16 October 2014, and the legal counsellor on 26 January 2015.

Regulation EOP

The EOP quantitative data is available together with information regarding the national procedures of *ordonanța de plată* and the *procedura cu privire la cererile de valoare redusă*. Table 6.2 provides information on the number of cases handled by Romanian courts since 2011.

The EOP information is divided between civil and commercial claims registered by the courts heaving jurisdiction in this area, the District Courts (DC), or the Higher General Courts (GC). Unfortunately, the set of data available on the EOP does not make a difference between the claims requesting the issuance of an EOP and applications for the delivery of a writ of execution (*încuviințarea executării silite*) for enforcement purposes.[1998] Creditors needed to obtain such a declaration of enforceability up until the amendment of the NCPC on 16 October 2014 and again from 5 February 2016. For statistical reasons, a difference between the two types of EOP applications would have been useful and desirable. The published case law gives some indication on the matter, but no sound data could be retrieved by the Statistics Office.

From the available statistics, it appears that all EOP cases are commercial – hence, they involve professionals. This is in fact not always the case, as can be seen in Section 6.7.2, though the B2B format is predominant in case law. One likely explanation of the manner the data is registered is linked to the way the EOP code was established. In the ECRIS system, the EOP code is part of the litigation between professionals (*Litigii cu profesioniștii – somația europeană de plată*), and is not included in civil case codes where at least one of the parties is not a professional.

	2011				2012				2013				2014			
	DC civ	*DC com*	*GC civ*	*GC com*	*DC civ*	*DC com*	*GC civ*	*GC com*	*DC civ*	*DC com*	*GC civ*	*GC com*	*DC civ*	*DC com*	*GC civ*	*GC com*
EOP	–	29	–	6	–	86	–	35	–	176	–	45	–	157	–	40
Ordonanța de plată	26,452	48,680	87	2,519	33,193	46,502	83	1,166	9,149	8,742	25	284	1,482	223	11	78
Cererile de valoare redusă	n/a	n/a	n/a	n/a	n/a	n/a	n/a	n/a	27,488	–	0	–	50,461	–	4	–

Table 6.2. Number of cases received by Romanian District Courts (DC) and Higher General Courts (GC) in civil (civ.) and commercial (com.) cases according to statistics provided by the Superior Council of Magistracy[1999]

1998 With the coming into force of Law No. 138/2014 on 19 October 2014, a writ of execution was no longer needed for the execution of enforceable judgments initiated after that date. Following the 2014 modification of the NCPC, the courts only handled requests for the issuance of EOP and ESCP judgments and objections to enforcement – *contestație la executare* – if the case. Subsequently, by way of Government Emergency Ordinance No. 1/2016, the requirement of a writ of execution issued by the court was reintroduced. The approval of the enforcement proceedings applied between 15 February 2013 and 21 October 2014, and again after 5 February 2016.

1999 Information on the number of cases was provided by the Office of Judicial Statistics of the Superior Council of Magistracy on 19 November 2014.

On an annual basis the information provided by the Superior Council of Magistracy can be read as follows:

	2011	2012	2013	2014
EOP	35	121	221	197
Ordonanţa de plată	77,738	80,944	19,236	1,794
Cereri de valoare redusă	n/a	n/a	27,488	50,465

Table 6.3. Consolidated annual data on the number of EOPs, Ordonanţa de plată, and Cereri de valoare redusă according to statistics provided by the Superior Council of Magistracy (2011–2014)

The clerk receiving an EOP application has two options: to register the request as a litigation between professionals even if only one party is a legal entity, or to register it under another code such as, for example, the national order for payment.[2000] Of course, this seems to create distortions with respect to the accuracy of statistical data, with possibly some C2C or C2B/B2C cases being lost in the registration process.

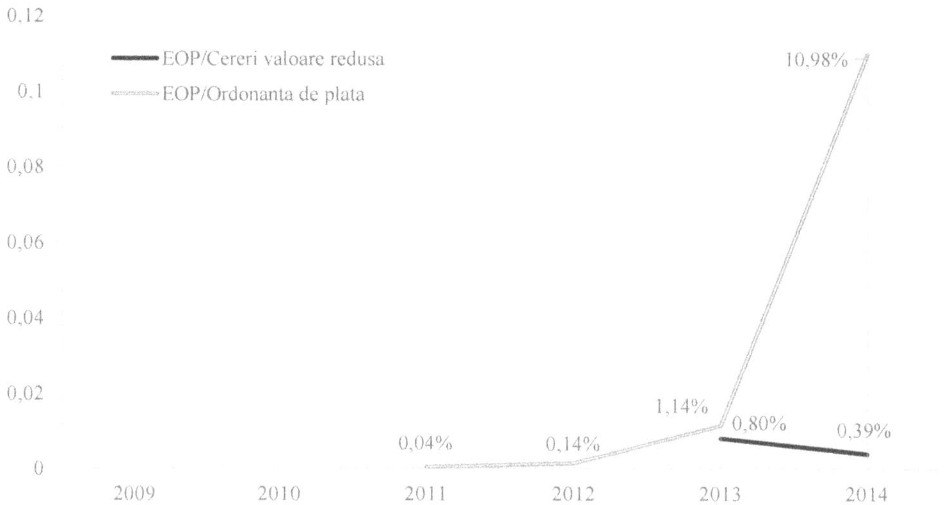

Fig. 6.1. Evolution of EOP cases in comparison to the *Ordonanţa de plată* and *Cereri de valoare redusă*

Looking at the aggregated numbers of cases (Fig. 6.1), EOPs represented barely 0.04% and 0.14% of the *Ordonanţa de plată* cases in 2011 and 2012, respectively. Following the entrance into force of the NCPC, the number of national order for payment procedures dropped, possibly also under the influence of the newly introduced small value claims procedure, which became immediately popular with parties and courts. Use of the EOP as opposed to the *Ordonanţa de plată* cases continued to grow, while use of the latter

[2000] On the way the EOP claims are registered, see Section 6.7.2.

decreased. Thus, in 2013 the EOP represented 1.14% of the national order for payment procedure cases and 0.80% of the small value claims, while in 2014 it reached 10.98% of the *Ordonanța de plată* to cases. The outcome is partly also a consequence of the fact that the national order for payment procedure is employed less often than in previous years. The situation is completely opposite in comparison to the *Cereri de valoare redusă*, where it decreased to 0.39%. The national procedure registered a more significant increase in the number of cases filed, which points to a particular preference for this instrument.

Regulation ESCP
Quantitative data on the use of the ESCP in Romania were not available from the Statistics Office of the *Consiliul Superior al Magistraturii*. This is partly due to the lack of a specific code for this procedure in the ECRIS system. Consequently, it is more difficult to trace the relevant cases, as they are registered under various codes.[2001] Section 6.7.2 provides only an indication of what the ESCP claims are in Romania, and the information provided cannot be generalised. In the future, it would be desirable to establish a specific ESCP registration code. This would also allow the Council to gather ESCP statistics, which would be valuable to analyse developments related to the use and application of this European procedure.

6.7.2. *Case Law*

6.7.2.1. Quantitative Data regarding Case Law

Information with regard to cases filed with the Romanian courts is public. The Portal of the Romanian Court provides information on EOP and ESCP claims and selected case law in the sections dedicated to Files (*Dosare*) and to Case Law (*Jurisprudenta*). The Case Law section assembles cases selected by the courts on the basis of their significance for the practice, the particularity of the problem they pose, and the originality of the solution adopted. They include complex cases or claims applying the new procedures. The Files section is set to provide information on all claims submitted to Romanian courts. However, the outcome of research on the EOP procedure differs from the quantitative data provided by the Superior Council of Magistracy (Table 6.4).

An examination of the data regarding cases available in the Files section make it immediately clear that EOP and ESCP claims are not always registered under the same code. The EOP has its own registration code, *Somația europeană de plată* (European Order for Payment), under the subject matter *Litigii cu profesioniști* (Litigation between professional parties); nonetheless, the claims are also registered under other codes such as *Ordonanță de plată* (Order for Payment),[2002] *Ordonanță președințială somația europeană de plată* (Order of the President of the Court European Order for Payment),[2003] *Somație de plată* (Notice/Order to pay),[2004] *Cerere cu valoare redusă* (Small Value Claim),[2005] *Pretenții*

[2001] On the way the ESCP claims are registered, see Section 6.7.2.
[2002] Judecătoria Arad, File No. 4112/55/2009.
[2003] Judecătoria Galați, File No. 14433/233/2011.
[2004] Judecătoria Hunedoara, File No. 7608/97/2011.
[2005] Judecătoria Târgu Cărbunești, File No. 1463/317/2014.

(Claims),[2006] and *Cerere necontencioasă somaţie europeană de plată* (Non-disputed claim European Order for Payment).[2007] This situation affects the research results.

EOP Data	2009	2010	2011	2012	2013	2014
Statistics-Superior Council of Magistracy	–	–	35	121	221	197
Portal. Just.ro	6	16	13	49	30	20

Table 6.4. Quantitative data on the EOP cases handled by Romanian courts according to the statistics provided by the Council of Magistracy in comparison to a study conducted on the Portal of the Romanian Courts

Further, ESCP claims are usually registered under the same identification code as the national small claims procedure (*Cerere cu valoare redusă*), which came into force in 2013. The inconsistent manner in which the claims are registered has a negative effect on the possibility of accurately identifying all the relevant case law in this area of cross-border litigation.

According to the number of cases identified on the Romanian *Judiciary Portal*, the EOP procedure is used much more frequently than the ESCP, with 249 EOP cases against nine ESCPs.[2008] On an annual basis, they are distributed as follows:

	2009	2010	2011	2012	2013	2014	2015
EOP	6	17	12	47	30	20	117
ESCP	2	0	2	1	1	0	3

Table 6.5. Annual distribution of EOP and ESCP cases as identified on the Judiciary Portal

They represent a mix of decisions on merits, requests for a writ of execution, and registrations of the enforceable title in an opened insolvency proceeding. The earliest decisions regarding both European procedures date back to 2009, and the courts handling EOP and ESCP claims are spread around the entire country. On a regional level, the 249 EOP cases identified are distributed as follows: 78 in Bucharest,[2009] 79 in

[2006] Judecătoria Sector 6, Bucureşti, File No. 15073/303/2012.

[2007] Judecătoria Sector 6, Bucureşti, File No. 28294/303/2011.

[2008] http://portal.just.ro/SitePages/acasa.aspx.

[2009] Judecătoria Sector 1, Bucureşti, Files No. 44676/299/2010, 50506/299/2012, 45573/299/2012, 60460/299/2012, 1281/299/2013, 1912/299/2013, 2203/299/2013, 5584/299/2013, 10989/299/2013, 50927/299/2013, 2323/299/2014, 32436/299/2014, 34756/299/2014, 45497/299/2014, 55900/299/2014, 122578/299/2015, 106612/299/2015, 42328/299/2015, 42329/299/2015, 42330/299/2015, 72435/299/2015, 82509/299/2015, 94288/299/2015, Decision No. 10700/02.06.2011; Judecătoria Sector 2, Bucureşti, Files No. 41968/300/2010, 38390/300/2010, 37136/300/2012, 71372/300/2015; Judecătoria Sector 3, Bucureşti, Files No. 40753/301/2011, 11606/301/2012, 38699/301/2012, 41477/301/2012, 42193/301/2012, 46119/301/2014, 57080/301/2014, 19381/301/2015, 19546/301/2015, 23798/301/2015, 24063/301/2015, 24066/301/2015; Judecătoria Sector 4, Bucureşti, Files No. 30550/4/2012, 10512/4/2014, 10551/4/2015, 10691/4/2015, 28251/4/2015, 38750/4/2015, 28253/4/2015, 28252/4/2015, 36238/4/2015; Judecătoria Sector 5, Bucureşti, Files No. 571/302/2009, 14067/302/2010, 21602/302/2010, 17915/302/2012, 38461/3/2012, 29847/302/2012, 21174/302/2014, 3700/302/2015; Judecătoria Sector 6, Bucureşti, Files

Transylvania,[2010] 53 in Wallachia and Dobrogea,[2011] and 39 in Moldova.[2012] Compared to the rest of the country, most EOP cases have been handled by courts in Bucharest and

No. 24931/303/2010, 28294/303/2011, 15073/303/2012, 14521/303/23013, 3183/303/2014; Tribunalul Bucureşti, Section VI, Files No. 23767/3/2009, 35668/3/2009, 12119/3/2010, 25382/3/2010, 56470/3/2010, 4088/3/2012, 25513/3/2013, 41220/3/2013, 14946/3/2014, 3427/3/2015, 10998/3/2015, 18247/3/2015, 35507/3/2015, 47366/3/2015, 42752/3/2015; Bucharest Court of Appeal, Decision No. 48/12 April 2012.

2010 Tribunalul Alba, Files No. 6327/107/2009 (no EOP was issued; the parties reached an agreement and the case was closed), 17/107/2009; Judecătoria Arad, Files No. 4112/55/2009, 13428/55/2011, 11881/55/2012, 16976/55/2013, 15348/55/2015, 12617/55/2015; Tribunalul Arad, File No. 1823/108/2010 (registration of an EOP issued in Italy as an enforceable title in an insolvency proceeding); Judecătoria Aiud, File No. 736/175/2015; Judecătoria Baia Mare, Files No. 4210/182/2015, 7391/182/2015, 7621/182/2015; Tribunalul Bihor, File No. 1782/111/2011; Judecătoria Bistriţa, File No. 1805/190/2013; Judecătoria Braşov, Files No. 12442/197/2011, 31929/197/2012; Judecătoria Cluj-Napoca, Files No. 19686/211/2010, 22003/211/2012, 8589/211/2013, 20459/211/2015, 22479/211/2015; Tribunalul Specializat Cluj, Files No. 177/1285/2015, 705/1285/2015, 1086/1285/2015; Judecătoria Gheorgheni, Files No. 2108/234/2015, 1176/234/2015, 1188/234/2015; Tribunalul Harghita, Files No. 3807/96/2012, 4144/96/2012; Tribunalul Hunedoara, Files No. 7608/97/2011, 1296/97/2013, 7672/97/2013, 1124/97/2015, 1315/97/2015, 1554/97/2015, 1722/97/2015, 1723/97/2015, 2077/97/2015, 2696/97/2015, 2703/97/2015, 2693/97/2015, 3013/97/2015, 4413/97/2015, 4082/97/2015; Judecătoria Lugoj, File No. 863/252/2013; Judecătoria Miercurea Ciuc, File No. 3481/258/2012; Tribunalul commercial Mureş, Files No. 509/1371/2012, 331/1371/2014, 598/1371/2014, 301/1371/2015, 760/1371/2015; Judecătoria Năsăud, Files No. 1058/265/2012, 319/265/2013; Judecătoria Odorheiul Secuiesc, File No. 3086/268/2015; Judecătoria Oradea, Files No. 20531/271/2010, 22655/271/2010, 808/271/2012, 18033/271/2013, 3148/271/2015, 3349/271/2015, 9062/271/2015; Judecătoria Oraviţa, File No. 1481/273/2012; Judecătoria Reşiţa, File No. 2895/290/2015; Judecătoria Salonta, File No. 1491/833/2015; Judecătoria Sibiu, Files No. 8064/306/2015, 8246/306/2015; Judecătoria Şimpleul Silvaniei, Files No. 1735/309/2012, 1544/309/2013; Judecătoria Târgu Mureş, Files No. 5756/320/2015, 6293/320/2015; Judecătoria Timişoara, Files No. 14586/325/2010, 14587/325/2010, 8177/325/2011; Timişoara Court of Appeal, Decisions No. 285/15.02.2011 (insolvency procedure in which the registration of an EOP as enforceable title issued by an Italian court is requested), 1047/A/29.10.2015; Judecătoria Vişeul de Sus, Files No. 172/336/2015, 531/336/2015, 1620/336/2015.

2011 Judecătoria Buzău, Files No. 801/200/2014, 7329/200/2015, 12919/200/2015; Tribunalul Călăraşi, File No. 272/116/2013; Judecătoria Constanţa, Files No. 12730/212/2012, 7262/212/2015, 14113/212/2015, 24856/212/2015, 29487/212/2015; Tribunalul Constanţa, Files No. 11530/118/2012, 8438/118/2014, 4969/118/2015, 5864/118/2015/A1, 7748/118/2015; Judecătoria Craiova, Files No. 19646/215/2010, 26180/215/2014, 4314/215/2015, 27433/215/2015; Judecătoria Giurgiu, Files No. 12121/236/2013, 5456/236/2015; Tribunalul Giurgiu, Files No. 141/192/2012, 143/192/2012, 144/192/2012, 145/192/2012, 147/192/2012, 149/192/2012; Judecătoria Târgu-Cărbuneşti, File No. 1463/317/2014; Tribunalul Ilfov, File No. 649/93/2013; Judecătoria Cornetu, Files No. 7402/1748/2010, 1542/1748/2012, 12197/1748/2012, 15120/1748/2012, 2385/1748/2013, 4862/1748/2013, 7777/1748/2013, 80/1748/2015, 3910/1748/2015; Judecătoria Buftea, Files No. 1297/94/2012, 15441/94/2012, 3043/94/2015; Judecătoria Petroşani, File No. 118/278/2012; Judecătoria Ploieşti, Files No. 34171/281/2012, 34172/281/2012, 291/281/2015, 9368/281/2015, 9369/281/2015; Tribunalul Prahova, File No. 7568/105/2012; Judecătoria Râmnicu Vâlcea, File No. 13294/288/2013; Judecătoria Brezoi, File No. 1807/198/2014; Judecătoria Slobozia, Files No. 5603/3132/2012, 1212/312/2013; Judecătoria Târgovişte, File No. 7261/315/2015; Judecătoria Tulcea, File No. 6820/327/2012.

2012 Judecătoria Bacău, Files No. 13451/180/2012, 1270/180/2015, 3884/180/2015, 10432/180/2015; Judecătoria Botoşani, Files No. 3466/193/2015, 3467/193/2015; Judecătoria Galaţi, Files No. 1062/233/2011, 11433/233/2011, 14422/233/2011, 7750/233/2012, 6228/233/2013, 12656/233/2014, 3942/233/2015, 14982/233/2015, 16859/233/2015; Tribunalul Galaţi, Files No. 378/121/2015, 381/121/2015, 382/121/2015, 384/121/2015, 385/121/2015, 387/121/2015, 388/121/2015, 389/121/2015, 390/121/2015, 391/121/2015; Judecătoria Iaşi, Files No. 15868/245/2013, 16017/245/2013, 33817/245/2015, 4218/245/2015, 21452/245/2015, 21930/245/2015; Tribunalul Iaşi, Files No. 8839/99/2012, 7460/99/2015; Tribunalul Neamţ, File No. 2531/103/2011; Judecătoria Oneşti, File No. 2492/270/2013; Judecătoria Suceava, Files No. 748/314/2014, 5628/314/2015.

the surrounding areas. This abundance of cases is possibly influenced by the importance of the city and surrounding areas in terms of international commercial activities, the capital status of Bucharest, and the extensive number of legal entities incorporated in this area. Other courts that tend to register more cases are situated in the border region of Transylvania (Timişoara, Arad, Oradea) or are important centres for trade (Cluj, Târgu Mureş), are ports on the Danube River (Galaţi, Giurgiu), or are on the Black Sea (Constanţa). Further, in the vast majority of cases the EOP is issued by a District Court (*judecătorie*) and involves a request for the issuance of the actual order.

In addition to cases published on the portal of Romanian courts, five EOP-related cases have been identified in two legal databases: Legalis and iDrept. These concern decisions of the commercial section of the Timisoara Court of Appeal (available also on the courts' portal);[2013] a decision by the *Tribunalul* Bucureşti;[2014] a decision on a conflict of competence in enforcement proceedings;[2015] and a second appeal decision of the High Court for Cassation and Justice on a judgment by the *Tribunalul* Hunedoara.[2016]

With regard to the nine ESCPs, three cases were handled by the *Judecătoria* Timişoara,[2017] three by Bucharest District Courts,[2018] one by the *Judecătoria* Baia Mare,[2019] one by the *Judecătoria* Lipova,[2020] and another by the *Judecătoria* Miercurea Ciuc.[2021] Two of these cases concern a request for the granting of a writ of execution for an ESCP issued in another Member State against a Romanian company.[2022] In addition to this, another ESCP has been identified in the iDrept database.[2023]

6.7.2.2. Case Classification

Most of the analysed claims are B2B cases (79.7% of the EOPs and 66.66% of the ESCPs). Of the nine ESCPs, only three involve a consumer. Two of these are B2C cases in which a law firm sought to recover amounts owing for its legal services from a Romanian natural person; and a C2B case involving a consumer and a low-cost aviation company. With regard to the EOPs, there are 45 B2C cases, 12 C2B cases, 5 C2C cases, and 1 independent professional 2B case. All but 1 C2B cases were submitted by foreign private

2013 Timişoara Court of Appeal, Commercial Section, Decision No. 285/15 February 2011, published also in Supliment (2011)1, *Revista Buletinul Curtilor de Apel.*

2014 Tribunalul Bucureşti, Section V, Decision No. 484/29 February 2012, *Revista Română de Executare Silită*, (2012)1, at 177–185.

2015 Cluj Court of Appeal, Section I Civile, Decision 3/F/9.01.2015.

2016 High Court for Cassation and Justice, Section II Civil, Decision No. 527/13 February 2014; Tribunalul Hunedoara, File No. 7608/97/2011.

2017 Judecătoria Timişoara, Files No. 19529/325/2015, 386/325/2009, 20227/325/2009.

2018 Judecătoria Sectorului 1, Bucureşti, Files No. 114629/299/2015, 47938/299/2013; Judecătoria Sectorului 5, Bucureşti, File No. 14260/302/2011.

2019 Judecătoria Baia Mare, File No. 6282/182/2012.

2020 Judecătoria Lipova, File No. 859/250/2015.

2021 As indicated in the Report of Activity for 2011 of Judecătoria Miercurea Ciuc, at 17 (available at http://portal.just.ro/258/SiteAssets/SitePages/informatii/BILANT%202011%20JMC.pdf).

2022 Judecătoria Timişoara, File No. 20227/325/2009 and Judecătoria Sectorului 5, Bucureşti, File No. 14260/302/2011.

2023 Tribunalul Sibiu, Decision No. 1330/C/11 December 2013.

parties against Romanian registered companies; 4 cases involve the same parties – thus, with a repeated claimant and defendant.

Information related to the type of contractual relationship from which the claims arose is not always mentioned explicitly on the courts' portal. From the available data, it appears that the EOP has been used for recovering money claims resulting from loan agreements (21 cases), legal representation agreements (12 cases), sale-purchase agreements (4 cases), transport agreements (2 cases), and insurance agreements (2 cases). The ESCPs were initiated in relation to a legal representation agreement (1 case), a service agreement (2 cases), transport agreements (3 cases), and for recovering interest and procedural costs related to an enforcement procedure (1 case).

6.7.2.3. Conduct of Proceedings

In the majority of cases, the claims were handled during public hearings, similar to national procedure trials, with the parties or one of the parties and the legal representatives sometimes present in court. According to collected case law, 40% of the ESCP cases and 84.1% of the EOP claims were trialled during public hearings. Although the data available cannot be generalised to all EOPs and ESCPs handled by Romanian courts, they nevertheless offer some indication as to how the courts have applied the European procedures. Files on the courts' portal reveal certain characteristics of the way cases are handled. The length of the proceedings for the issuing of an EOP (Form E) varies between one day and 24 months and 26 days from the moment the Application Form (Form A) was submitted. However, on average the claim is handled within a period of 3 months and 1.5 weeks. On a yearly basis, there has been a significant increase in the speed with which the courts issue an EOP. Thus, in recent years Romanian courts have managed to steadily reduce to almost 3 months or less the timeframe needed to issue the EOP.

	2009	2010	2011	2012	2013	2014	2015
Period necessary for the court to issue Form E	6.33 months	6.1 months	1.4 months	3.21 months	2.17 months	1.5 months	2.6 months

Table 6.6. Weighted average of the period a Romanian court requires to issue an EOP from the moment it receives Form A

If the application is rejected and Form D is issued, the timeframe necessary varies between two days and 14 months and three days from the moment the application was filed, with an average of 3 months and 2.5 weeks. On the evolution of the period necessary for the court to reject an application for an EOP, the information is relevant only for the period 2012–2015; for the other years, the number of cases is too scanty for the information to be significant.[2024] Table 6.7 shows a decrease in the amount of time the courts took to

2024 Of the 132 EOP cases, Form D was issued for 1 claim in 2011, 2 claims in 2010, and 1 claim in 2009.

reject the claim. The results are in line with the developments in cases in which the judge issued an EOP. However, the time needed by the court is long, and may be partly due to the fact that the judges required additional information or clarifications in order to decide the case.

	2012	2013	2014	2015
Period necessary for the court to issue Form D	5 months	2.44 months	2.5 months	1.14 months

Table 6.7. Weighted average of the time a Romanian court needs to decide to reject an application for an EOP (Form D)

The longer periods necessary for handling an EOP application are due in most cases to the fact the court requires the claimant (1) to submit copies of the documents indicated as evidence in the Application Form (Form A); (2) to provide translations of documents indicated as evidence; (3) to pay the court fees and submit evidence of payment; or (4) the judge orders several adjournments of the case for procedural reasons or for issuing the decision. These requests for the claimant to submit the evidence documents as well as their translations into Romanian if it is in another language represent requirements that are additional to the exhaustive elements set by Article 7 EOP and confirmed by the CJEU in the *Szyrocka* case.[2025] In practice, a significant number of Romanian judges continue to demand these documents if they are not submitted together with Form A.[2026] This persistence in requesting the filing of evidence and of translated documents may be for two reasons. The first reason is that all national procedures require submission of the evidence on which the judge can determine whether or not a claim is founded. The second reason may lie in the fact the procedure is not well known and understood by some judges. Compared to national procedures, the number of EOP cases is still very low and does not properly allow the courts to develop a practice in this area of law.[2027] The longer delays for issuing EOP or ESCP decisions are also influenced by the need to trial the claims in public sessions. It is only after the entrance into force of the NCPC that the courts have had the possibility of trialling European claims in chambers.[2028]

Much less can be said of the nine ESCP claims, since no case pattern can be deducted from the existing data. The length of the proceedings varies from more than 10 months in one situation to 1.5 months in another. Two ESCP cases concern requests for the execution of judgments issued by foreign courts, and are dealt with by the court within a period of 2 to 3 weeks. In one of the two ESCP cases that lasted more than 6 months, the judge made use of Form B to request more documents and information in order to decide the case. This prolonged the length of the court proceedings. No information is available as to the time necessary for the court to issue Form D. In two ESCP cases, it

2025 Case C-215/11, para. 30–32.

2026 See also Hess (2017), Chapter 5 para. 876.

2027 See Table 6.2 and Table 6.3, and Section 6.7.1 above.

2028 See also Section 6.2.2 on the trial in chambers.

appears that Form D was issued at the same time as the judgment.[2029] In one case the request was annulled.

In 9.23% of the EOP cases,[2030] there is an indication the court sent Form B to the claimant requesting clarifications, additional information, or documents, such as (1) to indicate the interest claimed and the period concerned; (2) to specify the amount of the claim, as well as interest, penalties, and costs; (3) to proceed to paying the court fees and deposit the proof of payment; (4) to submit the documents indicated as evidence, or their translations; and (5) for the claimant to fill in an application by using standard Form A (2 cases). The payment of court fees creates some difficulties for claimants located abroad. The proof of payment has to be submitted together with the application form in accordance with the national procedural rules.[2031] Foreign claimants often comply with this requirement only after the court sends them Form B indicating the account to which they can send the payment. However, there are cases in which the request for an EOP was subsequently rejected due to the court not receiving proof of payment within the set period. This happened in three of 12 cases in which the court had requested the claimant to pay the court fees and to submit proof.

In around 2.8% of the cases, the court sent Form C to the claimant requesting him to modify the EOP application.[2032] These proposals concerned (1) the renunciation of legal interest; (2) the amount of the principal; (3) the penalties; and (4) the total amount of the EOP. In each situation, the claimant accepted the court's proposal, and Form E was subsequently issued for the indicated amount.

The EOP was awarded in 158 of the 249 cases identified, thus for 63.45% of the claims. The Declaration of enforceability was released within a period ranging from 2 to 20 months (from the moment of registration of the application to the moment Form G was awarded). With respect to the manner in which Form G is issued, the practice is not unitary. In certain cases, the judge establishes on his own initiative a date on which to check whether service of the EOP and Forms A and F had been carried out correctly and no opposition received. If this is the case, he then issues Form G. On two occasions, it appears that the court issued Form G together with Form E.[2033] However, the information is very limited for most of the identified files, and it is not always clear whether Form G was eventually issued following the delivery of Form E and the lapse of the opposition time, or upon request. Of the 158 cases in which the EOP (Form E) was issued, only for 23.41% of them is there a clear indication that a Declaration of enforceability (Form G) was granted.[2034] In one case, neither Form E nor Form G was issued. According to information on the court's portal, the parties reached an agreement, and the court took note of it and then closed the case.[2035] This is a singular solution by the court, as the EOP is a single-sided procedure. The explanation is most probably that the judge made a

2029 Judecătoria Sectorului 1, Bucureşti, File No. 114629/299/2015; Judecătoria Lipova, File No. 859/250/2015.

2030 Twenty-three cases.

2031 Article 197 NCPC.

2032 Seven cases.

2033 Judecătoria Aiud, File No. 736/175/2015; Judecătoria Oradea, File No. 3148/271/2015.

2034 Thirty-seven cases.

2035 Tribunalul Alba, Commercial Section, File No. 6327/107/2009.

combined application of the EOP Regulation and of the national order for payment procedure.[2036]

An application for the issuance of an EOP was rejected (Form D) by the Romanian courts in 26.10% of the cases.[2037] The reasons for rejection were (1) jurisdiction grounds (7 cases); (2) non-compliance with the criteria set by the Regulation for the issuance of an EOP (7 cases); (3) the claim was unfounded (6 cases); (4) the claimant failed to reply within the timeframe established by the judge (4 cases); (5) the judge considered that additional proof or further verifications not compatible with the EOP procedure were necessary (3 cases);[2038] (6) non-payment of the court fees (3 cases);[2039] and (7) the claimant failed to submit the evidence regarding the claim and the interest, and to clarify the claim (2 cases). In addition, in some of the above-mentioned cases the court also requested the claimant to submit a certified translation of the documents filed with the application form. As to the remaining 33 rejected application, the portal provides no clear information on the reasons that led the court to take this decision. Some of the above rejection decisions are unexpected, and they undermine the Regulation's objectives. The judges go on to set requirements additional to the ones provided by Article 7 EOP to issue the order (e.g. to submit copies of evidence documents described in Section 10 of Form A together with their certified translations,[2040] or the EOP is turned into an adversarial trial, similar to the national procedure, with the debtor filing a statement of defence and the claimant required to answer it[2041]). These ways of handling EOP claims also disregard the CJEU *Szyrocka* judgment that clearly states 'Article 7 governs exhaustively the requirements to be met by an application for a European order for payment'.[2042] Other remarkable solutions where the court fails completely to understand the European procedure concern the rejections of EOP applications due to the fact the judge considers he needs to acquire additional proof and to undertake verifications regarding the debtor that would not be compatible with the European procedure. The judge deems that he has to proceed to physically analyse the evidence on which the claim is based, and follow a full evidentiary phase for evaluating the claim.

2036 Article 5 of Government Ordinance No. 5/2001 regarding the writ of payment (Official Gazette of Romania No. 422/30 July 2001).

2037 Sixty-five cases. In one case, the court issued the rejection decision, with the claimant having the right to challenge it within a period of 30 days of being served (Judecătoria Reşiţa, File 2895/290/2015). This interpretation of the Romanian court is in breach of the provisions of Article 11(2) EOP, and raises doubts as to the national court's understanding of the European procedure.

2038 Judecătoria Sectorului 1, Bucureşti, Files No. 50506/299/2012, 1281/299/2013, 1912/299/2013.

2039 In 2 out of the 3 cases, the foreign party filled in Section 5 – Bank details of Form A authorising the court to collect the court fee from a bank account and from a credit card. The court sent a reply informing the claimants that the court was unable to collect the court fee, and that they needed to make a wire transfer to the specific bank account of the Romanian public authority. The claims were subsequently dismissed because the parties failed to provide the courts with proof of payment. Thus, the claimants were either not able to pay or gave up trying to make the payment.

2040 For example, Judecătoria Năsăud, File No. 319/265/2013; Tribunalul Bucureşti, File No. 14946/3/2014; Judecătoria Buftea, File No. 1297/94/2012.

2041 For example, Judecătoria Şimleul Silvaniei, File No 1544/309/2013, Tribunalul Călăraşi, File No. 272/116/2013.

2042 Case C-215/11, para. 27–32.

However, the Regulation establishes that the application needs to be assessed in accordance with Article 8 EOP, and the judge can reject it only if one of the criteria set by Article 11(1) EOP is not met.

The debtor opposed the EOP in 24 of the 249 cases. This accounts for only 9.63% of the identified cases; hence, it does not justify the concerns expressed by Romanian scholars in relation to this mechanism. In one case, the opposition was filed after the 30-day period had lapsed. Following the opposition, in 20 of the 24 cases the proceedings continued according to the ordinary procedure. The court subsequently informed the claimant that he needed to formulate a new claim in compliance with the requirements of the NCPC, and of the need to pay the required court fees. In one case, proceedings were terminated because the claimant had filled in Appendix 2 of Form A, blocking transfer to the national procedure. What is striking for this case is that the information available seems to point to the fact that the court communicated to the debtor not only information provided for by Article 12(3)-(4) EOP but also the fact the claimant had explicitly requested that proceedings be terminated in the event of an opposition.[2043] If this is truly the case, the court proceeded in breach of the provision of Article 12(2) that expressly mentions the Appendices will not be part of the EOP to be communicated to the debtor. However, this is not the only remarkable development in relation to an EOP opposition. Two courts rejected the debtors' opposition.[2044] In the *Judecătoria Braşov* case, the judge even requested the claimant to submit written notes to the court expressing his position on the debtor's opposition in accordance with Article 17 EOP. *Tribunalul Hunedoara* had an even more unexpected solution to the claim when it not only rejected the opposition submitted by the debtor, foreign entity, but it also went on to issue Form G on the basis of Article 18 EOP. These applications of the Regulation are some of the most unfortunate for a debtor, and show a significant lack of some judges' understanding of the procedure. *Tribunalul Hunedoara*'s decision was subsequently subject to appellate proceedings. The Court of Appeal accepted the appeal formulated by the debtor, rejecting the claimant's non-admissibility exception, although the Regulation does not provide for a special procedural means allowing an enforceable EOP to be challenged.[2045] In its reasoning, the court rightfully indicates that the effect of the opposition is the transfer of the claim to the ordinary national proceedings, unless the claimant requests the procedure to terminate in such circumstances. The provisions of Article 17 cannot be interpreted by the court as establishing a special means of appeal. Thus, the court had wrongly awarded Form G. Further, the court legitimately points out that the review, as established by Article 20(1) EOP, is not a means of appeal, and the decision of the first court cannot be subject to a review on this basis. Following the opposition, the national procedure governs the trial and the means of appeal. The claimant filed a second appeal with the High Court for Cassation and

[2043] Judecătoria Cornetu, File No. 1542/1748/2012.

[2044] Judecătoria Braşov, File No. 31929/197/2012 and Tribunalul Hunedoara, File No. 7608/79/2011 (Decision No. 3032/CA/2012 later subject to a second appeal by the High Court of Cassation and Justice, Decision No. 527/13 February 2013).

[2045] Alba Iulia Court of Appeal, Section II Civil, Decision No. 5/27 February 2013.

Justice,[2046] which the High Court accepted, considering the solutions of the lower courts to be incorrect. The court upheld the fact that Form G was issued in breach of the provisions of Article 18(1) EOP. Instead, the District Court should have applied Article 17 EOP. The High Court goes further and dismisses the application of the appeal provisions, pointing to the fact that the court should have re-qualified the appeal request as a review in accordance with Article 20(2) EOP. It was considered that a new panel of District Court judges should re-trial the case and modify it in line with the reasoning of the High Court and the provisions of Articles 16–18 EOP. Although the District Court's decision was issued clearly with an incorrect application of the law and was in breach of the provisions of the Regulation, the requalification of the appeal as a review under Article 20(2) seems to give the provisions an extensive and far-reaching interpretation. In this case, the EOP cannot be considered to have been 'clearly wrongly issued', as the issuing of the order itself did not breach any of the Regulation's provisions. This concerns only the Declaration of enforceability. Such an extensive interpretation of the provisions of Article 20(2) EOP is not in line with the decision of the CJEU in the *Thomas Cook* case.[2047] Further, rejection of an opposition by the court raises concerns as to whether the debtors' procedural rights are being protected, and whether the European procedures are understood by some members of the judiciary. Undoubtedly, in this respect there is a need to provide additional training to the national judiciary.

In looking at the results regarding the application for an EOP and its enforcement, the following picture emerges from the available case law.

	No. of cases identified on *portal.just.ro*
EOP issued (Form E)	159
Rejection of the claim (Form D)	65
Opposition and closing of the case	4
Opposition and passage to ordinary procedure	20
Request for the execution of EOP	11
Contesting the execution of EOP	1
Contesting jurisdiction enforcement court	2
Declining jurisdiction in enforcement	5
Seeking EOP execution in insolvency proceedings	4
Extinction of the case	2
Settlement[2048]	1
Not clear	4

Table 6.8. Information regarding EOPs awarded and their execution according to data available on the Judiciary Portal

2046 High Court for Cassation and Justice, Section II Civil, Decision No. 527/13 February 2014.

2047 See the reasoning of the CJEU in Case C-245/14, para 44–52.

2048 See comments related to the case in which the parties reached an agreement within the EOP proceedings and the court took note of it, followed by the closing of the case.

A small number of cases contain unexpected requests or awards. For example, in one instance the court not only issued the EOP but also decided upon rescission of the sale-purchase agreement on which the claim was based.[2049] The decision is surprising, because the EOP is a single-sided procedure for the collection of uncontested monetary claims where the order is to be issued based on the information contained in a standard form. This does not create premises for the court to properly proceed to an analysis of the contract. In another EOP case, under the influence of the provisions of the national procedural rules, the court issued Form G with a right for the debtor to request its annulment within 10 days from communication.[2050] The Regulation does not rule on the possibility of requesting the annulment of Form G, and such an interpretation does not seem to be in line with the aims of the Regulation. Further, this does not correspond to information communicated by the Romanian Government. Another surprising application of the EOP Regulation was by a court that rejected a request made under the national order for payment procedure; it considered the European procedure should have been used instead. The judge failed to recognise the non-compulsory nature of the EOP procedure (Article 1(2) EOP).[2051] This application might have been influenced by a line of doctrine according to which the national order for payment procedure (*ordonanța de plată*) applies only to purely internal cases.[2052]

6.7.2.4. Representation of the Parties

In the analysis of the cases, it emerges that parties were not always represented by a lawyer or legal adviser. Thus, in the EOP cases at least one of the parties was represented in 32 cases, in 6 cases the party was represented by a debt-recovering company, and in 10 cases law firms were using the EOP to recover their legal fees. In one ESCP case, the creditor was represented by a law firm in the execution stage, and in another case the law firm was the creditor.

2049 Judecătoria Sectorului 3, București, File No. 11606/301/2012.

2050 Tribunalul București, Section VI Civil, File No. 23737/3/2009.

2051 Article 1(2) EOP: 'This Regulation shall not prevent a claimant from pursuing a claim (...) by making use of another procedure available under the law of a Member State'. Recital 10 EOP: 'The procedure established by this Regulation serves as an additional and optional means for the claimant, who remains free to resort to a procedure provided by national law'.

2052 See Section 6.3.1 above.

Representation in the application procedure	Number of EOP cases	Number of ESCP cases
Creditor	35	1
Debtor	6	0
Both parties are represented	4	0
Lawyers are creditors	12	1
Creditor represented by debt recovery company	11	0
Representation in the execution process		
Creditor	8	1
Debtor	0	0
Both parties are represented	1	0

Table 6.9. Representation of parties by a lawyer or legal adviser in EOP and ESCP procedures

Some parties and their representatives were repeated players. In the vast majority of the cases, the claimants were repeated players seeking to recover their debt, but some situations involved multiple claims between the same parties.

6.7.2.5. Amounts and Costs Claimed

Although the amount of the debt that creditors sought to recover was not always mentioned expressly, some cases provided this information. In EOP cases, the amount of the principle varied from €6,817,626 to €250; in ESCP cases, this varied between €1,550 and €145. In addition to the main claim, interest and costs were sometimes requested and awarded by the judge. In most circumstances, legal interest was requested for a determined period or until payment of the entire debt had been completed.

The costs generally awarded were the court fees, and in very few cases other costs such as lawyers' fees, notary fees, or translation fees. Penalties were awarded in three cases. In most circumstances where information is available, the courts applied a fixed court fee to the EOP claims identical to the one applicable to the *ordonanța de plată*.[2053] Only occasionally was this calculated on the basis of the value of the claim as appeared to be the intention of the Romanian authorities.[2054] A consistent application with regard to the amount of the court fee would be desirable in practice. ESCP case law provides no

[2053] Judecătoria Sectorului 5, București, Files No. 571/302/2009, 14067/302/2010, 21174/302/2014; Tribunalul București, File No. 38461/3/2012; Judecătoria Arad, File No. 4112/55/2009; Judecătoria Bistrița, File No. 1805/190/2013; Judecătoria Galați, File No. 12656/233/2014; Tribunalul Iași, File No. 8839/99/2012; Judecătoria Iași, Files No. 4218/245/2015, 16017/245/2013; Judecătoria Cornetu, File No. 12197/1748/2012.

[2054] Judecătoria Sectorului 3, București, File No. 57080/301/2014; Tribunalul Commercial Mureș, File No. 509/1371/2012; Judecătoria Șimpleul Silvaniei, File No. 1544/309/2013. On the position of the Romanian Government, see Section 6.5 above.

information as to any difficulty related to the payment of court fees; thus, no estimate can be made in this regard.

6.7.2.6. Service and Language Aspects

Information on service of the EOP was mainly in relation to language requirements. Only five cases mentioned that the EOP was served on defendants in their own language, these being Bulgarian, French, German, Hungarian and, respectively, Italian. Additionally, one case reports that the opposition form (Form F) and the Declaration of enforceability (Form G) were sent in Dutch, the language of the defendant, while in another, the EOP was translated into Italian in order to serve it on the debtor. In all other available references, service takes place using forms in Romanian. This practice prevents the foreign debtor from immediately understanding the content of the documents served, and jeopardises the party's right of access to justice. Furthermore, it is not in line with the provisions of the Service Regulation. According to descriptions in the EOP files studied, Romanian courts inform the debtor of the choice he has in paying or otherwise opposing the order, as well as regarding the information in Article 12 (4) EOP. Service seems to have been problematic in some of the identified cases, but the causes were not mentioned. The cases seldom presented a clear indication as to whether the Service Regulation was used if the debtor was located abroad. In a couple of cases where service needed to be carried out abroad, particular attention appears to have been given by the Romanian courts to compliance with domestic rules of the Member State where the communication was undertaken.[2055]

An ESCP case offers information on the service of the documents of the proceedings on the debtor. The judge postponed the judgment and indicated that the service procedure was to be renewed by the procedural agent and by registered post with an acknowledgement of receipt. The defendant was to be provided with a copy of Form A and of the documents submitted together with Form C. However, no indication was given regarding the language in which these had been served, though most probably it was Romanian, the language of the proceedings.

The verification undertaken by the judge, along with the renewed service, are important guarantees for the defendant's procedural rights and his access to justice. The translation of documents is often requested by Romanian judges. A reference in this respect appears mostly in EOP cases, in relation to EOP applications (12 cases), but also in enforcement proceedings (1 case). This concerns the standard forms and their content or/and the translation of the documents submitted, although these last ones should not be requested or made compulsory by the court for issuance of the EOP. One ESCP case makes implicit reference to the requirements in Article 21(2) ESCP. The bailiff is to provide the court with a translation in order to initiate the execution phase.

[2055] Judecătoria Buftea, File No. 3043/94/2015; Timişoara Court of Appeal, Section II Civil, Decision No. 1047/A/29 October 2015. In this last case, it is arguable whether the method of service used – postal service with the document deposited at the postal office for the defendant to collect – actually provided sufficient protection for the debtors' procedural rights. It appears from the particulars of the case that the actual service is based on a fiction of the domestic law in Italy that considers the service to have been carried out if the defendant does not collect the documents from the post office within a period longer than 30 days (*compiuta giacenza*).

6.7.2.7. Enforcement

A limited number of cases provide information on the enforcement in Romania of EOPs and ESCPs. Only 11 of the 137 EOP cases published were actually related to execution of the order. Another eight EOP cases concerned procedural aspects related to enforcement (e.g. obtaining the writ, contesting jurisdiction of the enforcement court). Additionally, two of the nine ESCP cases concern the execution of titles issued by courts in other Member States, and the procedures took place in chambers. The execution judge generally requested the bailiff to submit the EOP together with Form G and/or a certified translation in Romanian. The same demand was registered for one of the ESCP cases. In the other ESCP file, the judge approved enforcement regarding all assets of the debtor within its territorial jurisdiction for recovery of the debt and the costs of execution. In some EOP cases, the debtor raised an objection as to the court not having jurisdiction with regard to enforcement purposes, thereby seeking to prevent or delay execution of the enforceable title.

6.7.2.8. Influence of the National Procedures

As seen in published case law, there is a tendency for Romanian judges to supplement the requirements established by Article 7 EOP,[2056] even though this is contrary to the text of the Regulation and to the interpretation the CJEU issued on this provision.[2057] The principle of the active role of the judge in finding the truth, and allowing Romanian judges to request parties to present additional evidence within the national procedures, could contribute to this practice.[2058] In exceptional circumstances, these requirements involve written notes by the claimant, counterarguments to an opposition, or conclusions to the EOP procedure by the debtor. In these cases, the EOP is applied in a manner that resembles the national procedure. The analysis of EOP and ESCP case law shows that there is still a need to provide information and train the judiciary and the courts' administrative staff on the European procedures and the manner in which these instruments should be applied.

6.7.3. *EOP and ESCP Procedures: Empirical Findings*

6.7.3.1. Preliminary Aspects regarding Data Collection

The data analysed in this section was collected on the basis of surveys, interviews, information exchanges with legal professionals and an analysis of court files. The analysis was an alternative offered by some courts in response to the request to conduct interviews with judges and clerks on their experience with handling EOP and ESCP cases. This

2056 Although in the *Szyrocka* case (C-215/11), para. 36: 'Article 7 of Regulation No 1896/2006 must be interpreted as governing exhaustively the requirements to be met by an application for a European order for payment.' See also Hess (2017), Chapter 5, para. 876.

2057 Case C-215/11, points 27–32.

2058 Article 22(2) NCPC. See also Section 6.2 above.

approach was based on a restrictive interpretation by the courts of the provisions of the law granting access to information of public interest for research purposes in conjunction with the Regulation regulating the courts' internal activity.[2059] Law 544/2001 does not expressly regulate the possibility of conducting interview research with the judiciary and clerks. To obtain more information on the functioning of the EOP and the ESCP, a pragmatic approach was chosen. Two courts in Bucharest (the Hight General Court and the *Judecătoria Sector 2*) were selected and were sent a request to obtain access to their EOP and/or ESCP files for research purposes. When permission was obtained from the two courts, the files were consulted in the courts' archives.

Additionally, invitations to participate in the research were submitted to all six District Courts in Bucharest (*Judecătorii*) as well as to all national judges and clerks attending a training conference on civil and commercial cooperation organised by the National Institute of Magistracy (*Institutul Național al Magistraturii*).[2060] Subsequently, a request was transmitted to the Romanian judges participating in a training session on the EOP and the ESCP organised by the European Judicial Training Networks at the Judicial Academy in Slovakia.[2061] One individual judge who participated in an ERA course on these European procedures was directly invited to participate in the research, and to extend the request to other interested judges to share their experiences. The Bucharest District Court 6 sent the replies of the judges that had agreed to take part in the research, while the Bucharest District Court 1 agreed to inform its judges of the research conducted on the EOP and the ESCP. The number of responses from judges and clerks has overall been modest.[2062] In addition, documents relating to 26 EOP files and one ESCP case were analysed at the Bucharest High General Court and the *Judecătoria Sector 2*.

Lawyers' professional bodies also received an invitation for their members to participate in the research: namely, the Union of the National Romanian Bars (*Uniunea Națională a Barourilor din Romania*, U.N.B.R.),[2063] the 42 National Bar Organisations,[2064] and the National Institute for the Training of Lawyers (*Institutul Național pentru Pregătirea și Perfecționarea Avocaților*).[2065] Additional requests were sent to law firms

2059 Article 2 and Article 5 in conjunction with Article 11 Law No. 544/2001 regarding free access to information of public interest, as subsequently modified, Official Gazette of Romania No. 663/23 October 2001; Regulation regarding the internal activity of the courts (*Regulamentul de ordine interioară al instanțelor judecătorești*), approved by the Decision of the Supreme Council of Magistracy No. 387/2005 as subsequently modified.

2060 Practical exercises in implementing the judicial cooperation instruments in civil and commercial matters, Final Conference, Bucharest, Romania, 20–21 November 2014.

2061 European Payment Order, European Small Claims Procedure, Judicial Academy, Slovakia, 25–26 May 2015. The advance training encounter was set to discuss practical issues of recovering debts by means of the European payment order or in the small claims procedure, relevant case law and current problems related to these instruments.

2062 Eleven EOP surveys and four ESCP surveys were returned.

2063 Email exchanges from 9 July 2014 and Reply Address No. Nr. 156 – DIV – 2014 of 9 July 2014 (documents on file with the researcher).

2064 The invitations were dispatched electronically to all National Bars during the period 2–23 July 2014.

2065 A request was sent to the director of the institute on 22 July 2014. This request and several email exchanges did not result in any collaboration.

identified as having been using or offering advice to their clients on the EOP and/or the ESCP, according to the case law available on the judiciary portal.[2066] A small number of survey replies were collected.[2067] One lawyer was contacted following participation in the ESCP European Commission consultation. Two interviews were carried out with lawyers, one on the EOP procedure and the other on the ESCP. In relation to the EOP, additional information was collected by way of email exchanges with professionals and in personal discussions.

An invitation was also sent to the National Union of Bailiffs (*Uniunea Naţională a Executorilor Judecătoreşti*),[2068] which redirected the invitations to all Bailiffs Chambers organised within the jurisdiction of the fifteen Romanian Courts of Appeal.[2069] Hence, a modest number of replies and comments were able to be collected.[2070]

To complete the framework of professionals' experience, ECC Romania legal advisors were invited to share their perspectives regarding consumers' familiarity with the European uniform procedures. They replied to the ESCP survey and agreed to discuss their experiences in an interview focused mainly on the procedures about which they had advised some consumers following failed mediation procedures.

A significant number of extensive and repeated requests and invitations to provide information failed to elicit responses. Finally, an invitation to take part in this research was published on a dedicated private international law website.[2071]

This resulted in an overall number of 17 EOP survey responses,[2072] 10 ESCP survey responses,[2073] 2 interviews,[2074] and a volume of timely feedback and correspondence from Romanian practitioners.

6.7.3.2. Familiarity with European Procedures and Handling Practices

The outcome of the surveys showed that respondents generally have a high perception of their knowledge of the EOP and the ESCP (Figs. 6.2–6.3). The EOP and ESCP survey respondents generally rated their knowledge of the European procedure above

2066 http://portal.just.ro.

2067 Four EOP and two ESCP surveys were returned.

2068 A request for assistance in making the research visible for bailiffs was sent to the President of the Union on 3 July 2014.

2069 At the request of the President of the National Union of Bailiffs Chamber of Bailiffs organised within the jurisdiction of the Court of Appeal of Alba-Iulia, Court of Appeal of Bacău, Court of Appeal of Braşov, Court of Appeal of Bucureşti, Court of Appeal of Cluj-Napoca, Court of Appeal of Constanţa, Court of Appeal of Craiova, Court of Appeal of Galaţi, Court of Appeal of Iaşi, Court of Appeal of Oradea, Court of Appeal of Piteşti, Court of Appeal of Ploieşti, Court of Appeal of Suceava, Court of Appeal of Târgu Mureş, Court of Appeal of Timişoara.

2070 Two bailiffs replied to the EOP survey. In addition, two other bailiffs sent comments on their experience or lack of requests regarding the EOP and the ESCP.

2071 On 19 July 2015. See http://conflictoflaws.net/2015/surveys-on-european-order-for-payment-and-small-claims-procedures/.

2072 Survey responses were provided by 11 judges and clerks, 4 lawyers, 2 bailiffs.

2073 Survey responses were provided by 7 judges and clerks, 2 lawyers, and ECC Romania.

2074 Interviews were conducted with 2 lawyers.

level 3.[2075] No significant difference is registered between the various professional categories with regard to their own perception over their familiarity with the European procedure. With regard to knowledge held by potential users, a Eurobarometer study revealed that 88% of the respondents were not aware of the ESCP's existence.[2076]

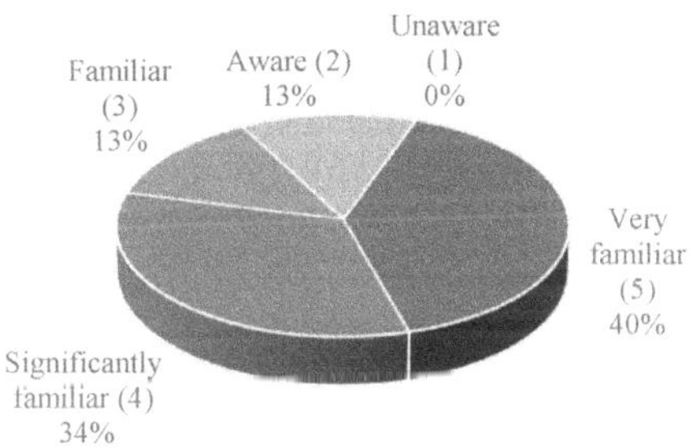

Fig. 6.2. Professionals' perception of their familiarity with the EOP (15 responses)

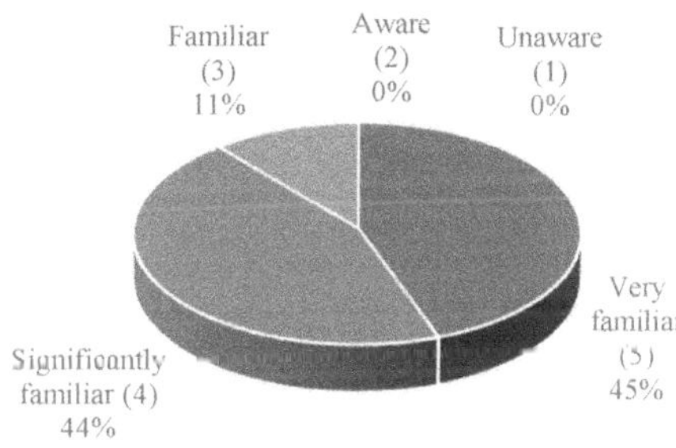

Fig. 6.3. Professionals' perception of their familiarity with the ESCP (9 responses)

The survey results were very likely influenced by two factors. First, most EOP survey respondents at some point had followed a training course on the procedure.[2077] The same appeared to be the case for half of the ESCP respondents. Nevertheless, in relation to the ESCP, respondents who mentioned having undergone some training did not rate their knowledge as being at the top end of the scale. One possible explanation could be that most of the respondents who actually participated in a training session did not have the opportunity to handle any ESCP applications in practice. This is not the case for the EOP, as the procedure was more often used. The courses or training sessions were organised by the professional organisation to which the responded belonged, by the law firm with whom they collaborated, or by a European programme. One judge indicated that he had familiarised himself with the EOP as a result of a professional exam in private international law. ECC Romania remarked that the ESCP procedure was not sufficiently well known to Romanian courts. The organisation requested the Ministry of Justice and the Superior Council of Magistracy to take action in this regard. Second, an aspect contributing to the practitioners' familiarity with the EOP and ESCP is whether they had received and handled applications or provided advice on the use of the instrument or made use of it for their own interest (i.e. law firms trying to use the EOP procedure to recover their due fees).[2078] At the same time, concrete information on the volume of EOP

2075 The 16 EOP surveys contain responses from 9 judges, 2 clerks, 3 lawyers, and 2 bailiffs. All but 2 respondents rated their knowledge of the procedure above level 3. The 10 ESCP surveys contained responses from 5 judges, 2 clerks, 2 lawyers, and ECC Romania. Only 1 respondent rated his knowledge of the ESCP procedure below level 3.

2076 Special Eurobarometer 395, *European Small Claims Procedure*, 2013, at 69.

2077 From the information provided, it is generally impossible to determine whether the courses took place prior to or immediately following the entrance into application of the Regulation or some period after the EOP became applicable. One of the responding bailiffs refers to a training course for bailiffs that was organised in 2012.

2078 Two respondents based their replies on their colleagues' experience.

and ESCP claims handled by respondents is only marginally available, and involves a handful of cases, especially concerning the ESCP.[2079]

As regards respondents' perception of general awareness of the European uniform procedures, the results are more modest (Figs. 6.4–6.5). None of the EOP respondents considered other legal professionals or parties to be 'very familiar' with the EOP. The ESCP survey results show that respondents perceived general awareness to be higher than for the EOP, and similarly at a lower level than their own (50% of the responses consider general knowledge of the ESCP to be at level 3 or 2, while personal familiarity was rated at that level only for 11% of the respondents).

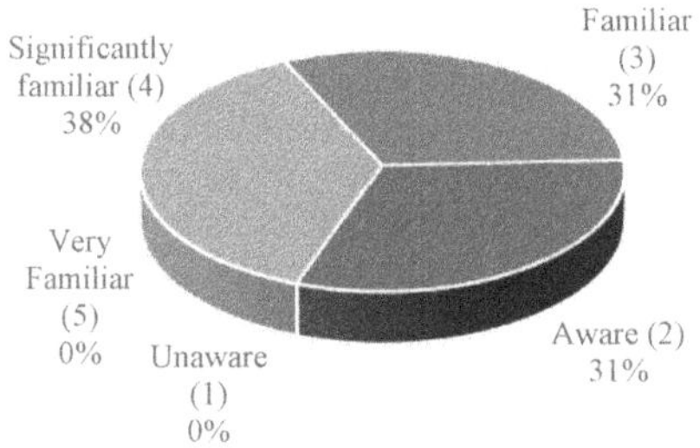

Fig. 6.4. Professionals' perception of general EOP awareness (16 responses)

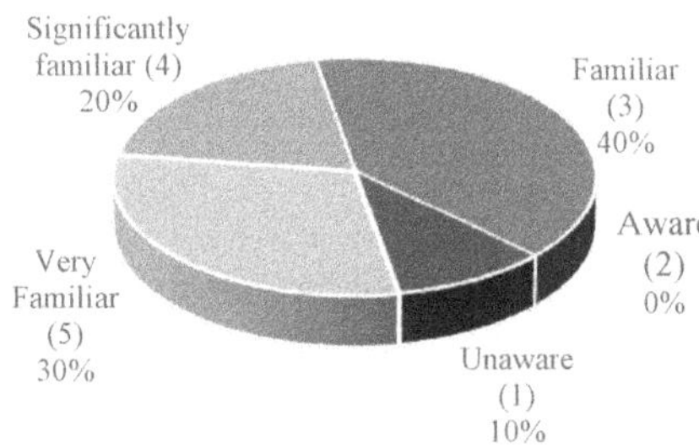

Fig. 6.5. Professionals' perception of general ESCP awareness (10 responses)

The way the claims are handled in practice and the limited knowledge and familiarity with the European uniform procedures are very likely among the reasons that the procedures are applied in a manner more closely resembling familiar domestic instruments.[2080] As EOP case law indicates, and the analysis of court files and replies confirms, courts and practitioners systematically add additional requirements to those established by Article 7 EOP for the submission of an application and the issuance of an order. The claims are sometimes handled in an adversarial format, although the Regulation provides for a single-sided primarily administrative procedure before the EOP is served on the defendant. The defendant's lawyers submit oppositions in a format identical to the domestic procedures, including procedural exceptions and defences on the substance of the claim instead of using Form F. These identified outcomes justify the lower rating of general awareness. Regarding the ESCP, ECC Romania encountered situations in which the courts competent to handle the claim were not familiar with the procedure, and actually proceeded to apply the national procedure, *procedura cu privire la cererile de valoare redusă*, instead of the European instrument.[2081] This practice was

2079 According to the ESCP survey, only two lawyers, a court clerk, and ECC Romania had actually handled such claims themselves. None of the responding bailiffs seem to have had an opportunity to enforce any ESCP judgments.

2080 See also Hess (2017), Chapter 5, para. 900.

2081 The organisation in question sent information to the Ministry of Justice and the Supreme Council of Magistracy, pointing to the lack of awareness regarding the ESCP Regulation, but it had no further information on courses the authorities had organised.

confirmed by other professionals, although such a transfer is not generally possible on the basis of the European procedure.

The manner in which the EOP and the ESCP are applied distances the procedures from their actual aim and the format adopted by the European legislator. This creates difficulties for the parties that choose these instruments over national procedures, and encourages them to give preference to domestic procedures that are better known to courts and practitioners (Figs. 6.6–6.7).

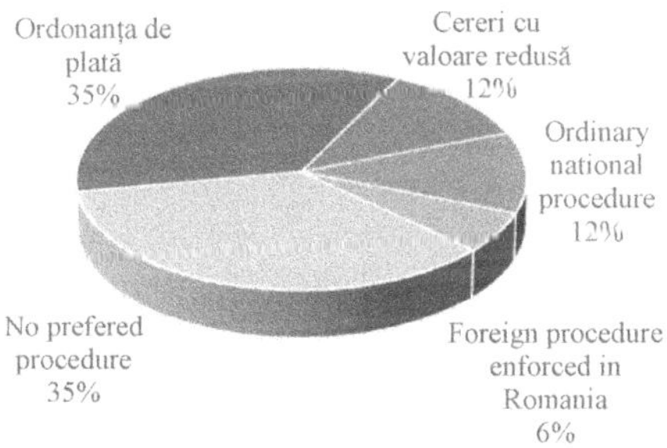

Fig. 6.6. National procedures chosen over the EOP (16 responses)

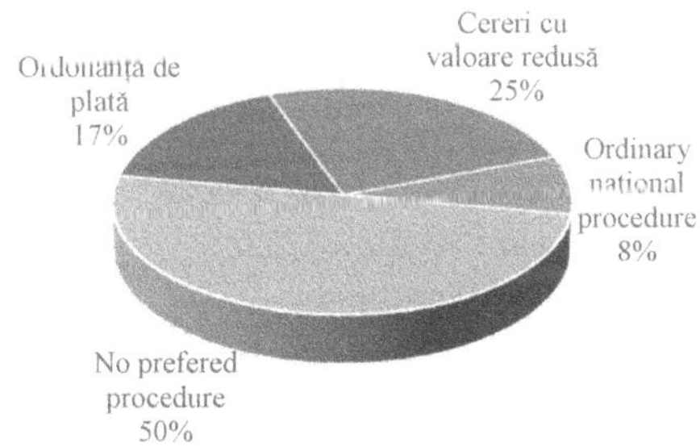

Fig. 6.7. National procedures chosen over the ESCP (12 responses)

The reasons provided by the respondents for these alternative choices are partly linked to the previous identified aspects, such as the limited familiarity of national practitioners with these European instruments, and the way the EOP and the ESCP have been applied. This could be an important reason preventing practitioners from using or advising the use of the European procedures to their clients. As remarked by a lawyer, they would not risk their clients' chances of success with a procedure of which the court did not have sufficient knowledge or that applied the EOP in a manner that did not correspond to the provisions of the Regulation. Additionally, in relation to execution of the judgment being carried out, some practitioners indicated that *ordonanţa de plată* or the *cererile cu valoare redusă* are better known by bailiffs and courts deliver the judgments faster. Information regarding the national procedures is more easily available, and efforts have been made so far by authorities to inform and train the practitioners in relation to these domestic instruments. Hence, national procedures remain better known and easier to apply and make use of than the European equivalents.

6.7.3.3. Case Classification

In the EOP procedure, most of the submitted cases involve B2B claims, and it appears to be the same for the ESCP procedure. Natural persons occasionally decide to use the European procedures or these are used against private parties. Action often seems to be lodged by private Romanian companies against private foreign companies and occasionally against natural persons. Only in a limited number of EOP cases has a foreign private company sought to bring proceedings before Romanian courts against local companies or private parties. Additionally, the analysed EOP files confirm that parties involved are sometimes repeated players, an aspect identified earlier in the case law. The number of ESCP files and case law unfortunately do not allow a similar analysis.

With regard to the type of contractual relationship, the results reveal that the EOP is most often used for claims related to sale-purchase agreements, service agreements, financial services and loan agreements, and guarantees or other collaterals. For the ESCP, claims are generally based on sale-purchase agreements (concluded sometimes via the internet), services agreements, rental agreements, aviation cases, and touristic package deals.

The empirical findings are in line with the outcome of the case law analysis.[2082]

6.7.3.4. Conduct of Proceedings and Encountered Difficulties

Handling of Cases

As to how EOP and ESCP cases are handled by Romanian courts and the division of tasks between the judges and the clerks, the results vary among the survey respondents. The involvement of the two groups of professionals in handling EOP and ESCP claims points towards the judges playing a more significant role. Judges do tend to rate their involvement in the handling of European uniform procedures and forms above level 3 (Fig. 6.8). This might be explained by the fact that assessing the claim is a task accomplished exclusively by the judge, an aspect that might be perceived as having greater weight in the handling of a case. Furthermore, the judge will instruct the clerk to fulfill certain tasks regarding the case, such as typing up the text of the decision in the required format. The file analysis reveals additional information on the type of tasks that judges and clerks undertake, and the interaction between the two professionals in handling the European uniform procedures. Hence, the clerks' activities in relation to the European procedures is identical to those usually carried out in all other national procedures.

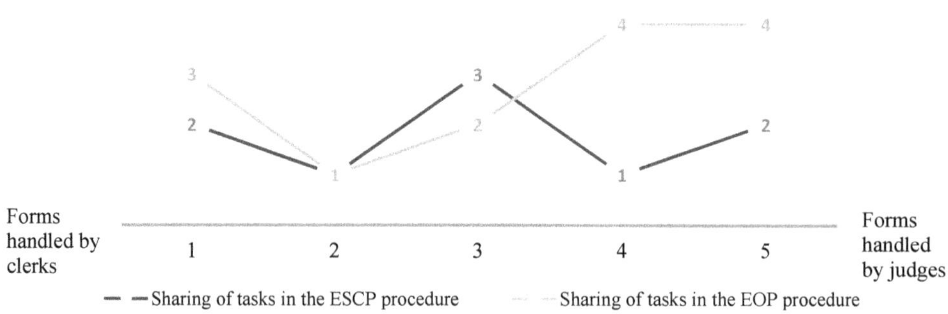

Fig. 6.8. Division of tasks between judges and clerks in the handling of EOP and ESCP forms (survey results)

2082 See Section 6.7.2.2 above.

The clerk usually checks that all the information and necessary documents are provided in the claim forms, and he informs the judge by drafting a report on the state of the claim. The judge then proceeds to order the necessary measures (e.g. sending a request to the party to complete the form by providing the missing information, payment of court fees). Further, the clerk is in charge of arranging service of the EOP on the defendant and of the standard forms between the parties in the ESCP, as well as communication of the judgment to the parties. The type of activity the clerks carry out and the collaboration they have with several judges allows them to gain a broader perspective on the handling of the European uniform procedures. The judges are allocated the cases randomly through a computerised system; hence, it is possible that they might receive one European uniform procedure claim a year or even less. In contrast, the clerks have the possibility of dealing with a higher number of such cases due to the administrative and support tasks they carry out. Thus, they are more likely to put some kind of work practice into place for the accomplishment of various tasks related to such cases (e.g. means of service to be used, requesting translation of standard forms/judgment for service purposes, communication of procedural documents to the parties within the requested time frame for the ESCP). However, it is clear from the data that both EOP and ESCP claims are treated in a manner similar to a national claim or are possibly confused with the domestic procedure. Respondents indicated that ESCP applications have been treated like ordinary requests by courts. Similarly, the EOP was considered in some cases to be an adversarial procedure, and the defendant was summonsed to court and requested to submit a statement of defence before the issuance of a decision. In requesting clarifications or completion of the application, the court sometimes appears to proceed by making use of the domestic procedure format rather than Form B. Generally, evidential documents are submitted along with EOP Form A or are requested by the courts. A translation is often included if the documents have been drafted in a foreign language, otherwise the court will request it. This also leads to additional procedural hearing dates, which results in delayed proceedings and additional costs. In such circumstances, the European procedures lose some of their essential characteristics.

These findings point to a problematic coordination between the Regulations and the national rules, as no specific rules or guidelines have been adopted thus far in order to facilitate application of the EOP and the ESCP in Romania. The limited familiarity of the legal practitioners and the lack of dedicated provisions can make application of the European provisions more difficult at times, especially as multiple interpretations of the legislation are possible. Nevertheless, most of the survey respondents did not perceive national rules as creating difficulties for application of the EOP and the ESCP (Figs. 6.9–6.10).

Respondents identified the following difficulties in applying the EOP: (1) the various interpretations that can be given to applicable legislation, and the multitude of available solutions the judges have to choose from; (2) a lack of special norms for application of these procedures (including continuation of the case following opposition in the EOP); (3) differences between the single-sided EOP model and the adversarial national order for payment; (4) the use of service methods that do not comply with the European procedure standards; (5) the use of forms is sometimes not considered sufficient (i.e. in accordance with domestic rules for the case to be closed, the judge must also draft a court resolution (*încheiere*) to be registered in the ECRIS system; the defendant does not make use of the standard form, but generally uses the reply format available for domestic procedures); and (6) the problem of compatibility of a judge who issued an EOP to handle the case following an opposition. These identified difficulties explain some of the findings regarding the manner in which the procedures are applied (e.g. the issue of the forms as well as a decision in the domestic format; the different court fee-related provisions that are applied for a similar claim, the multitude of hearing terms awarded). Identifying these problematic aspects for practitioners is a first step towards finding adequate solutions to facilitate the effective use of the European uniform procedures.

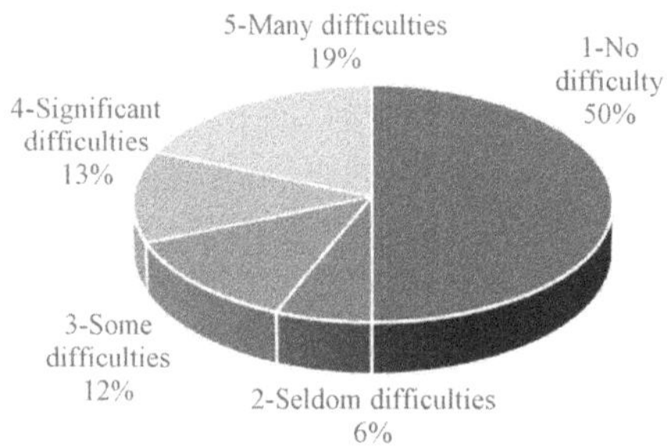

Fig. 6.9. National procedural rules create difficulties in the handling of EOP claims (16 responses)

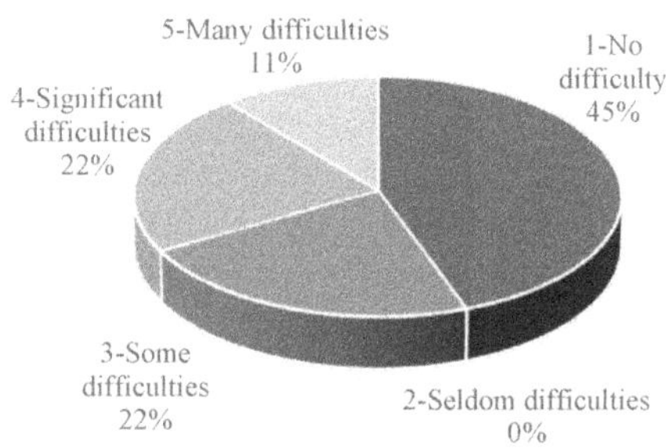

Fig. 6.10. National procedural rules create difficulties in the handling of ESCP claims (9 responses)

Forms

The use of standard forms appears to be challenging in practice. For both European procedures, more than 50% of the respondents indicated that completion of the forms creates problems for the parties.[2083] These difficulties are related to a series of requirements and information the claimant has to fill in, or to the lack of legal knowledge (Fig. 6.11).[2084]

Represented parties occasionally fail to lodge a claim using Form A, but instead make an application in the ordinary procedure format, though it contains all the information requested by the EOP.[2085] The lack of legal knowledge regarding the European procedures and the coordination of legislation creates a bottleneck for parties, especially when they do not employ professional legal services.

The use of EOP Form B to request completion and/or correction of the application form was referred to by approximately 41% of the respondents. The situation is very similar for the ESCP, with 40% of the respondents mentioning that Form B was used. As seen from the analysed files, in 34.6% of the cases the national judge requested completion and/or rectification of the application form. Additionally, the files revealed that courts

2083 This is 58.83% for the EOP (10 of 17 respondents) and 60% for the ESCP (6 of 10 respondents).

2084 The 'Other' type of difficulties concern the 'Date until when interest can be claimed' and 'Technical difficulties with filling in and saving the online questionnaire available on the e-Justice Portal' for the EOP procedure and the 'Incomplete information provided' for the ESCP.

2085 For example, Judecătoria Sectorului 2, Bucureşti, File No. 34340/300/2013.

were often inclined to make this request to the claimant in the format generally used for domestic procedures. This was the case with almost half of the requests concerned. Thus, a court resolution was used instead of Form B. The same appears to be the case in the ESCP file analysed. Although no express reason was provided as to why the court decided to proceed in this manner, the practice might have beeen determined by limited familiarity with the European procedure, difficulties in coordinating national practices with EOP and ESCP provisions, problems related to the ECRIS registration of the standard forms, or a combination of factors.

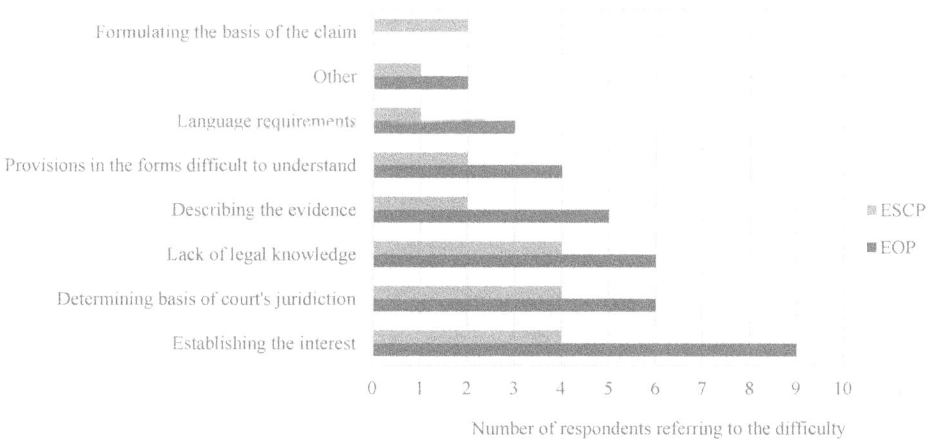

Fig. 6.11. Most common difficulties encountered by parties using the EOP and/or the ESCP

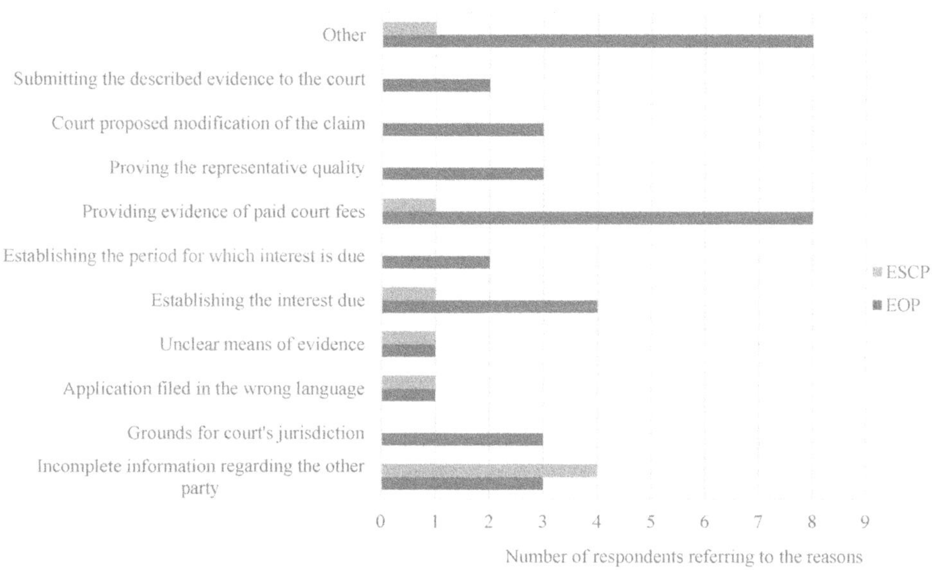

Fig. 6.12. Reasons for most requests for rectification and/or completion of the application form

Further, respondents indicated that Form B was used in less than 25% of the EOP and ESCP cases they were aware of or had handled.[2086] The number of answers is too small to generalise the findings, but nevertheless they provide some evidence that can be corroborated with the results of the file analyses. The files indicate that a consistent number of cases needed additional action from the claimant for completion and/or rectification. Some of these requests were actually unnecessary according to EOP and ESCP Regulations. Reasons that the courts request a completion and/or rectification of the claim are seen in Figure 6.12.[2087]

Courts and practitioners do seem keen to transfer additional requirements from familiar domestic procedures that resemble these harmonised instruments (e.g. requesting in the EOP the submission of described evidence, certification of the evidence for conformity with the original, the translation of evidence documents, and stating the legal grounds on which the claim is based).[2088] This actually only delays the handling of the claim, and shows a lack of understanding of the European instruments. In the ESCP procedure, there are indications that some Romanian judges requested the rectification of Form C because it was sent in a language different than that of the proceedings, or because the court noticed errors in the means of evidence put forward by the defendant. However, most respondents (87.5%) indicated that they had never encountered or requested the amendment of Form C.[2089] An interesting remark made by a judge and confirmed by an interviewed lawyer was that the defendants and/or their representatives rarely made use of standard Form C. Instead they chose to use the usual domestic statement of defence format. The situation was similar for Form F in the EOP procedure.[2090]

The analysis of the court files revealed that 42.3% of the EOP applications studied were rejected by the Romanian judges. However, these cases involved the same parties, with the claimant – in order to use the EOP – seeking several times to demonstrate that

2086 Nine of the 17 EOP survey respondents and 7 of the 10 ESCP respondents.

2087 The 'Other' reasons for requesting an amendment of the claim for the EOP refer to clarifying the amount of the costs claimed; *lis pendence* clarifications; requesting the claimant to fill in the information regarding his bank account details (point 5 in Form A, which has an optional character); certifying the submitted evidence documents for conformity with the original; clarifying the value of the principle; clearly stating the facts and legal grounds on which the claim is based; submitting an additional claim form for service on the defendant; and submitting two copies of evidence documents together with a translation by an authorised translator. Some of these requirements are clearly additional to the exhaustive elements set by Article 7 EOP and confirmed by the CJEU in the *Szyrocka* case. For the ESCP, this concerns the description of the object of the claim.

2088 See also Hess (2017), Chapter 5, para. 876 and 882.

2089 Eight of 10 respondents provided information on this aspect of the ESCP procedure, and 7 mentioned they were not aware of any request having been made for the rectification of Form C.

2090 In 6 cases concerning repeated players, the defence lawyers sent a full statement of defence invoking legal and factual arguments as a response to the EOP instead of making use of the standard opposition form. The claims were all handled by the same law firm, Tribunalul Bucureşti, Files No. 4787/3/20137419/3/2013, 7422/3/2013, 7426/3/2013, 7430/3/2013 Judecătoria Sectorului 2, Bucureşti, File No. 49185/300/2012. There is no indication whether this approach was determined by the lack of familiarity with the EOP or a consideration that the court might be more familiar with the national response format than with the European procedure form.

the defendant was living abroad.[2091] For the same reasons, the court rejected subsequent requests. This led artificially to a doubling of the volume of rejected claims compared to the outcome of the analysed case law.

According to the analysed court files, Romanian judges rejected the EOP claim because (1) the application did not concern a cross-border case (45.45%); (2) the application did not regard a pecuniary claim for a specific amount that had fallen due (36.36%); (3) the claimant failed to modify the claim within the time limit specified by the court (9%); and (4) no clear reason (9%). These grounds in most cases were in contrast to the ones indicated by case law.[2092]

As regards the use of Form D, in all but one case the court delivered its decision in the standard format.[2093] However, what is singular about the use of Form D in claims made by repeated players is that the judge issued Form D following an opposition submitted in a statement of defence format.[2094] The form was issued in what was supposed to be a handling of an opposed EOP in the ordinary procedure. Unfortunately, this type of handling of an opposed EOP demonstrates a deep lack of understanding and confusion with respect to the functioning of the European procedure. The EOP is not an adversarial procedure like the national order for payment. Additionally, the judgment issued following a transfer to the ordinary national procedure is not set to make use of the European standard forms.

With regard to Form E, most of the analysed files showed that the court issued the standard form. Nonetheless, in some cases the decisions were delivered in the domestic format or in both national and European formats. The reasons for this practice have already been mentioned.

The interpretation of the courts is not unitary as regards issuance of the Declaration of enforceability. In most cases, according to respondents and the analysed files, the court proceeded to declare the EOP enforceable upon the claimant's request. However, a significant number of respondents indicated that Form G was issued automatically by the court.[2095] The research has not been able to identify any special approach in relation to Form D in the ESCP procedure. From the limited information available, it appears that the court generally issued the certificate and sent a copy to the parties.

Finally, discussions with practitioners confirmed that the forms were not generally available on the courts' dedicated portals. Having the standard EOP and ESCP forms directly available from the courts or on their dedicated portals would contribute greatly to the visibility of the European procedures for parties and practitioners, and possibly encourage them to choose these instruments for cross-border litigation.

2091 See Tribunalul Bucureşti, Files No. 4787/3/2013, 7419/3/2013, 7422/3/2013, 7426/3/2013, 7430/3/2013, Judecătoria Sectorului 2, Bucureşti, File No. 49185/300/2012.

2092 See Section 6.7.2.3 above.

2093 In one case, the judge issued the decision in the format of a national judgment.

2094 Tribunalul Bucureşti, Files No. 4787/3/2013, 7419/3/2013, 7422/3/2013, 7426/3/2013, 7430/3/2013.

2095 During an interview, a lawyer mentioned that in one of the cases, the court issued Form G at the same time as Form E. This surprised the practitioner, but the court decided to wait and see whether the EOP would be opposed, and then only subsequently use the form to initiate enforcement proceedings against the debtor in a different Member State.

Language

According to collected empirical data, parties or practitioners did not seem to encounter significant difficulties with regard to the language or translation requirements in the EOP procedure. This was the case for almost 70.6% of the respondents. When language-related aspects arose because forms had not been submitted in the language of the proceedings, evidence documents were submitted in a foreign language, or service had to be carried out abroad, the court generally required the claimant to provide translations by an authorised translator. The court requested translations or the parties submitted translations on their own initiative in more than 42% of the EOP case files analysed. These translations concerned (1) the evidence documents or the evidence together with the application form; (2) requests for service purposes in accordance with the provisions of the Service Regulation; or (3) the serving of Form G. Although translation is absolutely necessary for service of the EOP and/or communication of Form G to another Member State in order to guarantee the defendant's procedural rights and access to justice, the court must not extend this to documents described as evidence in the application form. In requesting the translation of evidence documents, the Romanian judges imposed requirements additional to the ones established exhaustively in Article 7 EOP. Additionally, this added to the complexity of the procedure, increased the litigation costs and extended the proceedings' timeframe, aspects that the Regulation seeks to diminish and limit. From this perspective, application of the EOP appears problematic in practice, and it sometimes moves away from the purpose for which it was established.

As with the EOP, 80% of the ESCP respondents did not appear to have encountered language or translation-related difficulties. As mentioned earlier, a translation seemed to be requested each time the documents had not been drafted in the language of the proceedings. In relation to the service of documents, two different approaches have been observed: namely, communicating the copy of Form A and Form C to the defendant in Romanian, or requesting that the claimant provide translations of the documents to be served on the defendant in another Member State. This second approach is most often used; hence, the court does take notice of the ESCP and the provisions of its Service Regulation.

Service

Service of the EOP on the defendant is carried out in a variety of ways (Fig. 6.13). As indicated by the respondents and the analysed case files, the service methods are as follows.

The most frequently used methods of service for EOP and ESCP procedures are the service by post with acknowledgement of receipt and the method set by the Service Regulation through transmitting and receiving agencies. In addition, as shown in Figure 6.13, other methods often used are (1) personal service on the defendant or his representative attested by an acknowledgement of receipt; (2) service at the defendant's address on a member of his household or an employee; (3) deposit of the order at the post office or other competent authority, and placing a notification in the defendant's mailbox; and (4) service by procedural agent of the court.

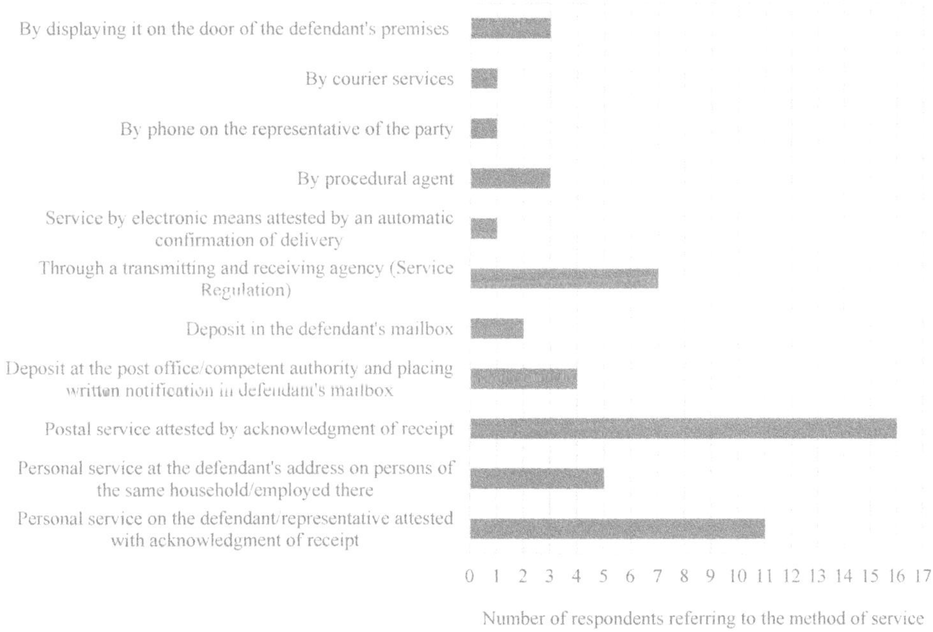

Fig. 6.13. Methods used to serve the EOP on the defendant

In addition to these methods that are provided by Article 13 or Article 14, Romanian procedural agents have proceeded to display a notification regarding the communicated document on the door of the defendant in accordance with national law (Article 163(3) NCPC). This action was sometimes triggered by the fact that the defendant's premises did not have a mail box in which to deposit the document, and because the procedural agent was faced with a repeated refusal by the defendant and/or his employees to receive the EOP documents. However, this method is not among the means provided by the Regulation, as it does not comply with the procedural standards set by the EOP. It does not provide sufficient guarantee that the defendant has been properly informed of the order issued against him with the possibility of opposition. Rightfully, foreign courts requesting service for the purpose of the EOP to be carried out in Romania have not considered the service to be valid when the documents are displayed on the door.[2096] In order to secure a balance between parties' interests and their right of access to justice, it would be desirable for the EOP to contain specific provisions that would prevent the defendant from making use of abusive tactics to prevent being served with an order issued by the court.

With regard to difficulties related to service of the EOP on the defendant, almost one-third of the respondents mentioned that they had not encountered such situations. The

[2096] Two Romanian lawyers referred to situations in which the Austrian court requested that the EOP be served on a Romanian defendant. The bailiff proceeded to display the document after several failed attempts to serve it at the premises of the defendant, after refusal by the defendant's employees to receive the document being served, and owing to the lack of a letter box that would have allowed the document to be deposited.

remaining two-thirds indicated that they were either aware of or not aware of problems regarding the EOP. The difficulties were often related to the service abroad or both abroad and in Romania. In relation to the ESCP service by post with acknowledgement of receipt, 50% of the respondents replied that they had encountered no problems. If difficulties arose in serving EOP or ESCP documents, these were generally related to the reasons in Figure 6.14 below.

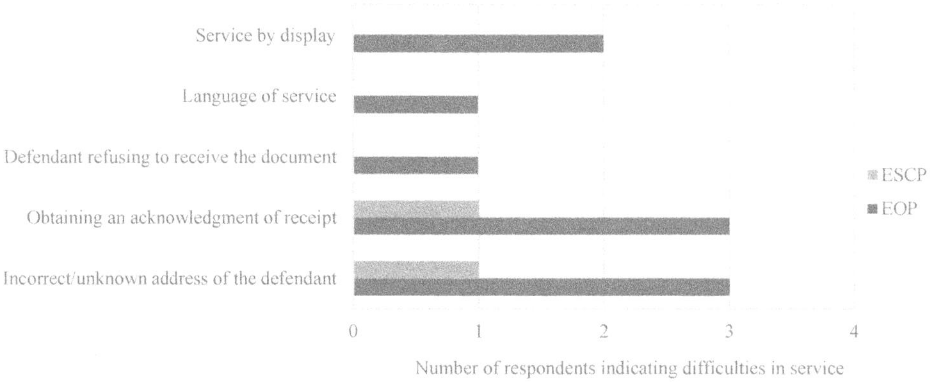

Fig. 6.14. Difficulties encountered in the serving of EOP or ESCP documents on the defendant

If difficulties are encountered, the period of time necessary to serve the documents in a valid manner stretches to 3 to 4 weeks or beyond 4 weeks.[2097] Furthermore, some practitioners indicated that the duration necessary was generally longer if the documents needed to be served abroad. If there were doubts about the validity of the service, the service was renewed. The claimant is required to provide proof of the defendant's domicile within the meaning of Brussels I*bis*, or to carry out the service through a procedural agent instead of by post (i.e. if the acknowledgement of receipt was not obtained). These measures are to provide additional procedural guarantees that the defendant is actually informed and aware of the proceedings. Hence, he is able to arrange for his defence. The analysed files revealed that courts verify the validity of the service of the EOP and the ESCP on the defendant, and whether this has been carried out in accordance with the minimum standards set by the Regulations. This is of particular importance for securing the defendants' access to justice. Although generally the Romanian courts are in charge of arranging the service, a particular practice in relation to the EOP and the ESCP sometimes comes up. The court communicates to the claimant that he needs to collect the document, and arrange for its translation and service on the defendant. In such circumstances, service is carried out by post with acknowledgement

[2097] The longest period necessary to serve an EOP was over 1 year. According to the documents in the case file, several attempts were made to serve the order on the defendant company, but no acknowledgement of receipt was obtained. Several of the companies addresses and information relating to the head-office in the trade registry were no longer valid. Thus, any attempt to carry out a valid service in accordance with the Regulation failed.

of receipt, and the court itself receives a copy of the communicated documents as well as proof that the claimant undertook the necessary steps to serve the EOP or ESCP standard forms on the defendant. This different approach to service in relation to the same procedures can lead to confusion for claimants.

Hearings

EOP and ESCP cases are handled during public hearings or in chambers in Romania, even though the procedures are designed to be carried out in written form. The use of public hearings or sessions in chambers is a consequence of the national legislation,[2098] limited familiarity with the European uniform procedures in some cases, and the fact that no specific provisions or guidelines have been adopted to coordinate the relation between the two levels of rules. From the analysis of the EOP files, it is clear that sometimes the judge confused the European procedure with other national provisions. The parties are summoned to a public hearing, and the procedure is not considered to have been discharged in a valid manner if the parties or their representatives do not respond when their names are called out by the court clerk. Additionally, the defendant is requested to submit a statement of defence, or in the event of a lack of discussion time during the public hearings, the parties and their representatives are requested to submit written notes or conclusions. The single-sided EOP is thus transformed into an adversarial procedure,[2099] similar to the national order for payment or the ordinary procedure. Even more alarming is the fact that this concerns not only claims registered in earlier years of the application of the EOP but also claims in a case as late as 2013. One lawyer acknowledged that in a case he had followed, the court summoned the parties to a hearing, but it was sufficient for him to oppose the claim during the hearing in order for the court to subsequently reject it. The EOP had not actually been issued.

For the ESCP, respondents indicated that hearings were organised because the courts confused the European procedure with the ordinary national procedure, and that this was due to a lack of familiarity with the instrument. Claimants generally did not seem to request the holding of a hearing. However, occasionally it appeared that the judge handled the claim during a hearing organised in chambers, due to the provisions of the national law that are held to be applicable by the court, even though the ESCP is primarily a written procedure.

Challenging Mechanisms (Opposition, Appeal, Review)

On the basis of responses to the EOP surveys,[2100] no generalisations can be made. Four respondents indicated that less than 25% of the cases had been opposed, while three others mentioned that between 51%-75% EOP had been opposed. From the analyses of

2098 See also Section 6.7.2.3 and 6.2.2 above.

2099 For example, in a hearing conducted in chambers, minutes regarding an EOP review were requested under Article 200 NCPC. In the operative part of the minutes, it is mentioned that the procedure was adversarial. See Tribunalul Bucureşti, Chambers Hearing Minutes (*Încheiere*) No. 543/03.09.2013, File No. 23275/3/2013.

2100 Only 7 of 16 respondents that filled in a survey provided information on the percentage of opposed EOP claims.

the 26 EOP files and the information provided by practitioners, only seven EOPs had been opposed (26.9% of the EOP cases), and six of these opposed cases were claims between the same parties. The defendant's lawyer had in none of them opposed the EOP by making use of Form F. Analyses of the case files revealed that the high opposition rates involved cases undertaken between the same parties who were repetitive players, and were not a variety of EOP cases received by the court. This represents an unnatural multifold increase in the opposition rate in comparison to other results based on published cases law. Due to these abnormal results and limited information from other sources, no triangulation is possible nor is an inference with regard to a possible overall national situation.

As to observance of the limitation period for submission of the opposition, only a few respondents indicated that they had come across situations in which the opposition was sent after the 30 days had lapsed. In two of these situations, the defendant requested reinstatement of the case within the 30-day period for the opposition and, surprisingly, the court granted it, probably in accordance with the national law. However, none of the respondents gave reasons as to why the Romanian judge proceeded in this manner.[2101]

The empirical data gathered does not provide in-depth information regarding ESCP appeal proceedings. Only one of the survey respondents mentioned that ESCP judgments had been appealed. None of the other respondents were able to provide information on the number of appeals. The only respondent who acknowledged the appeal proceedings mentioned that the whole procedure lasted less than 3 months from the registration of the claim until the appeal. This seems hard to believe, considering the time that procedures generally need. Other responses were probably based more on third-party information or on a personal guess. The reason ESCP appeals take longer than 6 months appears to stem from the fact that courts confuse the European procedure with the ordinary national procedure. Unfortunately, these findings cannot be triangulated with any statistical data or published case law in order to determine their validity. It would have been extremely useful to be able to obtain more information on this aspect of the ESCP procedure. It is hoped that future research will shed more light on the issue.

With regard to the review and its use in the EOP or ESCP procedure, most respondents replied that they were not aware of any cases in which the mechanism was used. This was the case for 43.75% of the EOP survey respondents and 71.42% of the ESCP.[2102] Further, 40% of the EOP respondents replied that no review requests had been lodged by defendants. Only 13.33% confirmed that the review had been used.[2103] As for the ESCP, the information is hardly relevant. One respondent replied that he had not been aware of

2101 The present information updated by the Romanian Government in relation to the EOP on the e-Justice Portal indicates that a reinstatement in the opposition time is possible before Romanian courts. See https://e-justice.europa.eu/content_european_payment_order-353-ro-en.do?member=1.

2102 This concerns information provided by 15 of the 17 EOP survey responses, and 7 of the 10 ESCP surveys returned to the researcher.

2103 Two respondents. Additionally, one of the EOP files studied refers to a review procedure (Tribunalul București, File No. 23275/3/2013). However, it is not a review procedure in the sense of Article 20 EOP, but a reassessment or review of the request (*cerere de reexaminare*) in accordance with Article 200 NCPC. The application was annulled by the court because the claimant had not provided the additional documents requested by the court within the set timeframe. The EOP claim was annulled owing to additional requirements that should have been complied with in accordance with the domestic procedural law (Articles 194–199 NCPC).

any review request, while another confirmed that he had known of such a procedure. This shows that the review procedure is not often used in relation to the EOP and the ESCP, an aspect confirmed also by the analysis of the available case law.[2104] The reasons given were not all actually related to the reasons provided by Article 20 EOP or Article 18 ESCP. These were (1) service of the EOP not having been carried out in accordance with the standards set by the Regulation; (2) force majeure; and (3) matters concerning the existence of the debt and its amount (the reason was also invoked for an ESCP). From the information available, the review was accepted in one EOP case on the grounds that the order had not been served in accordance with the Regulation's provisions. The choice of the national court pre-dates the ruling in *eco cosmetics* case, and is certainly not in line with the CJEU's restrictive interpretation of Article 20 EOP.

Representation

Representation is still commonly used in EOP and ESCP procedures, at least by one of the parties, as was also confirmed by the analysed case law.[2105] Of the respondents, 62.5% indicated that claimants had been represented in more than 50% of the EOP cases.[2106] The rate of representation, 50%, was slightly lower for EOP defendants.[2107] ESCP respondents indicated that 50% of the claimants and defendants had been represented in more than 50% of the cases.[2108]

The analysed case files highlight a higher level of representation of claimants in the European procedures. This was the case in 19 of the 26 EOP files (approx. 73% of the cases). Defendants were represented by a lawyer in only seven of the analysed cases (approx. 27% of the cases). Additionally, in 23% of the EOP cases both parties were represented. With regard to the ESCP, the level of representation was lower than for the EOP; in some cases the parties requested the assistance of a lawyer only to complete the standard application form, preferring then to appear in person, as representation by a legal practitioner might have resulted in procedural costs higher than the actual value of the claim.

Representation of the claimant or of the defendant did not completely eliminate the difficulties related to the filling in and use of the forms. In some circumstances, the lawyers also appeared not to be fully familiar with the instruments, and confused the requirements of the European uniform procedures with those of the corresponding special or ordinary domestic procedures.

Procedural timeframe

Based on the survey answers, it appears that a significant number of EOP decisions were issued within the expected timeframe – a period of 30 days for the issuance of the order. The results were more encouraging than those based on identified case law.[2109] The same

2104 See Section 6.7.2.3 above.

2105 See also Section 6.7.2.4 above.

2106 This concerns 5 of the 8 EOP survey respondents who replied to this question.

2107 This concerns 4 of the 8 EOP survey respondents who replied to this question.

2108 This concerns 3 of 6 ESCP survey respondents who replied to this question.

2109 See Section 6.7.2.3 above.

appears to be the case regarding the time necessary for the court to issue a rejection of the application (Form D).[2110] However, they are based on too limited a number of respondents and cases to be generalised. The collection of more detailed national statistics in relation to the EOP procedure would greatly contribute to a better insight into how it functions.

In comparing the outcome of the EOP survey and the file analysis, it becomes obvious that a significant number of claims are not being handled by the court within an average period of 30 days.[2111] The reasons for this longer handling period is provided by the empirical data, and relates to additional requests from the claimant: namely, (1) to submit the proof of having paid the court fees; (2) to submit the evidence documents, certified copies and translations of the documents; as well as (3) the high volume of cases the court has to handle;[2112] and (4) regularisation of the procedure following the entry into force of the new procedural code (NCPC). Some of these reasons that stretch the timeframe could be eliminated if the instrument were applied in accordance with the provision of the Regulation and the aim for which this instrument was adopted. Further, increasing judges' familiarity with the EOP would make them more at ease in proceeding to issue or refuse the request on the basis of the provisions of Article 8 EOP. This would probably make it less likely that judges would reject the EOP application on the basis of Article 200 NCPC, or request submission of the evidence described in standard Form A together with a translation.

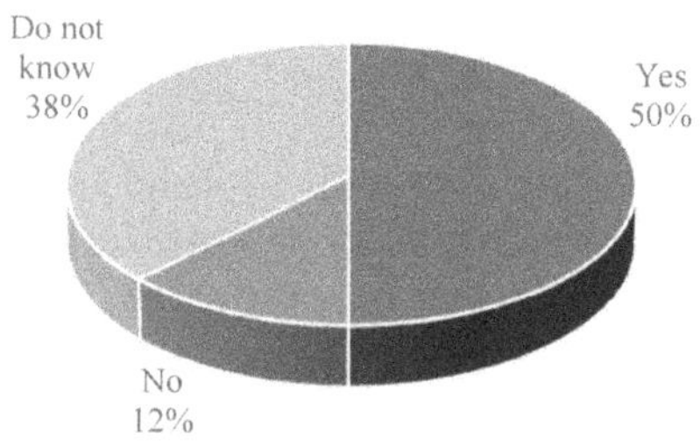

Fig. 6.15. EOP issued within 30 days (survey results)

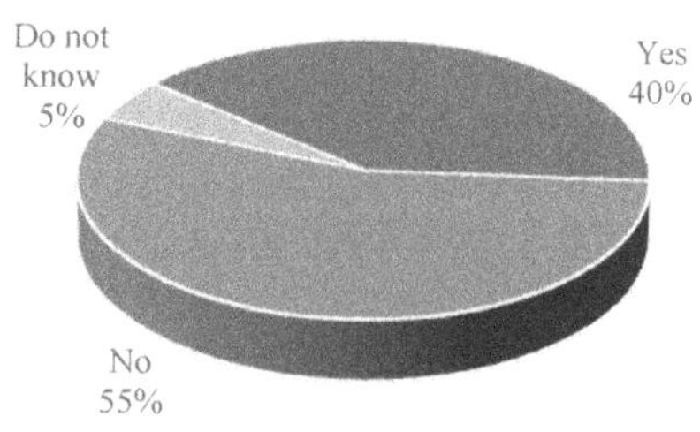

Fig. 6.16. EOP issued within 30 days (files analysis)

2110 In accordance with the case files studied, Form D was issued within a timeframe below 1 month in 3 cases (Tribunalul Bucureşti, Files No. 20307/3/2012, 20309/3/2012, 32450/3/2013), over 1 month in 1 case (Tribunalul Bucureşti, File No. 34717/3/2013), over 2 months in 1 case (Judecătoria Sectorului 2, Bucureşti, File No. 49185/300/2012), and 4 months (Tribunalul Bucureşti, File No. 23273/3/2013). The longer procedural timeframe for this case was due to an application of the EOP procedure in combination with national procedural requirements. See also Section 6.7.2.3 above.

2111 This includes situations in which the court issued Form E (the EOP) or Form D (rejecting the EOP application).

2112 There have been situations in which the request by the claimant's representative to obtain shorter procedural terms for the handling of the case was not possible. ECRIS's automatic allocation system was unable to accommodate the request due to the court's high workload. Judecătoria Sectorului 2, Bucureşti, File No. 34340/300/2013.

Article 9(1) EOP expressly establishes that the court is to make use of standard Form B in order for the claimant to complete or rectify the application if the requirements set by Article 7 are not met. Hence, certification of the documents, translation of evidence, and submission of documents are certainly not to be requested from the claimant. The judge has to decide on the basis of the EOP application form whether the claim appears to be founded. Additionally, clearer information for the parties on the court fees applicable to European procedures as well as precise information on the payment details would facilitate compliance with this requirement. It would also reduce the number of cases in which Form B is sent for this purpose. All of this would contribute to a further decrease in the time necessary for the issuance of an EOP.

With regard to the average period of time necessary from the lodging of From A to the moment of receiving Form G in the EOP procedure, the following outcome arises from the empirical data:

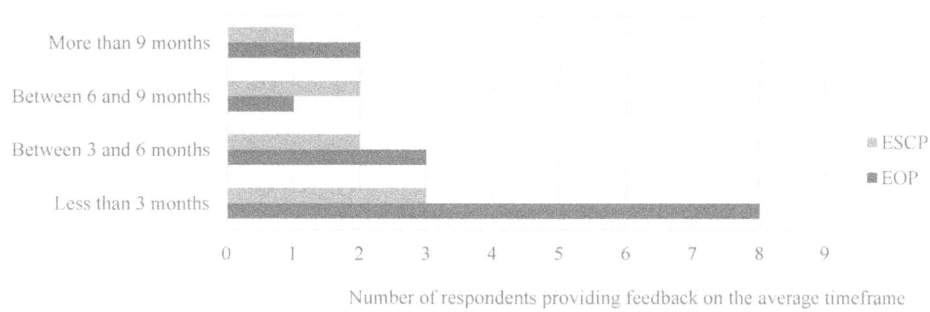

Fig. 6.17. Average time necessary to conclude an EOP or an ESCP procedure

In corroborating these results with the case files analysis, it was observed that the duration necessary for handling an EOP claim seems to be decreasing, while the duration regarding issuance of a national order for payment by the District Courts appears to have increased from 3.9 months in 2013 to 4.16 months in 2014. The reasons the EOP procedure took on average longer than 3 months to be finalised relates to (1) the carrying out of a valid service (including identifying the actual address of the defendants), especially when this is taking place abroad; (2) rectification of the application and the normal longer duration of court proceedings; and (3) the court setting multiple procedural terms and postponing the deliberation and issuance of a decision.[2113] As previously mentioned, Romanian judges pay significant attention to the verification of service to determine whether it has been carried out in a valid manner in order to guarantee the defendant's procedural rights. If there is any doubt, the procedure is renewed, even several times, which prolongs the EOP proceedings. Therefore, service remains a bottleneck issue. Facilitating access to information regarding parties' domicile, residence, or headquarters,

[2113] There are additional reasons identified by the respondents, such as increasing the timeframe of the EOP procedure, on top of the aspects mentioned earlier in relation to delays in issuance of the order and rejection of the application.

and cooperation between authorities in this respect, could greatly improve the cross-border service of documents in judicial proceedings. However, this does not appear to be likely in the near future.

With regard to the ESCP, respondents indicated that the judgment was generally issued within a period of 6 months, as can be seen from Figure 6.17. However, the timeframe for completion of the ESCP claim in the analysed file was above this desired result. The judgment was received by the Romanian claimant only within a period of 7 months and 2.5 weeks.

As pointed out previously in relation to the EOP, cross-border service is sometimes problematic and leads to a longer time being needed to accomplish the procedure. Unfortunately, national reports regarding the judiciary's activity in Romania provide no information regarding the average length of the national small claims procedures that could be used for comparative purposes.

This data gives some indication regarding the length of time the ESCP procedure could take. Nevertheless, the number of respondents and analysed files is too low to be able to determine any national trend in relation to this European procedure.

As to the average duration of ESCP appeal proceeding, 80% of the survey respondents estimated that it would take less than 3 months for the court to solve the request. However, none of the identified cases or the analysed file actually dealt with this procedural step; hence, the information cannot be verified further.

Costs, interest, penalties

In all the studied EOP and ESCP files, the courts proceeded to apply the fixed court fees that were applicable for the national *ordonanța de plată* and the *procedura cu privire la cererile de valoare redusă*.[2114] This practice was confirmed by the lawyer interviewed in relation to the EOP, as well as by the analysed case law.[2115] Contrary to this experience, one lawyer advising claimants on filing an ESCP mentioned that for both claims the court requested the payment of court fees determined based on the value of the claim in accordance with information provided by the Romanian authorities on the e-Justice Portal. The divergent practices of the courts as well as the difference between information available on dedicated European websites and the practice of the courts only creates uncertainties and difficulties for parties deciding whether to use these European procedures in cross-border litigation.

As well as costs, EOP and ESCP claimants requested the payment of interest, especially legal interest,[2116] up until the date that the debt was paid in full.

Contractual penalties were also requested in some EOP cases. In three of five cases, the claimant also requested interest, which the courts awarded. In a few EOP cases it was indicated that other costs were also awarded, such as lawyers' fees and the cost of certified translations.

2114 See discussion in Section 6.5.

2115 See Section 6.7.2.5.

2116 Additionally, in some EOP files, the claimant requested contractual interest (2 cases) or proceeded to request an amount he had calculated (2 cases).

6.7.3.5. Enforcement

Information regarding execution of the EOP and the ESCP in Romania is limited. This is partly due to the fact that only two bailiffs replied to the EOP survey, with an additional two providing comments on their experience with the European uniform procedures or lack thereof. Some information was provided by lawyers and judges. Considering the professional group to which most of the respondents belonged (judges, clerks, and lawyers), the results need to be considered with caution. The information provided by these groups on execution of the EOP and the ESCP could be fragmented, and concern only certain aspects of the enforcement process. Furthermore, as can be seen in Figures 6.18 and 6.19 below, in a significant number of cases respondents indicated they did not know what the situation was in practice. More research into these aspects of EOP and ESCP execution is necessary in the future.

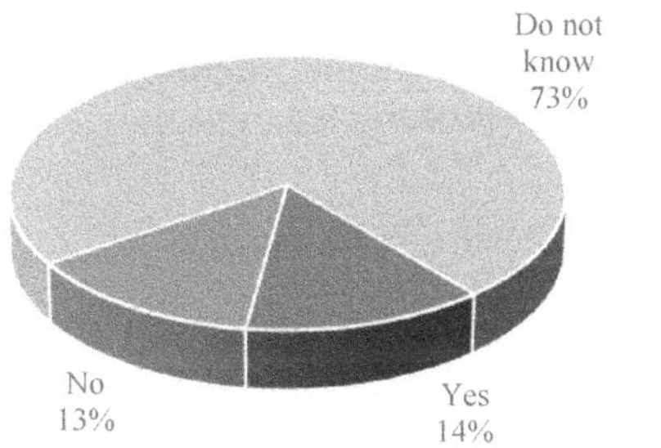

Fig. 6.18. Claimant experiencing difficulties in EOP enforcement following delivery of Form G (15 survey responses)

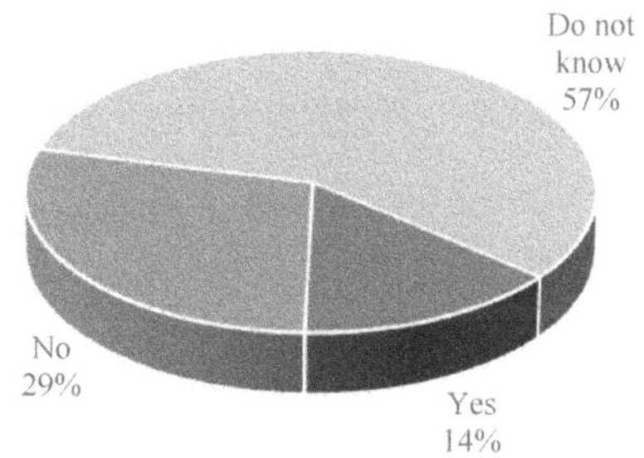

Fig. 6.19. Claimant experiencing difficulties in ESCP enforcement following delivery of Form D (7 survey responses)

According to respondents, among the difficulties claimants encountered in the EOP and ESCP execution processwere (1) obtaining information with regard to assets and the financial situation of the debtor (EOP and ESCP); (2) execution costs (EOP and ESCP); (3) identifying the authorities competent to carry out the execution (ESCP); (4) the execution process cannot be initiated prior to the defendant being served the enforceable title (ESCP); (5) choosing the execution method (ESCP); and (6) the execution has to be approved by the court (ESCP). Some of the above difficulties appeared to be particularly relevant for layperson claimants not having legal representation: for example, problems in identifying the competent authorities that would be able to carry out enforcement activities, or choosing the execution methods. Although the results are very limited and cannot be generalised, they provide an indication of possible additional information that might be made available more easily to parties making use of these procedures without engaging the services of a legal professional.

Respondents who replied in the affirmative to the question regarding similar difficulties between EOP and ESCP enforcement (Figs. 6.20–6.21) and the national judgment pointed to the fact that the execution procedure – regardless of the origin of the title – was identical as soon as it was enforceable in Romania. Hence, the bailiff follows the same execution procedure once the court approves the procedure's initiation.[2117]

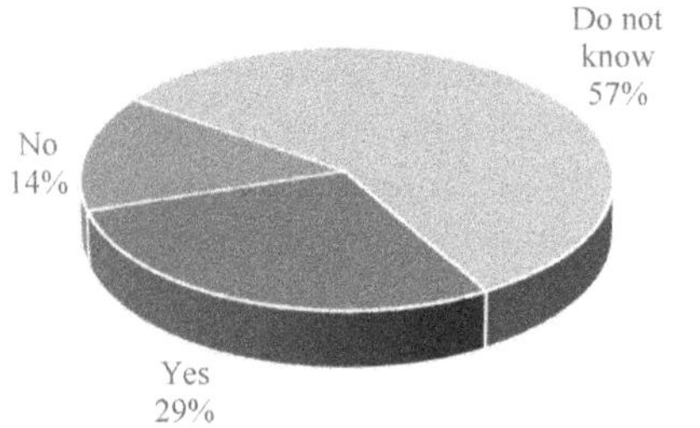

Fig. 6.20. EOP enforcement difficulties are similar to those experienced in national uncontested monetary claims enforcement (7 survey responses)

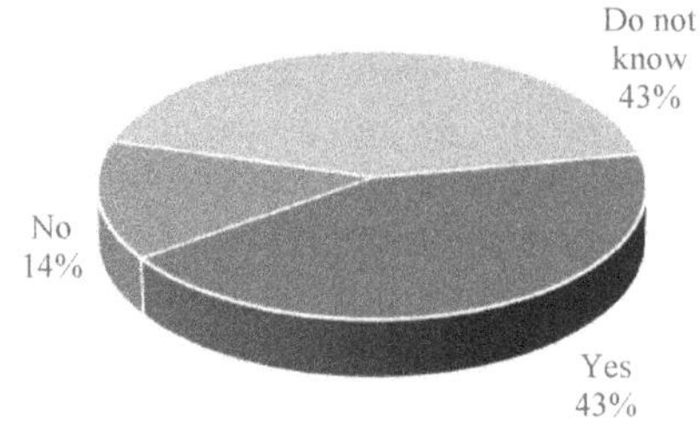

Fig. 6.21. ESCP enforcement difficulties are similar to those experienced in national small claims enforcement (7 survey responses)

Based on respondents' replies, creditors did not appear to refrain from enforcing proceedings in Romania (Figs. 6.22–6.23).[2118] This seems to have happened only in ESCP procedures, and was likely because the costs of successfully enforcing a judgment might easily have been higher than the amount the claimant was seeking to recover.

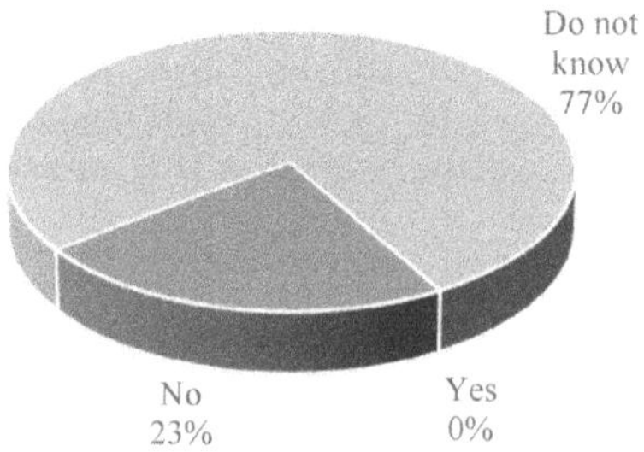

Fig. 6.22. Creditor decided not to pursue the EOP enforcement procedure (13 survey responses)

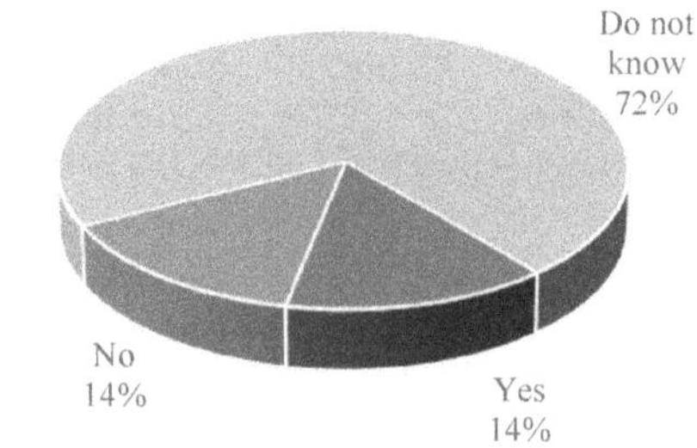

Fig. 6.23. Creditor decided not to pursue the ESCP enforcement procedure (7 survey responses)

The refusal of enforcement and the limitation or stay of enforcement mechanisms in EOP and ESCP procedures do not seem to have been applied in Romania. None of the respondents reported having encountered requests for a refusal of enforcement or for a

2117 For more information regarding the execution process, see Section 6.6.

2118 Results should be considered with caution, as most EOP respondents declared that they were not aware of this situation in practice. In addition, the number of responses is very modest, and does not allow generalisation.

limitation or stay of enforcement. Most practitioners were unable to provide any information in this respect. Furthermore, the analysed case files provided no further information.

The execution process is sometimes challenged by the defendant, and seems to be the case with EOPs (Fig. 6.24). The challenging of the execution activities is sometimes used by defendants in order to slow down the enforcement and create difficulties for the claimant, as the court has to rule on the objection raised in order for execution activity to continue. This practice was mentioned by some of the respondents as a tactic to delay execution of the EOP and the ESCP.

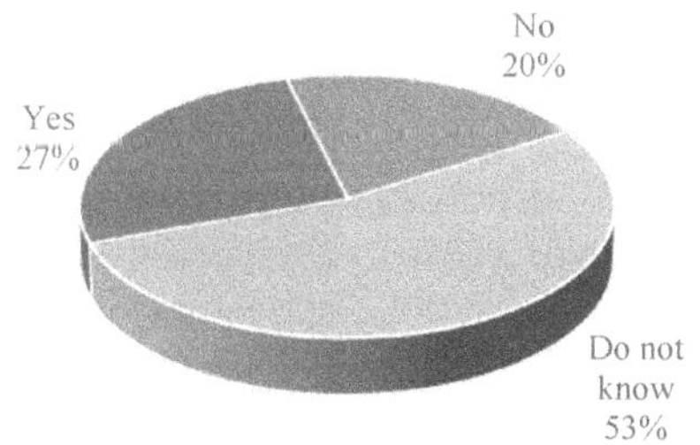

Fig. 6.24. EOP enforcement procedure was contested in Romania (15 survey responses)

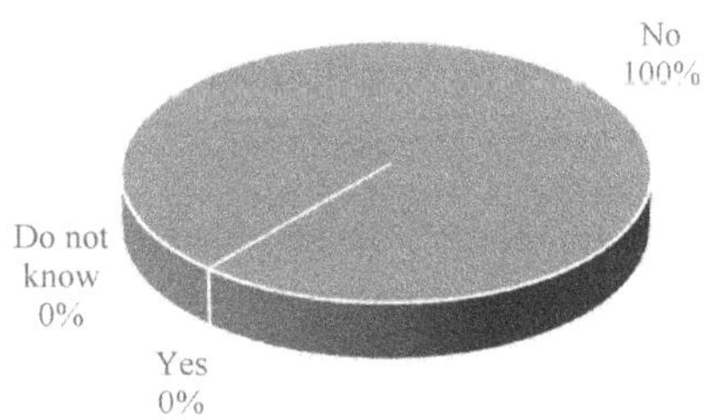

Fig. 6.25. ESCP enforcement procedure was contested in Romania (7 survey responses)

The various amendments of the NCPC since its entry into force in 2013 affected the enforcement procedure each time. This created a certain level of uncertainty for creditors, and increased the time necessary for the execution to be initiated. The issuance of a writ of execution by the court (*încuviințarea executării silite*) was reintroduced in February 2016.[2119] Furthermore, the type of enforcement activity chosen can also influence the time necessary to execute the European title. This is in particular the case for proceedings concerning immovable property, as certain procedural delays need to be followed.[2120] If assets that can be part of an execution process are lacking, enforcement will be delayed or made impossible. In accordance with the survey results, 33.33% of the respondents indicated that the length of the execution process was more than 1 month in EOP procedures.[2121] Similarly, 50% of the ESCP respondents indicated that the enforcement of ESCP judgments took between 1 and 2 months to pursue.[2122] Due to the very low number of practitioners who were able to respond to the survey questions, these results should be seen only as an indication of what the situation might be in practice. Further, according to additional feedback, there was an indication that enforcement might take as

[2119] See Section 6.6 above concerning amendment of the NCPC by Law No. 138/2014 and the Government Emergency Ordinance No. 1/2016.

[2120] See Articles 813–863 NCPC.

[2121] Three of 9 EOP respondents that replied to this survey question.

[2122] Three of 6 ESCP respondents that replied to this survey question.

long as one year to pursue. Unfortunately, in such situations the speedy execution of the European uniform procedures is no longer a reality.

With regard to Romanian bailiffs, one lawyer explained that he considered the enforcement officer to be more at ease with enforcing national orders for payment than with EOPs. This was because the bailiff was more familiar with the national procedure; hence, if execution is to be carried out in Romania against a Romanian party, it might be much easier to use the domestic instrument. According to the same respondent, the EOP would make more sense if the execution were to be carried out in several places in the EU (for example if accounts of the company or person are attached in more Member States and not only in Romania). Hence, at the national level there is still some reluctance to use newer procedures such as the European ones.

Data regarding the enforcement of Romanian EOP and ESCP titles in other Member States are scarce. Respondents generally declared that they were not aware of enforcement proceedings undertaken abroad (87% EOP respondents and 100% ESCP respondents).[2123] In relation to EOPs, one lawyer was following enforcement proceedings that were being initiated for an EOP in Italy in collaboration with local lawyers, as well as in Slovakia for a different EOP title. The Romanian lawyers had decided to contact local lawyers, as they had no knowledge of the enforcement procedure rules and practices in those countries.

With regard to the ESCP, the only information regarding execution of the judgment was provided by an analysed court file. In this case, the court issued Form D in Romanian and Italian, but this second version included the non-standard text in Romanian. The title was communicated to the defendant in this format, which does not comply with the requirements of the procedure to fully guarantee the party's understanding of the content of the decision. The service had to be carried out in Italy, and was carried out by post with acknowledgement of receipt. However, the case did not provide additional information as to whether the debtor actually paid the due amount to the creditor, which was a Romanian company.

6.7.3.6. Practitioners' assessment

Overall, respondents consider the EOP and the ESCP to be efficient solutions regarding uncontested monetary claims in a cross-border litigation procedure in terms of 'speediness, affordability, and protection of parties' right' compared to the national procedures available for this purpose (Figs. 6.26–6.27).

The reasons that the procedures are perceived to be efficient overall are that they require a relatively short time for their handling, the admission of evidence is less strict than in the national proceedings, and the procedures are based on standard forms. However, not all respondents provided additional information as to what determined their choice. The identified drawbacks that make the European procedures less appealing are (1) the confirmed limited familiarity of the court and practitioners with the proceedings; (2) the lack of coordination between EOP and ESCP provisions and national

2123 Thirteen of 15 EOP respondents and 7 ESCP respondents.

legislation; and (3) the complicated execution procedure, which should be simplified in order to facilitate EOP and ESCP enforcement.

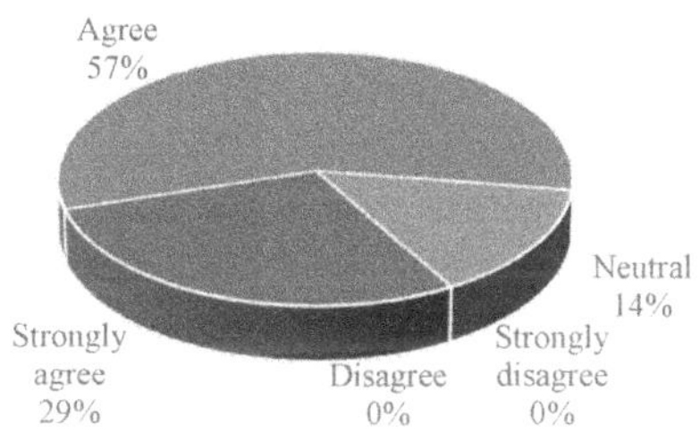

Fig. 6.26. Respondents consider the EOP an overall efficient solution (14 survey responses)

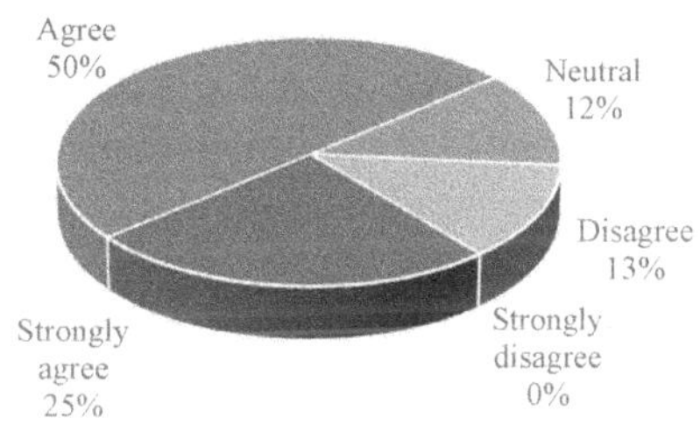

Fig. 6.27. Respondents consider the ESCP an overall efficient solution (8 survey responses)

With regard to the survey question on the effectiveness of the European uniform procedures for the recovery of uncontested or small value claims in cross-border litigation, the general position of the respondents was positive (Figs. 6.28–6.29).

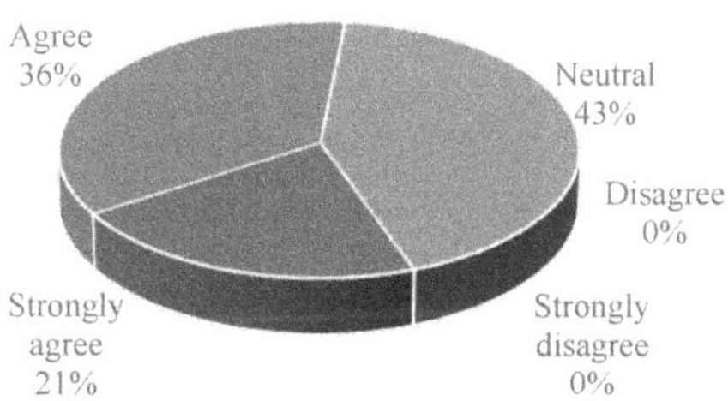

Fig. 6.28. Respondents consider the EOP an effective solution for the recovery of uncontested claims (14 survey responses)

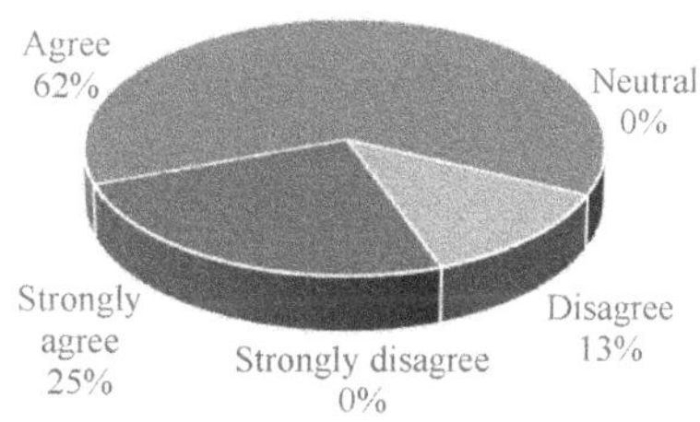

Fig. 6.29. Respondents consider the ESCP an effective solution for the recovery of small claims (8 survey responses)

Although most respondents decided not to explain their choice, the EOP and the ESCP were perceived as effective solutions because the debt was recovered; thus, the decision was executed, the claim was generally not contested by the defendant, and the timeframe within which the enforceable title was obtained was relatively short.

Notwithstanding the fact that practitioners consider the European uniform procedures to be effective solutions in cross-border litigation and efficient instruments in terms of speediness, procedural costs, and the guarantee of parties' procedural rights, obstacles to the successful application of the EOP and the ESCP were acknowledged. These were related to (1) courts' and practitioners' lack of familiarity with the European procedures; (2) coordination with national procedural rules (especially in the transfer to the ordinary procedure); (3) the excessive time necessary to obtain the title and then to pursue execution in comparison to what the procedures aim to achieve; (4) difficulties in complying with requirements regarding service abroad. These difficulties were also confirmed by the findings in case law and in the analysis of the files, as well as by the survey and interview responses.

To improve the way the EOP and the ESCP are applied, some of the respondents consider there is a need for more information and guidelines to be made available to practitioners. Guidelines should be made available online on the website of the Ministry of Justice as well as websites of the professional organisations. Further, practitioners need to become familiar with the procedures, and less hesitant with regard to the minimum control model they propose. Other proposed developments to improve application of the European procedures concern various stages of the proceedings. These are mainly related to the transfer to the ordinary procedure, to electronic service in the ESCP procedure, and to simplification of the national execution procedure. Regulation 2015/2421 amending the ESCP Regulation has already modified the service provision, encouraging the use of this means. The remaining two recommendations rest within the power of the Romanian and other national legislators. Further simplification of the execution procedure does not seem very likely, however, considering the latest NCPC amendments. It remains to be seen whether electronic service would have more chance of success and actually come to be applied in practice between the Member States.

6.7.4. *Overall assessment*

The EOP and the ESCP are to a certain extent known to Romanian courts and practitioners. Nevertheless, the way in which the procedures are applied in practice raises some concerns, and leads to a preference for the national procedures, as parties and practitioners seem to find them more clear.[2124]

The period of time necessary to obtain the needed enforcement titles appears to be decreasing, which is beneficial for parties deciding to make use of these European instruments. However, application of the EOP and the ESCP is usually complemented with national requirements, most of which are not compatible with the aims of the Regulations. Application of the EOP and the ESCP are at the cross-roads between European and national procedural requirements, and deviating from the Regulations' provisions does not encourage parties to choose and make use of these instruments in preference to national procedures. Practitioners themselves are sometimes reluctant to use these instruments if they are not certain that the competent courts are sufficiently familiar with the procedures and will proceed to apply them in accordance with their aim.

With regard to guaranteeing parties procedural rights, the courts seem to pay particular attention to observing the procedural standards set by the EOP and the ESCP as well as those of the domestic legislation. This risks making the procedure more difficult for the claimant, who has to comply with a number of additional requirements, some of which require his physical presence in court (e.g. providing certified translations at various stages of the proceedings, participating in hearings, requesting the certified decision to proceed to the execution, as he is only served a simple copy by the court). Hence, representation remains necessary although it is not mandatory according to the

2124 See also Hess (2017), Chapter 5, para. 900.

proceedings. The extensive use of legal representation is also influenced by the limited amount of information that is generally available to courts or on authorities' websites. A layperson will not easily find his way around, also because information is only available in Romanian if available at all. Furthermore, the institutional users (companies) seem to be the main parties interested in making use of these European uniform procedures in this Member State.

The results achieved by the EOP and ESCP procedures in Romania are promising for the facilitation of cross-border litigation. The data available do show some improvements, but these mainly relate to issuance of the decision and abolition of the exequatur. The execution process remains difficult and long, but changes in this area do not seem likely in the near future. Finally, application of the European procedures in general would benefit from a better national legislative framework and coordination between European and domestic norms. This would facilitate the courts' and parties' tasks, bring clarity, and contribute to the development of a stable practice involving Romanian courts. This might also encourage parties to choose these European instruments over available national procedures in cross-border cases.

Chapter 7

COMPARATIVE PERSPECTIVES ON THE FUNCTIONING OF THE EOP AND ESCP

The present chapter analyses the findings of the previous chapters on the EOP and the ESCP, focusing on the functioning of these European procedures in England and Wales (hereafter referred to jointly as England), France, Italy, and Romania. The analysed jurisdictions represent the two main legal traditions: common law (England) and civil law (France, Italy, and Romania). The chapter discusses the effects of the European harmonised procedures on cross-border litigation in the selected jurisdictions. Special attention is given to how these uniform instruments (1) are perceived within the national framework; (2) are implemented in the internal system of procedural rule; and (3) are interpreted and function in practice along with national special procedures that have a similar purpose. These aspects are considered in a comparative perspective, acknowledging the similarities and differences that exist between the analysed jurisdictions. Further, the chapter examines elements of the national procedural rules that influence the way in which the EOP and the ESCP are applied, as well as identifies additional reasons that contribute to the present state of the practice. Although this study is confined to four jurisdictions – England, France, Italy, and Romania – the outcome might provide common guidelines that also prove valid for other Member States.

7.1. Introduction: A Preliminary Comparative Outline

7.1.1. National Debt Recovery Procedures

To examine whether the European uniform procedures improve the process of cross-border litigation, it is necessary to consider the national procedures that are a functional equivalent to the EOP and the ESCP. In all analysed jurisdictions, national legislation contains specific proceedings for the recovery of contested or uncontested monetary claims, small value claims, or alternative summarised proceedings and/or simplified rules that the creditor can choose to apply when seeking to recover his debt. In certain cases, a specific court also exists to handle smaller and/or simple claims (e.g. *Giudice di pace* in Italy; *Juge de proximité* in France). Claimants who pursue the recovery of debts from debtors situated in another Member State have the possibility of choosing between national and European procedures. Furthermore, the rules regulating national procedures may in certain cases apply as well to the EOP and the ESCP.

Generally, the special debt recovery proceedings are handled by the lower or general national courts (e.g. *Tribunale* or *Giudice di pace* in Italy; *Judecătorie* or *Tribunal* in Romania; *District courts* in England; TGI, TI or *Juge de proximité*[2125] in France). The national proceedings available for the recovery of monetary claims differ significantly as to the parties' procedural duties, the sequence of procedural steps, and the observance of particular timeframes. It is essential that a creditor be aware of the particularities of national procedures when deciding whether to initiate court proceedings. The procedural rules that apply to a specific procedure may or may not imply compulsory legal representation,[2126] duties to perform certain procedural acts,[2127] an expected level of costs,[2128] and a predictable timeframe in which to obtain the enforceable title.[2129] Differences exist not only between different legal systems but may also concern various instruments a claimant may choose from within the same jurisdiction.

Taking into account the existing applicable national proceedings for the recovery of monetary claims, these can be grouped into four categories: namely, (1) order for payments procedures; (2) summary procedures regarding monetary claims; (3) small claims procedures; and (4) various simplified instruments. The characteristics of each category of proceedings are presented briefly in a subsequent section.

7.1.1.1. Order for Payment Procedures

Special procedures for the recovery of uncontested monetary claims exist in two of the three civil law jurisdictions:[2130] namely, France (*injonction de payer*) and Italy (*procedimento per ingiunzione*). The model adopted by these jurisdictions relies on a two-stage procedure. The first phase is single-sided, with the order being issued or the request rejected based only on the evidence and allegation put forward by the claimant. This stage of the national order for payment procedure differs from the EOP, where the European legislator chose a non-evidence-based model; hence, relying only on a description of the

2125 On 1 July 2017, the competence of these judges was transferred to the TI (*Tribunal d'instance*). See Section 4.2.1.

2126 For example, in Romania, a creditor deciding to use the *ordonanța de plată* or the *procedura cu privire la cererile de valoare redusă* is not subject to mandatory representation; in contrast, the same party seeking to initiate court proceedings in Italy has a duty to employ the services of a legal representative.

2127 For example, in France, the claimant has a duty to serve the *injonction de payer* on the defendant by employing the services of a bailiff. As opposed to this, in England, the court generally has the duty to serve the documents on the defendant.

2128 For example, when court fees are subject to being a fixed amount, are a variable amount, or there are no court charges (such as in France).

2129 This is the case in Romania, where the new Code of Civil Procedure establishes a duty on the court to issue the *ordonanța de plată* within a period of 45 days from the moment the claim was registered, or several procedural deadlines for specific stages of the proceedings for the *procedura cu privire la cererile de valoare redusă*.

2130 This type of procedure with its national particularities and differences is usually available within civil law countries. In common law countries, such as England, the summary judgments fulfill this function. See Kramer & Kakiuchi (2015), at 17 (available at http://papers.ssrn.com/sol3/papers.cfm?abstract_id=2610773).

proof, without analysing the evidence documents during the first stage of the proceedings. The trial becomes adversarial if the debtor opposes the order issued against him. Hereafter, the procedure continues as indicated in the rules of the ordinary procedure. In Romania, the legislator chose an adversarial model. The debtor is informed of the request, and is expected to participate in the trial. If the defendant does not submit a statement of defence, the judge will issue the order on the basis of the evidence submitted by the claimant.[2131] The national order for payment procedure (*ordonanța de plată*) resembles to a certain extent a summary procedure. In England, there is no specific national order for payment procedure. The ordinary default procedure is usually used for the recovery of money claims, or, alternatively, the parties opt for the summary procedure.[2132]

In all three jurisdictions, the order for payment procedures extend their application to cross-border cases. These are alternative instruments to the ordinary national procedure, and their applicability is not subject to a monetary threshold limitation. However, their application may involve specific types of monetary claims (i.e. France)[2133] or, alternatively, exclude from their scope certain types of debts (i.e. Romania).[2134]

Italian and Romanian orders for payment are not form-based procedures. The exception is France, where the claimant may use standard drafted forms. Additionally, special electronic applications are available in order to submit a national order for payment claim in France and Italy.[2135] In Romania, the claimant or his representative may choose to email the claim to the competent court. With the exception of Italy, representation by a lawyer is not mandatory.

In Romania and Italy, the judge has to issue the decision within a set period. This is 45 days and 30 days, respectively, from the moment the claim was registered. Furthermore, in France and Italy, an order for payment has to be served on the defendant within a set period in order to prevent it becoming void.[2136] This enables the defendant to oppose within a specific time limit the order that was issued against him. This varies per jurisdiction. If an opposition is submitted, the case has to continue as indicated in the national ordinary procedure; however, the transfer mechanism differs between jurisdictions. Hence, in France, the court automatically establishes a hearing date and summons the parties to appear in court, while in Italy, it is the defendant whose duty is to initiate proceedings, otherwise the *decreto ingiuntivo* remains valid and becomes

2131 See Section 6.3.1.

2132 See reply provided by the English Ministry of Justice regarding a study undertaken within the e-Codex project. Velicogna, Lupo & Mellone (2016), at 24. See also Section 3.2 above.

2133 In France, the procedure can be used by the creditor seeking to recover debts resulting from contracts or statutory acts, financial instruments (e.g. cheques, bills, promissory notes), assignment of professional debts, damages due to a crime that the offender had promised to pay (alternative measure established by the public prosecutor).

2134 In Romania, the national order for payment procedure cannot be used for the recovery of debts related to insolvency proceedings, labour and social security rights, enforcement of administrative, fiscal or customs acts, or criminal actions, or for the restitution of executed performances.

2135 This is the case with the IPWEB in France and Trial On-Line System in Italy, which allow practitioners to file applications and the courts to receive electronic documents regardless of whether based on the standard form or not.

2136 This is not the case in Romania, because the defendant is served at a prior stage with the documents of the proceedings. See Section 6.3.1.

enforceable. Alternatively, if the order is not opposed, the claimant may request the court to issue a writ of execution.

Costs of judicial proceedings for these instruments differ per jurisdiction and may include several types of fees at various stages. However, a common feature is that the filing fees are lower than for the ordinary national procedure.[2137]

7.1.1.2. Small Claims Procedures

In the analysed jurisdictions, a number of options are available for handling small value claims. One of the national approaches is to give competence for such claims to special courts or judges (i.e. *Giudice di pace* in Italy; *Juge de proximité* in France). In order to facilitate parties' access to justice, these courts are usually situated in the geographical proximity of the litigants. The case is trialled as indicated in the ordinary national procedure, but in a simplified, less formal format (e.g. in France, the claim is introduced by a simplified mechanism, *déclaration au greffe* or *saisine simplifiée*), and possibly includes a settlement attempt (e.g. in Italy, during the first hearing the Justice of the Peace will seek to achieve conciliation of the parties). The second solution is a specially adopted small value claim procedure. This is the case in England (*Small Claims Procedure*) and in Romania (*procedura cu privire la cererile de valoare redusă*). In addition to these procedures, since 2016 a small claim procedure, *Plateforme de Traitement des Petites Créances,* which is handled by bailiffs, has been available in France.[2138] In all three jurisdictions, the procedures are subject to a monetary threshold as well as to some material limitation. In England, the *Small Claims Procedure* applies to all claims whose value is below £10,000 (approx. €14,100) as well as to claims under £1,000 (approx. €1,410) for personal injury, and housing claims.[2139] The Romanian *procedura cu privire la cererile de valoare redusă* follows closely the ESCP guidelines, which served as a model for the national legislator. The procedure involves claims not exceeding RON10,000 (approx. €2,262.44). The scope of the procedure's application is less broad than that of the English *Small Claims Procedure*, and mirrors the ESCP Regulation. The French procedure is available for the recovery of claims up to a value of €4,000. Further, the English and Romanian procedures are adversarial, while the French procedure is an extrajudicial one that empowers the bailiff to negotiate a settlement with the debtor if he agrees to take part in the proceeding.[2140] The Romanian and French procedures are optional instruments, while the English one is a compulsory path for claims below the established threshold. This characteristic of the English procedure might contribute significantly to the high number of cases that are dealt with annually using this instrument.

2137 They are either fixed fees (i.e. Romania, France in commercial cases) or a percentage of the fees applicable in ordinary proceedings (i.e. Italy). The exceptions are the civil proceedings in France, where the claimant does not have to pay a court fee.

2138 See Section 4.3.4.

2139 A discretional application by the judge is possible for claims that are over the set limit by a small amount. See Section 3.3.6; Sorabji (2015), at 159.

2140 If a settlement cannot be reached, or the debtor is not willing to take part in the procedure, court proceedings can be initiated.

To initiate proceedings, all three national procedures make use of special standard forms. Claimants submit these to the court in England and Romania, or online to the bailiff in France, who will subsequently inform the defendant. The Romanian procedure, like the ESCP, is designed as a written proceeding. Hence, the judge is to decide the case on the basis of the forms filed by the parties and the written evidence submitted together with these, unless one of parties requests the court to organise a hearing or the court deems it necessary. In contrast, in the English procedure, the hearing is a central element. It is usually organised in a largely informal manner and takes place in the judge's chambers, unless a party requests that the court decide the claim in his absence, or both parties agree that the case is to be decided on the basis of the written submissions. In the English procedure, the judge adopts a more direct and inquisitorial approach, questioning the witnesses and the parties, and deciding on the appropriate evidence. Representation by a lawyer is not mandatory, as the procedures are meant to be carried out in person by the litigants.

As to the possibility of parties reaching a settlement, the English and Romanian systems chose a different approach, while the French procedure is focused on a settlement. The Romanian judge has no duty to achieve a settlement. As opposed to this approach, the English standard practice directions recommend that parties try to reach a settlement of the case or seek to narrow the issues before the hearing.[2141] In addition, a dedicated free court-based mediation scheme is available for all claims within the financial limits of the small track, and claims with a value below £5,000 (approx. €7,050) are referred to a mediator who informs the parties of the nature of the process and its benefits.[2142] Furthermore, in both jurisdictions an appeal is available against a judgment issued in the national small claims procedure. This secures a scrutiny of procedural as well as substantive errors.

The national approaches differ with regard to the winning party's recovery of the procedural costs. The Romanian legislator follows the same principle as in the ESCP; the loser pays, unless unnecessary or disproportionate costs are requested compared to the value of the claim. This approach is similar to the domestic principle followed by all court proceedings.[2143] The English CPR awards only the routine expenses,[2144] which is an incentive for the parties to appear in person before the English judge. Additionally, as regards court fees, filing costs for the English Small Claims Procedure are determined and vary in accordance with the value of the claim, while the Romanian legislator opted for two fixed fees applicable at determined thresholds. The French procedure is subject to fixed fees.

7.1.1.3. Summary Procedures regarding Monetary Claims

Special summary procedures that can be employed to recover monetary claims are available in England (*summary judgment*) and in Italy (*procedimento sommario di cognizione*).

2141 CPR PD 27, Appendix B.

2142 Use of the scheme, however, is not mandatory. See further Sorabji (2015), at 159.

2143 The losing party bears the costs of the proceedings, but the court can reduce, even *ex officio*, the reimbursement of costs related to lawyers' and experts' fees if there is an obvious lack of proportion between the value or complexity of the case or the activity carried out by the professional, and the circumstances of the case (Article 451(3)-(5) NCPC).

2144 The routine expenses (CPR 27.14) include, for example, court fees, costs of issuing the claim, travel expenses for witnesses, and loss of earnings capped at £90/day.

The aim of the summary proceedings in England is to facilitate and speed up proceedings for the creditor when no extensive trial appears necessary for the handling of the claim. This is the case when (1) the claimant has no real prospect of succeeding; (2) the defendant has no real prospect of successfully defending the claim; or (3) there is no other reason for the case to be disposed of at a trial.[2145] Both parties are involved in the proceedings from an early stage; hence, providing higher procedural guarantees for the defendant from the beginning of the proceedings. In Italy, this instrument is intended for less complex cases where the court can enter judgment immediately on the basis of the existing documents, or the evidence can be gathered promptly. Thus, the scope of application of these national procedures is broad. They are applicable in purely internal as well as in cross-border monetary claims in both jurisdictions.

In Italy, the claimant may request the use of this procedure; in England, both parties may choose to make use of the instrument at specific stages of the proceedings. Additionally, in England, the court on its own initiative can order the case to be handled in the summary procedure. In Italy, the judge can decide the opposite, switching the claim to the ordinary procedures if he considers it to be too complex for a simplified proceeding. In both jurisdictions, the parties are generally summonsed to a hearing, and the court issues a judgment on the basis of the presented arguments. The summary judgment usually has to do with the entire claim. Nonetheless, in England, the procedure can also be employed for a part of the claim.[2146] The decision issued by the court can be challenged by way of an appeal, otherwise it acquires *res judicata*.

The cost of the proceedings reflect the national rules. While court fees are reduced by 50% in the *procedimento sommario di cognizione*, in England they are determined by the value of the claim, as with the ordinary procedure.

7.1.1.4. Various Simplified Instruments

As well as the national instruments that can be categorised as orders for payment, summary procedures or small value claims, a number of additional simplified procedures are available and can be used in practice in the analysed jurisdictions for the collection of monetary claims, or to facilitate the handling of particular claims that fall under a specific monetary threshold. These additional simplified procedures can be classified as (1) default procedures; (2) interim decisions; (3) electronic monetary claims; and (4) other procedures.

Default Procedures

A default procedure as such is available only within the English procedural system, and aims to secure the claimant's access to justice if the defendant fails to respond to the claims. The form-based application implies in most cases a purely administrative act

[2145] CPR 24.2. On the interpretation of the phrase 'no real prospect of success', see Lord Wolf in *Swain v. Hillman*, Court of Appeal, [2001] 1 All English Law Reports (All ER) 91. Hence, 'real' has the meaning of realistic as opposed to fanciful prospects of success. The phrase does not mean 'real and substantial' prospect of success. On the test, see further Andrews (2008), at 86–87; Blackstone's Civil Practice 2015, at 568–569.

[2146] The remaining issues are handled in accordance with the common procedure (24 PD 10 CPR).

from the court, not involving any decision on the merits of the claims.[2147] The decision in most money claims is obtained without a hearing, and the title is immediately enforceable. The decision can be set aside by the judge if there are serious reasons or if it was issued in violation of the applicable rules. Although 'procedurally fragile' due to the power of the court to set it aside, the procedure is often used.

Interim Decisions
Interim orders or decisions enable the creditor to obtain an immediate provisional enforceable title before the actual conclusion of the trial. These are *interim payments* in England, *provvedimenti anticipatori di condanna* in Italy, and *ordonnance de référé* in France. They are not final decisions on the merits, but ensure that the creditor receives payment of the debt or of part of it that corresponds to the amount recognised or not contested by the defendant, if the court considers that it is highly likely the claimant will obtain an award for a specific amount in the trial (England), or if it appears that the existence of the obligation cannot be seriously denied (France). Interim decisions can be employed during ongoing procedures (Italy) or before the initiation of an actual trial (England and France). In France and Italy, the orders have the potential to acquire full enforceability if the parties decline to pursue the trial within which the orders were issued, or to initiate court proceedings regarding the same matter.

Electronic Monetary Claims
These types of procedure have to do with the English system, and involve Money Claim Online (MCOL) and the Claim Procedure Centre (CPC). Applications are filed electronically, and imply the use of standard forms. All applications are handled by one court: the Northampton County Court. MCOL deals with relatively simple money claims, while the CPC responds to the needs of institutions involved in the bulk recovery of claims (e.g. credit card companies, public utilities). They are applicable for specified debts of a value not higher than £100,000 (approx. €141,000). The procedures are written, and do not require a hearing. If the defendant admits the claim or does not reply, the court may issue a judgment in admission, or, accordingly, in default. If a defence is filed, MCOL or the CPC is transferred to the competent court and follows the rules of the ordinary claim procedure (e.g. track allocation, legal representation).

Other Procedures
Together with the above types of accelerated proceedings, two additional simplified instruments are made available to the creditor by English and French law. They concern ancillary monetary claims (*Part 8 Claim* in England) and orders related to the execution of an obligation other than monetary (*injonction de faire* in France).

7.1.1.5. Use in Practice

The variety of national procedures creates a diversity of solutions from which creditors may choose. Some of the analysed instruments in the above categories have acquired

[2147] See Section 3.3.1 above.

significant popularity within their national systems, and are regarded as effective solutions that are often chosen by litigating parties and their representatives. This is the case with the national order for payment procedures in France and Italy for the recovery of uncontested monetary debts. They allow the creditor to obtain a speedy order that may be enforced within a short period if it is not opposed by the debtor. In Romania, the preference of claimants for the national order for payments procedures registered a significant decrease following the coming into force of the new Code of Civil Procedure. This has coincided with the establishing of a new national simplified procedure, *procedura cu privire la cererile de valoare redusă*. The procedure appears to have gained a significant share of the claims whose value is below RON10,000 (approx. €2,262.44).

In recent years, submission of a national order for payment with the court in the analysed jurisdictions has been facilitated further by the adoption of electronic filing and handling systems. These developments promote access to justice and speed up the procedure, thus decreasing the time necessary for the court to register and handle a case.[2148] The reduced court fees in some of the jurisdictions (i.e. Italy and Romania) are an additional incentive to use these alternative procedures. As to the possibility for debtors to oppose the order issued against them, some concerns have been expressed, because only a small percentage of the orders are actually contested. This is the case in France and Italy.[2149] More available information should be provided as to the action the debtor can take, the costs he can expect to incur, and the nature of the procedure.

Small claims procedures are used frequently in England and Romania, where a significant number of cases are handled each year in accordance with these rules. In England, this is due also to the compulsory nature of the procedures, which are drafted in a manner that makes them user friendly considering the non-mandatory representation and the use of standard forms. Their adversarial nature secures that both parties can actively participate in the proceedings. Together with this, the speedy judgment,[2150] the reduced formalism,[2151] and the lower costs entailed in comparison to the ordinary procedure contribute to their success. The available appeal mechanisms safeguard parties' rights, offering litigants increased procedural guarantees.

In addition to these two popular types of national procedures, the default and the electronic monetary procedures in England, especially MCOL, have proven to be successful instruments for handling money claims. They account for around 70% and 13%, respectively, of the money claims filed in 2010 with the English courts.[2152]

Other available national procedures have produced more modest results. This is owing to a number of reasons that have their roots in the characteristics of the national systems, the interaction between various procedures, the available alternatives, and the provisions regulating their application.

2148 See for example the case in Italy, Section 5.3.1.

2149 See Sections 4.3.1 and 5.3.1.

2150 For example, in England, the average duration of a small claim was 32.4 weeks in 2015, and 23 weeks in 2013. See Section 3.3.6 and Sorabji (2015), at 159. In Romania, the court has to issue the judgment within 30 days from the moment it received all the necessary information.

2151 The mainly written procedure in Romania and the oral hearings taking place in the judge's chambers in England.

2152 See Sections 3.3.1 and 3.3.4. For references to the high use of MCOL, see O'Hare & Browne (2013), at 164.

7.1.2. *Uniform European Solutions within National Diversity*

Although the EOP and ESCP Regulations provide a uniform procedural framework that should ensure equal treatment for users,[2153] a significant number of aspects continue to be governed by the national procedural rules (e.g. service, costs of proceedings, way the procedure is handled, transfer to national ordinary procedure, appellate proceedings, enforcement). This maintains a certain national specificity regarding the way in which the EOP and the ESCP are applied.[2154]

Now several years into their application, a comparative study on the way the EOP and the ESCP are accommodated by the national procedural systems of several Member States can further our understanding of the way these instruments function. The solutions they provide in cross-border litigation compete with available domestic procedures. Their optional nature does not automatically favour their use, while their scope possibly overlaps that of other national instruments, or is more restrictive. Moreover, their certain reliance on national procedural rules impedes both the transparency and the predictability of the uniform provisions and the simplification the European legislator aimed to achieve. The particularities of the ways in which the European procedures are applied in various Member States create a sort of 'transplant effect'.[2155] Hence, certain EOP and ESCP provisions are applied in a manner that does not seem to correspond to the unified instruments the European legislator intended to establish, but resemble specific national procedures. These considerations appear to add to the complexity rather than to the simplification of the path a European creditor needs to undertake to recover his debt. In adopting a functional comparative approach, the analysis seeks to determine whether the European procedures serve the purpose for which they were established, and to what extent this has been achieved.

7.1.3. *Evaluation Criteria*

In analysing how the EOP and the ESCP function in the selected jurisdictions, this research uses a set of pre-determined criteria. These are used to assess whether the difficulties that are generally associated with cross-border litigation have been set aside by these uniform procedures, and whether they achieve their aims without trading off procedural justice. The evaluation criteria can be divided into three categories: these are (1) implementation, (2) effectiveness, and (3) efficiency.

In assessing the way in which the procedures were included in the national procedural systems, the following aspects are considered:

- the legislative actions undertaken by the national legislator;
- the accessibility of information regarding the EOP and the ESCP to interested parties and legal professionals;

[2153] Storskrubb (2008), at 214 and 229–230.

[2154] Kramer (2008a), at 282.

[2155] On the 'transplant effect', see further Arvind (2010), at 65–66, 78–79; Berrowitz, Pistor & Richard (2003), at 177–179.

- the relevance of the information on actually conducting court proceedings in the analysed jurisdiction; and
- the practitioners' level of knowledge with respect to these instruments.

The accessibility of information regarding the EOP and the ESCP is evaluated from the point of view of (i) the transparency of information as to the two European Regulations and the national rules that supplement various aspects of the proceedings; (ii) the availability of such sources of information for parties and practitioners; and (iii) the language in which this information is made available to the parties.

In analysing the effectiveness of the European procedures, the following aspects are examined:

- the level of simplification of proceedings;
- the procedural guarantees they provide for the parties; and
- the effective execution of the court's decision (in the Member State of origin or abroad).

The simplification offered by the EOP and the ESCP is assessed from the perspective of the procedural steps necessary in order to use the procedure, and the need to be actively involved in certain stages. In evaluating the procedural guarantees established by the European procedures, the researcher considers the means of service actively employed, the observance of language requirements related to the service and to the provision of translations, and consideration for the parties' procedural rights. In assessing the latter, the analysis focuses on the existence of actual means of appeal and review, their effectiveness when applied, the activities undertaken by the courts to verify that the defendant was properly informed of the procedure that was initiated against him, and was provided with sufficient data in order to undertake the actions that best fit his interests before the court.

The efficiency of the EOP and the ESCP in relation to national procedures and to aims the Regulations express are studied from the perspective of:

- the costs; and
- the time needed to conclude the procedure.

Section 7.2 below focuses in particular on the evaluation criteria related to the implementation of the EOP and the ESCP, considering the legislative actions undertaken in the analysed systems, the accessibility and relevance of the information regarding the European procedures, and the national rules that facilitate their application. The analysis also reflects on certain effectiveness and efficiency evaluation criteria. In addition, the level of simplification of the proceedings, the procedural guarantees they establish for the parties, as well as the costs of proceedings are examined from a legislative perspective. Building on this, Section 7.3 concentrates on an evaluation of the European instruments from the perspective of effectiveness and efficiency criteria. The effectiveness assessment (simplification, procedural guarantees, and execution of EOP and ESCP decisions) is conducted on the basis of case law findings and practitioners' perspectives. Statistical data on the application of the two European procedures give an indication of their effective use. Further, the level of practitioners' knowledge is also considered, studying the case law perspective as well as practitioners' opinions resulting from the empirical research carried out in the four jurisdictions. The cost efficiency of the EOP and the ESCP is examined in the light of practice-based information regarding costs implied by the application of these proceedings. The timeframe necessary to conduct an EOP or an ESCP case within the analysed jurisdiction is also considered. Finally, in Section 7.4, the comparative analysis assesses holistically the effectiveness and efficiency of the EOP and the ESCP, summing up elements of the evaluation criteria used in Sections 7.2 and 7.3. These emphasise the results achieved by the EOP and the ESCP in facilitating cross-border litigation as opposed to the functionally equivalent domestic procedures.

7.2. Implementation of the EOP and the ESCP

7.2.1. Legislative Approach

In integrating the European uniform procedures into the national procedural systems, Member States are free to choose their own approach and solutions: primarily, the choice of legal instruments. A regulation requires no specific additional legislative actions at the national level. The referral to domestic procedural rules when the Regulations contain no specific provision,[2156] as well as the explicit reference to national law in some provisions (e.g. methods of service in the EOP, the existence of an appeal mechanism for the ESCP judgment) have the potential to create disparities and to undermine the harmonised application of these European instruments. This may concern not only differences between Member States. At the domestic level, the choice made by the national legislator may undermine the uniform application of the procedure within that Member State. This may be the case when domestic courts within a single jurisdiction opt for discrepant applications of the European uniform procedures because they refer to different provisions of the national law for complementing the same rules set by the Regulations. Taking into consideration the provisions of the analysed European Regulations, the present section focuses on implementation of the path chosen in the four analysed jurisdictions.

7.2.1.1. Chosen Approaches in the Analysed Jurisdictions

In these jurisdictions, the national legislators opted for three different approaches. The French and English legislators chose to include specific EOP and ESCP provisions in the Code of Civil Procedure and in the Civil Procedure Rules, respectively, by amending them. In addition, guidelines were published to facilitate the application and use of the two instruments.[2157] The English Ministry of Justice states in an Explanatory Memorandum on the amendment of the Civil Procedure Rules that the new rules were necessary in order to 'ensure that the CPR is not inconsistent' with the

[2156] Article 26 EOP and Article 19 ESCP.

[2157] Articles 1382–1391 CPC regarding the ESCP, Articles 1425-1 to 1425-9 CPC on the EOP and Article 1425 CPC on court fees. Decree No. 2008-1346 of 17 December 2008. Part 78 CPR. See also Sections 3.5 and 5.5.

EOP and the ESCP.[2158] The French motivation is implicit, coordinating the provisions of the national rules with the necessary mechanisms for the application of the European Regulations.[2159]

The CPR Part 78 and Practice Directions along with the French CPC provisions set rules as to how the claims filed in accordance with the European uniform procedures should be treated by the courts, using when necessary the existing national mechanisms and procedural rules. Although both English and French provisions regarding the EOP and the ESCP are limited in the procedural aspects they tackle, the French rules appear more detailed and explicit in the actions that should be undertaken by the court or the parties in comparison to the English CPR provisions. The latter are limited in a number of situations to reassuming the provisions of the Regulations and/or referring the judge or the parties to other parts of the rules concerning aspects of the national procedure. Nevertheless, the adoption of specific domestic rules frame the EOP and the ESCP and their inclusion in the national procedural system and practice, thereby adding to the transparency of the norms. Being part of the main set of procedural rules contributes to the accessibility of information and to a unitary legislative approach.

In addition to the national procedural rules concerning the EOP and the ESCP, the French Ministry of Justice and Her Majesty's Court and Tribunal Service (HMCTS) issued guidelines. The HMCTS guidance leaflet (EX725) is dedicated to parties litigating in person and using one of the European uniform procedures. The document seeks to provide information in an accessible language for a layperson, and its contents repeat much of the explanatory material of the actual Regulations and their guidelines. Additional explanations are limited, and very often result in sending the party to other leaflets, but without providing clear details as to how the European procedures fit in the 'existing English procedures' or explaining the 'technical English legal terminology' or the activities that the parties actually need to carry out.[2160] In contrast to the English leaflet, the French guidelines are intended for the use of the courts (i.e. judges, clerks, and prosecutors).[2161] The documents offer a detailed explanation as to the provisions of the Regulations, the way these should be applied and interpreted, and clarifications on the filling in of certain points in the standard forms. The guidelines go on to create correlations in their interpretations between the provisions of the Regulations, the adopted provisions amending the CPC on the EOP and the ESCP, and other relevant national procedural rules. Their approach has the potential to facilitate a uniform interpretation of various aspects of the proceedings. The additional clarifications and correlations provided are highly relevant with regard to the way court proceedings are carried out. For parties using the European uniform procedures, however, the

2158 Explanatory Memorandum to the Civil Procedure (Amendment) Rules 2008, 2008 No. 2178 (L.10), at 1–2.

2159 See also Oudin (2009), at 17 and 27 (available at www.acj.si/en/project-results).

2160 HMCTS, Form EX725, 'Making a cross border claim in the EU. Using the European Order for Payment Procedure or European Small Claims Procedure'. See further criticism in Crifò (2016), at 86.

2161 Circulaire de la DACS C3 06–09 du 26 mai 2009, Official Gazette of the Ministry of Justice, 2009/4, 30 August 2009, Texte 16/51; Circulaire de la DACS C3 07–09 du 26 mai 2009, Official Gazette of the Ministry of Justice, 2009/4, 30 August 2009, Texte 17/51. The text of the guidelines is available at www.textes.justice.gouv.fr/art_pix/1_boj_20090004_0000_p000.pdf.

guidelines offer limited assistance. Hence, the two national approaches differ. The French Ministry of Justice opted to provide additional information and clarifications to professionals called to apply the European instruments, in contrast to the English authorities, who aimed to create comprehensible guidelines for those parties to whom the procedures are dedicated, taking into consideration the non-mandatory nature of legal representation.

In addition to the national procedural rules and the EOP and ESCP guidelines, various national French and English organisations provide parties with some degree of information (e.g. the Ministries of Justice websites, courts' websites, ECCs). However, in many instances, the details are too general for parties to actually be able to carry out court proceedings. The materials are more useful in making the existence of the procedures for cross-border litigation more visible, and in referring parties further to particular information on European dedicated websites (e.g. Judicial Atlas, e-Justice Portal).

Italy did not adopt any statute or legislation to coordinate application of the national procedural rules along with those of the European uniform procedures. Any coordination was left mainly to the interpretation of the courts (Justice of the Peace, *Tribunale*, or Court of Appeal). This approach resulted in certain difficulties for the courts, the legal professionals, and the parties, and led in practice to various solutions and a non-unitary application of the Regulations. The reduced number of cross-border claims in comparison to the number of domestic disputes for debt recovery, as well as the regulation nature of the European legislation, may have partly influenced this approach.[2162] The Italian Ministry of Justice issued a note for the clarification of particular aspects of the EOP procedure.[2163] In addition, the Ministry provided ad-hoc guidelines and replies to questions raised by the courts or by its various departments.[2164] No specific clarifications have been issued in relation to ESCP court proceedings. The communications sent to the European Commission on the basis of Article 29 EOP and Article 25 ESCP give additional indications as to the national applicable rules the Italian authorities considered appropriate for the functioning of the two Regulations. This patchy framework hardly contributes to the transparency and accessibility of the information, which is sometimes confined to a specific court or a Ministry department. Furthermore, it does not enhance the level of knowledge among professionals who may easily not be aware of the separate response issued by the Ministry of Justice. Finally, the information offered by ECC Italy on the European uniform procedures is of a general nature and does not provide support as to practical procedural aspects.[2165] A more functional approach to relevant information for conducting EOP and ESCP court proceedings could prove beneficial.

In Romania, the legislator and the Ministry of Justice have not adopted any internal legislation or guidelines as to the functioning of the EOP and the ESCP. Nonetheless, the procedures were mentioned by the Commission, which elaborated upon the new Code of

2162 See also Silvestri (2009), at 1 (available at www.acj.si/en/project-results).
2163 Nota 1° settembre 2010 – Regolamento CE 1896/2006.
2164 See Section 5.5.
2165 See Section 5.5.

Civil Procedure as being a considered source for the drafting of the legislative text, although the instruments have not been dedicated specific provisions.[2166] The reasons could be related to the direct applicability of the EOP and the ESCP Regulations within the national legal system. As in Italy, the aforementioned communications offer some indication of the Government's vision with respect to coordinating application of the national procedural rules in combination with the European procedures. Similar to the Italian situation, a significant interpretative duty is laid on the courts. In this situation, the judge needs not only to fill the interpretative gaps but also to coordinate the various communicated mechanisms and their updates following the application and amendment of the new CPC.[2167] Further, in Romania, the Ministry of Justice website provides no information that can actually be of use through the procedural stages of European procedures. In addition, the ECC Romania brochures make limited references to specific aspects that are relevant for application of the EOP or the ESCP. Their presentation is general and appears more geared to familiarise interested parties with the existence of these alternative cross-border procedures than to assist them through their various stages.

In addition to the national actions, the European Commission also published a specific EOP Guide and ESCP Guide on how to apply the instruments,[2168] and created a wizard application to help parties decide whether one of the two European procedures might be applicable to their case.[2169] All these initiatives aim to assist parties and practitioners in the use and application of these cross-border procedures. The guides generally explain their use and scope, giving details about the various stages. The ESCP Guide has adopted a more extensive step-by-step presentation of the characteristics, use, and stages of the proceedings. However, no specific national information is included in the text, although the ESCP Guide, largely intended for laypersons, offers more detailed information on sensitive matters such as jurisdiction rules, language and translation, assistance and information, and enforcement.

7.2.1.2. Explanation and Evaluation

The national approaches adopted in the four analysed jurisdictions are the result of various national attitudes towards the application of the European uniform procedures and legislative priorities. While it was considered necessary in England and France to

2166 The adoption of a new Code of Civil Procedure was driven by the need to comply with the requirements of modern justice, to facilitate access to justice, to provide predictability of the judicial act, and to facilitate the application of EU legislation. See Section 6.1.

2167 Additionally, the communicated information often takes a long time before it is updated and/or translated into all the languages on the e-Justice Portal. See Section 6.5.

2168 The EOP Guide contains more general information on the procedure (available at https://e-justice.europa.eu/content_order_for_payment_procedures-41-en.do), while the ESCP Guide explains the use and stages of the proceedings in a more detailed manner, providing additional explanations on a step-by-step basis (available at https://e-justice.europa.eu/content_small_claims-42-en.do). However, the Guides provide no information on the national specificities in each Member State regarding application of either of the European procedures.

2169 The wizard can be accessed from https://e-justice.europa.eu/content_dynamic_forms-155-en.do.

adopt provisions that would insure the consistency of national rules with the EOP and the ESCP, Italy and Romania seem to rely on the legislative characteristics of the European regulations. The incorporation of provisions referring to application of the European uniform procedures in the national code contributes to the visibility of the new instruments for professionals, and possibly for interested parties. The legislative approach undertaken by the English and French legislators offer a higher degree of transparency regarding national rules that are applicable within the EOP and ESCP proceedings in comparison to the Italian and the Romanian approach. The reason rests mainly in a perceived need to facilitate application of the EOP and the ESCP, and to prevent conflicting situations between the two levels of legislation. The guidelines' approach in Italy appears to be determined by the fact that the legislator is focused on resolving problems that are considered more urgent: namely, the lengthy national procedures, the excessive caseload burdening the court system, and the lack of resources.[2170] Although the practice is problematic, especially in relation to the EOP, the legislator has not considered it necessary to adopt legislative text with respect to the European uniform procedures, or to extend the guidelines provided in the general Note on the EOP. This approach could also be influenced by the small number of cases handled by the courts in accordance with the European procedures in comparison to purely domestic cases. In Romania, the nature of the European legislation – a Regulation – seems to have determined the chosen approach. The direct effect of the Regulations appeared sufficient for the application of the procedures in this jurisdiction. Additional reasons regarding the considered legislative priorities might have influenced this outcome (e.g. adopting a new Code of Civil Procedure that takes into consideration all main EU regulations in the area of European private international law).

In the analysed jurisdictions, the amendment of the codes relating to implementation of the European uniform procedures appears to better serve the need to facilitate access to information for the professionals and the parties. It contributes to a unitary approach of the law, provides transparency, and avoids a multiplication of the individual acts regulating different aspects of the court proceedings. A multitude of additional acts could create a complex national legislative framework that has the potential to impede easy access to information, in particular in cross-border situations when parties and professionals are not familiar with another Member State's procedural system. The users can be confused and find themselves lost between the various applicable acts without the help of a local lawyer. This is especially the case when information on EOP and ESCP procedures is not generally available or provided in a user-friendly format. If no national provisions or guidelines are adopted, the legislator's approach contributes very little to the transparency of the procedural rules applicable in the context of the European uniform procedures. In this case, the parties are confronted with the same difficulty as when needing to identify which national legal provisions apply within ordinary or special proceedings. Easy and clear information for users and practitioners as to the national rules complementing the European procedures are of key importance for

2170 Silvestri (2009), at 1 (available at www.acj.si/en/project-results).

diminishing complexity, facilitating application of these instruments, and encouraging parties to employ them in cross-border litigation. Additionally, if the national measures are not sufficient or result in divergent and confusing practices, the success of the alternative procedures can easily be compromised. Practitioners are likely less willing to advise their clients to make use of such alternative instruments. Instead, there is a tendency to continue to use domestic instruments, as they are best known, have established a predictable practice, and benefit from the clearer provisions that rule their application and functioning. For the parties, frequent referral to national rules that are not easily accessible preserves a state of legal insecurity.

As to the available information (e.g. leaflets, guidelines), the details they provide is usually of a more general nature. Often they present the procedure's main steps but do not give precise details of the steps that need to be followed in order to carry out court proceedings.[2171] Although these materials are relevant in terms of creating awareness about the alternative European procedures in cross-border litigation, their level of pertinence as regards actually undertaking court action is limited or lacking (e.g. how to pay court fees from abroad, details about making an electronic payment, duties the party is expected to fulfil during proceedings). Further action is necessary at the national as well as the European level in order to improve the standard of information available and increase the transparency of national relevant provisions for the parties as well as the legal practitioners called to apply the EOP and the ESCP or to offer advice for potential users. The lack of specific national provisions or guidelines on applying the Regulations has been shown to have significant consequences. Insufficient action to coordinate the two levels of norms and to adapt the national provisions in order to achieve an effective functioning of the European procedures has the potential to create divergent practices and legal uncertainty. This in particular is the case when it is not clear which domestic rules apply to the EOP and the ESCP (e.g. the transfer of an opposed EOP to the national ordinary procedure in Italy; the court establishing different court fees for proceedings in Romania).[2172] An additional aspect that appears to be influenced by the national legislative approach and the level of practitioners' knowledge is the tendency of courts to interpret and apply the European procedures in a manner that mirrors those domestic procedures that are perceived to be close to the scope of the Regulations.[2173] This phenomenon has different intensities, but its existence undoubtedly affects the uniform application of the provisions of the two Regulations within the analysed jurisdictions.

7.2.2. Stakeholders' Perception of the EU Solutions

In analysing the stakeholders' perception of the European uniform procedures, the elements considered were (1) the replies submitted by national entities and organisations

[2171] An exception in this regard involves the 2013 and 2014 ESCP guidelines, which adopted a more detailed, step-by-step approach to the information and to the procedural guidelines that the parties have to be aware of and consider before filing a claim, or during the various stages of the proceedings (available at https://e-justice.europa.eu/content_small_claims-42-en.do).

[2172] See further Section 7.3.2.

[2173] For a more detailed analysis of this aspect of the practice, see Sections 7.3.2 and 7.3.3.

to the public consultations; (2) the positions expressed by national governments during the negotiation processes; and (3) scholars' perspectives on application of the Regulations in coordination with national rules. These positions and points of view are of significance for understanding how the EOP and the ESCP are applied and function in England, France, Italy and Romania. This section focuses on the main common expectations, the principle positive results of the uniform procedures, and the most problematic aspects identified by national stakeholders in relation to the two European procedures.

7.2.2.1. The EOP

The national responses were mixed, varying from positive to more critical approaches questioning the coherence of the European framework and of the procedural model chosen. In particular, a number of aspects were debated by stakeholders in England, France, Italy, and Romania: namely, the reference to the Brussels I (now Brussels I*bis*) Regulation for jurisdiction rules, the definition of cross-border cases, the non-evidence hybrid model of the EOP Regulation, the use of standard forms, the EOP service provisions, the opposition mechanism and coordination with national procedural rules in the transfer of the national proceedings, and the abolition of exequatur.

Stakeholders consider the EOP an 'embryo' of a uniform procedure, still relying extensively on national procedural rules, though a decisive stage in the development of European law.[2174] The EOP has not reached the level of effectiveness of the homologous national instruments, and its use in practice does not yet match its theoretical importance.[2175]

7.2.2.2. The ESCP

The English, French, and Italian legislators have supported the proposal to adopt a European Regulation regarding small value claims, with Italian legislators even endorsing extension of its application to internal cases. Each of the jurisdictions considers the ESCP to be a useful tool. However, the national governments' enthusiasm does not match the actual situation in practice where the ESCP is still seldom used.[2176] Stakeholders in each country identified particular weaknesses that undermine the Regulation's intended simplicity. Some of the identified points of concern and of the criticism voiced regarding application of the European procedure have been addressed by Regulation 2015/2421 (e.g. increasing the threshold of the procedure, use of electronic means of communication, costs), and will likely contribute to improving the way in which this instrument functions.

Among the debated issues are the particular reliance on national procedural rules for a number of aspects (e.g. means of submitting the claim, evidence, appeal, costs,

[2174] Romano (2009), at 172; Legros (2007), at 15; Lopez de Tejada & d'Avout (2007), at 724–726 and 728–729.

[2175] See Section 7.3.1.

[2176] On the use of the ESCP in the analysed jurisdictions, see Section 7.3.1.

enforcement), the threshold, the use of standard forms, the holding of hearings, the assistance to be provided on the basis of Article 11 ESCP, the simplification of service rules, the lack of a common rule on appeal, the costs and immediate enforceability of the ESCP judgment.

7.2.2.3. Explanation and Evaluation

The stakeholders identified various points of concern that could result in a problematic application of the EOP or the ESCP within their national jurisdictions. These matters have their sources in the text of the Regulations or within the coordination and adaptation of the national rules to the application of the European procedures. Regulation 2015/2421 amending the EOP and ESCP Regulations has meanwhile addressed some of these concerns and has sought to clarify or improve the text of the provisions that were considered problematic or had raised concerns (e.g. the costs of proceedings, the transfer following opposition to the EOP, the threshold, the holding of hearings, and free assistance to parties in the ESCP). This action at the European level can potentially trigger additional changes within the Member States. It may improve actions at the implementation level, such as legislative measures or improving the access to relevant information and, subsequently, the standard of knowledge that practitioners and parties have of the alternative European procedures in cross-border litigation.[2177]

Scholars in France and Italy dedicated extensive analyses to the provisions of the European uniform procedures, and especially to the EOP. As is discussed further in Section 7.3, statistics and case law point to the EOP procedure as being used more often than the ESCP in the analysed jurisdictions.[2178] Some of the aspects the stakeholders expressed concerns about or criticised have materialised in practice, leading to a problematic application of the procedures, with implication for the parties' procedural rights and access to justice. Other points of concern remain at the theoretical level. Some of these will likely remain scholarly discussions (e.g. stretching the application of the EOP and the ESCP to purely internal cases by using jurisdiction clauses), but there are also aspects that have the potential to create future disparities in the way the EOP and the ESCP are applied in the Member States. This might be the case with national rules that could be interpreted as setting additional requirements for the application of the European uniform procedure, such as the opinion that a national foreclosure period should apply with regard to serving the EOP on the defendant.[2179] The lapse of such a period would result in the creditor not being able to enforce the title awarded to him and having to initiate new court proceedings. This would have an opposite effect to

[2177] See for example the results of the Special Eurobarometer 395, which show that 86% of the respondents had never heard of the ESCP procedure. Special Eurobraometer 395, *European Small Claims Procedure Report*, 2013, at 68.

[2178] As to the available statistics on the EOP and the ESCP, see Sections 3.7.1 for England, Section 4.7.1 for France, Section 5.7.1 for Italy, and Section 6.7.1 for Romania, as well Section 7.3.1 below.

[2179] See also Section 7.1.1 and Velicogna, Lupo & Onțanu (2017).

simplification of the proceedings, and would unnecessarily prolong court actions. A more detailed national legislative approach or set of guidelines would limit such risks and avoid similar interpretations that have the potential to undermine a harmonised application of the European procedures. From a practice perspective, there are indications that courts in the analysed jurisdictions continue to interpret some of the Regulation's provisions in the light of similar national alternative instruments.[2180] Hence, there seems to be a sort of 'transplant effect' reaction at the national level to the European procedures. This makes national legislative actions, accessibility of information and practitioners understanding of the EOP and ESCP mechanisms even more important. Increasing the level of knowledge of the existence and characteristics of the European procedures would contribute to their better application and use.

As well as the difficulties and concerns raised by national stakeholders, application of the EOP and the ESCP represent an important first step in making uniform procedures directly enforceable within all 27 Member States (except Denmark). The use of standard forms is part of the process of simplifying access to justice in cross-border litigation, and their standardised application by national courts is a key aspect in facilitating the use of the European procedures.[2181] The latest amendment to the Regulations provides some of the instruments that will contribute to the accessibility of national information. They request Member States to provide more detailed information that parties can make use of in conducting court proceedings. It rests now with the Member States to facilitate the task of the courts in applying the European procedures, as well as to establish the appropriate channels for informing parties on the use of these alternative instruments.

Finally, aspects remain that have not yet been addressed by the amended Regulation text, such as the variety of service methods for the EOP and the lack of a uniform appeal rule for the ESCP. They remain valid topics for future reviews of the European procedures, and should not be avoided, especially given their importance for guaranteeing parties' procedural rights and securing their access to justice.

7.3. The EOP and the ESCP in Practice: Influencing or Being Influenced?

7.3.1. The Reality of Available Statistics

7.3.1.1. EU Statistics

Statistical data on the use of the EOP and the ESCP are not generally available. The European Commission ESCP assessment report published in 2013 and the EOP report published in 2015 contain only limited information.[2182] The data provided by the

2180 See further Sections 4.7.2, 5.7.2, 6.7.2, and 7.3.2.

2181 Mellone (2014b), at 245–254.

2182 Report, Deloitte, Part I, COM(2013) 495 final, Brussels, 19.07.2013, at 63; Commission EOP Report, COM(2015) 495 final, Brussels, 13.10.2015.

Member States are not uniform. The statistics, as available from the European Commission reports, are reproduced in Tables 7.1 and 7.2. Some EOP and ESCP data series are incongruous and incomplete, although available or partially available at the national level, as the present study found (i.e. Italy and Romania). This makes assessing the functioning of the European uniform procedures more difficult. The European legislator does not have the proper tools to address the aspects that can facilitate or improve application of the procedures in Member States that are unable to provide national data on the functioning of the EOP and the ESCP. Any possible policy decisions can be based only on the details submitted by some of the Member States, and that potentially may also match the interests of the other countries.

7.3.1.2. National statistics

The annual published statistics on the activity of courts in England, France, Italy, and Romania contain no specific information on application of the EOP and the ESCP. Upon request, the Ministries of Justice or the Councils of the Judiciary were able to provide complete or partial data on the use of these European procedures. The incongruous format of the statistical data noticed in the EU reports comes back at the national level in the information the authorities are able to provide. This regards the format of the information (England, France, and Romania) as well as the annual series of statistics that are sometimes incomplete (Italy). In the gathering of statistical data in all four jurisdictions, one difficulty was seen to be the way in which EOP and ESCP cases are registered.

	No. applications	EOPs for enforcement	Applications returned for completion/ rectifications	Modification of application	No. oppositions	No. EOPs	Length of proceedings
France	335	–	118	–	+/– 16%	305	2 months
Italy[2183]	–	–	–	–	–	–	–
Romania	–	–	–	–	–	–	–
UK	208	108	No data England or Scotland 5 (Northern Ireland)	No data England or Scotland 1 (Northern Ireland)	No data for England or Scotland 5 (Northern Ireland)	No data England 1 (Scotland) 23 (Northern Ireland)	No data from any UK jurisdiction

Table 7.1. Statistical data on use of the EOP procedure in 2012[2184]

2183 The table indicates that there are no separate statistics for EOPs in Italy; these are treated together with national payment orders. See Commission EOP Report, COM(2015) 495 final, Brussels, 13.10.2015, at 15.

2184 Annex, Commission EOP Report, COM(2015) 495 final, Brussels, 13.10.2015.

	No. applications	No. ESCP judgments	No. competent courts	Length of proceedings	Lay judges
France	2009: 3 2010: 27 2011: 49 2012: 54[2185]	2009: n/a 2010: 5 2011: 26 2012: 20 (partial data)	District courts and commercial courts (TI and TC)	4.6 months	Yes
Italy[2186]	–	–	–	–	–
Romania[2187]	–	–	–	–	–
UK	526	526	181 civil county courts	n/a	No

Table 7.2. Indicators regarding application of the ESCP in the Member States[2188]

With some exceptions (France for the ESCP;[2189] Romania for the EOP[2190]), there is no specific code attributed to the procedures in the electronic registration system used by national courts. This leads to the data being compiled manually (i.e. England)[2191] or to a lack of statistics (i.e. Italy, Romania for the ESCP). This evidently has an impact on the reliability of the data and the information they present. According to national statistics, courts in all four jurisdictions received EOP and ESCP applications, as displayed in Table 7.3.

2185 The 2012 statistical data is only partial. See footnote 171, Deloitte Report, Part I, COM(2013) 495 final, Brussels, 19.07.2013, at 63.

2186 Italy's reply regarding the ESCP was received after the closing date of the report. It was not taken into account in the evaluation report. See footnote 185, Deloitte Report, Part I, COM(2013) 495 final, Brussels, 19.07.2013, at 66. However, in analysing the responses provided by the Ministry of Justice in the Review of the operation of Regulation (EC) No. 1896/2006 and Regulation (EC) No. 861/2007, Questionnaire Part II, Regulation 861/2007 establishing the European Small Claims Procedure, m-dg. DAG.01/07/2013.0086502. E (document on file with the researcher), it is clear that the Italian authorities were unable to provide most of the information requested, except for the number of competent courts (846 Justice of the Peace courts – Question 2 a) and the types of judges that handle ESCP applications (lay judges – Question 2 c)).

2187 No relevant information on these matters was provided by the Romanian Ministry of Justice for the European Commission's report.

2188 See Table 19: Indicators regarding ESCP applications in the Member States in Deloitte Report, Part I, COM(2013) 495 final, Brussels, 19.07.2013, at 66–67.

2189 Up until 2012, France was able to register EOP cases for statistical purposes. Since the implementation of the IPWEB for the registration and handling of national order for payment cases, the gathering of data on the EOP procedure is no longer exhaustive, because the new electronic system does not allow registration of this type of claim.

2190 A special code for registering EOP cases in the court system was established in 2011, permitting the distinction between the national and the European procedure and, thus, the collection of relevant statistics. Certain registration difficulties continue to exist and affect the accuracy of the data. See Section 6.7.1.

2191 Data compiled manually by the courts' staff that is not subject to quality verification by the statistics bureaus who cannot guarantee the soundness of the information. See also Section 3.7.1.

	Application to issue	2008	2009	2010	2011	2012	2013	2014
England	EOP	–	85	62	242	250	183	65
	ESCP	n/a	200	105	176	45	69	217
France	EOP	–	893	1093	960	343	–	–[2192]
	ESCP	n/a	n/a	21	48	73	69	108
Italy[2193]	EOP	–	–	–	–	–	–	–
	ESCP	n/a	–	–	–	–	–	–
Romania	EOP	–	–	–	35	121	221	197
	ESCP	n/a	–	–	–	–	–	–

Table 7.3. Annual statistical data on EOP and ESCP applications received by courts in the analysed Member States according to information provided by the Ministries of Justice/ Council for the Judiciary for the period 2008–2014

Comparing the data in the European Commission Reports and the statistics provided by national authorities, differences become obvious for France and Romania.[2194] The reasons are not clear as to why Romanian authorities did not provide information on the use of the EOP for the European Commission Report, or on the differences in the French data.

The information collected is more extensive for England and France. England also gathered data on the requests for EOP and ESCP enforcement, while French statistics contain additional information on the type of award (full or partial) and the number of oppositions and review requests, as well as on rejections and withdrawals of the applications, and the timeframe of the proceedings. This last aspect is particularly relevant for assessing the speediness of the European uniform proceedings compared to other available instruments. Data on enforcement in England became available due to national procedural circumstances that see courts involved in enforcement activities. Unfortunately, this is not replicated in Italy and Romania, although courts are also involved in enforcement activities.[2195]

The odd format of the data and the low level of available details across the four jurisdictions make a sound comparative analysis of the results impossible. The national

2192 The French Ministry of Justice indicated that no exhaustive EOP data are available for 2013–2014, because the IPWEB system does not allow the separate registration of EOP cases. See also Section 4.7.1.

2193 Some Italian courts were able to provide data on EOP cases handled during 2009-2010. See Section 5.7.1. There are no similar data regarding application of the ESCP procedure by the Italian Justice of the Peace offices.

2194 See emphasised data in Table 7.3.

2195 In Italy, bailiffs are court officials (see further Section 5.6.1). In Romania, the courts have to issue the writ of execution (*încuviințarea executătii silite*) before the bailiff can proceed to execution (on the amendments related to the court's involvement in the enforcement, see Sections 6.6.1 and 6.7.1).

data confirms the modest use of the European uniform procedures, though use of the EOP and the ESCP registered periods of growth, but also significant decreases from one year to the next. The reasons for this are not clear, though they may also have to do with the soundness of the data collected.

7.3.1.3. Explanation and Evaluation

The European Commission's reports as well as the national available data for the four analysed jurisdictions are unable to provide complete statistics on the application of the EOP and the ESCP. The available statistics do give some idea as to how often the two procedures are used, but the varying level of details and the missing blocks of information make them difficult to use for comparative purposes. One can only say that application of the EOP and the ESCP is still modest, even though it has been several years since the Regulations entered into force. Steps need to be taken to ensure future better statistics that would allow a sounder assessment of how the procedures function. These steps should (1) improve the collection of data by adopting individual registration codes for each of the instruments; (2) decide on the extent of the relevant information to be collected across the Member State for assessment purposes; and (3) verify the soundness of the data. In reaching a common understanding of the extent of data to be collected, the statistics can offer a deeper insight into how the European uniform procedures function, properly mirroring the evolution of their use across the jurisdictions. Collecting detailed information on their application and analysing the data can reveal promising results as well as difficulties in applying the European procedures (e.g. long procedural timeframe, competence problems, limited experience, and so on). These weaknesses can subsequently be addressed by way of appropriate measures and guidelines at the European and the national level. Additionally, sound statistics will offer information on courts receiving more EOP and ESCP application. This can facilitate the dissemination of expertise and handling practices between national courts, with less experienced courts benefitting from the knowledge already available. Finally, publishing data on the application of the EOP and the ESCP in annual national reports regarding the activity of the judiciary can contribute to practitioners' awareness of these alternative European procedures.

7.3.2. Case Law on European Uniform Procedures

7.3.2.1. Quantitative Data on Case Law

Judicial decisions in England, France, Italy, and Romania are generally not published automatically on national dedicated portals or in databases. It is a selection of judgments that is usually published based on their importance for the legal matters addressed, the novelty of the matter addressed, or the complexity of the subject analysed. This had an impact on the number of cases that became available for the study, as well as their typology (such as cases that were more controversial or problematic than simple straightforward EOP or ESCP awards).

	No. EOP cases	EOP issued	Average period necessary to issue EOP	Opposition	Review	EOP execution requests
France	21	9	1.5 months	8	2[2196]	8
Italy	38	34	19 days[2197]	17	1[2198]	1
Romania	249	159	3.3 months	24	1[2199]	24

Table 7.4. Statistical data on application of the EOP procedure according to available national case law

As to statistical data, the European uniform procedures might be identified or registered under domestic procedures.[2200] Other than this, in England, the publication of EOP and ESCP decisions is not a priority or considered important, as most claims are handled by the county courts, whose decisions are not binding on other courts. This adds an additional hurdle with regard to identifying cases whose transcription is a costly service. Under these circumstances, EOP case law became available in France, Italy, and Romania, while ESCP claims were identified in all four analysed jurisdictions (Tables 7.4 and 7.5).

	No. ESCP cases	ESCP issued	Average period necessary to issue ESCP judgment	Appeal	Review	ESCP execution requests
England	2	2	4 months and 1 week	0	0	1
France	4	4	2 months and 1.5 weeks	0	0	2
Italy	1	1	3 months and 1.1 weeks	0	0	0
Romania	9	6	6 months and 2 weeks	0	0	2

Table 7.5. Statistical data on the application of the ESCP according to available national case law

2196 The court in one case proceeded to issue Form G, even though the defendant had opposed the order. Therefore, the defendant sought to use the review mechanism. See CA Douai, Chambre 2, Section 2, 14 mars 2013, N° 12/02210.

2197 The result must be considered with caution, as information was available for only 2 of the 34 cases analysed.

2198 The EOP was opposed, and the court incorrectly issued Form G. See Tribunale di Mantova 7 July 2011, Case No. 1954/11.

2199 In relation to an opposed case, in which the court incorrectly issued Form G. See Decision No. 5/27 February 2013, Alba Iulia Court of Appeal, Section II Civil.

2200 For example, under the names of domestic procedures, or as part of other proceedings, in Romania, EOPs were registered under the following types of proceedings: enforcement actions, national order for payment procedure, ordinary procedure, and insolvency proceedings.

7.3.2.2. Case Classification

The majority of French, Italian, and Romanian EOP cases are B2B cases, and are seldom B2C, C2B or C2C cases. It is often a foreign company that initiates a claim against a local company. The English, French, and Italian ESCP cases are mostly C2B claims. In contast, the Romanian ESCP cases are mainly B2B cases. It seems Romanian consumers are less likely to initiate a cross-border claim, while companies appear to find it a useful tool to recover debts from foreign debtors. The EOP cases have revealed that some of the parties are repeat players (either both or one of them, especially the claimant).

The EOP and ESCP claims concerned a contractual relationship (e.g. sale-purchase agreements or services agreements) where assets or services were provided and the debtor did not pay the related invoices,[2201] or services that were not provided (i.e. ESCP aviation cases). A peculiar aspect of the ESCP is that the contracts were often concluded over the internet.

7.3.2.3. Conduct of Proceedings

Submission of the Application
EOP and ESCP applications are usually submitted by post or directly to the court. Available case law usually only addresses this aspect marginally. Exceptionally, this stage led to temporary difficulties in Italy in the EOP procedure, following a domestic reform of the compulsory electronic filing of a national order for payments after 30 June 2014. Some courts were confused as to whether the new rules also applied to the EOP.[2202] This finding already hints at the significant influence of the national procedure on the way the EOP and the ESCP are applied. This aspect re-emerges at various points in all four jurisdictions. Thus, there is a tendency for national courts to proceed in a manner that resembles corresponding national procedures. Other relevant examples are the engagements in negotiation prior to ESCP proceedings in a manner that is similar to the national small claims procedure in England, the treatment of the ESCP application as a *déclaration au greffe* in France, or the handling of EOP and ESCP applications in public or, occasionally, in-chamber hearings in Romania, as domestic proceedings are mostly conducted in hearings open to the public.[2203] The claimants were not usually aware of this national particularity prior to filing the standard application form (Form A), as none of the European portals provide information on these aspects of how the European uniform procedures are handled.

[2201] A remarkable particularity of the Romanian EOP cases is that a significant number of cases have to do with money claims based on legal representation agreements. See also Section 6.7.2.

[2202] Tribunale di Milano, Case No. 10488/8 April 2015. Subsequently, the Ministry of Justice issued a Ministry Guideline specifying that the new rules do not concern the EOP (Circolare dg_DAG.23/10/2015.0159552.U, Adempimenti di cancelleria relativi al Processo Civile Telematico, document on file with the researcher). See Section 5.7.2.

[2203] In some of the analysed cases, the parties and their representatives were present and took part in the proceedings, despite the fact that the European procedure does not require it. See Section 6.7.2.3.

Use of Standard Forms

Form A of the EOP and the ESCP are the standard forms most often employed. All other forms are used less often, or are replaced by national formats, or result in a combined use of standard forms and national formats.[2204] Case law provides no hints as to the difficulties claimants may have encountered in completing the EOP or ESCP application form (Form A). Form B is occasionally used to request additional information or clarification on some matters. This is more often the case in relation to EOP case law. Court requests can concern (1) clarifications or information to be provided from Form A (i.e. grounds of jurisdiction, interest claimed and the period for which this is claimed, the amount of costs and penalties claimed, information on the evidence to be used); (2) the compliance with national provisions on court fees and representation (i.e. payment of court fees, proof of proxy or power of attorney); or (3) additional requirements for the issuance of EOP or ESCP decisions (i.e. submission of evidence documents in the EOP procedure together with certified translations, submission of certified translations for all ESCP evidence documents filed). This last type of request for which Form B is incorrectly used by national courts points to a certain lack of knowledge and a tendency for judges to apply the European procedures in a manner that matches the national procedures, with which they are familiar and that they apply more often. Furthermore, this national practice conflicts with the provisions of Article 7 EOP and does not observe the ruling of the CJEU in the *Szyrocka* case.[2205] The payment of court fees is also problematic and can lead to procedural delays.[2206] Courts in none of the analysed jurisdictions are able to collect the court fee automatically on the basis of the information provided by the claimant in Form A.

EOP Form C is also used occasionally.[2207] The Italian and Romanian judges employed it to propose a reduction of the costs, interest, or penalties demanded by the claimant, or of the principle amount (in Romania). The result of the proposal is not known for all EOP cases where Form C was used (in some Romanian cases, the claimant accepted the court's proposal, and Form E was subsequently issued).

In the ESCP procedure, defendants always used Form C when opposing the claim.[2208] The form was usually served on the defendant together with a copy of Form A and of the evidence.

EOP Form D was used by Romanian courts, but some of the reasons for rejection were unexpected and did not comply with the provisions of the Regulation.[2209] The French, Italian, and Romanian judges issued the EOP (Form E) in most of the analysed

2204 For example, to register a decision in the court system in Romania, the judge also has to draft it in accordance with the domestic format. EOP Form E is not sufficient. This means additional time for a judge, who has to issue two documents instead of one as indicated in the Regulation.

2205 Case C-215/11.

2206 On the particularities and difficulties of paying court fees in Italy and Romania, see Sections 5.5 and 6.5.

2207 See further Sections 5.7.2 and 6.7.2.

2208 When the courts did not receive an answer from the claimant, they proceeded to issue the ESCP judgments on the basis of the evidence provided by the claimant.

2209 The reasons for rejection had to do with additional requirements set by the Romanian judges for the issuance of the EOP. See Section 6.7.2.

cases. Further, Form F was used by the defendant in a significant number of opposed EOPs. This appears to be the case in particular in France (88.8% of the cases) and Italy (42.2% of the cases).[2210] The French case law outcome is in contrast to the statistical data provided by the French Ministry of Justice and the European Commission Report indicating an approximately 16% level of opposition.[2211] These high opposition rates for French and Italian case law may be explained by (1) the basis on which the case law is selected for publication; and (2) the limited sample of published cases that concentrate mostly on the outcomes.

Information about issuing the Declaration of enforceability or the certification of the judgment as enforceable (Form G EOP or Form D ESCP) concerns a small number of case law instances (41 EOPs – 2 cases in France, 2 cases in Italy, and 37 cases in Romania, and 3 ESCPs – 1 Italian case,[2212] and 2 Romanian cases). An important aspect resulting from the case law analysis is the fact that both Form G and Form D are not issued in a uniform manner;[2213] in some cases, the court proceeds automatically to issue the standard declarations, while in other cases the interested party submits a request to the court.[2214] Additionally, Form G was issued incorrectly by the French, Italian, and Romanian courts in a few circumstances, which triggered the defendant to try to make use of the review mechanism in order to prevent enforcement, as is explained below.

Service and Language Aspects

Case law does not always provide information on the method of service chosen. However, for both European procedures the analysed cases indicate that the service methods used mirror national practices. This includes the entity or party responsible for the service. For example, in France the claimant requests a bailiff to serve the EOP on the defendant as in other national procedures; in Italy, the bailiff proceeds to serve ESCP documents by making use of the postal service with acknowledgement of receipt. If service needs to be carried out cross-border, EOP cases indicate that the Service Regulation is to be used.[2215] Most probably this is also the case in ESCP procedures, although the very small number of cases available did not address this issue. As to the documents served on the defendant, case law does not generally provide details. The Italian and Romanian EOP cases provided some information in this regard, mentioning that Form E was served together with a copy of Form A and Form F. However, nothing was said about the ESCP cases. Further, the judges proceeded to verify whether the EOP service had been carried out as

2210 Only 6.8% of the Romanian cases make reference to an opposition having been filed.

2211 See Table 7.1 above as well as Section 4.7.2 and Table 4.3: Quantitative data on EOP procedure and the outcome of the claims according to Ministry of Justice statistics.

2212 The Italian court issued a judgment in accordance with the nationally used format rather than with Form D, applying the procedure in a manner that matched national practices and procedural rules.

2213 This is the case, for example, in Romania.

2214 For the EOP, these different approaches might be triggered by the provisions of Article 18(2) EOP stating 'formal requirements for enforceability shall be governed by the law of the Member State of origin'. However, no confirmation of such interpretation is given by the available case law. See further Section 7.3.3.2.

2215 Romanian EOP case law provides this information.

indicated in the applicable rules. This is a significant procedural safeguard that protects the defendant's procedural rights and guarantees his access to justice.

The language in which the forms are served on the defendants or sent back to the court play a very important role in the successful application of the European procedures, in the protection of parties' rights, and for the procedural costs incurred. The courts do not translate *ex officio* the forms or documents served on the defendant; hence, the claimant has to provide a translation for service or communication purposes, or serve the forms on the foreign defendant in the language of the proceedings. For example, Romanian courts request the claimant to provide translations of the EOP or ESCP forms or awards; in one instance, a French defendant was served the EOP in German.[2216] Romanian courts are very conscious of the importance of this aspect for the defendant's access to justice. The language in which the defendant is served can immediately provide him with sufficient understanding of the action initiated against him, guaranteeing his right to act, if he chooses to, and securing a fair trial for the parties. In some EOP cases, the defendant transmitted Form F in another language (German) instead of the language of the proceedings (French and Italian, respectively). In these cases, the language had very serious consequences, as the courts did not take the opposition into consideration. They could not understand the documents they had received and did not recognise the EOP form. This resulted in additional court actions, with the defendant seeking the annulment of Form G; the result was a violation of the defendant's access to a fair trial, additional litigation costs, and longer procedural time. Some additional information as to language comes up in enforcement cases. It appears that for enforcement purposes, the creditor has to submit a translation of the EOP or the ESCP title issued by a court in another Member State. For example, Romanian judges requested a translation of the enforceable ESCP in order to issue a writ for the bailiff to proceed to the execution.

Hearings

ESCP case law indicates that the holding of a hearing can be influenced by the national practices with which the court is familiar. For example, in one English ESCP judgment a hearing was held to resolve the remaining issues the parties were not able to settle, just as in a domestic small claim. Additionally, in France a judge proceeded to summons the parties to a hearing according to the national proceedings. In spite of this, however, some courts are seeking to keep the ESCP as a written procedure as indicated in Article 5(1) ESCP.

Challenge Mechanisms (Opposition, Appeal, Review)

The activity to be undertaken by the judges/court and/or the parties after the EOP opposition differs between France, Italy, and Romania in accordance with the characteristics of each domestic procedure.[2217] The variety of approaches between

[2216] Luckily, the defendant appeared to know German, and was able to understand the documents he was served with.

[2217] For example, in France, the clerk will summons the parties to a hearing; in Romania, the court informs the claimant of the opposition and invites the party to formulate a claim in accordance with NCPC rules; in Italy, the activities differ based on the interpretation followed by the court concerned.

Member States or within one jurisdiction (i.e. Italy) can be quite complex for a non-repetitive user, as no relevant information on the actual practices regarding the transfer stage is available on the European dedicated portals, or in the national or European leaflets. The accessibility of such information is virtually non-existent for a layperson who is unfamiliar with the national system and has no knowledge of the language of the proceedings. In such circumstances, representation becomes necessary.

Case law reveals that the interpretation of the opposition provisions *per se* can be problematic at times. This is the case with some French and Romanian courts, where judges proceeded to reject the opposition.[2218] The decisions are striking because the national judges applied the EOP opposition mechanism in a manner that resembles the provisions applicable in well-known domestic procedures. In these unfortunate interpretations, the courts seem to be completely unfamiliar with the purpose of the EOP opposition and of the consequences this mechanism can generate. This finding is even more staggering because the judge proceeded to issue Form G declaring the EOP enforceable.[2219] These cases show a deep lack of understanding of the provision, and impinges upon the defendant's right to a fair trial and access to justice, making it impossible for the party to present his defence. Defendants sought to challenge the enforceable title either by making use of the review mechanism as established by Article 20 EOP (i.e. France), or by an appeal in accordance with domestic rules (i.e. Romania).[2220] In all these circumstances, the review was made use of as a safety brake to prevent the execution and to allow the court to declare the order null. In light of the CJEU's reasoning in the *eco cosmetics* case, the review mechanism seems not to have been properly applied. In Romania, for example, the national appeal mechanism should have sufficed, as the EOP was not *per se* 'clearly wrongly issued', and the breach of the Regulation's provisions concerned the way in which the Declaration of enforceability was issued by the first court and not the validity of the order. Hence, some national judges appear to have a different understanding of the way the review mechanism should apply in comparison to the CJEU's reasoning. The review or appellate mechanisms were not activated in any of the analysed ESCP cases.

Representation

Representation by a lawyer remains a common practice. In the published French, Italian, and Romanian EOP cases it was revealed that parties (one or both) are often represented by a lawyer or a legal entity undertaking debt recovery activities (i.e. Romania). Representation is used less often for ESCPs, where parties sometimes choose to appear in person (i.e. France and Romania). Consumers sometimes request assistance from ECC

2218 CA Douai Chambre 02, Section 02, 14 mars 2013, N° 12/02210 regarding the decision incorrectly issued by TC Lille for France. Judecătoria Brașov, File No. 31929/197/2012 and Tribunalul Hunedoara, File No. 7608/79/2011 (Decision No. 3032/CA/2012) for Romania.

2219 Tribunalul Hunedoara, File No. 7608/79/2011 (Decision No. 3032/CA/2012) for Romania. For the developments in the appellate proceedings against this decision, see further Section 6.7.2. CA Douai, Chambre 2, Section 2, 14 mars 2013, N° 12/02210 for France and Tribunale di Mantova 7 July 2011, Case No. 1964/11 for Italy.

2220 The Romanian High Court considered that the Court of Appeal should have re-qualified the request as a review, as indicated in Article 20(2) EOP.

offices in order to conduct an ESCP procedure in their home country or abroad (i.e. France and England). In some EOP cases, the parties and their representatives are repeat players. Occasionally, the lawyers themselves use the EOP procedure to recover debts related to their legal services and assistance fees. In exceptional circumstances, lawyers from different jurisdictions can be involved in the handling of one case (e.g. a lawyer in the country of residence of the party and a lawyer in the Member State of the court). This further increases the costs of the proceedings, an aspect that the Regulations seek to tackle through the use of standard forms and provisions regarding non-mandatory representation. The lawyer's services may also be sought at the enforcement stage if a title needs to the executed in another Member State (i.e. ESCP to be executed in Romania). The extent of the complexities the European procedures can reach during certain phases of the proceedings, and the duties set on the parties at the national level (e.g. the need to retrieve in person the enforceable title from the court, paying the court fees) sometimes make representation necessary in order to avoid greater costs (e.g. travelling to court to undertake a procedural act in person in a different Member State). Other reasons for maintaining a high interest in representation services could be the national practices,[2221] the parties' limited legal knowledge, and the difficulties they encounter when searching for the necessary information in a non-familiar legal system.

Procedural Timeframe

Case law does provide some information on the length of the proceedings. Although the outcome cannot be generalised to all national courts in these jurisdictions because of the reduced sample of cases analysed, they do give an indication, and this can be further triangulated for validation with other available data. For example, French case law indicates an average duration of 1.5 months for the judge to issue an EOP, which is in line with the European Commission EOP Report[2222] and with statistics provided by the French Ministry of Justice.[2223] The same verification can be carried out for French ESCP cases. Case law indicates a duration of 2.5 months, which is in line with statistics provided by the Ministry of Justice.[2224]

In general, case law points to a speedy handling of the European procedures by the national courts, with a timeframe that tends to approach the target set by the European Regulation in Article 12(1) EOP, or the 6-month period the European Commission was aiming to achieve in the ESCP procedure. The celerity of the proceedings is an important aspect when choosing between various available instruments and an element the claimant should consider.[2225] The reasons affecting the length of the court proceedings

2221 If representation is compulsory in domestic proceedings, the use of legal representation services might almost be an automatic choice for the party who is used to request assistance from a professional for any legal matters involving courts.

2222 Commission EOP Report, COM(2015) 495 final, Brussels, 13.10.2015, at 13.

2223 See Section 4.7.1, Table 4.3: Quantitative data on EOP procedure and the outcome of the claims according to Ministry of Justice statistics.

2224 See Section 4.7.1, Table 4.8: Quantitative data on ESCP procedures and the outcome of claims according to Ministry of Justice statistics.

2225 See also the discussion on the reasons that determine the choice or rejection of optional European procedures, in Fauvarque-Cosson & Behar-Touchais (2012), at 297.

are not obvious in all jurisdictions. However, where more information is available there is an indication that the limited knowledge and the treatment of the European procedure in accordance with national practices and requirements can influence the length of the procedure (i.e. Romania).[2226]

Amounts Claimed
Most EOP and ESCP cases provide information on the amount of the debt the creditor is seeking to recover. EOP amounts vary between some hundred to some million euros, while ESCP claims are always below the €2,000 threshold. Claimants usually request the payment of interest and the reimbursement of incurred litigation costs, but there are differences in the way interest and costs are approached by national courts. For example, in France and Romania, interest is awarded by the court from a specific date up until the debt has been paid in full (the amount of the interest is calculated by the bailiff at the execution stage); in Italy this amount is often mentioned expressly or concerns a specific period (e.g. from a specific date up until the submission of the claim).[2227] Further, the courts have a tendency to award the costs of the proceedings. In EOP cases, the costs awarded include court fees and, occasionally, other costs (e.g. translation fees, lawyers' fees). Penalties were rarely requested in the analysed case law. In ESCP cases, different approaches to costs can be observed in England and in Italy.[2228] The English judge assessed whether the costs were necessary and proportionate by analogy with the national small claims procedure test, while the Italian court awarded the total amount of costs requested (including the lawyer's legal assistance fees) although it amounted to one-third of the claim.[2229] The fact that in most of the analysed EOP and ESCP cases the judges awarded the costs or part of the incurred expenses is a positive outcome. The downside is the uncertainty related to the type of costs that are to be recovered (i.e. only court fees or also translation costs, legal representation fees), and whether these are more modest than or match the awards in other national procedures. The differences in cost recovery between domestic and European procedures can play a role in parties' procedure preferences. In this context, an autonomous interpretation of the provisions on the awarding of costs would favour their uniform application and eliminate uncertainties across the Member States.

7.3.2.4. Enforcement

A small number of EOP and ESCP cases offer some insight into enforcement matters.[2230] Regrettably, the information available concerns only a section of the analysed jurisdictions (France, Italy, and Romania for the EOP; England, France, and Romania for the ESCP). In some cases, the enforcement process dealt with insolvency and reorganisation proceedings, which required the creditor to register his title in the opened proceedings.

2226 See Section 6.7.2.3.
2227 Legal interest applies from the moment of the award up until the time the debt has been paid in full.
2228 See Sections 3.7.2.5 and 5.7.2.5.
2229 There is no indication that there was an assessment as to whether the costs could be considered disproportionate or incurred unnecessarily.
2230 All cases concern the enforcement of titles issued by courts in another Member State.

In EOP cases, the debtors often appear to try to prevent enforcement by contesting the execution procedure or the jurisdiction of the court, or by seeking a suspension of the execution activities. With both European procedures, the execution judges proceeded to verify compliance with the provisions of Article 21(2) EOP or Article 21(2) ESCP. For example, a Romanian judge requested the creditor to submit a translation of the EOP and Form G prior to obtaining the court's approval to proceed to execution of the enforceable title. Further, in an ESCP case, the verification (Article 21(2) ESCP) was deemed necessary in order to guarantee a fair trial in accordance with Article 6 ECHR. In general, no information on the means of enforcement emerged from the available case law. An exception is an EOP case in Italy where the EOP title was recognised as having the same legal effects as a domestic order for payment by the registration of a judicial hypothec (*ipoteca giudiziaria*), which allowed transfer of the asset's ownership from the debtor to the creditor on the basis of the debt title. Outcomes such as this confirm the effectiveness of the EOP. The recognition of such an execution measure on the basis of an EOP enforceable title is a strong indication regarding the function this procedure can fulfill in cross-border litigation. This has the potential to be a positive influence with regard to the use of the European instrument. Further, EOP and ESCP enforcement cases do not point to any additional problematic or difficult aspects related to the execution of titles issued by courts in other Member States.

7.3.2.5. Explanation and Evaluation

The number of identified EOP and ESCP cases points to their relatively scanty use. Occasional application of the European procedures leads to additional efforts and longer periods necessary for the decision to be issued and the enforceable title to be executed. The number of cases the courts receive often limits their possibility of establishing an actual handling practice. Parties' awareness of the procedures may also contribute to this modest outcome. Additionally, registration of the European uniform procedures under other domestic procedures makes it more difficult to identify the relevant cases, and limits their visibility.

Some characteristics of the European procedures (e.g. written procedures, use of standard forms, providing assistance to the parties in filling in the forms) are not common features of domestic procedures in all four analysed jurisdictions; thus, their application might create difficulties or lead to divergent interpretations. The national procedural rules and practices continue to influence significantly the way the EOP and the ESCP are applied (e.g. service, parties' role in the procedure, hearings, decisions issued in a domestic format instead of by means of a standard form, application of challenging mechanisms), preserving differences between the analysed jurisdictions. This is due not only to the application of domestic procedural rules that complement the Regulation but also to the influence national special procedures (i.e. order for payments procedures) can have on the way the European procedures are applied. The transplanting of requirements from special national procedures to the EOP and the ESCP sets additional criteria for the issuance of a court decision. This creates uncertainty as to the way the European procedures function and should be applied. Additionally, it demonstrates the limited experience and familiarity with the provisions and requirements of the European Regulations by practitioners and courts in different Member States. The differences existing between the way the European uniform procedures are applied across the analysed jurisdictions creates additional complexity for potential users, especially if information on national particularities is not easily accessible by interested parties prior to initiating court proceedings.

The EOP and ESCP procedures simplify some of the parties' tasks, and offer a certain uniform framework for cross-border litigation. However, other elements on which the application of these procedures is based maintain an unexpected level of complexity (e.g. diversity of national rules regulating the service, conservative approach to accepting or considering standard forms in languages other than the language of the proceedings, the various court fees, and the various duties the parties have under domestic law).

The lack of institutionalised assistance for parties using these European uniform procedures, and in particular the ESCP, creates difficulties for consumers. This can have consequences with regard to parties securing easy access to justice. Alternatively, the use of legal representation can be a solution, but the recovery of costs including lawyers' fees might not always be possible in all national courts (i.e. England). This can have important implications for the efficiency the European procedures strive to achieve in cross-border litigation. The full or partial award of costs likely influences the use of the European uniform procedures in comparison to other domestic instruments. An autonomous interpretation of costs awards would favour a uniform approach across the Member States and would limit existing disparities. As to guarantees of the parties' procedural rights and access to justice, some cases highlight the particular attention that national judges pay to compliance with EOP and ESCP service standards, verifying the activities undertaken and requesting additional action if necessary. These steps can secure high procedural standards, thus protecting parties' procedural rights.

Although case law findings cannot be generalised across the analysed jurisdiction, there seems to be some evolution towards handling the European procedures – especially the EOP – within shorter periods. A speedier handling may increase the interest of possible parties in choosing these instruments over domestic procedures. This evolution can be influenced by a number of aspects such as the growing familiarity of certain judges and clerks with the Regulations, and compliance with the set procedural timeframes. The speediness of enforcement depends very much on the need to make use of various execution methods, the challenging process, and the familiarity of the bailiffs and courts with the European procedures. No actual assessment of the length of this final procedural step can be made on the basis of the information offered by case law. Furthermore, there is no indication of the rate of success of the creditor obtaining full repayment of his debt (except for the Italian EOP case where the judge consented to the registration of a judicial hypothec). In order to carry out a comparative analysis of the effectiveness of the EOP and the ESCP, more detailed and more extensive information regarding the enforcement stage should be made available.

Case law shows that the application of the European uniform procedures has not yet reached its maximum potential. The procedures – especially the ESCP – are still underused and not sufficiently well known. It is essential to increase the awareness of potential users, to enhance courts' and practitioners' knowledge of the instruments, and to make practical information available. This will have a positive impact on the functioning of the procedures, facilitating their use and creating confidence in a smooth, straightforward implementation. It might also lessen the apparent tendency of national courts to apply the instruments in a way that resembles national special procedures. A more harmonised application of the EOP and ESCP has the potential to encourage their sole use in cross-border litigation.

7.3.3. *Empirics*

7.3.3.1. Familiarity with European Procedures and Handling Practices

Respondents sharing their views on how the EOP and the ESCP function generally report having a high level of familiarity with them (from 'Familiar' to 'Very familiar').[2231] This is most often above the level of general national awareness, as estimated by respondents. A remarkable finding is the fact that the jurisdictions that amended their procedural rules with special provisions for application of the European uniform procedures (England and France) register the highest level of general unawareness. A legislative action can be expected to contribute to better general awareness and visibility. However, the limited opportunities some national courts and practitioners have in applying the EOP and, even more so, the ESCP, might have mitigated the positive effect in practice. In all four analysed jurisdictions, parties and practitioners maintain their preference for domestic special procedures. These procedures are well known, parties are familiar with them, and courts are accustomed to applying them. Generally, this results in easier application and clearer expectations as to the way the claim is to be handled. A number of additional elements specific to each jurisdiction contribute as well to maintaining this preference.[2232] Furthermore, in the jurisdictions where no implementation rules or guidelines have been adopted to coordinate application of the European uniform procedures in conjunction with the national procedural rules, practitioners encounter diverse interpretations or divergent practices. This, for example, is the case of transfer following an opposition to an EOP in Italy, or the issue of public hearings in Romania.[2233] A difficult use of the EOP and the ESCP, and a different approach towards the way the European procedures should be applied within the same jurisdiction or across the Member State, does not incentivise parties to choose these alternative procedures over familiar domestic instruments that they can later enforce on the basis of the Brussels I*bis* Regulation. A more unitary approach to applying the EOP and the ESCP should be aimed for at the national and the EU level.

2231 Forty-four percent in England, 83% in France, 71% in Italy, and 87% in Romania.

2232 For example, a preference for national standard forms in England, electronic handling of the domestic order for payment in Italy, and not wanting to risk using a procedure with which courts are not sufficiently familiar in Romania. See Sections 3.7.3.2, 4.7.3.2, 5.7.3.2, and 6.7.3.2.

2233 See further Section 7.3.2.

7.3.3.2. Case Classification

The outcome of the empirical research confirms the findings in case law. As envisaged by the European legislator, the EOP is most often used in B2B cases in the analysed jurisdictions, while the ESCP is often used in C2B claims. The exception is Romania, where the procedure also appeals to claimants who are legal entities (B2B and B2C). The ESCP threshold maintains a certain relevance for Romanian companies, while consumers' awareness of and interest in initiating cross-border claims remains minimal. Another reason might be that the expected litigation and enforcement costs are simply too high to be considered worth the effort. It is hoped that the increase in the ESCP threshold will make the procedure more attractive to businesses in other European jurisdictions as well.

The typology of the EOP and the ESCP mainly confirms the case law findings.[2234] Additionally, EOP claims often concern disputes in relation to financial or loan agreements, and tenancy and lease agreements, while the ESCP is also used in disputes related to holiday packages and car lease agreements.

7.3.3.3. Conduct of Proceedings and Encountered Difficulties

Handling of Cases

The division of tasks between judges and court staff in handling EOP and ESCP claims is influenced by a number of factors that are characteristic of each analysed jurisdiction (i.e. legislation on the activity of judiciary, court functioning rules, internal organisational practices). For instance, this results in a more active involvement of the French clerks in handling the forms, or very active Romanian judges compared to their colleagues in the other analysed jurisdictions.[2235] Generally, the clerks' activities are at the forefront of handling the European uniform procedure. They are in charge of administrative tasks such as the registration of claims, the verification of the forms and of the payment of court fees, the communications to parties, and the issuance of Declarations of enforcement. For this reason, the clerks' familiarity with the European uniform procedures and their standard forms is of outmost importance, particularly as the forms can occasionally be filed or returned to the court in a language other than that of the proceedings. In such circumstances, the clerk should be able to recognise the form regardless of the language in which it is drafted, otherwise there might be significant consequences for the parties, as shown in EOP case law and empirical findings in France and Italy.[2236] The fact that in some jurisdictions the same clerk receives and registers the EOP or the ESCP claims can favour a concentration of expertise. This creates an opportunity for courts to handle a higher number of European procedures and, subsequently, to create handling practices that facilitate the carrying out of administrative

2234 See Section 7.3.2.2.

2235 Regrettably, similar information is not available for England, due to the very limited number of respondents.

2236 See also Sections 7.3.2, 4.7.3.4, and 5.7.3.4.

tasks. Following registration, the file is forwarded to an assigned judge to proceed to assess the merits of the EOP or ESCP claim.

Another significant aspect of the way EOP and ESCP claims are handled is the tendency practitioners have in all four jurisdictions to apply these instruments as domestic procedures, by combining national requirements with the European instruments.[2237] This has a significant impact on the functioning of the procedures, especially the EOP, as the model chosen by the European legislator has little in common with the domestic order for payments. Hence, the European procedures may be applied at times in a format that is more national than uniform. This is in contrast to the simplification the European procedures were designed to achieve, and is certainly not encouraging for a potential user who is facing the same requirements and constraints as when choosing a well-known domestic instrument. Nevertheless, the national procedural rules do not create barriers *per se* with regard to the handling of the European uniform procedures. Their incorrect application and flawed understanding on the part of courts and practitioners is closely connected to limited familiarity and experience, and/or to lack of guidelines or dedicated legislation that could facilitate the coordination between the two levels of legislation (i.e. Italy and Romania). Tackling the need for better training and available practical information will facilitate the use and application of the instruments.

Forms

Standard forms are not commonly employed in handling national procedures.[2238] The EOP and ESCP standard forms are not generally available from local courts or on their websites in England, France, Italy, and Romania. This does not improve awareness of the availability of these alternative procedures. The use of standard forms is to a certain extent problematic in all four analysed jurisdictions, especially for lay parties. The use of these standard forms can be seen as unnatural for French, Italian, or Romanian practitioners and courts, as it is not a common element of their national procedures, while for the English, their format seems odd and unfamiliar compared to national forms. Consequently, well-known domestic formats continue to be chosen over European procedures' standard forms.[2239] The limited experience on the part of practitioners and courts does not help their confidence when handling EOP and ESCP forms. The forms appear to be a bottleneck for unrepresented lay users and businesses, as they experience difficulties in understanding the provisions of the claim form and in filling in some of its sections (e.g. selecting the basis for the court jurisdiction, formulating the basis of the claim, describing the evidence, establishing the interest and/or the amount due). Collected data confirm case law findings on the occasional use of EOP or ESCP Form B by French, Italian, and Romanian courts. These requests concern less than 25% of the applications, and often have to do with the difficulties parties experience in filling in Form A, or with the provisions of national procedural rules (e.g. submission of proxy proof or representation agreement, submission of proof of payment of court fee in Italy and Romania). In addition, as indicated in case law, Form B is at times incorrectly

2237 See also Section 7.3.2.3.

2238 Except for England and, marginally, in Romania, on the small claims procedure inspired by the ESCP.

2239 See also Section 7.3.2.3.

employed to supplement the Regulations' provisions with requirements set by familiar national procedures.[2240] Courts in all four jurisdictions appear keen to assess the EOP claim on the basis of submitted evidence, which means handling EOP and EOP claims in a manner similar to the domestic procedure. Such an application breaches the provisions of the European Regulations and ignores the CJEU ruling in the *Szyrocka* case. Judges should avoid transplanting additional requirements set by special national procedures onto the European uniform procedures, as it delays proceedings and the delivery of an enforceable title. Occasionally, the courts in Italy and Romania request the rectification and/or completion of Form C in the ESCP procedure, seeking clarifications regarding evidence or compliance with language requirements, but this is not a generalised approach. The use of EOP Forms C, D, E, and F is at times disregarded for national decision formats with whom courts and practitioners are familiar.[2241] When it comes to EOP Form G and ESCP Form D allowing creditors to proceed to the enforcement, the empirical data confirm the case law findings. The courts do not proceed in a unitary format across the analysed jurisdictions and at times within the same Member State. For example, in England and Italy the creditor has to request them, while in Romania the courts issue them automatically.[2242] These different approaches are a consequence of the national procedural rules and practices (i.e. service practices involving the creditor, domestic approach to issuance of a writ of execution).[2243] These various national approaches to the issuance of the Declaration of enforceability may lead to difficulties for the interested parties to the extent they are not able to find information on the process; hence, a non-repetitive claimant or a foreign lawyer may very well not be aware of the way a court will proceed or whether they are supposed to play an active role and demand that the court issue the forms. More clarity on these practical aspects will certainly facilitate the use of the European procedures and speed up certain procedural steps.

Language

The empirical research in England, France, Italy, and Romania did not reveal extensive language difficulties related to use of the forms. EOP and ESCP forms are usually submitted to the court in the language of the proceedings, and the creditors seek as much as possible to litigate claims in their home Member State. If consumers have to submit the claim to a court in another Member State, some ECC offices might be able to assist them (i.e. France, Italy). Other claimants may choose to rely on the services of a local lawyer, which diminishes the extent of the procedural 'casualties' due to language requirements. Claimants are likely to experience language problems in communicating

2240 See Section 7.3.2.3.

2241 The domestic format of the decision might at times be a consequence of national rules or practices. For example, in Romania, the judge has to issue standard Form E as well as a decision in accordance with domestic formats for good order and for registration in the court's electronic system, ECRIS. Another example is Form F. Although the standard form is sufficient to prevent the order becoming enforceable, the defendants, and in particular their representatives, are sometimes keen to file a statement of defence in the domestic format (e.g. Italy and Romania).

2242 France has a mixed approach; some courts issue them automatically, and others proceed upon request.

2243 In Italy, the claimant is responsibile for the service; thus, unless receiving a request and the proof of service, the judge cannot issue Form G, as in France; see further Sections 4.7.3.4 and 5.7.3.4.

with the courts if they do not have a command of the language of the proceedings, and do not have the benefit of legal assistance. Further, the data available indicates that forms and evidence are not often filed in another language. If forms and/or documents received are in a language other than that of the proceedings, the court will immediately request that the form be resubmitted in the correct language or/and a translation of all documents be drafted in that language. Requesting the translation of all evidence documents in the ESCP procedure, regardless of whether these appear to be necessary to give a judgment, or of all EOP-related evidence, is an abusive practice, and is particularly burdensome for the creditor who has to advance the costs. Furthermore, for enforcement purposes, the courts and bailiffs do not appear to handle or accept requests based on forms and documents drafted in a language other than their own.[2244] This can be explained by a number of interacting factors such as the limited language competences, legislative requirements or, sometimes, over-formalism.

Language is of particular importance for guaranteeing the defendant's access to a fair trial. Empirical findings show that there is a certain practice of serving or communicating the forms or decisions in the language of the proceedings together with additional identical standard forms in the language of the Member State where service is carried out. This is particularly the case in France and Italy, and only occasionally in Romania, where courts pay particular attention to compliance with language requirements involving service taking place abroad. The use of standard forms instead of translations reduces the claimant's costs, but it is questionable whether all of this can be considered sufficient information for the defendant to decide on the appropriate action to take. He will certainly be able to understand which procedure is used against him, but not able to understand those descriptive parts of the claim that might be of key importance for guaranteeing his procedural rights and a fair trial. The data available does not provide detailed information on whether the defendant is always aware of the possibility of refusing to accept documents he cannot understand. Further, translations might be necessary for the communication or notification of the enforceable title on the debtor (i.e. France, Italy, Romania). However, this is not always clear from the EOP and the ESCP Guides,[2245] as the interested party is only informed that he might need to translate the title into the official language or languages of the Member State where enforcement is to take place, or into one of the languages acceptable for execution purposes. For example, France is the only analysed jurisdiction that accepts forms in four other languages besides French. As positive as this aspect can seem for the simplification of enforcement in terms of costs and procedural timeframe, it is certainly not clear how well this functions in practice, whether bailiffs are generally able to actually handle forms in all five indicated languages (English, French, German, Italian, and Spanish). The information creates in parties a justified expectation that forms are always accepted

2244 Court requests made in a language other than that of the proceedings were seldom accepted and handled in the analysed jurisdictions (i.e. France, see Section 4.7.3.4).

2245 *Practice Guide for the Application of the Regulation on the European Order for Payment*, European Commission, Directorate General for Justice, 2011; European Commission, *Practice guide for the application of the European Small Claims Procedure under Regulation (EC) No 861/2007 of the European Parliament and of the Council of 11 July 2007 establishing a European Small Claims Procedure*, 2013.

in any of the five languages, a situation that might not correspond to reality in practice simply because of courts' or bailiffs' lack of linguistic abilities. Although more limited than in domestic procedures, translation remains necessary at various stages of the EOP and ESCP procedures. Regulation 2015/2421 seeks to further reduce the costs of translation for enforceable ESCPs by setting a duty on the courts to use Form D in any EU official language. The same strategy should be considered for EOP Form G.

Service

The empirical data reveal that a variety of methods are used to serve the EOP on the defendant, some of which are specific to a particular national system.[2246] The diversity of methods makes it difficult at times for the claimant or for the authority in charge to determine the means accepted as valid in another Member State. The information available is not always updated (e.g. on the European Judicial Network in Civil and Commercial Matters website) or available for all Member States in all official languages (e.g. the e-Justice Portal).[2247] The claimant or his representative has to find other sources of information or employ a local lawyer, which increases the costs of the proceedings and the procedural timeframe. Also, it makes it significantly more difficult for a claimant to know prior to initiating the procedure whether he is expected to play an active role in serving the EOP on the defendant. The choice of methods to be used is influenced by the national procedural rules and validity requirements. Often, the most widely used domestic means are also chosen in EOP cases.[2248] These are the postal service and personal service on the defendant attested by a document signed by the professional in charge of the service or by the party. Both methods secure a high level of certainty that the defendant received the documents of the proceedings. Service by post involves fewer costs in comparison to service carried out by a local bailiff, but may prove problematic if the acknowledgement of receipt is not returned.[2249] This difficulty is also encountered in the ESCP procedure.

As to the entity or person responsible for serving the EOP, the analysed systems are evenly divided between courts being in charge of service (England and Romania) and claimants having to request a bailiff to proceed to serving the order (France and Italy). These national differences may also lead to confusion in ESCP procedures, as French findings reveal.[2250] However, only a small number of respondents indicated having difficulties in serving EOP or ESCP forms on the defendant. If difficulties do arise in the actual service, it appears they often concern cross-border service, and relate to an incorrect address for the defendant, the language in which service is carried out, or

2246 For example, service by first-class post or a similar service in England; service at the office of the bailiff in France; P.E.C. in Italy; by email or by displaying it on the door or the premises of the defendant in Romania.

2247 On 1 October 2016, national information regarding service was available on the e-Justice Portal for 19 Member States. Additionally, not all language versions of the existing information are in place (https://e-justice.europa.eu/content_service_of_documents-371-en.do).

2248 See also Velicogna, Lupo & Onţanu (2017).

2249 This could also be related to differences between postal services in various Member States.

2250 See Section 4.7.3.4.

obtaining the acknowledgement of receipt. As a consequence, service requires longer periods for the minimum standards to be observed. The Service Regulation provisions apply if service has to be carried out in another Member State.

Hearings

Very little information on ESCP hearings is available. The number of ESCP cases is low, and few professionals have had significant experience (i.e. English respondents were not able to provide any data, while most French and Italian respondents were not aware of hearings having been held). Romania is the only jurisdiction where EOP and ESCP hearings are handled in public or in chambers, but this is a consequence of the domestic procedural rules and the lack of specific implementation provisions.[2251]

Hearings seem to be organised more as a result of the confusion between the European procedures and domestic similar procedures, or due to national procedural rules that are automatically applied when registering a claim (i.e. France, Italy). There are also courts that do not immediately organise a hearing if it is not necessary for giving the judgment. Further, parties do not seem particularly eager to request that a hearing be held, nor the courts to organise them. ESCP case law confirms this approach. Hence, the procedure remains in general a written one, as envisaged by the European legislator. This does not seem to worry parties or their representatives, as the written format is not seen to be a limitation of their right to be heard or to a fair trial.

Challenging Mechanisms (Opposition, Appeal, Review)

The challenging mechanisms set by the European procedures appear to be seldom applied in practice. Few respondents in the analysed jurisdictions had actually used them.

The EOPs are not often opposed by defendants. Most respondents in France, Italy, and Romania indicated the opposition rate to be below 25% of the cases they knew of or had handled.[2252] The length of the EOP opposition period (30 days from service) seems to be sufficiently long for defendants to respond in cross-border litigation, and practitioners referred to very few instances of opposition being filed after the limit had lapsed. The aspects that actually created difficulties were the handling of the opposition and the transfer of the claim to the ordinary procedure, a factor also indicated by case law findings. However, the empirical research emphasises this problematic aspect particularly in relation to Italy, where uncertainties persist due to various streams of interpretation.[2253] A uniform approach would favour certainty, and the national legislator should consider it. This is the case in England and in France, where the legislator chose an implementation and coordination approach that favours more clarity.

The ESCP appeal is seldom used in France, Italy, and Romania, while the English respondents were not aware of any request having been filed. The existence of the

[2251] However, the parties are not always summonsed to appear before the judge, as both procedures are meant to be written ones.

[2252] The data for England are not conclusive, as only one respondent was able to provide feedback on the use of opposition, and rated it slightly higher than in the other jurisdictions.

[2253] See further Section 5.7.3.4.

mechanism is subject to national rules, which leads to different procedural approaches and timeframes. This does not favour a simplified and uniform application of the ESCP appeal across the EU. No statistical data are available, so the findings cannot be triangulated for validation purposes. The gathering of more detailed information on the ESCP appeal would be a welcome undertaking in future research projects.

The EOP and ESCP review tools remain uncommon means of challenging.[2254] As ECC France remarked, the European uniform procedures do not often reach this level. An interesting finding on the EOP review mechanism is that these requests are not based on criteria set by Article 20, but on other factors, such as the existence of the debt and the calculation of interest, the lack of the court's competence to hear the claim, the service not complying with the standards set by the Regulation, or the defendant not receiving the EOP.[2255] These findings are confirmed by case law on the use of the ESCP review mechanism (e.g. Romanian case).[2256] The way the mechanism is interpreted indicates there is some confusion at the national level. In some of the jurisdictions, this application might be influenced by the existence of national tools bearing the same name (France and Romania), which can create confusion. Additionally, the effect may also be triggered by a lack of understanding of the mechanism by parties and practitioners. This might explain the incorrect application of the review by courts that agreed to proceed on criteria other than that set by Articles 18 ESCP or 20 EOP. It is worrying that the Regulations' provisions are not observed, especially as the CJEU followed a strict interpretation of the Article 20 EOP provisions in the *eco cosmetics* and *Flight Refund Ltd* cases. The national courts appear more inclined to transfer acceptable domestic criteria to the European mechanism. It is hoped that the new Article 18 ESCP will bring more certainty in the way this mechanism should be understood and applied.

Representation

Representation continues to be common, though it is not mandatory. EOP claimants usually choose to make use of legal services in France, Italy, and Romania.[2257] The empirical findings confirm the case law and the Ministry of Justice data where available. Defendants also make use of representation, but less often than claimants. This could be because EOPs are seldom opposed; hence, the use of representation is not immediately obvious. In ESCPs, representation is less often used than for EOPs, and at times it may involve only certain stages of the procedure (i.e. completion of Form A). The small value of the claim compared to the lawyer's fees can act as disincentive for the parties. The ESCP empirical data is limited, making it difficult to form a complete picture of the national practices regarding representation. Overall, the extensive use of lawyers' services in the European uniform procedures can be influenced by a number of factors. Apart from parties being accustomed to relying on the services of a lawyer in all four analysed jurisdictions, obtaining the necessary information in order to apply the EOP

2254 For the ESCP, the review was requested only in England and Romania according to the information provided by practitioners.

2255 See further Sections 3.7.3.4, 4.7.3.4, 5.7.3.4, and 6.7.3.4.

2256 See Section 6.7.3.4.

2257 This appears to be the case in England as well, but the data sample is too small to provide a broader perspective of the actual situation.

or/and the ESCP can involve significant time and effort. This is even more the case if the claim has to be submitted to a court in another Member State. Certain technical requirements of the forms (i.e. jurisdiction, interest) or compliance with national provisions (i.e. paying court fees, service, obtaining copies for communication require physical presence, translation requirements) are not easily complied with by a lay party appearing in person. Furthermore, no institutionalised legal assistance is available for parties to guide them in filling in the forms, to clarify how the EOP or the ESCP function, or to offer the necessary practical information. This means that parties need to rely on the services of a local lawyer. Although the use of a lawyer entails costs for the user, in the medium and long term, however, it can also have a positive influence with respect to the application of the European uniform procedures: for instance, it can help to raise awareness on the part of courts and practitioners. An example in this regard is the comment made by an Italian clerk who had noticed that while in the first years following the entrance into force of the EOP, most requests were filed by foreign claimants, lately more applications were being registered by local lawyers. The fact of local lawyers advising their clients to employ the procedures certainly helps to establish local practices with regard to the instruments. Increased familiarity also favours speedier handling of the claim and guarantees better protection of parties' procedural rights.

ECC offices in England, France, Italy, and Romania have also provided assistance for consumers, which is much needed in practice. It is hoped that the clarifications brought in by Regulation 2015/2421 will facilitate parties' access to free assistance and to the establishment of an institutionalised service in each Member State.

Procedural Timeframe

French, Italian, and Romanian courts generally appear to issue EOPs within 30 days, or within a timeframe just above the 30 days, as confirmed by case law and the statistical data available. For England, the outcome is not conclusive.[2258] In France and Romania, the procedure takes longer because of organisational shortcomings (i.e. limited number of staff), the backlog of cases, or requests for claimants to submit evidence documents and translations. The request for additional documents by courts constitutes an incorrect application of the Regulation, and should be avoided. This would speed up some of the EOP cases, giving judges more time for other cases, and thus decreasing the backlog.

The timeframe required to obtain EOP Form G is more than 3 months in all four analysed jurisdictions. The data indicate a slightly faster handling in France, with times under 3 months to complete the procedure. A number of aspects prolong proceedings above 3 months. In addition to reasons identified in France and Romania, delays are the result of difficulties in obtaining information about the defendant (i.e. address of the party),[2259] carrying out the service, and limited knowledge, all of which require more time and effort on the part of the clerks and judges. Increasing the judiciary's knowledge of the EOP will contribute to a better and faster handling of the claims.

2258 No triangulation is possible due to the lack of detailed statistics and published case law.

2259 Easier access to information between authorities and professionals involved in the handling of the EOP claim is not likely to happen in the near future, owing to differences between national legislations and concerns regarding personal data privacy.

For the ESCP, the empirical data available indicate judgments are often obtained within 6 months. Proceedings can take a bit longer in France and Romania. However, this outcome must be viewed with caution, as only a handful of respondents in all four jurisdictions were able to provide feedback. Almost no information is available on the time necessary to handle an appeal or on how this compares to domestic appeals. The English and Romanian practitioners' estimate of the appeal timeframe cannot be triangulated with case law or statistics, thus making it difficult to fully estimate the ESCP timeframe and the procedure's efficiency in comparison to national instruments.

Costs, Interests, Penalties

When it comes to court fees, each of the analysed national systems has its own arrangement.[2260] Though certain steps have been taken to make more detailed court fee information available on the e-Justice Portal, practical aspects are mostly missing (i.e. account details for paying court fees, wire transfers, not possible for all courts, more difficulties in receiving payments from abroad). Not being able to pay the court fees and to submit proof to the court can sometimes have serious consequences for claimants (i.e. Form B-based request to provide proof of payment led to cases being closed in Italy or struck off in Romania). More practical information on means of payment should be made available on the e-Justice Portal, as information on national websites or in the legislation is often available only in the official language of the Member State concerned. This makes it difficult for parties to find the relevant information, and hinders their access to justice. Other costs (i.e. service, translation, bailiffs' fees, lawyers' fees) must be advanced by the claimant, but may or may not be recovered in the EOP or the ESCP procedures. This is due to the divergent domestic interpretations of the Regulations' provisions on costs (i.e. some Italian judges are reluctant to award costs related to legal services) or due to assessments based on national interpretations of proportionality (i.e. recovery of ESCP lawyers' fees in England). Interested parties are actually unable to have clear upfront details on these various national approaches to the recovery of advanced procedural costs. This fragmentation further prevents a uniform application of the Regulations.

As to requests and the calculation of interest, practices differ between analysed jurisdictions. For example, interest requests were sometimes not considered by French judges, while the way interest is calculated differs between Italy and Romania.[2261] The e-Justice Portal should contain detailed information on the legal interest applicable in each Member State. Without the assistance of a local lawyer, a lay party will find it difficult to identify this information and request interest, especially if parties did not agree beforehand on a contractual interest applicable for late payments.

[2260] In France, court fees apply only in commercial litigation; England taxes procedures on the basis of the value of the claim; Romania notified the European Commission of a similar approach, but in practice it is not uncommon for courts to apply a fixed fee, as for similar domestic procedures; Italy applies fixed court fees.

[2261] In Italy, interest can be requested and is calculated up until the date of the submission of the claim, after this moment, and until repayment of the debt's legal interest applies. In Romania, requested interest is awarded up until the debt has been paid in full.

7.3.3.4. Enforcement

Only a handful of bailiffs in the four analysed jurisdictions were able to provide feedback on the execution of EOP and ESCP judgments; hence, the bailiffs' perspective in this study is limited. Courts and lawyers in England, France, Italy, and Romania provided some feedback on enforcement, but the information did not offer extensive insights into the execution process, largely because many practitioners had not had any practical experience with this stage of the EOP or the ESCP. Additional research on the enforcement of European uniform procedures is desirable, as the present findings can only hint at the situation in practice. The broader participation of bailiffs would be welcome, as they are directly responsible for the actual execution process.

English, French, Italian, and Romanian respondents referred to difficulties in the enforcement process. These are related mainly to insufficient practical information necessary for the execution process (e.g. identifying the national competent authority, difficulties in finding information about the debtor's assets and financial situation, and choosing the method of enforcement), high enforcement costs, and additional procedural steps that needed to be taken at the national level in order to initiate the execution (e.g. having to request issuance of the Declaration of enforceability, providing translations). Lay parties appearing in person are likely more exposed to these problems, especially when the process has to be pursued in another Member State. Information available on enforcement has slightly improved lately, and more details have become available on the e-Justice Portal. However, for the moment these do not involve all Member States and not all official languages are covered.[2262] This impedes the creditor's access to justice, as enforcement is a key element of the process. Long delays in initiating the execution process can seriously diminish chances of the debt being recovered, an aspect that can affect the effectiveness and efficiency of the European uniform procedures. An execution process that is easy to carry out can encourage possible claimants to make use of EOP or ESCP procedures.

The method of execution chosen influences the time necessary to enforce a European uniform procedure,[2263] as well as a series of procedural actions (i.e. serving of the title on the debtor, translations). According to respondents in the four jurisdictions, the execution can often take on average from around 1 month to 3–4 months based on the means of execution and assets involved. However, because some bailiffs have a limited knowledge of the procedures, the enforcement stage can be prolonged.[2264] A slow enforcement of the EOP or ESCP judgment certainly diminishes advantages that the procedures can provide. It is not sufficient for the claimant to obtain a speedy decision. The execution mechanisms should further facilitate the use of the European uniform procedures, otherwise access to justice is jeopardised at this last stage. Although it does not happen extensively,

2262 As of 1 October 2016 (https://e-justice.europa.eu/content_procedures_for_enforcing_a_judgment-299-en.do).

2263 Execution procedures involving immovable property require a longer period due to various procedural steps that need to be undertaken.

2264 Bailiffs may refuse to take up an enforcement request for a procedure with which they are unfamiliar, or they will be extra cautious in verifying the title and the required steps.

creditors sometimes decide not to pursue enforcement because of the practical difficulties, the high execution costs, and/or the insolvency of the debtor. The debtors at times challenge the execution activities in seeking to prevent enforcement, but this usually has to do with the execution process and not with the soundness of the enforceable title. Furthermore, an EOP or ESCP enforcement has seldom been rejected, and the instances had to do with the bailiffs' scant knowledge of the procedure and forms (Italy and France). At this point, the mechanism involving a limitation or stay of enforcement has apparently never been used.

7.3.3.5. Practitioners' Assessment

Views are divided on the efficiency of the European uniform procedures in terms of 'speediness, affordability and protection of parties' rights'. While respondents in Italy and Romania were more positive regarding the European procedures, views were more divergent in England and France. Additionally, English, French, Italian, and Romanian practitioners appreciated the EOP more than the ESCP, which is less often used. This preference appears to be based on the speed with which EOP proceedings are handled, its affordability, and the less restrictive requirements compared to national procedures. Practitioners were more reserved regarding the ESCP. The €2,000 threshold was considered too low compared to the costs the procedure can entail, although the raising of the threshold to €5,000 by Regulation 2015/2421 might increase creditors' interest in this procedure. The limited familiarity and practical experience on the part of courts, lawyers, and bailiffs affects the procedures' efficiency. This in turn has a negative influence on the speed with which claims are handled and decisions executed, on the costs the parties have to bear, and on parties' access to justice.

In terms of the effectiveness of the solution proposed, respondents tended to rate the EOP and the ESCP as effective instruments if the debt was actually recovered by the creditor. The EOP was more often used and better known, and scored higher than the ESCP. Its effectiveness was also linked by respondents to the timeframe within which an order was obtained, the low opposition rate, and the use of standard forms.

A number of obstacles to the application of the European uniform procedures remain. Respondents referred in this regard to the limited familiarity of parties and practitioners and, occasionally, to the lack of practical experience of the latter,[2265] the lack of sufficiently detailed information about various practical aspects (e.g. court fees, continuation of the procedure following opposition, enforcement), and problematic service. Some of the identified obstacles were more closely related to national procedural rules (i.e. impossibility of recovering court fees from foreign claimants in Italy, coordination with national legislation, means available to pay court fees). To address some of these obstacles, sufficiently detailed information and guidelines should be made available at the national and the European level (i.e. e-Justice Portal). For respondents, the availability of practical information on the procedures is crucial. The creation of national step-by-step guides for

2265 The number of cases received is too low to allow practitioners to develop expertise in handling EOP or ESCP claims.

practitioners who only occasionally apply these instruments can facilitate the process. This would address national particularities, and facilitate the coordination between domestic rules and the provisions of the European Regulations. Better coordination and clarification as to which rules should complement the Regulations would contribute to their coherent and unitary application. Together with this, it is necessary to provide additional training for courts and practitioners, and to organise free assistance for parties. A simplification of the national execution process for the European uniform procedures seems unlikely to be considered. At present, there is no political interest in proceeding to or in achieving any form of unification or harmonisation of the domestic enforcement mechanisms. Regulation 2015/2421 addresses some points of improvement referred to by the respondents (e.g. increasing the ESCP threshold (England and Italy), using e-mail addresses to serve documents of the proceedings or the decision (England and Romania)). It remains to be seen, however, whether these points are sufficient to boost the use of this procedure from July 2017.

7.3.3.6. Evaluation and Explanation

Practitioners participating in this research were in most cases familiar with the European uniform procedures, but for practitioners in general the procedures were not widely known.[2266] Parties were also not familiar with the procedures unless they had previously employed them. Hence, most courts and practitioners had received no EOP or ESCP requests. Thus, as previously indicated, this did not give them an opportunity to develop any expertise or to establish handling practices that could facilitate and speed up the application of these European procedures. Organising coordinated information campaigns at the European and the national level as well as creating dedicated material on practical and crucial domestic aspects can improve parties' and practitioners' awareness. Training courts and practitioners to handle EOP and ESCP claims will extend their expertise and contribute to a unitary understanding of the Regulations' provisions, and of the way these instruments should be applied across the EU. Further, in order to optimise available resources, national legislators should consider the possibility of concentrating these written procedures in a smaller number of national courts.[2267] This can help involved courts gain a high level of expertise and allow them to develop handling practices. Additionally, this will contribute to procedural guarantees being observed and to the European uniform procedures being handled more efficiently in terms of streamlining the procedural timeframe and limiting litigation costs that result from incorrect additional requirements.[2268] This can have a positive influence on how the European uniform procedures function, and encourage potential litigants to use these alternative instruments. A positive experience can also lead to repeated use of the procedures as well as to attracting new users. The increase in the ESCP threshold can also make the procedure more interesting for businesses.

[2266] A situation also seen in the case law analysis; see Section 7.3.2.
[2267] See also Contini (2014), at 331.
[2268] See also Section 7.3.2.

As previously emphasised, domestic procedures continue to have a significant influence on the manner in which the procedures are applied, although national procedural rules are not necessarily an obstacle for their application. This leads to inappropriate interpretations that do not correspond to the aims of the Regulations (i.e. judges requesting the submission of evidence in an EOP proceeding, requesting the ESCP claimant to serve documents of the proceeding on the defendant).[2269] Further, it creates an unnecessary burden for the claimants, adding an extra layer to procedures that are presented as being simple and less costly EU alternatives to domestic procedures. Legislative actions geared towards better accommodating the European uniform procedures within domestic procedural systems together with training have the potential to prevent the instruments from being applied incorrectly. The level of knowledge that courts and practitioners have reflects upon the level of procedural simplification the Regulations manage to secure within the analysed jurisdictions, as well as the litigation timeframe and costs.

Free assistance for parties not using legal representation as well as more detailed practical information, should be made available at the national level.[2270] Information that can offer general as well as practical advice on EOP and ESCP usage should be established as part of national administration, court systems, or professional organisations in accordance with national legislation.[2271] This assistance should involve practical aspects and include support in obtaining information on the procedures and the situations in which these can be used, information and advice on the way the standard forms have to be filled in, identifying the competent court and its contact details, the way court fees have to be paid, determining the applicable interest rates and, possibly, offering language support. Translation requirements and costs play an important role in the application of the European uniform procedures and the protection of parties' procedural rights. Information on languages accepted for procedural and enforcement purposes continues to create incorrect expectations (i.e. France).[2272] The e-Justice Portal should make it clearer which languages are relevant for submission of the application based on the country in which the competent court is situated. The fact that the claimant can select any of the official languages of the EU to generate the online standard claim form can lead to confusion. It creates a false expectation that the claim can be submitted in any of the languages to be chosen from.[2273] Service information is another aspect that needs to be urgently addressed, as it impinges upon parties' procedural rights and their access to justice. Updated information must become available in all official EU languages on the e-Justice Portal. Further, future possible reviews of the EOP Regulation should

[2269] *Ibidem.*

[2270] For example, citizens in various Member States (including Italy, England) are unable to find the information necessary to start the ESCP. See Special Eurobarometer 395, *European Small Claims Procedure Report*, 2013, at 80–81.

[2271] A solution that fits within the national system should be chosen. An alternative arrangement should be considered if the court staff cannot assist parties due to concerns related to the principle of impartiality.

[2272] See Section 4.7.3.4.

[2273] See final step of the online standard Form A available on the e-Justice Portal 'Please select the language in which you wish to generate the pdf form' (visited on 1 September 2016). For prior criticism, see Onţanu & Pannebakker (2012), at 174.

investigate the possibility of diminishing the number of accepted service methods in order to facilitate users' tasks, as well as reducing the complexity of the present checks that courts are required to carry out in assessing the validity of the service.

The European uniform procedures are not often challenged. As case law has also indicated, the EOP opposition is easy to make use of, but the transfer to the national ordinary procedure and the coordination with national procedural rules in certain jurisdictions (i.e. Italy) creates difficulties and uncertainties for claimants. A clearer approach by the national legislator or authorities would certainly facilitate access to justice, but this remains an aspect that national authorities should address. As to the ESCP, the present diversity of approaches adds an additional layer of complexity to a procedure that aims to be simple and fast. A uniform approach would be desirable. Unfortunately, Regulation 2015/2421 was unable to secure a consensus in this regard; furthermore, the practical information available on challenging a decision is not sufficient. More detailed references should be made available on the e-Justice Portal or on national dedicated websites. In addition, the review mechanism is not always applied appropriately or understood well by practitioners. Its infrequent use and its possible confusion with national mechanisms hinder its proper application.

The limited information available on the EOP and ESCP enforcement stage makes it extremely difficult to evaluate the success of this last stage of the procedures. More explicit practical information on domestic enforcement rules and requirements should be made available in all official languages to facilitate this process, which remains deeply rooted in the national legislations and traditions. Otherwise, enforcement matters will remain a serious bottleneck in terms of costs, timeframe necessary, identification of assets, and procedural steps if the debtor does not comply with the decision.

Overall, practitioners valued the EOP procedure more highly than the ESCP. The limited familiarity and practical experience on the part of courts, lawyers, and bailiffs influences the way the European instruments are applied in terms of speed, affordability, and the protection of parties' procedural rights. Furthermore, the success of the execution process has an impact on the perceived effectiveness of the procedures. Achieving better coordination between the provisions of the Regulations and the domestic procedural rules together with a concentration of the European uniform procedures in a smaller number of national courts appears to be the way forward in making full use of the potential these instruments offer in cross-border litigation.

7.4. Effectiveness and Efficiency of the European Uniform Procedures

In general, the EOP and ESCP Regulations and judicial cooperation between EU Member States still have to overcome a number of bottlenecks.

First, a successful implementation of the EOP and the ESCP within the national procedural systems is a prerequisite for an effective and efficient application of the European uniform procedure. EOP and ESCP Regulations set a uniform procedural framework, but continue to rely on national procedural rules in numerous aspects (e.g. service methods, court fees, activities parties are expected to undertake, challenging mechanisms, etc.). Looking at the specific criteria set in Section 7.1.3 to evaluate implementation of the European uniform procedures within the four analysed jurisdictions, the following aspects are identified:

- the process of incorporating specific legal rules on the application of the European uniform procedures into national procedural rules (England and France) or the adoption of dedicated guidelines or clarification papers (England, France, and – to some extent – Italy) offers a higher degree of transparency and certainty as to provisions applicable in relation to the European procedures. Unclear coordination can lead to problematic interpretations of some procedural aspects (e.g. filing of EOPs in Italy following domestic reforms, application of the review mechanism) and divergent application of the European uniform procedures across the analysed jurisdictions (e.g. automatic delivery or issuance upon request of the Declaration of enforceability). This can hamper a successful application of the European uniform procedures, as parties will not be willing to take risks with uncertain procedures or confusing practices that could diminish their chances of recovering their debt or that involve long procedural timeframes and significant costs;
- it is not always clear which national rules apply in conjunction with the European uniform procedures, and the related text is not always easily accessible, especially for foreign parties (e.g. transfer of EOP following opposition in Italy, applicable court fees in Romania). This prolongs a state of legal insecurity for the parties and for professionals called to apply the European uniform procedures. Interaction and coordination between the two levels of legislation is extremely important, as difficulties at this stage can compromise the successful and speedy application of the procedures, which are designed to be fast, simple, and less costly than others;
- the availability of information on aspects that are important for the application of the EOP and the ESCP is crucial for the procedures to function. This should concern not only general information, as is mostly available at the European (e.g. e-Justice Portal, EOP and ESCP Guidelines) and the national level (e.g. Consumer Organisation, Ministry of Justice, Courts' Portals), but also specific information on practical aspects necessary to apply the European procedures in each jurisdiction. Unclear or misleading information (e.g. details as to competent courts, available methods for the payment of court fees, obtaining the Declaration of enforceability) can prolong the European procedures and add to procedural costs (e.g. additional legal services, translation costs) unnecessarily, thereby influencing the effectiveness (level of simplification of the procedures), and efficiency (costs and time to conclude a European procedure) of the EOP and the ESCP. National and European actions are necessary to improve the information available and to increase the transparency of relevant national rules, including in other EU official languages. Insufficient action to coordinate the two levels of legislation jeopardises a harmonious application of the European uniform procedures;
- the practical experience of courts and practitioners, as indicated in the available statistics and case law, as well as in European Commission Reports, is not extensive, and this affects their knowledge of and familiarity with the instruments. This can further influence the effectiveness and efficiency with which the European procedures are applied (time to conclude the European procedures).

The outcome of the comparative research emphasises that even optimally drafted European procedures might create difficulties if they are highly dependent upon national implementation and application, and if clear actions are required to properly address these issues.

Second, in analysing the effectiveness of the EOP and the ESCP against the set evaluation criteria, the following aspects are revealed:

- sometimes the additional request the court makes or the tasks the claimant has to comply with mirror requirements of domestic procedures. This adds additional steps that the party needs to follow in order to make successful use of the European uniform procedures. This affects the simplification the procedures seek to achieve in cross-border litigation.
- in the assessment of the procedural guarantees the EOP and the ESCP provide for the parties, the data show that courts pay significant attention to verifying that the defendants are informed of the procedures initiated against them. In all four jurisdictions, the case law and the empirical data point to the use of service methods securing a high degree of certainty that the documents have reached the defendant (i.e. personal service on the debtor, service by post with acknowledgement of receipt). Further, the French, Italian, English, and Romanian courts proceed to a verification of whether the service methods used comply with the standards set by EOP and ESCP Regulations. To secure protection of the defendant's procedural rights, the service is renewed if there are doubts as to whether the debtor was informed of the proceedings. This action is of particular importance for guaranteeing access to justice;
- the language and translation requirements for the service of documents and for enforcement purposes are handled differently in each of the four jurisdictions. As to the observance of language requirements, Romanian judges are the most attentive to language provisions when serving the standard forms on the defender. Other practices, such as communicating additional identical standard forms in the official language of the place where service is performed (France, Italy, and – occasionally – Romania) can offer hints regarding the nature of the procedure, but do not comply with the language requirements set by the ESCP or the Service Regulations. This means that protection of the party's procedural rights is diminished. The language and translation requirements can have a significant influence on the cost of the European procedures (in terms of efficiency), but are also of key importance for guaranteeing parties' procedural rights and a fair trial. These should not be traded off for economic reasons;
- As to the application of challenging mechanisms, their effect at the moment appears to remain slightly more theoretical. Their limited use and the limited familiarity many practitioners have with the European procedures may lead at times to difficulties in applying these safety mechanisms (e.g. rejection of EOP oppositions in Romania, use of the EOP review mechanism in France). Furthermore, the fact the ESCP is disciplined differently across the analysed jurisdictions does not favour a simple uniform approach. The existence of challenging mechanisms *per se* is an important guarantee for the parties' procedural rights, but the way these are structured and applied can have a negative impact on the effectiveness of the procedures;
- in terms of enforcement and successful execution of the EOP and the ESCP judgments, the data available are too limited to provide a sound assessment of the effectiveness of the procedures, though it appears that survey and interview respondents are more

inclined to rate the procedures as effective if the debt is successfully recovered. The research is unable to assess the level of successful enforcement of the EOP and the ESCP titles. Additionally, national statistics on enforcement requests are not generally collected (except in England).

As the comparative research reveals, application of the EOP and the ESCP leads to mixed results in terms of effectiveness. Therefore, it has to be acknowledged that simplification is at best partial, and that parties' rights are protected and guaranteed only to a certain extent; hence, further improvements are essential in order to prevent the EOP and the ESCP and their challenging mechanisms from being applied incorrectly.

Third, in assessing the efficiency of the EOP and the ESCP against the evaluation criteria, the following aspects must be mentioned:

- in terms of cost efficiency, the EOP and the ESCP are set to diminish certain costs associated with cross-border litigation (e.g. translation, lawyers, travelling), though not completely eliminating them. Some of these expenses cannot be eliminated, as they are related to procedural guarantees (e.g. serving EOP or ESCP forms in a language the party is able to understand) or involve complicated domestic rules that apply in connection with the European uniform procedures.[2274] Additional tensions are added by the fact that some domestic courts are not willing to award certain costs (e.g. lawyers' fees in EOP and ESCP procedures). In such circumstances, parties are more inclined to continue using domestic procedures, which allow them to secure full award of the costs. Excessive costs due to various requirements of the proceedings (e.g. representation, actions to pay court fees, uncertainties as to the application of procedures, enforcement) can hinder access to justice, especially if these reach disproportionate levels, deterring parties from initiating or continuing court proceedings or enforcement. Achieving a balance between efficient application of the EOP and the ESCP in terms of procedural costs and timeframe, and compliance with procedural guarantees is highly desirable;
- the time necessary to deal with EOP and ESCP claims generally appears to be on the decrease towards a handling within 30 days for the EOP and 6 months for the ESCP: hence, less than in many domestic procedures applicable for similar purposes. However, sometimes the proceedings are unnecessarily prolonged by additional requirements based on an incorrect understanding of the provisions of the European uniform procedures. The necessary enforcement period varies, and is based on the type of mechanism chosen, the number of pre-enforcement steps required (e.g. collecting the Declaration of enforceability from the court, translating the title, serving of the title on the debtor), and the actual execution time. The empirical data, however, are insufficient, and offer only a hint in this respect.

The EOP and the ESCP set the basis for procedures that can facilitate cross-border litigation. However, their application has not yet achieved its full potential, although the EOP is more popular and more often used than the ESCP. The possibility of creditors

[2274] No institutionalised free assistance is given to parties using the ESCP (it is hoped this will change with the entrance into force of Regulation 2015/2421). In such circumstances, the parties need to rely on local lawyers in order to identify and have easy access to information relevant for the application of the procedures.

obtaining a decision within a short period is a reality, as is a simplification of this stage of the proceedings.

The EOP and the ESCP have taken certain steps forward by creating a uniform framework. Nevertheless, more coordinated actions need to be taken to improve their application in terms of effectiveness and efficiency, and of building on the experience of courts and practitioners.

One of the first moves to enhance the application and functioning of the procedures should be to make the necessary practical information easily accessible across the Member States. Clear national guidelines on the interaction between the domestic rules and EOP and ESCP Regulations should be made available. The present EU Guides are not sufficient. Furthermore, it is essential to set up appropriate training programmes for all categories of practitioners involved in the handling of EOP and ESCP claims. In addition, since the use of the European uniform procedures continues to remain modest in comparision to the domestic procedures available for similar purposes, the national legislator and/or Ministries of Justice should seriously consider concentrating these written procedures in a smaller number of courts. This will allow a better use of resources (e.g. training, ICT) and favour the creation of expertise and handling practices that in turn can contribute to a speedy and sound handling of EOP and ESCP claims (i.e. achieving the objectives they set in terms of enforcement as well as guaranteeing the protection of parties' procedural rights). Concentration might also facilitate the collection of better and more detailed statistical data on the use of the European procedures. In this respect, the national data systems should be properly equipped to register these applications separately. Sound and complete statistical data can offer valuable information on the functioning of the European procedures, highlighting the strong procedural points as well as any difficulties encountered in their application. Known difficulties are easier to address, and good practices are able to be shared. In addition, the increase in the ESCP threshold has the potential to make the procedure more interesting for legal entities and to raise awareness on the part of potential users.

Finally, legislative actions are strongly desired in relation to the EOP and ESCP Regulations. Reliance on national procedural rules should be less extensive in order to achieve a better harmonised framework (e.g. smaller number of service methods in the EOP procedure, uniform approach to appeal in the ESCP procedure), and the text of the EOP and ESCP Regulations should be better coordinated. Regulation 2015/2421 clarifies certain mechanisms or rules only in relation to the ESCP procedures (e.g. payment of court fees, language of the certificate, review, information to be provided by Member States). Furthermore, and also in relation to the EOP procedure, free legal assistance would be beneficial to parties needing general information on the scope of the procedure, on the competent courts, and on filling in the forms. Although legislative action by the European Commission in the immediate future does not appear to be likely, measures at the European and national level to improve the EOP and the ESCP information should be easier to achieve. These would already contribute to improving the efficiency of the European procedures in terms of costs and procedural delays. They would also simplify the claimant's position at the outset by providing him with a full overview of the procedural steps he actively needs to pursue and the rules he is required to observe.

Chapter 8

CONCLUSIONS

'L'Europe ne se fera pas d'un coup, ni dans une construction d'ensemble: elle se fera par des réalisations concrètes créant d'abord une solidarité de fait', Robert Schumann[2275]

8.1. Introduction

The present chapter analyses the results of the enactment and application of two of the three current European uniform procedures. The third procedure, the European Account Preservation Order (EAPO), only became applicable on 18 January 2017,[2276] and is therefore only incidentally addressed.

As described in Chapter 1, the analysis was carried out in four European jurisdictions: England and Wales (hereafter England), France, Italy, and Romania. The main research question was whether the EOP and the ESCP improved cross-border litigation in terms of securing effective enforcement mechanisms while protecting parties' procedural rights. In order to answer this, the following sub-questions were addressed in Chapters 3–7:

1) Which national instruments serve a purpose similar to that of the EOP and the ESCP, and how do they function in practice?
2) How are the European uniform procedures implemented within the legal framework of the analysed national systems?
3) How are these European procedures perceived and applied in practice?
4) To what extent do the EOP and the ESCP succeed in providing effective alternative instruments in cross-border litigation?
5) Do the European uniform procedures offer sufficient guarantees for the parties' procedural rights?

2275 Declaration of 9 May 1950, Quai d'Orsay (available at http://europa.eu/about-eu/basic-information/symbols/europe-day/schuman-declaration/index_fr.htm).

2276 Regulation (EU) No 655/2014 of the European Parliament and of the Council of 15 May 2014 establishing a European Account Preservation Order procedure to facilitate cross-border debt recovery in civil and commercial matters, OJ L 189/59, 27.6.2014.

A complementary question is based on the answers to the main question, investigating whether the template established by the European uniform procedures represents a model for future procedures aimed at simplifying cross-border enforcement and harmonising civil procedures.

The analysis considers and refers to the EAPO procedure whenever it is considered to contribute to the discussion generated by the follow-up question.

The chapter first concludes on the findings reported in previous chapters, and then addresses the follow-up question concerning developments and future projects in the area of European civil justice.

Chapters 2–7 discuss and assess the application of the EOP and the ESCP, looking at their implementation and interaction with domestic rules and procedures. Chapter 2 explores the main features of the first two European uniform procedures, focusing on their standards and characteristics, and on their interaction with domestic procedural rules. Chapters 3–6 present a multi-level comparative and empirical analysis of the implementation and application of the EOP and the ESCP within the national procedural systems of England, France, Italy, and Romania. These chapters also explore their functioning within the national procedural systems, and in relation to domestic procedures that serve a similar purpose. The analysis offers insights into the implementation process and the choices made by national legislators and/or ministries, as well as into the stakeholders' perception of the European uniform procedures. Next, the way the European procedures are applied and function in England, France, Italy, and Romania is investigated. Statistical data and case law are scrutinised together with empirical data collected from courts, practitioners, and the ECC network. The findings offer valuable information on the way these two European procedures function in practice, and on whether they manage to secure the protection they seek to offer to parties. Chapter 7 is comparative. It aggregates the national findings to assess whether the EOP and ESCP procedures improve the process of cross-border litigation in providing an effective and efficient enforcement mechanism, and in guaranteeing parties' procedural rights. Their effectiveness is analysed from two perspectives: the process of obtaining an enforceable decision and the success of the enforcement process. Their efficiency is evaluated in terms of procedural costs and timeframe (i.e. court proceedings and execution process).

Sections 8.2 and 8.3 address the follow-up question that builds on the conclusion regarding the effectiveness and the efficiency of the EOP and the ESCP. They also examine the implication of the legal standards they establish for future developments aimed at simplifying cross-border enforcement and harmonising civil procedure in the European Union. In concluding the chapter, Section 8.4 considers additional ongoing developments and their importance for simplifying cross-border enforcement, facilitating parties' access to justice, and consolidating the area of European civil justice.

8.2. Improving Cross-Border Litigation: Application of the European Uniform Procedures

8.2.1. *Use in Practice*

The statistical data available at the EU and the national level show that the European uniform procedures are seldom used. The EOP and the ESCP have not yet reached their maximum potential in cross-border litigation, and parties' limited awareness of them contributes to this. Sounder and more detailed national statistics are sorely needed, and if made available will certainly provide better information on how the procedures function. This will also increase the comparability of the collected data. Better national statistics will help identify more courts experienced in handling EOP and ESCP claims, and allow an investigation of possible best practices as well as their dissemination together with acquired expertise. Courts receiving more EOP and ESCP cases will then be able to develop practices to facilitate and speed up the treatment of claims.[2277]

The relatively limited use of these instruments is confirmed by case law and by empirical data, which also reveal that the EOP is more successful in practice than the ESCP. As initially envisaged by the European legislator, the EOP procedure is more appealing for legal entities, while consumers (except for Romania) more often choose the ESCP. For instance, a report in 2016 revealed that 70% of responding small and medium-size businesses in England had problems relating to late payment by customers (72% of cases in the last 5 years). However, the businesses were afraid to use official procedures.[2278] Perhaps consumers have a similar attitude towards court litigation, which might contribute to the infrequent use of the procedures. In such circumstances, it is possible that alternative dispute resolutions can offer a better solution.[2279]

The recent (14 June 2017) increase in the ESCP threshold to €5,000 might also pique companies' interest in this instrument.

The way the EOP and the ESCP are used and applied is analysed on a basis of chosen evaluation criteria (as discussed in Chapter 7, Section 7.1.3).

8.2.2. *Implementation in the National Systems and Practice*

In relation to applying the EOP and the ESCP, a significant number of aspects require that domestic procedural rules be implemented as well. Therefore, domestic legislation has an important influence on the manner in which the European procedures are applied. This makes their implementation within the national procedural system a key pre-requisite for their successful application.[2280] The absence of such an action at the national

2277 See also Contini (2014), at 331.

2278 Federation of Small Businesses, *Tied Up. Unravelling the Dispute Resolution Process for Small Firms*, Report, 2016 (available at www.fsb.org.uk/docs/default-source/fsb-org-uk/tied-up-unravelling-the-dispute-resolution-process-for-small-firms.pdf?sfvrsn=0).

2279 See further Section 8.4.4.

2280 See also Samyn (2015), at 186.

level might undermine the use of the procedures altogether, along with their appeal to parties and to professionals representing parties in cross-border claims.[2281] In Italy and Romania, due to the lack of implementation guidelines, the complexity of correlating rules, inadequate coordination, and uncertainty as to which national rules apply in connection with the European procedures strongly influence their use and application.[2282] Scholars have come to similar conclusions in other jurisdictions as well, where implementation rules are missing (e.g. Belgium).[2283] These findings are confirmed by the results of the 2017 European Commission study evaluating the impact of national procedural laws and practices on the free circulation of judgments.[2284] The adoption of dedicated procedural rules and/or guidelines to facilitate and coordinate the application of domestic and European provisions offers certainty and consistency as to how the EOP and the ESCP should be applied. This simplifies the tasks of courts and practitioners as well as those of potential parties in understanding their role in the proceedings. No unitary approach exists between Member States on how the EOP and ESCP Regulations are to be accommodated within their national procedural systems. As well as publishing guidelines, the English and French legislators adopted specific provisions amending their procedural rules. The Italian Ministry of Justice opted for ad-hoc guidelines and clarifications on the EOP. The Romania legislator relies on the direct effect of the regulations. These diverse approaches to EOP and ESCP implementation in national procedural systems can be confusing for lay users as well as for legal practitioners not familiar with a particular Member State's procedural system or with the norms adopted for this purpose. This is in particular the case if relevant information is not easily accessible or not available in all official EU languages.[2285] Furthermore, the lack of a uniform approach at the national level leads to diverse interpretations of the European uniform procedures. The Regulations seek to prevent this complexity by adopting uniform instruments, but they are only partly successful, because they rely significantly on domestic rules. The lack of dedicated provisions or guidelines hinders users as well as practitioners wishing to handle such claims or to offer advice on them. This is the case for local as well as foreign users, since both may encounter difficulties in determining which domestic provisions are applicable in EOP or ESCP procedures.

A significant number of practitioners who took part in the research indicated that they were fairly well versed in the EOP and the ESCP, and in the way the procedures function. Nevertheless, the level of overall knowledge regarding the procedures remains relatively low despite them having been available for almost ten years.

2281 Samyn (2013), at 186.

2282 For example, the transfer of an opposed EOP to the ordinary procedure, the duties of the parties, the means available to pay ESCP court fees, and the review procedure in Italy; the trial of EOP and ESCP requests in public hearings, the various national mechanisms in accordance with which review is to be handled in Romania. See further Sections 5.5, 5.7.2 – 5.7.4 for Italy and Sections 6.7.2 – 6.7.4 for Romania.

2283 Voet (2015), at 156; Samyn (2015), at 323.

2284 Hess (2017), Chapter 5.3–4 and 6 (para. 882, 890, 898, 900, 910, 915, 945).

2285 Specific information on national procedural law is not easily available across the EU. The references to domestic rules on the e-Justice Portal and other dedicated websites are often too general for interested parties to be able to use them. This makes the services of a legal practitioner necessary, although representation is not mandatory according to the Regulations.

8.2.3. *Application*

Considering the relatively limited use of the EOP and the ESCP in the four jurisdictions, and the modest familiarity of most national practitioners with the procedures, one might wonder whether such instruments are even necessary.

The research has revealed that the national procedures influence the manner in which the EOP and the ESCP are handled, as well as the timeframe necessary to obtain a decision. The limited experience and understanding that practitioners have of the European procedures have led in practice to a reverse transplant situation. The procedures are applied in a manner that mirrors domestic instruments that resemble or have a purpose similar to that of the EOP or the ESCP. Hence, the parties have to comply with additional requirements for EOP or ESCP judgments. In all four jurisdictions, the courts often have a conservative approach to the language of the proceedings, and are keen to examine the evidence documents, although this is not required by the format of the procedure (i.e. EOP), or to receive certified translations of all submitted documents. Such situations annul or diminish the simplification that the European procedures were designed to bring to cross-border litigation. Additionally, this can result in longer procedural timeframes, additional costs, and negative outcomes for the claimant. All these factors contribute to an increase rather than a decrease in the costs of litigation, which are often an important element upon which the decision to initiate a court claim rests. As Reimann points out '[E]ven if a matter is deemed important enough, and even if the chances of success are considered high, a party may not be able or willing to bear the cost of litigation'.[2286] In such circumstances, parties are doubtful about the ability of the European uniform procedures to truly reduce costs and to speed up and simplify cross-border litigation.

As EOP and ESCP application is still in the process of being calibrated to national procedural systems and practice, the potential of these procedures in cross-border litigation must not be ignored. The EOP and the ESCP establish a common procedural framework for cross-border uncontested and small value claims. Additionally, they can provide simplified alternatives when national special procedures are not applicable (e.g. Money Claim Online in England). The introduction of standard forms generally facilitates the use and handling of the European uniform procedures, although limited familiarity with them may at times impede their uniform application. The claims are handled in a written format without involving the automatic summonsing of the parties before the judge as is done in many national procedures. This facilitates access to justice for parties resident abroad, and reduces litigation costs associated with such a requirement. The period necessary for the court to issue an EOP or an ESCP decision appears on average to be decreasing in the analysed jurisdictions; the goal is 30 days for the EOP, and observing the various ESCP time-related steps.[2287] The European uniform procedures represent a significant improvement in this regard in cross-border litigation, as was also pointed out in the European Commission's dedicated reports and

[2286] Reimann (2012), at 4. See also Tulibacka, Sanz & Blomeyer (2016), at 19.

[2287] No data in this regard is available for England.

evaluations.[2288] However, European and national legislators should not ignore the fact that certain procedural aspects remain under the influence of the national procedural rules, and need to be properly addressed in order to preserve *l'effet utile* of the EOP and ESCP. This involves, for example, the service methods, which must comply with the standards set by the Regulations, the parties' active role in the proceedings,[2289] the holding of hearings, the format in which the decision is issued,[2290] or the challenging mechanisms.[2291] The differences identified in the application of the European uniform procedures maintain a certain complexity. Without detailed information on how to conduct the proceedings or a common understanding of how the Regulations should be interpreted and applied, potential users as well as professionals will continue to prefer better-known domestic procedures.

8.2.4. Guarantees of Parties' Procedural Rights

The EOP and ESCP Regulations provide in principle a reasonable basis on which to guarantee parties' procedural rights (e.g. means of service providing a high level of certainty, trial within a reasonable time, procedural safeguards to challenge the decision). In practice, however, applying some of these guarantees can be problematic, especially for the defendant. This is not necessarily due to a lack of diligence on the part of national courts. For example, by verifying the activities undertaken to serve defendants, judges seek to secure compliance with service standards as set by the EOP and the ESCP, as well as by domestic procedural rules. However, problems arise due to the wide variety of methods covered by the EOP Regulations, and to courts not receiving the acknowledgement of receipt in the ESCP procedures. Some service methods, especially those indicated in Article 14 EOP, cannot provide a full guarantee that the defendant is actually aware of the proceedings, as was revealed in the *eco cosmetics* case. Furthermore, the manner in which the challenging mechanisms are applied differ across the analysed systems, making parties vulnerable; this is because the levels of protection vary, although in principle they should provide a level playing field. For example, the ESCP approach to appeal does not favour simplification, or a similar standard of protection for parties' procedural rights. The application of the review mechanism is also not satisfactory, and sometimes too narrow to provide the necessary protection. Additionally, practice shows it is in fact rarely used, and practitioners confuse it at times with national mechanisms (i.e. in France). This of course affects the level of guaranteed protection.

2288 Hess (2017), Chaper 5.3–4 (para. 905); Deloitte Report, Part I, COM(2013) 495 final, Brussels, 19.07.2013, at 66; Commission EOP Report, COM(2015) 495 final, Brussels, 13.10.2015, Annex.

2289 Such as whether the claimant has to arrange for service of the decision on the defendant.

2290 For example, in Romania, it is not sufficient for the judge to issue the standard form provided by the Regulation; he also has to draft a decision in accordance with the domestic format for registration purposes.

2291 For example, an appeal might or might not be available to challenge the ESCP judgment, or there might be more than one appellate proceeding in place.

8.2.5. *Effectiveness of the Enforcement Process*

The limited information available regarding the last stage of the enforcement process makes it difficult to evaluate the effectiveness of the EOP and ESCP. Without denying the importance of the development brought by the instruments in eliminating the exequatur, the entrance into force of the Brussels *Ibis* generalised the abolition of exequatur to all civil and commercial decisions falling within its scope. Direct execution certainly facilitates and simplifies access to justice. As the empirical research revealed, the success of the execution has an impact on the perceived effectiveness of the European uniform procedures; however, the level of the success rate is impossible to assess on the basis of available data. Further research is essential in this regard.

Finally, information on the e-Justice Portal with regard to enforcement remains at a general level,[2292] resulting in additional costs and delays that create a serious bottleneck.

8.2.6. *Recommendations*

Additional action is necessary in order to address the identified differences in the application of the European uniform procedures across justice systems. In the short and medium term, this situation can be mitigated by:

- securing a clearer approach to implementing the European uniform procedures, and to helping courts and professionals gain a better knowledge of the instruments. This would limit, if not completely eliminate, incorrect applications of the Regulations;
- making sufficiently detailed, updated, and pertinent information easily accessible at the EU and the national level;
- creating national guidelines to clarify which steps need to be taken and which national rules apply in connection with the EOP and ESCP, and making it clear when parties are required to have an active involvement in the proceedings. This would further speed up application of the European procedures and guarantee appropriate information for the parties.

In the long term, the European uniform procedures should rely less extensively on national procedural rules.

In order to improve the protection of parties' procedural rights, certain actions are recommended:

- eliminating service methods that cannot guarantee that the defendant has actually been informed of the proceedings;
- a uniform approach to challenging mechanisms in the EOP and the ESCP (i.e. appeal and review) and to their national application is necessary to sustain a high standard of protection of parties' procedural rights and to provide a level playing field;
- in some countries, national authorities must take additional steps to clarify the manner in which the transfer of opposed EOPs to the ordinary procedures should be

[2292] Additional information on execution matters can be found on the www.europe-eje.eu website. However, this contains information for only 9 European jurisdictions (Belgium, France, Germany, Hungary, Italy, Luxembourg, The Netherlands, and Scotland).

carried out. Divergent interpretations and practices with regard to applicable national procedural rules create confusion and complexity;
- a common challenging mechanism should be provided by the Regulations for situations where the titles are issued in breach of the legal provisions, and the defendants are unable to make use of the means already available (i.e. opposition or appeal) or of the restrictive criteria set for a review request;
- increased availability of practical information on service means and on challenging mechanisms in order to secure access to a fair trial.

Because the harmonisation of enforcement is unlikely to happen in the near future, more detailed practical information on domestic procedural rules as well as steps to be undertaken by a creditor need to be made available in order to improve and facilitate enforcement in cross-border litigation.

8.3. EOP and ESCP Models: Implications for Future Procedures

8.3.1. Legal Basis

The EOP and the ESCP are part of the horizontal procedural harmonisation undertaken at the EU level in a piecemeal approach. This has led to fragmentation in the area of civil justice, and to parallel EU instruments that may at times lack sufficient connection and cohesion.[2293]

The limiting of the procedures to cross-border litigation is a consequence of the legal basis on which the EOP and ESCP Regulations were adopted (Article 67 TCE, now Article 81 TFEU). Article 81 TFEU remains the prevailing legal basis with regard to adopting legislation that seeks mainly to harmonise civil procedures.[2294] This is possibly a disadvantage for their use, as cross-border cases as defined by the two Regulations are far fewer than cases that can involve a foreign element (e.g. accident that happened abroad, enforcement of assets situated abroad). Hence, the EAPO,[2295] the latest European uniform civil procedure, is likewise limited to cross-border claims. This will likely affect any future measures aimed at harmonising civil procedure rules, unless the European legislator and Member States are willing to extend the present interpretation of what is considered a cross-border case.

8.3.2. Optional Nature

The optional nature of the EOP and the ESCP, as well as of the EAPO, appears to be an easier way to harmonisation, as it is less '*intrusive*' of the national legal systems, creating

[2293] Hess (2013), at 275.

[2294] See also discussion on Article 81 TFEU in Mańko (2015), at 11 and subsequent; Cortés & Mańko (2016), at 42–44.

[2295] Regulation (EU) No 655/2014 of the European Parliament and of the Council of 15 May 2014 establishing a European Account Preservation Order procedure to facilitate cross-border debt recovery in civil and commercial matters, OJ L 189/59, 27.6.2014.

a parallel alternative to coexisting domestic procedures.[2296] Harmonisation through optional instruments is a slower process, but allows consensus and certainty to grow and to be tested in practice with regard to the benefits of the process.[2297] The Regulations establish an additional layer of procedural rules that exist alongside national procedural rules and mechanisms. They do not directly aim to modify or amend national rules, but might sometimes lead to the adoption of national procedures that have a similar purpose and that also apply to purely domestic claims (e.g. the adoption of a small claims procedure in Romania).

8.3.3. *Written Procedures*

With a view to simplifying and speeding up litigation, and to reducing its related costs, the EOP and the ESCP are written procedures based on standard forms. The European legislator also favoured this approach for the EAPO, and its standard forms are available online in all EU official languages (e-Justice Portal). The EOP and ESCP standard forms offer litigating parties an easy system of filling in or ticking boxes, which minimises translation requirements, as well as provide guidance as to what type of information the party should provide. The EAPO follows the ESCP approach in the design of the standard forms. Similar forms or improved versions of the existing dynamic forms are likely to be considered for future procedures designed to simplify cross-border enforcement and to harmonise civil procedure within the EU. The use of standard forms could be considered further in the process of establishing common European minimum procedural standards.[2298]

Standard forms and the possibility of filling them in online are key elements with regard to developments that seek to achieve the electronic submission of claims in cross-border litigation. The first steps have already been taken under the umbrella of the e-Codex project piloting electronic filing of EOPs and ESCPs between several participating Member States.[2299] In the effort to digitalise civil procedures and to extend the use of ICT means, future developments relating to standard forms could also include translation functions to further facilitate parties' access to justice and communication between courts and their users.[2300]

8.3.4. *Harmonisation and Reliance on National Rules*

Although they establish a uniform framework, the EOP and the ESCP depend to a great extent on applicable domestic rules. This makes the manner in which the two levels of legislation interact with each other of crucial importance for their respective successful

2296 See also Mańko (2015), at 16; Fauvarque-Cosson & Behar-Touchais (2012), at 487; Fauvarque-Cosson & Behar-Touchais (2012a), at 49 and subsequent.

2297 See Fauvarque-Cosson & Behar-Touchais (2012), at 486–487.

2298 See Tulibacka, Sanz & Blomeyer (2016), at 33.

2299 See Velicogna & Lupo (2017), Section 4.4; Steigenga & Velicogna (2017), Section 2.

2300 See Tulibacka, Sanz & Blomeyer (2016), at 34.

application. The same interaction and need for implementation is also important in relation to the EAPO.[2301]

The EOP and ESCP Regulations took an important step in establishing genuine European civil procedures, making a shift in the approach to harmonisation in cross-border debt collection. However, the extensive referral to domestic rules and methods results in divergent applications of procedures that are meant to establish a level playing field. This is a downside of the EOP and ESCP template. This identified weakness needs to be properly addressed at the national and the European level, and considered carefully in the drafting of new procedural instruments. Nevertheless, the template should be seen in the broader context of the novelty these instruments bring – together with the time needed for their calibration[2302] – to the existing procedural environment as well as to their being discovered by parties and practitioners.

As the present study reveals, European and national legislators need to acknowledge the importance of the interrelation and the need for coordination when choosing this legislative template. Adopting implementing measures is necessary to facilitate the application of these procedures and to bring certainty and clarity to the rules that courts are required to adhere to when handling European procedures. Legislative actions that rely on a far-reaching harmonisation approach and that cover legislative gaps such as those identified in the EOP and the ESCP Regulations may be a welcome development as a European procedural model. However, the envisaged template does not appear to be a feasible one in the present political climate, and it might be difficult to achieve from an EU competence perspective. It would be very difficult – if not impossible – to adopt harmonised rules for all the procedural elements necessary to successfully implement the European uniform procedures. Such measures would likely go beyond the grounds of the principles of proportionality and subsidiarity. Furthermore, the Member States and the European institutions have not arrived at a consensus on the adoption of further harmonisation instruments in the area of civil justice. It is also questionable whether in virtue of the *effet utile* the European legislator would be able to set a duty on Member States or request them to adopt specific internal legislation to accommodate European uniform procedures that rely on domestic rules for their functioning.

In order to achieve better coordination between the two levels of legislation, alternative actions should be considered by European and national legislators. Like the EOP and the ESCP, the EAPO relies on a model that depends to a significant extent on domestic legislation; hence, the near decade of applying the EOP and ESCP could serve as a useful experiential basis to help increase both the application of such instruments and the knowledge that national practitioners have of them.

2301 For example, an estimation of whether the evidence is sufficient to issue a preservation order (Article 7 EAPO); establishing mechanisms by which an applicant can request and obtain information on bank accounts held by his debtor in a Member State (Article 14 EAPO); liability of the bank for failure to comply with the obligations under the Regulation (Article 26); amounts exempted from preservation (Article 31 EAPO); ranking of the preservation order (Article 32 EAPO).

2302 Kramer (2016a), at 97.

In this regard, legislators have to be aware that additional measures will subsequently be necessary to address the need for coordination between the European and the national provisions.

8.3.5. Guarantees of Procedural Rights

The EOP and ESCP procedural template puts in place specific mechanisms to balance parties' rights and to secure a fair trial, as indicated in Article 6 ECHR and Article 47 of the Charter. The procedures seek to offer the claimant simpler, speedier, less costly instruments to recover his debt, while providing a high level of procedural guarantees for the defendant, and an easy way to challenge them if he chooses.

With the abolition of the exequatur and the grounds of refusal generally associated with this procedure (except for irreconcilability), the EOP and the ESCP allow for fewer possible checks at the enforcement stage, thus shifting them entirely to the court of origin. Hence, the Regulations rely on other mechanisms to provide a similar level of protection of procedural rights and to secure a fair trial. These include (1) the use of service methods that offer a high degree of certainty that the documents have reached the defendant;[2303] (2) specific language requirements; (3) free assistance with regard to the ESCP procedure; (4) making information on certain procedural aspects available; and (5) establishing challenging mechanisms. Other mechanisms are based on the provisions of other regulations, in particular the Service Regulation and to a lesser extent the Brussels I*bis* Regulation. As to jurisdiction rules, the EOP offers a higher standard of protection to consumers who are defenders, who are sued only before courts in the Member State of their domicile. Regrettably, the ESCP does not rely on a similar provision, but on the Brussels I*bis* Rules.[2304] However, if the jurisdiction rules are violated or there are other problematic aspects regarding the observance of parties' procedural rights, the EOP and the ESCP offer less protection in terms of grounds of refusal for enforcement purposes. For this reason, the way the safety checks put in place by the EOP and the ESCP function is of crucial importance for securing a fair trial and enhancing mutual trust.

Combining the provisions of the European uniform procedures with national choices continues to prolong a certain degree of uncertainty as to the valid rules applicable, especially as information provided on dedicated websites is often too general and too slowly updated in all the official EU languages. Unfortunately, the EAPO also maintains a national approach to a significant number of procedural aspects.[2305]

[2303] If postal service or electronic service is not successful in the ESCP procedure, the service methods established by Article 13 or 14 of the EOP apply (Article 13(4) Regulation 2015/2421).

[2304] See the discussion in Kramer (2008a), at 267–268.

[2305] For example, jurisdiction (Article 6 EAPO); estimation of sufficient evidence to issue a preservation order (Article 7 EAPO); form of security acceptable (Article 12 EAPO); additional type of liability or grounds regarding the creditor's liability (Article 13(3) EAPO); establishing mechanisms by which an applicant can request and obtain information on bank accounts held by his debtor in a Member State (Article 14 EAPO); amounts exempted from preservation (Article 31 EAPO); ranking of the preservation order (Article 32 EAPO).

Although it is not a new mechanism, the communication of standard forms in a language the defendant understands or in the official language of the Member State where service is to be carried out (Article 6(3) ESCP and Article 8(1) Service Regulation) does facilitate access to justice. This is of particular importance in cross-border European uniform procedures that seek to provide the creditor with an enforceable title within a short time. In consideration of the importance of providing the defendant with sufficient information on the procedure initiated against him, the EAPO has opted for an approach similar to the ESCP (Article 28(5) in conjunction with Article 49 (1) EAPO). It expressly establishes the need to translate the documents if these are in a language the party does not understand or are drafted in a language other than the official language of the place where service is to be carried out.

Free assistance to parties in filling in the forms, obtaining general information on the scope of the Regulation, and determining the competent court is of significant importance in cross-border procedures in which representation is not mandatory. In practice, free assistance has not been established at court level due to impartiality concerns. Furthermore, professional or consumer organisations are not usually officially endorsed to provide assistance. Empirical findings and the present research reveal that non-repetitive users encounter difficulties in finding their way to the European uniform procedures and in communicating with courts in other Member States. This raises concerns with regard to guaranteeing parties' access to justice. The EAPO does not include this mechanism, but the choice might be related to the fact that the instrument is not designed for consumers, and legal entities are more likely to rely on legal advice services.

The single-sided or adversarial type of procedure has shaped the existing challenging mechanisms to secure a fair trial, as indicated in Article 6 ECHR and Article 47 of the Charter. These give defendants in the European uniform procedures mainly a general opportunity to challenge the claims filed against them. However, ESCP appeal proceedings are not uniformly addressed within this procedure, and remain the individual choice of each of the 27 Member States. This makes ESCP parties vulnerable, and subject to varying degrees of protection across the EU, a situation that must be avoided with respect to future European procedural instruments aimed at simplifying cross-border enforcement. Along with these general mechanisms, special challenging means for exceptional situations are in place. Although the review (Article 20 EOP, Article 18 ESCP) sets a uniform framework, the way the procedure is applied is governed by national procedural law; thus, various ways of applying this tool exist. Furthermore, Regulation 2015/2421 amended the ESCP review to address identified issues, but disconnected it from the EOP formulation. This challenging mechanism has not been used in the EAPO Regulation, as the European legislator focused on other remedies (e.g. the revocation).

Finally, access to sufficiently detailed information on all the guarantees put into place by the European uniform procedures is a key element with regard to how these mechanisms will function, and to securing a fair trial for parties.

8.3.6. *Procedural Standards*

The aim of the uniform framework established by the EOP and the ESCP is to overcome impediments related to cross-border litigation as well as to reduce uncertainties. The common minimum standards of civil procedure adopted within this framework are intended to improve certainty as to the applicable rules and requirements, and to enhance mutual trust between Member States. These standards have to do with provisions regarding proportionate levels of court fees (not exceeding that of national ordinary/special procedures); guarantees of defendants' rights (information on the proceeding, service methods offering a high level of certainty that the party was informed of proceedings, challenging mechanisms); avoidance of undue delay (timeframes for procedural steps); access to free legal advice and information on the procedure (for the ESCP); non-mandatory representation; the loser-pays principle (for the ESCP); and abolition of the exequatur for enforcement purposes. The established EOP and ESCP standards are to guarantee the protection of parties' procedural rights within the meaning of Article 6 ECHR and Article 47 Charter in a legal framework that abolished the checks related to exequatur and grounds of refusal, such as public policy.

The EOP and the ESCP set various procedural standards in order to guarantee a fair trial and access to justice. Some of these standards aim to ensure that the defendant is properly informed of his rights, and that he understands the consequences of the initiated procedure, especially if the European provisions are forced to rely on national procedural rules for their application. This is the case, for example, regarding methods of service considered to be valid, the information on the consequences of the EOP, or the availability of an appeal. Other procedural standards are intended to speed up the handling of claims, to lower the costs of proceedings, and to facilitate enforcement. Their significance for EU cross-border litigation is confirmed by their subsequent consideration in instruments adopted later (i.e. EAPO), and in ongoing projects investigating the future of European civil procedure and the potential of establishing common minimum standards of civil procedure, and the European Rules of Civil Procedure. However, the standards set by the EOP and ESCP Regulations leave a significant number of aspects to be determined by national procedural rules (e.g. determining the competent court, service methods, court fees, accepted languages, challenging mechanisms). In practice, this leads to situations where aspects expressly regulated by the EOP and ESCP Regulations are interpreted and applied differently across the Member States, due to differences in the domestic rules (e.g. valid service method in the EOP, level of court fees, challenging mechanisms).[2306] This includes the situation in which the European uniform procedures are applied in observance of their own minimum procedural standards. The EAPO procedure adopts the EOP and ESCP approach in terms of establishing procedural standards that are to guarantee a proper application of the procedure, as well as referring explicitly or implicitly to national rules regarding a significant number of aspects. These references are meant not only to fill the gaps existing within the European uniform procedures but are also related to the fact that the three instruments are meant to

[2306] See Sections 3.7, 4.7, 5.7, 6.7.

function within a national court system that has its own particularities. Furthermore, it would be very difficult – if not impossible – to adopt harmonised rules for all the procedural aspects necessary to apply the European uniform procedures. It is very likely such measures would go beyond the grounds of the principles of proportionality and subsidiarity. However, fewer gaps and references to national procedural rules (e.g. service methods, availability of challenging mechanisms, additional national actions for that part of the debt not covered by the decision, additional type of liability for the creditor, rank of the preservation order) could improve the uniform interpretation and functioning of the European procedures across Member States. Future legislation should take this aspect into account with a view to achieving a better outcome in the use and application of EU common procedural standards.

8.3.7. *Enforcement*

Enforcement of the European uniform procedures should be seen as a two-step process: namely, obtaining the enforceable title and actually executing the decision. The EOP and the ESCP have managed to improve users' perspectives significantly with regard to obtaining a judicial decision within a shorter timeframe. For example, as indicated in the ESCP Report, the duration of the litigation decreased to an average of 5 months from up to 2 years and 5 months, and to only a few months for the EOP, as indicated in the EOP Report.[2307] These findings are supported by information collected in England, France, Italy, and Romania.[2308] The use of EOP and ESCP standard forms has also contributed to this (e.g. the possibility of filling them in online, the automatic translation of the standard text of the forms into any official language of the European Union). The actions undertaken at the European level in order to digitalise the submission and handling of claims in cross-border litigation (e.g. pilot projects such as e-Codex) further benefit and facilitate the treatment of the European claims.[2309] The use of forms and the possibility of filling them in online is a pre-requisite for developments that could lead to the full electronic handling of European uniform procedures.

The timeframes set by the EOP and the ESCP for the various stages of the proceedings contribute to speeding up the process. Specific time limits in which to accomplish certain steps have a positive effect on the speed with which the procedures are handled, although practical difficulties and limited familiarity have led in practice to delays. Statistical data and case law show the tendency of national courts to handle the European uniform procedures with the shortest delay possible, in an attempt to abide by the timeframe set by the Regulations. Although modestly used, the EOP and ESCP procedures establish a model that has the resources to provide parties with an enforceable title within a relatively short time. The EAPO follows this approach as well, setting specific procedural delays aimed at securing a speedy and efficient preservation of bank account funds, but also at protecting the defendant's rights.

2307 Commission ESCP Report, at 2; Commission EOP Report, at 7 and 13–15.

2308 For a comparative perspective on the four analysed jurisdictions, see Sections 7.3.2 and 7.3.3. On e-Codex, see Section 8.4.3 on digitalisation.

2309 See further Section 8.4.3.

For the EOP and ESCP model, the execution stage remains an 'Achilles heel'. Although enforcement may be – and often is – problematic in purely domestic cases, and poses difficulties for creditors, further steps are necessary to improve the final phase of the European procedures. Non-enforcement or slow enforcement increases the risk of them losing their effectiveness, and thus resulting in a denial of access to justice.[2310] Apart from some specific provisions as to automatic recognition and enforcement, and the rules regarding stay, limitation, and rejection of enforcement, the execution process is not harmonised, and remains entirely regulated by domestic legislation. This is problematic, since national enforcement rules and methods are generally not well known to practitioners and parties from other Member States.[2311] As empirical evidence has revealed, users tend to consider the European uniform procedures effective only if the debt is actually recovered. Hence, a title obtained in a simplified and speedy procedure – but that provides little certainty as to the possible success in recovering the debt – is of little use. Elimination of the exequatur did away with the administrative stage related to recognition and enforcement of decisions issued by courts in other Member States, eliminating some of the related costs. Nevertheless, problems related to the execution of enforceable titles remain. As legislative action to harmonise this aspect of civil procedure in cross-border claims appears unlikely to be a priority in the near future, other approaches need to be considered.

8.3.8. Recommendations

In order to maximise the benefits established by the EOP and ESCP procedural models, certain additional actions are recommended. At the European level, the following actions should be considered further and endorsed:

- the European legislator should set a duty on Member States to communicate information to the Commission on all procedural aspects for which the text requires application of the national procedural rules or coordination with them. Regulation 2015/2421 amending the ESCP has broadened the list of information to be provided for this procedure, and the EAPO also follows a more generous approach to making relevant national information available;
- draft implementation guidelines or recommendations for Member States in order to support the integration of such European procedures within national legal systems and practice;
- make detailed and clear information available on the e-Justice Portal as to what steps are to be taken to use the European uniform procedures; guides and interactive wizards can help interested parties find their way to the suitable procedure. The e-Justice Portal offers users two types of wizards, but they focus on the Regulations' provisions rather than on the national procedural rules applicable in correlation with the European procedures. One wizard offers guidance in helping parties decide

2310 In the light of ECtHR case law, Hornsby Case (ECtHR, *Hornsby v. Greece*, 18357/91, ECHR 1997-II, para. 40), access to justice 'would be illusory if a Contracting State's domestic legal system allowed a final, binding judicial decision to remain inoperative to the detriment of the party'.

2311 Hess (2013), at 278.

whether to use the EOP or the ESCP for their claim.[2312] The second wizard provides information on competent national authorities with regard to certain steps in the EOP and ESCP procedures (e.g. court having jurisdiction, enforcement authority). This is a helpful instrument, but the tool's features need to be further refined and the options become fully operational. The searches often leave the lay user with several possible competent authorities but without any additional criteria or information that would guide him in making an appropriate choice.[2313] Based on these interactive EU wizards, the development of similar tools should be considered for the procedural steps that need to be taken within Member State systems in applying the EOP and the ESCP;

- offer more dedicated training to practitioners prior to the entrance into force of European uniform procedures in order to raise awareness among those professionals most likely to apply the instruments; European procedures might be quite different from available national functional equivalents;
- continue to encourage dialogue between professionals, and share national information and practices by way of professional organisations (e.g. EJN, ECC-net, Enterprise Europe Network, CCBE) in order to create a synergy that can lead to common understanding and practices from a bottom-up approach.

At the national level, it is recommended to:

- adopt national legislation to implement European uniform procedures in order to properly complement the provisions of these Regulations and coordinate the application of national procedural rules in the framework set by the Regulations;
- create national step-by-step guidelines on the European uniform procedures for practitioners;
- consider concentrating the claims in a smaller number of national courts and/or assigning the cases to specialised judges in order to favour the creation of expertise and court practices that could contribute to a uniform interpretation and application of the procedures;
- interpret the provisions of the European instruments in line with their aim and purpose in order to preserve their *effet utile*;
- enhance cooperation between practitioners who have more experience, and encourage the sharing of constructive solutions and good practices.[2314]

With regard to the coordination required between the European and the national provisions, the following possibilities should be considered:

- a legislative or a soft law approach to provide the necessary mechanisms for the application of the procedures. This can be chosen based on what best suits a particular

[2312] Available under the Dynamic forms section of the e-Justice Portal (https://e-justice.europa.eu/content_dynamic_forms-155-en.do).

[2313] Additional features have been added to the wizards with regard to the authority competent for enforcement, for refusal of enforcement, and for stay or limitation of enforcement, but these searches are not yet functional; interested parties have not been able to obtain any reply on the matter (available at https://e-justice.europa.eu/content_european_payment_order-353-en.do?clang=en, last visited 30 March 2017).

[2314] See also Onţanu (2017).

national system. Only in this manner can the EOP and ESCP template be a valuable model for possible future procedures intended to simplify cross-border enforcement and harmonise civil procedures within the EU;

- in the long term, an evolution of the model towards European instruments that are more independent of domestic rules and methods would be desirable, rather than leaving it up to Member States to choose from a wide range of approaches. This could also involve a closer convergence of national procedural rules with common procedural solutions and mechanisms. However, this might not fit in with the present diversity of national approaches, or be considered appealing by Member States or the European legislator.

In order to improve enforcement and to eliminate related bottlenecks, the following actions should be considered:

- in the short to medium term, help practitioners and users to become more familiar with the enforcement laws of various Member States. This can be done by making the necessary information easily accessible (i.e. authorities in charge of enforcement, applicable rules, costs, duties). Detailed information is crucial for non-repetitive users in cross-border claims. This approach would certainly facilitate the use of the European uniform procedures, also increasing the prospects of successful debt recovery;
- in the long term, legislative actions should be considered.

8.4. European Procedural Instruments: Avenues for Further Developments

8.4.1. Enhanced Judicial Cooperation on Civil Procedure

Rules relating to European uniform procedures rely to a significant extent on national frameworks. Their functioning in practice and their implementation and accommodation within these national systems and practice is of considerable importance. In this context, national case law can play a significant role in the way European procedures are applied and interpreted across Member States. Case law can be inspiring for judges having to deal with the same matter or having difficulty in applying a certain provision relating to a European procedure. It can enable the creation of a common understanding of the way uniform rules and procedures should be applied, and increase mutual trust, as judges and practitioners will be able to find out more easily about each other's work and views.

The process of developing European portal-based access to national case law has already been launched, and includes creating databases in the area of cross-border litigation accessible through the EUR-Lex and e-Justice Portals. A few initiatives can be singled out: the JURE collection containing national judgments related to jurisdiction, recognition, and enforcement in civil and commercial matters,[2315] the National case-law

[2315] The database was created by the European Commission, and also includes case law on relevant international conventions (i.e. 1968 Brussels Convention, 1988 Lugano Convention) (available at http://eur-lex.europa.eu/collection/n-law/jure.html).

web page dedicated to EU case law,[2316] and the e-Justice ECLI research engine.[2317] In all three, the decisions are generally available in their original language, and sometimes – when provided by the Member State of origin – a summary in English, French, or German (JURE), key words on the topic of the case in English and French (National case-law), or occasionally an abstract or key words in English or France (e-Justice ECLI research engine). Additionally, a new research project in which the present author will participate intends to set up an English-language database for national and CJEU cases in relation to the European Enforceement Order (EEO), and for the EOP, the ESCP, and the EAPO.[2318] The database will be made publicly available, and will be linked to the e-Justice Portal in order to facilitate access to information for courts and practitioners, to raise awareness with regard to these European instruments, and to support informed choices in cross-border enforcement.

To include a complete translation of national cases in such databases would be costly and time consuming. A more practical approach might be a direct exchange of information between courts under the umbrella of the existing judicial cooperation network. Furthermore, certain regulations encourage judges to communicate with their counterparts in other Member States.

In this regard, the European Judicial Training Network in civil and commercial matters (EJN-civil) provides support through national contact points for each Member State.[2319] Future consideration could be given to extending this cooperation by supplying more specific information on civil procedural law matters and a more decentralised approach. This could involve direct contact persons at the court level, who could offer support to their colleagues in other Member States in the decision making process by offering information on their case law on the application of European legislation, uniform procedures, and enforcement.[2320]

The use of keywords for published cases together with the possibility of directly contacting the court that issues the decision through its own contact person could enhance the use of available information on the national applications of European legislation. Judges would be able to request support from or offer it to colleagues in other Member States. This would enhance cooperation and enable practitioners to become

2316 http://eur-lex.europa.eu/collection/n-law/n-case-law.html.

2317 At the moment, the ECLI engine includes case law from 10 Member States (Czech Republic, Germany, Greece, Spain, France, Croatia, Italy, Netherlands, Slovenia, and Finland) (available at https://e-justice.europa.eu/content_ecli_search_engine-430-en.do). More information on the European Case Law Identifier (ECLI) can be found at https://e-justice.europa.eu/content_european_case_law_identifier_ecli-175-en.do?clang=en.

2318 Informed Choices in Cross-Border Enforcement, European Commission Action Grant, JUST-JCOO-CIVI-AG-2016.

2319 The EJN-civil was established by the Council Decision 2001/470/EC of 28 May 2001 and started operating on 1 December 2002. This legal basis was modified in 2009. All Member States except Denmark participate in the EJN-civil (more information is available at https://e-justice.europa.eu/content_about_the_network-431-en.do?clang=en).

2320 See in this regard point 4.1, Communication from the Commission to the European Parliament, the Council and the European Economic and Social Committee and the Committee of the Regions, *The EU Justice Agenda for 2020 – Strengthening Trust, Mobility and Growth within the Union*, COM(2014) 144 final.

acquainted with the justice system and legislation of other Member States; this in turn would help boost confidence in each other's legal systems, encourage legal professionals to share best practices, and foster mutual trust.

8.4.2. Coherence across Civil Procedure Instruments and Architecture

Legislative developments in the area of EU procedural law have increased tremendously since the entrance into force of the Amsterdam Treaty. Many instruments addressing specific areas of cross-border litigation – some of them overlapping – have been adopted over the last two decades.[2321] However, despite these instruments covering a significant range of procedural matters, European civil procedure is still in its infancy.[2322] The law-making process has been sectorial, developing to a certain extent in an ad-hoc manner based on policy priorities, and is the result of political compromise.[2323] As noted by Hess, a better coordination of European instruments and a more systematic approach would be desirable.[2324]

As a legislative technique, regulations have prevailed over directives and occasional Council decisions. The instruments concerning various aspects of civil procedure rely on diverse levels of harmonisation, ranging from a traditional private international law approach aiming to coordinate the different systems of the Member States to harmonised European procedures. As Kramer notes, this is 'part of a political reality, where limited competence and compromise come into play'.[2325]

Furthermore, in some of the adopted instruments, the same concepts or mechanisms might be interpreted differently, or rely on different criteria for their application,[2326] or have an ambiguous meaning.[2327] This mirrors the incidental manner in which the instruments were adopted and the political compromise that needed to be reached before they could become a part of European legislation. Bringing clarity, uniformity of meaning, and application criteria into the terminology used by European procedural instruments can eliminate confusion and allow for their smoother application.

In order to be in line with the EU 2020 Justice Agenda, it is time to reflect on how to better coordinate existing European procedural instruments and national procedural rules; to consolidate this area of law; to improve the implementation of these instruments;

2321 See on this Hess (2016), at 3–4; A European Framework for private international law: current gaps and future perspectives, European Parliament Study, 2012, PE462.487.

2322 Kramer (2016a), at 120; Crifò (2016), at 96.

2323 Kramer (2016a), at 120; Kramer (2013), at 26.

2324 Hess (2016), at 18.

2325 Kramer (2017).

2326 For example, the situations in which a review can be requested as indicated in Article 20 EOP and in the amended Article 18 ESCP; the criteria in accordance with which a case is considered to be a 'cross-border case' in accordance with the EOP, ESCP, Brussels I*bis*. See *inter alia*, Berthe (2014), at 307.

2327 The notion of domicile and habitual residence under Article 3(1) ESCP and Article 3(1) EOP can create legal uncertainty. The notion of 'domicile' is defined by Article 50 and 60 Brussels I or Article 62 and 63 Brussels I*bis*, but the concept of 'habitual residence' in the ESCP procedure is not defined. See Oro Martinez (2016), at 129–130.

and to proceed to an in-depth evaluation of how these procedures function in practice. Increasing coherence will certainly improve their impact.

8.4.3. Digitalisation

At the EU level, e-Justice has been on the agenda of the European policy maker for over a decade, but any advancements depend significantly on national information and achievements and developments in information and communication technology (ICT), as well as on the willingness of Member States to be involved.[2328] The extent to which ICT is used across Member States in judicial proceedings differs widely.[2329] Digitalisation and the use of ICT are crucial for developing new tools designed to facilitate access to legal information and justice. Some of the actions undertaken to enhance the use of ICT seek to achieve the online submission of claims and the electronic handling of cases, to broaden access to information in national registers that are relevant for legal actions, and to link national ADR platforms through an online dispute resolution platform. The EU and several Member States are working to create the necessary legal framework to enable the use of electronic means for cross-border procedural purposes (e.g. adopting specific provisions for the use of electronic means of filing claims, for communication purposes, for the taking of evidence, for electronic signatures, for electronic access to court files), and for building the necessary technical infrastructure.[2330] Additionally, the EU has actively been encouraging the electronic transmission of documents, the use of videoconferencing, and the setting up and interconnection of national databases and registers on various matters (e.g. insolvency, incorporation registries, property registries).[2331] All these actions are intended to help speed up court proceedings and enforcement, to reduce the costs of certain procedural steps, and to facilitate access to relevant information.

The 2014–2018 European e-Justice Strategy[2332] and the Multiannual European e-Justice Action Plan[2333] emphasise the key role the e-Justice Portal plays. Steps are being taken to make the portal a 'one-stop-shop in the area of justice': namely, the main tool for providing access to information on cross-border procedures and national legislation necessary for the application of European instruments for legal professionals, European

[2328] European e-Justice is based on decentralisation and interoperability. See Velicogna (2017); Kramer (2016), at 353.

[2329] For a critical presentation of empirical ICT experiences in EU Member States, see Contini & Lanzara (2014); Contini & Lanzara (2009); Velicogna (2008); Velicogna (2007); Fabri & Contini (2003); Fabri & Contini (2001).

[2330] Contini & Lanzara (2014), at xiii; Contini (2014), at 331; Velicogna (2014), at 309–311.

[2331] For example, Council Recommendation, *Promoting the use of and sharing of best practices on cross-border videoconferencing in the area of justice in the Member States and at EU level*, OJ C 250/1, 31.7.2015, European Commission, *e-Justice Action Plan 2014–2018*, OJ C182/2, 14.6.2014, Regulation (EU) No 1382/2013 of the European Parliament and of the Council of 17 December 2013 establishing a Justice Programme for the period 2014 to 2020, OJ 354/73, 28.12.2013.

[2332] European Commission, Draft Strategy on European e-Justice 2014–2018, OJ C376/06, 21.12.2013.

[2333] European Council, Multiannual European e-Justice Action Plan 2014–2018, OJ C182/2, 14.6.2014.

citizens, and businesses.[2334] Moreover, in order to improve access to justice, future tools will be integrated into the e-Justice Portal. These will include a single access point via the interconnection of national registers relevant for justice purposes, which will link existing national infrastructures in order to facilitate cooperation with the judiciary and legal practitioners, and to improve communication between judicial authorities via a platform for the secure exchange of information.[2335]

The European uniform procedures as well as the online dispute resolution tool (ODR) can benefit enormously from enhanced ICT use. The EOP, the ESCP, and the EAPO contain provisions able to support the electronic handling of these claims (e.g. online filling in of dynamic forms, electronic service). However, complete electronic handling is not yet largely available for these instruments, although it has been piloted among Member States taking part in the e-Codex project.[2336] Further national and European developments are necessary to make the online handling of European uniform procedures widely available. The limited national infrastructure and interoperability as well as the size of the e-Codex infrastructure cannot yet allow full online access to a multitude of users filing and handling European court proceedings on a general basis.[2337] This piloting of full electronic handling has also pointed to the many complexities and challenges that lie ahead in the digitalisation of cross-border claims (e.g. security of data, recognition of parties), but also to its potential for European justice.[2338] This experience creates the synergies for further actions investigating possible solutions to enhance judicial cooperation, to build interoperability between national systems and available instruments, and to facilitate parties' access to justice. ICT's importance in enhancing access to justice in cross-border litigation, a new functionality for the e-Justice Portal is currently being developed to allow citizens to file EOP applications electronically with the competent courts in the Member States participating in the pilot.[2339]

2334 See https://e-justice.europa.eu/home.do. The Portal provides, *inter alia*, information on European and national procedures; a judicial atlas for the European uniform procedures; a wizard to help interested creditors determine which European procedure to use; the standard forms related to European uniform procedures and other instruments; and the possibility of filling in standard forms online and making use of the automatic translation of the forms' standard text. See also, Steigenga & Velicogna (2017), Section C.1.

2335 See also Veligona (2016).

2336 This stands for 'e-Justice Communication via Online Data Exchange'. The project was launched under the multiannual European e-Justice Action Plan 2009–2013 to work on the dematerialisation of cross-border judicial procedures and communication between judicial authorities. Twenty Member States became actively involved in the project. The online handling of EOPs and ESCPs has been piloted among Austria, Estonia, Germany, Greece, Italy, Malta, and Poland, with the country acting as a sending or a receiving country, or both, for EOP and/or ESCP claims. For a broader perspective on the development of the e-Codex solution and its effects, see *inter alia*, Veligona (2016); Velicogna & Lupo (2017), Section 4.4; Steigenga & Velicogna (2017), Section 2; Velicogna & Steigenga (2016) (available at https://ssrn.com/abstract=2914362); Project for electronic processing of the European Order for Payment Procedure, EPSA Award (available at www.epsa-projects.eu/index.php?title=Porject_for_electronic_processing_of_the_European_order_for_payment_procedure&oldid=4762).

2337 On the electronic process of the EOP and ESCP, see Kramer (2016), at 358–360; Velicogna & Lupo (2017), Section 5.2.

2338 See Steigenga & Velicogna (2017); Velicogna & Steigenga (2016); Velicogna (2015).

2339 See *inter alia* Steigenga & Velicogna (2017), Section 2; Veligona (2016); Velicogna & Steigenga (2016).

Other initiatives that are being developed on the basis of the e-Codex building blocks and experience are me-Codex,[2340] e-Sens,[2341] FAL 2,[2342] Pro-Codex,[2343] and API for Justice.[2344, 2345] Such evolution in digitalisation will be relevant not only for European uniform procedures (EOP, ESCP, and EAPO) and cross-border legal actions in family and criminal matters but also in facilitating access to justice on a broader scale, as well as in relation to other European instruments (e.g. service of documents, taking of evidence, ADR/ODR). Additionally, they can facilitate access to national procedural steps relevant for cross-border litigation, such as the payment of court fees (e-payment), the electronic identification of parties and signatures, the handling of documents, and the handling of metadata.

8.4.4. *Alternative Dispute Resolution*

In addition to European court procedures able to facilitate cross-border litigation, the European legislator has sought to develop extrajudicial schemes (mediation, alternative dispute resolution, and online dispute resolution)[2346] and collective-action instruments.[2347] Recently, steps have also been taken to reinforce the use of alternative dispute mechanisms within European court procedures. Regulation 2015/2421 amending the ESCP has enhanced the court settlement provisions by expressly attributing to the settlement the same value as an ESCP judgment.[2348] The European Commission has

2340 Me-Codex stands for 'Maintenance of e-Codex'. Me-Codex is to ensure a swift and sustainable transition of the e-Codex project towards a long-term sustainability of its building blocks by an agency.

2341 E-Sens stands for 'Electronic Simple European Networked Services', and aims to consolidate building blocks developed by previous large-scale projects (e.g. e-Signature, e-Identity, e-Delivery, e-Documents).

2342 FAL 2 stands for 'Find a Lawyer 2' project. In the e-Codex project, FAL 2 is to provide the necessary mechanism to ensure that the person claiming to be a lawyer is indeed a qualified lawyer in his home jurisdiction.

2343 Pro-Codex stands for 'Connecting legal practitioners' national applications with e-Codex infrastructure', and it is a project that began investigating the possibilities of creating conditions to make e-Codex interoperable with applications used by legal professionals at the national level.

2344 This project aims to open up the infrastructure for cross-border legal services provided by e-Codex and the European e-Justice Portal by means of an API (Application Programming Interface), thus making it possible for third parties to build applications that use the e-Codex services.

2345 See *inter alia* Velicogna & Lupo (2017), Section 5.2; Steigenga & Velicogna (2017); Velicogna & Steigenga (2016); Veligona (2016).

2346 Directive 2008/52/EC of the European Parliament and of the Council of 21 May 2008 on certain aspects of mediation in civil and commercial matters, OJ L136/3, 24.5.2008; Directive No 2013/11/EU of the European Parliament and of the Council of 21 May 2013 on alternative dispute resolution for consumer disputes and amending Regulation (EC) No 2006/2004 and Directive 2009/22/EC (Directive on consumer ADR), OJ L165/63, 18.6.2013; Regulation (EU) No 524/2013 of the European Parliament and of the Council of 21 May 2013 on online dispute resolution for consumer disputes and amending Regulation (EC) No 2006/2004 and Directive 2009/22/EC (Regulation on consumer ODR), OJ L165/1, 18.6.2013.

2347 Commission Recommendation of 11 June 2013 on common principles for collective redress mechanisms in the Member States for injunctions against and claims on damages caused by violations of EU rights, COM(2013) 3539/3. On the complex background of the recommendation, see Voet (2017); Hodges (2014), at 67; Stadler (2013), at 483.

2348 Article 23a in conjunction with Recitals 18 and 19 Regulation 2015/2421.

acknowledged the need to complement court access to justice with additional out-of-court mechanisms,[2349] and to encourage their use when parties are able to resolve their dispute without pursuing a full court trial.

Alternative dispute mechanisms can provide less costly options for low-value claims, especially for consumers. Although the European procedures have contributed to speeding up proceedings and decreasing costs, they may not appear to be user-friendly enough to persuade consumers to make use of them, since the costs of court actions continue to remain relatively high, especially as consumers are generally not repeat players.[2350]

Alternative means of dispute resolution have been partly successful in some jurisdictions where well-functioning mechanisms are in place, and here the alternatives provide good solutions. In other jurisdictions, developments thus far have been modest. Further investigation and research in this area is necessary in order to gain a better understanding of the aspects that might guarantee the successful use of these mechanisms.

The diversity of national alternative dispute resolution mechanisms also needs to be considered. The new alternative dispute resolution directive (ADR) and the regulation on online dispute resolution (ODR) comprise the framework geared to actively enhance the use of out-of-court means in cross-border and domestic disputes involving consumers. The consumer ADR Directive establishes a duty on Member States to enable consumers and traders to submit their claims to dispute resolution. The ODR Regulation focuses on consumer contracts concluded online. This mechanism offers consumers a cost-free possibility of filing an electronic complaint, of identifying national ADR mechanisms, of transmitting the complaint, and of providing management of the case electronically, as well as translations and electronic forms for the ADR entity (i.e. to submit information and the ADR result). The ODR platform became operational in February 2016.[2351] Although these instruments are still young in the plethora of existing European procedures and national mechanisms, they have the power to increase consumers' access to justice while securing a set of quality criteria to govern the service offered. It is hoped that a significant number of users will make successful use of this tool.

The benefits of the various forms of out-of-court dispute resolutions established by recent EU legislation are largely undisputed, but further steps are required to connect them more effectively to European court proceedings. The European uniform procedures and the ADR/ODR are not directly or expressly connected to each other, apart from some implicit references (Article 12(3) ESCP, Article 7(2)(a)(v) ODR Regulation). A more connected approach would be a welcome development.[2352] For example, one

2349 European Commission Staff Working Paper, Impact Assessment, Proposal for a Directive on Alternative Dispute Resolution for Consumer Disputes, and the Proposal for a Regulation on Online Dispute Resolution for Consumer Disputes, SEC(2011) 1408 final.

2350 See discussion in Hodges (2016), Section A.

2351 See https://webgate.ec.europa.eu/odr/main/index.cfm?event=main.home.chooseLanguage.

2352 On the argument that the ESCP should encourage parties to attempt ADR/ODR solutions, see Cortés & Mańko (2016), at 58.

improvement could be the possibility for the ODR platform to divert consumers with cross-border disputes that are not suitable for an ADR proceeding to the competent national courts or to the ESCP.[2353]

However, the use and development of out-of-court dispute resolution mechanisms should not be a trade-off involving the quality of justice. Professionals taking part in this process need to remain highly qualified and make decisions that uphold the rule of law.[2354]

With regard to collective redress instruments, the Commission Recommendation establishes basic principles that Member States take into account when adopting horizontal compensatory or injunctive collective redress mechanisms. However, Member States have no obligation to implement such tools. The Recommendation seeks to respect national traditions, and provides a series of safeguards to discourage parties from bringing in unmeritorious claims.[2355] The text includes many exceptions that allow Member States to maintain their existing instruments. Hence, it does not favour a common approach towards collective redress, or encourage a level playing field. The topic is still on the discussion table, as in the next few years the Commission is set to revisit the situation and analyse developments in the Member States. However, resistance to a harmonised collective redress tool may persist on the part of systems that have a successful national procedure as well as of Member States that are against collective actions. New means probably need to be investigated. ADR mechanisms might be able to provide some answers, but more discussions are necessary in this area of civil justice.[2356]

8.4.5. Towards European Civil Procedure Principles and Rules

The groundwork for the harmonisation of European procedural law was set by the Storme Commission in the 1990s,[2357] and gradually continued after the entrance into force of the Amsterdam Treaty. To date, the process of harmonisation has evolved in a piecemeal manner,[2358] with more than a dozen instruments being adopted. The EU has been shaping this policy area bit by bit, adopting new procedural instruments, amending existing ones, and exploring the possibility of 'a legislative proposal setting out common minimum standards of civil procedure law'.[2359] Over the past few years, scholars have shown increased interest in the harmonisation of civil procedures, with some identifying the lack of harmonised rules in the EU as the 'missing link' in the enforcement of private rights.[2360] Despite varying levels of criticism, a consensus exists on the need for

2353 *Ibidem*, at 61.
2354 See Hodges (2016), Section C.4.
2355 Opt-in mechanism only, the loser-pays rule, prohibition regarding punitive damages and contingency fees.
2356 See Hodges (2014), at 67.
2357 Storme (1994).
2358 Tulibacka, Sanz & Blomeyer (2016), at 22; Kramer (2013), at 19–24.
2359 Radev (2015), at 2.
2360 Schwartze (2000), at 135; Kramer (2014), at 223.

and the desirability of further harmonisation to provide 'for a coherent and systematic set of rules of European procedural law'.[2361] Scholars' initiatives in this area have been matched by interest on the part of the European Commission and the European Parliament.

A number of recent projects have also gained ground. In November 2013, the European Commission Discussion paper on EU Civil Law for the *Assises de la Justice* underlined the need to reinforce mutual trust through procedural integration.[2362] Furthermore, the European Parliament is conducting an exploratory project on the establishment of common minimum standards of civil procedure.[2363] The European Parliamentary Research Service carried out an in-depth analysis of the EU legal basis and possible legislative approach to harmonising civil procedure at the EU level.[2364] Further, the service commissioned a study on 'Common minimum standards of civil procedure' to assess whether action at the EU level is necessary and to examine potential obstacles to further developments in the area, as well as looking at the potential added value of introducing such standards.[2365] The study is in favour of a systemic approach to minimum standards of civil procedure, establishing an 'umbrella instrument' containing principles that apply to cross-border as well as to domestic cases. The application of procedural standards to both cross-border and national procedures is singled out as important for mutual trust between judicial authorities and for an effective enforcement of decisions. However, it would maintain a parallel system of principles and standards, preserving a difference that can be noted in relation to European uniform procedures applicable only in cross-border claims. Common minimum standards can be a valuable support for national courts in interpreting and applying EU legislation – thus giving a uniform interpretation to provisions of the European procedures – since the existing instruments are not interpreted equally across the Member States.[2366] At the same time, common principles or standards can ensure that the European uniform procedures are applied in a manner that complies with the highest standards of protection of fundamental rights and a fair trial.

The set of common minimum standards as an expression of general principles proposed by the study can be grouped into four categories:
(1) principles relating to access to a court and to justice,
(2) principles relating to ensuring fairness in the proceedings,
(3) principles relating to ensuring the efficiency of the proceedings, and
(4) principles relating to ensuring a just and effective outcome.[2367]

2361 See *inter alia* Kramer (2013), at 26; Hess (2012), at 171; Storme (2012), at 379–386.
2362 European Commission, 'Discussion Paper 1: EU Civil Law', *Assises de la Justice*, 21–22 November 2013, Brussels.
2363 Radev (2015).
2364 Mańko (2015).
2365 Tulibacka, Sanz & Blomeyer (2016).
2366 Tulibacka, Sanz & Blomeyer (2016), at 53.
2367 *Ibidem*, at 19–20.

A significant number of the principles contained in the above categories are key to applying European uniform procedures effectively, to guaranteeing a fair balance between parties' rights, and to securing access to justice. These concern, for example:
- access to free legal advice and information within the context of the procedure;
- proportionate costs of litigation;
- loser-pays principle and security of costs;
- judicial expertise;
- transparency of proceedings, including language requirements;
- equality of arms/fair balance between parties;
- guarantees of defendants' rights, including securing appropriate information on the proceeding for the defendant, service, and challenging mechanisms;
- judicial control over the process;
- avoidance of undue delay;
- effective enforcement.

Furthermore, the principles individualised in the study can contribute to enhancing judicial cooperation, coherence, and digitalisation through encouraging developments that facilitate access to information (e.g. through the dedicated e-Justice Portal) and improve the handling of procedures (e.g. use of standard forms available online, use of ICT, and possible developments regarding translation functions for the content of standard forms).

In October 2013, the European Law Institute (ELI) and the International Institute for the Unification of Private Law (UNIDROIT) held a first exploratory workshop on a joint project on 'European Rules of Civil Procedure'.[2368] The project aims to adapt the Principles of Transnational Civil Procedure adopted in 2004 by the American Law Institute (ALI) and UNIDROIT to the European legal context. Five working groups were set up in 2014, focusing on Provisional and Protective Measures, Access to Information and Evidence, Service and Due Notice of Proceedings, Lis Pendens and Res Judicata, and Obligations of the Parties and Lawyers.[2369] In 2015, three more working groups were established: namely, Costs, Judgments, and a horizontal working group on the Structure of Civil Proceedings that will coordinate and ensure coherence of the rules.[2370] The ELI-UNIDROIT project could represent a useful tool against a 'fragmentary and haphazard growth of European civil procedural law'[2371] and 'a blueprint for the EU civil justice' to 'further access to justice and support good law-making'.[2372] Its aims are more ambitious than that of the Storme working group, as it seeks to develop rules of civil procedure that can tackle current problems in cross-border and domestic litigation (e.g. costs, service of proceedings), and fill existing gaps. Full harmonisation might be difficult to achieve quickly in this area, however, although the European Rules of Civil Procedure might

2368 An outline of the first workshop on the project 'From Transnational Principles to European Rules of Civil Procedure' is available at http://conflictoflaws.net/2013/the-eli-unidroit-project-from-transnational-principles-to-european-rules-of-civil-procedure-1st-exploratory-workshop/.

2369 See also Hazelhorst (2016).

2370 The last group is an overarching working group, see further Kramer (2014), at 218–238.

2371 Overview available at www.unidroit.org/work-in-progress-studies/current-studies/transnational-civil-procedure.

2372 Kramer (2014), at 237.

make it a possibility in the long term through the convergence of European and national rules. While the working groups – consisting of academics and practitioners – conduct the work independently, regular consultation is taking place with the European Parliament and the Commission, which could increase the impact of the work after its completion.

It remains to be seen how these desirable developments will evolve, and how the European legislator will adopt rules to help legal systems converge more efficiently.

8.5. Final Remarks

The EOP and the ESCP are the fruits of developments that were unimaginable a couple of decades ago. The present research has sought to investigate their functioning and achievements in cross-border litigation. Although they have not yet attained their full potential, and difficulties remain in their application, the instruments represent the seeds of uniform European civil procedures. They have laid the foundation for further steps towards harmonisation.

Analysing the way these first procedures function provides valuable information on the way such instruments are applied, on their weaknesses and strong points, and on areas where focus should be concentrated when new instruments are being adopted.

National traditions play an important role in the way courts and practitioners handle EOP and ESCP claims. To this end, it is necessary to provide better training to practitioners so that they will know how to apply these instruments when necessary, and should be considered in relation to future similar initiatives in the area of European law. A great deal more must be done to make the procedures familiar to parties and practitioners. This effort has to be doubled by appropriate and clear information relating to the various stages of EOP and ESCP application by national courts. Furthermore, a better linkage between available EU instruments (court or out-of-court procedures) in the area of civil justice should be considered by the European legislator.[2373] Together, these actions can lead to further improved results in the application of European uniform procedures.

The achievement of the EOP and the ESCP in terms of establishing new procedural models can be seen as an intermediary step. However, the outcome of this research into their application across four jurisdictions draws attention to the importance of proper integration, coordination, and information details that rely to a great extent on domestic procedural rules, and on choices made by national authorities. It might take considerable time to design the perfect procedural template, but the EOP and the ESCP provide a sound experiential basis on which to construct future instruments for the purpose of cross-border litigation.

2373 See also Hess (2013), at 275.

SAMENVATTING

Inleiding

Een adequate toegang tot de rechter en effectieve handhavingsmechanismen zijn essentieel in een Europese Unie die gebaseerd is op rechtsstatelijkheid en die beoogt de rechten van haar burgers die voortvloeien uit de vier fundamentele vrijheden te beschermen. Met name bij grensoverschrijdend procederen krijgen partijen echter vaak te maken met obstakels, zoals verschillen in het toepasselijk recht, lange procedures en disproportioneel hoge kosten.

Inmiddels is op EU-niveau op het gebied van justitiële samenwerking in burgerlijke zaken een aantal instrumenten tot stand gebracht om de grensoverschrijdende geschilbeslechting en rechtshandhaving te vergemakkelijken. Het onderhavige onderzoek richt zich op de Europese betalingsbevelprocedure (EBB) en de Europese procedure voor geringe vorderingen (EPGV). Met de EBB- en EPGV-Verordeningen zijn de eerste autonome Europese procedures tot stand gebracht. Zij hebben eenvormige regels gecreëerd voor niet-betwiste en geringe vorderingen in grensoverschrijdende zaken. Beide instrumenten zijn gebaseerd op het beginsel van wederzijdse erkenning en vereisen geen exequatur in de fase van tenuitvoerlegging. De procedures vormen een alternatief voor de nationale procedures van de lidstaten en beogen grensoverschrijdende geschilbeslechting te vereenvoudigen, te versnellen en goedkoper te maken. Hoewel met de eenvormige Europese procedures een eenvormig procesrechtelijk kader in het leven is geroepen, blijft het nationale procesrecht nog steeds relevant, zoals voor hoe de procedure moet worden ingeleid, wat de hoogte van de griffierechten is, welke beroepsmogelijkheden openstaan in de EPGV en hoe de tenuitvoerlegging dient plaats te vinden. Ondanks het uitgangspunt dat de procedures in alle lidstaten op dezelfde wijze worden toegepast, kunnen hierdoor toch verschillen ontstaan.

Doel, onderzoeksvraag en methodologie

Dit onderzoek heeft tot doel het functioneren van de eerste twee eenvormige Europese procedures bijna tien jaar na hun introductie in kaart te brengen. Het beoogt te evalueren in hoeverre de EBB en de EPGV hebben bijgedragen aan het vergemakkelijken van de toegang tot de rechter en het versterken van het noodzakelijke wederzijdse vertrouwen tussen de rechtssystemen van de lidstaten in het kader van het vrije verkeer van vonnissen.

De analyse geeft waardevolle inzichten in de werking en de effectiviteit van deze Europese instrumenten, voor zowel nationale als Europese belanghebbenden, die het academische debat naar een hoger plan te tillen.

De vraag die in dit onderzoek centraal staat is hoe de eerste generatie eenvormige Europese procedures – de EBB en de EPGV – de grensoverschrijdende geschilbeslechting verbeteren. Hierbij wordt gekeken naar enerzijds het waarborgen van effectieve handhavingsmechanismen, en anderzijds de bescherming van de procedurele rechten van de betrokken partijen. In vervolg op de bevindingen naar aanleiding van de hoofdvraag, wordt de vraag gesteld of de EBB en de EPGV als blauwdruk kunnen worden gebruikt voor toekomstige Europese procedures die eveneens tot doel hebben de grensoverschrijdende rechtshandhaving te vereenvoudigen en het burgerlijk procesrecht te harmoniseren.

De studie richt zich op vier Europese rechtsstelsels: Engeland en Wales (hierna: Engeland), Frankrijk, Italië en Roemenië. Zij maakt gebruik van juridisch-dogmatisch en sociaalwetenschappelijke onderzoeksmethoden. Om te bepalen op welke wijze de EBB en de EPGV de grensoverschrijdende geschilbeslechting bevorderen, is gebruikgemaakt van functionele rechtsvergelijking. Voor het juridisch onderzoek zijn primaire en secundaire rechtsbronnen bestudeerd, waaronder wetshistorie, richtlijnen, beleidsdocumenten, literatuur en nationale en Europese rechtspraak. Het empirische onderzoek is gebaseerd op de 'mixed methods'-methode, waarbij voor de dataverzameling zowel kwantitatieve als kwalitatieve benaderingen zijn gevolgd. Voor het kwantitatieve onderzoek is gebruikgemaakt van officiële statistieken en van kwantitatieve data die zijn verzameld door middel van een eigen enquête, die is ingevuld door verschillende praktijkjuristen, zoals rechters, advocaten, gerechtsdeurwaarders en werknemers van het Europees Consumenten Centrum. Het kwalitatieve onderzoek is gebaseerd op de antwoorden op de open vragen uit de enquête, alsmede op semigestructureerde interviews en op e-mailwisselingen met praktijkjuristen.

Het empirisch onderzoek beschrijft de wijzen waarop advocaten en gerechten de EBB en de EPGV toepassen, en zet de knelpunten en voordelen van deze eenvormige Europese procedures uiteen. Daarbij beoogt het empirische onderzoek overeenkomsten en verschillen in de toepassing van deze procedures in de verschillende rechtssystemen in kaart te brengen. Vervolgens zijn de empirische bevindingen aangevuld door, ten eerste, analyses van Europese en nationale databestanden over het gebruik van deze Europese procedures. De Europese databestanden in de periode van het onderhavige onderzoek ter beschikbaar gekomen. De verwerkte nationale statistische gegevens zijn uniek. Deze studie is de eerste die ongepubliceerde bestanden op een gedetailleerde wijze rapporteert. In de tweede plaats zijn de empirische bevindingen aangevuld door jurisprudentie-onderzoek. Door gebruik van triangulatie wordt beoogd de validiteit van de onderzoeksbevindingen van het empirisch onderzoek te vergroten.

De eenvormige Europese procedures vanuit Europees perspectief

Hoofdstuk 2 richt zich op de eigenschappen van de EBB en de EPGV binnen de Europese context. In dit hoofdstuk worden de politieke achtergronden geschetst die hebben geleid tot de vaststelling van deze eenvormige Europese procedures. Vervolgens wordt de aandacht verlegd naar de kenmerken van de procedures, de normen die zij in het leven roepen voor grensoverschrijdende geschilbeslechting en de wisselwerking met nationaal procesrecht. De analyse toont het belang aan van de inbedding van de EBB en de EPGV in het nationale rechtssysteem, alsook de uitdagingen die hiermee gepaard gaan. De informatie die door de lidstaten openbaar wordt gemaakt, zoals welke gerechten bevoegd zijn, welke communicatiemiddelen worden aanvaard, welke rechtsmiddelen openstaan en hoe de tenuitvoerlegging plaatsvindt, blijkt voor partijen en advocaten die van de procedures gebruikmaken niet altijd toereikend te zijn. Het is voor hen vaak nodig om aanvullende inlichtingen te vergaren. Hoewel Europese websites en consumentenorganisaties ook algemene en specifieke informatie beogen te verschaffen over de geschilbeslechting in de verschillende lidstaten, verloopt de informatieverstrekking nog niet feilloos. Op nationaal niveau en door de nationale rechtspraktijk zal op dit punt nog veel werk verzet moeten worden.

De juridische beroepsbeoefenaars uit de onderzochte lidstaten zijn niet altijd bekend met de procedurele systematiek en de specifieke regels van de EBB en de EPGV, zoals de herzieningsprocedure en de betekening per post met ontvangstbevestiging. De procedures vergen soms een andere aanpak dan de nationale procedures waarmee zij gewoonlijk werken. Met betrekking tot de EBB-Verordening heeft de uniforme uitleg van het Hof van Justitie van de Europese Unie (verder HvJ) de eenvormige toepassing in de lidstaten vergemakkelijkt. Voor de EPGV ontbreken deze richtsnoeren van het HvJ vooralsnog. Het is nu aan de nationale wetgevers en gerechten om het gebruik van de Europese procedures te vereenvoudigen en te garanderen dat deze op een eenvormige en coherente wijze worden toegepast.

In de volgende hoofdstukken wordt onderzocht hoe de eenvormige Europese procedures zijn ingepast in het nationale procesrecht en hoe zij in de praktijk functioneren. De geanalyseerde rechtsstelsels – Engeland, Frankrijk, Italië en Roemenië – vertegenwoordigen elk een verschillend institutioneel en procedureel kader waarbinnen de EBB en de EPGV de geschilbeslechting eenvoudiger, sneller en goedkoper zouden moeten maken. De eenvormige Europese procedures zouden, ongeacht het nationale procesrechtelijke stelsel, een gelijk speelveld moeten creëren voor grensoverschrijdende geschilbeslechting. De praktijk en rechtspraak laten echter zien dat de inbedding in het nationale recht en de uniforme toepassing een hele uitdaging is.

De eenvormige Europese procedures vanuit nationaal perspectief

In de hoofdstukken 3–6 wordt een meerlagige rechtsvergelijkende en empirische analyse gemaakt van het functioneren van de eenvormige Europese procedures. De analyse richt zich op de implementatie van de EBB en de EPGV binnen het nationale procesrechtelijke stelsel en de praktijk, alsmede op de percepties en verwachtingen met betrekking tot de procedures van belanghebbenden en rechtsgeleerden en het gebruik van de procedures in de praktijk. Hiervoor is gebruikgemaakt van statistieken, rechtspraak en empirische data.

In Engeland lijken de EBB en de EPGV een bescheiden bekendheid te genieten. Gedegen kennis over en begrip van deze procedures blijkt onder praktijkjuristen beperkt aanwezig en volgens de beschikbare statistieken worden de procedures slechts op kleine schaal ingezet. De invoering van de Civil Procedure Rules 78 (CPR78), waarin de EBB en de EPGV zijn ondergebracht, lijkt weinig effect te hebben gehad op de bekendheid van de procedures en de bereidheid om in grensoverschrijdende geschillen voor deze procedures te kiezen, in plaats van voor een nationale procedure. Door de CPR78 hebben de instrumenten echter wel aan zichtbaarheid gewonnen bij rechters en andere praktijkjuristen. Omdat de rechtspraak over de procedures schaars is, kunnen juridische professionals niet goed inschatten hoe de gerechten bepaalde regels zullen uitleggen en toepassen. Hierdoor blijft aan de eenvormige Europese procedures enige onzekerheid kleven, vooral in vergelijking tot de vertrouwde nationale procedures. Uit de analyse van het Engelse recht komt meermaals naar voren dat Engelse rechters geneigd zijn om de Verordeningen te interpreteren in het licht van de hun bekende nationale procedures en praktijk. In sommige gevallen worden de bepalingen aangevuld met vereisten uit het nationale recht die eigenlijk niet in overeenstemming zijn met de doelstellingen van de Europese instrumenten, zoals het vereiste dat voor een EBB bewijsmiddelen worden overgelegd en de voorwaarde in het kader van de EPGV dat alle bewijsdocumenten die niet in het Engels zijn opgesteld, worden vertaald. Praktijkjuristen lijken overigens meer belangstelling te hebben voor de EBB dan voor de EPGV. Het gebruik van beide procedures voor grensoverschrijdende geschillen zou kunnen worden vergemakkelijkt en gestimuleerd door de bekendheid van de instrumenten te vergroten en door meer informatie te verstrekken, die moet worden afgestemd op de behoeften van partijen en juridische beroepsbeoefenaars. Door het aangekondigde vertrek van het Verenigd Koninkrijk uit de Europese Unie zijn de prioriteiten echter elders komen te liggen, waardoor het vrijwel onmogelijk zal zijn om aanvullende maatregelen te nemen om het functioneren van de eenvormige Europese procedures te bevorderen.

Hoewel de Franse gerechten en juridische beroepsbeoefenaars over het algemeen op de hoogte zijn van het bestaan van zowel de EBB als de EPGV, lijken zij beter op de hoogte van de vaker gebruikte EBB-procedure. De wijze waarop deze procedures worden toegepast, wordt soms aanzienlijk beïnvloed door het nationale procesrecht, bijvoorbeeld wanneer de vereisten voor het verstrekken van een titel worden aangevuld met die van bekende nationale procedures. De rechters blijven erop gebrand om het bewijs, dat op grond van de EBB-Verordening in het verzoekschrift moet worden vermeld, te beoordelen. Hoewel de coördinatie tussen de bepalingen van de Verordeningen en de nationale rechtsregels niet altijd duidelijk is, wordt het gebruik van de EBB en de EPGV wel vereenvoudigd door de invoering van speciale bepalingen in het Franse burgerlijk procesrecht en de publicatie van specifieke richtsnoeren. Hiermee wordt ten aanzien van verschillende procedurele aspecten rechtszekerheid gecreëerd, zowel voor de partijen als voor de gerechten en beroepsbeoefenaars. Daarnaast blijkt dat degenen die van de procedure gebruikmaken, en dan vooral niet-professionele partijen, vaak problemen ervaren bij het invullen van de standaardformulieren. De ondersteuning die wordt geboden aan consumenten en bedrijven die de procedures gebruiken, zou beter georganiseerd en bekendgemaakt kunnen worden. Het aantal zaken waarin sprake is van vertegenwoordiging door een juridische professional is nog altijd hoog en partijen en juridische beroepsbeoefenaars blijven een voorkeur houden voor de nationale procedures, waarmee zij meer vertrouwd zijn. In de praktijk blijken zij echter wel geïnteresseerd te zijn in de toepassing van de eenvormige Europese procedures, en dan vooral de EBB-procedure. De statistieken laten een stijgende lijn zien in het gebruik van de EBB en de EPGV en ook in de snelheid waarmee de vorderingen worden afgehandeld. Door het bewustzijn te vergroten en partijen en praktijkjuristen te voorzien van specifieke informatie en nationale richtsnoeren, zal het gebruik van de procedures verder worden bevorderd en vergemakkelijkt.

In Italië zijn de meeste gerechten en juridische beroepsbeoefenaars op de hoogte van de Europese procedures. Dat is met name het geval bij de EBB, dat vaker wordt gebruikt dan de EPGV. Bij de wijze waarop de eenvormige Europese procedures worden gehanteerd en de afstemming met het nationale recht kunnen zich echter wel problemen voordoen. Om een doeltreffende toepassing van de EBB en de EPGV te garanderen, moeten rechters de leemten in de regelgeving opvullen, wat geen gemakkelijke opgave is. Nationale procedures, die gelijkenissen vertonen met de Europese procedures, zijn hierdoor van grote invloed op de wijze waarop de eenvormige procedures worden toegepast en aangevuld. De bemoeienis van het Ministerie van Justitie is tot op heden minimaal geweest; deze heeft slechts een beperkt aantal procedurele problemen opgelost of verhelderd. Aangezien niet duidelijk is welke nationale bepalingen in relatie tot de Europese procedures moeten worden toegepast, loopt de toepassing van de Verordening in de praktijk uiteen. Dit wordt pijnlijk duidelijk wanneer wordt gekeken naar de voortzetting van het proces nadat de verweerder verzet heeft aangetekend tegen een EBB. Uit de rechtspraak blijkt dat de uitleg van de rechters op dit punt aanzienlijk uiteenloopt. Verder zijn de nationale bepalingen niet altijd verenigbaar met de doelstellingen van de Verordeningen; zij vereisen dat de eiser fysiek aanwezig is om proceshandelingen te verrichten. De instrumenten wordt hiermee geen dienst bewezen; partijen worden zo niet gestimuleerd om gebruik te maken van de procedures en het gevolg is dat de voorkeur in de praktijk nog altijd uitgaat naar de nationale procedures. Uit de rechtspraak en empirische data blijkt wel dat de EBB en de EPGV het gemakkelijker maken om binnen korte tijd een beslissing te verkrijgen – en dat in een rechtsstelsel dat bekend staat om zijn langdurige procedures. De EBB en de EPGV zouden daarom baat hebben bij een duidelijker nationaalrechtelijk kader, waardoor de bestaande praktijken en interpretaties worden geünificeerd en de toepassing van de instrumenten wordt vereenvoudigd. Daarnaast zouden specifieke trainingen van juridische professionals kunnen helpen om de bekendheid van de instrumenten te vergroten en de toepassing ervan te verbeteren.

De Roemeense gerechten en juridische beroepsbeoefenaars zijn tot op zekere hoogte bekend met de EBB en de EPGV. Niettemin roept de wijze waarop de Europese procedures in de praktijk worden toegepast wel vragen op, en blijft er een voorkeur bestaan voor nationale procedures, die in de ogen van partijen en praktijkjuristen duidelijker zijn. Het tijdbestek dat nodig is om een executoriale titel te verkrijgen lijkt korter te worden, hetgeen gunstig is voor partijen die besluiten om de instrumenten te gebruiken. De EBB-procedure en de EPGV worden doorgaans aangevuld met voorwaarden die worden gesteld in het nationale recht, welke vaak niet in overeenstemming zijn met de doelstellingen van de Verordeningen. Juridische professionals zijn soms terughoudend in het gebruik van de instrumenten, vooral wanneer zij er niet van overtuigd zijn dat de bevoegde rechter voldoende op de hoogte is van de procedures. Ten aanzien van de procedurele rechten van de partijen kan worden opgemerkt dat de gerechten bijzonder gespitst zijn op de naleving van de procedurele standaarden die zijn neergelegd in de EBB en EPGV, maar ook in het nationale recht. Hierdoor bestaat het risico dat de procedure ingewikkelder wordt voor de eisende partij, aangezien deze moet voldoen aan allerlei aanvullende voorwaarden, zoals het fysiek aanwezig zijn in de rechtszaal – bijvoorbeeld om deel te nemen aan een geplande hoorzitting, of om een gecertificeerde beslissing te verkrijgen ten behoeve van de tenuitvoerlegging. In combinatie met het feit dat er weinig gedetailleerde informatie wordt verstrekt, maken deze omstandigheden het voor een leek niet gemakkelijk om zijn weg te vinden in de procedures. Het zal voor hem hierdoor veelal noodzakelijk zijn om zich in rechte te laten vertegenwoordigen. De belangstelling voor het gebruik van de procedures lijkt in Roemenië vooral aanwezig bij institutionele gebruikers (ondernemingen). De dataverzameling laat zien dat zich enige verbeteringen hebben voorgedaan in het vereenvoudigen van grensoverschrijdende geschilbeslechting, maar deze betreffen vooral het uitvaardigen van een beslissing en de afschaffing van het exequatur. Het proces van tenuitvoerlegging is echter nog altijd ingewikkeld en duurt relatief lang. In het algemeen zou de toepassing van de Europese procedures gebaat zijn bij een duidelijker nationaal wettelijk kader en een betere coördinatie tussen Europese en nationale rechtsnormen. Dit zou de werklast van de gerechten en partijen verlichten, helderheid scheppen en bijdragen aan de ontwikkeling van een bestendige praktijk. Op deze manier zouden partijen bovendien kunnen worden gestimuleerd om voor een van deze instrumenten te opteren, in plaats van voor een procedure die in het nationale recht voorhanden is.

Vergelijkende evaluatie

In hoofdstuk 7 worden de nationale bevindingen uit de hoofdstukken 3–6 met elkaar vergeleken. De analyse heeft tot doel om op basis van opgestelde criteria – die betrekking hebben op tot de uitvoering, doelmatigheid en efficiëntie – te bepalen of de EBB en de EPGV het proces van grensoverschrijdende geschilbeslechting bevorderen door enerzijds effectieve handhavingsmechanismen te bieden en anderzijds de procedurele belangen van de partijen te beschermen.

De analyse van de nationale rechtssystemen toont aan dat de EBB en de EPGV op verschillende wijzen zijn geïmplementeerd. De Engelse en Franse wetgevers bieden in vergelijking tot Italië en Roemenië meer transparantie wat betreft de nationale regels die van toepassing zijn in verhouding tot de Europese procedures. Italië en Roemenië lijken daarentegen te vertrouwen op de juridische eigenschappen van de Europese Verordeningen. Met de aanpassingen die in de nationale wetgevingen zijn doorgevoerd ten behoeve van de implementatie van de eenvormige Europese procedures, lijkt te worden ingespeeld op de behoefte van juridische professionals en partijen aan een betere toegang tot informatie. In de beschikbare informatie over de Europese procedures, zoals brochures en richtlijnen, ontbreekt het echter vaak aan gedetailleerde informatie over de precieze stappen die moeten worden ondernomen om te kunnen procederen. Hierdoor is de betekenis van het materiaal voor het daadwerkelijk aanhangig maken van een geschil – op zijn minst – beperkt. Om de transparantie van de relevante nationale bepalingen te vergroten, zal op zowel nationaal als Europees niveau moeten worden ingegrepen. Het feit dat specifieke nationale wetsbepalingen en richtsnoeren ontbreken, heeft als belangrijke consequentie dat de wijze van toepassing op nationaal niveau verschilt. Hiermee blijft de rechtsonzekerheid over het gebruik van de eenvormige Europese procedures in stand.

Wat betreft de doelmatigheid is het beeld dat de EBB en de EPGV laten zien niet eenduidig. In het algemeen kan worden gesteld dat er voor een effectieve toepassing van de Verordeningen nog enkele knelpunten zullen moeten worden opgelost. In aanvullende vereisten die wel door de rechters worden gesteld, zijn vaak voorwaarden uit nationale procedures te herkennen. Dit heeft consequenties voor het doel van de eenvormige Europese procedures om grensoverschrijdende geschilbeslechting te vereenvoudigen. Wat betreft de procedurele waarborgen die in de Verordeningen worden geboden, laat de dataverzameling zien dat rechters uitgebreid nagaan of de gedaagde in kennis is gesteld van het feit dat een procedure tegen hem aanhangig is gemaakt. Uit het onderzoek blijkt dat in de rechtsstelsels verschillend wordt omgegaan met de vereisten die worden gesteld aan de taal en de vertaling van de documenten die worden betekend of die nodig zijn in de fase van tenuitvoerlegging. De Roemeense rechters blijken op dit punt het zorgvuldigst te werk te gaan. Deze vereisten kunnen niet alleen van grote invloed zijn op de kosten (en daarmee de efficiëntie) van de Europese procedures, maar zijn ook van essentieel belang om de procedurele rechten van partijen te waarborgen. Om deze laatstgenoemde reden zouden zij niet afgeruild mogen worden tegen economische voordelen. Dat een partij een rechtsmiddel kan instellen, lijkt vooral een theoretische mogelijkheid. Het feit dat weinig gebruik wordt gemaakt van de rechtsmiddelen en de omstandigheid dat de kennis van de juridische professionals op dit punt beperkt is, kunnen de toepassing van deze veiligheidsmechanismen in sommige situaties bemoeilijken. Dit wordt geïllustreerd door de verweerschriften tegen de EBB die in Roemenië worden geweigerd en de wijze waarop in Frankrijk gebruik wordt gemaakt van de mogelijkheid om heroverweging te verzoeken van de EBB. Ook de omstandigheid dat de benaderingen ten aanzien van de beroepsmogelijkheid in de EPGV per land verschillen, draagt niet bij aan een eenvormige en eenvoudige toepassing van dit mechanisme. Over het afdwingen en succesvol ten uitvoer leggen van een EBB of een EPGV-uitspraak is niet genoeg informatie beschikbaar, zodat over de doelmatigheid van de procedures op dit punt geen gefundeerd oordeel kan worden geveld. De resultaten uit de enquête en de interviews lijken er echter op te wijzen dat de respondenten de procedures eerder als effectief beschouwen wanneer zij erin zijn geslaagd de vordering te innen.

Op basis van het onderzoek kan worden gesteld dat de vereenvoudiging van de grensoverschrijdende inning van vorderingen hoogstens gedeeltelijk is geslaagd, en dat de rechten van de partijen tot op zekere hoogte worden beschermd, maar dat aanpassingen nodig zijn om ervoor te zorgen dat de Verordeningen en de mechanismen in deze instrumenten op de juiste wijze worden toegepast.

Wanneer de Verordeningen naar maatstaven van kostenefficiëntie worden beoordeeld, dan blijkt dat sommige kosten die gepaard gaan met grensoverschrijdende geschilbeslechting, zoals kosten voor vertalingen, juridische bijstand en reizen, weliswaar worden verminderd, maar niet geheel worden geëlimineerd. Sommige kosten kunnen niet worden geëlimineerd omdat zij betrekking hebben op procedurele waarborgen, zoals de betekening van documenten die zijn opgesteld in een taal die de wederpartij kan begrijpen, of het gevolg zijn van een ingewikkelde regel van nationaal procesrecht, die in verband met de eenvormige Europese procedures wordt toegepast. Excessieve kosten, die het gevolg zijn van de verschillende vereisten die in de procedures worden gesteld, kunnen de toegang tot de rechter belemmeren, met name wanneer zij disproportionele hoogten bereiken en de partijen ervan weerhouden om een rechtszaak aanhangig te maken of om een beslissing af te dwingen. Om partijen ervan te overtuigen om voor deze procedures te kiezen, is het wenselijk dat een balans wordt bereikt tussen enerzijds de efficiënte toepassing van de EBB en de EPGV wat betreft de proceskosten en doorlooptijd, en anderzijds het naleven van de gestelde procedurele waarborgen. Wat betreft de tijdsefficiëntie kan een dalende trend worden waargenomen in de termijn waarbinnen de Europese procedures worden afgehandeld: deze gaat richting dertig dagen voor de EBB en zes maanden voor de EPGV. Daarmee kennen deze procedures een kortere doorlooptijd dan veel vergelijkbare nationale procedures. In sommige gevallen wordt de duur van de Europese procedures echter onnodig verlengd doordat de rechter, als gevolg van een onjuist begrip van de Verordeningen, aanvullende eisen stelt.

Over het geheel genomen blijkt dat schuldeisers door middel van de EBB en de EPGV in staat worden gesteld om in een kort tijdbestek een beslissing te verkrijgen en dat de Verordeningen deze fase van de procedure hebben vereenvoudigd. Ondanks het feit dat zij slechts op beperkte schaal worden ingezet in vergelijking tot nationale procedures, vormen de EBB en de EPGV een referentiepunt voor andere procedures die grensoverschrijdende geschilbeslechting proberen te vergemakkelijken. Nationale wetgevers zullen de optie om deze schriftelijke procedures te concentreren in een kleiner aantal gerechten daarom serieus in overweging moeten nemen. Hiermee wordt bevorderd dat de beschikbare bronnen (zoals trainingen en IT) op een betere manier worden ingezet en dat er op dit terrein expertise en gebruiken ontstaan, die kunnen bijdragen aan een snelle en deugdelijke toepassing van de EBB en EPGV. Ten slotte is het wenselijk dat de wetgever actie onderneemt. Om het geharmoniseerde kader te verbeteren – bijvoorbeeld door het aantal mogelijkheden voor betekening te reduceren en een uniforme benadering ten aanzien van het beroep in de EPGV te creëren – zouden de procedures minder afhankelijk moeten zijn van het nationale procesrecht en zouden de teksten van de EBB- en EPGV-Verordeningen beter op elkaar afgestemd moeten worden. In Verordening nr. 2015/2421 zijn voor de EPGV enkele mechanismen en regels verduidelijkt, zoals de betaling van griffierechten, de taal waarin het certificaat moet zijn opgesteld, de heroverweging en de informatie die door de lidstaten verstrekt dient te worden, maar deze verhelderingen strekken zich niet uit tot de EBB. Zo zou bijvoorbeeld kosteloze rechtsbijstand voor de partijen een gunstig effect hebben op de EBB-procedure. Door op Europees en nationaal niveau maatregelen te treffen om de informatie over de EBB en de EPGV voor partijen en juridische beroepsbeoefenaars beter beschikbaar te maken, kan worden bijgedragen aan de efficiëntie van de eenvormige Europese procedures (minder kosten en procedurele vertragingen). Verder kan de positie van de eiser worden vergemakkelijkt door hem aan het begin een totaaloverzicht te geven van alle te nemen procedurele stappen en de procedurele regels die hij dient na te leven.

Concluderende opmerkingen

In hoofdstuk 8 wordt ingegaan op de vraag welke gevolgen de juridische normen, die zijn vastgesteld in het kader van de EBB en de EPGV, zullen hebben op toekomstige ontwikkelingen die gericht zijn op de vereenvoudiging van grensoverschrijdende rechtshandhaving en de harmonisatie van het procesrecht binnen de Europese Unie. Onderzocht wordt welke elementen uit de EBB en de EPGV als model kunnen worden gebruikt voor toekomstige procedures. Hierbij moet worden gedacht aan de juridische basis, het optionele karakter van de instrumenten, de vorm van de schriftelijke procedure, de harmoniserende aanpak en de afhankelijkheid van nationaal procesrecht, de waarborgen ter bescherming van de procedurele rechten van partijen, de procedurele normen die zij tot stand brengen en de benadering ten aanzien van tenuitvoerlegging.

Het hoofdstuk sluit af met een uiteenzetting van de ontwikkelingen die op het onderhavige terrein gaande zijn – nauwere justitiële samenwerking op het gebied van het burgerlijk procesrecht, de ontwikkeling van een coherente aanpak tussen de procesrechtelijke instrumenten en digitalisering, alternatieve geschilbeslechting en de beginselen en regels van Europees civiel procesrecht – en hun betekenis voor de vereenvoudiging van grensoverschrijdende rechtshandhaving, de vergemakkelijking van de toegang tot de rechter en de bestendiging van het Europees burgerlijk recht.

ANNEX

EOP: Sample Survey[2374]

Dear Sir/Madam,

This questionnaire is part of the research project entitled *'Securing Quality in Cross-Border Enforcement: Towards European Principles of Civil Procedure?'*, financed by The Netherlands Organisation for Scientific Research (NWO).

With this questionnaire, the researcher is seeking to determine (1) how familiar practitioners are with handling monetary claims by means of the European Order for Payment (EOP); (2) the nature of the interaction between this European uniform procedure and the national procedural rules and legal mechanisms to enforce claims; and (3) how these procedures function in the enforcement of cross-border claims.

The research project is being carried out in several jurisdictions (England and Wales, France, Italy, and Romania), and involves professionals who are called to apply the procedures or to offer related advice to potential parties (e.g. judges, clerks, lawyers, and bailiffs).

The survey focuses on the EOP procedure. Your professional expertise and opinion regarding this European instrument will provide valuable information on its use and on how it functions, and will constitute an essential element of the present project.

Participation is anonymous, and your personal details will remain confidential. The information provided will be used within the researcher's PhD thesis and in possible additional publications.

Thank you for agreeing to participate. For additional information regarding the project, or for clarifications regarding the questionnaire, please do not hesitate to contact the researcher.

Sincerely,

Alina Onţanu LL.M., PhD Candidate

Prof. Dr. Xandra Kramer

E.A. Onţanu is a PhD Candidate in the Department of Private International Law and Comparative Law of Erasmus School of Law, Erasmus University Rotterdam. Contact: *ontanu@law.eur.nl*, telephone: +31 10 408 1504.

X.E. Kramer is a professor in the Department of Private International Law and Comparative Law of Erasmus School of Law, Erasmus University Rotterdam, and is a visiting professor at the Catholic University of Leuven (2013–2014); www.xandrakramer.eu.

2374 The present survey is a sample of the questionnaires used to conduct empirical research. Each linguistic version has been adapted to the national legislative framework of the jurisdiction in which the research was conducted. Hence, small differences exist between the surveys in different languages. Furthermore, the present sample does not entirely preserve the online formatting of the survey.

Your participation in this research will remain anonymous, and personal details are confidential. The researcher will use this information only if it is necessary to request clarifications or for follow-up questions.

Identification information

* If more than one person is involved in responding to subsequent questions, please fill in all the relevant personal information.

Name:
Position:
Institution:
Number of years of professional experience:
Number of years in this position:

Please provide contact person details and an e-mail address for follow-up questions:

I am interested in receiving information on the results of this study in England and Wales:
○ Yes;
○ No.

1. General awareness

1. How familiar are you with the European Order for Payment (EOP) procedure?
Please indicate the number (i.e. tick the box) you consider appropriate to rate your familiarity with the EOP procedure (5 = 'very familiar with the procedure;' 1 = 'unaware of the procedure').

○ 1 ○ 2 ○ 3 ○ 4 ○ 5

Please specify whether you have participated in any course and/or information-related meetings regarding EOP and/or Part 78 – European Procedures (European Order for Payment provisions) of the Civil Procedure Rules (Part 78 – EOP).

2. On the basis of your experience, is the EOP/Part 78 – EOP a well-known procedure in your country? Please indicate the number (i.e. tick the box) you consider appropriate to rate general awareness of the procedure (5 = 'well-known procedure'; 1 = 'unknown procedure'). If you are unable to answer this question, please tick the N/A box.

○ 1 ○ 2 ○ 3 ○ 4 ○ 5 ○ N/A

3. How involved are judges and members of the administrative staff in handling EOP/Part 78 – EOP forms?
Please indicate the number (i.e. tick the box) you consider appropriate to rate judges' and court staffs' involvement in handling an EOP/Part 78 – EOP procedure (5 = 'the forms of the procedure handled entirely by a judge'; 1 = 'the forms of the procedure are handled entirely by the court's administrative staff'). If you are unable to answer this question, please tick the N/A box.

O 1 O 2 O 3 O 4 O 5 O N/A

4. Please provide information on the type of tasks the judges and members of the court's administrative staff perform, and on their interaction in handling an EOP/Part 78 – EOP (i.e. when is a judge involved in handling an EOP, the situations in which members of the court's administrative staff consult with the judge in handling an EOP).

6. Do national procedural rules create any difficulties in the handling of EOP/Part 78 – EOP claims? Please indicate the number (i.e. tick the box) you consider appropriate to rate the level of difficulties created in this regard (5 = 'many difficulties'; 1 = 'no difficulties').

O 1 O 2 O 3 O 4 O 5

Please specify what type of difficulties the national procedural rules create in the handling of an EOP/Part 78 – EOP procedure.

7. Are different national procedures preferred in cross-border claims?
O Yes;
O No;
O I do not know.

If 'Yes', please specify which national procedures are preferred and which are the reasons for this practice.

2. Case law-related information

1. What were the most frequent types of cases filed in accordance with the EOP/Part 78 – EOP in England and Wales?
Please choose the three most frequent types of cases for which parties chose to use this European procedure.

- ○ sales contracts;
- ○ service contracts;
- ○ loan contracts;
- ○ financial contracts;
- ○ real estate contracts;
- ○ other contracts. Please specify:

2. Based on the EOP/Part 78 – EOP cases you handled, did parties experience any difficulties in filling in the EOP forms (EOP Regulation Annex I PD 78)?
(If the answer to this question is 'No', please go directly to question 6.)

- ○ Yes;
- ○ No.

3. What elements created the most difficulties for parties filling in EOP forms?
Please choose the three most common difficulties encountered by parties using this European procedure.

- ○ provisions in the forms difficult to understand;
- ○ basis of court's jurisdiction;
- ○ language requirements;
- ○ lack of legal knowledge;
- ○ establishing the interest on the amount due;
- ○ describing the evidence;
- ○ other. Please specify:

4. Based on your experience with the EOP/Part 78 – EOP, can you specify whether any of the difficulties you selected for question 3 were specific to a certain category of parties (e.g. consumers, national private companies, multinationals)?
Please indicate the reasons that determine them.

5. Based on your experience with the EOP/Part 78 – EOP, were the difficulties you selected for question 3 specific to a particular type of case (e.g. sales contract, service contract)?
Please indicate the reasons that determine this.

6. Did you or the parties experience language- or translation-related difficulties in applying this procedure (e.g. language in which the forms were filled in, documents served)?
○ Yes;
○ No.

If 'Yes', please specify the difficulties experienced and how they were resolved.

7. Are you aware of any cases in which a request for rectification and/or completion of the application form (Form A) was made?
(If the answer to this question is 'No', please go directly to question 9.)
○ Yes;
○ No.

8. What were the reasons behind most requests for rectification and/or completion of the application form (Form A)?
○ incomplete information on the other party/their representative;
○ grounds for the court's jurisdiction;
○ cross-border nature of the case;
○ application form filed in the wrong language;
○ no description of evidence;
○ establishing interest on the amount due;
○ court proposed modification of the application form;
○ other. Please specify:

9. On the basis of your experience, is the 30-day period provided in Article 12 EOP Regulation (Annex I PD 78 CPR) generally observed in practice for the issuing of an EOP?
○ Yes;
○ No;
○ I do not know.

If 'No', please indicate why the issuance of an EOP (Annex I PD 78 CPR) takes longer.

10. Who is in charge of serving the EOP on the defendant?
○ the court;
○ the claimant.

11. What are the methods of service used to serve the EOP on the defendant (Article 13 and 14 EOP Regulation, Annex I PD 78 in conjunction with PD 78.4)?
Please tick the boxes that correspond to the methods of service used by courts and claimants in serving the European order for payment on the defendant.

	Court	Claimant
Personal service on the defendant/representative attested with acknowledgement of receipt	○	○
Personal service attested by a document signed by the person who effected service	○	○
Personal service at the defendant's address on persons belonging to the same household	○	○
Postal service attested by acknowledgement of receipt	○	○
First-class post or similar service	○	○
Fax/other means of electronic communication	○	○
Deposit of the order in the defendant's mailbox	○	○

Other means. Please specify:

12. Based on the EOP/Part 78 – EOP cases you have handled, did you encounter any difficulties regarding service of the EOP on the defendant?
(If the answer to this question is 'No', or 'I do not know', please go directly to question 16.)

○ Yes;
○ No;
○ I do not know.

13. What were the most common difficulties or problems encountered in the service of documents in the EOP/ Part 78 – EOP procedure?

○ address of the defendant not correct;
○ language in which the EOP is served;
○ obtaining an acknowledgement of service (Article 13 EOP Regulation, Annex I PD78);
○ other. Please specify:

14. Were the difficulties mentioned in question 13 regarding service of the EOP:

○ in England and Wales;
○ cross-border in other EU Member States;
○ both in England and Wales and cross-border in other EU Member States.

Please explain:

15. Based on your experience with the EOP/Part 78 – EOP, how were the difficulties mentioned in question 13 resolved in practice?

16. Based on your practical experience in handling EOP/Part 78 – EOP cases, how long did it take to serve the EOP on the defendant after the court had issued the EOP (Form E)?
- O less than 1 week;
- O between 1 and 2 weeks;
- O between 2 and 3 weeks;
- O between 3 and 4 weeks;
- O more than 4 weeks.

17. If service of the EOP on the defendant took longer than 2 weeks, was this due to difficulties identified in question 13 above?
- O Yes;
- O No;
- O I do not know.

If 'No', please specify why service of the EOP on the defendant took longer than 2 weeks.

3. Review

1. Based on your experience with the EOP/Part 78 – EOP, were any review requests made by the defendants regarding courts' decisions (Article 20 EOP Regulation (Annex I PD 78) in conjunction with Part 78.8 – EOP)?
(If the answer to this question is 'No', or 'I do not know', please go directly to Section 4)
- O Yes;
- O No;
- O I do not know.

If 'Yes', please specify the reasons invoked for reviewing the EOP.

2. Based on your experience with the EOP/Part 78 – EOP, were the requests to review the EOP/ Part 78 – EOP decisions accepted by the court?
(If the answer to this question is 'I do not know', please go directly to Section 4.)

- O Yes;
- O No;
- O I do not know.

If 'Yes', please specify the reasons held to be justified in accepting a request for review.

3. If 'No', what were the reasons that determined the rejection of the request to review formulated by the defendant?

4. Were oral hearings held in accordance with Part 23 CPR (Part 78.8 – EOP and PD 78.6.1 – 6.2 – EOP)?

- O Yes;
- O No;
- O I do not know.

If 'Yes', please provide additional information (e.g. number of cases, reasons for holding an oral hearing, means used to hold the hearing, procedure to organise them, timeframe for their arrangement, etc.).

4. Enforcement of judicial decision

1. What steps were taken in the enforcement process following the lapse of the opposition period (Article 16(2) in conjunction with Article 18(1) of the EOP Regulation, Annex I PD 78 CPR)?

○ the court declared the EOP enforceable, and sent Forms E and G to the claimant;
○ at the claimant's request, the court declared the EOP enforceable, and sent Forms E and G to the claimant;
○ other. Please specify:

2. Following delivery of the EOP enforceable title to the claimant, were there any problems or difficulties related to the enforcement?
(If the answer to this question is 'No', or 'I do not know', please go directly to question 5.)

○ Yes;
○ No;
○ I do not know.

3. What were the general difficulties or problems encountered in the process of enforcing the EOP in England and Wales?
Please choose the three most common difficulties encountered by claimants in the enforcement of this European procedure.

○ finding the competent authority;
○ needing to provide a translation of the EOP/Declaration of enforceability;
○ the costs of enforcement;
○ obtaining information about the defendant's assets and financial situation;
○ selecting the method of enforcement;
○ other. Please specify:

4. Were the EOP enforcement difficulties similar to those experienced in the enforcement of uncontested national monetary claims?

○ Yes;
○ No;
○ I do not know.

Please explain:

5. Are you aware of any cases in which enforcement proceedings were abandoned by the claimant due to enforcement problems?

- ○ Yes;
- ○ No;
- ○ I do not know.

If 'Yes', please provide additional information (e.g. percentage of cases in which enforcement was abandoned, reasons why enforcement was abandoned, etc.).

6. Was any EOP issued by a court in other Member States refused enforcement based on the provisions of Article 22 EOP Regulation (Annex I PD 78) in conjunction with Part 78.10 – EOP and PD 78.8.1 – 8.3?

- ○ Yes;
- ○ No;
- ○ I do not know.

If 'Yes', please provide additional information (e.g. reasons for refusing enforcement, Member States involved, area of law the case concerned, etc.).

7. Was the enforcement of any EOP issued by a court of another Member State limited or stayed according to Article 23 EOP Regulation (Annex I PD 78) in conjunction with Part 78.11 – EOP and PD 78.9.1 – 9.2?

- ○ Yes;
- ○ No;
- ○ I do not know.

If 'Yes', please provide additional information (e.g. area of law the case concerned, reasons for stay/limitation of enforcement, Member State involved, etc.).

8. Were any oral hearings held according to Part 23 CPR read in conjunction with Part 78.10–78.11 – EOP and PD 78–6.1 – 6.2?

- O No;
- O Yes;
- O I do not know.

If 'Yes', please provide additional information (e.g. number of cases, reasons for holding an oral hearing, means used to hold the hearing, procedure to organise them, timeframe for their arrangement. etc.).

9. Did you have any information on the enforcement of EOP judgments issued by courts in England and Wales in other Member States?

- O Yes;
- O No.

If 'Yes', please provide any relevant additional information (e.g. Member States, area of law, difficulties encountered, reasons for refusal, limitation or stay of enforcement, etc.).

5. Case law-related information

1. How many cases has your court/organisation handled since the EOP procedure became applicable on 12 December 2008.

Total number of cases:

If possible, please provide information regarding each year for the period 2008–2014:

2. In how many cases handled by your court/ organisation were the EOP procedure applications rejected or withdrawn?

Total number of cases:

If possible, please provide information regarding each year for the period 2008–2014:

3. How often were the categories in the table below involved in an EOP/Part 78 – EOP procedure as claimant?
If accurate information is not available, please estimate a percentage based on your personal experience.

Consumer

National private company

National public company

Multinational

NGO

Other. Please specify:

4. How often were the categories in the table below involved in an EOP/Part 78 – EOP procedure as defendant?
If accurate information is not available, please estimate a percentage based on your personal experience.

Consumer

National private company

National public company

Multinational

NGO

Other. Please specify:

5. In how many cases were the claimants assisted by a lawyer/legal counsellor?
- ○ less than 25% of the cases;
- ○ between 25% and 50% of the cases;
- ○ between 51% and 75% of the cases;
- ○ more than 75% of the cases.

6. In how many cases were the defendants assisted by a lawyer/legal counsellor?
- ○ less than 25% of the cases;
- ○ between 25% and 50% of the cases;
- ○ between 51% and 75% of the cases;
- ○ more than 75% of the cases.

7. In how many cases was the claimant requested to rectify and/or to complete the application form (Form A)?

- O in less than 25% of the cases;
- O between 25% and 50% of the cases;
- O between 51% and 75% of the cases;
- O in more than 75% of the cases.

8. How often were EOP/ Part 78 – EOP claims opposed by the defendants?

- O in less than 25% of the cases;
- O between 25% and 50% of the cases;
- O between 51% and 75% of the cases;
- O in more than 75% of the cases.

9. In how many cases was the opposition to an EOP/Part 78 – EOP filed after the 30-day opposition period had lapsed (Article 16(2) EOP Regulation, Annex I PD 78)?

10. In how many cases did the defendant request a review of the EOP/Part 78 – EOP decision?

Total number of cases:

If possible, please provide information regarding each year for the period 2008–2014:

11. In how many cases did the court accept the request for review formulated by the defendant?

Total number of cases:

If possible, please provide information regarding each year for the period 2008–2014:

12. On the basis of your experience, what was the average timeframe necessary to conclude an EOP/Part 78 – EOP claim (from the moment the application form, Form A, was submitted to the court to the issuance of the Declaration of enforceability, Form G)?

- O less than 3 months;
- O between 3 and 6 months;
- O between 6 and 9 months;
- O more than 9 months.

If procedures lasted longer than 3 months, please indicate the main reasons that determined this outcome.

13. On the basis of your experience, what was the average timeframe necessary to enforce an EOP/ Part 78 – EOP in England and Wales (from the moment of the issuance of Form G to the actual execution of the EOP)?

- ○ less than 1 month;
- ○ between 1 and 2 months;
- ○ between 2 and 3 months;
- ○ between 3 and 4 months;
- ○ more than 4 months.

If procedures lasted longer than 1 month, please indicate the main reasons that determined this outcome.

14. In how many cases was the enforcement of an EOP issued by a court of another Member State refused in accordance with Article 22 EOP Regulation (Annex I PD 78) in conjunction with Part 78.10 – EOP and PD 78.8.1 – 8.3?

Total number of cases:

If possible, please provide information regarding each year for the period 2008–2014:

15. In how many cases was the enforcement of an EOP issued by the court of another Member State limited or stayed in accordance with Article 23 EOP Regulation (Annex I PD 78) in conjunction with Part 78.11 – EOP and PD 78.9.1 – 9.2?

Total number of cases:

If possible, please provide information on each year for the period 2008–2014:

6. Evaluation of the EOP procedure

Please indicate to what extent you agree or disagree with the statements below.

1. The EOP/Part 78 – EOP procedure can be considered overall an efficient solution regarding uncontested monetary claims in a cross-border litigation procedure in terms of *speed*, *affordability*, and *protection of parties' rights* in comparison to national procedures available for this purpose.

○ Strongly disagree ○ Disagree ○ Neutral ○ Agree ○ Strongly agree

Please explain your choice:

2. The EOP/Part 78 – EOP procedure can be considered overall an effective solution regarding the recovery of uncontested monetary claims in cross-border litigation.

○ Strongly disagree ○ Disagree ○ Neutral ○ Agree ○ Strongly agree

Please explain your choice:

3. There are remaining obstacles that impede the successful application of the EOP procedure/ Part 78 – EOP.

○ Strongly disagree ○ Disagree ○ Neutral ○ Agree ○ Strongly agree

Please explain your choice:

4. Do you have any recommendations or suggestions that may help to improve the application of the EOP procedure/Part 78 – EOP?

Thank you very much for answering this questionnaire.

ESCP: Sample Survey[2375]

Dear Sir/Madam,

This questionnaire is part of the research project entitled '*Securing Quality in Cross-Border Enforcement: Towards European Principles of Civil Procedure?*' financed by The Netherlands Organisation for Scientific Research ('NWO').

With this questionnaire, the researcher is seeking to determine (1) how familiar practitioners are with handling monetary claims by means of the European Small Claims Procedure (ESCP); (2) what is the nature of the interaction between this European uniform procedure and the national rules and legal mechanisms to enforce claims; and (3) how these procedures function in the enforcement of cross-border claims.

The research project is being carried out in several jurisdictions (England and Wales, France, Italy, Romania), and involves professionals who are called to apply the procedures or to offer related advice to potential parties (e.g. judges, clerks, lawyers, and bailiffs).

The survey focuses on the ESCP. Your professional expertise and opinion regarding this European instrument will provide valuable information on its use and on how it functions, and will constitute an essential element of the present project.

Participation remains anonymous, and your personal details will remain confidential. The information provided will be used within the researcher's PhD thesis and in possible additional publications.

Thank you for agreeing to participation. For additional information regarding the project, or for clarifications regarding the questionnaire please do not hesitate to contact the researcher.

Sincerely,

Alina Onţanu LL.M., PhD Candidate

Prof. Dr. Xandra Kramer

E.A. Onţanu is a PhD Candidate in the Department of Private International Law and Comparative Law of Erasmus School of Law, Erasmus University Rotterdam. Contact: ontanu@law.eur.nl, telephone: +31 10 408 1504

X.E. Kramer is a professor in the Department of Private International Law and Comparative Law of Erasmus School of Law, Erasmus University Rotterdam; and is a visiting professor at the Catholic University Leuven (2013–2014); www.xandrakramer.eu

[2375] The present survey is a sample of the questionnaires used for conducting empirical research. Each linguistic version has been adapted to the national legislative framework of the jurisdiction in which the research was conducted. Hence, small differences exist between different languages surveys. Furthermore, the present sample does not preserve entirely the online formatting of the survey.

Your participation in this research will remain anonymous, and personal details are confidential. The researcher will use this information only if it is necessary to request clarifications or for follow-up questions.

Identification information

* If more than one person is involved in responding to subsequent questions, please fill in all the relevant personal information.

Name:
Position:
Institution:
Number of years of professional experience:
Number of years in this position:

Please provide contact person details and an e-mail address for follow-up questions:

3. I am interested in receiving information on the results of this study in England and Wales:
○ Yes;
○ No.

1. General awareness

1. How familiar are you with the European Small Claims Procedure (ESCP)?
Please indicate the number (i.e. tick the box) you consider appropriate to rate your familiarity with the ESCP procedure (with 5 = 'very familiar with the procedure'; 1 = 'unaware of the procedure').

○ 1 ○ 2 ○ 3 ○ 4 ○ 5

Please specify whether you have participated in any course and/or information related meetings regarding ESCP and/or Part 78 – European Procedures (European Small Claims Procedure provisions) of the Civil Procedure Rules (Part 78 – ESCP).

2. On the basis of your experience, is the ESCP/Part 78 – ESCP a well-known procedure in your country?
Please indicate the number (i.e. tick the box) you consider appropriate to rate general awareness of the procedure (5 = 'well known procedure'; 1 = 'not known'). If you are unable to answer this question, please tick the N/A box.

O 1 O 2 O 3 O 4 O 5 O N/A

3. How involved are judges and members of the court's administrative staff in the handling of the ESCP/Part 78 – ESCP forms for claims filed according to this procedure?
Please indicate the number (i.e. tick the box) you consider appropriate to rate judges' involvement in handling of an ESCP/Part 78 – ESCP (5 = 'forms procedure entirely handled by a judge'; 1 = 'the forms are handled entirely by members of the court's administrative staff"). If you are unable to answer this question, please tick the *N/A* box.

O 1 O 2 O 3 O 4 O 5 O N/A

4. Please provide information on the type of tasks performed by the judges and members of the court's administrative staff perform, and on their interaction in handling an ESCP/Part 78 – ESCP (i.e. when is a judge involved in handling the ESCP, situations in which members of the court's administrative staff consult with the judge in handling of the ESCP).

5. Do national procedural rules create any difficulties in the handling of ESCP/Part 78 – ESCP claims?
Please indicate the number (i.e. tick the box) you consider appropriate to rate the level of difficulties created in this regard (5 = 'many difficulties'; and 1 = 'no difficulties').

O 1 O 2 O 3 O 4 O 5

Please specify what type of difficulties the national procedural rules create in the handling of an ESCP/Part 78 – ESCP.

6. Are different national procedures preferred in cross-border claims?
O Yes;
O No;
O I do not know.

If 'Yes', please specify which national procedures are preferred and which are the reasons for this practice.

2. Case law-related information

1. What were the most frequent type of cases filed in accordance with the ESCP/Part 78 – ESCP in England and Wales?
Please choose the three most frequent types of cases for which parties chose to use this European procedure.
- O sales contracts;
- O service contracts;
- O rent contracts;
- O holiday package contracts;
- O aviation contracts (i.e. flight cancelation, flight delay, reimbursement of tickets price);
- O other contracts. Please specify:

2. Based on the ESCP/Part 78 – ESCP cases you handled, did parties experience any difficulties in filling in the ESCP forms (ESCP Regulation Annex II PD 78)?
(If the answer to this question is No, please go directly to question 6.)
- O Yes;
- O No.

3. What elements created the most difficulties for the parties filling in the ESCP forms?

Please choose the three most common difficulties encountered by parties using this European procedure.
- O provisions in the forms difficult to understand;
- O basis of court's jurisdiction;
- O language requirements;
- O lack of legal knowledge;
- O establishing the interest on the amount due;
- O formulating the basis of the claim;
- O establishing the evidence to be put forward and the points of the claims it supports;
- O other. Please specify:

4. Based on your experience with the ESCP/Part 78 – ESCP, can you specify whether any of the difficulties you selected for question 3 were specific to a certain category of parties (e.g. consumers, national private companies, multinationals)?
Please indicate the reasons that determine them.

5. Based on your experience with the ESCP/Part 78 – ESCP, were the difficulties you selected for question 3 specific to a particular type of case (e.g. sales contract, service contract, rental contract)?
Please indicate the reasons that determine them.

6. Did you or the parties experience language- or translation-related difficulties in applying this procedure (e.g. due to language in which the forms were filled in, additional information sent by the parties)?

- O Yes;
- O No.

If 'Yes', please specify what were the difficulties experienced and how they were solved.

7. Are you aware of any cases in which a request for rectification and/or completion of the claim form (Form A) was made?

(If the answer to this question is 'No', please go directly to question 9.)

- O Yes;
- O No.

8. What were the reasons behind most requests for rectification and/or completion of the application form (Form A)?

○ incomplete information on the other party/their representative;
○ grounds for the court's jurisdiction;
○ application filed in the wrong language;
○ formulating the basis of the claim;
○ establishing interest on the amount due;
○ establishing the evidence to be put forward and the points of the claims it supports;
○ other. Please specify:

9. Are you aware of any cases in which a request for rectification of the answer form (Form C) was made?

(If the answer to this question is 'No', please go directly to question 11.)

○ Yes;
○ No.

10. What were the reasons behind the request for rectification of the answer form (Form C)?

○ explaining the reasons why the claim is not accepted;
○ answer form filed in the wrong language;
○ establishing interest on the amount due;
○ other. Please specify:

11. On the basis of your experience, were there any problems related to the service of documents, particularly with regard to the service of documents by post within the meaning of Article 13 of the ESCP Regulation (Annex II PD 78)?

(If the answer to this question is No, or I do not know, please go directly to question 15.)

○ Yes;
○ No;
○ I do not know.

12. What were the most common difficulties or problems encountered in the service of documents in the ESCP/Part 78 – ESCP procedure?

- ○ address of the defendant not correct;
- ○ language in which the ESCP claim was served;
- ○ obtaining an acknowledgement of service (Article 13 ESCP Regulation, Annex II PD 78);
- ○ other. Please specify:

13. Were the difficulties mentioned in question 12 regarding service of the ESCP documents:

- ○ in England and Wales;
- ○ cross-border into other EU Member States;
- ○ both in England and Wales and cross-border into other EU Member States.

Please explain:

14. Based on your experience with the ESCP/Part 78 – ESCP, how were the difficulties mentioned in question 12 resolved in practice?

15. Based on your practical experience in handling ESCP/Part 78 – ESCP cases, how long did it take to serve the ESCP claim upon the defendant (copy Form A and Form C)?

- ○ less than 1 week;
- ○ between 1 and 2 weeks;
- ○ between (more than) 2 and 3 weeks;
- ○ between (more than) 3 and 4 weeks;
- ○ more than 4 weeks.

16. If service of the ESCP claim on the defendant took longer than 2 weeks, was this due to the difficulties mentioned in question 12 above?

- ○ Yes;
- ○ No;
- ○ I do not know.

If 'No', please specify why service of the ESCP claim on the defendant took longer than 2 weeks.

17. Based on the provisions of Article 5(1) and Article 8 of the ESCP Regulation (Annex II PD 78) in conjunction with PD 78.17.1–2, were there any court hearings held?

- O Yes;
- O No;
- O I do not know.

If 'Yes', please specify why a court hearing was held in the ESCP/Part 78 – ESCP claim.

3. Appeal

1. Based on your experience with the ESCP/Part 78 – ESCP, were there any requests for the appeal of ESCP judgments (Article 17 ESCP Regulation, Annex II PD 78 in conjunction with Part 78.14 – ESCP, PD 78.13.1, and PD 27.8.1 – 8.3)?

- O Yes;
- O No;
- O I do not know.

2. Did the court accept the requests to appeal ESCP/Part 78 – ESCP judgments?

- O Yes;
- O No;
- O I do not know.

Please provide information on the general outcome of the appeal procedure.

4. Review

1. Based on your experience with the ESCP/Part 78 – ESCP, were any review requests made by the defendants regarding courts' decisions (Article 28 ESCP Regulation, Annex II PD 78 in conjunction with Part 78.19 – ESCP and PD 78.18.1 – 18.2)?
(If the answer to this question is 'No' or 'I do not know', please go directly to Section 5.)
- O Yes;
- O No;
- O I do not know.

If 'Yes', please specify the reasons invoked for reviewing the ESCP judgment.

2. Based on your experience with the ESCP/Part 78 – ESCP, were the requests to review the ESCP judgments accepted by the court?
(If the answer to this question is I do not know, please go directly to Section 5.)
- O Yes;
- O No;
- O I do not know.

If 'Yes', please specify the reasons held to be justified in accepting a request for review.

3. If 'No', what were the reasons that determined the rejection of the request to review formulated by the defendant?

4. Were oral hearings held in accordance with Part 23 CPR (Part 78.19 – ESCP and PD 78.18.1 – 18.2)?
- O Yes;
- O No;
- O I do not know.

If 'Yes', please provide additional information (e.g. number of cases, reasons for holding an oral hearing, means used to holding the hearing, procedure to organise them, timeframe for their arrangement, etc.):

5. Enforcement of judicial decision

1. Following the delivery of the certificate concerning an ESCP judgment, were there any problems or difficulties related to the enforcement?
(If the answer to this question is 'No', or 'I do not know', please go directly to question 4.)
- O Yes;
- O No;
- O I do not know.

2. What were the general difficulties or problems encountered in the process of enforcing the ESCP judgments in England and Wales?
Please choose the three most common difficulties or problems encountered by claimants in the enforcement of this European procedure.
- O finding the competent authority;
- O needing to provide a translation of the ESCP judgment;
- O the costs of enforcement;
- O obtaining information about the defendant's assets and financial situation;
- O selecting the method of enforcement;
- O other. Please specify:

3. Were the enforcement difficulties similar to those experienced in the enforcement of national small claims judgments?
- O Yes;
- O No;
- O I do not know.

Please explain:

4. Are you aware if any cases in which enforcement proceedings were abandoned by the claimant due to enforcement problems?

- ○ Yes;
- ○ No;
- ○ I do not know.

If 'Yes', please provide additional information (e.g. percentage of cases in which enforcement was abandoned, reasons for which enforcement was abandoned, etc.).

5. Was any ESCP judgment issued by a court in other Member State refused enforcement based on the provisions of Article 22 ESCP Regulation (Annex II PD 78) in conjunction with Part 78.21 – ESCP and PD 78.20.1 – 20.2?

- ○ Yes;
- ○ No;
- ○ I do not know.

If 'Yes', please provide additional information (e.g. the reasons for refusing enforcement, Member States involved, area of law the case concerned, etc.).

6. Was the enforcement of any ESCP judgment issued by a court of another Member Sate limited or stayed according to Article 23 ESCP Regulation (Annex II PD 78) in conjunction with Part 78.22 – ESCP and PD 78.21.1 – 21.4?

- ○ Yes;
- ○ No;
- ○ I do not know.

If 'Yes', please provide additional information (e.g. the reasons for stay/limitation of enforcement, Member States involved, area of law the case concerned, etc.).

7. Were any oral hearings held according to Part 23 CPR in conjunction with Part 78.21 – 78.22 – ESCP and PD 78–18.1 – 18.2?

- ○ Yes;
- ○ No;
- ○ I do not know.

If 'Yes', please provide additional information (e.g. number of cases, reasons for holding an oral hearing, means used to hold the hearing, procedure to organise them, timeframe for their arrangement, etc.).

8. Do you have any information on the enforcement of ESCP judgments issued by England and Wales courts in other Member States?
- ○ Yes;
- ○ No.

If 'Yes', please specify as far as possible (e.g. Member States, area of law, difficulties encountered, reasons for refusal, limitation or stay of enforcement, etc.).

6. Case law-related information

1. How many cases has your court/organisation handled since the ESCP procedure became applicable on 1 January 2009?

Total number of cases:

If possible, please provide information regarding each year for the period 2009–2014:

2. How many cases have been dismissed or withdrawn since the ESCP procedure became applicable on 1 January 2009?

Total number of cases:

If possible, please provide information regarding each year for the period 2009–2014:

3. How many cases have been settled since the ESCP procedure became applicable on 1 January 2009?

Total number of cases:

If possible, please provide information regarding each year for the period 2009–2014:

4. How often were the categories in the table below involved in an ESCP/Part 78 – ESCP as claimant?
If accurate information is not available, please estimate a percentage on the basis of your personal experience.

Consumer

National private company

National public company

Multinational

NGO

Other. Please specify:

5. How often were the categories in the table below involved in an ESCP/Part 78 – ESCP as defendant?

If accurate information is not available, please estimate a percentage on the basis of your personal experience.

Consumer

National private company

National public company

Multinational

NGO

Other. Please specify:

6. In how many cases were the claimants assisted by lawyer/legal counsellor?
- less than 25% of the cases;
- between 25% and 50% of the cases;
- between 51% and 75% of the cases;
- more than 75% of the cases.

7. In how many cases were the defendants assisted by lawyer/legal counsellor?
- less than 25% of the cases;
- between 25% and 50% of the cases;
- between 51% and 75% of the cases;
- more than 75% of the cases.

8. In how many cases was the claimant requested to rectify and/or to complete the claim form (Form A)?

- ○ in less than 25% of the cases;
- ○ between 25% and 50% of the cases;
- ○ between 51% and 75% of the cases;
- ○ in more than 75% of the cases.

9. In how many cases was the defendant requested to rectify and/or to complete the answer form (Form C)?

- ○ in less than 25% of the cases;
- ○ between 25% and 50% of the cases;
- ○ between 51% and 75% of the cases;
- ○ in more than 75% of the cases.

10. Based on your experience with the ESCP/Part – 78 ESCP, what was the average timeframe within which service of documents on the defendant was carried out within this procedure?

11. In how many cases did the parties request an oral hearing in accordance with Article 5(1) and Article 8 of the ESCP Regulation (Annex II PD 78) in conjunction with PD 78.17.1 – 17.2?

Total number of cases:

If possible, please provide information regarding each year for the period 2009–2014:

12. In how many cases did the court hold an oral hearing?

Total number of cases:

If possible, please provide information regarding each year for the period 2009–2014:

13. Were there any cases in which the court decided on its own motion to hold an oral hearing in an ESCP/Part 78 – ESCP claim? Please explain.

Total number of cases:

If possible, please provide information regarding each year for the period 2009–2014:

14. On the basis of your experience, what was the average timeframe necessary to conclude an ESCP/Part 78 – ESCP claim (from the moment the application form, Form A, was submitted to the court to the issuance of the court decision)?

- ○ less than 3 months;
- ○ between 3 and 6 months;
- ○ between (more than) 6 and 9 months;
- ○ more than 9 months.

If procedures lasted longer than 6 months, please indicate what were the main reasons that determined this outcome.

15. In how many cases was the answer form, Form C, returned to the court after the 30-day period had lapsed (Article 5(3) ESCP Regulation, Annex II PD 78)?

16. How many requests for the appeal of an ESCP judgment were registered (Article 17 ESCP Regulation, Annex II PD 78 in conjunction with Part 78.14 – ESCP, PD 78.13.1 and PD 27.8.1 – 8.3 ESCP)?

Total number of cases:

If possible, please provide information regarding each year for the period 2009–2014:

17. How many requests for the appeal of an ESCP judgment were accepted by the court (Article 17 ESCP Regulation, Annex II PD 78 in conjunction with Part 78.14 – ESCP, PD 78.13.1 and PD 27.8.1 – 8.3 ESCP)?

Total number of cases:

If possible, please provide information regarding each year for the period 2009–2014:

18. On the basis of your experience, what was the average timeframe necessary to resolve an ESCP/Part 78 – ESCP appeal?

- ○ less than 3 months;
- ○ between 3 and 6 months;
- ○ between (more than) 6 and 9 months;
- ○ more than 9 months.

19. In how many cases did the defendant request a review in accordance with Article 18 ESCP Regulation (Annex II PD 78) in conjunction with Part 78.19 – ESCP?

Total number of cases:

If possible, please provide information regarding each year for the period 2009–2014:

20. In how many cases did the court accept the request for review formulated by the defendant?

Total number of cases:

If possible, please provide information regarding each year for the period 2009–2014:

21. On the basis of your experience, what was the average time period necessary to enforce an ESCP/Part 78 – ESCP judgment in England and Wales (following the issuance of the certificate, Form D)?

- ○ less than 1 month;
- ○ between 1 and 2 months;
- ○ between (more than) 2 and 3 months;
- ○ between (more than) 3 and 4 months;
- ○ more than 4 months.

If procedures lasted longer than 1 month, please indicate the main reasons that determined this outcome.

22. In how many cases was the enforcement of an ESCP judgment issued by the court of another Member refused in accordance with Article 22 ESCP Regulation (Annex II PD 78) in conjunction with Part 78.20 – ESCP and PD 78.20.1 – 20.2?

Total number of cases:

If possible, please provide information regarding each year for the period 2009–2014:

23. In how many cases was the enforcement of an ESCP judgment issued by the court of another Member State limited or stayed in accordance with Article 23 ESCP Regulation (Annex II PD 78) in conjunction with the Part 78.22 – ESCP and PD 78.21.1 – 21.4?

Total number of cases:

If possible, please provide information on a yearly basis:

7. Evaluation of the ESCP

Please indicate to what extent you agree or disagree with the statements below.

1. The ESP/Part 78 – ESCP procedure can be considered overall an efficient solution regarding small monetary claims in cross-border litigation terms of *speed*, *affordability* and *protection of parties' rights* in comparison to other national procedures available for this purpose.

○ Strongly disagree ○ Disagree ○ Neutral ○ Agree ○ Strongly agree

Please explain your choice:

2. The ESP/Part 78 – ESCP procedure can be considered overall an effective solution in cross-border small claims litigation.

○ Strongly disagree ○ Disagree ○ Neutral ○ Agree ○ Strongly agree

Please explain your choice:

3. There are remaining obstacles that impede the successful application of the ESCP/Part 78 – ESCP.

○ Strongly disagree ○ Disagree ○ Neutral ○ Agree ○ Strongly agree

Please explain your choice:

4. Do you have any recommendations or suggestions that may help to improve the application of the ESCP/Part 78 – ESCP?

Thank you very much for answering this questionnaire.

BIBLIOGRAPHY

A

Adenas (2005)

M. Andenas, 'National Paradigms of Civil Enforcement: Mutual Recognition or Harmonization in Europe?', M. Andenas, B. Hess and P. Oberhammer (eds.), *Enforcement Agency. Practice in Europe*, British Institute of International and Comparative Law, 2005, pp. 7–23

Amrani-Mekki (2011)

S. Amrani-Mekki, 'Règlement (CE) n° 1896/2006 du 12 décembre 2006 instituant une procédure européenne d'injonction de payer', in L. Cadiet, E. Jeuland, S. Amrani-Mekki (eds.), *Droit processuel civil de l'Union européenne*, LexisNexis, 2011, pp. 249–259

Andersson (2005)

T. Andersson, 'Harmonization and mutual recognition: How to handle mutual distrust', M. Andenas, B. Hess and P. Oberhammer (eds.), *Enforcement Agency Practice in Europe*, British Institute of International and Comparative Law, 2005, pp. 245–251

Andrews (2008)

N. Andrews, *The Modern Civil Process. Judicial and Alternative Forms of Dispute Resolution in England*, Mohr Siebeck, 2008

Andrews (2012)

N. Andrews, 'Case Management and Procedural Discipline: Fundamentals of Essential New Technique', *Beijing Conference Paper* (September 2012)

Andrews (2013)

N. Andrews, *Andrews on Civil Processes, Court Proceedings and Principles*, Volume 1, Intersentia, 2013

Arvind (2010)

T.T. Arvind, 'The 'Transplant Effect" in Harmonization', *International Civil Law Quarterly*, 59(2010)1, pp. 65–88

Asprella (2008)

C. Asprella, 'Il "procedimento europeo per le controversie di modesta entità"', *Giurisprudenza di merito*, (2008)1, pp. 29–42

B

Baldwin (2003)

J. Baldwin, *Small Claims in the County Courts in England and Wales. The Bargain Basement of Civil Justice?*, Oxford University Press, Reprinted 2003

Baldwin & Cunnington (2004)

J. Baldwin and R. Cunnington, 'The crisis in enforcement of civil judgments in England and Wales', *Public Law*, 2004, pp. 305–350

Balena (2012)

G. Balena, *Istitutizoni di diritto processuale civile*, 2nd Edition, Cacuci Editore, 2012

Barbu (2014)

M. C. Barbu, *Noul Cod de procedură civilă. Jurisprudență rezumată*, C.H. Beck, București, 2014

Bastianon (2008)

S. Bastianon, 'Prime osservazioni sul Regolamento CE n. 1896/2006 che istituisce un procedimento europeo di ingiunzione di pagamento', *Giurisprudenza di merito, Osservatorio sulla procedura civile* 476, (2008)11, pp. 2871–2883

Bauvin, Ghera & Mecarelli (2012)

J.-F. Bauvin, T. Ghera and G. Mecarelli, 'Dématérialisation des procédures judiciaires: regards sur l'arrêté du 28 août 2012, *Droit et Procédures*, 2012, 65(9), pp. 222–228

Bello (2010)

L. Bello, *Small Claims, Big Claims – Consumers' Perception of the Small Claims Process*, Consumers Focus, 2010, pp. 29–59

Beraudo & Beraudo (2011)

J.-P. Beraudo and M.-J. Beraudo, 'Injonction de payer européenne et procédure européenne de règlement des petits litiges', *JurisClasseur Europe Traité*, Fasc. 2820, 2011, pp. 1–24

Berglund (2009)

M. Berglund, *Cross-Border Enforcement of Claims in the EU. History, Present Time and Future*, Wolters Kluwer, 2009

Berrowitz, Pistor & Richard (2003)

D. Berrowitz, K. Pistor and J.-F. Richard, 'The Transplant Effect', *The American Journal of Comparative Law*, 51(2003)1, pp. 163–203

Berthe (2014)

A. Berthe, 'L'impact du règlement Bruxelles I bis sur les règlements T.E.E., I.P.E. et R.P.L.', in E. Guinchard (ed.), *Le nouveau règlement Bruxelles I bis*, Bruylant, 2014, pp. 295–316

Bertoli (2008)

P. Bertoli, 'Verso un diritto processuale civile comunitario uniforme: l'ingiunzione europea di pagamento e le controversie di modesta entità', *Rivista di diritto internazionale privato e processuale*, 44(2008)2, pp. 395–428

Biavati (2013)

P. Biavati, *Argomenti di diritto processuale civile*, 2nd Edition, Bononia University Press, 2013

Biavati (2011)
P. Biavati, 'Droit italien', in chapter by S. Amrani-Mekki, 'Règlement (CE) n° 1896/2006 du 12 décembre 2006 instituant une procédure européenne d'injonction de payer', in L. Cadiet, E. Jeuland and S Amrani-Mekki (eds.), *Droit processuel civil de l'Union européenne*, LexisNexis, 2011, pp. 387–469

Biavati (2010)
P. Biavati, 'Art. 1. (Oggetto)', in P. Biavati, 'Reg. CE N. 1896/2006 del Parlamento Europeo e del Consiglio che Istituiesce un Procedimento Europeo d'Ingiunzione di Pagamento. Commentario a cura di Paolo Biavati', *Le Nuove Leggi Civile Commentate*, CEDAM, (2010)2

Bina (2008)
M. Bina, 'Il procedimento europeo per le controversie di modesta entità (Reg. CE N. 861/2007)', *Rivista di diritto processuale*, 73(2008)6, pp. 1630–1643

Bochove & Onţanu (2013)
L. M. van Bochove and E. A. Onţanu, Noot bij: Hof van Justitie. (2012, December 13), Szyrocka/SiGer Technologie GmbH, Zaaknr. C-215/11, *Tijdschrift voor Consumentenrecht en handelspraktijken* (TvC), (2013)6, pp. 285–293

Boeije (2010)
H. Boeije, *Analysis in Qualitative Research*, SAGE Publications, 2010

Bonato (2007)
G. Bonato, 'L'ambito di applicazione del procedimento europeo d'ingiunzione di pagamento e la nozione di controversia transfrontaliera', in A. Carratta (ed.), *Verso il procedimento ingiuntivo europeo*, Dott. A. Giuffrè Editore, Milano 2007, pp. 171–234

Boroi & Stancu (2015)
G. Boroi and M. Stancu, *Drept procesual civil*, 2nd Edition, Editura Hamangiu, 2015

Boroi & Theohari (2014)
G. Boroi and D.-N. Theohari, 'Sinteza principalelor modificări şi completări aduse Codului de procedură civilă prin Legea nr. 138/2014', in *Noul Code de procedură civilă şi 12 legi uzuale*, Legislaţie, Editura Hamangiu, updated at 20 October 2014

Boucard (2009)
F. Boucard, 'Pourvoi en cassation. Le contrôle de cassation. Contrôle de l'application de la loi', *JurisClasseur Procédure civile*, Fasc. 756, 2009

Boursier (2010)
M.-E. Boursier, 'Opposition', *Répertoire de procédure civile Dalloz*, 2010

Bove (2010)
M. Bove, *Il procedimento sommario di cognizione di cui agli articoli 702-bis ss. c.p.c.*, 29 April 2010

Bozeşan (2014)
V. Bozeşan, *Ordonanţa de plată şi cererile de valoare redusă. Comentarii şi jurisprudenţă potrivit noului Code de procedură civilă*, Editura Hamangiu, Comentarii practice, 2014

Briggs (2016)
Lord Justice Briggs, *Civil Court Structure Review: Final Report*, July 2016 (available at https://www.judiciary.gov.uk/wp-content/uploads/2016/07/civil-courts-structure-review-final-report-jul-16-final-1.pdf).

Briggs (2015)
Lord Justice Briggs, *Civil Court Structure Review: Interim Report*, December 2015

Bryman (2012)
A. Bryman, *Social Research Methods*, 4th Edition, Oxford University Press, 2012

Bugada (2011)
A. Bugada, 'Référé prud'homal: pas d'autorité de la chose jugée au principal sur la compétence', *Revue Procédures*, 2011(4), Commentaires 140

C

Cadiet (2011)
L. Cadiet, 'Introduction to French Civil Justice System and Civil Procedure', *Ritsumeikan Law Review*, 28(2011), pp. 331–338

Cadiet (2009)
L. Cadiet, *Code de Procédure Civile 2009*, 28th Edition, Comments to Article 1422, pp. 849–850

Cadiet (2005)
L. Cadiet, 'The New French Code of Civil Procedure (1975)', in C.H. van Rhee (ed.), *European Traditions in Civil Procedure*, Ius Commune Europaeum 54, Intersentia Metro, 2005, pp. 49–68

Cadiet & Amrani-Mekki (2008)
L. Cadiet and S. Amrani-Mekki, 'Civil Procedure', in G. A. Bermann and E. Picard (eds.), *Introduction to French Law*, Wolters Kluwer Law & Business, 2008, pp. 161–181

Cadiet & Jeuland (2013)
L. Cadiet, E. Jeuland, *Droit judiciaire privé*, 8th Edition, Manuel, Lexis Nexis, 2013

Caglioti (2015)
G. W. Caglioti, 'Controversie Europee di modesta entità. Criticità relative alla trasmissione della domanda in formato telematico, notifiche e comunicazione atti e mutamento di rito', *Filo diritto*, 26 June 2015 (available at www.filodiritto.com/articoli/2015/06/criticit-relative-alla-trasmissione-della-domanda-in-formato-telematico-notifiche-e-comunicazione-atti-e-mutamento-di.html)

Caglioti (2014)
G. W. Caglioti, 'Regolamento CE 1896/2006 – Procedimento Europeo di ingiunzione di pagamento e relative opposizione: regime fiscale', *Filo diritto*, 17 February 2014, (available at www.filodiritto.com/articoli/2014/02/regolamento-ce-18962006-procedimento-europeo-di-ingiunzione-di-pagamento-e-relativa-opposizione-regime-fiscale/)

Caglioti (2014a)
G. W. Caglioti, 'Gratuito patrocinio: controversie di modesta entità regolamento CE 861/2007 aspetti fiscali', *Filo diritto*, 07 August 2014 (available at www.filodiritto.com/articoli/2014/07/gratuito-patrocinio-controversie-di-modesta-entit-regolamento-ce-8612007-aspetti-fiscali.html)

Campeis & De Pauli (2007)
G. Campeis and A. De Pauli, 'Prime riflessioni sul procedimento europeo di ingiunzione di pagamento (Regolamento n. 1896/2006/CE)', *Giustizia civile*, (2007) Supplemento, P II, pp. 355–377

Caponi (2009)
R. Caponi, 'Consentito al giudice un solo tipo di passaggio dalla trattazione semplificata a quella ordinaria', *Guida al diritto, Il Sole-24 Ore*, 16(2009)50, pp. 52–54

Cappelletti, Merryman & Perillo (1967)
M. Cappelletti, J. H. Merryman and J. M. Perillo, *The Italian Legal System. An Introduction*, Stanford Univeristy Press, 1967

Caprioli (2013)
É. Caprioli, 'Communication par voie électronique des injonctions de payer', *Communication Commerce électronique*, 2013(3), Commentaires 37

Carnevali & Resca (2014)
D. Carnevali and A. Resca, 'Pushing at the Edge of Maximum Manageable Complexity: The Case of 'Trial Online' in Italy, in F. Contini and G. F. Lanzara (eds.), *The Circulation of Agency in E-Justice. Interoperability and Infrastructures for European Transborder Judicial Proceedings*, Spinger, 2014, pp. 161–183

Carnevali & Resca (2013)
D. Carnevali and A. Resca, 'The case of Trial On-Line in Italy', in F. Contini, G. F. Lanzara (eds.), *Building Interoperability for European Civil Proceedings Online*, ClueB, 2013, pp. 273–316

Carpi, Colesanti & Taruffo (2015)
F. Carpi, V. Colesanti, and M. Taruffo (dir.), *Commentario Breve al Codice di Procedura Civile*, 8th Edition, Wolters Kluwer CEDAM, 2015

Carratta (2007)
A. Carratta, 'Il procedimento ingiuntivo europeo e la "comunitarizzazione" del diritto processuale civile', *Rivista di diritto processuale*, 42(2007)6, pp. 1519–1540

Carratta (2007a)
A. Carratta, 'Il nuovo procedimento ingiuntivo europeo fra luci ed ombre', in A. Carratta (ed.), *Verso il procedimento ingiuntivo europeo*, Dott. A. Giuffrè Editore, Milano 2007, pp. 1–38

Casal (2013)
N. Casal, 'Agents de l'exécution. Attributions', *JurisClasseur Procédure civile*, Fasc. 2180, 2013

Castellaneta (2009)
M. Castellaneta, 'All'attore la possibilità di scelta tra rito europeo e il meccanismo del codice di procedura civile', *Giuda al diritto – Il sole-24 ore*, Dossier 1, 16(2009)1, pp. 66–68

Castellaneta (2009a)
M. Castellaneta, 'Un Sistema alternative alle regole interne limitato ai crediti di carattere monetario', *Giuda al diritto – Il sole-24 ore*, Dossier 1, 16(2009)1, pp. 6–9

Castellaneta (2009b)
M. Castellaneta, 'Tempi e mezzi per attivare il procedimento: in Italia per la domanda utile solo la Posta', *Giuda al diritto – Il sole-24 ore*, Dossier 1, 16(2009)1, pp. 87–99

Cataldi (2011)
M. Cataldi, 'L'opposizione all'ingiunzione europea di pagamento e la prosecuzione del procedimento: prime decisioni di meritò, *Il Corriere giuridico*, (2011)8, pp. 1129–1136

Cataldi (2009)
M. Cataldi, 'Il procedimento monitorio: le condizioni di ammissibilità', in B. Capponi (ed.), *Il procedimento d'ingiunzione*, Zanichelli Editore, 2009, pp. 75–104

Caubet (2013)
J. Caubet, 'The "Juge de proximité" in France', in E. von Bóné, *The Justice of the Peace in Europe*, Erasmus School of Law, Erasmus University Rotterdam, 2013

Cayrol (2013)
N. Cayrol, 'Référé civil', *Répertoire de procédure civile*, Dalloz, 2013C

Chainais (2010)
C. Chainais, 'L'injonction de payer française, modèle d'une protection juridictionnelle monitoire', *in Justice et droit du procès. Du légalisme procédural à l'humanisme processuel, Mélanges en l'honneur de Serge Guichard*, Dalloz 2010, pp. 621–650

Chainais & Tapie (2009)
C. Chainais and G. Tapie, 'L'injonction de payer: maniement et remaniements', *Recueil Dalloz*, 2009(13), pp. 860–862

Charlet (2013)
V. Charlet, 'La pratique de l'injonction de payer européenne: expression du talent des huissiers de justice en France?', in J. Attard, M. Dupuis et al. (eds.), *Un recouvrement de créances sans frontières?*, Larcier, 2013, pp. 29–45

Comite & Liguori (2014)
A Comite and S. Liguori (eds.), *Codice di Procedura civile esplicato*, Simone Edizioni Giuridiche, XI Edition, 2014

Constanda (2016)
A. Constanda, 'Titlul IX. Procedura ordonanței de plată', in G. Boroi (coordin.*), Noul Cod de procedură civilă. Comentariu pe articole*, Editura Hamangiu, Volume II, 2016, pp. 897–918

Constanda (2016a)
A. Constanda, 'Art. 1016. Cuprinsul cererii', in G. Boroi (coordin.), *Noul Cod de procedură civilă. Comentariu pe articole*, Editura Hamangiu, Volume II, 2016, pp. 905

Constanda (2016b)
A. Constanda, 'Art. 1018. Determinarea dobânzii', in G. Boroi (coordin.), *Noul Cod de procedură civilă. Comentariu pe articole*, Editura Hamangiu, Volume II, 2016, pp. 907–909

Constanda (2016c)
A. Constanda, 'Art. 1021. Contestarea creanței', in G. Boroi (coordin.), *Noul Cod de procedură civilă. Comentariu pe articole*, Editura Hamangiu, Volume II, 2016, pp. 912–913

Constanda (2013)
A. Constanda, 'Art. 1013. Domeniu de aplicare', in G. Boroi (coordin.), *Noul Cod de procedură civilă. Comentariu pe articole*, Editura Hamangiu, Volume II, 2013, pp. 1300–1303

Constanda (2013a)
A. Constanda, 'Art. 1016. Cuprinsul cererii', in G. Boroi (coordin.), *Noul Cod de procedură civilă. Comentariu pe articole*, Editura Hamangiu, Volume II, 2013, pp. 1304–1305

Contini (2014)
F. Contini, 'Let Agency Circulate: Architectures and Strategies for Pan-European e-Justice', in F. Contini and G. F. Lanzara (eds.), *The Circulation of Agency in E-Justice. Interoperability and Infrastructures for European Transborder Judicial Proceedings*, Spinger, 2014, pp. 331–354

Contini & Lanzara (2014)
F. Contini and G. F. Lanzara, 'Introduction: The Challenge of Interoperability and Complexity in European Civil Proceedings Online', in F. Contini and G. F. Lanzara (eds.), *The Circulation of Agency in E-Justice. Interoperability and Infrastructures for European Transborder Judicial Proceedings*, Spinger, 2014, pp. xiii-xxi

Contini & Lanzara (2009)
F. Contini and G.F. Lanzara (eds.), *ICT and Innovation in the Public Sector – European Studies in the Making of E-Government*, Palgrave, 2009

Correa Delcasso (2005)
J. P. Correa Delcasso, 'La Proposition de règlement instituant une procédure européenne d'injonction de payer', *Revue International de droit comparé*, 2005(1), pp. 144–170

Coze (2006)
H. Coze, 'Injonction de payer électronique', *Revue Procédures*, 2006(8), Commentaires 185

Crifò (2016)
C. Crifò, '"Trusted with a Muzzle and Enfranchised with a Clog": The British Approach to European Civil Procedure', in B. Hess, M. Bergström and E. Storskrubb (eds.), *EU Civil Justice Current Issues and Future Outlook*, Swedish Studies in European Law, Volume 7, Hart Publishing, 2016, pp. 81–96

Crifo (2011)
C. Crifò, 'Europeanisation, Harmonisation and Unspoken Premises; The Case of Service Rules in the Regulation on a European Small Claims Procedure (Reg. No. 861/2007), *Civil Justice Quarterly*, 30(2011)3, pp. 283–303

Crifò (2009)
C. Crifò, 'Civil Procedure in the European Order: An Overview of the Latest Developments, D. Dwyer (ed.), *The Civil Procedure Rules Ten Years On*, Oxford University Press, 2009, pp. 373–441

Crifò (2009a)
C. Crifò, *Cross-Border Enforcement of Debts in the European Union, Default Judgments, Summary Judgments and Orders for Payment*, Kluwer Law International, 2009

Crifò (2007)
C. Crifò, 'Europeanisation, Harmonisation and Unspoken Premises: The Case of Service Rules in the Regulation on a European Small Claims Procedure (Reg. No. 861/2007)', *Civil Justice Quarterly*, 30(2011)3, pp. 283–303

Crifò (2005)
C. Crifò, 'First Steps towards the Harmonisation of Civil Procedure: the Regulation creating a European Enforcement Order for Uncontested Claims', *Civil Justice Quarterly*, 24(2005)2, pp. 200–223

Cultrera (2008)
M. R. Cultrera, 'Il procedimento d'ingiunzione europeo. Le ragioni della scelta regolamentare', *Le nuove leggi civili commentate*, 2008, pp. 705–717

Cuniberti & Rueda (2016)
G. Cuniberti and I. Rueda, Commentaries to Article 41, in U. Magnus and P. Mankowski, *Brussels I bis Regulation – Commentary*, Otto Schmidt, 2nd Edition, 2016, pp. 845–849

Cuniberti, Normand & Cornette (2011)
G. Cuniberti, C. Normand, and F. Cornette, *Droit international de l'exécution. Recouvrement des créances civiles et commerciales*, L.G.D.J., 2011

Cortes Dieguez (2008)
J. P. Cortes Dieguez, 'Does the proposed European procedure enhance the resolution of small claims?', *Civil Justice Quarterly*, 27(2008)1, pp. 83–97

Cortés & Mańko (2016)
P. Cortés and R. Mańko, 'Developments in European Civil Procedures, P. Cortés (ed.), *The New Regulatory Framework for Consumer Dispute Resolution*, Oxford University Press, 2016, pp. 41–62

Couchez & Lagarde (2011)
G. Couchez and X. Lagarde, *Procédure civile*, 16th edition, Dalloz Sirey, 2011

Cupşan-Morar (2010)
D.-F. Cupşan-Morar, 'Somaţia de plată europeană. Somaţia şi ordonanţa de plată în dreptul român', *Dreptul*, (2010)3, pp. 156–177

D

D'Alessandro (2011)
E. D'Alessandro, 'Il procedimento monitorio europeo con particolare riferimento alla fase di opposizione ex. Art. 17 Reg. n. 1896/2006', *Il giusto processo civile*, (2011)3, pp. 719–738

D'Alessandro (2010)
E. D'Alessandro, 'Choosing Among the Three Regualtions Creating a European Enforcement Order (EEO Regulation, EOP Regulation, ESCP Regultion): *Practical Guidelines*', *Int'l Lis – Rivista di diritto processuale internazionale e arbitrato internazionale*, (2009/2010)1, pp. 39–50

D'Alessandro (2009)
E. D'Alessandro, 'Impugnazione lunga e breve in due fasi e possibilità di ricorrere in Cassazione', *Giuda al diritto – Il sole-24 ore*, Dossier 1, 16(2009)1, pp. 84–86

D'Alessandro (2009a)
E. D'Alessandro, 'In assenza di previsioni della disciplina comunitaria scatta il diritto del Paese nel quale c'è il processo', *Giuda al diritto – Il sole-24 ore*, Dossier 1, 16(2009)1, pp. 79–83

D'Alessandro (2008)
E. D'Alessandro, *Il procedimento uniforme per le controversie di modesta entità. Regolamento comunitario dell'11 luglio 2007, n.861*, G. Giappichelli Editore-Torino, 2008

D'Ambra (2009)
D. D'Ambra, 'Conciliation et médiation – droit interne', in S. Guinchard (dir.), *Droit et pratique de la procédure civile. Droit interne. Droit communautaire*, Dalloz Action, 6th Edition, 2009, pp. 675–689

David (2009)
A. David, 'Il procedimento europeo di ingiunzione di pagamento. L'esecuzione del titolo', *Giurisprudenza di merito*, Osservatorio sulla procedura civile, 64(2009)2, pp. 406–414

Dănăilă (2016)
V. Dănăilă, 'Art. 244 Cercetarea procesului', in G. Boroi (coordin.) *Noul Cod de procedură civilă. Comentariu pe articole*, Editura Hamangiu, Volume I, 2016, pp. 644–646

Dănăilă (2016a)
V. Dănăilă, 'Art. 1027. Caracterul alternativ', in G. Boroi (coordin.), *Noul Cod de procedură civilă. Comentariu pe articole*, Editura Hamangiu, Volume II, 2016, pp. 922–924

Dănăilă (2016b)
V. Dănăilă, 'Art.1030. Desfăşurarea procedurii', in G. Boroi (coordin.), *Noul Cod de procedură civilă. Comentariu pe articole*, Editura Hamangiu, Volume II, 2016, pp. 928–933

Dănăilă (2016c)
V. Dănăilă, 'Titlul X. Procedura cu privire la cererile cu valoare redusă', in G. Boroi (coordin.), *Noul Cod de procedură civilă. Comentariu pe articole*, Editura Hamangiu, Volume II, 2016, pp. 919–936

Défossez (2006)
M. Défossez, 'Titre exécutoire', *JurisClasseur Procédure civile*, Fasc. 345, 2006

Deleanu (2013)
I. Deleanu, *Tratat de procedură civilă*, Universul Juridic, Volume I and II, 2013

Deleanu (2013a)
I. Deleanu, 'Noua reglementare privind taxele judiciare de timbru', *Pandectele Române*, (2013)11, pp. 45–64

de Roo & Jagtenberg (1994)
A. de Roo and R. Jagtenberg, *Settling labour disputes in Europe*, Kluwer Law International, 1994

Després (2012)
I. Després (dir.), *Code de Procédure Civile*, Dalloz, 103e edition, Dalloz, 2012

Di Cola (2007)
L. Di Cola, 'L'efficacia dell'ingiunzione di pagamento europea', in A. Carratta (ed.), *Verso il procedimento ingiuntivo europeo*, Dott. A. Giuffrè Editore, Milano 2007, pp. 235–295

Didone (2010)
A. Didone, *Le ordinanze anticipatorie di condanna e il nuovo procedimento sommario*, Giuffrè Editore, 2nd Edition, 2010

Di Frederico (2012)
G. Di Frederico, 'Rappresentazione sintetica del complesso degli uffici giudiziari, delle loro relazioni funzionali e della loro dimensione organizzativa' in Giuseppe Di Frederico (ed.), *Ordinamento Giudiziario. Uffici giudiziari, CSM e governo della magistratura*, 2nd edition, CEDAM, 2012, pp. 1–12

Di Giacomo (2015)
V. Di Giacomo, *Il nuovo processo civile telematico*, Giuffrè Editore, 2015

di Napoli (2015)
E. di Napoli, 'Una concreta applicazione (fra le poche note) del procedimento europeo sulle controversie di modesta entità', Aldricus blog, 18 September 2015 (available at http://aldricus.com/2015/09/18/una-concreta-applicazione-fra-le-poche-note-del-procedimento-europeo-sulle-controversie-di-modesta-entita/)

Dinu (2013)
C. C. Dinu, *Procedura ordonanței de plată*, Universul Juridic, 2013

Dinu (2011)
C. C. Dinu, 'Procedura cu privire la cererile cu valoare redusă în contextul noului Cod de procedură civilă', *Revista Română de Drept Privat*, (2011)3, pp. 68–78

Dinu & Stanciu (2015)
M. Dinu and R. Stanciu, *Executarea silită în noul Cod de procedură civilă*, Editura Hamangiu, 2015

Dockers (2010)
K. Dockers, 'Het Europees Betalingsbevel EBB - De praktijk en de visie van de gerechtsdeurwaarder', *Tijdschrift voor Internationaal Privaatrecht*, 9(2010)2, pp. 111–121

Douchy-Odot (2013)
M. Douchy-Oudot, 'Médiation et conciliation', *Répertoire de procédure civile Dalloz*, 2013

Douchy-Odot (2013a)
M. Douchy-Oudot, 'Jugement par défaut et opposition', *JurisClasseur Procédure civile*, Fasc. 540, 2013

Douchy-Oudot (2012)
M. Douchy-Oudot, 'Tribunal d'instance. Compétence', *JurisClasseur Procédure civile*, Fasc. 320, 2012

Douchy-Oudot (2012a)
M. Douchy-Oudot, 'Tribunal d'instance. Procédure', *JurisClasseur Procédure civile*, Fasc. 330, 2012

Douchy-Odot (2008)
M. Douchy-Oudot, 'La force exécutoire à dimension européenne', *Revue Procédures*, 2008(8), pp. 14–18

Duagi (2013)
G. Duagi, 'Executarea creanţelor în spaţiul intra-comunitar', *Revista de drept commercial*, (2013)3, pp. 56–62

F

Fabri & Contini (2003)
M. Fabri and F. Contini, *Judicial Electronic Data Interchange In Europe: Applications, Policies and Trends*, Lo Scarabeo, Bologna, 2003

Fabri & Contini (2001)
M. Fabri and F. Contini, *Justice and technology in Europe: How ICT is changing the judicial business*, Kluwer Law Intl, 2001

Farina (2012)
M. Farina, *Titoli esecutivi europei ed esecuzione forzata in Italia*, Aracne Editrice, 2012

Fattaccini (2009)
C. Fattaccini, 'Pourvoi en cassation', in S. Guinchard (dir.), *Droit et pratique de la procédure civile. Droit interne. Droit communautaire*, Dalloz Action, 6th Edition, 2009, pp. 1320–1377

Fauvarque-Cosson & Behar-Touchais (2012)
B. Fauvarque-Cosson and M. Behar-Touchais, *Mise en œuvre des instruments optionnels européens en droit privé*, Collection Trans Europe Experts, Volume 5, 2012

Fauvarque-Cosson & Behar-Touchais (2012a)
B. Fauvarque-Cosson and M. Behar-Touchais, Implementation of Optional Instruments within European Civil Law, Study, European Parliament, Directorate-General for Internal Policies, January 2012, PE462.425

Fauvarque-Cosson & Fournier (2012)
B. Fauvarque-Cosson and A. Fournier, 'France' in J. M. Smits (ed.), *Elgar Encyclopedia of Comparative Law*, 2nd Edition, Edward Elgar Publishing Limited, 2012, pp. 344–348

Ferrand (2010)
F. Ferrand, 'La procédure européenne de règlement des petits litiges, concurrente des procédures nationales? Comparaison avec les procédures française et allemande', *Supplément de Droit et procédures, Actes du VIIIe colloque Droit et Procédures*, Partie II, 63(2010)10

Ferrand (2005)
F. Ferrand, 'Injonction de payer européenne', *Derecho del comercio intenacional. Temas y actualidades, Litigio judicial international*, 2005, pp. 880–893

Ferrand (2005a)
F. Ferrand, 'Mahnverfahren Allemande, Injonction de payer Française et projets Communautaires: Remarques Comparatives', in B. Bachmann, S. Breidenbach et al. (eds.), *Grenzüberschreitungen Beiträge zum Internationalen Verfahrensrecht und zur Schiedsgerichtsbarkeit. Festschrift für Peter Schlosser zum 70. Geburtstag*, Mohr Siebeck, 2005, pp. 175–195

Ferrand (2001)
F. Ferrand, 'La procédure d'injonction de payer en droit français', in W. H. Rechberger and G. E. Kodek (eds.), *Order for Payment in the European Union/ Mahnverfahren in der Europäischen Union/ L'Injonction de Payer dans l'Union Européenne*, Kluwer Law International, 2001, pp. 131–143

Finocchiaro (2009)
G. Finocchiaro, 'Con l'introduzione delle norme processuali uniche fatto un balzo in avanti per l'armonizzazione europea', *Giuda al diritto – Il sole-24 ore*, Dossier 1, 16(2009)1, pp. 21–64

Fiorini (2008)
A. Fiorini, 'Facilitating Cross-Border Debt Recovery – The European Order for Payment and Small Claims Regulations', *International and Comparative Law Quarterly*, 57(2008)2, pp. 449–465

Florescu (2013)
G. Florescu, *Somaţia europeană de plată. Analiza unor probleme practice prin prisma dispoziţiilor Noului Cod de Procedură Civilă*, 2013 (available at www.euroquod.ro/ue/files/pubs/somatie2013.pdf)

Fodor & Popa (2013)
M. Fodor and S. Popa, 'Procedura ordonanţei de plată în reglementarea Noului Cod de procedură civilă', *Dreptul*, (2013)3, pp. 80–107

Foulon & Strickler (2011)
M. Foulon and Y. Strickler, 'Le décret n° 2011–1043 du 1er septembre 2011 et la procédure en la forme des référés', *Recueil Dalloz*, 39 (2011), pp. 2668–2672

Fradeani (2007)
F. Fradeani, 'I presupposti per la concessione dell'ingiunzione di pagamento europea', in A. Carratta (ed.), *Verso il procedimento ingiuntivo europeo*, Dott. A. Giuffrè Editore, Milano 2007, pp. 119–170

Fricero (2012)
N. Fricero, 'Procédure civile', *Recueil Dalloz*, 4 (2012)

Frenţiu (2014)
G. C. Frenţiu, 'Unele consideraţii referitoare la cererea de apel potrivit noului Cod de procedură civilă şi altor acte normative recente', *Dreptul*, (2014)4, pp. 21–32

Frenţiu & Băldean (2013)
G. C. Frenţiu and D.-L. Băldean, *Noul Cod de procedură civilă comentat şi adnotat*, Editura Hamangiu, 2013

G

Gavriş (2016)
D. M. Gavriş, 'Art. 626. Rolul statului în executarea silită', in G. Boroi (coordin.), *Noul Cod de procedură civilă. Comentariu pe articole*, Editura Hamangiu, Volume II, 2016, pp. 354-356

Gavriş (2016a)
D. M. Gavriş, 'Art. 670. Cheltuieli de executare', in G. Boroi (coordin.), *Noul Cod de procedură civilă. Comentariu pe articole*, Editura Hamangiu, Volume II, 2016, pp. 435-439

Gavriş (2016b)
D. M. Gavriş, 'Art. 712. Condiţii de admisibilitate', in G. Boroi (coordin.), *Noul Cod de procedură civilă. Comentariu pe articole*, Editura Hamangiu, Volume II, 2016, pp. 489-493

Gerardo & Mutarelli (2011)
M. Gerardo and A. Mutarelli, *Procedimento sommario di cognizione ex art. 702bis c.p.c.: primo bilancio operativo*, 1 July 2011 (available at www.judicium.it/wp-content/uploads/saggi/201/Gerardo-Mutarelli.pdf)

van Gerven (1995)
W. van Gerven, 'Bridging the Gap between Community and National Laws: towards a Principle of Homogeneity in the field of Legal Remedies?', *Common Market Law Review*, 32(1995), pp. 679–702

Ghera (2012)
T. Ghera, 'La dématérialisation des procédures judiciaires au sein de l'Union européenne, vecteur de transcendance des particularismes nationaux. Synthèse du rapport de la Commission dématérialisation des procédures judiciaires, Institut sur l'évolution des professions juridiques (IEPJ)', *Droit et procédures*, 65(2012)11, pp. 279–286

Gheorghe (2013)
C. Gheorghe, 'Discuţii privind procedura specială a ordonanţei de plată în reglementarea noului Cod de procedură civilă', *Dreptul*, (2013)3, pp. 35–43

Glyn Watkin (1997)
T. Glyn Watkin, *The Italian Legal Tradition*, Ashgate Dartmouth, 1997

Graziadei (2006)
M. Graziadei, 'Comparative Law as the Study of Transplants and Receptions', in M. Reimann and R. Zimmermann (eds.), *The Oxford Handbook of Comparative Law*, Oxford University Press, 2006, pp. 441–476

Graziosi (2011)
C. Graziosi, 'Alcuni tratti pratici dell'ingiunzione di pagamento europea', *Rivista trimestrale di diritto e procedura civile*, 65(2011)1, pp. 229–255

Gruau (2013)
Brandine Gruau, 'Recouvrement de créance', *Bulletin des Transport et de la Logistique*, (2013)3450

Guez (2012)
P. Guez, 'Tribunal de commerce. Compétence des tribunaux de commerce. Règles générales', *JurisClasseur Procédure civile*, Fasc. 401, 2012

Guinchard (2016)
E. Guinchard, 'Réforme législative adoptée pour le règlement RPL et réforme jurisprudentielle à venir pour le règlement IPE?', *Revue trimestrielle de droit européen*, (2016)2, pp. 435–446

Guinchard (2015)
E. Guinchard, 'Cour de justice, 3e ch., 4 septembre 2014, eco cosmetics GmbH & Co. KG c/ Virginie Laetitia Barbara Dupuy et Raiffeisenbank St. Georgen reg. Gen. mbH c/ Tetyana Bonchyk, aff. Jointes C-119/13 et C-120/13, ECLI:EU:C:2014:2144', in F. Picod (dir.), *Jurisprudence de la CJUE 2014. Décisions et commentaires*, Bruylant, 2015, pp. 873–881

Guinchard (2014)
E. Guinchard, Vers une réforme faussement technique du règlement RPL et superficielle du règlement IPE?', *Revue trimestrielle de droit européen*, (2014)2, pp. 479–485

Guinchard (2013)
E. Guinchard, 'Le règlement des petits litiges: un premier bilan plutôt décevant', in J. Attard, M. Dupuis et al. (eds.), *Un recouvrement de Créances sans Frontières?*, Larcier, 2013, pp. 65–91

Guinchard (2013a)
E. Guinchard, 'Première jurisprudence européenne sur la première procédure civile européenne', *Revue trimestrielle de droit européen*, 2013(2), pp. 335–338

Guinchard (2012)
E. Guinchard, 'Règlement (CE) n° 1896/2006 du Parlement européen et du Conseil du 12 décembre 2006 instituant une procédure européenne d'injonction de payer', in G. de Leval and J. F. van Drooghenbroeck (eds.), *La jurisprudence du code judiciaire commentée, Droit judiciaire européen et international*, Volum V, La Charte, 2012, pp. 559–588

Guinchard (2010)
E. Guinchard, 'L'injonction de payer européenne à la recherche de son succès', *Supplément de Droit et Procédures, Actes du VIIIe colloque Droit et Procédures*, Partie II, 2010, 63(10), pp. 46–50

Guinchard (2008)
E. Guinchard, 'L'Europe, la procédure civile et le créancier: l'injonction de payer européenne et la procédure européenne de règlement des petits litiges', *Revue trimestrielle de droit commercial*, 2008(3), pp. 465–483

Guinchard (2007)
E. Guinchard, 'La procédure civile européenne est née. Vive le créancier! Présentation de l'injonction de payer européenne et de la procédure pour les demandes de faible importance', in G. de Leval and F. Georges (eds.), *Le droit judiciaire en mutation. En hommage à Alphonse Kohl*, Anthémis, 2007, pp. 8–16

Guinchard (2006)
E. Guinchard, 'Commentaire sur la proposition de règlement instituant une injonction de payer européenne', *Les Petites Affiches*, 2006 (98), pp. 4–17

Guinchard, Chainais & Ferrand (2012)
S. Guinchard, C. Chainais, and F. Ferrand, *Procédure civile. Droit interne et droit de l'Union européenne*, 31e edition, Dalloz Précis, 2012

Guzzi (2006)
S. Guzzi, 'La proposta di regolamento istituente il procedimento di ingiunzione europeo: prime osservazioni', *Diritto del commercio internazionale*, (2006)1, pp. 137–155

H

Haibach (2005)
G. Haibach, 'The Commission Proposal for a Regulation Establishing a European Small Claims Procedure: An Analysis', *European Review of Private Law*, (2005)4, pp. 593–601

Haye & Prevett (2003)
N. Haye and G. Prevett, 'England and Wales', in S. R. Grubbs (ed.), *International Civil Procedure*, World Law Group Member Firms, Kluwer Law International, 2003, pp. 179–200

Hazelhorst (2016)
M. Hazelhorst, *Free Movement of Civil Judgments in the European Union and the Right to a Fair Trial*, Thesis Erasmus School of Law, 2016/ Free Movement of Civil Judgments in the European Union and the Right to a Fair Trial, Springer Asser Press, 2017

Hérons & Le Bars (2012)
J. Hérons and T. Le Bars, *Droit judiciaire privé*, 5th edition, Montchretien, 2012

Hess (2017)
B. Hess (Scientific Coord.), *An Evaluation Study of National Procedural Laws and Practices in Terms of their Impact on the Free Circulation of Judgments and on the Equivalence and Effectiveness of the Procedural Protection of Consumers under EU Consumer Law*, Mutual Trust and Free Circulation of Judgments, Stand 1, JUST/2014/RCON/PR/CIVI/0082, 2017

Hess (2016)
B. Hess, 'The State of Civil Justice Union', in B. Hess, M. Bergström and E. Storskrubb (eds.), *EU Civil Justice. Current issues and Future Outlook*, Hart Publishing, 2016, pp. 1–19

Hess (2016a)
B. Hess, *Harmonized Rules and Minimum Standards in the European Law of Civil Procedure, In-Depth Analysis for the Juri Committee*, European Parliament, PE 556.971, 2016

Hess (2013)
B. Hess, 'The European Small Claims Procedure in the Context of the European Law of Civil Procedure', *Le temps et le droit, Hommage au Professeur Closset-Marchal*, Bruylant, 2013, pp. 267–281

Hess (2012)
B. Hess, 'Procedural Harmonisation in a European Context', in X. E. Kramer and C.H. van Rhee (eds.), *Civil Litigation in a Globalising World*, The Hague: Asser Press, 2012, pp. 159–174

Hess (2005)
B. Hess, 'Comparative Analysis of the National Reports', M. Andenas, B. Hess and P. Oberhammer (eds.), *Enforcement Agency Practice in Europe*, British Institute of International and Comparative Law, 2005, pp. 25–46

Hess & Raffelsieper (2015)
B. Hess and K. Raffelsieper, 'Debtor protection within Regulation 1896/2006: Current gaps in European procedural law', *Praxis des Internationalen Privat- und Verfahrensrechts* (IPRax), (2015)5, pp. 46–51

Hodges (2014)
C. Hodges, 'Collective Redress: A Breakthrough or a *Damp Squibb*?', *Journal of Consumer Policy* (2014) 37, pp. 67–89

Hodges (2016)
C. Hodges, 'Consumer Redress: Implementing the Vision', *University of Leicester School of Law Research Paper* No. 16-27, 2016, section A

Hodges (2016a)
C. Hodges, 'Proposed Modernisation of Courts in England & Wales: IT and the Online Court', *International Journal of Procedural Law*, 6(2016)1, pp. 149–163

Hoonakker (2012)
P. Hoonakker, *Procédures civiles d'exécution. Voies d'exécution. Procédures de distribution*, Larcier, 2012

I

Idot (2013)
L. Idot, 'Compléments susceptibles d'être apportés au formulaire d'injonction de payer', Note 108, *Europe*, 23(2013)2

J

Jackson (2010)
Sir R. Jackson, *Review of Civil Litigation Costs*, Final Report, 2010

James (2009)
M. James, *Litigation with a Foreign Aspect. A Practical Guide*, Oxford University Press, 2009

Jeuland (2007)
E. Jeuland, 'La procédure européenne d'injonctiond e payer est arrivée', *La Semaine Juridique*, Edition générale, Droit judiciaire privé, 139, (2007)14, pp. 22–27

Jeuland & Manin (2004)
E. Jeuland and F. Manin, 'Les incertitudes du référé injonction de faire en droit de sociétés', *Revue sociétés*, 2004(1), pp. 1–17

Juilon (2009)
J. Juillon, 'Appel', in S. Guinchard (dir.), *Droit et pratique de la procédure civile. Droit interne. Droit communautaire*, Dalloz Action, 6th Edition, 2009

Juilon (2009a)
J. Juillon, 'Opposition', in S. Guinchard (dir.), Droit et pratique de la procédure civile. Droit interne. Droit communautaire, Dalloz Action, 6th Edition, 2009

Jolowicz (2001)
J. A. Jolowicz, 'Order for Payment: English Law', in W. H. Rechberger and G. E. Kodek (eds.), *Orders for Payment in the European Union/Mahnverfahren in de Europäischen Union/ L'Injonction de Payer dans l'Union Européene*, Kluwer Law International, 2001, pp. 115–120

Jolowicz (2000)
J.A. Jolowicz, *On Civil Procedure*, Cambridge University Press, 2000

Jolowicz (1992)
J. A. Jolowicz, 'Vue générale du droit anglais', in J. A. Jolowicz (ed.), *Droit Anglais*, 2e edition, Précis Dalloz, 1992, pp. 1–17

K

Kačevska (2012)
Kačevska et al., *Practical Application of European Union Regulations relating to European Union Level Procedures in Civil Cases: the Experience in Baltic States*, No. TM 2012/04/EK, Riga, Vilnius, Talin, 2012

Kay (2015)
Maurice Kay (ed.-in-chief), *Blackstone's Civil Practice* ('Blackstone's Civil Practice 2015'), Oxford University Press, 2015

Kramer (2017)
X. E. Kramer 'Judicial cooperation in civil matters', in F. Amtenbrink, D. Curtin, B. de Witte, P. J. Kuijper, A. McDonnell, S. Van den Bogaert (eds.), *Law of the European Union*, Kluwer International Law (forthcoming 2017)

Kramer (2016)
X. E. Kramer, 'Access to Justice and Technology: Transforming the Face of Cross-Border Civil Litigation and Adjudication in the EU', in K. Benyekhlef, J. Bailey, J. Burkell and F. Gélinas (eds.), *eAccess to Justice*, University of Ottawa Press, 2016, pp. 351–375

Kramer (2016a)
X. E. Kramer, 'European Procedures on Debt Collection: Nothing or Noting? Experiences and Future Prospects', in B. Hess, M. Bergström, and E. Storskrubb (eds.), *EU Civil Justice: Current Issues and Future Outlook*, Hart Publishing, Oxford, 2016, pp. 97–121

Kramer (2015)
X. E. Kramer, Commentaries to Articles 39–44 in A. Dickinson and E. Lein (eds.), *The Brussels I Regulation Recast*, Oxford University Press, 2015, pp. 417–420

Kramer (2014)
X. E. Kramer, 'The Structure of Civil Proceedings and why it matters: exploratory observations on future ELI-Unidroit European Rules of Civil Procedure', *Uniform Law Review*, 19(2014), pp. 218–238

Kramer (2013)
X. E. Kramer, *Procedural Matters. Construction and Deconstructivism in European Civil Procedure*, Erasmus Law Lecures 33, Eleven International Publishing, 2013

Kramer (2011)
X. E. Kramer, 'Small Claim, Simple Recovery? The European Small Claims Procedure and its Implementation in the Member States', *ERA Forum* (2011)12, pp. 119–133

Kramer (2011a)
X. E. Kramer, 'Abolition of the exequatur under the Brussels I Regulation: effecting and protecting rights in the European judicial area', *Nederlands Internationaal Privaatrecht*, (2011)4, pp. 633–641

Kramer (2010)
X. E. Kramer, 'Enhancing Enforcement in the European Union. The European Order for Payment and its Implementation in the Member States, particularly in Germany, the Netherlands and England', C.H. van Rhee and A. Uzelac (eds.), *Enforcement and Enforceability: Tradition and Reform*, Intersentia, 2010, pp. 17–39

Kramer (2008)
X. E. Kramer: 'The European Small Claims procedure: Striking the Balance Between Simplicity and Fairness in European Litigation', *Zeitschift für Europäisches Privatrecht*, (2008)2, pp. 355–373

Kramer (2008a)
X. E. Kramer, 'A Major Step in Harmonization of Procedural Law in Europe: The European Small Claims Procedure. Accomplishments, New Features and Some Fundamental Questions of European Harmonization', in A.W. Jongbloed (ed.), *The XIIIth World Congress of Procedural Law: The Belgian and Dutch Reports*, Intersentia, 2008, pp. 253–283

Kramer (2007)
X. E. Kramer, *Eenvormige Europese procedures voor de inning van vorderingen. De Europese betalingsbevelprocedure en de Europese procedure voor geringe vorderingen*, Kluwer Deventer, 2007

Kramer & Kakiuchi (2015)
X. Kramer and S. Kakiuchi, Relief in Small and Simple Matters in an Age of Austerity, *General Report for the XV World Congress of Procedural Law*, 2015, pp. 121–225 (http://papers.ssrn.com/sol3/papers.cfm?abstract_id=2610773)

Kramer & Onţanu (2014)
X. E. Kramer and E. A. Onţanu, 'The Dutch Perspective on Cross-Border Small Claims Litigation: Guarded Optimism and Pragmatism. A Normative and Empirical Approach', in N. Neuwhal and S. Hammamoun, *The European Small Claim Procedure and the Philosophy of Small Change/ La procedure européenne des petites créances ou la gestion d'un changement progressif*, Les Éditions Thémis, 2014, pp. 7–35

Kramer & Onţanu (2013)
X. E. Kramer, E. A. Onţanu, 'The functioning of the European Small Claims Procedure in the Netherlands: normative and empirical reflections', *Nederlands Internationaal Privaatrecht* (NIPR), 2013(3), pp. 319–328

Kramer & Sujecki (2006)
X. E. Kramer and B. Sujecki, 'De Europese betalingsbevelprocedure. Een kritische beschouwing', *Nederlands International Privaatrecht*, 2006, pp. 1–8

Kramer, Tuil, Tillema, Hazelhorst & Onţanu (2012)
X. E. Kramer, M. L. Tuil, I. Tillema, M. I. Hazelhorst, E. A. Onţanu, *Verkrijging van een executoriale titel in incassozaken*, WODC, Ministerie van Veiligheid & Justitie, 2012 (available at www.wodc.nl/onderzoeksdatabase/executoriale-titel.aspx)

Kunda & Gonçalvse de Melo Marinho (2010)
I. Kunda and C. M. Gonçalvse de Melo Marinho, *Practical Handbook on European Private International Law', Improving the knowledge on new EU regulations of the members of the national Judiciary networks in civil and commercial matters in the MS of the EU Project*, Civil Justice Programme 2010

L

Laboragine (2011)
O. Laboragine, 'Procedimento sommario di cognizione: prime esperienze applicative', *Foro italiano*, 2011, V, c.59

Lacabarats (2009)
A. Lacabarats, 'Référé' in S. Guinchard (dir.), *Droit et pratique de la procédure civile. Droit interne. Droit communautaire*, Dalloz Action, 6th Edition, 2009, pp. 652–665

Larionescu & Trantea (2009)
L. C. Larionescu and G. Trantea, 'Notele scrise şi principiul contradictorialităţii', *Curierul Judiciar*, (2009)12, pp. 692–699

Lauvergnat (2013)
L. Lauvergnat, 'Requête en injonction de payer devant le président du tribunal de grande instance', *Revue Procédures*, (March) 2013, pp. 35–36

Lawless, Robbennolt & Ulen (2010)
R. M. Lawless, J. K. Robbennolt, and T. S. Ulen, *Empirical Methods in Law*, Aspen Publishers, 2010

Leandro (2009)
A. Leandro, 'Il procedimento europeo per le controversie di modesta entità', *Rivista di diritto internazionale*, (2009)1, pp. 65–93

Lebeau (2012)
D. Lebeau, 'Tribunal de commerce. Procédure ordinaire. Introduction de l'instance', *JurisClasseur Procédure civile*, Fasc. 410, 2012

Legros (2007)
C. Legros, 'Commentaire du règlement CE n° 1896/2006 instituant une procédure d'injonction de payer européenne', *Les Petites Affiches*, 2007(151), pp. 8–15

Leş (2015)
I. Leş, *Noul Cod de procedură civilă, Comentariu pe articole*, 2nd Edition, Editura C.H. Beck, 2015

Leş (2014)
I. Leş, *Tratat de drept procedural civil. Principii şi instituţii generale. Judecata în faţa primei instanţe*, Universul Juridic, Volume I, 2014

Leş (2009)
I. Leş, 'Cererea de chemare în judecată în unele reglementări comunitare', *Curierul Judiciar*, (2009)1, pp. 24–27

Leş (2009a)
I. Leş, 'Reglementări naţionale şi comunitare privitoare la soluţionarea cererilor cu valoare redusă', *Revista Română de Drept Privat*, (2009), pp. 13–28

Leş & Spinei (2013)
I. Leş and S. Spinei, 'Reprezentarea şi asistarea părţilor prin avocat sau consilier juridic în lumina Noului Cod de procedură civilă', *Dreptul*, 5(2013), pp. 13–17

de Leval (1998)
G. de Leval, *Subject of the proceedings, The execution of court decisions in civil cases*, Council of Europe Publishing, September 1998

de Leval (1996)
G. de Leval, 'Une harmonisation des procédures d'exécution dans l'Union européenne est-elle concevable?', *Civil Procedure in Europe*, Kluwer, 1996, pp. 595–626

Lewis (2006)
P. Lewis, 'The consumer's court? Revising the theory of the small claims procedure', *Civil Justice Quarterly*, 25(2006)1, pp. 52–69

Linton (2016)
M. Linton, 'Abolishing of Exequatur, All in the Nature of Mutual Trust!', in B. Hess, M. Bergström and E. Storskrubb (eds.), *EU Civil Justice. Current issues and Future Outlook*, Hart Publishing, 2016, pp. 257–282

Lombardini (2008)
I. Lombardini, 'Verso l'armonizzazione del diritto processuale civile nell'Unione europea: il procedimento europeo d'ingiunzione di pagamento (Regolamento CE n. 1896 del 2006)', *Studium iuris*, 14(2008)1, pp. 18–26

Lopez de Tejada (2014)
M. Lopez de Tejada, 'Effets d'une opposition à l'injonction de payer européenne', *Revue critique de droit international privé*, (2014)1, pp. 135–145

Lopez de Tejada & d'Avout (2007)
M. Lopez de Tejada and L. d'Avout, 'Les non-dits de la procédure européenne d'injonction de payer', *Revue critique de droit international privé*, 2007, 96(4), pp. 717–748

Loznean (2015)
V. Loznean, 'Procedura ordonanţei de plată', in I. Leş (coord.), *Tratat de drept procesual civil*, Volume II, Editura Universul Juridic, 2015, pp. 380–396

Loznean (2015a)
V. Loznean, 'Procedura cu privire la cererile cu valoare redusă', in I. Leş (coord.), *Tratat de drept procesual civil*, Volume II, Editura Universul Juridic, 2015, pp. 397–405

Lucaciuc (2014)
S. I. Lucaciuc, *Contestaţia la executare în reglementarea noului Cod de procedură civilă*, Editura Hamangiu, 2014

Lupoi (2014)
M. A. Lupoi, *Civil Procedure in Italy*, Wolters Kluwer Law & Business, 2014

Lupoi (2012)
M. A. Lupoi, *Civil Procedure in Italy*, Wolters Kluwer Law & Business, 2012

Lupoi (2012a)
M. A. Lupoi, 'Recent developments in Italian Civil Procedure', *Civil Procedure Review*, (2012)1, pp. 25–51

Lupoi (2011)
M. A. Lupoi, 'Civil Enforcement in Italy: A Comparative Perspective', in R. Stürner and M. Kawano (eds.), *Comparative Studies on Enforcement and Provisional Measures*, Mohr Siebeck, 2011, pp. 90–101

Lupoi (2010)
M. A. Lupoi, 'Art. 3. (Controversie transfrontaliere)', in P. Biavati (ed.), 'Reg. CE N. 1896/2006 del Parlamento Europeo e del Consiglio che Istituiesce un Procedimento Europeo d'Ingiunzione di Pagamento. Commentario a cura di Paolo Biavati', *Le Nuove Leggi Civile Commentate*, CEDAM, (2010)2

Lupoi (2010a)
M. A. Lupoi, 'Art. 21 (Esecutione)', in P. Biavati (ed.), 'Reg. CE N. 1896/2006 del Parlamento Europeo e del Consiglio che Istituiesce un Procedimento Europeo d'Ingiunzione di Pagamento. Commentario a cura di Paolo Biavati', *Le Nuove Leggi Civile Commentate*, CEDAM, (2010)2, pp. 456–458

Lupoi (2010b)

M. A. Lupoi, 'Art. 22 (Rifiuto dell'esecuzione)', in P. Biavati (ed.), 'Reg. CE N. 1896/2006 del Paralamento europeo e del Consiglio che istitutisce un procedimento europeo d'ingiunzione di pagamento', *Le Nuovo Leggi Civili Commentate*, 33(2010)2, pp. 458–461

Lupoi (2010c)

M. A. Lupoi, 'Art. 23 (Limitazione o sospensione dell'esecuzione)', in P. Biavati (ed.), 'Reg. CE N. 1896/2006 del Paralamento europeo e del Consiglio che istitutisce un procedimento europeo d'ingiunzione di pagamento', *Le Nuovo Leggi Civili Commentate*, 33(2010)2, pp. 461–463

Lupoi (2010d)

M. A. Lupoi, *Sommario* (ma non troppo), 23 July 2010, point 3 (available at pwww.judicium.it/wp-content/uploads/saggi/106/Lupoi.pdf)

Lupoi (2008)

M. A. Lupoi, 'Di crediti non contestati e procedimento di ingiunzione: le ultime tappe dell'armonizzazione processuale in Europa', *Rivista trimestrale di diritto e procedura civile*, 62(2008)1, pp. 171–206

M

Madge (2004)

N. Madge, 'Small claims in the county court', *Civil Justice Quarter*ly, 23(2004)3, pp. 201–224

Mandrioli & Carratta (2015)

C. Mandrioli and A. Carratta, *Diritto Processuale Civile. L'esecuzione forzara. I procedimenti sommari, cautelari e camerali*, 24th Edition, G. Giappichelli Editore, Volume IV, 2015

Mandrioli & Carratta (2014)

C. Mandrioli and A. Carratta, *Diritto processuale civile, Il processo ordinario di cognizione*, G. Giappichelli Editore-Torino, 24th Edition, Volume II, 2014

Mańko (2015)

R. Mańko, *Europeanisation of civil procedure. Towards common minimum standards?, In-depth Analysis*, European Parliament Research Service, June 2015

Mańko (2014)

R. Mańko, *European Small Claims Procedure. Legal analysis of the Commission's proposal to remedy weaknesses in the current system*, European Parliamentary Research Service, June 2015, PE559.499

Marinelli (2009)

M. Marinelli, 'Note sul Regolamento CE n. 1896/2006 in tema di procedimento ingiuntivo europeo', in V. Colesanti, C. Consolo, G. Gaja and F. Tommaseo (eds.), *Il diritto processuale civile nell'avvicinamento giuridico internazionale. Omaggio ad Aldo Attardi*, Cleup, 2009, Tomo I, pp. 579–606

Măstăcăneanu (2012)

A. Măstăcăneanu, *Cererile cu valoare redusă în NCPC. Prezentare generală*, published on 12 August 2012 (available online on www.juridice.ro)

Marchand (2011)
X. Marchand, 'Recours en révision. Procédure', *JurisClasseur Procédure civile*, Fasc. 747, 2011

Mellone (2014)
M. Mellone, 'Les procédures européennes pour les petits litiges et pour l'ordre de paiement et les moyens informatiques de communication: la perspective italienne', in N. Neuwahl and S. Hammamoun (eds.), *The European Small Claims Procedure and the Philosophy of Small Change (La procédure européenne des petites créances ou la gestion d'un changement progressif)*, Les Éditions Thémis, 2014, pp. 79–102

Mellone (2014a)
M. Mellone, 'L'onere della notifica nell'ingiunzione di pagamento europea: il difficile rapporto tra modello processuale europeo e norme nazionali', *Il Diritto dell'Unione Europea*, (2014)2, pp. 273–292

Mellone (2014b)
M. Mellone, 'Legal Interoperability in Europe: An Assessment of the European Payment Order and the European Small Claims Procedure' in F. Contini and G. F. Lanzara (eds.), *The Circulation of Agency in e-Justice: Interoperability and Infrastructure for European Transborder Judicial Proceedings*, Springer, 2014, pp. 254–264

Mellone (2012)
M. Mellone, 'Legal interoperability: the case of the European Payment Order and of European Small Claims Procedure', *Building Interoperability for European Civil Proceedings Online*, Research Conference-Bologna, 15–16 June 2012 (available at www.irsig.cnr.it/BIEPCO/documents/case_studies/EuropeanSmallClaim_Mellone.pdf)

Mellone & Pancaldi (2008)
M. Mellone and A. Pancaldi, 'Il nuovo regolamento comunitario sulle controversie di modesta entità', *Il Diritto dell'Unione europea*, 13(2008)2, pp. 281–317

Miguet (2012)
J. Miguet (updated by O. Staes), 'Procédure d'injonction de payer', *JurisClasseur Procédure civile*, Fasc. 990, 2012

Miguet (2012a)
J. Miguet, 'Procedure d'injonction de faire', *JurisClasseur Procédure civile*, Fasc. 991, 2012

Milan (2009)
D. Milan, 'L'ingiunzione di pagamento europea', in A. Bonomi (ed.), *Diritto internazionale privato e cooperazione giudiziaria in materia civile*, G. Giappichelli Editore-Torino, 2009, pp. 293–343

Milan (2009a)
D. Milan, 'Il procedimento europeo per le controversie di modesta entità', in A. Bonomi (ed.), *Diritto internazionale privato e cooperazione giudiziaria in materia civile*, G.Giappichelli Editore-Torino, 2009, pp. 65–93

Milan (2006)
D. Milan, 'Prime riflessioni sul regolamento comunitario sull'ingiunzione di pagamento europea', *Il foro padano*, 62 (2006), pp. 157–172

Mondini (2014)
A. Mondini, 'Il regolamento europeo d'ingiunzione di pagamento al vaglio della Corte di Giustizia', Giurisprudenza comunitaria e straniera, *Il Foro Italiano*, Parte Quarta, 2014, pp. 271–283

Mondini (2009)
A. Mondini, 'Con l'opposizione al decreto ingiuntivo europeo la causa prosegue seguendo il rito ordinario – Trascurata la posizione del creditore che non ha facoltà di integrare l'istanza', *Giuda la diritto – Il Sole-24 Ore*, (2009)46, pp. 41–59

Moţiu (2009)
F. A. Moţiu, 'Somaţia europeană de plată – o nouă provocare pentru jurişti', *Pandectele Române*, (2009)2, pp. 17–28

Moţiu (2009a)
F. A. Moţiu, 'Reexaminare somaţiei europene de plată', *Pandectele Române*, (2009)6, pp. 9–17

Moţiu (2009b)
F. A. Moţiu, 'Opoziţia la somaţia europeană de plată', *Pandectele Române*, (2009)3, pp. 67–77

Munoz-Perez & Sommer (2013)
B. Munoz-Perez and J.-M. Sommer, 'L'injonction de faire: une procédure efficace?', *Infostat Justice. Bulletin d'information statistique*, (2013)120

N

Negrilă (2016)
C. Negrilă, Art. 466. Apelul principal. Obiectul', in G. Boroi (coordin.), *Noul Cod de procedură civilă. Comentariu pe articole*, Editura Hamangiu, Volume II, 2016, pp. 36–37

Negri (2012)
M. Negri, 'Art. 186-bis-Ordinanza per il pagamento di somme non contestate', in L. P. Comoglio, C. Consolo, B. Sassani and R. Vaccarella (eds.), *Commentario del Codice di Procedura Civile*, III, Tomo primo, 2012, pp. 386

Negri (2012a)
M. Negri, 'Art. 186-ter-Instanza di ingiunzione', in L. P. Comoglio, C. Consolo, B. Sassani, and R. Vaccarella (eds.), *Commentario del Codice di Procedura Civile*, III, Tomo primo, 2012, pp. 428–429

Nelken (2002)
D. Nelken, 'Legal Transplants and Beyond: Of Disciplines and Metaphors', in A. Harding and E. Örücü (eds.), *Comparative Law in the 21st Century*, Kluwer Law International, 2002, pp. 29–34

Ng (2012)
G. Y. Ng, 'European Payment Order and European Small Claim Online Simulation UK-Italy, *Building Interoperability for European Civil*, Conference Bologna, 15–16 June 2012 (available at www.irsig.cnr.it/BIEPCO/documents/case_studies/EPO_Simulation_Gar_Yein.pdf)

Neuberger (2012)
Lord Neuberger, *Docketing: Completing Case Management's Unfinished Revolution*, Ninth Lecture in Implementation Programme, London, 9 February 2012

Niboyet (2008)
M.-L. Niboyet, '2006–2007: normalisation et nouveau souffle de la communautarisation', *Chroniques, Jurisprudence & Législation, Droit et patrimoine*, 2008 (167), pp. 100–112

Nicolì (2012)
A. Nicolì, 'Gli organi giudicanti' in G. Di Frederico (ed.), *Ordinamento Giudiziario. Uffici giudiziari, CSM e governo della magistratura*, 2nd edition, CEDAM, 2012, pp. 13–120

Nioche (2011)
M. Nioche, 'Règlement (CE) n° 861/2007 du 11 juillet 2007 instituant une procédure européenne de règlement des petits litiges', in L. Cadiet, E. Jeuland, and S. Amrani-Mekki (eds.), *Droit processuel civil de l'Union européenne*, LexisNexis, 2011, pp. 277–298

Normand (2013)
J. Normand (updated by L. Llahi), 'Juge de l'exécution. Difficultés d'exécution', *JurisClasseur Procédure civile*, Fasc. 2080, 2013

Nourissat (2013)
C. Nourissat, 'Opposition à une "IPE" et comparution du défendeur au sens du règlement "Bruxelles I"', *Revue Procédures*, (2013)8–9, pp. 15–16

Nourissat (2013a)
C. Nourrisat, 'L'injonction de payer européene', *Revue Procédures*, (2013)6, note 184

Nourissat (2009)
C. Nourissat, 'L'"IPE" et les "petits litiges" intègrent le Code de procédure civile', *Revue Procédures*, 2009(March), Commentaires 82, pp. 17–18

Nourissat (2007)
C. Nourissat, 'Le règlement (CE) n° 1896/2006 du 12 décembre 2006 instituant une procédure européenne d'injonction de payer', *Revue Procédures*, Étude 10, 2007, pp. 5–9

Nourissat (2005)
C. Nourissat, 'Droit civil de l'Union européenne: panorama 2004', *Recueil Dalloz Sirey*, 2005(9), pp. 608–615

Noviello (2011)
D. Noviello, 'I moduli standard di domanda e di replica nel regolamento small claims', in M. A. Lupoi (ed.), *Tutele e procedure giudiziarie europee: principi fondamentali e applicazioni pratiche*, Maggioli Editore, 2011, pp. 329–342

O

O'Hare & Browne (2013)
J. O'Hare and K. Browne, *Civil Litigation*, 16th Edition, Sweet & Maxwell Thomson Reuters, 2013

Onţanu (2017)
E. A. Onţanu, 'Incorporating European Uniform Procedures into the National Procedural System and Practice. Best Practices a Solution for Harmonious Application', in X. E. Kramer and B. Hess (eds.), *From Common Rules to Best Practices in European Civil Procedure* (forthcoming in 2017)

Onţanu & Pannebakker (2012)
E. A. Onţanu and E. Pannebakker, 'Tackling Language Obstacles in Cross-Border Litigation: the European Order for Payment and the European Small Claims Procedure Approach', *Erasmus Law Review*, 5(2012)3, pp. 169-186

Oro Martinez (2016)
C. Oro Martinez, 'The Small Claims Regulation: On the Way to an Improved European Procedure?', in B. Hess, M. Bergström, and E. Storskrubb (eds.), *EU Civil Justice: Current Issues and Future Outlook*, Hart Publishing, Oxford, 2016

Orsal (2006)
F. Orsal, *Proposition de Règlement instituant une procédure européenne pour les demandes de faible importance. Réactions de la CCIP présenté au nom de la Commission du droit de l'entreprise et adopté à l'Assemblée générale*, Rapport de 9 mars 2006

Oudin (2009)
M. Oudin, 'Simplified Debt Collection Procedures in French Law', *Simplification of Debt Collection in the EU Project*, (JLS/2009/JCIV/AG/003-30-CE) (available at www.acj.si/en/project-results)

Örücü (2012)
E. Örücü, 'Methodology of comparative law', in J. M. Smits (ed.), *Elgar Encyclopedia of Comparative Law*, 2nd Edition, Edward Elgar, 2012, pp. 560–576

Örücü (2002)
E. Örücü, 'Unde Venit, Quo Tendit Comparative Law?, in A. Harding and E. Örücü (eds.), *Comparative Law in the 21st Century*, Kluwer Law International, 2002

P

Payan (2014)
G. Payan, 'La procédure d'injonction de payer européenne: entre efficacité et insécurité', *Ius & actores*, (2014)2

Payan (2014a)
G. Payan, 'L'irrégularité de la notification d'une injonction de payer européenne: la réponse de la CJUE', *Ius & actores*, (2014)2

Payan (2013)
G. Payan, 'Opposition à une injonction de payer européenne et notion de "comparution du défendeur": interprétation combinee des Règlements (CE) n° 1896/2006 et (CE0 n° 44/2001 par la CJUE', *Lexbase Hebdo* n°539, édition privée, 12 September 2013, n°Lexbase: N8451BT8

Payan (2012)
G. Payan, *Droit européen de l'exécution en matière civile et commerciale*, Bruylant, 2012

Pearl & Goodman (2010)
P. Pearl and A. Goodman, *Small Claims Procedure in the Country Court. A Practical Guide to Mediation and Litigation*, Wildy, Simmonds and Hill Publishing, 2010

Penasa (2015)
L. Penasa, 'Il rimedio a disposizione dell'ingiunto nel caso di dichiarazione di esecutività dell'IPE non validamente notificata: la Corte di giustizia rinuncia a una soluzione unitaria e rinvia ai diritti nazionali', *Int'l Lis*, (2015)1, pp. 73–74

Perrot (2006)
R. Perrot, *Institutions judiciaires*, Montchrestien, 12e édition, 2006

Perrot (2004)
R. Perrot, 'Les procédures civiles d'exécution en France et les perspectives européennes', *Revue Hellénique de Droit International*, 57(2004)2, pp. 363–376

Perrot (1991)
R. Perrot, 'Injonction de payer: recours en cassation contre l'ordonnance devenue exécutoire (le problème né de la supression du visa par le juge)', *Revue trimestrielle de droit civile*, 1991, Chroniques

Picciotto & Carlisi (2010)
A. Picciotto and M. Carlisi, 'Entra in vigore il Regolamento n. 1896 del 2006: la competitività del sistema Europa passa anche attraverso la rapida esazione dei crediti transfrontalieri', *Giurisprudenza di Merito*, 42(2010)2, pp. 304–332

Picod & Davo (2010)
Y. Picod and H. Davo, *Droit de la consummation*, 2nd Edition, Sirey Université, 2010

Piedelièvre (2007)
S. Piedelièvre, 'Litiges transfrontaliers et mise en œuvre des mesures d'exécution', *Revue de droit bancaire et financier*, 2007 (September-October), Commentaires 190, pp. 52–53

della Pietra (2011)
G. della Pietra, 'Paupertas et simplicitas: spunti di semplificazione dalle controversie di modesta entità', in M. A. Lupoi (ed.), *Tutele e procedure giudiziarie europee: principi fondamentali e applicazioni prati*che, Maggioli Editore 2011, pp. 313–328

Pîrvu (2009)
L. N. Pîrvu, 'Procedurile soluţionării cererilor în legătură cu somaţia europeană de plată', *Dreptul*, (2009)4, pp. 150–161

Popovici (2015)
S. Popovici, *Executarea silită transfrontalieră. Instrument de consolidare a creditului*, Editura C.H. Beck, Bucureşti, 2015

Porcelli (2013)
G. Porcelli, 'Il regolamento CE n. 805 del 2004 sul titolo esecutivo europeo per i crediti non contestati e n. 1896 del 2006 sul procedimento di ingiunzione europeo', in P. Biavati and

M. A. Lupoi (eds), *Regole europee e giustizia civile*, Bonomia University Press, 2nd edition, 2013, pp. 131–154

Porcelli (2011)
G. Porcelli, 'L'ambito di applicazione dei regolamenti processuali comunitari: vantaggi e limiti della tutela europea', in M. A. Lupoi (ed.), *Tutele e procedure giudiziarie europee: principi fondamentali e applicazioni pratiche*, Maggioli Editore, 2011, pp. 245–266

Porcelli (2007)
G. Porcelli, 'Ingiunzione di pagamento europea e "mercato interno": un concetto da riformare?', in A. Carratta (ed.), *Verso il procedimento ingiuntivo europeo*, Dott. A. Giuffrè Editore, Milano 2007, pp. 87–170

Porcelli (2006)
G. Porcelli, 'La "nuova" proposta di procedimento europeo d'ingiunzione di pagamento', *Rivista trimestrale di diritto e procedure civile*, 40(2006)4, pp. 1259–1289

Porchia (2009)
O. Porchia, 'Il procedimento europeo di ingiunzione di pagamento: il regolamento comunitario 1896/2006', B. Capponi (ed.), *Il procedimento d'ingiunzione*, Zanichelli Editore, Torino, 2009, pp. 55–74

Pozzi (2008)
V. Pozzi, 'Il rito bagatellare europeo', *Rivista trimestrale di diritto e procedura civile*, 62(2008)2, pp. 611–629

Pozzo (2012)
B. Pozzo, 'Italy', in J. M. Smits (ed.), *Elgar Encyclopedia of Comparative Law*, 2nd Edition, Edward Elgar Publishing Limited, 2012, pp. 453–461

Prechal & Shelkoplyas (2004)
S. Prechal and N. Shelkoplyas, 'National Procedures, Public Policy and EU Law. From Van Schijndel to Eco Swiss and Beyond', *European Review of Private Law*, 12(2004)5, pp. 589–611

R

Radev (2015)
E. Radev, *Working document on establishing common minimum standards for civil procedure in the European Union – the legal basis*, European Parliament, Committee on Legal Affairs, PE572.853v01-00

Reimann (2012)
M. Reimann, 'Cost and Fee Allocation in Civil Procedure: A Synthesis', in M. Reimann (ed.), *Cost and Fee Allocation in Civil Procedure. A Comparative Study*, Springer, 2012

van Rhee (2000)
C.H. van Rhee, 'Civil Procedure: A European Ius Commune?', *European Review of Private Law*, 8(2000)4, pp. 589–611

van Rhee & Uzelac (2009)
C.H. van Rhee and A. Uzelac, 'Introduction', in C.H. van Rhee and A. Uzelac (eds.), *Access to Justice and the Judiciary: Towards New European Standards of Affordability, Quality and Efficiency of Civil Adjudication*, Intersentia, 2009, pp. 1–12

Rivais (2014)
R. Rivais, 'Les malheurs du plaideur européen', *Le Monde*, Friday 31 January 2014

Rivas (2012)
C. Rivas, 'Coding and Analysing Qualitative Data', in C. Seale (ed.), *Researching Society and Culture*, 3rd Edition, SAGE Publications, 2012

Romano (2015)
A. A. Romano, 'Una deludente sentenza della Corte di giustizia in materia di ingiunzione di pagamento europea', *Rivista di Diritto Processuale*, (2015)3, pp. 806–812

Romano (2009)
A. A. Romano, *Il procedimento europeo di ingiunzione di pagamento*, Giuffrè Editore, 2009

Rota (2011)
F. Rota, 'Droit italien', in Chapter 2 by M. Nioche, 'Règlement (CE) nº 861/2007 du 11 juillet 2007 instituant une procedure européenne de règlement des petits litiges', L. Cadiet, E. Jeuland and S. Amrani-Mekki (eds.), *Droit processuel civil de l'Union européenne*, LexisNexis, 2011, pp. 294–298

du Rusquec (2014)
E. du Rusquec (updated by M. Défossez), 'Mesures conservatoires. Dispositions communes', *JurisClasseur Voies d'exécution*, Fasc. 501, 2014

S

Salomone (2013)
E. Salomone, 'Il Regolamento CE n.861/2007 sul procedimento per le controversie di modesta entita e le ADR nell'ambito dell'Unione europea', in P. Biavati and M. A. Lupoi (eds.), *Regole europee e giustizia civile*, Bononia University Press, 2nd Edition, 2013, pp. 197–218

Salvati (2014)
A. Salvati, 'Prove e procedimenti sommari', *Officina del Diritto*, (2014)38

Sandbrook (2011)
C. Sandbrook, *Enforcement of a Judgment*, 11th Edition, Thomson Reuters, 2011

Samyn (2015)
L. Samyn, 'Betalingsbevelprocedure en Verordening Geringe Vorderingen', in B. Allemeersch and Th. Kruger (eds.), *Handboek Europees Burgerlijk Procesrecht*, Intersentia, 2015, pp. 295-324

Samyn (2013)
L. Samyn, *De uitdagingen van het Europees (internationaal) procesrecht voor het Belgisch procesrecht*, Thesis, Law Faculty, Antwerpen University, 2013

Savu (2007)
C. Savu, 'Noua reglementare privind procedura europeană a somației de plată', *Revista Română de Drept Comunitar*, (2007)3, pp. 76–85

Schwartze (2000)
A. Schwartze, 'Enforcement of Private Law: The Missing Link in the Process of European Harmonization', *European Review of Private Law*, 8(2000)1, pp. 135–146

Seatzu (2008)
F. Seatzu, 'Il procedimento d'ingiunzione di pagamento nel Regolamento comunitario n. 1896/2006', in *Studi in onore di Vincenzo Starace*, Volume II, Editoriale Scientifica Srl, 2008, pp. 1601–1621

Silvestri (2014)
E. Silvestri, 'Goals of Civil Justice When Nothing Works: The Case of Italy', in A. Uzelac (ed.), *Goals of Civil Justice and Civil Procedure in Contemporary Judicial Systems*, Springer International Publishing Switzerland, 2014, pp. 79–103

Silvestri (2014a)
E. Silvestri, 'Italy: Civil Procedure in Crisis' in C.H. van Rhee and Fu Yulin (eds.), *Civil Litigation in China and Europe. Essays on the Role of the Judge and the Parties*, Springer, 2014, pp. 235-255

Silvestri (2010)
E. Silvestri, 'The Devil is in the Details: Remarks on Italian Enforcement Procedures', C.H. van Rhee and A. Uzelac, *Enforcement and Enforceability – Tradition and Reform*, Intersentia, 2010, pp. 207-215

Silvestri (2009)
E. Silvestri, 'Italian Report' in *Simplification of Debt Collection in the EU*, Project (JLS/2009/JCIV/AG/003–30-CE), (available at www.acj.si/en/project-results)

Sime (2014)
S. Sime, *A practical approach to Civil Procedure*, 17th edition, Oxford University Press, 2014

Smith (2006)
D. Smith, 'England and Wales' in J.M. Smits (ed.), *Edgar Encyclopedia of Comparative Law*, Edward Elgar Publishing, 2006

Smith & Bull (2012)
D. Smith and W. Bull, 'England and Wales', in J. Smits (ed.), *Edgar Encyclopedia of Comparative Law*, 2nd Edition, Edward Elgar, 2012, pp. 294–298

Soldi (2014)
A. M. Soldi, *Manuale dell'esecuzione forzata*, 4th Edition, CEDAM, 2014

Solignac (2003)
M. P. Solignac au nom de la Commission juridique, *Vers des procédures européennes de recouvrement des créances. Réactions de la CCIP au Livre vert de la Commission européenne*, adopté à l'Assemblée générale du 22 mai 2003, Rapport

Sorabji (2015)
J. Sorabji, 'Austerity's Effect on English Civil Justice', *Erasmus Law Review*, (2015)4, pp. 159–173

Sorabji (2014)
J. Sorabji, *English Civil Justice after the Woolf and Jackson Reforms. A Critical Analysis*, Cambridge University Press, 2014

Spicer (2012)
N. Spicer, 'Combining Qualitative and Quantitative Methods, in C. Seale (ed.), *Researching Society and Culture*, 3rd Edition, SAGE Publications, 2012

Spineanu-Matei (2016)
O. Spineanu-Matei, 'Art. 483. Obiectul şi scopul recursului. Instanţa competentă', in G. Boroi (coordin.), *Noul Cod de procedură civilă. Comentariu pe articole*, Editura Hamangiu, Volume II, 2016, pp. 121–128

Stadler (2013)
A. Stadler, 'The Commission's Recommendation on Common Principles of Collective Redress and Private International Law Issues', *Netherlands Journal of Private International Law*, (2013)4, pp. 483–488

Spinei (2012)
S. Spinei, 'Romanian Civil Procedure: The Reform Cycles', in X. E. Kramer and C. H. van Rhee (eds.), *Civil Litigation in a Globalising World*, T.M.C Asser Press Springer, 2012, pp. 365–367

Steigenga & Velicogna (2017)
E. Steigenga and M. Velicogna, 'Envisioning the Next Step in e-Justice: In Search of the Key to Provide Easy Access to Cross-Border Justice for All Users', in X. E. Kramer and B. Hess (eds.), *From Common Rules to Best Practices in European Civil Procedure* (forthcoming in 2017)

Steiner (2010)
E. Steiner, *French Law: A Comparative Approach*, Oxford University Press, 2010

Storme (2012)
M. Storme, 'Closing Comments: Harmonisation or Globalisation of Civil Procedure?', in X. Kramer and C. H. van Rhee (eds.) *Civil Litigation in a Globalising World*, The Hague: Asser Press, 2012, pp. 379-387

Storme (1994)
M. Storme (ed.), *Approximation of Judiciary Law in the European Union*, Martinus Nijhoff Publishers, 1994

Storme
M. Storme, *Le rapport entre les Règlement européens en matière de procedure (en particulier celle relative aux petites créances) et le droit judiciaire interne belge* (available at https://www.academia.edu/11398039/Le_rapport_entre_les_Re_glements_europe_ens_en_matie_re_de_proce_dure_en_particulier_celle_relative_aux_petites_cre_ances_et_le_droit_judiciaire_interne_belge)

Storskrubb (2016)
E. Storskrubb, 'Mutual Recognition as a Governance Strategy for Civil Justice', in B. Hess, M. Bergström and E. Storskrubb (eds.), *EU Civil Justice. Current issues and Future Outlook*, Hart Publishing, 2016, pp. 299–318

Storskrubb (2008)
E. Storskrubb, *Civil Procedure and EU Law: a Policy Area Uncovered*, Oxford University Press, 2008

Storto (2009)
A. Storto, ' Lo svolgimento e i possibili esiti della fase senza contraddittorio', in B. Capponi (ed.), *Il procedimento d'ingiunzione*, Zanichelli Editore, 2009, pp. 317–364

T

Tabacu (2013)
A. Tabacu, *Citarea şi comunicarea actelor de procedură civilă*, Universul Juridic, 2013

Tabacu (2009)
A. Tabacu, 'Procedura cu privire la cererile cu valoare redusă şi mijloacele procedurale de asigurare a celerităţii în procesul civil, potrivit proiectului noului Cod de procedură civilă', *Revista Română de Drept Privat*, (2009)4, pp. 235–250

Tăbârcă (2013)
A. Tăbârcă, *Drept procesual civil, Teoria generală*, Universul Juridic, Volume I, 2013

Tăbârcă (2013a)
M. Tăbârcă, *Drept procesual civil, Procedura contencioasa in faţa primei instanţe. Procedura necontencioasă judiciară. Proceduri special*, Universul Juridic, Volume II, 2013

Taruffo (2008)
M. Taruffo, 'Harmonizing civil litigation in Europe?', in F. Cafaggi and H. Muir-Watt (eds.), *Making European Private Law. Governance Design*, Edgar Publishing, 2008, pp. 136–170

Tedoldi & Merlo (2009)
A. Tedoldi and C. Merlo, 'Notificazione del decreto ingiuntivo', in B. Capponi (ed.), *Il procedimento d'ingiunzione*, Zanichelli Editore, 2009, pp. 463–600

Theohari & Eftimie (2016)
D. N. Theohari and M. Eftimie, 'Art. 21. Încercarea de împăcare a părţilor', in G. Boroi (coordin.), *Noul Cod de procedură civilă. Comentariu pe articole*, Editura Hamangiu, Volume I, 2016, pp. 60–63

Theohari (2016)
D. N. Theohari, 'Art. 227. Prezenţa personală a părţilor în vederea soluţionării amiabile a litigiului', in G. Boroi (coordin.), *Noul Cod de procedură civilă. Comentariu pe articole*, Editura Hamangiu, Volume I, 2016, pp. 618–620

Theohari, Ilie, Bîrlog & Cristea (2012)
D. N. Theohari, C. M. Ilie, M. A. Bîrlog, and B. Cristea, *Acţiunile civile şi taxele judiciare de timbru. Legea nr. 146/1997 comentată*, Editura Hamangiu, Bucureşti, 2012

Tinel (2007)
I. Tinel, 'Country Report France', in J. Albert (dir.), *Study on the Transparency of Costs of Civil Judicial Proceedings in the European Union*, 2007, Executive Summary (available at https://e-justice.europa.eu/content_costs_of_proceedings-37-fr-en.do)

Titirigă (2014)
R. Titirigă, 'Small Claims Litigation in Romania: The EU as a Normative Power Enhancing Access to Justice', in N. Neuwahl and S. Hammamoum, *The European Small Claims Procedure and the Philosophy of Small Change/ La procédure européenne des petites créances ou la gestion d'un changement progressif*, Les Éditions Thémis, 2014

Tenereiro & Seoane (2003)
M. Tenereiro and J. Alegre Seoane, 'The Creation of A European Judicial Area in Civil and Commercial Matters: What can the EU do?', M. Storme (ed.), *Procedural Laws in Europe. Towards Harmonisation*, Antwerp-Apeldoorn Maklu, 2003, pp. 461–472

Tiscini (2010)
R. Tiscini, *L'accertamento del fatto nei procedimenti con struttura sommaria*, 29 April 2010, point 9 (available at www.judicium.it/wp-content/uploads/saggi/48/tiscini%20I.pdf)

Tulibacka (2009)
M. Tulibacka, 'Europeanization of Civil Procedure: In Search of a Coherent Approach', *Common Market Law Review*, 46(2009), pp. 1527–1565

Tulibacka, Sanz & Blomeyer (2016)
M. Tulibacka, M. Sanz, and R. Blomeyer, *Common Minimum Standards of Civil Procedure*, European Added Value Assessment, Annex I, PE581.385, June 2016

Turner (2009)
R. Turner, '"Actively": The Word that Changed the Civil Courts', in D. Dwyer (ed.), *The Civil Procedure Rules Ten Years On*, Oxford University Press, 2009

V

Valle (2009)
C. Valle, 'Notificazione del decreto ingiuntivo', in B. Capponi (ed.), *Il procedimento d'ingiunzione*, Zanichelli Editore, 2009, pp. 435–462

Văcărelu & Ognean (2014)
S. S. Văcărelu and A. O. Ognean, 'Romania: Procedural Reforms: Plus Ça Change, Plus C'est La Même Chose', in C.H. Rhee and Fu Yulin (eds.), *Civil Litigation in China and Europe. Essays on the Role of the Judge and the Parties*, Springer, 2014, pp. 299-331

Velicogna (2017)
M. Velicogna, 'e-Justice in Europe: From National Experiences to EU Cross-Border Service Provision', in L. Alcaide Muñoz and M.P.R. Bolívar (eds.), *International e-Government Development. Policy, Implementation and Best Practices*, Palgrave Macmillan (forthcoming 2017)

Velicogna (2016)
M. Velicogna et al., 'D7.6 Architectural Hands on Material (Update of D7.4)', *e-Codex Deliverable*, 2016

Velicogna (2015)
M. Velicogna, 'e-CODEX and the Italian Piloting Experience', *IRSIG-CNR Working Paper*, V. 1.0., 2015, (available at SSRN: https://ssrn.com/abstract=2726515)

Velicogna (2008)
M. Velicogna, 'Use of Information and Communication Technologies (ICT) in European Judicial Systems', *CEPEJ Studies No. 7*, Council of Europe, 2008

Velicogna (2007)
M. Velicogna, 'Justice Systems and ICT. What can be learned from Europe?, *Utrecht Law Review*, 3(2007)1 – Special on Adjudication in a Globalizing Context, pp. 129–147

Velicogna & Steigenga (2016)
M. Velicogna and E. Steigenga, 'Can Complexity Theory Help Understanding Tomorrow e-Justice?', Conference on Complex Systems, Law and Complexity Session, 20–23 September 2016 (available at https://ssrn.com/abstract=2914362)

Velicogna & Lupo (2017)
M. Velicogna and G. Lupo, 'From Drafting Common Rules to Implementing Electronic European Civil Procedures: the Rise of e-Codex', in X. E. Kramer and B. Hess (eds.), *From Common Rules to Best Practices in European Civil Procedure* (forthcoming in 2017)

Velicogna, Lupo & Mellone (2016)
M. Velicogna, G. Lupo, and M. Mellone, 'Notification and Service of Documents in National and European Civil Procedures', *e-Justice Communication via Online Data Exchange*, e-Codex, WP7 2016

Velicogna, Lupo & Onţanu (2017)
M. Velicogna, G. Lupo, and E. A. Onţanu, 'Simplifying access to justice in cross-border litigation, the national practices and the limits of the EU procedures. The example of the service of documents in the order for payment claims', *International Journal of Procedural Law*, 7(2017)1

Velicogna, Lupo & Onţanu (2015)
M. Velicogna, G. Lupo, and E. A. Onţanu, 'Simplifying Access to Justice in Cross-Border Litigation, the National Practices and the Limits of the EU Procedures. The Service of Documents Example', *Annual 2015 Conference of the European Group for Public Administration, Permanent Study Group XVIII: Justice and Court Administration*, 26–28 August 2015, Toulouse, France

Verde (2009)
V. Verde, 'La prova nel procedimento ingiuntivo', in B. Capponi (ed.), *Il procedimento d'ingiunzione*, Zanichelli Editore, 2009, pp. 105–190

Véricel (2013)
M. Véricel, 'Le retour (provisoire) des juridictions et juges de proximité en matière civile. À propos de la loi du 24 décembre 2012', *La Semaine juridique*, Édition générale, 2013(6), pp. 230–233

Véricel (2008)
M. Véricel, *Les juridictions et juges de proximité. Leur rôle concret en matière d'accès à la justice des petits litiges civils*, CERCRID (University of Staint Etienne), 2008

Vinckel (2013)
F. Vinckel, 'Droit d'exécution. Présentation générale', *JurisClasseur Procédure civile*, Fasc. 2010, 2013

Voet (2017)
S. Voet, '"Where the Wild Things Are" Reflections on the State and Future of European Collective Redress', M. Loos and A. Keirse (eds.), Forthcoming in a book in the Ius Commune Europaeum series, Intersentia, 2017 (available at https://papers.ssrn.com/sol3/papers.cfm?abstract_id=2913010)

Voet (2015)
S. Voet, 'Relief in Small and Simple Matters in Belgium', *Erasmus Law Review*, (2015)4, pp. 147–158

Vuitton (2011)
X. Vuitton, 'Référés spéciaux. Référé aux fins d'obtention d'une mesure d'instruction à future. Référé provision. Référé injonction de faire', *JurisClasseur Procédure civile*, Fasc. 474, 2011

Vuitton (2011a)
X. Vuitton, 'Référé. Ordonnance. Caractéristiques. Exécution provisoire. Voies de recours et de contestations. Mesures', *JurisClasseur Procédure civile*, Fasc. 474, 2011

Vuitton (2013)
X. Vuitton, 'Tribunal de grande instance. Procédure ordinaire. Saisine. Fixation et distribution de l'affaire', *JurisClasseur Procédure civile*, Fasc. 218, 2013

Vuitton & Vuitton (2013)
J. Vuitton and X. Vuitton, 'Pourvoi en cassation. Délais. Forme. Effets', *JurisClasseur Procédure civile*, Fasc. 754, 2013

Vuitton & Vuitton (2013a)
J. Vuitton and X. Vuitton, 'Pourvoi en cassation. Décisions susceptibles de pourvoi', *JurisClasseur Procédure civile*, Fasc. 752, 2013

W

2015 White Book
2015 White Book, Volume 2, Section 3L, Sweet & Maxwell Thomson Reuters, pp. 2014

2012 White Book
2012 White Book Part 78 – European Procedure, Annotation 78.12.1

Woolf (1996)
Lord Woolf, *Access to Justice: Final Report to the Lord Chancellor on the Civil Justice System in England and Wale*, 1996

Y

Yin (2011)
R. K. Yin, *Qualitative Research from Start to Finish*, The Guilford Press, 2011

Z

Zidaru (2013)
G.-L. Zidaru, 'Unele aspect privind regularizarea cererii de chemare în judecată şi noua reglementare a taxelor judiciare de timbru', *Revista Română de Drept Privat* (Romanian Review of Private Law), 2013(3), pp. 149–173

Zucconi Galli Fonseca (2009)
E. Zucconi Galli Fonseca, 'La provvisoria esecutività del decreto ingiuntivo', *Rivista trimestrale di diritto e procedura civile*, 43(2009)1, pp. 175–207

Zuckerman (2013)
A. Zuckerman, *Zuckerman on Civil Procedure. Principles of Practice*, 3nd Edition, Sweet & Maxwell, 2013

Zweigert & Kötz (1998)
K. Zweigert and H. Kötz, *Introduction to Comparative Law*, translated from German by Tony Weir, 3rd Edition, Clarendon Press, Oxford, 1998

TABLE OF CASES

Judgements of the Court of Justice of the European Union

Case Number	Parties	ECLI number
C-215/11	*Iwona Szyrocka v SiGer Technologie GmbH case*	ECLI:EU:C:2012:794
C-245/14	*Thomas Cook Belgium NV v. Thurner Hotel GmbH*	ECLI:EU:C:2015:715 and ECLI:EU:C:2015:442 (opinion)
C-215/11	*Iwona Szyrocka v. SiGer Technologie GmbH*	ECLI:EU:C:2012:400 (opinion)
C119/13 and C120/13	*Eco Cosmetics GmbH & KG v. Virginie Laetitia Barbara Dupuy, Raiffeissenbank St. Georgen reg. Gen mbH v. Tetyang Bonchyk*	ECLI:EU:C:2014:2144 and ECLI:EU:C:2014:248 (opinion)
C-144/12	*Goldbet Sportwetten GmbH v. Massimo Sperindeo*	ECLI:EU:C:2013:393 ECLI:EU:C:2013:136
C-324/12	*Novotech-Zala*	ECLI:EU:C:2013:205
C-94/14	*Flight Refund Ltd. V. Deutsche Lufthansa AG*	ECLI:EU:C:2016:148 ECLI:EU:C:2015:723 (opinion)
C-21/17	*Catlin Europe SE v O.K. Trans Praha spol. s.r.o., 18 January 2017,*	Application

Judgements of the European Court of Human Rights

Parties	Application number	Reported
Döry v. Sweden	28394/95	ECLI:CE:ECHR:2002:1112 JUD002839495
Golder v. UK	4451/70	ECHR (1975) A18
Hornsby v. Greece	18357/91	ECHR (1997)
Notar v. Romania	42860/98	ECHR (2004)
Weissman and others v. Romania	63945/00	ECHR (2006)

National Case law

Austria

Judgment of Bezirksgericht Schwechat of 12 October 2014, 4C 580/11v – 10

England and Wales

Campbell v Mylchreest [1999] P.I.Q.R. Q17, Auld L.J.
Regency Rolls Ltd v Carnall [2000], EWCA Civ 379
Orford v Rasmi Electronics Ltd [2000] EWCA Civ 1672
Colley v. Council for Licensed Conveyancers at [32], [2001] EWCA Civ 1137; [2002] 1 WLR 160
Swain v. Hillman, Court of Appeal, [2001] 1 All English Law Reports (All ER) 91
E.D.&F. Man Liquid Products Ltd v Patel [2003] CPLR 384;
Smith v. Brough (2005) ([2005] EWCA Civ 26)
Messer Griesheim GmbH v Goyal MG Gases PVT Ltd [2006], EWHC 79, QB (Comm)
Mullock v Price [2009], EWCA Civ 1222, [2010] at [2]
Paseana Ltd v Lextrex Holdings Ltd. [2010] EWCA Civ 1539;
Credit Suisse International v Ramot Plana OD [2010] EWHC 2759 (Comm).
Puchala v Thomas Cook Airlines Limited, 12th May 2015, Chichester County Court, District Judge Ellis (Unreported) (transcript on file with the researcher)

France

Cass. 2e civ., 23 January 1991, No. 89–18747
Cass., Ch. comm., 27 Nov. 2012, n°11–17.185, ECLI:FR:CCASS:2012:CO01177
Cass., Ch. Comm., 28 janvier 2014, N° de pourvoi 112–25008, ECLI:FR:CCASS: 2014: CO00116, Bulletin 2014, IV, n° 26
CA Colmar, Chambre 3 civile, Section A, 16 décembre 2013, N° 3 A 12/00029
CA Dijon, 1re Chambre civile, 9 juin 2015, N° 14/01155
CA Douai, Chambre 02, Section 02, 14 mai 2013, N° 12/02093;
CA Douai Chambre 02, Section 02, 14 mars 2013, N° 12/02210;
CA Douai, Chambre 2, Section 2, Arrêt du 14 mars 2013, N° 2011/00619
CA Grenoble, Chambre commerciale, 30 juin 2011, N° 11/01943
CA Nîmes, 10 mai 2012, N° 11/01267
CA Paris, Pôle 1, Chambre 1, 26 mai 2011, N° 10/18208
CA Paris, Pôle 1, Chambre 1, 26 mai 2011, N° 10/18209
CA Poitiers, Chambre 2 Civile, 23 février 2010, N° 08/01986
CA Riom, Chambre des référes, 19 septembre 2013, N° 13/00025
CA Riom, 1re Chambre civile, 7 avril 2014; N° 13/01233
CA Versailles, Chambre 14, 31 mars 2010, N° 09/01176
CA Versailles, Chambre 12, 9 décembre 2014, N° 13/01145
TI de Chalon sur Saône, G 1ère instance 11 13–868, 10 juin 2014
TC Créteil, Chambre 2, 18 mars 2013, N° 2012F00900

TC Créteil, 1re Chambre, 28 janvier 2013, N° 2012F00683
TC Créteil, 1re Chambre, 11 février 2014, N° 2012F00518
TC Créteil, Chambre 2, 8 mars 2011, N° 2010F00947
TC Lille, 23 février 2012, N° 2011/00619
TC Nanterre, Chambre 6, 9 novembre 2011, N° 201 1F00195
TC Nanterre, Chambre 4, 10 avril 2015, N° 2013F03851
TC Nanterre, Chambre 4, 19 décembre 2012, N° 2010F03902
TC Nanterre, Chambre 2, 23 février 2011, N° 2010F04309
Juridiction de proximité Angers, 6 Décembre 2010 N° 91.10–438, Vielle Société By Lifestyle 4 U Gmbh (not published).

Italy

Cassazione 25 maggio 2005, n. 11023
Cassazione 2 aprile 2010, n. 8126
Corte Costituzionale, Sentenza n. 120, 20 maggio 1976
Corte Costituzionale, Sentenza n. 157, 4 giugno 2014
Corte di Appello di Trieste, Sezione 1 Civil, Case No. 189/2013, Decision issued on 13 May 2014
Tribunale di Cagliari Order, 6 November 2009
Tribunale di Firenze, 25 November 2009
Tribunale di Firenze, Sezione 3, Decision No. 1734/2013
Tribunale di Forli Case No. 2192/2011, Decision issued 22 Janaury 2013
Tribunale di Forli, Case No. 45/24 January 2013
Tribunale di Forli, Case No. 450/2012, Decision issued 17 June 2013
Tribunale di Genova, 28 January 2014
Tribunale di Mantova 7 July 2011, Case No. 1964/11
Tribunale di Mantova 14 July 2011
Tribunale di Milano 18 July 2011
Tribunale di Milano 28 October 2010
Tribunale di Milano, Case No. 76746/2013
Tribunale di Milano, Case No. 10488/8 April 2015
Tribunale di Mondovì, Order of 10 November 2009
Tribunale di Mondovì Order, of 5 November 2009
Tribunale di Napoli, 4 December 2009
Ufficio Giudice di Pace di Parma, Sezione 1, Procedimento No. 7667/2013, Sentenza No. 347/2014 di 6/02/2014 (available at https://aldricus.files.wordpress.com/2015/09/2015-06-30-ester.pdf)
Tribunale di Piacenza 18 September 2010
Tribunale di Roma, Sezione XII, Decision of 17 May 2012
Tribunale di Roma, Sezione XII, Decision of 12 September 2012
Tribunale di Roma, Sezione XII, Case No. 23097/18 November 2013
Tribunale di Roma, Sezione XII, Case No. 35042/13 March 2013
Tribunale di Rovereto, Decision No. 688/2012
Tribunale di Rovereto, Decision No. 511/2012
Tribunale di Taranto, Sezione II, Decision No. 5949/15 September 2016
Tribunale di Trieste, Case No. 565/23 February 2009

Tribunale di Trieste 29 March 2009
Tribunale di Trieste, Case No. 3/17 April 2009
Tribunale di Trieste, Case No. 4/5 June 2009
Tribunale di Trieste, Case No. 5/5 June 2009
Tribunale di Trieste, Case No. 6/5 June 2009
Tribunale di Trieste 15 June 2009
Tribunale di Trieste, Case No. 9/17 June 2009
Tribunale di Trieste Case No. 9/2009
Tribunale di Trieste, Case No. 10/2009
Tribunale di Trieste, Decision No. 3617/15 December 2009
Tribunale di Trieste, Case No. 1819/ 3 June 2010
Tribunale di Trieste, Case No. 3294/29 October 2012
Tribunale di Trieste, Case No. 6617/26 August 2015
Ufficio del Giudice di Pace di Trieste, Decision 4710/10 January 2015
Tribunale di Varese, Order of 18 November 2009
Tribunale di Varese 12 November 2010
Tribunale di Verona, Case No. 7443/26 May 2012

Romania

Înalta Curte de Casaţie şi Justiţie Decision No. 527/13 February 2014
Alba Iulia Curte de Appel (Court of Appeal) Decision No. 5/27 February 2013, Section II Civil
Cluj Court of Appeal, Section I Civile, Decision 3/F/9.01.2015
Timişoara Curte de Apel (Court of Appeal) Decision No. 285/15.02.2011
Timişoara Curte de Appel (Court of Appeal, commercial section) Decision No. 285/15 February 2011
Tribunalul Alba File No. 6327/107/2009 (no EOP was issued; the parties reached an agreement and the case was closed), 17/107/2009;
Tribunalul Arad File No. 1823/108/2010
Tribunalul Bihor: File No. 1782/111/2011;
Tribunalul Bucureşti, Section V, Decision No. 484/29 February 2012, Revista Română de Executare Silită, (2012)1
Tribunalul Bucureşti, Section VI: Files No. 23767/3/2009, 35668/3/2009, 12119/3/2010, 25382/3/2010, 56470/3/2010, 4088/3/2012, 25513/3/2013, 41220/3/2013, 14946/3/2014
Tribunalul Specializat Cluj: Files No. 177/1285/2015, 705/1285/2015, 1086/1285/2015
Tribunalul Călăraşi: File No. 272/116/2013
Tribunalul Constanţa: Files No. 11530/118/2012, 8438/118/2014, 4969/118/2015, 5864/118/2015/A1, 7748/118/2015
Tribunalul Galaţi: Files No. 378/121/2015, 381/121/2015, 382/121/2015, 384/121/2015, 385/121/2015, 387/121/2015, 388/121/2015, 389/121/2015, 390/121/2015, 391/121/2015
Tribunalul Giurgiu: Files No. 141/192/2012, 143/192/2012, 144/192/2012, 145/192/2012, 147/192/2012, File No. 149/192/2012
Tribunalul Harghita: Files No. 3807/96/2012, 4144/96/2012;

Tribunalul Hunedoara: Files No. 1296/97/2013, 7672/97/2013, 7608/79/2011, 1124/97/2015, 1315/97/2015, 1554/97/2015, 1722/97/2015, 1723/97/2015, 2077/97/2015, 2696/97/2015, 2703/97/2015, 2693/97/2015, 3013/97/2015, 4413/97/2015, 4082/97/2015
Tribunalul Iaşi: Files No. 8839/99/2012, 15868/245/2013, 16017/245/2013, 7460/99/2015
Tribunalul Ilfov: File No. 649/93/2013
Tribunalul Mureş: Files No. 509/1371/2012, 331/1371/2014, 598/1371/2014, 301/1371/2015, 760/1371/2015
Tribunalul Neamţ: File No. 2531/103/2011;
Tribunalul Prahova: File No. 7568/105/2012
Judecătoria Oradea, Civil Section, Civil Judgment No. 3164/2011, (available online at http://portal.just.ro/271/Lists/Jurisprudenta/DispForm.aspx?ID=31)
Judecătoria Arad: Files No. 4112/55/2009, 13428/55/2011, 11881/55/2012, 16976/55/2013, 15348/55/2015, 12617/55/2015;
Judecătoria Aiud: File No. 736/175/2015
Judecătoria Bacău: File No. 13451/180/2012, 1270/180/2015, 3884/180/2015, 10432/180/2015
Judecătoria Baia Mare: Files No. 6282/182/2012, 4210/182/2015, 7391/182/2015, 7621/182/2015;
Judecătoria Bistriţa: File No. 1805/190/2013
Judecătoria Botoşani, Decision No. 96/16 January 2014, Files No. 3466/193/2015, 3467/193/2015
Judecătoria Braşov: Files No. 12442/197/2011, 31929/197/2012
Judecătoria Brezoi: File No. 1807/198/2014
Judecătoria Buftea: Files No. 1297/94/2012, 15441/94/2012, 3043/94/2015
Judecătoria Buzău: Files No. 801/200/2014, 7329/200/2015, 12919/200/2015
Judecătoria Cluj-Napoca: Files No. 19686/211/2010, 22003/211/2012, 8589/211/2013, 20459/211/2015, 22479/211/2015
Judecătoria Constanţa: Files No. 12730/212/2012, 7262/212/2015, 14113/212/2015, 24856/212/2015, 29487/212/2015
Judecătoria Cornetu: Files No. 7402/1748/2010, 1542/1748/2012, 12197/1748/2012, 15120/1748/2012, 2385/1748/2013, 4862/1748/2013, 7777/1748/2013, 80/1748/2015, 3910/1748/2015
Judecătoria Craiova: Files No. 19646/215/2010, 26180/215/2014, 4314/215/2015, 27433/215/2015;
Judecătoria Giurgiu: Files No. 12121/236/2013, 5456/236/2015
Judecătoria Galaţi, Files No. 14433/233/2011, 1062/233/2011, 11433/233/2011, 14422/233/2011, 7750/233/2012, 6228/233/2013, 12656/233/2014, 3942/233/2015, 14982/233/2015, 16859/233/2015
Judecătoria Gheorgheni: Files No. 2108/234/2015, 1176/234/2015, 1188/234/2015;
Tribunalul Harghita: Files No. 3807/96/2012, 4144/96/2012
Judecătoria Giurgiu: File No. 12121/236/2013;
Judecătoria Hunedoara: File No. 7608/97/2011
Judecătoria Iaşi: Files No. 15868/245/2013, 16017/245/2013,33817/245/2015, 4218/245/2015, 21452/245/2015, 21930/245/2015
Judecătoria Lugoj: File No. 863/252/2013;
Judecătoria Miercurea: File No. 3481/258/2012;
Judecătoria Năsăud: Files No. 1058/265/2012, 319/265/2013;
Judecătoria Odorheiul Secuiesc: File No. 3086/268/2015
Judecătoria Oneşti: File No. 2492/270/2013
Judecătoria Oradea: Files No. 20531/271/2010, 22655/271/2010; 808/271/2012, 18033/271/2013, 3148/271/2015, 3349/271/2015, 9062/271/2015

Judecătoria Oraviţa: File No. 1481/273/2012;
Judecătoria Petroşani: File No. 118/278/2012;
Judecătoria Ploieşti: Files No. 34171/281/2012, 34172/281/2012,, 291/281/2015, 9368/281/2015, 9369/281/2015
Judecătoria Râmnicu Vâlcea: File No. 13294/288/2013
Judecătoria Reşiţa: File No. 2895/290/2015
Judecătoria Salonta: File No. 1491/833/2015
Judecătoria Sibiu: Files No. 8064/306/2015, 8246/306/2015
Judecătoria Şimpleul Silvaniei: Files No. 1735/309/2012, 1544/309/2013
Judecătoria Slobozia: Files No. 5603/3132/2012, 1212/312/2013
Judecătoria Suceava: Files No. 748/314/2014, 5628/314/2015
Judecătoria Târgu Cărbuneşti, File No. 1463/317/2014
Judecătoria Târgovişte: File No. 7261/315/2015
Judecătoria Târgu Mureş: Files No. 5756/320/2015, 6293/320/2015
Judecătoria Timişoara: Files No. 14586/325/2010, 14587/325/2010, 8177/325/2011
Judecătoria Tulcea District Court: File No. 6820/327/2012
Judecătoria Vişeul de Sus: Files No. 172/336/2015, 531/336/2015, 1620/336/2015
Judecătoria Sector 1, Bucureşti: Files No. 44676/299/2010, 50506/299/2012, 45573/299/2012, 60460/299/2012, 1281/299/2013, 1912/299/2013, 2203/299/2013, 5584/299/2013, 10989/299/2013, 50927/299/2013, 2323/299/2014, 32436/299/2014, 34756/299/2014, 45497/299/2014, 55900/299/2014, 122578/299/2015, 106612/299/2015, 42328/299/2015, 42329/299/2015, 42330/299/2015, 72435/299/2015, 82509/299/2015, 94288/299/2015, Decision No. 10700/02.06.2011.; Judecătoria Sector 2, Bucureşti: Files No. 41968/300/2010, 38390/300/2010, 37136/300/2012, 71372/300/2015; Judecătoria Sector 3, Bucureşti: Files No. 40753/301/2011, 11606/301/2012, 38699/301/2012, 41477/301/2012, 42193/301/2012, 46119/301/2014, 57080/301/2014, 19381/301/2015, 19546/301/2015, 23798/301/2015, 24063/301/2015, 24066/301/2015; Judecătoria Sector 4, Bucureşti: Files No. 30550/4/2012, 10512/4/2014, 10551/4/2015, 10691/4/2015, 28251/4/2015, 38750/4/2015, 28253/4/2015, 28252/4/2015, 36238/4/2015; Judecătoria Sector 5, Bucureşti: Files No. 571/302/2009, 14067/302/2010, 21602/302/2010, 17915/302/2012, 38461/3/2012, 29847/302/2012, 21174/302/2014, 3700/302/2015; Judecătoria Sector 6, Bucureşti: Files No. 24931/303/2010, 28294/303/2011, 15073/303/2012, 14521/303/23013, 3183/303/2014; Tribunalul Bucureşti, Section VI: Files No. 23767/3/2009, 35668/3/2009, 12119/3/2010, 25382/3/2010, 56470/3/2010, 4088/3/2012, 25513/3/2013, 41220/3/2013, 14946/3/2014, 3427/3/2015, 10998/3/2015, 18247/3/2015, 35507/3/2015, 47366/3/2015, 42752/3/2015; Bucharest Court of Appeal, Decision No. 48/12 April 2012

CURRICULUM VITAE

Elena Alina Onţanu was born in 1984 in Bucharest, Romania. She graduated in 2007 in Romanian law (University of Bucharest Law School), in French and European law (Maîtrise and Master 1, University of Paris I Panthéon-Sorbonne), and in management of public administrations (Academy of Economic Studies Bucharest). She obtained her LL.M in 2008 in International, Comparative, and European Law (Master 2, University Toulouse 1 Capitole).

After completing her master studies, Alina worked as an intern in the Office of Judge Camelia Toader at the Court of Justice of the European Union in Luxembourg. Following the internship, from 2008 to 2011, she worked as a financial law lawyer with a leading Romanian law firm, Nestor Nestor Diculescu Kingston Petersen. In September 2011, Alina began her doctoral research at Erasmus University Rotterdam. Since October 2016, she has been a researcher at the Research Institute on Judicial Systems – National Research Council (IRSIG-CNR) in Bologna.

While working on her PhD, she was a visiting scholar at Clare College, Cambridge University (2012), IRSIG-CNR (2014), and at the Max Planck Institute Luxembourg for International, European and Regulatory Procedural Law (2015). In addition to her doctoral research, she has contributed to various other research projects carried out by Erasmus University Rotterdam, IRSIG-CNR, and the Max Planck Institute Luxembourg.

Alina often works on multidisciplinary projects, conducting comparative and empirical research. Her research interests focus on European uniform procedures and civil litigation, national special procedures for debt recovery, securing access to justice in a transnational context, protection of parties' procedural rights, cross-border enforcement, digitalisation of civil procedure, quality of justice, and the EU Justice Scoreboard. She has acquired significant international work experience through collaborating with researchers and professionals from different countries.

From September 2017, Elena Alina Onţanu works as an assistant professor of Private International Law at Erasmus University Rotterdam.

IUS COMMUNE EUROPAEUM

A peer-reviewed book series in which the common foundations of the legal systems of the Member States of the European Union are the central focus.

The *Ius Commune Europaeum* series includes horizontal comparative legal studies as well as studies on the effect of treaties within the national legal systems. All the classic fields of law are covered. The books are published in various European languages under the auspices of METRO, the Institute for Transnational Legal Research at Maastricht University.

Recently published:
Volume 147: *Legal Certainty in Real Estate Transactions: A Comparison of England and France*, B. Du Marais and D. Marrani (eds.)
Volume 148: *Scarcity and the State I. The Allocation of Limited Rights by the Administration*, P. Adriaanse, F. van Ommeren, W. den Ouden and J. Wolswinkel (eds.)
Volume 149: *Optional Instruments of the European Union. A Definitional, Normative and Explanatory Study*, W.A. Bull
Volume 150: *The European Union and National Civil Procedure. A Smooth Process or a Rocky Road for Member States?*, A. Nylund and B.H. Krans (eds.)
Volume 151: *Different Paths Towards Sustainable Biofuels? A Comparative Study of the International, EU, and Chinese Regulation of the Sustainability of Biofuels*, T. Yue
Volume 152: *Regulation of Cross-Border Establishment in China and the EU. A Comparative Law and Economics Approach*, G. Shen
Volume 153: *The French Contract Law Reform: a Source of Inspiration?*, S. Stijns and S. Jansen (eds.)
Volume 154: *Convergence in European Consumer Sales Law. A Comparative and Numerical Approach*, C. Goanţă
Volume 155: *Quality and Speed in Administrative Decision-Making: Tension or Balance?*, C. Backes, M. Eliantonio and S. Jansen (eds.)
Volume 156: *Letter of Intent in International Contracting*, E. Pannebakker
Volume 157: *Revisiting Procedural Human Rights*, A. Uzelac and C.H. van Rhee (eds.)
Volume 158: *Waves in Contract and Liability Law in Three Decades of Ius Commune*, A. Keirse and M. Loos (eds.)

www.ingramcontent.com/pod-product-compliance
Ingram Content Group UK Ltd.
Pitfield, Milton Keynes, MK11 3LW, UK
UKHW051925100926
8556IPUK00022B/1367

9 781780 686097